ENDEAVOUR SURVEYORS LTD

Chrissie Davis, Princ...
www.endeavoursur...
Chrissie@endeavours...
Tel: 07723 026269   07545 597112

Yacht and Small Craft Surveyor specialising in GRP and Wooden Yachts,

Survey Reports available:-

Pre purchase Condition Report

Pre Purchase Structural Report

Insurance Surveys

Damage and Repair Reports

Valuations

Free Quotations,

I travel to all areas,

Full colour reports with pictures, sent out as a bound hard copy and free CD version, fast and efficient service

2010/MA104/e

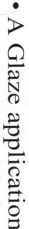

Make a **winning** decision

Your choice of marine electronics is one of the most important decisions you will have to make as a boat owner, next to choosing the boat itself of course.

When you buy Raymarine equipment, you are buying into world-class performance, top-notch integration, and the latest proven design technologies. Years of research and development, and customer feedback have resulted in the 'simple-on-the-outside, sophisticated-on-the-inside' design philosophy that is behind all our intuitive easy-to-use equipment.

Worldwide support and warranty

That's why Raymarine has a worldwide network of product-trained distributors and service dealers and offers a comprehensive warranty to handle the unexpected… wherever you decide to go.

For product information, visit your local stockist or go to **www.raymarine.co.uk**

Raymarine®
…world leaders in marine electronics.

REEDS
EASTERN
ALMANAC
2010

ADLARD COLES NAUTICAL

EDITORS Andy Du Port and Rob Buttress

Free updates are available at www.reedsalmanac.co.uk

Published by Adlard Coles Nautical 2009

Copyright © Nautical Data Ltd 2001–2003

Copyright © Adlard Coles Nautical 2004–2009

IMPORTANT SAFETY NOTE AND LEGAL DISCLAIMER

This Almanac is intended as an aid to navigation only and to assist with basic planning for your passage. The information, charts, maps and diagrams in this Almanac should not be relied on for navigational purposes and should always be used in conjunction with current official hydrographic data. Whilst every care has been taken in its compilation, this Almanac may contain inaccuracies and is no substitute for the relevant official hydrographic charts and data, which should always be consulted in advance of, and whilst, navigating in the relevant area. Before setting out you should also check local conditions with the harbourmaster or other appropriate office responsible for your intended area of navigation.

Before using any waypoint or coordinate listed in this Almanac it must first be plotted on an appropriate official hydrographic chart to check its usefulness, accuracy and appropriateness for the prevailing weather and tidal conditions.

To the extent that the editors or publishers become aware that corrections are required, these will be published on the website www.reedsalmanac.co.uk. Readers should therefore regularly check the website for any such corrections. Data in this Almanac is corrected up to Weekly Edition 26/2009 of Admiralty Notices to Mariners.

The publishers, editors and their agents accept no responsibility for any errors or omissions, or for any accident, loss or damage (including without limitation any indirect, consequential, special or exemplary damages) arising from the use or misuse of, or reliance upon, the information contained in this Almanac.

The decision to use and rely on any of the data in this Almanac is entirely at the discretion of, and is the sole responsibility of, the Skipper or other individual in control of the vessel in connection with which it is being used or relied upon.

Adlard Coles Nautical
36 Soho Square
London, W1D 3QY
Tel: +44 (0)207 758 0200
Fax: +44 (0)207 758 0222/0333
Email: info@reedsalmanac.co.uk
www.reedsalmanac.co.uk

Almanac manager
Chris Stevens

Cartography
Chris Stevens, Garold West

Cover photograph
Lowestoft Haven Marina
www.lowestofthavenmarina.co.uk

ISBN 978 1 4081 1368 4 – Reeds Eastern
Almanac 2010

A CIP catalogue record for this book is available from the British Library.

Printed in the UK.

ADVERTISEMENT SALES
Enquiries about advertising should be addressed to:
MS Publications,
2nd Floor, Ewer House,
44-46 Crouch Street,
Colchester, Essex CO3 3HH.
Tel: +44 (0)1206 506223
Fax: +44 (0)1206 500228

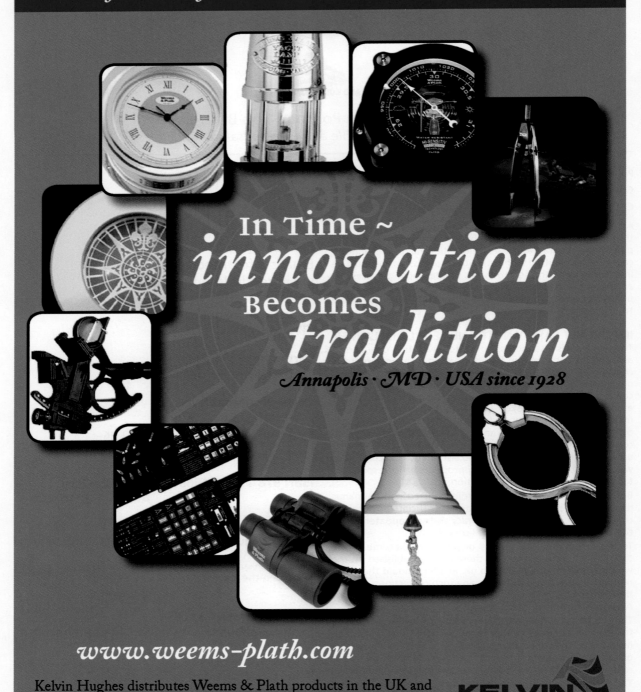

Reference Contents

I am your Lifejacket.

When we are on the water,

I will make you feel safe.

And when we are in the water,

I will keep you alive.

I will stop you from panicking.

I will keep you afloat.

Even in rough weather.

Even if you are unconscious,

I will support and protect you

until help arrives.

All this I will do for you

if you do one thing for me.

Please, put me on.

Navigational Contents

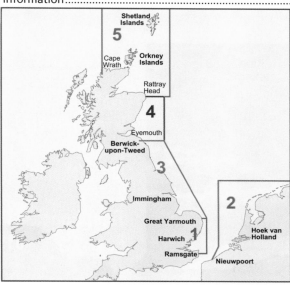

Bembridge Harbour

Isle of Wight

PONTOON BERTHS AND TROT MOORINGS AT COMPETITIVE RATES

Contact

Website
www.bembridgeharbour.co.uk
E-mail
chris@bembridgeharbour.co.uk

Telephone: 01983872828
Fax: 01983872922

2010/MA97/e

We Discovered the Difference

Sir Anthony Greener

"I hope we are at the end of a very long road and I would like to thank you and Pantaenius for your outstanding service and support. It has been an exemplary (and very unusual) experience for a client."

Mr. David Evans

"Why would I ever try to buy the cheapest insurance? I now have a self-satisfied glow that I made the right decision by buying the BEST insurance. This was brought about by listening to a friend who had a claim with yourselves. His claim was equally well handled by Pantaenius and that experience persuaded me that what I needed was the best, not the cheapest!"

Dr. H. Chadwick

"I would like to thank Pantaenius and especially yourself for the way in which you have dealt with things, as losing one's boat, especially in such dangerous circumstances is quite a traumatic event. I was very grateful for both the immediate help and advice that I received and the subsequent help with managing the situation and the rapid settlement of the insurance issues."

Mr. Dave Leaning

"Thanks for all your help throughout this claim, one reads all sorts of insurance horror stories in the yachting press but I don't think I could possibly have received any better service. It made a difficult process painless."

Why don't you contact us

PANTAENIUS
Yacht Insurance

Germany · United Kingdom · Monaco · Denmark · Austria · Spain · Croatia · Sweden · USA*

ine Building · Victoria Wharf · Plymouth · Devon PL4 0RF · Phone +44-1752 22 36 56 · Fax +44-1752 22 36 37 · info@pantaenius.co.uk
Authorised and regulated by the Financial Services Authority

2010/MA3/e

www.pantaenius.co.uk

* Pantaenius America Ltd. is a licensed insurance agent in the state of New York as well as in other states. It is an independent corporation incorporated under the laws of New York and is a separate and distinct entity from any entity of the Pantaenius group.

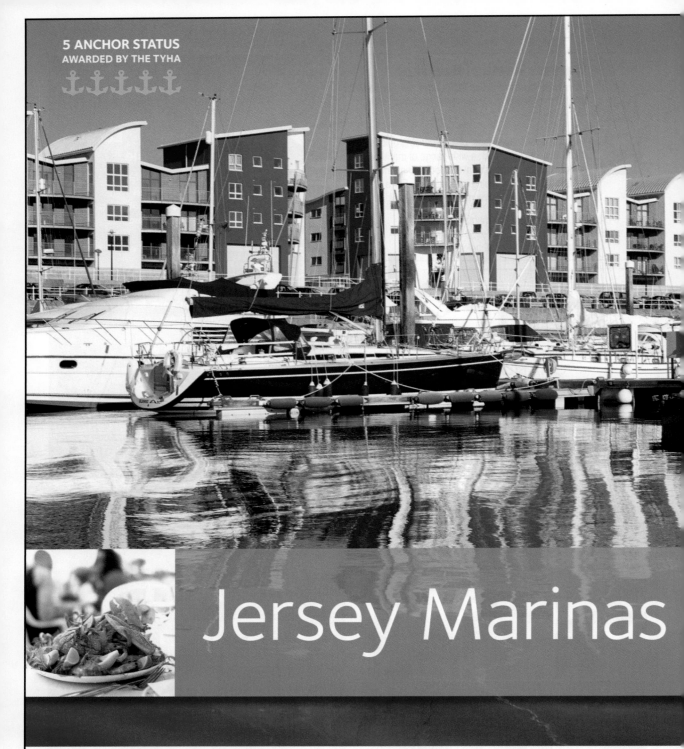

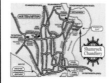

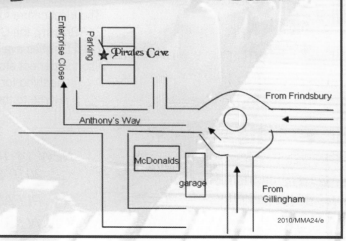

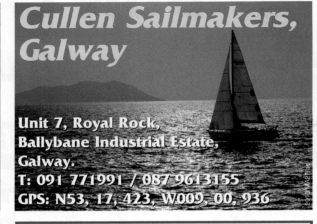

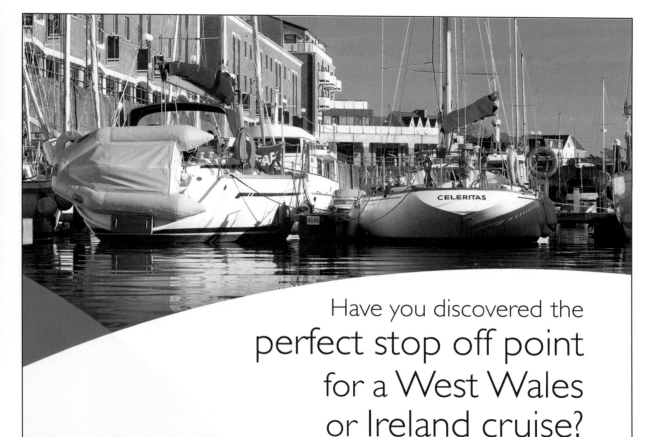

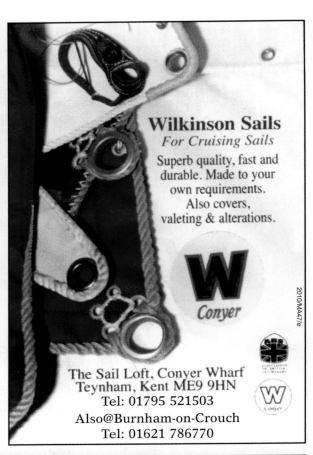

next time you visit Rye,
why not bring your boat...

Visitor's berths are available from £14 per night including power, water, shower and toilet facilities.
Permanent moorings are also available.
The yearly charge for a 9 metre boat is just £1,005.71.
Contact the Harbour Office for more details.

Rye Harbour Office, New Lydd Road, Camber, Rye, East Sussex TN31 7QS. Tel: 01797 225225.

Email: rye.harbour@environment-agency.gov.uk
Website: www.environment-agency.gov.uk/harbourofrye

2010/MA18/e

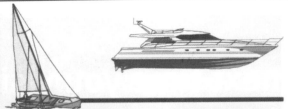

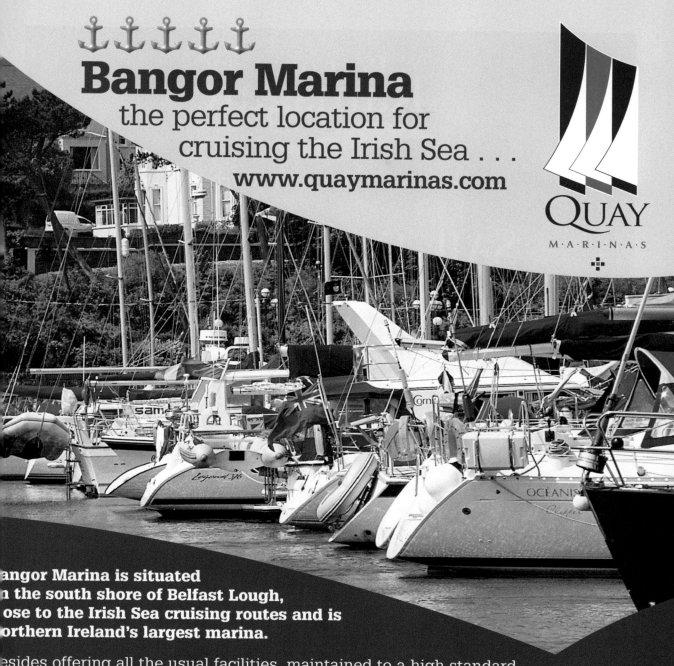

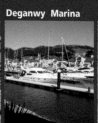

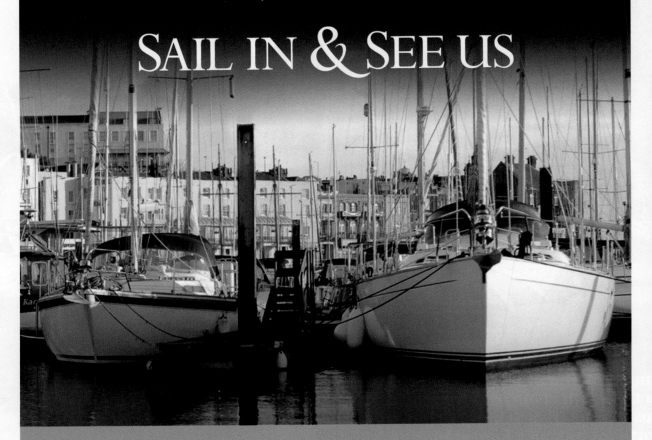

Port of Ramsgate
Royal Harbour Marina

SAIL IN & SEE US

Have you considered a permanent mooring at the Royal Harbour Marina, Ramsgate?

- Kent's premier marina offering safe mooring 365 days a year with superb facilities
- 24 hour security, CCTV and foot patrols
- 40 tonne boat hoist
- Good road access

Please visit our website at www.portoframsgate.co.uk for our fees and charges

Contact us on: 01843 572100 or email portoframsgate@thanet.gov.uk

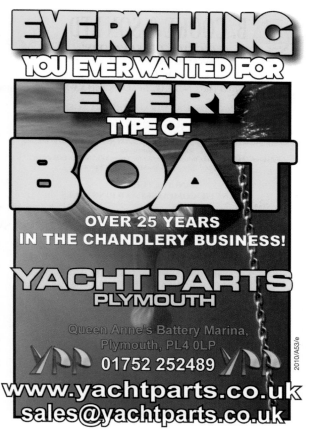

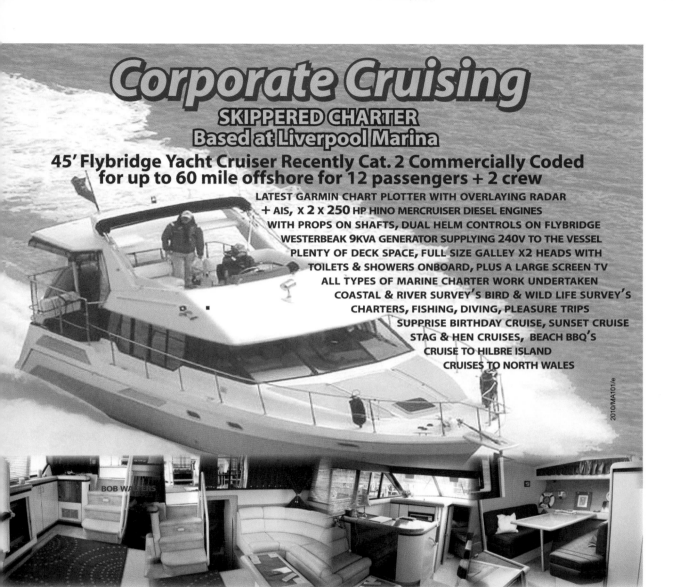

Sailing HOLIDAYS IN IRELAND

CALL US NOW FOR 2010

KILRUSH MARINA & BOATYARD
+353-65-9052072

BANGOR MARINA
028 9145 3297

CARLINGFORD MARINA
+353-4293-7307

FENIT HARBOUR MARINA
+353-66-7136231

DINGLE MARINA
+353-66-9151629

MALAHIDE MARINA
+353-1-845412*

LAWRENCE COVE MARINA
+353-27-75044

DUBLIN CITY MOORINGS
+353-1-818 330

SALVE MARINE
+353-21-831145

DUN LAOGHAIRE MARINA
+353-1-2020040

DONEGAL · LARNE · BELFAST · SLIGO · GALWAY · R. Shannon · Lough Derg · DUBLIN · LIMERICK · ROSSLARE · KILLARNEY · CORK

CASTLEPARK MARINA
+353-21-4774959

WATERFORD CITY MARINA
+353-51-309900

KILMORE QUAY MARINA
+353-53-29955

Sail in Ireland and enjoy the experience of a lifetime

Further information: Sailing Holidays in Ireland, Trident Hotel, Kinsale, Co. Cork, Ireland. Tel +353-21-477 2927.

www.sailingireland.com   www.irelandwatersports.net   Email:sailirl@indigo

ADLARD COLES NAUTICAL
WEATHER FORECASTS
BY FAX & TELEPHONE

Coastal/Inshore	2-day by Fax	5-day by Phone
Anglia	09065 222 345	09068 969 645
East	09065 222 344	09068 969 644
North East	09065 222 343	09068 969 643
Scotland East	09065 222 342	09068 969 642
National (3-5 day)	09065 222 340	09068 969 640

Offshore	2-5 day by Fax	2-5 day by Phone
English Channel	09065 222 357	09068 969 657
Southern North Sea	09065 222 358	09068 969 658
Northern North Sea	09065 222 362	09068 969 662
North West Scotland	09065 222 361	09068 969 661

09068 CALLS COST 60P PER MIN. 09065 CALLS COST £1.50 PER MIN.

Reference data

0.1 THE ALMANAC

• Acknowledgements

The Editors thank the many official bodies and individuals for information and advice given in the compilation of this Almanac. These include: UKHO, Trinity House, Northern Lighthouse Board, HM Nautical Almanac Office, HMSO, HM Revenue & Customs, Meteorological Office, BBC, IBA, MCA, RNLI, PLA, ABP, Koninklijke Nederlandse Redding Maatschappij (KNRM), countless Harbourmasters and our many individual Harbour Agents.

• Permissions

Chartlets, tidal stream diagrams and curves are reproduced from Admiralty charts and publications (ALL, ASD, ATT and ALRS) by permission of the UKHO (Licence No GB DQ – 001 – Adlard Coles) and the Controller of HMSO.

UK and foreign tidal predictions are supplied by and with the permission of UKHO and by the German and Dutch HOs with permission to use the tidal predictions stated:

BSH (German HO): Helgoland. (Authorisation 11123/2008-07).

Rijkswaterstaat, Netherlands: Vlissingen, Hoek van Holland.

Vlaamse Hydrografie, Belgium: Zeebrugge.

Extracts from the *International Code of Signals 1969* and *Meteorological Office Weather Services for Shipping* are published by permission of the Controller of HMSO.

Ephemerides are derived from HM Nautical Almanac by permission of HM Nautical Almanac Office and the Council for the Central Laboratory of the Research Councils.

• Disclaimer

No National HO has verified the information in this product and none accepts liability for the accuracy of reproduction or any modifications made thereafter. No National HO warrants that this product satisfies national or international regulations regarding the use of the appropriate products for navigation.

Chartlets in this Almanac are not intended for navigational use, only for reference. Always consult fully updated navigational charts for the latest information.

• Improvements

This edition contains many hundreds of corrections. Tide Tables for 6 new Standard Ports (Margate, Harwich, River Tees, Rosyth, Invergordon and Zeebrugge) have been included, and many of the harbour chartlets have been fully revised.

Readers' suggestions for improving the content or layout are always most welcome, especially those based on experience and practical use at sea. Not every suggestion can be implemented, but all are carefully considered.

Please send your comments, by email if possible, to: updates@reedsalmanac.co.uk. Otherwise a note to Adlard Coles Nautical (see page v) will be forwarded to the relevant Editor.

• Notifying errors

Although the Almanac has been very carefully compiled from countless sources, a few errors may still occur. Please let us know if you spot any.

• Harbour Agents

Our harbour agents provide invaluable local information which may not appear in official sources. Vacancies are advertised on our website www.reedsalmanac.co.uk. If you would like to earn a free copy of Reeds Nautical Almanac every year, please apply to Adlard Coles Nautical (page v) with a brief summary of your nautical qualifications.

• Sources of corrections

This Almanac is corrected to Weekly edition No. 26/2009 of Admiralty Notices to Mariners.

Corrections to Admiralty charts and publications can be downloaded from the UKHO website or obtained from Admiralty Chart Agents (ACA) and certain Port Authorities.

• Updates

Free monthly updates, from January to June, can be downloaded at www.reedsalmanac.co.uk/updates. Please register online if you would like to receive an email reminder when the updates are available for download.

0.2 ABBREVIATIONS AND SYMBOLS

The following more common abbreviations and symbols feature in Reeds Almanacs. Other Admiralty chart symbols are on the flap of the inside back cover. Chart 5011 (a booklet) is the complete reference for Symbols and Abbreviations on charts.

@	Internet café/access
AB	Alongside berth
ABP	Associated British Ports
AC, ⏢	Shore power (electrical)
AC, ACA	Admiralty Chart, AC Agent
ACN	Adlard Coles Nautical (Publisher)
Aff Mar	Affaires Maritimes
AIS	Automatic Identification System
aka	Also known as
ALL	Admiralty List of Lights
ALRS	Admiralty List of Radio Signals
Al	Alternating light
AM	Amplitude Modulation
ANWB	Association of road & waterway users (Dutch)
Appr	Approach(es)
ASD	Admiralty Sailing Directions (Pilot)
ATM	Automatic telling machine, cashpoint
ATT	Admiralty Tide Tables
ATT	Atterisage (landfall/SWM) buoy
Auto	Météo Répondeur Automatique
B.	Bay, Black
Bar, ⌂	Licensed bar, Public house, Inn
BH	Boat Hoist (+ tons)
Bkwtr	Breakwater
BMF	British Marine Federation
BMS	Bulletin Météorologique Spécial
Bn, bcn(s)	Beacon, beacon(s)
BSH	German Hydrographic Office/chart(s)
BST	British Summer Time (= DST)
Bu	Blue
BWB	British Waterways Board
By(s)	Buoy, buoys
BY, ⚓	Boatyard
C.	Cape, Cabo, Cap
C	Crane (+ tons)
©	National Coastwatch Institution station
ca	Cable (approx 185m)
Cas	Castle
CD	Chart datum (vertical)
CEVNI	Code Européen de Voies de la Navigation Intérieure (inland waterways signs etc)
cf	Compare, cross-refer to
CG	Coastguard
CH, ⌂	Chandlery
chan	Channel (navigational)
Ch	Channel (VHF)

Ch, ⌖	Church
Chy	Chimney
COG	Course Over the Ground
Col	Column, pillar, obelisk
CPA	Closest Point of Approach
CROSS	Centre Régional Opérationnel de Surveillance et Sauvetage (= MRCC)
CRS	Coast Radio Station
D	Diesel (supply by hose)
Dec	Declination (of the Sun)
dest	Destroyed
DF, D/F	Radio Direction Finding
DG	De-gaussing (range)
DGPS	Differential GPS
Dia	Diaphone (fog signal)
discont	Discontinued
Dn(s)	Dolphin(s)
DR	Dead Reckoning
DSC	Digital Selective Calling
DST	Daylight Saving Time
DW	Deep Water (route)
DYC	Dutch Yacht Chart(s)
DZ	Danger Zone (buoy)
E	East
ECM	East cardinal mark (buoy/beacon)
ED	Existence doubtful, European Datum
EEA	European Economic Area
EI	Electrical repairs
Ⓔ	Electronic repairs
Elev	Elevation
Ent	Entrance, entry, enter
EP, △	Estimated position
ETA	Estimated Time of Arrival
ETD	Estimated Time of Departure
F	Fixed light
f	Fine (eg sand)
F&A	Fore and aft (berth/mooring)
Fcst	Forecast
FFL	Fixed and Flashing light
Fl	Flashing light
FM	Frequency Modulation
Foc	Free of charge
Fog Det lt	Fog Detector light
Freq, Fx	Frequency
FS	Flagstaff, Flagpole
ft	Foot, feet
Ft	Fort
FV	Fishing vessel
FW, ⚓	Fresh water supply
G	Gravel, Green
Gas	Calor Gas
Gaz	Camping Gaz
GC	Great Circle
GDOP	Geometrical Dilution of Precision (GPS)
GHA	Greenwich Hour Angle
GLA	General Lighthouse Authority
GMDSS	Global Maritime Distress & Safety System
grt	Gross Registered Tonnage
Gy	Grey
H, h, Hrs	Hour(s)
H−, H+	Minutes before/after the whole hour
H24	Continuous
HAT	Highest Astronomical Tide
HF	High Frequency
HFP	High Focal Plane (buoy)
HIE	Highlands & Islands Enterprise
HJ	Day service only, sunrise to sunset
HM	Harbour Master
HMRC	HM Revenue & Customs
HMSO	Her Majesty's Stationery Office
HN	Night service only, sunset to sunrise
HO	Office hours, Hydrographic Office
(hor)	Horizontally disposed (lights)
hPa	Hectopascal (= 1millibar)
HT	High Tension (overhead electricity line)
HW	High Water
HX	No fixed hours
IALA	International Association of Lighthouse Authorities
iaw	In accordance with
ICAO	International Civil Aviation Organisation
IDM	Isolated Danger Mark (buoy/beacon)
IHO	International Hydrographic Organisation
IMO	International Maritime Organisation
INMARSAT	International Maritime Satellite Organisation
intens	Intensified (light sector)
IPTS	International Port Traffic Signals
IQ	Interrupted quick flashing light
IRPCS	International Regulations for the Prevention of Collisions at Sea
Is, I	Island, Islet
ISAF	International Sailing Federation
Iso	Isophase light
ITU	International Telecommunications Union
ITZ	Inshore Traffic Zone (TSS)
IUQ	Interrupted ultra quick flashing light
IVQ	Interrupted very quick flashing light
JRCC	Joint Rescue Co-ordination Centre
kn	knot(s)
Kos	Kosangas
kW	Kilowatts
L	Lake, Loch, Lough, Landing place
Lat	Latitude
LAT	Lowest Astronomical Tide
Lanby, ⊂	Large automatic navigational buoy
LB, ⬩	Lifeboat, inshore lifeboat
Ldg	Leading (light)
LF	Low frequency
L Fl	Long flash
LH	Left hand
L/L	Latitude/Longitude
LNG	Liquefied Natural Gas
LNTM	Local Notice To Mariners
LOA	Length overall
Long	Longitude
LPG	Liquefied Petroleum Gas
LT	Local time
Lt(s), ✫ ✩	Light(s)
⚓	Light float, minor
Lt V, ⊂	Light vessel; Lt float, major; Lanby
M	Moorings, nautical (sea) mile(s), Mud
m	Metre(s)
Mag	Magnetic, magnitude (of Star)
mb	Millibar (= 1 hectopascal, hPa)
MCA	Maritime and Coastguard Agency
ME	Marine engineering repairs

Météo	Météorologie (weather)
MHWN	Mean High Water Neaps
MHWS	Mean High Water Springs
MHz	Megahertz
ML	Mean Level (tidal)
MLWN	Mean Low Water Neaps
MLWS	Mean Low Water Springs
MMSI	Maritime Mobile Service Identity
Mo	Morse
Mon	Monument, Monday
MRCC	Maritime Rescue Co-ordination Centre
MSI	Maritime Safety Information
N	North
Navi	Navicarte (French charts)
NB	Nota Bene, Notice Board
NCI, ©	National Coastwatch Institution
NCM	North Cardinal Mark (buoy/beacon)
NGS	Naval Gunfire Support (buoy)
NM	Notice(s) to Mariners
nps	Neap tides
NP	Naval Publication (plus number)
NT	National Trust (land/property)
Obscd	Obscured
Obstn	Obstruction
Oc	Occulting light
ODAS	Ocean Data Acquisition System (buoy)
Or	Orange
OT	Other times
OWF	Offshore wind farm
P	Petrol (supply by hose), Pebbles
(P)	Preliminary (NM)
PA	Position approximate
Pax	Passenger(s)
PC	Portuguese chart
PD	Position doubtful
PHM	Port-hand Mark (buoy/beacon)
PLA	Port of London Authority
PO, ✉	Post Office
prom	Prominent
PSSA	Particularly Sensitive Sea Area
Pt(e), Pta	Point(e), Punta
⚓	Pump-out facility
Q	Quick flashing light
QHM	Queen's Harbour Master
R	Red, Restaurant ✕, River, Rock
Racon	Radar transponder beacon
Ramark	Radar beacon
RCD	Recreational Craft Directive
RDF	Radio Direction Finding
RG	Emergency RDF station
RH	Right hand
Rk, Rky	Rock, Rocky
RMG	Reeds Marina Guide
RNLI	Royal National Lifeboat Institution
ROI	Republic of Ireland
R/T	Radiotelephony
Ru	Ruins
RYA	Royal Yachting Association
S	South, Sand
S, St, Ste	Saint(s)
SAMU	Service d'Aide Médicale Urgente (ambulance)
SAR	Search and Rescue
SC	Sailing Club, Spanish chart
SCM	South Cardinal Mark (buoy/beacon)
SD	Sailing Directions, Semi-diameter (of sun)
SD	Sounding of doubtful depth
sf	Stiff
Sh	Shells, Shoal
SHM	Simplified Harmonic Method (tides),
SHM	Starboard-hand Mark (buoy/beacon)
SHOM	French Hydrographic Office/Chart
Si	Silt
SIGNI	Signalisation de la Navigation Intérieure
SM	Sailmaker
✕	Shipwright (esp wooden hulls)
SMS	Short Message Service (mobile texting)
SNSM	Société Nationale de Sauvetage en Mer
so	Soft (eg mud)
SOG	Speed Over the Ground
SOLAS	Safety of Life at Sea (IMO Convention)
sp	Spring tides
SPM	Special Mark (buoy/beacon)
SR	Sunrise
SRR	Search and Rescue Region
SS	Sunset, Signal Station
SSB	Single Sideband (Radio)
Stbd	Starboard
subm	Submerged
SWM	Safe Water Mark (buoy/beacon)
(T), (Temp)	Temporary
tbc	To be confirmed
tbn	To be notified
TD	Temporarily discontinued (fog signal)
TE	Temporarily extinguished (light)
tfn	Till further notice
Tr, twr	Tower
T/R	Traffic Report (tells the CG your route etc)
TSS	Traffic Separation Scheme
≠	In transit with, ie ldg marks/lts
u/mkd	Unmarked (feature/hazard)
UQ	Ultra Quick flashing light
UT	Universal Time (= approx GMT)
Var	Variation (magnetic)
Vel	Velocity
(vert)	Vertically disposed (lights)
Vi	Violet
VLCC	Very large crude carrier (Oil tanker)
VNF	Voie Navigable de France (canals)
VQ	Very Quick flashing light
VTS	Vessel Traffic Service
W	West, White
WCM	West Cardinal Mark (buoy/beacon)
⏉	Wind turbine
wef	With effect from
WGS	World Geodetic System (GPS datum)
WIP	Work in progress
Wk, ⚓	Wreck
WPT, ⊕	Waypoint
Wx	Weather
WZ	Code for UK coastal navigation warning
Y	Yellow, Amber, Orange
YC, ⚑	Yacht Club

0.3   PASSAGE PLANNING FORM

DATE .... FROM ....ETD .... VIA .... TO .... ETA ....

TIMES OF SUNRISE .... SUNSET .... MOON RISE .... MOONSET .... WATCH SYSTEM ☐

CHARTS ☐   DOCUMENTS ☐   CUSTOMS ☐   PAY DUES ☐   CG (T/R) ☐   FUEL ☐   WATER ☐   FOOD ☐

WEATHER FORECAST ....

DEPARTURE PORT VHF .... HM ☎ ....

BRIDGE TIMES ....

LOCK/GATE TIMES..

BAR CROSSING TIMES ....

DEPARTURE WINDOW ....

DEPARTURE PROCEDURE ....

....

VTS DETAILS ....

....

....

STANDARD PORT, TIDES (SP/NP, HW/LW TIMES & HEIGHTS)

....

....

DEPARTURE PORT TIDES (HW/LW TIMES & HEIGHTS) ....

TIDAL STREAMS ON DEPARTURE ....

....

....

EN ROUTE

TIDAL STREAM ANALYSIS ....

....

....

....

....

TIDAL GATES (TIMES) ....

TIDE RACES ....

....

TRAFFIC SEPARATION SCHEMES ....

PROHIBITED AREAS/DANGERS ....

PRINCIPAL LIGHTS/MARKS ....

....

LEG DETAILS

FROM	TO	WPT	TRK°M	DIST	TIME	REMARKS

DESTINATION PORT VHF .... HM ☎ ....

ARRIVAL PROCEDURE ....

....

BAR CROSSING TIMES ....

LOCK/GATE/SILL TIMES ....

BRIDGE TIMES ....

ACCESS WINDOW ....

ALTERNATE PORT VHF .... HM ☎ ....

ARRIVAL PROCEDURE ....

....

BAR CROSSING TIMES ....

LOCK/GATE/SILL TIMES ....

BRIDGE TIMES ....

ACCESS WINDOW ....

0.4 PASSAGE PLANNING

Before you start to navigate you need to plan: where you are going, how to get there and what factors may influence the plan. To most people this is commonsense; it is also the law. Guidance is given to small craft skippers in the MCA's *Pleasure Craft Information Pack* at www.mcga.gov.uk/c4mca/mcga-safety_information.htm.

SOLAS V Regulation 34 requires that all passages outside sheltered waters should be pre-planned. At the least, the following should be considered:

- **Limitations of the vessel.** Seaworthiness; suitably equipped and provisioned (food, water, fuel).
- **Limitations of the crew.** Experience, ability and stamina.
- **Navigational dangers**. Awareness and avoidance; use of up-to-date charts and publications.
- **Tides.** Times and heights; best use of tidal streams.
- **Weather.** Suitability for passage; forecast updates.
- **Contingency plan.** Deteriorating weather; gear failure; accident or injury.
- **GPS.** Equipment failure; ability to navigate 'manually'.
- **Information ashore.** Shore contact; CG66 - Voluntary Identification Scheme.

Although the passage plan need not be recorded on paper, in the event of legal action a written plan is clear proof that planning has been done. It can also be referred to during the passage. A suggested passage planning form is on the previous page. When completed this would constitute a reasonable passage plan. The blank form may be photocopied and modified to suit individual needs.

Before completing the form:

- Decide the aim; it is not always obvious.
- Gather the facts; time consuming but essential.
- Assess all available information.
- Formulate the plan; think of all contingencies.

0.5 HORIZONTAL DATUMS

GPS uses the World Geodetic System 84 datum (WGS84). With the exception of much of the coast of Ireland and the west coast of Scotland, Admiralty charts of UK waters have now been converted to WGS84. All harbour chartlets in this Almanac are referenced to WGS84.

GPS fixes can be plotted directly onto charts which are referenced to WGS84 but not onto charts which are still referenced to another datum. Before plotting WGS84 coordinates read from the GPS receiver, they must be converted to the datum of the chart in use. The datum used is always printed on the chart, normally under 'SATELLITE-DERIVED POSITIONS' which gives the Lat/Long corrections (which can amount to several hundred metres) to be applied.

Most receivers contain many datums. The navigator has two options:

- Set the receiver to WGS84. Before plotting positions, manually apply the corrections given on the chart. This option is advised by UKHO.
- Set the receiver to the datum of the chart in use. The datum corrections will automatically be applied by the receiver's software. This method is convenient but not the most accurate due to the random nature of the differences and software limitations.

0.6 COMMUNICATIONS

Radio Telephony (R/T)

VHF gives a range about 30-40M depending on the aerial heights of both the shore station and the yacht.

Give your position in Lat/Long or as the yacht's bearing and distance **from** a charted object, eg 'My position 225° Start Point 4M' means you are 4M SW of the Start Point. Use the 360° True bearing notation and the 24 hour clock (0000 to 2359), specifying UT, LT etc.

VHF sets may be Simplex, ie transmit and receive on the same frequency, so that only one person can talk at a time; Semi-Duplex, ie transmit and receive on different frequencies; or Duplex, ie simultaneous semi-duplex, so that conversation is normal.

Marine VHF frequencies are in the band 156·00 –174·00 MHz. Frequencies are known by their international channel number (Ch), as shown below.

Channels are grouped according to three main purposes, but some can be used for more than one purpose.

- ***Public correspondence:*** (via Coast Radio Stations). Ch 26, 27, 25, 24, 23, 28, 04, 01, 03, 02, 07, 05, 84, 87, 86, 83, 85, 88, 61, 64, 65, 62, 66, 63, 60, 82, 78, 81. All channels can be used for duplex.

- ***Inter-ship:*** Ch 06, 08, 10, 13, 09, **72**, 73, 69, **77**, 15, 17. These are all simplex channels. It is as well to remember the **recommended** channels so that, if called on Ch 16, you can nominate an inter-ship working channel without delay.

- ***Port Operations:***
Simplex: Ch 12, 14, 11, 13, 09, 68, 71, 74, 69, 73, 17, 15.
Duplex: Ch 20, 22, 18, 19, 21, 05, 07, 02, 03, 01, 04, 78, 82, 79, 81, 80, 60, 63, 66, 62, 65, 64, 61, 84.

The following channels have one specific purpose:

Ch 0 (156·00 MHz): SAR ops, not available to yachts.

Ch 10 (156·50 MHz), **23** (161·750 MHz), **84** (161·825 MHz) and **86** (161·925 MHz): MSI broadcasts. The optimum channel number is stated on Ch 16 in the announcement prior to the broadcast itself.

Ch 13 (156·650 MHz): Inter-ship communications relating to safety of navigation; a possible channel for calling a merchant ship if no contact on Ch 16.

Ch 16 (156·80 MHz): Distress, Safety and calling. Ch 16, in parallel with DSC Ch 70, will be monitored by ships, CG rescue centres (and, in some areas, any remaining Coast radio stations) for Distress and Safety until further notice. Yachts should monitor Ch 16. After an initial call, stations concerned **must** switch to a working channel, except for Distress and Safety matters.

Ch 67 (156·375 MHz): Small craft safety channel used by all UK CG centres, accessed via Ch 16.

Ch 70 (156·525 MHz): Digital Selective Calling for Distress and Safety purposes under GMDSS.

Ch 80 (157·025 MHz): Primary working channel between yachts and UK marinas.

Ch M (157·85 MHz): Secondary working channel, formerly known as Ch 37, but no longer.

Ch M2 (161·425 MHz): for race control, with Ch M as standby. YCs may apply to use Ch M2.

0.7   DISTRESS CALLS

Distress signal - MAYDAY

Distress only applies to a situation where a vessel or person is in *grave and imminent danger and requires immediate assistance*. A MAYDAY call should usually be sent on VHF Ch 16 or MF 2182 kHz, but any frequency may be used if help would thus be obtained more quickly.

Distress, Urgency and Safety messages from vessels at sea are free of charge. A Distress call has priority over all other transmissions. If heard, cease all transmissions that may interfere with the Distress call or messages, and listen on the frequency concerned.

Brief your crew so they are all able to send a Distress message. The MAYDAY message format (below) should be displayed near the radio. Before making the call:

- Switch on radio (check main battery switch is ON)
- Select HIGH power (25 watts)
- Select VHF Ch 16 (or 2182 kHz for MF)
- Press and hold down the transmit button, and say slowly and distinctly:

- **MAYDAY MAYDAY MAYDAY**
- **THIS IS** ....
  (name of boat, spoken three times)
- **MAYDAY** ....
  (name of boat spoken once)
- **MY POSITION IS** ....
  (latitude and longitude, true bearing and distance *from* a known point, or general location)
- **Nature of distress** ....
  (sinking, on fire etc)
- **Help required** ....
  (immediate assistance)
- **Number of persons on board** ....
- **Any other important, helpful information** ....
  (you are taking to the liferaft; distress rockets are being fired etc)
- **OVER**

On completion of the Distress message, release the transmit button and listen. The boat's position is of vital importance and should be repeated if time allows.

Vessels with GMDSS equipment should make a MAYDAY call on Ch 16 *after* sending a DSC Distress alert on VHF Ch 70 or MF 2187·5 kHz.

0.7.1   MAYDAY acknowledgement

In coastal waters an immediate acknowledgement should be expected, as follows:

> **MAYDAY** ....
> (name of station sending the Distress message, spoken three times)
>
> **THIS IS** ....
> (name of station acknowledging, spoken three times)
>
> **RECEIVED MAYDAY**

If an acknowledgement is not received, check the set and repeat the Distress call.

If you hear a Distress message, write down the details and,

if you can help, acknowledge accordingly - but only after giving an opportunity for the nearest Coastguard station or some larger vessel to do so.

0.7.2   MAYDAY relay

If you hear a Distress message from a vessel, and it is not acknowledged, you should pass on the message as follows:

> **MAYDAY RELAY** ....
> (spoken three times)
>
> **THIS IS** ....
> (name of vessel re-transmitting the Distress message, spoken three times), followed by the intercepted message.

0.7.3   Control of MAYDAY traffic

A MAYDAY call imposes general radio silence until the vessel concerned or some other authority (eg the nearest Coastguard) cancels the Distress. If necessary the station controlling Distress traffic may impose radio silence as follows:

> **SEELONCE MAYDAY,** followed by its name or other identification, on the Distress frequency.
>
> If some other station nearby believes it necessary to do likewise, it may transmit:
>
> **SEELONCE DISTRESS,** followed by its name or other identification.

0.7.4   Relaxing radio silence

When complete radio silence is no longer necessary, the controlling station may relax radio silence as follows, indicating that restricted working may be resumed:

> **MAYDAY**
>
> **ALL STATIONS, ALL STATIONS, ALL STATIONS**
>
> **THIS IS** ....
> (name or callsign)
>
> The time ....
>
> The name of the vessel in distress ....
>
> **PRUDONCE**

Normal working on the Distress frequency may then be resumed, having listened carefully before transmitting. Subsequent calls from the casualty should be prefixed by the Urgency signal (0.8).

If Distress working continues on other frequencies these will be identified. For example, PRUDONCE on 2182 kHz, but SEELONCE on VHF Ch 16.

0.7.5   Cancelling radio silence

When the problem is resolved, the Distress call must be cancelled by the co-ordinating station using the prowords SEELONCE FEENEE as follows:

> **MAYDAY**
>
> **ALL STATIONS, ALL STATIONS, ALL STATIONS**
>
> **THIS IS** ....
> (name or callsign)
>
> The time ....
>
> The name of the vessel in distress ....
>
> **SEELONCE FEENEE**

0.8   URGENCY AND SAFETY CALLS

Urgency signal - PAN PAN

The radio Urgency prefix, consisting of the words PAN PAN spoken three times, indicates that a vessel, or station, has *a very urgent message concerning the safety of a ship or person*. It may be used when urgent medical advice is needed.

This is an example of an Urgency call:

> PAN PAN, PAN PAN, PAN PAN
>
> ALL STATIONS, ALL STATIONS, ALL STATIONS
>
> THIS IS YACHT SEABIRD, SEABIRD, SEABIRD
>
> Two nine zero degrees Needles lighthouse two miles
>
> Dismasted and propeller fouled
>
> Drifting east north east towards Shingles Bank
>
> Require urgent tow
>
> OVER

PAN PAN messages take priority over all traffic except Distress, and are sent on Ch 16 or 2182 kHz. They should be cancelled when the urgency is over.

If the message is long (eg a medical call) or communications traffic is heavy, it may be passed on a working frequency after an initial call on Ch 16 or 2182 kHz. At the end of the initial call you should indicate that you are switching to a working frequency.

If you hear an Urgency call react in the same way as for a Distress call.

0.8.1   Safety signal - SÉCURITÉ

The word SÉCURITÉ (pronounced SAY-CURE-E-TAY) spoken three times, indicates that the station is about to transmit an important navigational or meteorological warning. Such messages usually originate from a CG Centre or a Coast Radio Station, and are transmitted on a working channel after an announcement on the distress/calling channel (Ch 16 or 2182 kHz).

Safety messages are usually addressed to 'All stations', and are often transmitted at the end of the first available silence period. An example of a Sécurité message is:

> SÉCURITÉ, SÉCURITÉ, SÉCURITÉ ....
>
> THIS IS ....
> (CG Centre or Coast Radio Station callsign, spoken three times)
>
> ALL STATIONS ....
> (spoken three times) followed by instructions to change channel, then the message.

0.9   GMDSS

The Global Maritime Distress and Safety System (GMDSS) is a sophisticated, but complex, semi-automatic, third-generation communications system. Although not compulsory for yachts, its potential for saving life, particularly when far offshore and out of VHF range, is so great that every yachtsman should consider it. Equipment costs continue to fall. Training courses, leading to the award of the Short Range Certificate (SRC) of Competence, are widely available.

0.9.1   Purpose

GMDSS enables a coordinated SAR operation to be mounted rapidly and reliably anywhere at sea. To this end, terrestrial and satellite communications and navigation equipment is used to alert SAR authorities ashore and ships in the vicinity to a Distress incident or Urgency situation. GMDSS also promulgates MSI (Maritime Safety Information).

0.9.2   Sea areas

For the purposes of GMDSS, the world's sea areas are divided into 4 categories (A1-4), defined mainly by the range of radio communications. These are:

A1	An area within R/T coverage of at least one VHF Coastguard or Coast radio station in which continuous VHF alerting is available via DSC. Range: 20–50M from the CG/CRS.
A2	An area, excluding sea area A1, within R/T coverage of at least one MF CG/CRS in which continuous DSC alerting is available. Range: approx 50–250M from the CG/CRS.
A3	An area between 70°N and 70°S, excluding sea areas A1 and A2, within coverage of HF or an Inmarsat satellite in which continuous alerting is available.
A4	An area outside sea areas A1, A2 and A3, ie the polar regions, within coverage of HF.

In each category certain types of radio equipment must be carried. In A1 areas VHF DSC; A2 areas MF or HF DSC; A3 areas SatCom; A4 MF/HF.

0.9.3   Digital Selective Calling

DSC is a vital component of GMDSS. It is so called because information is sent by a burst of digital code; selective because it can be addressed to a specific DSC-equipped vessel or to a selected group of vessels.

In GMDSS every vessel and shore station has a 9-digit number, or MMSI (Maritime Mobile Service Identity), which is in effect an automatic, electronic callsign.

DSC is used to transmit Distress alerts from ships, and to receive Distress acknowledgements from ships or shore stations. DSC is also used to send Urgency and Safety alerts; to relay Distress alerts; and for routine calling and answering. A thorough working knowledge is needed. A typical VHF/DSC Distress alert might be sent as follows:

- Briefly press the (red, guarded) Distress button. The set automatically switches to Ch 70 (DSC Distress channel). Press again for 5 seconds to transmit a basic Distress alert with position and time. The radio then reverts to Ch 16.

- If time permits, select the nature of the distress from the menu, eg Collision, then press the Distress button for 5 seconds to send a full Distress alert.

A CG/CRS should automatically send an acknowledgement on Ch 70 before replying on Ch 16. Ships in range should reply directly on Ch 16. When a DSC Distress acknowledgement has been received, or after about 15 seconds, the vessel in distress should transmit a MAYDAY message by voice on Ch 16, including its MMSI.

Fig 0(4) *Distress and life saving signals*

(1) Signals to be used by Ships, Aircraft or Persons in Distress

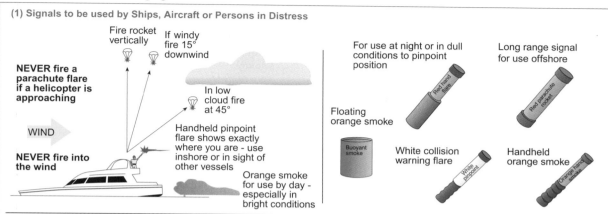

Fire rocket vertically

If windy fire 15° downwind

In low cloud fire at 45°

NEVER fire a parachute flare if a helicopter is approaching

WIND

NEVER fire into the wind

Handheld pinpoint flare shows exactly where you are - use inshore or in sight of other vessels

Orange smoke for use by day - especially in bright conditions

For use at night or in dull conditions to pinpoint position

Long range signal for use offshore

Red hand flare

Red parachute rocket

Floating orange smoke

Buoyant smoke

White collision warning flare

White pinpoint

Handheld orange smoke

Orange hand smoke

(2) Replies from life-saving stations etc. to distress signals made by ships or persons

Orange smoke signal

White star rocket - three single signals fired at intervals of about one minute

Meaning
'You are seen - assistance will be given as soon as possible'

(3) Surface to Air Signals

Message	International Code of Signals		ICAO Visual Signals
'I require assistance'	**'V'**	$\boxtimes$ (· · · —)	V
'I require medical assistance'	**'W'**	$\blacksquare$ (· — — —)	X
'No' or 'negative'	**'N'**	(— ·)	N
'Yes' or 'affirmative'	**'C'**	(— · — · ·)	Y
'Proceed in this direction'		↑	

(4) Air to Surface replies

'Message understood'

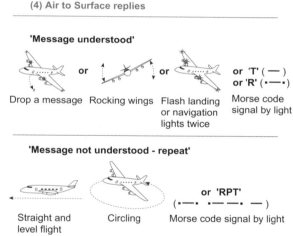

or   or   or 'T' (—)
                    or 'R' (· — ·)

Drop a message   Rocking wings   Flash landing or navigation lights twice   Morse code signal by light

'Message not understood - repeat'

or 'RPT'
(· — · · — · — —· —)

Straight and level flight   Circling   Morse code signal by light

(5) Air to Surface Direction Signals

Sequence of 3 manœuvres meaning proceed in this direction

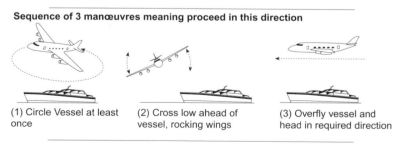

(1) Circle Vessel at least once

(2) Cross low ahead of vessel, rocking wings

(3) Overfly vessel and head in required direction

Your assistance is no longer required

Cross low astern of vessel rocking wings

Note: as an alternative to rocking wings, the aircraft engine pitch or volume may be varied

(6) Surface to Air replies

'Message understood - I will comply'

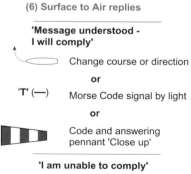

Change course or direction

or

'T' (—)   Morse Code signal by light

or

Code and answering pennant 'Close up'

'I am unable to comply'

'N' (— ·)   Morse Code signal by light

or

International flag 'N'

0.10 WEATHER BROADCASTS IN THE UK

BBC Radio 4 Shipping forecast

BBC Radio 4 broadcasts shipping forecasts at:

0048 LT[1]	LW, MW, FM
0520 LT[1]	LW, MW, FM
1201 LT	LW only
1754 LT	LW, FM (Sat/Sun)

[1] Includes weather reports from coastal stations

Frequencies

LW		198 kHz
MW	Tyneside:	603 kHz
	London:	720 kHz
	Aberdeen:	1449 kHz
FM	England:	92·4–94·6 MHz
	Scotland:	91·3–96·1 MHz
		103·5–104·9 MHz

Contents of the Shipping forecast

The forecast contains:

A summary of gale warnings in force at time of issue; a general synopsis of weather systems and their expected development over the next 24 hours; and a forecast of wind direction/force, weather and visibility in each sea area for the next 24 hours.

Gale warnings are also broadcast at the earliest juncture in Radio 4 programmes after receipt, as well as after the next news bulletin. Sea area **Trafalgar** is only included in the 0048 forecast.

Strong Wind Warnings are issued by the Met Office whenever winds of Force 6 or more are expected over coastal waters up to 5M offshore.

Shipping forecasts cover large sea areas, and rarely include the detailed variations that may occur near land. The Inshore waters forecast (see 0.10.1) can be more helpful to mariners on coastal passages.

Weather reports from coastal stations follow the 0048 and 0520 forecasts. They include wind direction and force, present weather, visibility, and sea-level pressure and tendency, if available. The stations are shown below in 0.10.1 and in Fig 0(2).

0.10.1 BBC Radio 4 Inshore waters forecast

A forecast for inshore waters (up to 12M offshore) around the UK and N Ireland, valid until 1800, is broadcast after the 0048 and 0520 coastal station reports.

It includes a general synopsis, forecasts of wind direction and force, visibility and weather for stretches of inshore waters.

These are defined by well-known places and headlands from Cape Wrath clockwise via Orkney, Shetland, Rattray Head, Berwick-upon-Tweed, Whitby, Gibraltar Point, North Foreland and Selsey Bill.

Reports of actual weather at the stations below are only broadcast after the 0048 inshore waters forecast: Boulmer, *Bridlington*, Sheerness, St Catherine's Pt*, *Lerwick*, Wick*, Aberdeen and Leuchars.

These stations are shown in Fig 0(2). Asterisk* denotes an automatic station. Stations in italics also feature in the 0048 and 0520 shipping forecasts.

0.10.2 Terms used in weather bulletins

Speed of movement of pressure systems

Slowly	< 15 knots
Steadily	15–25 knots
Rather quickly	25–35 knots
Rapidly	35–45 knots
Very rapidly	> 45 knots

Visibility

Good	> 5 miles
Moderate	2–5 miles
Poor	1000 metres–2 miles
Fog	Less than 1000 metres

Timing of gale warnings

Imminent:	Within 6 hrs from time of issue
Soon:	6–12 hrs from time of issue
Later:	>12 hrs from time of issue

Barometric pressure changes (tendency)

Rising or falling slowly: Pressure change of 0·1 to 1·5 hPa/mb in the preceding 3 hours.

Rising or falling: Pressure change of 1·6 to 3·5 hPa/mb in the preceding 3 hours.

Rising or falling quickly: Pressure change of 3·6 to 6 hPa/mb in the preceding 3 hours.

Rising or falling very rapidly: Pressure change of more than 6 hPa/mb in the preceding 3 hours.

Now rising (or falling): Pressure has been falling (rising) or steady in the preceding 3 hours, but at the observation time was definitely rising (falling).

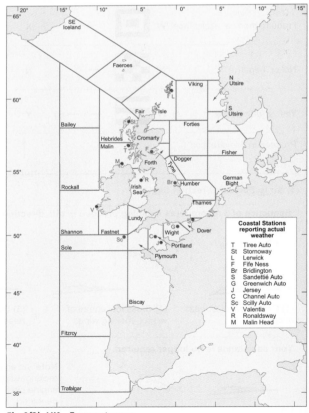

Fig 0(2) UK - Forecast areas

Coastal Stations reporting actual weather

T	Tiree Auto
St	Stornoway
L	Lerwick
F	Fife Ness
Br	Bridlington
S	Sandettié Auto
G	Greenwich Auto
J	Jersey
C	Channel Auto
Sc	Scilly Auto
V	Valentia
R	Ronaldsway
M	Malin Head

0.11 NAVTEX

Navtex uses a dedicated aerial, receiver and LCD screen or integral printer. The user inserts the required station(s) and message categories into the receiver. MSI is automatically displayed or printed. Interference between stations is avoided by time sharing and by limiting the range of transmitters to about 300M. Coverage of Europe is excellent. Navtex information applies only to the geographic area for which each station is responsible. Navtex is especially valuable if there is a language problem, where out of range of other sources, or otherwise occupied.

Two frequencies are used, 518 kHz and 490 kHz:
518 kHz messages are always in English and occasionally in the national language as well.

490 kHz (for clarity shown in red throughout this section) is used abroad for transmissions in the national language. In the UK it is used for inshore waters forecasts extended outlook and actual weather reports as shown in 0.11.3. 490 kHz and 518 kHz stations have different identification letters.

0.11.1 Message categories

A*	Navigational warnings
B*	Meteorological warnings
C	Ice reports
D*	SAR info and Piracy attack warnings
E	Weather forecasts
F	Pilot service
G	AIS
H	LORAN
I	Spare
J	SATNAV
K	Other electronic Navaids
L	Navwarnings additional to **A**
M-U	Spare
V-Y	Special services – as allocated
Z	No messages on hand

* These categories cannot be rejected by the receiver.

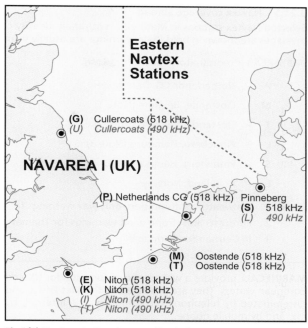

Fig 0(3) Navtex stations/areas – North Sea

0.11.4 Message numbering

Each message is prefixed by a group of four characters:

The 1st character is the ident of the station (eg **E** for Niton). The 2nd is the message category, see 0.11.1. The 3rd and 4th are message serial numbers from 01 to 99, then re-starting at 01. The serial number 00 is used for urgent messages which are always printed.

Messages which are corrupt or have already been printed are rejected. Weather messages, and certain other message types, are dated and timed. All Navtex messages end with NNNN.

0.11.2 UK 518 kHz stations

The times (UT) of weather messages are in bold; the times of an extended outlook (a further 2 or 3 days beyond the shipping forecast period) are in italics.

E – Niton	_0040_	0440	**0840**	1240	1640	**2040**
Thames clockwise to Fastnet, excluding Trafalgar.						
G – Cullercoats	_0100_	0500	**0900**	1300	1700	**2100**
Fair Isle clockwise to Thames, excluding N and S Utsire, Fisher and German Bight.						

0.11.3 UK 490 kHz stations

These provide forecasts for UK inshore waters (to 12M offshore), a national 3 day outlook for inshore waters and, at times in bold, reports of actual weather at the places listed below. To receive these reports select message category 'V' (0.11.1) on your Navtex receiver. Times (UT) of transmissions are listed in chronological order.

Actual Met data includes: Sea level pressure (mb), wind direction and speed (kn), weather, visibility (M), air and sea temperatures (°C), dewpoint temperature (°C) and mean wave height (m).

I – Niton	The Wash to St David's Head	0120	0520	**0920**	1320	1720	**2120**
Sandettie Lt V and other places westwards along the English Channel.							
U – Cullercoats	C. Wrath & Shetland to N Foreland	0320	0720	**1120**	1520	1920	**2320**
Sandettie Lt V, Manston, Shoeburyness, Weybourne, Donna Nook or Bridlington, Boulmer, Leuchars, Aberdeen, Lossiemouth, Wick, Kirkwall, Lerwick, Foula, K7 Met buoy, Sule Skerry.							

See overleaf for Navtex coverage abroad

0.11.5 Navtex coverage abroad

Selected Navtex stations in Metarea I, with their identity codes and transmission times are listed below. Times of weather messages are shown in **bold**. Gale warnings are usually transmitted 4 hourly.

METAREA I (Co-ordinator – UK)	Transmission times (UT)					
P – **Netherlands CG**, Den Helder	**0230**	0630	1030	**1430**	1830	2230
M – **Oostende**, Belgium (Note 1)	0200	0600	1000	1400	1800	2200
T – **Oostende**, Belgium (Note 2)	0310	**0710**	1110	1510	**1910**	2310
L – **Pinneberg**, Hamburg (Note 3)	0150	0550	0950	1350	1750	2150
S – **Pinneberg**, Hamburg	**0300**	**0700**	**1100**	**1500**	**1900**	**2300**
L – **Rogaland**, Norway	0150	0550	0950	**1350**	1750	2150

Note 1 No weather information, only Nav warnings for NavArea Juliett.

   2 Forecasts and strong wind warnings for Thames and Dover, plus nav info for the Belgian coast.

   3 In German for German Bight.

MARINECALL provides a wide range of forecasts for UK and European waters. They are produced by the Met Office and disseminated by telephone recordings, on the internet, by fax, and by mobile phone.

For further information contact:

Marinecall Customer Services, iTouch (UK) Ltd, Avalon House, 57-63 Scrutton Street, London EC2A 4PF.

☎ 0871 200 3985 (M-F 0900-1700); 📠 0870 600 4229. www.marinecall.co.uk marinecall@itouch.co.uk

Cost. 09068 calls cost 60p/min. 09065 faxes £1.50/min. SMS 25p/text.

0.12 WEATHER BY TELEPHONE

Dial ☎ **09068 96 96** + the required two digit area number on Fig 0(4), in green for inshore waters or red for offshore. These forecasts are updated up to 3 times a day and contain 5 main components as shown below:

- **Inshore and offshore forecasts for 48 hours**
- **Local waters forecast for days 1–5**
- **National forecast for days 6–10**
- **Outlook for one month ahead**

0.13 WEATHER BY FAX

Included are a 48 hours inshore and offshore forecast; a local area 1-5 day tabular forecast; a national forecast for days 6-10; plus synoptic charts valid for 48 hours and 2-5 days.

Fax forecasts contain the same data as those listed under 0.12, but are updated thrice daily. The Advance forecast (📠 09065 @ £1.50/min) contains slightly more detail than the Standard forecast (📠 09060 @ £1/min). The Fax numbers in Fig 0(4) are for the Advance service.

To obtain a forecast dial 📠 09065 22 23 plus the 2 digit area number in Fig 0(4), either green for inshore waters or red for offshore. After dialling press the Start or Receive button to start the transmission; be prepared for a slight delay as the data is downloaded to your fax machine.

0.13.1 Marinecall FaxDirect

Discounts to regular users of the Advance services include, for example over 3 months: 1 fax/week costs £38.76 inc VAT; 3 faxes/week £102.23; and 7 faxes/week £211.50.

Forecasts, updated 4 times/day, cover a 6 hrs period and include wind speed/direction, cloud cover, temperature, visibility and significant weather for the European areas below. These forecasts are also available online; see 5.9.

For Tel forecasts dial ☎ 09064 700 + 3 digits below.

For Fax forecasts dial 📠 09065 501 + 3 digits.

Area		☎	📠
NE France	(Dunkerque – Deauville)	421	611

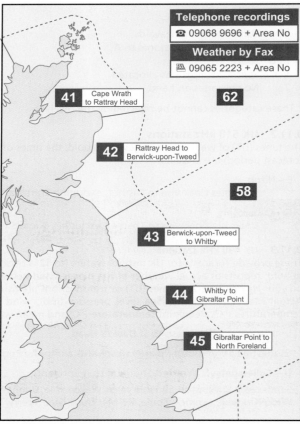

Telephone recordings
☎ 09068 9696 + Area No

Weather by Fax
📠 09065 2223 + Area No

41 Cape Wrath to Rattray Head

62

42 Rattray Head to Berwick-upon-Tweed

58

43 Berwick-upon-Tweed to Whitby

44 Whitby to Gibraltar Point

45 Gibraltar Point to North Foreland

Fig 0(4) Inshore and Offshore forecast areas and codes by Phone and Fax

Marinecall can be used from any landline or mobile network within the UK and Channel Islands. For international services join the Marinecall Club.

0.13.2 4-digit codes

Over 200 such codes give quicker, cheaper access to a required area or port by reducing the preamble. They apply to Tel and Fax messages for UK and Europe. Dial ☎ 09068 96 96 or 🖷 09065 22 23, and the 2 digit area code, ie the offshore areas 57-62 shown in red in Fig. 0(4). Add the 4-digit code, eg 6360 for Oban, as soon as the call connects or you are prompted to do so. A full listing of 4-digit codes is in the Marinecall Handbook or visit www.marinecall.co.uk.

For European coastal locations dial ☎ 09068 96 96 or 🖷 09065 22 23, and the 2 digit area code; add the 4-digit code as stated above. For example for Oostende 58 2939 or for Calais 57 2909.

Other 2-digit Area codes include:

> **West Denmark** Area code 58: Thyborøn 2938.
>
> **Netherlands/Belgium** Area code 58: West Terschelling 2940; Westkapelle 2941; Oostende 2939. **France**: Dunkerque 2942.
>
> **North France** Area code 57: Calais 2909; Le Touquet 2910; Dieppe 2911; Le Havre 2912; Cherbourg 2913; St Malo 2914; Ile de Bréhat 2915; Ouessant 2916.

0.14 WEATHER BY MOBILE PHONE

Mobile phones that have Internet access can receive the BBC Shipping Forecast as long as they have signal coverage. Texting the word WEATHER to 81010 results in a link to a BBC shipping forecast mobile site.

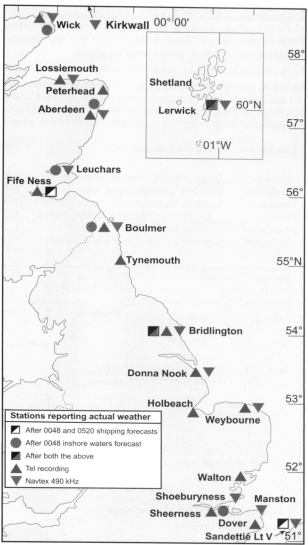

Fig 0(5) Stations reporting actual weather via BBC Radio 4 or telephone recordings

0.15 BROADCASTS BY HM COASTGUARD

HM CG Centres routinely broadcast MSI (Maritime Safety Information) every 3 hours at the times in the Table below. The broadcast channel is pre-stated on Ch 16.

Each broadcast contains one of 3 different Groups of MSI:

Group A, the full broadcast, contains the Shipping forecast, a new Inshore waters forecast and 24 hrs outlook, Gale warnings, a Fisherman's 3 day forecast (1 Oct-31 Mar*), Navigational (WZ) warnings and Subfacts & Gunfacts where

appropriate ‡. Times of 'A' broadcasts are in bold.

Group B contains a new Inshore waters forecast, plus the previous outlook, and Gale warnings. 'B' broadcast times are in plain type.

Group C is a repeat of the Inshore forecast and Gale warnings (as per the previous Group A or B) plus new Strong wind warnings. 'C' broadcast times are italicised.

‡ Subfacts and Gunfacts are broadcast (occas) by Aberdeen CG.

Coastguard	Shipping forecast areas	Inshore areas	Broadcast times LT							
			B	C	A	C	B	C	A	C
Thames	Dover, Wight, Thames, Humber	5, 6	0110	*0410*	**0710**	*1010*	1310	*1610*	**1910**	*2210*
Yarmouth	Humber, German Bight, Dogger, Tyne	3–5	0150	*0450*	**0750**	*1050*	1350	*1650*	**1950**	*2250*
Humber*	Same as Yarmouth CG	3–5	0150	*0450*	**0750**	*1050*	1350	*1650*	**1950**	*2250*
Forth	Tyne, Forth, Cromarty, Forties, Fair Is	1, 2	0130	*0430*	**0730**	*1030*	1330	*1630*	**1930**	*2230*
Aberdeen‡*	Same as Forth CG	1, 2	0130	*0430*	**0730**	*1030*	1330	*1630*	**1930**	*2230*
Shetland*	Cromarty, Viking, Fair Isle, Faeroes	1, 16	0110	*0410*	**0710**	*1010*	1310	*1610*	**1910**	*2210*

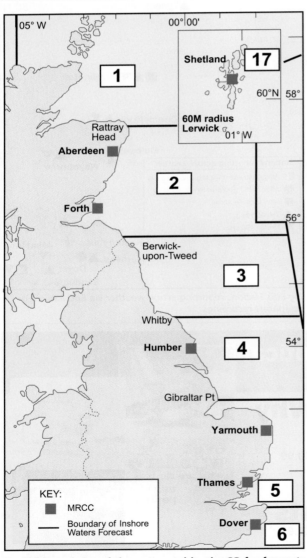

Fig 0(6) Boundaries of the areas used by the CG for forecasts covering inshore waters.

0.15.1 Remote transmitters

MSI broadcasts are transmitted via remote aerial sites geographically selected to give optimum coverage. Their positions and the VHF broadcast channel to be used are listed below.

Thames CG
Shoeburyness	23	51°31'N 00°47'E
Bradwell (R Blackwater)	86	51°44'N 00°53'E
Walton-on-the-Naze	23	51°51'N 01°17'E
Bawdsey (R Deben)	84	52°00'N 01°25'E

Yarmouth CG
Lowestoft	23	52°29'N 01°46'E
Great Yarmouth	86	52°36'N 01°43'E
Trimingham (Cromer)	23	52°55'N 01°21'E
Langham (Blakeney)	86	52°57'N 00°57'E
Guy's Head (Wisbech)	23	52°48'N 00°13'E

Humber CG
Easington (Spurn Hd)	86	53°39'N 00°06'E
Flamborough Hd*	*2226kHz*, 23	54°07'N 00°05'W
Ravenscar	86	54°24'N 00°30'W
Hartlepool	23	54°42'N 01°10'W
Cullercoats (Blyth)	86	55°04'N 01°28'W
Newton	23	55°31'N 01°37'W

Forth CG
St Abbs/Cross Law	86	55°54'N 02°12'W
Craigkelly (Burntisland)	23	56°04'N 03°14'W
Fife Ness	84	56°17'N 02°35'W
Inverbervie	23	56°51'N 02°16'W

Aberdeen CG
Greg Ness*	*2226kHz*, 86	57°08'N 02°03'W
Windyheads Hill	23	57°39'N 02°14'W
Rosemarkie (Cromarty)	86	57°38'N 04°05'W
Noss Head (Wick)	84	58°29'N 03°03'W
Durness (Loch Eriboll)	23	58°34'N 04°44'W

Shetland CG
Wideford Hill (Kirkwall)	86	58°59'N 03°01'W
Fitful Head (Sumburgh)	23	59°54'N 01°23'W
Lerwick (Shetland)	84	60°08'N 01°08'W
Collafirth*	*1770kHz*, 86	60°32'N 01°23'W
Saxa Vord (Unst)	23	60°50'N 00°50'W

0.16 DUTCH WEATHER BROADCASTS

Netherlands Coastguard
VHF weather broadcasts Fig 0(7)

Forecasts for Dutch coastal waters (7 areas up to 30M offshore) and inland waters (IJsselmeer, Markermeer and Oosterschelde) are transmitted in **English** and Dutch at 0805, 1305, 1905, 2305 LT on the VHF channels shown below, **without** prior announcement on Ch 16 or DSC 70.

Westkapelle	Ch 23	Hoorn	Ch 83
Woensdrecht	Ch 83	Wezep	Ch 23
Renesse	Ch 83	Kornwerderzand	Ch 23
Scheveningen	Ch 23	West Terschelling	Ch 83
Schoorl	Ch 83	Schiermonnikoog	Ch 23
Den Helder	Ch 23	Appingedam	Ch 83

Gale warnings are broadcast on receipt and at 0333, 0733, 1133, 1533, 1933 and 2333 UT.

MF weather broadcasts

Forecasts for areas Dover, Thames, Humber, German Bight, Dogger, Fisher, Forties and Viking is broadcast in **English** by Scheveningen at 0940 and 2140 UT on 3673 kHz. Gale warnings for these areas are broadcast in **English** on receipt and at 0333, 0733, 1133, 1533, 1933 and 2333 UT.

0.16.1 Radio Noord-Holland (FM)

Coastal forecasts for northern areas, gale warnings and wind strength are broadcast in Dutch, Mon-Fri at 0730, 0838, 1005, 1230 and 1705LT; Sat/Sun 1005, by:

Wieringermeer 93.9 MHz and **Haarlem** 97.6 MHz.

0.16.2 Omroep Zeeland (FM)

Coastal forecasts for southern areas, synopsis, gale warnings and wind strength are broadcast in Dutch, Mon-Fri at 0715, 0915, 1215 and 1715LT; Sat/Sun 1015, by:

Philippine 97.8 MHz and **Goes** 101.9 MHz.

0.17 BELGIAN WEATHER BROADCASTS

Coast Radio Stations

Oostende Radio broadcasts in **English** and Dutch on VHF Ch 27 and 2761 kHz: Strong wind warnings on receipt and at 0820 and 1720 UT, together with a forecast for sea areas Thames and Dover.

Antwerpen Radio broadcasts in **English** and Dutch on VHF Ch 24 for the Schelde estuary: Gale warnings on receipt and at every odd H+05. Also strong wind warnings (F6+) on receipt and at every H+03 and H+48.

Fig 0(7) Netherlands CRS broadcasts, showing the boundaries and names of coastal areas referred to above

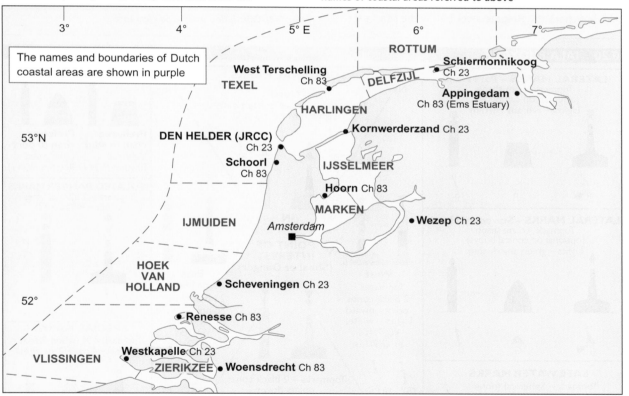

0.18 AUTOMATIC IDENTIFICATION SYSTEM (AIS)

AIS was originated to monitor SOLAS traffic in key areas (in the Minches, for example, to safeguard the marine environment), and in choke points (for example, the Dover Strait). It is also widely used to assist in collision avoidance by automatically and continuously identifying, tracking and displaying other vessels' movements.

Each ship's course and speed vector is shown by a tadpole-like symbol on an AIS screen or overlaid on radar, chart plotter or PC. This data may also appear in a text box as heading, COG & SOG, range, CPA (in some sets); Lat/Long, ship's name (derived from its MMSI), and her status - under power or sail, anchored, constrained by draught, restricted in her ability to manoeuvre, not under command, fishing, etc. Range scales are usually 1, 2, 4, 8, 16 and 32M.

AIS must be fitted in passenger ships and all commercial vessels >300 GRT.

AIS is not mandatory for leisure craft, but it is worth considering. Accurate and continuous display of a target's COG and SOG removes any doubts when these parameters are derived solely from basic radar information. Receive-only equipment (basically a VHF dual frequency transceiver, aerial, GPS input and a mini-computer) is available for small craft. Note: AIS is not a radar despite what some advertisements may imply!

Caveats: Some ships do not switch on their AIS; some only display 3 lines of text, not a plot; in busy areas only the strongest signals may be shown; AIS may distract a bridge watchkeeper from his radar watch (yachts may therefore not be detected); unlike eyes and radar, AIS does not yet feature in IRPCS; GPS/electronic failures invalidate AIS.

0.19 CALCULATING CLEARANCES BELOW OVERHEAD OBJECTS

A diagram often helps when calculating vertical clearance below bridges, power cables etc. Fig 0(8) shows the relationship to CD. The height of such objects as shown on the chart is usually measured above HAT, so the actual clearance will almost always be more. The height of HAT above CD is given at the foot of each page of the tide tables. Most Admiralty charts now show clearances above HAT, but check the **Heights** block below the chart title.

To calculate clearances, insert the dimensions into the following formula, carefully observing the conventions for brackets:

> Masthead clearance = (Height of object above HAT + height of HAT above CD) minus (height of tide at the time + height of the masthead above waterline)

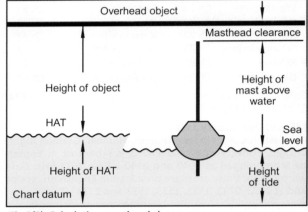

Fig 0(8) Calculating masthead clearance

0.20 IALA BUOYAGE

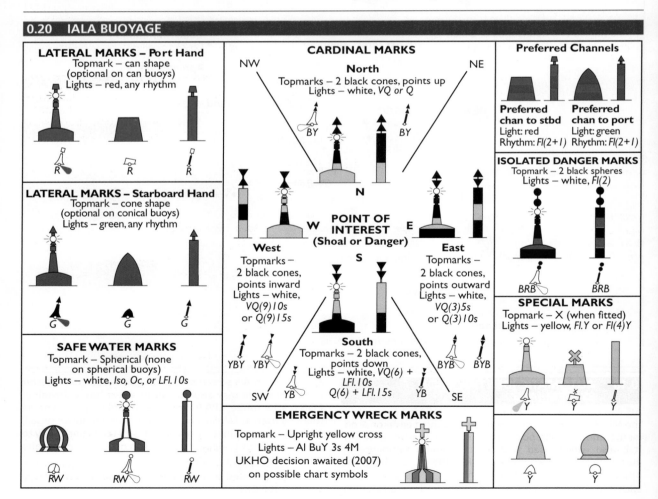

0.21 HM COASTGUARD - CONTACT DETAILS OF CG CENTRES

EASTERN REGION

DOVER COASTGUARD
50°08′N 01°20′E. DSC MMSI 002320010
Langdon Battery, Swingate, Dover CT15 5NA.
☎ 01304 210008. 📠 01304 225762.
Area: Beachy Head to Reculver Towers (51°23′N 01°12′E).
Operates Channel Navigation Information Service (CNIS).

THAMES COASTGUARD
51°51′N 01°17′E. MMSI 002320009
East Terrace, Walton-on-the-Naze CO14 8PY.
☎ 01255 675518. 📠 01255 679415.
Area: Reculver Towers to Southwold (52°19′N 01°40′E).

LONDON COASTGUARD
51°30′N 00°03′E. MMSI 002320063
Thames Barrier Navigation Centre, Unit 28,
34 Bowater Road, Woolwich, London SE18 5TF.
☎ 02083 127382. 📠 02083 098196.
Area: River Thames from Shell Haven Pt (N bank) & Egypt Bay (S bank) up-river to Teddington Lock.

YARMOUTH COASTGUARD
52°37′N 01°43′E. MMSI 002320008
Haven Bridge House, North Quay,
Great Yarmouth NR30 1HZ.
☎ 01493 851338. 📠 01493 331975.
Area: Southwold to Haile Sand Fort (SW of Spurn Hd).

†HUMBER COASTGUARD
54°06′N 00°11′W. MMSI 002320007
Lime Kiln Lane, Bridlington, E Yorkshire YO15 2LX.
☎ 01262 672317. 📠 01262 400779.
Area: Haile Sand Fort to the Scottish border.

SCOTLAND (& NORTHERN IRELAND) REGION

FORTH COASTGUARD
56°17′N 02°35′W. MMSI 002320005
Fifeness, Crail, Fife KY10 3XN.
☎ 01333 450666. 📠 01333 450703.
Area: English border to Doonies Pt (57°01′N 02°10′W).

†ABERDEEN COASTGUARD
57°08′N 02°05′W. MMSI 002320004
Marine House, Blaikies Quay, Aberdeen AB11 5PB.
☎ 01224 592334. 📠 01224 575920.
Area: Doonies Pt to Cape Wrath, incl Pentland Firth.

†SHETLAND COASTGUARD
60°09′N 01°08′W. MMSI 002320001
Knab Road, Lerwick ZE1 0AX.
☎ 01595 692976. 📠 01595 693634.
Area: Orkney, Fair Isle and Shetland.

NOTE: †Monitors DSC MF 2187.5 kHz.

0.22 DUTCH COASTGUARD

The national SAR agency is: SAR Commission, Directorate Transport Safety (DGG), PO Box 20904, 2500 EX The Hague, Netherlands.

The Netherlands CG at Den Helder, co-located with the Navy HQ, coordinates SAR operations as the Dutch JRCC for A1 and A2 Sea Areas. (JRCC = Joint Rescue Coordination Centre – marine & aeronautical.)

Callsign is *Netherlands Coastguard*, but *Den Helder Rescue* is used during SAR operations.

The JRCC keeps a listening watch H24 on DSC Ch 70, and MF DSC 2187·5 kHz (but not on 2182 kHz); MMSI 002442000. Coastguard Operations can be contacted H24 via:

In emergency:
☎ + 31 9000 111 or dial 112.

Operational telephone number:
☎ + 31 223 542300. 📠 + 31 223 658358; ccc@kustwacht.nl If using a mobile phone, call 9000 111, especially if the International emergency number 112 is subject to delays.

Admin/info (HO)
☎+ 31 223 658300. 📠+31 223 658303. info@kustwacht.nl PO Box 10000, 1780 CA Den Helder.

Remote CG stations are shown on Fig. 0(7). Working channels are VHF 23 and 83.

0.22.1 Medical advice
Call initially on Ch 16, DSC Ch 70 or 2187·5 kHz (MMSI 002442000). Working chans are VHF Ch 23 & 83 or MF 2824 kHz (transmit), 2520 kHz (receive).

0.22.2 Resources
The Dutch Lifeboat Ass'n (KNRM) manages 26 lifeboat stations and 13 inshore lifeboat stations along the coast. The 60 lifeboats include 13m LOA water-jet, rigid inflatables capable of 36 kn. Helicopters, fixed wing aircraft and ships of the RNLN can be called upon; also Air Force helos at Leeuwarden. The area of activity extends across the Dutch Continental Shelf and into the Waddenzee, IJsselmeer and estuaries of Zuid Holland and Zeeland.

0.23 BELGIAN COASTGUARD

The Belgian Coastguard coordinates SAR operations from Oostende MRCC, callsign *Coastguard Oostende*. The MRCC and *Oostende Radio* (Coast Radio Station) both keep listening watch H24 on Ch 16, 2182 kHz and DSC Ch 70 and 2187·5 kHz.

Coastguard stations

MRCC OOSTENDE
☎ +32 59 701000; 📠 +32 59 703605. MMSI 002050480.

MRSC Nieuwpoort
☎ +32 58 230000; 📠 +32 58 231575.

MRSC Zeebrugge
☎ +32 50 550801; 📠 +32 50 547400.

RCC Brussels (Point of contact for COSPAS/SARSAT)
☎ +32 2 7200338; 📠 +32 2 7524201.

Coast radio stations

OOSTENDE Radio
☎ 59 702438; 📠 59 701339.
Ch 16, DSC Ch 70 and MF DSC 2187·5 kHz.
MMSI 002050480.

Antwerpen Radio (remotely controlled by Oostende CRS) MMSI 002050485. Ch 16, DSC Ch 70.

0.23.1 Resources
Offshore and inshore lifeboats are based at Nieuwpoort, Oostende and Zeebrugge.

The Belgian Air Force provides helicopters from Koksijde near the French border. The Belgian Navy also participates in SAR operations as required.

Flags & ensigns – Lights & shapes

 UK WHITE ENSIGN
 UK BLUE ENSIGN
 UK RED ENSIGN
 AUSTRALIA

 BASQUE FLAG
 BELGIUM
 BERMUDA
 CANADA

 CYPRUS
 DENMARK
 EU
 FINLAND

 FRANCE
 GERMANY
 GREECE
 GUERNSEY

 IRELAND
 ISRAEL
 ITALY
 LIBERIA

 MALTA
 MONACO
 MOROCCO
 NETHERLANDS

 NEW ZEALAND
 NORWAY
 PANAMA
 POLAND

 PORTUGAL
 SOUTH AFRICA
 SPAIN
 SWEDEN

 SWITZERLAND
 TUNISIA
 TURKEY
 USA

0.25 LIGHTS AND SHAPES

Vessels being towed and towing

Vessel towed shows sidelights (forward) and sternlight

Tug shows two masthead lights, sidelights, sternlight, yellow towing light

Towing by day — Length of tow more than 200m

Towing vessel and tow display diamond shapes. By night, the towing vessel shows three masthead lights instead of two as for shorter tows

Motor sailing

Cone point down, forward. At night the lights of a power-driven vessel underway

Vessel fishing

All-round red light over all-round white, plus sidelights and sternlight when making way

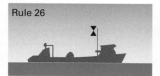

Fishing/Trawling

A shape consisting of two cones point to point in a vertical line one above the other

Vessel trawling

All-round green light over all-round white, plus sidelights and sternlight when making way

Vessel restricted in her ability to manoeuvre

All-round red, white, red lights vertically, plus normal steaming lights when making way

Three shapes in a vertical line: ball, diamond, ball

Not under command

Two all-round red lights, plus sidelights and sternlight when making way

Two balls vertically

Dredger

All round red, white, red lights vertically, plus two all-round red lights (or two balls) on foul side, and two all-round green (or two diamonds) on clear side

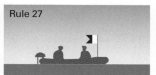

Divers down

Letter 'A' International Code

Constrained by draught

Three all-round red lights in a vertical line, plus normal steaming lights. By day — a cylinder

Pilot boat

All-round white light over all-round red, plus sidelights and sternlight when underway, or anchor light

Vessel at anchor

All-round white light; if over 50m, a second light aft and lower

Ball forward

Vessel aground

Anchor light(s), plus two all-round red lights in a vertical line

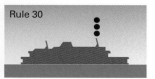

Three balls in a vertical line

0.26 NAVIGATION LIGHTS

LIGHTS FOR TYPICAL YACHT WITH 3 OPTIONAL VARIANTS

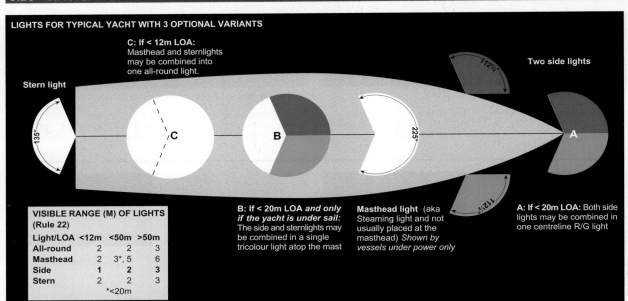

C: If < 12m LOA: Masthead and sternlights may be combined into one all-round light.

Two side lights

Stern light

112½°

225°

135°

112½°

VISIBLE RANGE (M) OF LIGHTS (Rule 22)			
Light/LOA	<12m	<50m	>50m
All-round	2	2	3
Masthead	2	3*, 5	6
Side	1	2	3
Stern	2	2	3
		*<20m	

B: If < 20m LOA *and only if the yacht is under sail:* The side and sternlights may be combined in a single tricolour light atop the mast

Masthead light (aka Steaming light and not usually placed at the masthead) *Shown by vessels under power only*

A: If < 20m LOA: Both side lights may be combined in one centreline R/G light

PLAN VIEWS OF LIGHTS FOR SAILING VESSELS UNDERWAY AND UNDER SAIL ONLY
Note: If motor-sailing, the lights appropriate for a power-driven vessel must be shown, as below

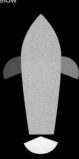

Sailing vessel <7m shows, if practicable, side and sternlights; if not, a white light to prevent collision. Rule 25 d i

Sailing vessel <20m may show:

Either tricolour light atop the mast. Rule 25 b

Or combined centreline side lights plus stern light. Rule 25 a

Sailing vessel >20m Separate sidelights and sternlight. Rule 25 a

Sailing vessel under sail may show (in addition to other lights) two all-round lights, red over green, near the top of the mast, **but never** at the same time as a tricolour light atop the mast. Rule 25 c

PLAN VIEWS OF LIGHTS FOR POWER-DRIVEN VESSELS UNDERWAY AND SAILING CRAFT UNDER POWER

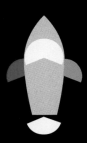
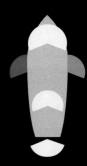

<7m and <7 knots (all-round light and, if practicable, side lights). Rule 23 d ii

<12m (combined masthead & sternlight). Rule 23 d i

<20m (sidelights combined in one centreline light). Rule 21 b

>20m showing masthead, stern and separate sidelights. Rule 21 a, b, c

>50m with two masthead lights, the aft one higher. Rule 23 a i & ii

Times are in UT - add 1 hour in non-shaded areas to convert to BST

0.27 SUNRISE/SET TIMES 2010

The table shows times of Sunrise (SR) and Sunset (SS) for every 4th day as the times of Sunrise and Sunset never change by more than 8 minutes (and often by only 1–3 minutes) between the given dates.

The table is based on Longitude 0°, so longitude corrections are required. To calculate this add 4 minutes of time for every degree West of Greenwich; subtract if East.

LATITUDE 56°N

Day	JANUARY Rise	Set	FEBRUARY Rise	Set	MARCH Rise	Set	APRIL Rise	Set	MAY Rise	Set	JUNE Rise	Set
1	08 31	15 36	07 55	16 33	06 52	17 34	05 31	18 38	04 17	19 39	03 22	20 34
4	08 30	15 40	07 49	16 39	06 44	17 40	05 23	18 44	04 10	19 45	03 19	20 38
7	08 29	15 44	07 43	16 46	06 37	17 47	05 15	18 50	04 03	19 51	03 17	20 42
10	08 26	15 49	07 37	16 53	06 29	17 53	05 08	18 56	03 57	19 57	03 15	20 44
13	08 24	15 54	07 30	16 59	06 21	17 59	05 00	19 02	03 51	20 03	03 14	20 47
16	08 20	16 00	07 23	17 06	06 13	18 05	04 52	19 09	03 46	20 08	03 13	20 49
19	08 16	16 06	07 16	17 12	06 05	18 11	04 45	19 15	03 40	20 14	03 13	20 50
22	08 12	16 12	07 09	17 19	05 57	18 18	04 38	19 21	03 36	20 19	03 13	20 51
25	08 07	16 18	07 02	17 25	05 50	18 24	04 30	19 27	03 31	20 24	03 14	20 51
28	08 02	16 24	06 54	17 32	05 42	18 30	04 23	19 33	03 27	20 29	03 16	20 50
31	07 57	16 31			05 34	18 36			03 23	20 33		

Day	JULY Rise	Set	AUGUST Rise	Set	SEPTEMBER Rise	Set	OCTOBER Rise	Set	NOVEMBER Rise	Set	DECEMBER Rise	Set
1	03 18	20 49	04 04	20 08	05 04	18 55	06 03	17 36	07 07	16 20	08 07	15 31
4	03 21	20 47	04 09	20 02	05 10	18 47	06 09	17 28	07 13	16 13	08 11	15 29
7	03 24	20 45	04 15	19 55	05 16	18 39	06 15	17 20	07 19	16 07	08 16	15 27
10	03 28	20 42	04 21	19 49	05 21	18 31	06 21	17 12	07 26	16 01	08 20	15 26
13	03 32	20 39	04 27	19 42	05 27	18 23	06 27	17 05	07 32	15 56	08 23	15 25
16	03 36	20 35	04 33	19 35	05 33	18 15	06 33	16 57	07 38	15 51	08 26	15 25
19	03 41	20 31	04 38	19 28	05 39	18 07	06 39	16 50	07 44	15 46	08 28	15 26
22	03 46	20 26	04 44	19 20	05 45	18 00	06 45	16 43	07 50	15 41	08 30	15 27
25	03 51	20 21	04 50	19 13	05 51	17 52	06 52	16 36	07 56	15 37	08 31	15 29
28	03 56	20 16	04 56	19 05	05 57	17 44	06 58	16 29	08 01	15 34	08 32	15 31
31	04 02	20 10	05 02	18 57			07 04	16 22			08 31	15 35

0.28 MOONRISE/SET TIMES 2010

The table gives the times of Moonrise (MR) and Moonset (MS) for every 4th day; interpolation is necessary for other days. The aim is simply to indicate whether the night in question will be brightly moonlit, partially moonlit or pitch black – depending, of course, on the level of cloud cover. The table is based on Longitude 0°. To correct for longitude, add 4 minutes of time for every degree West; subtract if East. ** Indicates that the phenomenon does not occur.

LATITUDE 56°N

Day	JANUARY Rise	Set	FEBRUARY Rise	Set	MARCH Rise	Set	APRIL Rise	Set	MAY Rise	Set	JUNE Rise	Set
1	16 39	09 07	20 27	08 20	19 22	06 37	22 51	05 41	23 53	05 20	23 42	07 36
4	21 27	10 02	** **	08 56	23 56	07 18	01 15	07 30	01 02	08 39	00 05	11 18
7	00 24	10 35	03 37	10 06	02 31	08 46	03 01	10 56	01 48	12 22	00 35	15 00
10	04 34	11 31	06 09	12 53	04 37	11 55	03 42	14 38	02 17	16 04	01 25	19 02
13	07 34	13 53	07 05	16 37	05 24	15 38	04 10	18 23	03 00	20 05	03 52	21 57
16	08 44	17 34	07 33	20 18	05 52	19 21	04 57	22 24	04 59	23 22	08 19	23 03
19	09 14	21 16	08 04	** **	06 29	23 18	07 07	00 39	09 05	00 23	12 47	23 41
22	09 42	** **	09 20	02 50	08 08	01 47	11 18	03 01	13 32	01 08	17 05	00 12
25	10 43	03 51	12 56	05 27	12 03	03 54	15 49	03 01	17 56	01 48	20 25	01 54
28	13 57	06 59	17 47	06 25	16 45	04 43	20 20	03 43	21 42	03 12	21 48	05 18
31	18 53	08 07			21 23	05 22			23 25	06 20		

Day	JULY Rise	Set	AUGUST Rise	Set	SEPTEMBER Rise	Set	OCTOBER Rise	Set	NOVEMBER Rise	Set	DECEMBER Rise	Set
1	22 23	09 02	21 14	11 40	21 04	14 25	22 18	14 47	00 25	14 11	02 34	13 00
4	22 53	12 41	22 24	15 31	** **	16 49	01 16	15 52	04 56	14 55	06 57	14 12
7	23 52	16 36	00 18	18 21	03 49	17 48	05 56	16 35	09 23	16 19	09 59	17 04
10	01 29	19 51	04 51	19 29	08 34	18 31	10 32	17 46	12 03	19 26	11 08	20 53
13	05 52	21 09	09 35	20 10	12 59	19 50	13 35	20 32	13 03	23 11	11 43	** **
16	10 30	21 49	14 00	21 13	15 38	22 44	14 44	** **	13 36	01 35	12 20	02 55
19	14 53	22 41	17 04	23 43	16 38	01 12	15 19	02 38	14 16	05 15	13 40	06 41
22	18 22	** **	18 17	02 08	17 11	04 50	15 54	06 17	15 48	08 59	16 58	09 20
25	19 54	03 04	18 52	05 49	17 47	08 30	17 07	10 03	19 18	11 20	21 25	10 26
28	20 32	06 48	19 23	09 27	19 05	12 14	20 06	12 46	23 39	12 18	00 20	11 08
31	21 02	10 25	20 25	13 14			** **	13 56			04 40	12 12

0.29 INTERNATIONAL CODE OF SIGNALS

Code flags, phonetic alphabet, Morse code, single-letter signals. IALA BUOYAGE SYSTEM 'A'. INTERNATIONAL PORT TRAFFIC SIGNALS.

A – Alpha
I have a diver down; keep well clear at slow speed
· —

*B – Bravo
I am taking in, or discharging, or carrying dangerous goods
— · · ·

*C – Charlie
Yes
— · — · —

*D – Delta
Keep clear of me; I am manoeuvring with difficulty
— · ·

*E – Echo
I am altering course to starboard
·

F – Foxtrot
I am disabled; communicate with me
· · — ·

*G – Golf
I require a pilot. When made by fishing vessels 'I am hauling in nets'
— — ·

*H – Hotel
I have a pilot on board
· · · ·

*I – India
I am altering my course to port
· ·

J – Juliett
I am on fire and have dangerous cargo aboard; keep well clear of me
· — — —

K – Kilo
I wish to communicate with you
— · —

L – Lima
You should stop your vessel instantly
· — · ·

*M – Mike
My vessel is stopped and making no way through the water
— —

N – November
No
— ·

O – Oscar
Man overboard

P – Papa
Vessel about to put to sea. By fishing vessels 'My nets are caught fast'

Q – Quebec
My vessel is 'healthy' and I request free pratique
— — · —

R – Romeo
· — ·

*S – Sierra
My engines are going astern
· · ·

*T – Tango
Keep clear of me; I am engaged in pair trawling
—

U – Uniform
You are running into danger
· · —

V – Victor
I require assistance
· · · —

W – Whiskey
I require medical assistance
· — —

X – X-ray
Stop carrying out your intentions and watch for my signals
— · · —

Y – Yankee
I am dragging my anchor
— · — —

*Z – Zulu
I require a tug. By fishing vessels 'I am shooting nets'
— — · ·

1 Wun · — — — —

2 Too · · — — —

3 Tree · · · — —

4 Fow-er · · · · —

INTERNATIONAL PORT TRAFFIC SIGNALS

No	Lights		Main message
1		Flashing	Serious emergency – all vessels to stop or divert according to instructions
2		Fixed or Slow Occulting	Vessels shall not proceed (*Note:* Some ports may use an exemption signal, as in 2a below)
3			Vessels may proceed. One-way traffic
4			Vessels may proceed. Two-way traffic
5			A vessel may proceed only when she has received specific orders to do so. (*Note:* Some ports may use an exemption signal, as in 5a below)

Exemption signals and messages

No	Lights		Main message
2a		Fixed or Slow Occulting	Vessels shall not proceed, except that vessels which navigate outside the main channel need not comply with the main message
5a			A vessel may proceed when she has received specific orders to do so, except that vessels which navigate outside the main channel need not comply with the main message

Auxiliary signals and messages

White and/or yellow lights, displayed with the main lights	Local meanings, as promulgated in local port orders

5 Fife · · · · ·

6 Six — · · · ·

7 Sev-en — — · · ·

8 Ait — — — · ·

9 Nin-er — — — — ·

0 Zero — — — — —

Code and answering pennant

First Substitute   Second Substitute   Third Substitute

0.30 AREA INFORMATION

The 5 geographic Areas are arranged as follows:

A map of the area showing the positions of harbours, principal lights, emergency RDF stations, CG Centres with their boundaries, magnetic variation and a distance table.

Tidal stream chartlets showing hourly rates and set.

Lights, buoys and waypoints listing characteristics of selected lights, their daytime appearance, fog signals, Racons and position. Arcs of visibility and alignment of leading lights are true bearings as seen from seaward. Lights are white unless otherwise stated. Any colours are shown between the bearings of the relevant arcs.

Passage information is threaded between the harbours in each Area and briefly describes the coast, offlying dangers, tidal gates, tide races, selected anchorages, recommended routes and any local weather patterns.

Special notes giving data specific to that country or Area.

0.31 HARBOUR INFORMATION

Below the **harbour name**, the County or Unitary Council (or foreign equivalent) is given, followed by the lat/long of the harbour entrance for use as the final waypoint.

The **harbour ratings**, which are inevitably subjective, grade a port for ease of access, facilities and attractiveness as a place to visit, based on the following criteria:

Ease of access:
- ✿✿✿   *Can be entered in gales from most directions and at all states of tide, by day or night.*
- ✿✿   *Accessible in strong winds from most directions; possible tidal or pilotage constraints.*
- ✿   *Only accessible in calm, settled conditions by day with little or no swell; possible bar and difficult pilotage.*

Facilities available:
- ⬭⬭⬭   *Good facilities for vessel and crew.*
- ⬭⬭   *Most domestic needs catered for, but limited boatyard facilities.*
- ⬭   *Possibly some domestic facilities, but little else.*

Attractiveness:
- ✿✿✿   *An attractive place; well worth visiting.*
- ✿✿   *Average for this part of the coast.*
- ✿   *Holds no particular attraction.*

Chart numbers show Admiralty (AC), Imray, Stanford (Stan) and foreign charts, all smallest scale first, and Admiralty Leisure Folios (56XX). Some ACs are available as Leisure Editions (prefix: SC), printed on wet strength paper and with additional useful information on the back of each chart.

Tde tables and tidal curves are given for Standard Ports and the differences for Secondary Ports.

Harbour chartlets are based on AC or relevant foreign charts.

They are not intended to be used for navigation, although great care has been taken to ensure that they accurately portray the harbour. The publisher and editors disclaim any responsibility for resultant accidents or damage if they are so used. The largest scale official chart, properly corrected, should always be used.

Drying areas and the 5m depth contour are coloured as follows: Dries ▨   <5m ▨   >5m

Due to their scale, chartlets do not always cover the whole area referred to in the text nor do they show every depth, mark, feature or the approach waypoint (⊕).

Shelter assesses how protected a harbour is from wind, sea, surge and swell. It warns of access difficulties and advises on safe berths and anchorages.

Navigation gives the lat/long of an approach waypoint with its bearing and distance to the harbour entrance or next significant feature; some waypoints may be off the harbour chartlet. Approach channels, buoyage, speed limits and hazards are also described.

Access times, if quoted, are based on a nominal 1·5m draft, plus a safety margin, for an average tide. Any significant swell may affect these times. Lock and bridge opening times are in local time.

Wrecks around the UK which are of archaeological or historic interest are protected by law. Sites are listed under the nearest harbour or in Passage Information. Unauthorised interference, including anchoring and diving on such sites, may lead to a substantial fine.

Lights and Marks describe, in more detail than is shown on the chartlets, any unusual characteristics of marks, their appearance by day and features not listed elsewhere.

IPTS (International Port Traffic Signals) are shown at 0.29.

R/T lists VHF channels related to the port, marina or VTS. Callsigns, if not obvious, are in *italics*.

Telephone gives any area code in brackets (which is not repeated for individual telephone numbers unless different or additional codes apply). International calls from/to the UK are described in Special Notes, as are national numbers for marine emergencies abroad including Ambulance, Fire, Police. In the EU 112 is the main emergency number; in the UK it is 999.

Facilities describe man-made features: pontoons, ⚓s, quays, pile moorings, etc at harbours, YCs and marinas (see also the free **Reeds Marina Guide**) followed by commercial services. Most YCs welcome bona fide crews who belong to a recognised club and arrive by sea. Town facilities are listed, with rail, ferry and air links.

The overnight cost of a visitor's alongside berth (AB), *at the previous year's rates*, is the average charge per metre LOA (unless otherwise stated) during high season, usually June to Sept. It includes harbour dues, if applicable, and VAT. The cost of pile moorings, ⚓s or ⚓s, where these are the norm, may also be given. Shore electricity is usually free abroad, but extra in the UK.

The number of ❶ berths is a marina's estimate of how many visitors may be accommodated at any one time. It is always advisable to call the marina beforehand.

Slipways. Access and launch/recovery fees per day, eg Slip HW±2 (£6.00), are given where possible for craft <6.5m LOA.

0.32 FACILITIES FOR DISABLED PEOPLE

RYA Sailability operates under the RYA's auspices to open up sailing and its related benefits to disabled sailors. Facilities include car parking, wheelchair ramps to buildings and pontoons and purpose-built toilets and showers. Facilities for those with sight or hearing disabilities are becoming more widely available. Standard symbols (♿ ♨ ▨ ▨) are used.

0.33   ENVIRONMENTAL GUIDANCE

- Comply with regulations for navigation and conduct within Marine Nature Reserves, Particularly Sensitive Sea Areas (PSSA) and National Water Parks.
- In principle never ditch rubbish at sea, keep it on board and dispose of it in harbour refuse bins.
- Readily degradable foodstuffs may be ditched at sea when >3M offshore (>12M in the English Channel).
- Foodstuffs and other materials which are not readily degradable should never be ditched at sea.
- Sewage. If you do not have a holding tank, only use the onboard heads when well offshore. A holding tank should be fitted as soon as possible as many countries require them. Pump-out facilities (⊅) are shown in the text. Do not pump out holding tanks until more than 3M offshore.
- Do not discharge foul water into a marina, anchorage or moorings area and minimise on washing-up water.
- Deposit used engine oil and oily waste ashore at a recognised facility. Do not allow an automatic bilge pump to discharge oily bilge water overboard.
- Dispose of toxic waste, (eg some antifoulings, cleaning chemicals, old batteries) at an approved disposal facility.
- Row ashore whenever possible – to minimise noise, wash and disturbance. Land at recognised places.
- Respect wild birds, plants, fish and marine animals. Avoid protected nesting sites and breeding colonies.
- Do not anchor or dry out on vulnerable seabed species, eg soft corals, eel grass.

0.34   DISTANCES (M) ACROSS THE NORTH SEA

Approximate distances in nautical miles are by the most direct route, avoiding dangers and allowing for TSS.

Norway to France / UK	Bergen	Stavanger	Lindesnes	Skagen	Esjberg	Sylt (List)	Brunsbüttel	Helgoland	Bremerhaven	Willhelmshaven	Delfzijl	Den Helder	IJmuiden	Scheveningen	Roompotsluis	Vlissingen	Zeebrugge	Oostende	Nieuwpoort	Dunkerque
Lerwick	210	226	288	403	428	442	517	470	510	500	493	486	497	505	551	550	552	555	562	588
Kirkwall	278	275	323	438	439	452	516	467	507	497	481	460	473	481	515	514	516	519	526	545
Wick	292	283	323	437	428	440	498	449	489	479	458	433	444	451	485	484	486	489	496	514
Inverness	356	339	381	485	461	462	529	479	519	509	487	460	471	478	513	512	514	517	524	542
Fraserburgh	288	266	296	410	383	384	451	404	444	434	412	385	396	403	430	429	431	434	441	456
Aberdeen	308	279	298	411	371	378	433	382	432	412	386	353	363	369	401	400	402	405	412	426
Dundee	362	329	339	451	394	401	448	396	436	426	395	352	359	364	390	389	385	388	395	412
Port Edgar	391	355	362	472	409	413	457	405	445	435	401	355	361	366	391	390	386	389	396	413
Berwick	374	325	320	431	356	361	408	355	395	385	355	310	315	320	342	341	337	340	347	364
Hartlepool	409	353	340	440	340	331	367	312	352	342	302	241	243	247	266	265	261	264	271	288
Grimsby	463	395	362	452	324	318	342	291	332	325	288	187	182	185	199	198	190	191	201	198
Kings Lynn	485	416	379	466	330	333	343	292	344	336	283	184	183	183	197	195	187	188	198	195
Lowestoft	508	431	380	453	308	300	295	262	284	271	218	118	104	98	95	99	87	87	89	106
Harwich	540	461	410	483	330	331	320	287	309	296	243	147	126	114	94	100	84	77	80	80
Brightlingsea	558	479	428	501	348	349	338	305	327	314	261	165	144	105	108	106	92	88	86	87
Burnham/Crouch	567	488	437	510	357	358	347	314	336	323	270	174	151	112	109	115	99	92	93	95
London Bridge	620	543	490	560	400	408	395	361	382	374	320	222	199	149	153	149	134	125	126	114
Sheerness	580	503	450	520	360	367	353	319	340	334	280	180	157	109	113	109	94	85	86	74
Ramsgate	575	498	446	516	368	346	339	305	323	315	262	161	144	121	89	85	77	65	58	42
Dover	588	511	459	529	378	359	352	328	336	328	275	174	155	132	101	92	79	65	58	44

Eastern England

Ramsgate to Berwick-upon-Tweed

E England

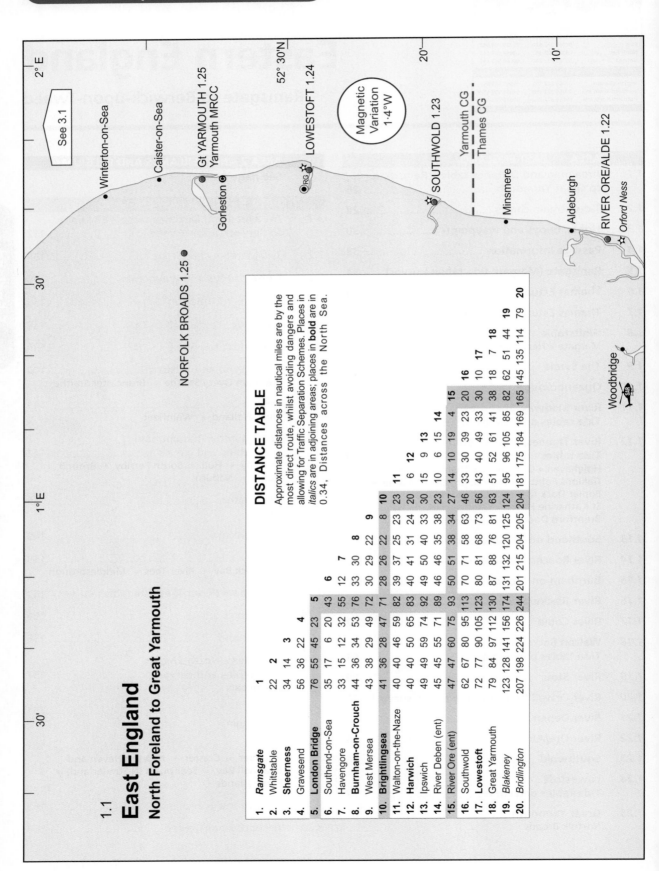

1.1

East England
North Foreland to Great Yarmouth

Winterton-on-Sea

Caister-on-Sea

Gt YARMOUTH 1.25
Yarmouth MRCC
Gorleston

LOWESTOFT 1.24

52° 30'N

NORFOLK BROADS 1.25

Magnetic Variation 1·4°W

SOUTHWOLD 1.23

Yarmouth CG
Thames CG

Minsmere

Aldeburgh

RIVER ORE/ALDE 1.22
Orford Ness

Woodbridge

See 3.1

2° E — 1°E — 30' — 30' — 20' — 10'

DISTANCE TABLE

Approximate distances in nautical miles are by the most direct route, whilst avoiding dangers and allowing for Traffic Separation Schemes. Places in *italics* are in adjoining areas; places in **bold** are in 0.34. Distances across the North Sea.

	1	2	3	4	5	6	7	8	9	10	11	12	13	14	15	16	17	18	19	20
1. *Ramsgate*	1																			
2. Whitstable	22	2																		
3. **Sheerness**	34	14	3																	
4. Gravesend	56	36	22	4																
5. **London Bridge**	76	55	45	23	5															
6. Southend-on-Sea	35	17	6	20	43	6														
7. Havengore	33	15	12	32	55	12	7													
8. **Burnham-on-Crouch**	44	36	34	53	76	33	30	8												
9. West Mersea	43	38	29	49	72	30	29	22	9											
10. **Brightlingsea**	41	36	28	47	71	28	26	22	8	10										
11. Walton-on-the-Naze	40	40	46	59	82	39	37	25	23	23	11									
12. **Harwich**	40	40	50	65	83	40	41	31	24	20	6	12								
13. Ipswich	49	49	59	74	92	49	50	40	33	30	15	9	13							
14. River Deben (ent)	45	45	55	71	89	46	46	35	38	23	10	6	15	14						
15. **River Ore (ent)**	47	47	60	75	93	50	51	38	34	27	14	10	19	4	15					
16. Southwold	62	67	80	95	113	70	71	58	63	56	33	30	39	23	20	16				
17. **Lowestoft**	72	77	97	105	123	80	81	68	73	66	43	40	49	33	30	10	17			
18. Great Yarmouth	79	84	97	112	130	87	88	76	81	63	51	52	61	41	38	18	7	18		
19. *Blakeney*	123	128	141	156	174	131	132	120	125	124	95	96	105	85	82	62	51	44	19	
20. *Bridlington*	207	198	224	226	244	201	215	204	205	204	181	175	184	169	165	145	135	114	79	20

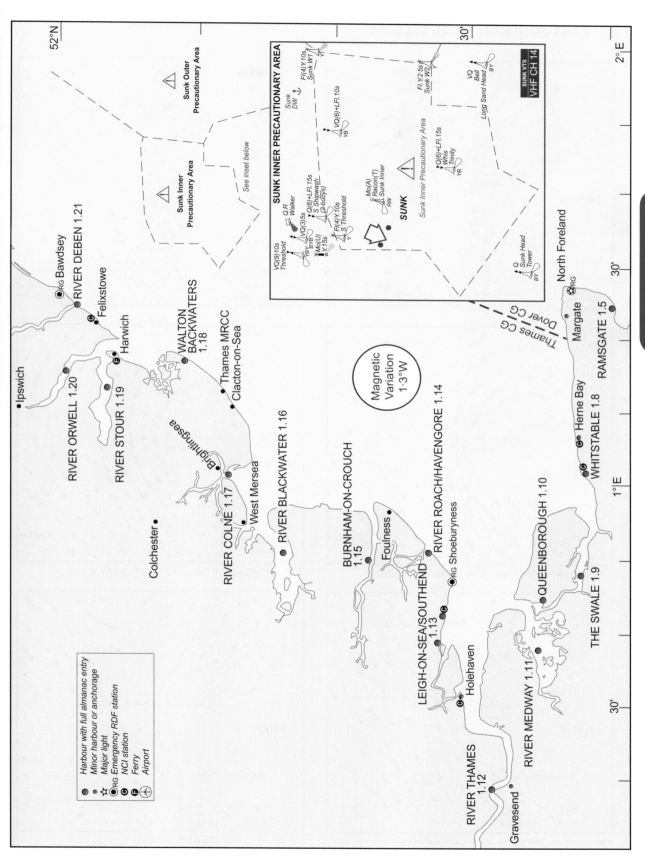

SUNK INNER PRECAUTIONARY AREA

Sunk Outer
Precautionary Area

Sunk Inner
Precautionary Area

See inset below

Sunk
DW

Fl(4)Y.10s
Sunk W1
Y

VQ(6)+LFl.10s
YB

Fl.Y.2.5s
Sunk W2
Y

VQ
Bell
Long Sand Head
BY

Q.R
Walker

VQ(3)5s
YB BYB

Q(6)+LFl.15s
S Shipwash
(2-buoys)

Mo(U)
Y.15s

Fl(4)Y.10s
S Threshold
Y

Q(6)+LFl.15s
Whis
Trinity
YB

Mo(A)
Racon(T)
Sunk Inner
RW

SUNK

VQ(9)10s
Threshold

Q
Sunk Head
Tower
BY

SUNK VTS
VHF CH 14

52°N

30'

2°E

30'

1°E

30'

30'

52°N

● Ipswich

RIVER ORWELL 1.20

RG Bawdsey
RIVER DEBEN 1.21

G Felixstowe

Harwich

RIVER STOUR 1.19

Brightlingsea

WALTON
BACKWATERS
1.18

Thames MRCC
Clacton-on-Sea

● Colchester

RIVER COLNE 1.17

West Mersea

RIVER BLACKWATER 1.16

BURNHAM-ON-CROUCH
1.15

Foulness

RIVER ROACH/HAVENGORE 1.14

RG Shoeburyness

LEIGH-ON-SEA/SOUTHEND
1.13
G

Magnetic
Variation
1·3°W

QUEENBOROUGH 1.10

Herne Bay
G

WHITSTABLE 1.8
G

RAMSGATE 1.5

Margate
North Foreland
RG

Thames CG
Dover CG

THE SWALE 1.9

RIVER MEDWAY 1.11

Holehaven

G

RIVER THAMES
1.12

Gravesend

Harbour with full harbour entry
Minor harbour or anchorage
Major light
RG Emergency RDF station
NCI station
Ferry
Airport

1.2 EAST ENGLAND TIDAL STREAMS

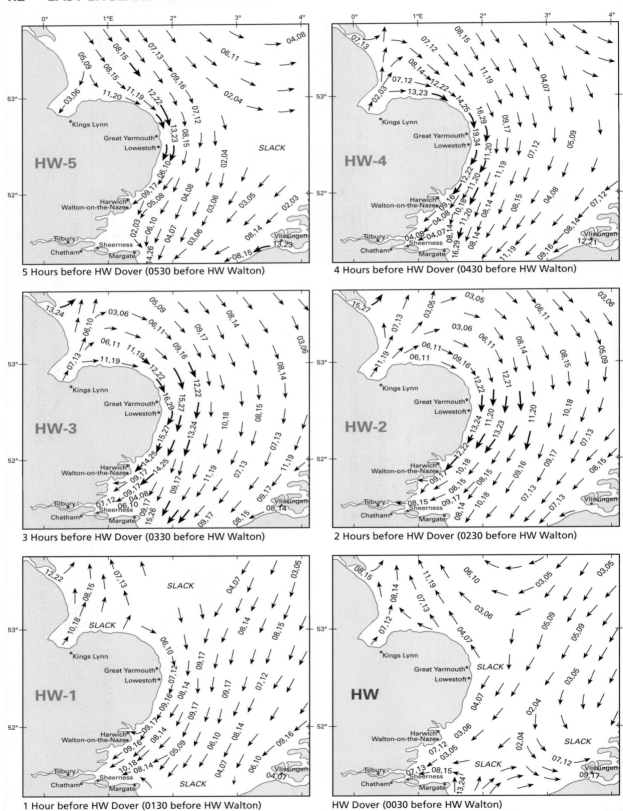

5 Hours before HW Dover (0530 before HW Walton)

4 Hours before HW Dover (0430 before HW Walton)

3 Hours before HW Dover (0330 before HW Walton)

2 Hours before HW Dover (0230 before HW Walton)

1 Hour before HW Dover (0130 before HW Walton)

HW Dover (0030 before HW Walton)

Thames Estuary 1.6 Eastward 2.2 Northward 3.2

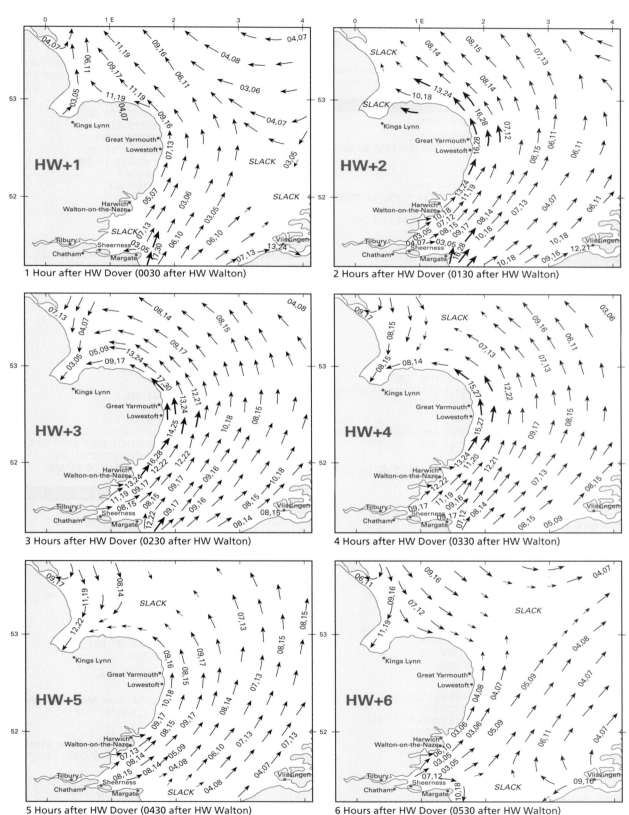

1 Hour after HW Dover (0030 after HW Walton)

2 Hours after HW Dover (0130 after HW Walton)

3 Hours after HW Dover (0230 after HW Walton)

4 Hours after HW Dover (0330 after HW Walton)

5 Hours after HW Dover (0430 after HW Walton)

6 Hours after HW Dover (0530 after HW Walton)

1.3 LIGHTS, BUOYS AND WAYPOINTS

Bold print = light with a nominal range of 15M or more. CAPITALS = place or feature. *CAPITAL ITALICS* = light-vessel, light float or Lanby. *Italics* = Fog signal. ***Bold italics*** = Racon. See 0.2 for Abbreviations.

IMPORTANT NOTE. Regular changes are made to Thames Estuary buoyage. Check Notices to Mariners for the latest information.

THAMES ESTUARY – SOUTHERN
(Direction of buoyage generally East to West)

APPROACHES to THAMES ESTUARY
Foxtrot 3 ⟞ 51°24'·20N 02°00'·40E; Fl 10s 12m **15M**; *Racon (T) 10M*; *Horn 10s.*
Falls Hd ⟨ Q; 51°28'·23N 01°49'·89E.
Drill Stone ⟨ Q (3) 10s; 51°25'·88N 01°42'·89E.
Thanet Offshore Windfarm Met ⟨ Fl (5) Y 20s; 51°25'·53N 01°38'·60E.
NE Spit ⟨ VQ (3); *Racon (T) 10M;* 5s; 51°27'·93N 01°29'·89E.
East Margate ⟨ Fl R 2·5s; 51°27'·03N 01°26'·40E.
Elbow ⟨ Q; 51°23'·23N 01°31'·59E.
Foreness Pt Outfall ⟨ Fl R 5s; 51°24'·61N 01°26'·02E.
Longnose ⟨ 51°24'·15N 01°26'·08E.
Longnose Spit ⟨ Fl R 2·5s 5m 2M; 51°23'·93N 01°25'·68E.

MARGATE and GORE CHANNEL
SE Margate ⟨ Q (3) 10s; 51°24'·05N 01°20'·40E.
S Margate ⟨ Fl G 2·5s; 51°23'·83N 01°16'·65E.
Hook Spit ⟨ QG; 51°24'·08N 01°12'·18E.
E Last ⟨ QR; 51°24'·07N 01°11'·92E.

HERNE BAY
Beltinge Bay Bn ⟨ Fl Y 5s; 51°22'·73N 01°08'·63E.
Landing Stage ⟨ Q 18m 4M, (isolated); 51°22'·91N 01°06'·89E.
N Pier Hd ⟨ 2 FR (vert); 51°22'·43N 01°07'·27E.

WHITSTABLE
Whitstable Street ⟨; 51°24'·00N 01°01'·54E. (See The Swale.)
Oyster ⟨ Fl (2) R 10s; 51°22'·14N 01°01'·16E.
W Quay Dn ⟨ Fl G 5s 2m.
S Quay ⟨ Dir lt 122°; Dir Fl WRG 3s 7m: vis: 117·5°-G-120·5°-W-123·5°- R-126·5°; 51°21'·76N 01°01·70E.

THE SWALE
Whitstable Street ⟨ Fl R 2s; 51°24'·00N 01°01'·54E.
Columbine ⟨ Fl G 2s; 51°24'·26N 01°01'·34E.
Columbine Spit ⟨ Fl (3) G 10s; 51°23'·86N 01°00'·03E.
Ham Gat ⟨ Q G; 51°23'·08N 00°58'·32E.
Pollard Spit ⟨ Q R; 51°22'·98N 00°58'·57E.
Sand End ⟨ Fl G 5s; 51°21'·43N 00°55'·90E.
Receptive Point ⟨ Fl G 10s; 51°20'·86N 00°54'·41E.
Queenborough Spit ⟨ Q (3) 10s; 51°25'·81N 00°43'·93E.
South Oaze ⟨ Fl R 2s; 51°21'·34N 00°56'·01E.

QUEENS CHANNEL and FOUR FATHOMS CHANNEL
E Margate ⟨ Fl R 2·5s; 51°27'·03N 01°26'·40E.
Spaniard ⟨ Q (3) 10s; 51°26'·23N 01°04'·00E.
Spile ⟨ Fl G 2·5s; 51°26'·43N 00°55'·70E.

PRINCES CHANNEL
Tongue Sand E ⟨ VQ (3) 5s; 51°29'·48N 01°22'·21E.
Tongue Sand N ⟨ Q; 51°29'·68N 01°22'·03E.
Princes Outer ⟨ VQ (6) + L Fl 10s; 51°28'·89N 01°20'·43E.
Princes North ⟨ Q G; 51°29'·25N 01°18'·35E.
Princes South ⟨ Q R; 51°28'·74N 01°18'·26E.
Princes No.1 ⟨ Fl (4) G 15s; 51°29'·23N 01°16'·02E.
Princes No.2 ⟨ Fl (2) R 5s; 51°28'·81N 01°13'·08E.
Princes No.3 ⟨ Fl (2) G 5s; 51°29'·33N 01°13'·10E.
Princes No.4 ⟨ Fl (3) R 10s; 51°28'·83N 01°09'·90E.
Princes No.5 ⟨ Fl (3) G 10s; 51°29'·39N 01°10'·00E.
Princes Mid ⟨ Fl Y 5s; 51°29'·19N 01°09'·00E.

Shivering Sand Twr N ⟨ Q; 51°30'·01N 01°04'·76E.
Shivering Sand Twr S ⟨ Q (6) + L Fl 15s; *Bell;* 51°29'·75N 01°04'·83E.
Princes No.8 ⟨ Fl (2) R 5s; 51°29'·15N 01°03'·87E.
Princes Inner ⟨ Fl Y 2·5s; 51°29'·59N 01°03'·47E.

FOULGER'S GAT and KNOB CHANNEL
The N Edinburgh Channel is not buoyed. Fisherman's Gat is a commercial ship channel; Foulger's Gat, suitable for leisure craft, is marked at each end with SWMs.

Long Sand Inner ⟨ Mo 'A' 15s; 51°38'·80N 01°25'·60E.
Long Sand Outer ⟨ L Fl 10s; 51°35'·90N 01°26'·00E.
Shingles Patch ⟨ Q; 51°33'·01N 01°15'·37E.
N Shingles ⟨ Fl R 2·5s; 51°32'·79N 01°14'·25E.
Tizard ⟨ Q (6) + L Fl 15s; 51°32'·93N 01°12'·90E.
Mid Shingles ⟨ Fl (2) R 5s; 51°31'·96N 01°11'·98E.
NE Knob ⟨ QG; 51°32'·03N 01°10'·00E.
NW Shingles ⟨ VQ; 51°31'·26N 01°09'·73E.
SE Knob ⟨ Fl G 5s; 51°30'·89N 01°06'·41E.
Knob ⟨ Iso 5s; *Bell;* 51°30'·69N 01°04'·28E.

OAZE DEEP
Oaze Deep ⟨ Fl (2) G 5s; 51°30'·03N 01°00'·70E.
Red Sand Trs N ⟨ Fl (3) R 10s; *Bell;* 51°28'·73N 00°59'·32E.
N Oaze ⟨ QR; 51°30'·03N 00°57'·65E.
Oaze ⟨ Fl (4) Y 10s; 51°29'·06N 00°56'·93E.
W Oaze ⟨ Iso 5s; 51°29'·06N 00°55'·43E.
Oaze Bank ⟨ Q G 5s; 51°29'·36N 00°56'·95E.
Cant ⟨ (unlit); 51°27'·77N 00°53'·36E.
East Cant ⟨ QR; 51°28'·53N 00°55'·60E.

MEDWAY, SHEERNESS
Medway ⟨ Mo (A) 6s; 51°28'·83N 00°52'·81E.
No. 1 ⟨ Fl G 2·5s; 51°28'·55N 00°50'·50E.
No. 2 ⟨ Q; 51°28'·33N 00°50'·52E.
No. 7 ⟨ Fl G 10s; 51°27'·91N 00°47'·52E.
No. 9 ⟨ Fl G 5s; 51°27'·74N 00°46'·61E.
No. 11 ⟨ Fl (3) G 10s; 51°27'·51N 00°45'·80E.
Grain Hard ⟨ Fl G 5s; 51°26'·98N 00°44'·17E.
Isle of Grain ☆ Q WRG 20m W13M, R7M, G8M; R & W ◇ on R twr; vis 220°-R-234°- G-241°-W-013°; 51°26'·70N 00°43'·38E.
Queenborough Spit ⟨ Q (3) 10s; 51°25'·81N 00°43'·93E.

RIVER THAMES

SEA REACH, NORE and YANTLET
No. 1 ⟨ Fl Y 2·5s; *Racon (T) 10M;* 51°29'·45N 00°52'·57E.
No. 2 ⟨ Iso 5s; 51°29'·40N 00°49'·75E.
No. 3 ⟨ L Fl 10s; 51°29'·33N 00°46'·54E.
No. 4 ⟨ Fl Y 2·5s; 51°29'·61N 00°44'·18E.
No. 5 ⟨ Iso 5s; 51°29'·95N 00°41'·44E.
No. 6 ⟨ Iso 2s; 51°30'·03N 00°39'·83E.
No. 7 ⟨ Fl Y 2·5s; *Racon (T) 10M;* 51°30'·10N 00°37'·04E.
Nore Swatch ⟨ Fl (4) R 15s; 51°28'·28N 00°45'·55E.
Mid Swatch ⟨ Fl G 5s; 51°28'·68N 00°44'·16E.
W Nore Sand ⟨ Fl R 10s; 51°29'·41N 00°40'·85E.
East Blyth ⟨ Fl (2) R 10s; 51°29'·72N 00°37'·80E.
Mid Blyth ⟨ Q; 51°30'·08N 00°32'·38E.

LEIGH-ON-SEA and SOUTHEND-ON-SEA
Leigh ⟨; 51°31'·07N 00°42'·56E.
Southend Pier E End ⟨ 2 FG (vert) 7m; *Horn Mo (N) 30s, Bell (1)*
SE Leigh ⟨ Q (6) + L Fl 15s; 51°29'·42N 00°47'·07E.

GRAVESEND
Shornmead ⟨ Fl (2) WR 10s 12m 11/7M , W11M, W7M, R11M; vis 070°-W-084°-R(Intens)-089°-W(Intens) -094°- W - 250°; 51°26'·92N 00°26'·24E.

Northfleet Upper ☆ Oc WRG 10s 30m **W16M**, R12M, G12M; vis:126° - R - 149°- W - 159°- G - 268° - W -279°; 51°26'·93N 00°20'·06E.

Plot waypoints on chart before use

THAMES TIDAL BARRIER

Span B (51°29'·73N 00°02'·23E) is used for small craft/yachts Eastbound and Span G (51°29'·91N 00°02'·21E) is used for small craft/yachts Westbound. Spans B, C, D, E, F & G are navigable. Spans C to F are for larger vessels. All spans display a F GR ⚡. A Green ⟶ indicates span open for navigation. A **Red X** indicates span closed to navigation. In low visibility F lights are shown either side of those spans which are displaying a Green ⟶.

THAMES ESTUARY – NORTHERN

KENTISH KNOCK
Kentish Knock ⚲ Q (3) 10s; *Whis*; 51°38'·08N 01°40·43E.
S Knock ⚲ Q (6) + L Fl 15s; *Bell*; 51°34'·13N 01°34'·29E.

KNOCK JOHN CHANNEL
No. 7 ⚐ Fl (4) G 15s; 51°32'·03N 01°06'·40E.
No. 5 ⚐ Fl (3) G 10s; 51°32'·49N 01°07'·75E.
No. 4 ⚑ QR 10s; 51°32'·33N 01°07'·90E.
No. 2 ⚑ Fl (3) R 10s; 51°33'·11N 01°09'·85E.
No. 3 ⚲ Q (6) + L Fl 15s; 51°33'·23N 01°09'·70E.
No. 1 ⚐ Fl G 5s; 51°33'·75N 01°10'·72E.
Knock John ⚑ Fl (2) R 5s; 51°33'·61N 01°11'·37E.

BLACK DEEP
No. 12 ⚑ Fl (4) R 15s; 51°33'·83N 01°13'·50E.
No. 11 ⚐ Fl (3) G 10s; 51°34'·33N 01°13'·40E.
No. 10 ⚑ Fl (3) R 10s; 51°34'·74N 01°15'·60E.
No. 9 ⚲ Q (6) + L Fl 15s; 51°35'·13N 01°15'·09E.
No. 8 ⚲ Q (9) 15s; 51°36'·36N 01°20'·43E.
No. 7 ⚐ QG. 51°37'·08N 01°17'·69E.
No. 6 ⚑ Fl R 2·5s; 51°38'·53N 01°24'·41E.
No. 5 ⚲ VQ (3) 5s; 51°39'·53N 01°23'·00E.
No. 4 ⚑ Fl (2) R 5s; 51°41'·42N 01°28'·49E.
Long Sand Bcn ⚊ ; 51°41'·48N 01°29'·49E.
No. 3 ⚐ Fl (3) G 15s; 51°42'·41N 01°26'·48E.
No. 1 ⚐ Fl G 5s, 51°44'·03N 01°28'·09E.
No. 2 ⚑ Fl (4) R 15s; 51°45'·63N 01°32'·20E.
Sunk Head Tower ⚲ Q; *Whis*; 51°46'·63N 01°30'·51E.
Black Deep ⚑ QR.51°47'·50N 01°35'·64E.
Trinity ⚲ Q (6) + L Fl 15s; *Whis*; 51°49'·03N 01°36'·39E.
Long Sand Head ⚲ VQ; *Bell*; 51°47'·90N 01°39'·42E.

FISHERMANS GAT
Outer Fisherman ⚲ Q (3) 10s; 51°33'·89N 01°25'·01E.
Fisherman No. 1 ⚐ Fl G 2·5s; 51°34'·53N 01°23'·57E.
Fisherman No. 2 ⚑ Fl R 2·5s; 51°34'·35N 01°23'·01E.
Fisherman No. 3 ⚐ Fl G 5s; 51°34'·72N 01°22'·94E.
Fisherman No. 4 ⚑ Fl (2) R 5s; 51°35'·25N 01°21'·35E.
Fisherman No. 5 ⚐ Fl (2) G 5s; 51°35'·52N 01°21'·75E.
Inner Fisherman ⚑ Q R; 51°36'·07N 01°19'·87E.

BARROW DEEP
SW Barrow ⚲ Q(6) + L Fl 15s; *Bell*; 51°32'·29N 01°00'·31E.
Barrow No. 14 ⚑ Fl R 2·5s; 51°31'·83N 01°00'·43E.
Barrow No. 13 ⚐ Fl (2) G 5s; 51°32'·82N 01°03'·07E.
Barrow No. 12 ⚐ Fl (2) R 5s; 51°32'·77N 01°04'·13E.
Barrow No.11 ⚐ Fl (3) G 10s; 51°34'·08N 01°06'·70E.
Barrow No. 9 ⚲ VQ (3) 5s; 51°35'·34N 01°10'·30E.
Barrow No. 8 ⚑ Fl (2) R 5s; 51°35'·03N 01°11'·40E.
Barrow No. 6 ⚑ Fl (4) R 15s; 51°37'·30N 01°14'·69E.
Barrow No. 5 ⚐ Fl G 10s; 51°40'·03N 01°16'·20E.
Barrow No. 4 ⚲ VQ (9) 10s; 51°39'·88N 01°17'·48E.
Barrow No. 3 ⚲ Q (3) 10s; *Racon (M)10M*; 51°42'·02N 01°20'·24E.
Barrow No. 2 ⚑ Fl (2) R 5s; 51°41'·98N 01°22'·89E.

WEST SWIN and MIDDLE DEEP
Blacktail (W) ⚊ ; 51°31'·46N 00°55'·19E.
Maplin ⚐ Q G; *Bell*; 51°33'·66N 01°01'·59E.

W Swin ⚑ QR; 51°33'·40N 01°01'·97E.
Maplin Edge ⚐ Fl G 2.5s; 51°35'·33N 01°03'·64E.
Maplin Bank ⚑ Fl (3) R 10s; 51°35'·50N 01°04'·70E.

EAST SWIN and KING'S CHANNEL
NE Maplin ⚐ Fl G 5s; *Bell*; 51°37'·43N 01°04'·90E.
W Hook Middle ⚑ 51°39'·18N 01°07'·97E.
S Whitaker ⚐ Fl (2) G 10s; 51°40'·23N 01°09'·05E.
N Middle ⚲ Q; 51°41'·03N 01°11'·88E.
W Sunk ⚲ Q (9) 15s; 51°44'·33N 01°25'·80E.
Gunfleet Spit ⚲ Q (6) + L Fl 15s; *Bell*; 51°45'·33N 01°21'·70E.

WHITAKER CHANNEL and RIVER CROUCH
Whitaker ⚲ Q (3) 10s; *Bell*; 51°41'·43N 01°10'·51E.
Whitaker No. 6 ⚲ Q; 51°40'·69N 01°08'·06E.
Swin Spitway ⚲ Iso 10s; *Bell*; 51°41'·95N 01°08'·35E.
Ron Pipe ⚑ 51°40'·51N 01°03'·62E.
Swallow Tail ⚐ 51°40'·51N 01°04'·70E.
Ridge ⚑ Fl R 10s; 51°40'·13N 01°04'·87E.
Foulness ⚑ Fl (2) R 10s; 51°39'·85N 01°03'·81E.
Sunken Buxey ⚲ Q; 51°39'·54N 01°00'·59E.
Buxey No. 1 ⚲ VQ (6) + L Fl 10s; 51°39'·18N 01°01'·01E.
Buxey No. 2 ⚲ Q; 51°38'·98N 01°00'·15E.
Outer Crouch ⚲ Q (6) + L Fl 15s; 51°38'·38N 00°58'·48E.

GOLDMER GAT and WALLET
NE Gunfleet ⚲ Q (3) 10s; 51°49'·93N 01°27'·79E.
Wallet No. 2 ⚑ Fl R 5s; 51°48'·88N 01°22'·99E.
Wallet No. 4 ⚑ Fl (4) R 10s; 51°46'·53N 01°17'·23E.
Wallet Spitway ⚑ L Fl 10s; *Bell*; 51°42'·86N 01°07'·30E.
Knoll ⚲ Q; 51°43'·88N 01°05'·07E.
Eagle ⚐ QG; 51°44'·13N 01°03'·82E.
N Eagle ⚲ Q; 51°44'·71N 01°04'·32E.
NW Knoll ⚑ Fl (2) R 5s; 51°44'·35N 01°02'·17E.
Colne Bar ⚐ Fl (2) G 5s; 51°44'·61N 01°02'·57E.
Bench Head ⚐ Fl (3) G 10s; 51°44'·69N 01°01'·10E.

RIVER BLACKWATER
The Nass ⚲ VQ (3) 5s 6m 2M; 51°45'·83N 00°54'·83E.
Thirslet ⚐ Fl (3) G 10s; 51°43'·73N 00°50'·39E.
No. 1 ⚐ ; 51°43'·44N 00°48'·02E.

RIVER COLNE and BRIGHTLINGSEA
Inner Bench Head No. 2 ⚑ Fl (2) R 5s; 51°45'·96N 01°01'·74E.
Colne Pt No. 1 ⚐ Fl G 3s; 51°46'·01N 01°01'·92E.
No. 8 ⚑ Fl R 3s; 51°46'·90N 01°01'·30E.
No. 9 ⚐ Fl G 3s; 51°47'·36N 01°01'·07E.

Ldg lts 041°. Front, FR 7m 4M; W ☐, R stripe on post; vis: 020°-080°; 51°48'·39N 01°01'·20E. Rear, 50m from front, FR 10m 4M; W ☐, R stripe on post. FR lts are shown on 7 masts between 1·5M and 3M NW when firing occurs.

WALTON BACKWATERS
Pye End ⚑ L Fl 10s; 51°55'·03N 01°17'·90E.
No. 2 ⚑ Fl (2) 5s; 51°54'·62N 01°16'·80E.
Crab Knoll No. 3 ⚐ Fl G 5s; 51°54'·41N 01°16'·41E.

HARWICH APPROACHES
(Direction of buoyage North to South)

MEDUSA CHANNEL
Medusa ⚐ Fl G 5s; 51°51'·23N 01°20'·35E.
Stone Banks ⚑ FlR 5s; 51°53'·19N 01°19'·23E.
Pennyhole ⚐ ; 51°53'·55N 01°18'·00E (Mar–Sep).

CORK SAND and ROUGH SHOALS
S Cork ⚲ Q (6) + L Fl 15s; 51°51'·33N 01°24'·09E.
Roughs Tower SE ⚲ Q (3) 10s; 51°53'·64N 01°28'·94E.
Roughs Tower NW ⚲ Q (9) 15s; 51°53'·61N 01°29'·06E.
Cork Sand ⚲ Fl (3) R 10s; 51°55'·51N 01°25'·42E.

HARWICH CHANNEL

Sunk Inner ⌐ Iso 3s 11m 12M, *Racon T*; *Horn 30s*; 51°51'·03N 01°34'·89E.
S Threshold ⚲ Fl (4) Y 10s; 51°52'·20N 01°33'·14E.
S Shipwash ⚲⚲ 2 By(s) Q (6) + L Fl 15s; 51°52'·71N 01°33'·97E.
Outer Tidal Bn ⚲ Mo (U) 15s 2m 3M; 51°52'·85N 01°32'·34E.
E Fort Massac ⚲ VQ (3) 5s; 51°53'·36N 01°32'·79E.
W Fort Massac ⚲ VQ (9) 10s; 51°53'·36N 01°32'·49E.
Walker ⌐ QR; 51°53'·79N 01°33'·90E.
N Threshold ⚲ Fl Y 5s; 51°54'·49N 01°33'·47E.
SW Shipwash ⚲ Q (9)15s; 51°54'·75N 01°34'·21E.
Haven ⚲ Mo (A) 5s; 51°55'·76N 01°35'·56E.
W Shipwash ⌐ Fl (2) R 10s; 51°57'·13N 01°35'·89E.
NW Shipwash ⌐ Fl R 5s; 51°58'·98N 01°37'·01E.
Harwich App (HA) ⚲ Iso 5s; 51°56'·75N 01°30'·66E.
Cross ⚲ Fl (3) Y 10s; 51°56'·23N 01°30'·48E.
Harwich Chan No. 1 ⚲ Fl Y 2·5s; *Racon (T)10M*; 51°56'·13N 01°27'·06E.
Harwich Chan No. 3 ⚲ Fl (3) Y 10s; 51°56'·04N 01°25'·54E.
Harwich Chan No. 5 ⚲ Fl (5) Y 10s; 51°55'·96N 01°24'·01E.
Harwich Chan No. 7 ⚲ Fl (3) Y 10s; 51°55'·87N 01°22'·49E.
S Bawdsey ⚲ Q (6) + L Fl 15s; *Whis*; 51°57'·23N 01°30'·19E.
Washington ▲ QG; 51°56'·52N 01°26'·59E.
Felixstowe Ledge ▲ Fl (3) G 10s; 51°56'·30N 01°23'·72E.
Wadgate Ledge ⚲ Fl (4) G 15s; 51°56'·16N 01°21'·99E.
Platters ⚲ Q (6) + L Fl 15s; 51°55'·64N 01°20'·97E.
Rolling Ground ▲ QG; 51°55'·55N 01°19'·75E.
Beach End ▲ Fl (2) G 5s; 51°55'·62N 01°19'·21E.
Cork Sand Yacht Bn ⚲ VQ 2M; 51°55'·21N 01°25'·20E.
Rough ⚲ VQ; 51°55'·19N 01°31'·00E.
Pitching Ground ⌐ Fl (4) R 15s; 51°55'·43N 01°21'·05E.
Inner Ridge ⌐ QR; 51°55'·38N 01°20'·20E.
Deane ⌐ L Fl R 6s; 51°55'·36N 01°19'·28E.
Landguard ⚲ Q; 51°55'·45N 01°18'·84E.

RIVERS STOUR AND ORWELL

RIVER STOUR and HARWICH

Shotley Spit ⚲ Q (6) + L Fl 15s; 51°57'·21N 01°17'·69E.
Shotley Marina Lock E side Dir lt 339·5° 3m 1M (uses Moiré pattern); Or structure; 51°57'·46N 01°16'·60E.
Guard ⌐ Fl R 5s; *Bell*; 51°57'·07N 01°17'·86E.

RIVER ORWELL and IPSWICH

Suffolk Yacht Harbour. Ldg lts Front Iso Y 1M; 51°59'·73N 01°16'·09E. Rear Oc Y 4s 1M.

HARWICH TO ORFORDNESS

FELIXSTOWE, R DEBEN and WOODBRIDGE HAVEN

Woodbridge Haven ⌐ Mo(A)15s; 51°58'·20N 01°23'·85E.
Deben ⌐; 51°59'·30N 01°23'·53E.

RIVERS ORE and ALDE

Orford Haven ⚲ L Fl 10s; *Bell*. 52°01'·62N 01°28'·00E.

OFFSHORE MARKS

S Galloper ⚲ Q (6) L Fl 15s; *Racon (T)10M*; 51°43'·98N 01°56'·43E.
N Galloper ⚲ Q; 51°49'·84N 01°59'·99E.
S Inner Gabbard ⚲ Q (6) + L Fl 15s. 51°49'·92N 01°51'·89E.
N Inner Gabbard ⚲ Q; 51°59'·20N 01°56'·00E.
Outer Gabbard ⚲ Q (3) 10s; *Racon (O)10M*; 51°57'·83N 02°04'·19E.
NHR-SE ▲ Fl G 5s; 51°45'·39N 02°39'·89E.

SHIPWASH and BAWDSEY BANK

E Shipwash ⚲ VQ (3) 5s; 51°57'·08N 01°37'·89E.
NW Shipwash ⌐ Fl R 5s; 51°58'·98N 01°37'·01E.
N Shipwash ⚲ Q 7M; *Racon (M) 10M*; *Bell*; 52°01'·73N 01°38'·27E.
S Bawdsey ⚲ Q (6) + L Fl 15s; *Whis*; 51°57'·23N 01°30'·22E.
Mid Bawdsey ▲ Fl (3) G 10s; 51°58'·88N 01°33'·59E.
NE Bawdsey ▲ Fl G 10s; 52°01'·73N 01°36'·09E.

CUTLER and WHITING BANKS

Cutler ▲ QG; 51°58'·51N 01°27'·48E.
SW Whiting ⚲ Q (6) + L Fl 10s; 52°00'·96N 01°30'·69E.
Whiting Hook ⌐ Fl R 10s; 52°02'·98N 01°31'·82E.
NE Whiting ⚲ Q (3) 10s; 52°03'·61N 01°33'·32E.

ORFORDNESS TO WINTERTON

(Direction of buoyage is South to North)
Orford Ness ☆ 52°05'·03N 01°34'·46E; Fl 5s 28m **20M**;
W ○ twr, R bands. F WRG 14m **W17M**, R13M, **G15M** (same twr). vis: R shore-210°, 038°-R-047°-G-shore; *Racon (T) 18M*.
FR 13m 12M vis: 026°- 038° over Whiting Bank.
Aldeburgh Ridge ⌐ QR; 52°06'·72N 01°36'·95E.

SOUTHWOLD

Southwold ☆ 52°19'·63N 01°40'·89E; Fl (4) WR 20s 37m **W16M, R12M, R14M**; vis 204°-R (intens)- 215°-W-001°.

LOWESTOFT and APPR VIA STANFORD CHANNEL

E Barnard ⚲ Q (3) 10s; 52°25'·14N 01°46'·38E .
Newcome Sand ⚲ QR; 52°26'·28N 01°46'·97E.
S Holm ⚲ VQ (6) + L Fl 10s; 52°27'·05N 01°47'·15E.
Stanford ⌐ Fl R 2·5s; 52°27'·35N 01°46'·67E.
SW Holm ▲ Fl (2) G 5s; 52°27'·87N 01°46'·99E.
Claremont Pier ⚲ Fl R 5s 5m 3M; 52°27'·89N 01°44'·87E.
Outer Hbr S Pier Hd ⚲ Oc R 5s 12m 6M; *Horn (4) 60s*; Tfc sigs; 52°28'·29N 01°45'·36E.
N Newcome ⌐ Fl (4) R 15s; 52°28'·39N 01°46'·37E.
Lowestoft ☆ 52°29'·22N 01°45'·35; Fl 15s 37m **23M**; W twr; part obscd 347°- shore;

LOWESTOFT NORTH ROAD and CORTON ROAD

Lowestoft Ness SE ⚲ Q (6) + L Fl 15s; 52°28'·84N 01°46'·25E.
Lowestoft Ness N ⚲ VQ (3) 5s; *Bell*; 52°28'·89N 01°46'·23E.
W Holm ▲ Fl (3) G 10s; 52°29'·80N 01°47'·09E.
NW Holm ▲ Fl (4) G 15s; 52°31'·93N 01°46'·70E.

GREAT YARMOUTH APPROACH via HOLM CHANNEL

E Newcome ⌐ Fl (2) R 5s; 52°28'·51N 01°49'·21E.
Corton ⚲ Q (3) 10s; *Whis*; 52°31'·13N 01°51'·39E.
E. Holm ⌐ Fl (3) R 10s; 52°30'·64N 01°49'·72E.
S Corton ⚲ Q (6) + L Fl 15s; *Bell*; 52°32'·70N 01°49'·50E.
NE Holm ⌐ Fl R 2·5s; 52°32'·30N 01°48'·20E.
Holm ▲ Fl G 2·5s; 52°33'·53N 01°47'·96E,
Holm Sand ⚲ Q. 52°33'·36N 01°46'·85E.

GREAT YARMOUTH and GORLESTON

W Corton ⚲ Q (9) 15s; 52°34'·59N 01°46'·62E.
Brush Sector ⚲ Dir Oc WRG 10s 7m 1M; 248·5°-G-250·5°-Alt GW-252·5°-W-257·5°-R-258·5°; metal framework tower; 52°34'·30N 01°44'·00E.
Gorleston South Pier Hd ⚲ Fl R 3s 11m 11M; vis: 235°-340°; *Horn (3) 60s*; 52°34'·33N 01°44'·28E.
N Pier Hd ⚲ QG 8m 6M; vis: 176°-078°; 52°34'·38N 01°44'·38E.

1.4 PASSAGE INFORMATION

Reference books include: *East Coast Rivers* – latest edition 2004 (NDL/Harber) from the Swale to Lowestoft. The Admiralty NP 28 *Dover Strait Pilot* and NP54 *North Sea (West) Pilot*. The area is well covered by Admiralty Leisure Folios: 5606 covers the Thames Estuary from Ramsgate to Tower Bridge, 5607 the northern Thames Estuary to Orford Ness, and 5614 from Orford Ness northwards.

More Passage Information is threaded between the harbours of this Area.

THE THAMES ESTUARY

(AC 1183, 1975) To appreciate the geography of the Thames Estuary there is a well-known analogy between its major sandbanks and the fingers and thumb of the left hand, out-stretched palm-down: With the thumb lying E over Margate Sand, the index finger covers Long Sand; the middle finger represents Sunk Sand and the third finger delineates West and East Barrow; the little finger points NE along Buxey and Gunfleet Sands.

The intervening channels are often intricate, but the main ones, in sequence from south to north, are:

- between the Kent coast and thumb – Four Fathoms, Horse, Gore and South Chans; sometimes known as the overland route due to relatively shallow water.
- between thumb and index finger – Queens and Princes Chans leading seaward to Knock Deep.
- between index and middle fingers – Knob Chan leading to Knock Deep via the Edinburgh Chans across Long Sand and the Shingles. Knock John Chan and Black Deep, the main shipping channels which are restricted to vessels drawing more than 6m.
- between middle and third fingers – Barrow Deep.
- between third and little fingers – W and E Swin, Middle Deep and Whitaker Chan leading seaward to King's Chan.
- between little finger and the Essex coast – The Wallet and Goldmer Gat.

The sandbanks shift constantly in the Thames Estuary. Up-to-date charts showing the latest buoyage changes are essential, but it is unwise to put too much faith in charted depths over the banks; a reliable echosounder is vital. The main chans carry much commercial shipping and are well buoyed and lit, but this is not so in lesser chans and swatchways which are convenient for yachtsmen, particularly when crossing the estuary from N to S, or vice versa. Unlit, unmarked minor chans should be used with great caution, which could indeed be the hallmark of all passage-making in the Thames Estuary. Good visibility is needed to pick out buoys/marks, and to avoid shipping.

CROSSING THE THAMES ESTUARY

▶ *Study the tides carefully and understand them, so as to work the streams to best advantage and to ensure sufficient depth at the times and places where you expect to be, or might be later. In principle it is best to make most of the crossing on a rising tide, ie departing N Foreland or the vicinity of the Whitaker buoy at around LW. The stream runs 3kn at sp in places, mostly along the chans but sometimes across the intervening banks. With wind against tide a short, steep sea is raised, particularly in E or NE winds.* ◀

Making N from N Foreland to Orford Ness or beyond (or vice versa) it may be preferable to keep to seaward of the main banks, via Kentish Knock and Long Sand Head buoys, thence to N Shipwash lt buoy 14M further N.

Bound NW from N Foreland it is approximately 26M to the Rivers Crouch, Blackwater or Colne. A safe route is through either the Princes Channel or Fisherman's Gat, thence S of the Tizard,

Knob and West Barrow banks to the West Swin, before turning NE into Middle Deep and the East Swin. This is just one of many routes which could be followed, depending on wind direction, tidal conditions and confidence in electronic aids in the absence of marks.

A similar, well-used route in reverse, ie to the SE, lies via the Wallet Spitway, to the Whitaker lt buoy, through Barrow Swatchway to SW Sunk bn; thence via the N Edinburgh Chan, toward the E Margate lt buoy keeping E of Tongue Sand tr. Beware shoal waters off Barrow and Sunk Sands.

London VTS can give navigational help to yachts on VHF Ch 69; Thames CG at Walton-on-the-Naze can also assist. *London VTS* has radar coverage between the Naze and Margate, eastward to near the Dutch coast.

NORTH FORELAND TO LONDON BRIDGE

N Foreland has a conspic lt ho (AC 1828), with buoys offshore. ▶ *From HW Dover –0120 to +0045 the stream runs N from The Downs and W into Thames Estuary. From HWD + 0045 to + 0440 the N-going stream from The Downs meets the E-going stream from Thames Estuary, which in strong winds causes a bad sea. From HWD –0450 to –0120 the streams turn W into Thames Estuary and S towards The Downs. If bound for London, round N Foreland against the late ebb in order to carry a fair tide from Sheerness onward.* ◀

For vessels drawing less than 2m the most direct route from North Foreland to the Thames and Medway is via South Chan, Gore Chan, Horse Chan, Kentish Flats, Four Fathom Chan and Cant; but it is not well marked particularly over the Kentish Flats. Beware of Kentish Flats wind farm (30 turbines) with submarine cables to Herne Bay. An alternative, deeper route is East of Margate Sand and the Tongue, via the Princes Channel to the Oaze Deep. The N & S Edinburgh Channels are unmarked but navigable with caution. ▶ *W-going streams begin at approx HW Sheerness –0600 and E-going at HW Sheerness +0030.* ◀

Margate or Whitstable afford little shelter for yachts. The Swale provides an interesting inside route S of the Isle of Sheppey with access to Sheerness and the R Medway. If sailing from N Foreland to the Thames, Queenborough offers the first easily accessible, all-tide, deep-water shelter. The Medway Chan is the main appr to Sheerness from the Warp and the Medway Fairway buoy.

CROSSING FROM THAMES/ORWELL TO BELGIUM OR THE NETHERLANDS

(ACs 1408, 1406, 1610, 1630, 1872, 1183) Up to date charts are *essential*. The southern North Sea is an extremely busy area with several large and complex Traffic Separation Schemes and associated Precautionary Areas which should be avoided if at all possible. Where practicable, navigate outside the schemes using any available ITZs, and always cross a TSS on a heading at 90° to the traffic flow in accordance with the Collision Regulations. However, from the Thames to Zeebrugge the most direct route crosses the Nord Hinder South TSS in the vicinity of F3 light float which is a focal point for dense crossing traffic. The very busy area around West Hinder would then have to be negotiated. A longer but much safer route (or if bound for Dunkerque, Oostende or Nieuwpoort) via S Falls, Sandettié and Dyck minimises time spent in the TSS.

From the Orwell (or adjacent rivers) to the Netherlands, it may be best to pass north of the Sunk Inner and Sunk Outer TSS/Precautionary Areas before setting course for Hoek van Holland. From S Shipwash make for N Inner Gabbard before setting course for NHR-S to cross the North Hinder TSS to NHR-SE, then pass S of the Maas-West TSS leaving MW1, MW3 and MW5 buoys to port before shaping up for MV-N buoy.

▶ *Care must be taken throughout with the tidal streams, which may be setting across the yacht's track.* ◀ The whole area is relatively shallow, and in bad weather seas are steep and short. *(See also Area 2.)*

1.5 RAMSGATE

Kent **51°19´·51N 01°25´·50E** ✦✦✦♠♠♠♠✿✿✿

CHARTS AC 5605, 323, 1828, 1827; Imray C30, C8, C1; Stan 9, 5, 20.

TIDES +0030 Dover; ML 2·7; Duration 0530

Standard Port DOVER (◄—)

Times				Height (metres)			
High Water		Low Water		MHWS	MHWN	MLWN	MLWS
0000	0600	0100	0700	6·8	5·3	2·1	0·8
1200	1800	1300	1900				
Differences RAMSGATE							
+0030	+0030	+0017	+0007	−1·6	−1·3	−0·7	−0·2
RICHBOROUGH							
+0015	+0015	+0030	+0030	−3·4	−2·6	−1·7	−0·7

HW Broadstairs = HW Dover +0037 approx.

SHELTER Options: (a) Inner Marina, min depth 3m. Access approx HW ±2 via flap gate and lifting bridge; (b) W Marina, in 3m, access H24; (c) E Marina, in 2m, access H24. Larger vessels can berth on outer wavebreak pontoons of both W and E marinas.

NAVIGATION WPT 51°19´·43N 01°27´·70E, 270°/1·45M to S bkwtr. Commercial shipping uses the well-marked main E-W chan dredged 7·5m. *Due to silting, depths may be significantly less than shown; parts of Eastern Marina almost dry at LWS.* Latest information may be obtained from Port Control.

For ent/dep yachts must use the Recommended Yacht Track on the S side of the main buoyed chan. Ent/dep under power, or advise Port Control if unable to motor. Ent/dep Royal Hbr directly; cross the turning basin without delay *keeping close to the W Pier to avoid shoal patch alongside E Pier.* Holding area to the S of the S bkwtr must be used by yachts to keep the hbr ent clear for freight vessels. Beware Dike Bank to the N and Quern Bank close S of the chan. Cross Ledge and Brake shoals are further S. Speed limit 5kn. See www.portoframsgate.co.uk

LIGHTS AND MARKS Ldg lts 270°: front Dir Oc WRG 10s 10m 5M; rear, Oc 5s 17m 5M. N bkwtr hd = QG 10m 5M; S bkwtr hd = VQ R 10m 5M. At E Pier, **IPTS** (Sigs 2 and 3) visible from seaward and from within Royal Hbr, control appr into hbr limits (abeam Nos 1 & 2 buoys) and ent/exit to/from Royal Hbr. In addition a Fl Orange lt = ferry is under way; no other vessel may enter Hbr limits from seaward or leave Royal Hbr. Ent to inner marina controlled by separate IPTS to stbd of ent. Siren sounded approx 10 mins before gate closes; non-opening indicated by red ball or light.

R/T Listen and contact *Ramsgate Port Control* on Ch 14 when intending to enter or leave Royal Hbr. Only when in Royal Hbr call *Ramsgate Marina* Ch 80 for a berth. Ramsgate Dock Office can be called on Ch 14 for information on Inner Marina Lock.

TELEPHONE (Code 01843) Marina Office 572110, Hbr Office 572100; Broadstairs HM 861879; MRCC (01304) 210008; Marinecall 09068 500 455/456; Police 231055; Dr 852853; Ⓗ 225544.

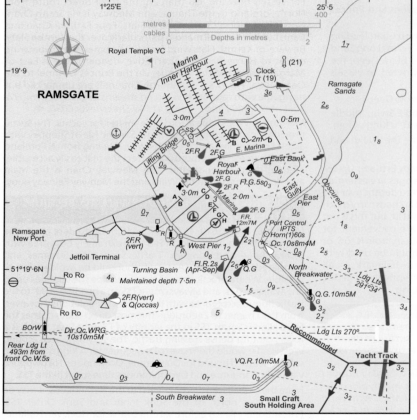

FACILITIES Note: No animals are allowed in Ramsgate Harbour, including the marinas. **Marinas** (510+300Ⓥ) £2.30, ☎ 572100, portoframsgate@ thanet.gov.uk, D, P, FW, ⬚D, BH (40 ton), Ⓔ, ME, El, ✕, Slip £28/craft <5tons, CH, ACA, Gaz, SM, Ⓠ; **Royal Hbr** P & D (0600-2200). **Royal Temple YC** ☎ 591766, Bar. **Town:** Gas, Gaz, ⷲ, R, Bar, ✉, Ⓑ, ⇌.

ADJACENT HARBOUR

SANDWICH, Kent, **51°16´·83N 01°21´·20E**. AC 1827 1828. Richborough differences above; ML 1·4m; Duration 0520. HW Sandwich Town quay is HW Richborough +1. Access HW ±1 at sp for draft 2m to reach Sandwich; arrive off ent at HW Dover. Visitors should seek local knowledge before arriving by day; night ent definitely not advised. The chan is marked by small lateral buoys and beacons. Visitors' berths on S bank of the River Stour at Town Quay ☎ (01304) 612162. Limited turning room before the swing bridge (opens 1H notice ☎ 01304 620644 or Mobile 0860 378792), 1·7m clearance when closed. Facilities: Slip HW±2; ⷲ, R, Bar, ✉, Ⓑ, ⇌, ✈ (Manston).

Marina (50 + some visitors), £2.20, ☎ 613783 (max LOA 18m, 2·1m draft), BH (15 ton), ✕, Slip, FW, SM, CH, ME, Gas; D & P (cans from garage).

Sandwich Sailing and Motorboat Club ☎ 617650 and **Sandwich Bay Sailing and Water Ski Clubs** offer some facilities. The port is administered by Sandwich Port & Haven Commissioners.

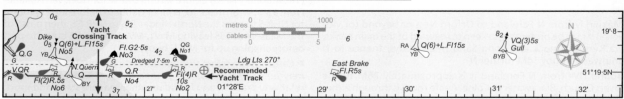

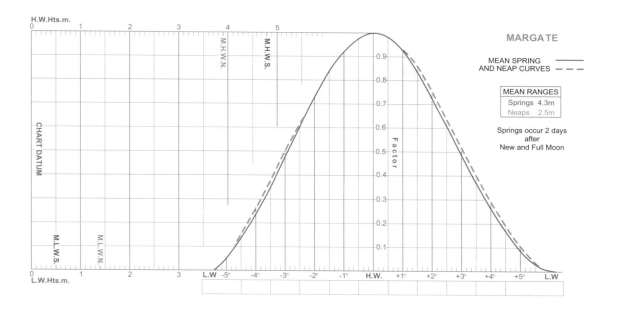

TIME ZONE (UT)
For Summer Time add ONE hour in **non-shaded areas**

MARGATE   LAT 51°23'N   LONG 1°23'E
TIMES AND HEIGHTS OF HIGH AND LOW WATERS

Dates in red are **SPRINGS**
Dates in blue are **NEAPS**

YEAR **2010**

JANUARY

Time	m		Time	m
1 0612	0.6	**16** 0020	4.5
1203	4.8	0651	0.7
F 1819	0.8	SA 1244	4.4
		1850	1.0
2 0024	4.7	**17** 0052	4.6
0700	0.5	0724	0.7
SA 1253	4.9	SU 1315	4.5
1906	0.8	1918	1.0
3 0112	4.8	**18** 0127	4.6
0748	0.3	0752	0.6
SU 1344	4.9	M 1350	4.5
1954	0.8	1945	1.0
4 0200	4.8	**19** 0202	4.6
0835	0.3	0820	0.6
M 1436	4.8	TU 1425	4.4
2042	0.9	2016	1.0
5 0249	4.8	**20** 0236	4.6
0922	0.3	0850	0.7
TU 1530	4.7	W 1459	4.3
2128	0.9	2051	1.0
6 0337	4.8	**21** 0307	4.5
1009	0.4	0923	0.7
W 1623	4.6	TH 1529	4.2
2216	1.0	2128	1.1
7 0426	4.7	**22** 0337	4.4
1100	0.6	0958	0.8
TH 1715	4.4	F 1600	4.1
☽ 2307	1.2	2208	1.2
8 0519	4.5	**23** 0415	4.3
1157	0.8	1036	1.0
F 1811	4.2	SA 1642	4.0
		☽ 2259	1.3
9 0004	1.3	**24** 0506	4.2
0620	4.3	1125	1.1
SA 1259	1.0	SU 1741	3.9
1911	4.0		
10 0113	1.4	**25** 0007	1.4
0736	4.1	0609	4.0
SU 1401	1.1	M 1235	1.3
2019	4.0	1905	3.9
11 0242	1.4	**26** 0123	1.4
0849	4.1	0727	4.0
M 1504	1.2	TU 1409	1.3
2129	4.1	2022	4.0
12 0353	1.2	**27** 0255	1.3
0953	4.2	0857	4.1
TU 1605	1.2	W 1523	1.2
2227	4.2	2135	4.1
13 0447	1.0	**28** 0412	1.0
1049	4.2	1007	4.4
W 1656	1.2	TH 1626	1.0
2311	4.3	2239	4.4
14 0534	0.8	**29** 0510	0.7
1135	4.3	1104	4.6
TH 1739	1.1	F 1722	0.9
2348	4.4	2330	4.6
15 0614	0.7	**30** 0601	0.5
1212	4.4	1155	4.8
F 1817	1.1	SA 1811	0.8
●		○	
		31 0016	4.8
		0648	0.3
		SU 1245	4.9
		1857	0.7

FEBRUARY

Time	m		Time	m
1 0101	4.9	**16** 0106	4.7
0733	0.2	0724	0.6
M 1334	5.0	TU 1326	4.5
1941	0.7	1926	0.9
2 0146	5.0	**17** 0140	4.7
0817	0.2	0751	0.6
TU 1422	4.9	W 1359	4.5
2023	0.7	1957	0.8
3 0231	5.0	**18** 0211	4.7
0858	0.2	0821	0.6
W 1508	4.8	TH 1427	4.5
2105	0.8	2030	0.9
4 0315	5.0	**19** 0238	4.6
0937	0.4	0852	0.6
TH 1552	4.6	F 1455	4.4
2147	0.9	2103	1.0
5 0358	4.8	**20** 0305	4.5
1018	0.6	0923	0.8
F 1636	4.4	SA 1522	4.3
◐ 2232	1.1	2137	1.1
6 0445	4.5	**21** 0341	4.4
1104	0.9	0958	0.9
SA 1726	4.1	SU 1602	4.2
2324	1.2	2222	1.2
7 0541	4.2	**22** 0431	4.3
1206	1.2	1044	1.1
SU 1825	3.9	M 1657	4.0
		◐ 2332	1.3
8 0028	1.4	**23** 0535	4.1
0658	4.0	1156	1.3
M 1318	1.4	TU 1824	3.8
1936	3.8		
9 0213	1.5	**24** 0053	1.4
0823	3.9	0702	3.9
TU 1434	1.5	W 1341	1.4
2100	3.9	1957	3.9
10 0336	1.3	**25** 0237	1.2
0938	4.0	0845	4.1
W 1553	1.4	TH 1505	1.3
2207	4.1	2121	4.1
11 0435	1.0	**26** 0356	0.9
1042	4.2	0956	4.4
TH 1647	1.3	F 1613	1.1
2255	4.3	2226	4.4
12 0521	0.7	**27** 0454	0.6
1128	4.3	1053	4.6
F 1728	1.2	SA 1708	0.9
2332	4.4	2316	4.7
13 0558	0.7	**28** 0544	0.4
1201	4.4	1143	4.7
SA 1803	1.1	SU 1755	0.8
		○ 2359	4.9
14 0004	4.5		
0630	0.7		
SU 1228	4.4		
● 1833	1.0		
15 0034	4.6		
0658	0.6		
M 1255	4.5		
1859	0.9		

MARCH

Time	m		Time	m
1 0629	0.2	**16** 0010	4.6
1229	4.9	0626	0.6
M 1838	0.7	TU 1230	4.5
		1835	0.9
2 0042	5.0	**17** 0041	4.7
0710	0.1	0652	0.6
TU 1315	4.9	W 1259	4.6
1920	0.6	1905	0.8
3 0125	5.1	**18** 0113	4.7
0750	0.2	0721	0.5
W 1358	4.9	TH 1328	4.6
2001	0.6	1938	0.8
4 0208	5.1	**19** 0143	4.7
0826	0.3	0752	0.6
TH 1439	4.7	F 1355	4.5
2041	0.7	2012	0.8
5 0249	5.0	**20** 0212	4.6
0902	0.5	0823	0.6
F 1517	4.6	SA 1424	4.5
2121	0.8	2046	0.9
6 0330	4.8	**21** 0244	4.6
0938	0.7	0855	0.6
SA 1555	4.4	SU 1458	4.4
2202	1.0	2122	1.0
7 0413	4.5	**22** 0323	4.5
1019	1.0	0932	1.0
SU 1641	4.1	M 1541	4.2
☽ 2250	1.2	2210	1.1
8 0505	4.2	**23** 0414	4.3
1116	1.4	1023	1.2
M 1741	3.9	TU 1638	4.0
2352	1.4	◐ 2318	1.2
9 0624	3.9	**24** 0521	4.1
1234	1.6	1144	1.4
TU 1855	3.7	W 1806	3.9
10 0138	1.5	**25** 0039	1.2
0755	3.8	0659	4.0
W 1401	1.7	TH 1325	1.4
2024	3.8	1938	3.9
11 0311	1.3	**26** 0225	1.1
0915	3.9	0833	4.2
TH 1534	1.5	F 1446	1.3
2136	4.0	2103	4.2
12 0411	1.1	**27** 0336	0.8
1018	4.2	0941	4.5
F 1627	1.3	SA 1554	1.1
2227	4.2	2205	4.5
13 0456	0.9	**28** 0433	0.5
1102	4.3	1037	4.7
SA 1707	1.1	SU 1647	0.9
2306	4.4	2254	4.7
14 0531	0.8	**29** 0521	0.3
1136	4.4	1125	4.8
SU 1740	1.0	M 1733	0.8
2340	4.5	2337	4.9
15 0601	0.7	**30** 0603	0.2
1203	4.5	1208	4.8
M 1809	0.9	TU 1815	0.6
●		○	
		31 0018	5.0
		0642	0.2
		W 1249	4.8
		1857	0.6

APRIL

Time	m		Time	m
1 0101	5.1	**16** 0044	4.7
0719	0.3	0653	0.6
TH 1329	4.8	F 1257	4.6
1939	0.6	1920	0.7
2 0144	5.1	**17** 0118	4.7
0756	0.4	0726	0.6
F 1408	4.7	SA 1330	4.6
2020	0.6	1957	0.7
3 0225	4.9	**18** 0154	4.7
0831	0.6	0800	0.7
SA 1444	4.6	SU 1406	4.5
2059	0.8	2036	0.8
4 0305	4.7	**19** 0233	4.6
0905	0.9	0837	0.8
SU 1520	4.4	M 1446	4.4
2139	0.9	2118	0.8
5 0346	4.4	**20** 0317	4.5
0943	1.2	0921	1.0
M 1603	4.2	TU 1535	4.3
2223	1.1	2210	0.9
6 0435	4.1	**21** 0411	4.3
1034	1.5	1019	1.2
TU 1659	4.0	W 1638	4.1
◐ 2320	1.3	◐ 2314	1.1
7 0547	3.8	**22** 0521	4.2
1152	1.7	1142	1.4
W 1809	3.8	TH 1755	4.0
8 0047	1.5	**23** 0035	1.0
0719	3.7	0655	4.1
TH 1315	1.8	F 1306	1.4
1937	3.8	1916	4.1
9 0227	1.3	**24** 0205	0.8
0835	3.9	0814	4.3
F 1452	1.6	SA 1421	1.2
2055	4.0	2037	4.3
10 0328	1.1	**25** 0311	0.6
0936	4.1	0919	4.5
SA 1552	1.4	SU 1528	1.0
2149	4.2	2139	4.5
11 0414	0.9	**26** 0406	0.5
1023	4.3	1014	4.6
SU 1634	1.2	M 1622	0.9
2231	4.4	2228	4.7
12 0451	0.8	**27** 0453	0.4
1100	4.4	1101	4.6
M 1708	1.0	TU 1709	0.8
2308	4.5	2312	4.8
13 0521	0.7	**28** 0534	0.4
1131	4.4	1142	4.7
TU 1739	0.9	W 1753	0.7
2340	4.6	○ 2355	4.9
14 0550	0.7	**29** 0613	0.4
1159	4.5	1221	4.7
W 1810	0.8	TH 1837	0.6
●			
15 0011	4.6	**30** 0038	5.0
0620	0.6	0651	0.3
TH 1227	4.6	F 1301	4.7
1843	0.8	1920	0.6

Chart Datum: 2·5 metres below Ordnance Datum (Newlyn). HAT is 5·2 metres above Chart Datum; see 0.19

TIME ZONE (UT)
For Summer Time add ONE hour in **non-shaded areas**

MARGATE LAT 51°23'N LONG 1°23'E
TIMES AND HEIGHTS OF HIGH AND LOW WATERS

Dates in red are SPRINGS
Dates in blue are NEAPS

YEAR 2010

E England

MAY

Time	m	Time	m
1 0121 / 0729 / SA 1340 / 2002	4.9 / 0.6 / 4.6 / 0.6	**16** 0059 / 0706 / SU 1314 / 1946	4.7 / 0.7 / 4.6 / 0.6
2 0203 / 0806 / SU 1417 / 2042	4.8 / 0.8 / 4.5 / 0.7	**17** 0141 / 0746 / M 1357 / 2030	4.7 / 0.8 / 4.6 / 0.6
3 0243 / 0840 / M 1455 / 2120	4.6 / 1.0 / 4.4 / 0.9	**18** 0227 / 0830 / TU 1444 / 2117	4.7 / 0.9 / 4.5 / 0.7
4 0324 / 0916 / TU 1537 / 2200	4.3 / 1.2 / 4.4 / 1.0	**19** 0316 / 0920 / W 1536 / 2209	4.6 / 1.0 / 4.4 / 0.7
5 0410 / 1000 / W 1627 / 2250	4.1 / 1.4 / 4.1 / 1.2	**20** 0413 / 1021 / TH 1635 / ◑ 2310	4.4 / 1.2 / 4.3 / 0.7
6 0508 / 1106 / TH 1725 / ◑ 2358	3.9 / 1.6 / 3.9 / 1.3	**21** 0524 / 1130 / F 1740	4.3 / 1.2 / 4.3
7 0625 / 1222 / F 1831	3.8 / 1.7 / 3.9	**22** 0025 / 0638 / SA 1240 / 1849	0.8 / 4.3 / 1.3 / 4.3
8 0122 / 0739 / SA 1334 / 1950	1.3 / 3.8 / 1.6 / 3.9	**23** 0139 / 0747 / SU 1349 / 2004	0.7 / 4.3 / 1.2 / 4.4
9 0226 / 0842 / SU 1446 / 2059	1.2 / 4.0 / 1.5 / 4.1	**24** 0241 / 0850 / M 1458 / 2109	0.7 / 4.4 / 1.1 / 4.5
10 0317 / 0934 / M 1543 / 2148	1.0 / 4.1 / 1.3 / 4.2	**25** 0336 / 0948 / TU 1558 / 2202	0.6 / 4.4 / 1.0 / 4.6
11 0401 / 1016 / TU 1628 / 2228	0.9 / 4.3 / 1.1 / 4.4	**26** 0424 / 1037 / W 1648 / 2250	0.7 / 4.5 / 0.9 / 4.7
12 0440 / 1052 / W 1707 / 2305	0.8 / 4.4 / 1.0 / 4.5	**27** 0507 / 1120 / TH 1735 / ○ 2335	0.7 / 4.5 / 0.8 / 4.7
13 0517 / 1125 / TH 1746 / 2341	0.8 / 4.5 / 0.9 / 4.6	**28** 0549 / 1159 / F 1821	0.7 / 4.5 / 0.6
14 0553 / 1157 / F 1825 ●	0.7 / 4.5 / 0.8	**29** 0020 / 0629 / SA 1239 / 1905	4.7 / 0.8 / 4.6 / 0.6
15 0018 / 0629 / SA 1234 / 1905	4.7 / 0.7 / 4.6 / 0.7	**30** 0103 / 0709 / SU 1318 / 1948	4.7 / 0.8 / 4.6 / 0.6
		31 0144 / 0747 / M 1357 / 2027	4.6 / 0.9 / 4.5 / 0.7

JUNE

Time	m	Time	m
1 0224 / 0821 / TU 1435 / 2102	4.5 / 1.0 / 4.5 / 0.8	**16** 0222 / 0828 / W 1440 / 2112	4.8 / 0.8 / 4.7 / 0.4
2 0303 / 0853 / W 1515 / 2138	4.3 / 1.2 / 4.4 / 0.9	**17** 0315 / 0919 / TH 1531 / 2202	4.7 / 0.9 / 4.7 / 0.5
3 0345 / 0932 / TH 1559 / 2218	4.2 / 1.3 / 4.3 / 1.0	**18** 0412 / 1012 / F 1623 / 2257	4.6 / 1.0 / 4.6 / 0.5
4 0433 / 1021 / F 1648 / ◑ 2307	4.0 / 1.4 / 4.4 / 1.1	**19** 0512 / 1108 / SA 1718 ◐	4.4 / 1.1 / 4.5
5 0528 / 1122 / SA 1740	3.9 / 1.5 / 4.0	**20** 0000 / 0611 / SU 1208 / 1819	0.6 / 4.3 / 1.2 / 4.4
6 0013 / 0627 / SU 1230 / 1835	1.2 / 3.9 / 1.6 / 4.0	**21** 0106 / 0713 / M 1313 / 1928	0.7 / 4.2 / 1.2 / 4.4
7 0124 / 0728 / M 1336 / 1936	1.2 / 3.9 / 1.5 / 4.0	**22** 0207 / 0816 / TU 1427 / 2039	0.8 / 4.2 / 1.2 / 4.4
8 0222 / 0827 / TU 1443 / 2042	1.1 / 4.0 / 1.4 / 4.1	**23** 0305 / 0920 / W 1537 / 2140	0.9 / 4.2 / 1.1 / 4.4
9 0315 / 0922 / W 1546 / 2141	1.1 / 4.1 / 1.2 / 4.2	**24** 0359 / 1018 / TH 1634 / 2235	1.0 / 4.3 / 1.0 / 4.4
10 0404 / 1011 / TH 1638 / 2230	1.0 / 4.3 / 1.0 / 4.4	**25** 0449 / 1106 / F 1724 / 2324	1.0 / 4.3 / 0.8 / 4.5
11 0449 / 1055 / F 1725 / 2316	0.9 / 4.4 / 0.9 / 4.5	**26** 0534 / 1147 / SA 1810 ○	1.0 / 4.4 / 0.7
12 0531 / 1137 / SA 1809 ●	0.9 / 4.5 / 0.7	**27** 0009 / 0615 / SU 1225 / 1853	4.5 / 1.0 / 4.5 / 0.6
13 0000 / 0612 / SU 1220 / 1853	4.7 / 0.8 / 4.6 / 0.6	**28** 0050 / 0655 / M 1301 / 1933	4.5 / 0.9 / 4.6 / 0.6
14 0045 / 0654 / M 1304 / 1938	4.8 / 0.8 / 4.7 / 0.5	**29** 0127 / 0731 / TU 1338 / 2009	4.5 / 1.0 / 4.6 / 0.7
15 0132 / 0740 / TU 1352 / 2025	4.8 / 0.8 / 4.7 / 0.5	**30** 0203 / 0803 / W 1415 / 2041	4.5 / 1.0 / 4.6 / 0.7

JULY

Time	m	Time	m
1 0240 / 0832 / TH 1453 / 2111	4.4 / 1.0 / 4.5 / 0.8	**16** 0305 / 0905 / F 1515 / 2143	4.8 / 0.8 / 4.9 / 0.3
2 0319 / 0906 / F 1532 / 2144	4.3 / 1.1 / 4.4 / 0.8	**17** 0356 / 0951 / SA 1602 / 2230	4.7 / 0.9 / 4.8 / 0.5
3 0359 / 0946 / SA 1611 / 2222	4.2 / 1.2 / 4.3 / 0.9	**18** 0446 / 1039 / SU 1652 / ◑ 2322	4.5 / 1.0 / 4.7 / 0.7
4 0441 / 1033 / SU 1644 / ◑ 2306	4.0 / 1.3 / 4.2 / 1.1	**19** 0539 / 1133 / M 1748	4.3 / 1.1 / 4.5
5 0530 / 1128 / M 1743	3.9 / 1.4 / 4.1	**20** 0024 / 0636 / TU 1235 / 1856	0.9 / 4.1 / 1.3 / 4.3
6 0001 / 0627 / TU 1234 / 1839	1.2 / 3.9 / 1.5 / 4.0	**21** 0130 / 0741 / W 1359 / 2014	1.1 / 4.0 / 1.3 / 4.2
7 0118 / 0730 / W 1345 / 1945	1.3 / 3.9 / 1.4 / 4.0	**22** 0237 / 0856 / TH 1523 / 2125	1.2 / 4.0 / 1.2 / 4.2
8 0231 / 0834 / TH 1506 / 2059	1.2 / 4.0 / 1.3 / 4.1	**23** 0344 / 1004 / F 1625 / 2229	1.2 / 4.1 / 1.0 / 4.3
9 0331 / 0937 / F 1612 / 2204	1.1 / 4.2 / 1.1 / 4.3	**24** 0441 / 1056 / SA 1716 / 2322	1.2 / 4.3 / 0.8 / 4.4
10 0425 / 1034 / SA 1706 / 2257	1.0 / 4.3 / 0.8 / 4.5	**25** 0526 / 1137 / SU 1800	1.1 / 4.4 / 0.7
11 0515 / 1124 / SU 1754 / ● 2346	0.9 / 4.5 / 0.6 / 4.7	**26** 0004 / 0605 / M 1211 / ○ 1838	4.4 / 1.0 / 4.5 / 0.6
12 0601 / 1209 / M 1841	0.8 / 4.6 / 0.5	**27** 0038 / 0640 / TU 1243 / 1913	4.5 / 1.0 / 4.6 / 0.6
13 0034 / 0647 / TU 1255 / 1927	4.8 / 0.8 / 4.8 / 0.3	**28** 0108 / 0713 / W 1317 / 1944	4.5 / 0.9 / 4.6 / 0.6
14 0123 / 0733 / W 1342 / 2013	4.9 / 0.7 / 4.9 / 0.3	**29** 0140 / 0741 / TH 1352 / 2012	4.5 / 0.9 / 4.7 / 0.6
15 0214 / 0819 / TH 1429 / 2058	4.9 / 0.7 / 4.9 / 0.2	**30** 0214 / 0809 / F 1428 / 2040	4.5 / 0.9 / 4.7 / 0.7
		31 0249 / 0842 / SA 1502 / 2110	4.4 / 0.9 / 4.6 / 0.7

AUGUST

Time	m	Time	m
1 0320 / 0917 / SU 1533 / 2144	4.3 / 1.0 / 4.4 / 0.8	**16** 0413 / 1010 / M 1623 / ◑ 2240	4.4 / 0.9 / 4.7 / 0.8
2 0350 / 0956 / M 1607 / 2220	4.2 / 1.2 / 4.3 / 1.0	**17** 0502 / 1100 / TU 1717 / 2338	4.2 / 1.1 / 4.4 / 1.1
3 0426 / 1042 / TU 1652 / ◑ 2304	4.0 / 1.3 / 4.2 / 1.2	**18** 0600 / 1201 / W 1829	4.0 / 1.3 / 4.1
4 0518 / 1144 / W 1749	3.9 / 1.4 / 4.0	**19** 0052 / 0708 / TH 1337 / 1954	1.4 / 3.9 / 1.4 / 4.0
5 0008 / 0638 / TH 1258 / 1901	1.3 / 3.8 / 1.4 / 4.0	**20** 0213 / 0833 / F 1510 / 2113	1.5 / 3.9 / 1.2 / 4.1
6 0145 / 0757 / F 1429 / 2031	1.4 / 3.9 / 1.3 / 4.1	**21** 0336 / 0946 / SA 1614 / 2222	1.4 / 4.1 / 1.0 / 4.2
7 0303 / 0912 / SA 1550 / 2145	1.2 / 4.1 / 1.0 / 4.3	**22** 0432 / 1038 / SU 1704 / 2313	1.2 / 4.3 / 0.8 / 4.4
8 0406 / 1018 / SU 1647 / 2242	1.1 / 4.3 / 0.8 / 4.6	**23** 0514 / 1119 / M 1743 / 2351	1.1 / 4.4 / 0.7 / 4.5
9 0501 / 1110 / M 1737 / 2333	0.9 / 4.5 / 0.5 / 4.8	**24** 0549 / 1152 / TU 1817 ○	1.0 / 4.5 / 0.6
10 0549 / 1155 / TU 1824 ●	0.8 / 4.7 / 0.3	**25** 0019 / 0621 / W 1222 / 1847	4.5 / 0.9 / 4.6 / 0.6
11 0020 / 0633 / W 1239 / 1909	4.9 / 0.7 / 4.9 / 0.2	**26** 0044 / 0650 / TH 1253 / 1914	4.5 / 0.9 / 4.7 / 0.6
12 0108 / 0717 / TH 1323 / 1952	4.9 / 0.6 / 5.0 / 0.1	**27** 0113 / 0718 / F 1326 / 1939	4.5 / 0.8 / 4.7 / 0.6
13 0156 / 0800 / F 1408 / 2033	4.9 / 0.6 / 5.1 / 0.2	**28** 0144 / 0747 / SA 1359 / 2008	4.5 / 0.8 / 4.7 / 0.6
14 0243 / 0843 / SA 1452 / 2113	4.8 / 0.6 / 5.0 / 0.3	**29** 0214 / 0818 / SU 1429 / 2038	4.5 / 0.8 / 4.6 / 0.7
15 0328 / 0925 / SU 1536 / 2154	4.6 / 0.8 / 4.9 / 0.5	**30** 0239 / 0853 / M 1457 / 2109	4.4 / 0.9 / 4.6 / 0.8
		31 0306 / 0927 / TU 1529 / 2142	4.2 / 1.0 / 4.4 / 1.0

Chart Datum: 2·5 metres below Ordnance Datum (Newlyn). HAT is 5·2 metres above Chart Datum; see 0.19

MARGATE LAT 51°23′N LONG 1°23′E

TIMES AND HEIGHTS OF HIGH AND LOW WATERS

TIME ZONE (UT)
For Summer Time add ONE hour in **non-shaded areas**

Dates in red are **SPRINGS**
Dates in blue are NEAPS

YEAR 2010

SEPTEMBER

Time	m		Time	m
1 0343	4.1	**16**	0521	3.9
1008	1.2		1133	1.3
W 1614	4.2	TH 1804		4.0
☽ 2223	1.2			
2 0433	4.0	**17**	0014	1.6
1109	1.3		0634	3.8
TH 1713	4.1	F 1312		1.4
2327	1.4		1932	3.9
3 0550	3.8	**18**	0143	1.7
1226	1.4		0803	3.8
F 1831	3.9	SA 1447		1.2
			2053	4.0
4 0111	1.5	**19**	0317	1.5
0725	3.8		0916	4.0
SA 1404	1.3	SU 1550		1.0
2014	4.0		2159	4.2
5 0239	1.3	**20**	0411	1.3
0851	4.0		1009	4.3
SU 1528	0.9	M 1639		0.8
2128	4.3		2246	4.4
6 0347	1.1	**21**	0452	1.1
0959	4.3		1050	4.4
M 1626	0.6	TU 1716		0.7
2226	4.6		2322	4.5
7 0442	0.9	**22**	0527	1.0
1050	4.6		1125	4.5
TU 1716	0.4	W 1747		0.6
2316	4.8		2351	4.5
8 0529	0.7	**23**	0558	0.9
1134	4.8		1156	4.6
W 1802	0.2	TH 1814		0.6
●		○		
9 0001	4.9	**24**	0016	4.5
0613	0.6		0626	0.8
TH 1216	5.0	F 1226		4.7
1844	0.1		1839	0.6
10 0045	4.9	**25**	0043	4.6
0655	0.6		0654	0.8
F 1259	5.1	SA 1257		4.7
1924	0.1		1907	0.6
11 0129	4.9	**26**	0111	4.6
0738	0.6		0725	0.7
SA 1343	5.1	SU 1329		4.7
2003	0.2		1937	0.6
12 0213	4.8	**27**	0138	4.5
0820	0.6		0759	0.8
SU 1427	5.0	M 1359		4.6
2042	0.4		2008	0.7
13 0254	4.6	**28**	0206	4.4
0902	0.7		0833	0.8
M 1510	4.8	TU 1430		4.5
2120	0.7		2039	0.9
14 0335	4.4	**29**	0238	4.3
0946	0.9		0908	0.9
TU 1555	4.6	W 1506		4.4
2203	1.0		2113	1.0
15 0422	4.2	**30**	0317	4.2
1034	1.1		0952	1.0
W 1648	4.3	TH 1553		4.2
☽ 2258	1.3		2158	1.2

OCTOBER

Time	m		Time	m
1 0409	4.0	**16**	0550	3.8
1052	1.2		1229	1.3
F 1653	4.1	SA 1901		3.8
☽ 2306	1.4			
2 0527	3.8	**17**	0055	1.8
1207	1.2		0717	3.8
SA 1817	4.0	SU 1406		1.3
			2016	3.9
3 0049	1.5	**18**	0237	1.6
0658	3.9		0836	3.9
SU 1344	1.1	M 1509		1.1
1956	4.1		2118	4.1
4 0212	1.3	**19**	0338	1.4
0824	4.1		0931	4.2
M 1503	0.8	TU 1558		0.9
2108	4.4		2207	4.3
5 0322	1.1	**20**	0421	1.2
0933	4.4		1015	4.3
TU 1601	0.5	W 1636		0.8
2205	4.7		2246	4.4
6 0419	0.9	**21**	0457	1.0
1025	4.7		1053	4.4
W 1651	0.3	TH 1708		0.7
2254	4.8		2318	4.5
7 0506	0.7	**22**	0530	0.9
1108	4.9		1126	4.5
TH 1735	0.2	F 1738		0.7
● 2337	4.9		2345	4.5
8 0550	0.6	**23**	0601	0.8
1150	5.0		1156	4.6
F 1816	0.2	SA 1807		0.7
		○		
9 0017	4.9	**24**	0010	4.6
0633	0.5		0632	0.6
SA 1234	5.1	SU 1228		4.6
1855	0.3		1837	0.7
10 0059	4.8	**25**	0039	4.6
0717	0.5		0706	0.7
SU 1318	5.1	M 1301		4.6
1934	0.4		1909	0.7
11 0140	4.7	**26**	0110	4.6
0800	0.5		0741	0.7
M 1403	4.9	TU 1336		4.6
2013	0.6		1942	0.8
12 0221	4.6	**27**	0144	4.5
0843	0.7		0819	0.7
TU 1446	4.7	W 1413		4.5
2051	0.9		2017	0.9
13 0301	4.4	**28**	0222	4.4
0925	0.8		0859	0.8
W 1531	4.6	TH 1455		4.4
2132	1.2		2057	1.1
14 0345	4.2	**29**	0305	4.3
1011	1.0		0946	0.9
TH 1622	4.4	F 1544		4.3
☽ 2223	1.5		2148	1.2
15 0441	4.0	**30**	0400	4.1
1106	1.2		1043	1.0
F 1734	3.9	SA 1645		4.2
2335	1.7	☽ 2259		1.4
		31	0513	4.0
			1152	1.0
		SU 1808		4.1

NOVEMBER

Time	m		Time	m
1 0025	1.4	**16**	0113	1.7
0630	4.0		0728	3.8
M 1321	0.9	TU 1406		1.2
1932	4.2		2025	4.0
2 0141	1.3	**17**	0233	1.6
0749	4.2		0842	4.0
TU 1433	0.7	W 1459		1.1
2041	4.4		2119	4.1
3 0251	1.1	**18**	0335	1.4
0901	4.4		0933	4.1
W 1531	0.5	TH 1546		1.0
2139	4.6		2204	4.3
4 0351	1.0	**19**	0420	1.2
0956	4.6		1015	4.3
TH 1622	0.4	F 1626		0.9
2229	4.7		2241	4.4
5 0443	0.8	**20**	0459	1.0
1043	4.8		1052	4.4
F 1707	0.4	SA 1704		0.9
2312	4.7		2312	4.4
6 0529	0.7	**21**	0536	0.9
1127	4.9		1127	4.5
SA 1748	0.4	SU 1738		0.8
● 2352	4.7	○ 2342		4.5
7 0614	0.6	**22**	0612	0.8
1212	4.9		1202	4.6
SU 1829	0.5	M 1812		0.8
8 0033	4.7	**23**	0015	4.6
0659	0.5		0649	0.7
M 1258	4.9	TU 1240		4.6
1910	0.6		1847	0.8
9 0115	4.7	**24**	0052	4.6
0744	0.5		0728	0.6
TU 1342	4.8	W 1320		4.7
1950	0.8		1924	0.8
10 0156	4.6	**25**	0132	4.6
0827	0.6		0809	0.6
W 1426	4.6	TH 1403		4.6
2029	1.0		2005	0.9
11 0236	4.5	**26**	0214	4.5
0908	0.8		0853	0.6
TH 1509	4.4	F 1449		4.6
2107	1.2		2051	1.0
12 0319	4.3	**27**	0302	4.4
0950	0.9		0940	0.7
F 1556	4.1	SA 1539		4.4
2151	1.4		2144	1.2
13 0408	4.1	**28**	0356	4.3
1038	1.1		1033	0.7
SA 1654	3.9	SU 1639		4.3
☽ 2251	1.6	☽ 2248		1.3
14 0504	3.9	**29**	0457	4.3
1141	1.2		1136	0.8
SU 1807	3.8	M 1751		4.2
			2357	1.3
15 0001	1.7	**30**	0603	4.2
0608	3.8		1251	0.8
M 1300	1.3	TU 1902		4.2
1920	3.8			

DECEMBER

Time	m		Time	m
1 0105	1.3	**16**	0110	1.6
0713	4.2		0711	3.9
W 1400	0.7	TH 1359		1.2
2008	4.3		2006	3.9
2 0215	1.2	**17**	0224	1.5
0827	4.3		0822	3.9
TH 1459	0.7	F 1455		1.2
2109	4.4		2106	4.0
3 0324	1.1	**18**	0334	1.3
0929	4.5		0927	4.1
F 1553	0.7	SA 1547		1.1
2204	4.5		2158	4.2
4 0422	0.9	**19**	0427	1.1
1022	4.6		1017	4.2
SA 1642	0.7	SU 1633		1.0
2252	4.5		2243	4.3
5 0513	0.8	**20**	0512	0.9
1111	4.7		1101	4.4
SU 1727	0.7	M 1715		1.0
● 2335	4.6		2322	4.5
6 0601	0.6	**21**	0554	0.8
1158	4.7		1143	4.5
M 1811	0.9	TU 1754		0.9
		○		
7 0017	4.6	**22**	0000	4.6
0647	0.6		0634	0.6
TU 1243	4.7	W 1225		4.7
1853	0.8		1833	0.9
8 0058	4.6	**23**	0041	4.7
0731	0.6		0716	0.5
W 1327	4.6	TH 1309		4.8
1934	0.9		1915	0.8
9 0138	4.6	**24**	0124	4.7
0813	0.6		0759	0.4
TH 1408	4.5	F 1354		4.8
2012	1.1		1959	0.8
10 0217	4.5	**25**	0209	4.7
0851	0.7		0844	0.4
F 1448	4.4	SA 1442		4.7
2045	1.2		2047	0.9
11 0257	4.4	**26**	0256	4.7
0927	0.8		0929	0.4
SA 1529	4.2	SU 1532		4.6
2120	1.3		2136	1.0
12 0339	4.3	**27**	0345	4.6
1004	0.9		1016	0.5
SU 1615	4.1	M 1626		4.5
2203	1.4		2229	1.1
13 0425	4.2	**28**	0437	4.5
1048	1.1		1110	0.6
M 1706	3.9	TU 1726		4.5
☽ 2257	1.6	☽ 2325		1.2
14 0516	4.0	**29**	0534	4.4
1145	1.2		1214	0.7
TU 1803	3.8	W 1828		4.2
15 0002	1.6	**30**	0027	1.3
0610	3.9		0639	4.3
W 1256	1.3	TH 1323		0.9
1904	3.8		1931	4.1
		31	0138	1.3
			0755	4.2
		F 1427		1.0
			2039	4.1

Chart Datum: 2·5 metres below Ordnance Datum (Newlyn). HAT is 5·2 metres above Chart Datum; see 0.19

1.6 THAMES ESTUARY

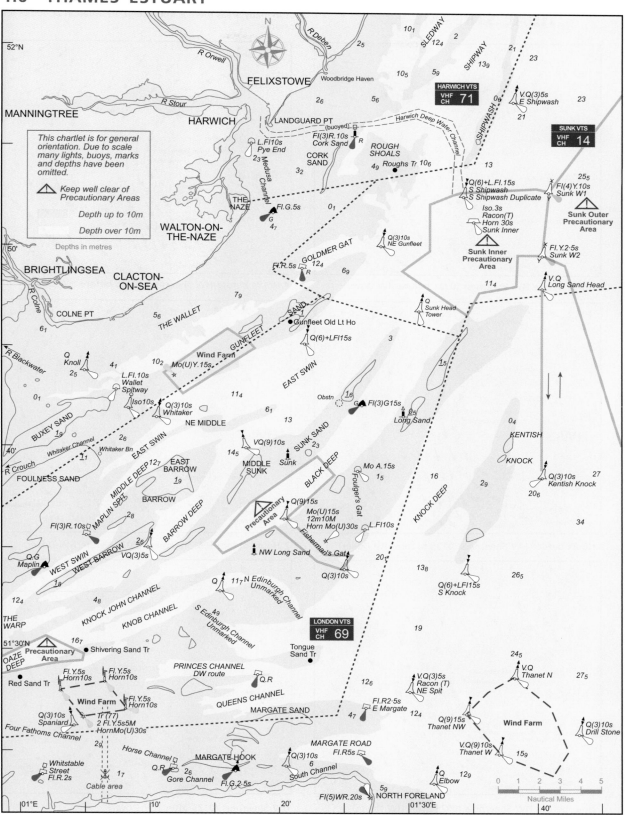

E England

1.7 THAMES ESTUARY TIDAL STREAMS

Due to very strong rates of tidal streams in some areas, eddies may occur. Where possible, some indication of these is shown, but in many areas there is insufficient information or eddies are unstable.

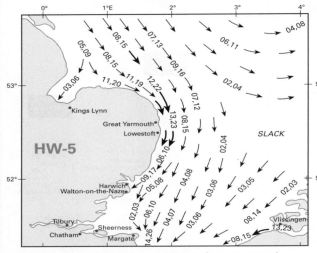

5 Hours before HW Sheerness (0335 before HW Dover)

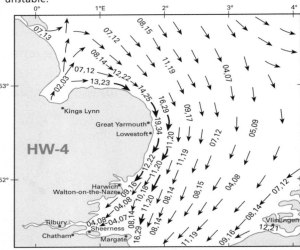

4 Hours before HW Sheerness (0235 before HW Dover)

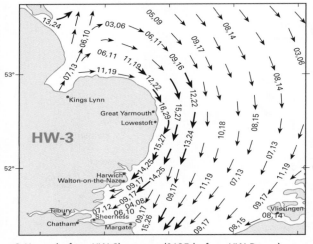

3 Hours before HW Sheerness (0135 before HW Dover)

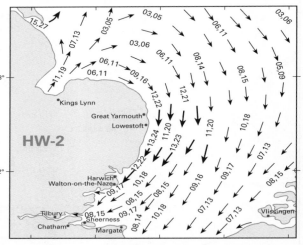

2 Hours before HW Sheerness (0035 before HW Dover)

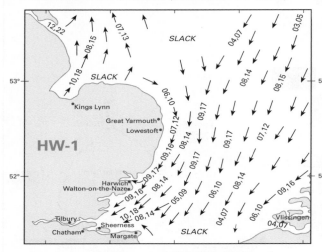

1 Hour before HW Sheerness (0025 after HW Dover)

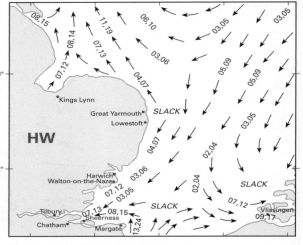

HW Sheerness (0125 after HW Dover)

Due to very strong rates of tidal streams in some areas, eddies may occur. Where possible, some indication of these is shown, but in many areas there is insufficient information or eddies are unstable.

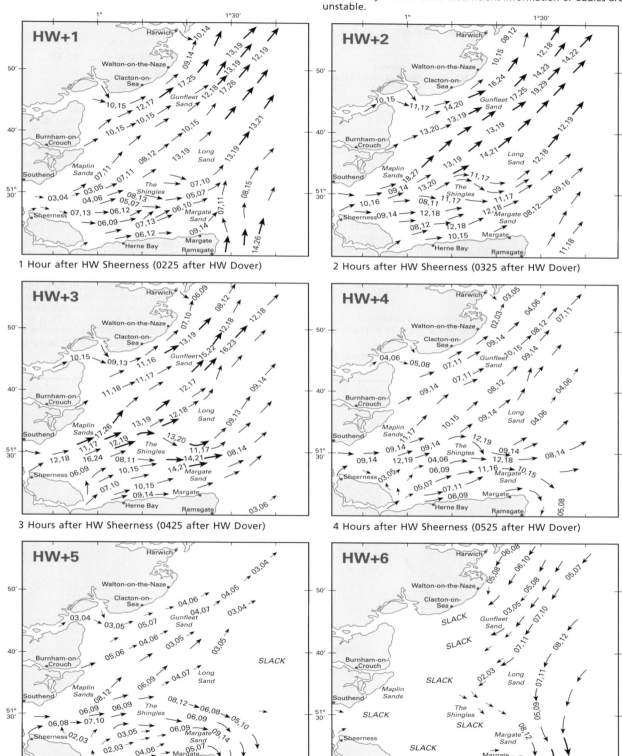

1 Hour after HW Sheerness (0225 after HW Dover)

2 Hours after HW Sheerness (0325 after HW Dover)

3 Hours after HW Sheerness (0425 after HW Dover)

4 Hours after HW Sheerness (0525 after HW Dover)

5 Hours after HW Sheerness (0600 before HW Dover)

6 Hours after HW Sheerness (0500 before HW Dover)

E England

1.8   WHITSTABLE

Kent **51°21'·86N 01°01'·46E** ✹✹⚓⚓✿✿✿

CHARTS AC 5606, 1607, 2571; Imray C1; Stanfords 5, 8.

TIDES +0135 Dover; ML 3·0; Duration 0605

Standard Port MARGATE (←)

Times				Height (metres)			
High Water		Low Water		MHWS	MHWN	MLWN	MLWS
0100	0700	0100	0700	4·8	3·9	1·4	0·5
1300	1900	1300	1900				
Differences HERNE BAY							
+0034	+0022	+0015	+0032	+0·6	+0·4	+0·1	0·0
WHITSTABLE APPROACHES							
+0042	+0029	+0025	+0050	+0·6	+0·6	+0·1	0·0

SHELTER Good, except in strong winds from NNW to NE. Hbr dries up to 0·4m; access HW±1 for strangers. Yacht berths are limited since priority is given to commercial shipping. Fender board needed against piled quays or seek a mooring to NW of hbr (controlled by YC).

NAVIGATION WPT 51°22'·65N 01°01'·10E, 345°/0·83M to W Quay dolphin. From E keep well seaward of Whitstable Street, a hard drying sandspit, which extends 1M N from the coast; shoals a further 1M to seaward are marked by Whitstable Street NCM lt buoy. From W avoid Columbine and Pollard Spits.

Appr (not before half flood) via Oyster PHM lt buoy to harbour entrance or in W sector of Dir lt.

LIGHTS AND MARKS Off head of W Quay on a dolphin, ⚡ Fl G 5s, covers the approaches. At the head of the hbr a Dir lt, Fl WRG 3s 7m, leads 122° into hbr ent.

R/T Call *Whitstable Harbour Radio* VHF Ch **09** 12 16 (Mon–Fri:

0830–1700 LT. Other times: HW –3 to HW+1). Tidal info is available on request.

TELEPHONE (Code 01227) HM 274086, www.canterbury.gov.uk, MRCC (01255) 675518; Marinecall 09068 969645; Police 770055; Dr 594400.

FACILITIES Hbr ☎ 274086, AB £10.00, FW, D.

Whitstable YC ☎ 272942, M, R, Slip HW ±3, L, FW, Bar.

Services: ME, C, CH, ACA, SM, Gas, Ⓔ.

Town: ⊠, P, 🛒, R, Bar, ✉, Ⓑ, ⇌, ✈ Lydd/Manston.

MINOR HARBOURS WEST OF NORTH FORELAND
MARGATE, Kent, **51°23'·43N 01°22'·65E**. AC 5606,1 827, 1828, 323; Imray Y7, C1; Stanfords 5, 8. HW+0045 on Dover; ML 2·6; Duration 0610; Standard Port (←). Small hbr drying 3m, inside bkwtr (Stone Pier) FR 17m 4M; exposed to NW'lies. Appr's: from E, via Longnose NCM buoy, keeping about 5ca offshore; from N, via Margate PHM lt buoy; from W via Gore Chan and S Chan to SE Margate ECM lt buoy. Facilities: Margate YC ☎ (01843) 292602, Ⓒ, Bar.

Town, 10 Slips all HW±2, check suitability with Foreshore Office ☎ (01843) 577529, D & P (cans), R, 🛒, Bar, ✉, Ⓑ, ⇌, ✈ Manston.

HERNE BAY, Kent, **51°22'·40N 01°07'·22E**. AC 5606, 1607. Tides see 1.8. Close E of Pavillion (old pier), 400m long bkwtr 'Neptunes Arm' gives well sheltered drying ⚓'ge for craft <8m. Exposed to strong NE'lies at HW springs when Thames Barrier closed as seas may then top the bkwtr. 3 Slips (HW±2½ to HW±3). Foreshore Mngr ☎ (01227) 266719. Herne Bay SC ☎ (01227) 375650. Lts: QW 8m 4M is 6ca offshore (former pier hd); bkwtr hd 2FR (vert); pier hd 2FG (vert); R bn on B dolphin, Fl Y 5s, is approx 1M ENE of bkwtr hd. Reculvers twrs are conspic 3M to the E.

Town, D & P (cans), Ⓔ, R, 🛒, Bar, ✉, Ⓑ, ⊠, ⇌, ✈ Lydd/Manston.

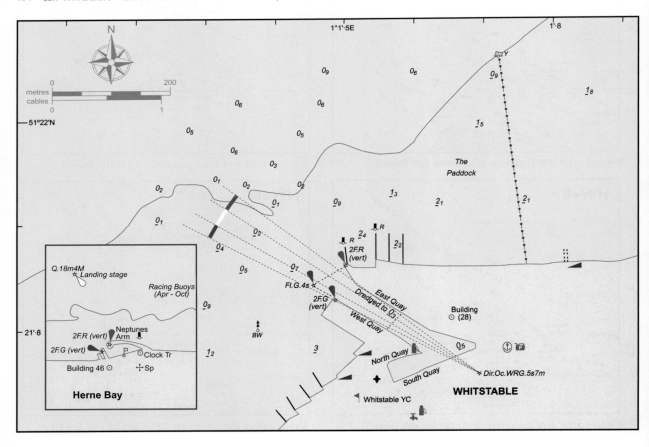

1.9 THE SWALE
Kent ✿✿✿▵▵▵✿✿

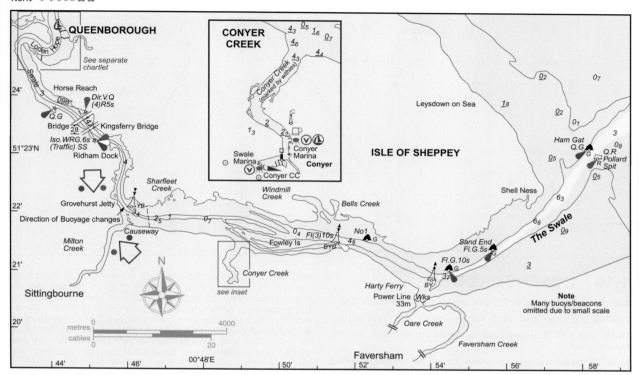

CHARTS AC 5606, 2482, 2571, 2572, 1834, 3683; Imray Y18, C1; Stanfords 5, 8.

TIDES Queenborough +0130 Dover; Harty Ferry +0120 Dover; ML (Harty Ferry) 3·0; Duration 0610. Faversham HW differences are −0·2m on Sheerness; no other data.

Standard Port SHEERNESS (→)

Times				Height (metres)			
High Water		Low Water		MHWS	MHWN	MLWN	MLWS
0200	0800	0200	0700	5·8	4·7	1·5	0·6
1400	2000	1400	1900				

Differences R. SWALE (Grovehurst Jetty)
−0007	0000	0000	+0016	0·0	0·0	0·0	−0·1

Grovehurst Jetty is close N of the ent to Milton Creek.

SHELTER Excellent in the Swale, the 14M chan between the Isle of Sheppey and the N Kent coast, from Shell Ness in the E to Queenborough in the W. Yachts can enter the drying creeks of Faversham, Oare, Conyer, and Milton. Beware wrecks at ent to Faversham Creek. Many moorings line the chan from Faversham to Conyer Creeks. See 1.10 for Queenborough, all-tide access.

NAVIGATION E ent WPT: Whitstable Street lit PHM, 51°24'·00N 01°01'·54E, at ent to well marked buoyed chan. Speed limit 8kn. The middle section from 1·5M E of Conyer Creek to 0·5M E of Milton Creek is narrowed by drying mudbanks and carries least depths of 0·4m. At Milton Creek direction of buoyage changes. There are numerous oyster beds in the area. Kingsferry Bridge (see opposite) opens for masted craft on request, but subject to railway trains; temp anchs off SW bank. The power lines crossing SE of the br have a clearance of 30m. W ent is marked by Queenborough Spit ECM buoy, Q (3) 10s, 1M S of Garrison Pt, at 51°25'·81N 00°43'·93E.

LIGHTS AND MARKS See chartlet and 1.3. In W Swale the following lights intended for large coasters using the narrow chan:

No 5 Bn Oc WRG 6s; vis: 161°-G-166°-W-167°-R-172°. Round Loden Hope bend: two Q WG and one Q WRG on bns; keep in G sectors. See 1.10 chartlet. Horse Reach ldg lts 113°: front QG 7m 5M; rear Fl G 3s 10m 6M. Dir lt 098°, VQ (4) R 5s 6m 5M. Kingsferry Bridge: Dir WRG, 142°-G-147°-W-148°-R-153° 9m. Lts on bridge: two x 2 FG (vert) on SW buttresses; two x 2 FR (vert) on NE. Road bridge has a vertical clearance of 28m.

Kingsferry Bridge traffic sigs:
No lts	= Bridge down (3·35m MHWS).
Al Q ●/●	= Centre span lifting.
F ●	= Bridge open (29m MHWS).
Q ●	= Centre span lowering. Keep clear.
Q ○	= Bridge out of action.

Request bridge opening on VHF Ch 10 (or Ch 74 if no response).

R/T Call: *Medway VTS* VHF Ch **74** 16 22 (H24); Kingsferry Bridge Ch 10 (H24).

TELEPHONE (Code 01795) HM (Medway Ports Ltd) 596593; MRCC (01255) 675518; Marinecall 09068 969645; Police 477055; Dr or Ⓗ via Medway Navigation Service 663025.

FACILITIES FAVERSHAM: Services: BY, AB £5, M, ⬡, FW, Ⓔ, ME, El, ⚒, C (40 ton); SM, D, C (25 ton).
Town 🛒, R, Bar, Gas, ✉, Ⓑ, ⇌, ✈ Gatwick.

OARE CREEK: Services: AB, M, C (8 ton), ME, El, ⚒, CH; Hollow Shore Cruising Club, Bar.

CONYER CREEK: Swale Marina ☎ 521562; AB(dredged 2m) £13/craft, FW, ⬡, D, P, Gas, BH (30 ton), ME, ⚒, C (30ton), Slip, ⚓, ▢;
Conyer CC. Conyer Marina ☎ 521711 AB £7.50, CH, SM, Rigging, BY, ME, ⚒, El, Ⓔ, Slip, D.

MILTON CREEK (Sittingbourne): Crown Quay M, FW.
Town 🛒, R, Bar, ✉, Ⓑ, ⇌, ✈ (Gatwick); also the Dolphin Yard Sailing Barge Museum.

E England

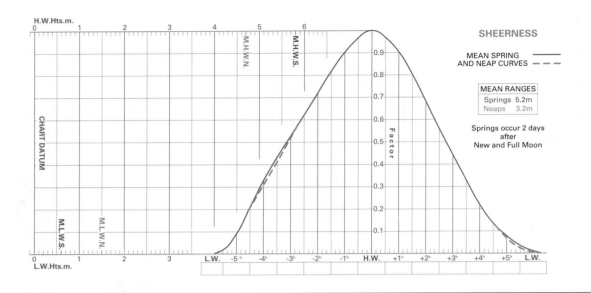

1.10 QUEENBOROUGH

Kent (Isle of Sheppey) **51°25'·04N 00°44'·19E** ✿✿✿✿♦♦♦✿✿

CHARTS AC 5606, 1834, 2572, 3683; Imray C1, Y18; Stanford 8.

TIDES Use 1.11 Sheerness, 2M to the N. +0130 Dover; ML 3·0; Duration 0610

SHELTER Good, except near HW in strong N'ly winds. The first

deep-water refuge W of N Foreland, accessible at all tides from Garrison Pt (1.11); or from the Swale (1.9) on the tide. An all-tide pontoon/jetty (5m depth at end) on E bank is for landing/short stay only; both sides of the jetty are foul. 2 pairs Gy ⚓s (raft up to 6 craft <10m each) on E side, N & S of all-tide landing & the hard/drying causeway; also single visitors Y ⚓s Nos 14-26 for craft <10m, with HM's permission craft >10m berth on W side of Concrete Lighter. When ⚓s are full the hbr controller will offer spare buoys. Smaller R buoys (numbered) are for locals. ⚓ is discouraged due to commercial traffic. Speed limit 8kn.

NAVIGATION WPT: see 1.11 for appr via Garrison Pt. Enter the river at Queenborough Spit ECM buoy, Q (3) 10s, 51°25'·75N 00°43'·93E. The chan narrows between drying banks and moorings. See 1.9 if approaching from the Swale.

LIGHTS AND MARKS Lights as chartlet. Note: No 5 Bn Dir Oc WRG 6s, vis 161°-G-166°-W-167°-R-172°, on river bend covers the appr chan. All-tide landing 2 FR (vert). Concrete lighter Fl G 3s.

R/T Monitor *Medway VTS* VHF Ch **74** for tfc info. Call Ch 08 *Sheppey One* (Q'boro HM) for berths, also water taxi at weekends only (£1.20 to landing).

TELEPHONE (Code 01795) HM ☎ 662051; MRCC (01255) 675518; Marinecall 09068 969645; Police 477055; Dr 583828; Ⓗ (01634) 830000 (Gillingham).

FACILITIES HM/Hbr Controller, ⚓ £9 <11m, inc 2 tokens for all-tide-landing turnstile, FW on all-tide landing jetty.

Queenborough YC Wed, Fri, Sat evenings, Sat, Sun lunchtimes, M, R, Bar, ♿, 🚿, 🚮;

The Creek ☎ 07974 349018, (HW±1½) Slip, Scrubbing berth (FW, 🔌, D (cans)).

Services: Slip, BY, ME, El, ✕, C (10 ton); Gas

Town P & D (cans), 🛒, R, Bar, ✉, ➔, ✈ (Gatwick).

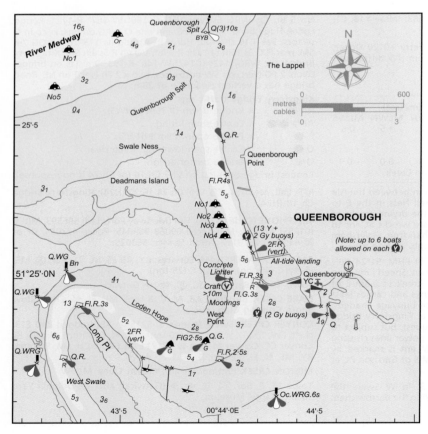

1.11 RIVER MEDWAY (SHEERNESS TO ROCHESTER)

Kent **51°27'·03N 00°44'·50E** (Off Garrison Pt) ❀❀❀❀🔱🔱🔱❀❀❀

CHARTS AC 5606, 1835, 1834, 1185, 2482, 3683; Imray C1, Y18; Stanfords 5, 8.

TIDES +0130 Dover; ML 3·1; Duration 0610

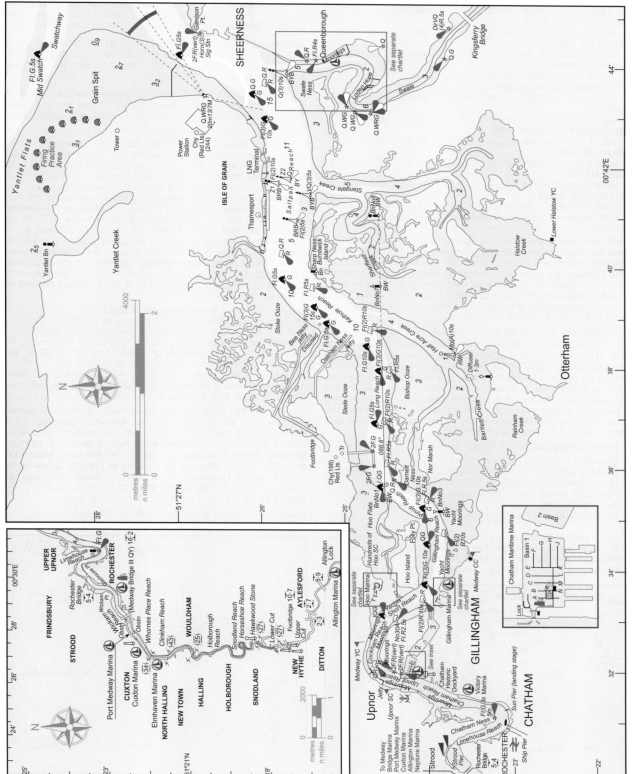

Standard Port SHEERNESS (→)

Times				Height (metres)			
High Water		Low Water		MHWS	MHWN	MLWN	MLWS
0200	0800	0200	0700	5·8	4·7	1·5	0·6
1400	2000	1400	1900				
Differences BEE NESS							
+0002	+0002	0000	+0005	+0·2	+0·1	0·0	0·0
BARTLETT CREEK							
+0016	+0008	No data		+0·1	0·0	No data	
DARNETT NESS							
+0004	+0004	0000	+0010	+0·2	+0·1	0·0	−0·1
CHATHAM (Lock Approaches)							
+0010	+0012	+0012	+0018	+0·3	+0·1	−0·1	−0·2
UPNOR							
+0015	+0015	+0015	+0025	+0·2	+0·2	−0·1	−0·1
ROCHESTER (STROOD PIER)							
+0018	+0018	+0018	+0028	+0·2	+0·2	−0·2	−0·3
WOULDHAM							
+0030	+0025	+0035	+0120	−0·2	−0·3	−1·0	−0·3
NEW HYTHE							
+0035	+0035	+0220	+0240	−1·6	−1·7	−1·2	−0·3
ALLINGTON LOCK							
+0050	+0035	No data		−2·1	−2·2	−1·3	−0·4

NOTE: Sheerness tidal predictions are given below.

SHELTER There are 4 marinas down-river of Rochester Bridge and 5 above. Sheerness is solely a commercial hbr. See 1.10 for Queenborough and access to/from The Swale. Lower reaches of the Medway are exposed to strong NE winds, but Stangate and Half Acre Creeks are secure in all winds and give access to lesser creeks. There are good ⚓s in Sharfleet Creek; from about HW−4 it is possible to go via the 'back-door' into Half Acre Creek. Speed limit is 6kn W of Folly Pt (Hoo Island).

NAVIGATION WPT 51°28'·80N 00°52'·92E, Medway SWM buoy, 253°/4·5M to No 11 SHM buoy, then follow recommended route 240°/1M to Grain Hard SHM buoy. The wreck of the *Richard Montgomery* is visible 2M NE of estuary ent and a Military Wreck depth 2₂ in Kethole Reach. There is a huge area to explore, although much of it dries to mud. Some minor creeks are buoyed. The river is well buoyed/marked up to Rochester and tidal up to Allington Lock (21·6M). Above Rochester bridge the river shoals appreciably and in the upper reaches there is only about 1m at LW; access approx HW±3.

Bridge Clearances (HAT), going up-river:

Rochester	5·4m
Medway (M2)	16·2m
New Hythe (footbridge)	10·7m
Aylesford (pedestrian)	2·3m
Aylesford (road)	2·7m
Maidstone bypass (M20)	8·9m

LIGHTS AND MARKS See 1.3 and chartlet for details of most lts. NB: not all buoys are shown due to small scale. Isle of Grain lt Q WRG 20m 13/7/8M 220°-R-234°-G-241°-W-013°. Power stn chy (242m) Oc and FR lts. Tfc Sigs: Powerful lt, Fl 7s, at Garrison Pt

means large vessel under way: if shown up river = inbound; if to seaward = outbound.

R/T Call: *Medway VTS* VHF Ch **74** 16 (H24). Monitor Ch 74 underway and Ch 16 at ⚓. Radar assistance is available on request Ch 22. Ch **80** M for marinas: Gillingham, Hoo (H24), Chatham Maritime (H24), Medway Bridge (0900-1700LT) and Port Medway (0800-2000LT). Link calls via Thames Radio Ch 02, 83.

TELEPHONE (Codes 01795 Sheerness; 01634 Medway) HM (01795) 596593; MRCC (01255) 675518; Marinecall 0891-500455; Police (01634) 827055, (01795) 661451; Dr via Medway Navigation Service (01795) 663025.

FACILITIES (☎ code 01634, unless otherwise stated) All moorings are run by YCs or marinas. Landing (only) at Ship Pier and Town Quay (Rochester). Slips at Commodores Hard, and Gillingham.

Marinas from seaward to Rochester Bridge:
Gillingham Marina (252+12Ⓥs) ☎ 280022, pre-book. £2·00 locked basin (access via lock (width 6m) HW±4½), £1·40 tidal basin HW±2, P, ME, El, Ⓔ, ✕, Gas, Gaz, CH, BH (65 ton), ⚓, C (1 ton), 🍽, Bar. Note: effects of cross-tide, esp. the ebb, off the lock ent are reduced by a timber baffle at 90° to the stream (close W of the lock). An angled pontoon deflects the stream and is also the fuel berth; the outboard end is lit by 2FR (vert). **Medway Pier Marine** ☎ 851113, D, FW, Slip, C (6 ton), BY, Ⓔ; **Hoo Marina** (120 AB inc Ⓥ) £2·35, ☎ 250311, 🔄, ✕, ✕, ME, SM, CH, El, Ⓔ, D (cans), C (16 ton), access to W basin HW±2½; HW±3 to E basin (via sill 1m above CD); an unlit WCM buoy marks chan ent; 4 waiting buoys in river. **Chatham Maritime Marina** – see inset on previous page – ☎ 899200, (300 AB), access via lock H24 and sill 1.3m below CD (1.5m at MLWS), £3.20. C(15T), P, D, 🔄, Wi-fi. **Victory Marina** ☎ 07785 971797, Ⓥ, FW, 〰️.

Marinas (Up-river from Rochester Bridge)
Medway Bridge Marina (160+4 visitors) ☎ 843576, £1.20, Slip, D, P, ME, El, Ⓔ, ✕, C (3 ton), BH (10 ton), Gas, Gaz, SM, CH, 🍽, R, Bar; **Port Medway Marina** (50) ☎ 720033, BH (16 ton), C, ⚓; **Cuxton Marina** (150+some Ⓥ) ☎ 721941, Slip, ME, El, Ⓔ, ✕, BH (12 ton), CH; **Elmhaven Marina** (60) ☎ 240489, ME, El, ✕, C; **Allington Lock** operates HW−3 to +2, ☎ (01622) 752864. **Allington Marina** (120) ☎ (01622) 752057, above the lock; CH, ME, El, ✕, P, D, Slip, C (10 ton), FW, Gas, Gaz.

YACHT CLUBS Sheppey YC (Sheerness) ☎ 663052; **Lower Halstow YC** ☎ (01227) 458554; **Medway Cruising Club** (Gillingham) ☎ 856489, Bar, M, L, FW; **Hoo Ness YC** ☎ (01634) 250052, Bar, R, M, L, FW; **Hundred of Hoo SC** ☎ (01634) 250102; **Medway Motor Cruising Club** ☎ 827194; **Medway Motor YC** ☎ 01622 737647; **Medway YC** (Upnor) ☎ 718399; **Upnor SC** ☎ 718043; **Royal Engineers YC** ☎ 844555; **RNSA** (Medway) ☎ (01634) 200970; **Rochester CC** ☎ 841350, Bar, R, M, FW, L, 🔄; **Strood YC** ☎ 718261, Bar, M, C (1·5 ton), FW, L, Slip.

Towns: All facilities R, 🍽, 🔄, ✉, 🚂, ✈ (Gatwick).

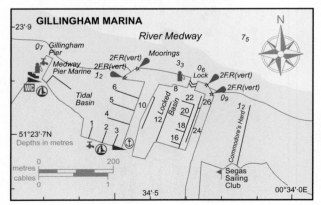

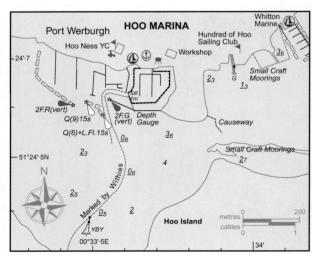

TIME ZONE (UT)
For Summer Time add ONE hour in **non-shaded areas**

SHEERNESS LAT 51°27'N LONG 0°45'E
TIMES AND HEIGHTS OF HIGH AND LOW WATERS

Dates in red are **SPRINGS**
Dates in blue are **NEAPS**

YEAR 2010

E England

JANUARY

Day	Time m	Time m	Time m	Time m
1 F	0020 5.6	0639 0.7	1243 5.9	1857 0.8
2 SA	0107 5.7	0733 0.5	1333 6.0	1945 0.8
3 SU	0152 5.8	0824 0.4	1421 6.1	2031 0.8
4 M	0237 5.9	0913 0.3	1509 6.0	2115 0.8
5 TU	0322 5.8	0959 0.3	1556 5.9	2157 0.9
6 W	0408 5.7	1043 0.5	1645 5.7	2239 1.1
7 TH	0456 5.6	1127 0.7	1737 5.4	2324 1.2
8 F	0550 5.4	1215 0.9	1833 5.2	
9 SA	0018 1.4	0651 5.2	1313 1.2	1935 5.0
10 SU	0126 1.5	0801 5.0	1421 1.3	2043 4.9
11 M	0243 1.5	0915 4.9	1528 1.4	2151 4.9
12 TU	0359 1.4	1024 5.1	1630 1.4	2252 5.1
13 W	0507 1.2	1122 5.2	1721 1.3	2342 5.2
14 TH	0600 1.1	1210 5.4	1803 1.2	
15 F ●	0024 5.3	0642 0.9	1251 5.5	1839 1.1
16 SA	0101 5.4	0719 0.9	1327 5.5	1912 1.1
17 SU	0133 5.5	0751 0.8	1359 5.5	1944 1.0
18 M	0203 5.5	0822 0.8	1431 5.5	2017 1.0
19 TU	0233 5.5	0852 0.8	1502 5.5	2049 1.0
20 W	0304 5.5	0922 0.8	1534 5.4	2121 1.1
21 TH	0336 5.4	0951 0.9	1607 5.3	2152 1.2
22 F	0409 5.3	1018 1.0	1644 5.1	2224 1.3
23 SA ◑	0448 5.2	1049 1.2	1727 5.0	2304 1.4
24 SU	0536 5.0	1133 1.3	1823 4.8	
25 M	0003 1.6	0640 4.8	1241 1.5	1936 4.7
26 TU	0130 1.6	0804 4.8	1429 1.5	2057 4.8
27 W	0310 1.5	0928 5.0	1551 1.3	2209 5.1
28 TH	0425 1.2	1039 5.3	1657 1.1	2312 5.4
29 F	0532 0.8	1154 5.6	1755 0.9	
30 SA ○	0005 5.6	0633 0.6	1234 5.9	1847 0.8
31 SU	0053 5.8	0726 0.3	1322 6.1	1935 0.7

FEBRUARY

Day	Time m	Time m	Time m	Time m
1 M	0138 6.0	0814 0.1	1407 6.2	2018 0.6
2 TU	0220 6.1	0858 0.1	1451 6.1	2059 0.6
3 W	0302 6.1	0939 0.2	1534 6.0	2136 0.7
4 TH	0344 6.0	1016 0.4	1617 5.7	2211 0.9
5 F ◐	0427 5.7	1050 0.7	1701 5.4	2248 1.1
6 SA	0514 5.4	1127 1.0	1750 5.1	2333 1.3
7 SU	0611 5.1	1216 1.3	1849 4.8	
8 M	0037 1.5	0724 4.8	1330 1.6	2002 4.6
9 TU	0210 1.6	0850 4.7	1454 1.7	2123 4.6
10 W	0342 1.5	1009 4.9	1606 1.6	2232 4.9
11 TH	0457 1.2	1026 5.1	1704 1.4	2324 5.1
12 F	0549 1.0	1155 5.3	1748 1.2	
13 SA	0006 5.3	0627 0.9	1233 5.5	1823 1.1
14 SU ●	0041 5.4	0700 0.8	1306 5.5	1855 1.0
15 M	0112 5.5	0731 0.7	1336 5.6	1926 0.9
16 TU	0141 5.6	0800 0.7	1405 5.6	1958 0.8
17 W	0210 5.6	0831 0.7	1435 5.6	2031 0.8
18 TH	0240 5.6	0900 0.7	1505 5.5	2100 0.9
19 F	0310 5.6	0926 0.8	1537 5.4	2126 1.0
20 SA ◑	0342 5.5	0946 1.0	1611 5.3	2151 1.1
21 SU	0419 5.3	1009 1.1	1651 5.1	2228 1.2
22 M ◐	0505 5.1	1051 1.3	1742 4.9	2325 1.4
23 TU	0607 4.9	1200 1.5	1855 4.6	
24 W	0054 1.5	0734 4.8	1358 1.6	2026 4.7
25 TH	0249 1.4	0908 4.9	1531 1.4	2148 5.0
26 F	0411 1.1	1026 5.3	1640 1.2	2254 5.3
27 SA	0523 0.7	1127 5.7	1741 0.9	2347 5.7
28 SU ○	0622 0.4	1218 6.0	1832 0.7	

MARCH

Day	Time m	Time m	Time m	Time m
1 M	0033 5.9	0711 0.2	1304 6.1	1917 0.6
2 TU	0116 6.1	0755 0.1	1347 6.2	1958 0.5
3 W	0157 6.2	0835 0.1	1427 6.1	2037 0.5
4 TH	0238 6.1	0912 0.2	1507 6.0	2113 0.6
5 F	0318 6.0	0944 0.5	1546 5.7	2145 0.8
6 SA	0359 5.8	1013 0.8	1625 5.4	2218 1.0
7 SU ◑	0443 5.4	1046 1.1	1708 5.1	2258 1.2
8 M	0537 5.0	1130 1.5	1801 4.7	2355 1.5
9 TU	0649 4.6	1240 1.8	1917 4.4	
10 W	0138 1.7	0820 4.5	1419 1.9	2048 4.4
11 TH	0319 1.5	0944 4.7	1538 1.7	2203 4.7
12 F	0431 1.2	1044 5.1	1638 1.4	2257 5.0
13 SA	0521 1.0	1128 5.3	1722 1.2	2338 5.3
14 SU	0559 0.9	1205 5.5	1759 1.1	
15 M ●	0013 5.4	0632 0.8	1237 5.5	1831 0.9
16 TU	0044 5.5	0702 0.7	1307 5.6	1903 0.8
17 W	0114 5.6	0733 0.7	1336 5.7	1936 0.8
18 TH	0143 5.7	0804 0.6	1406 5.7	2010 0.8
19 F	0214 5.7	0835 0.7	1437 5.6	2041 0.9
20 SA	0246 5.6	0901 0.8	1509 5.5	2107 0.9
21 SU	0320 5.6	0922 1.0	1544 5.4	2135 1.0
22 M	0400 5.4	0949 1.1	1625 5.1	2214 1.1
23 TU ◑	0449 5.2	1037 1.3	1718 4.9	2315 1.3
24 W	0554 5.0	1152 1.6	1831 4.7	
25 TH	0049 1.4	0720 4.8	1342 1.7	2003 4.7
26 F	0236 1.2	0853 5.0	1510 1.4	2126 5.0
27 SA	0357 0.9	1008 5.4	1619 1.2	2231 5.4
28 SU	0506 0.6	1107 5.7	1719 0.9	2323 5.7
29 M	0601 0.4	1156 5.9	1809 0.7	
30 TU ○	0009 5.9	0647 0.2	1241 6.0	1853 0.6
31 W	0052 6.1	0729 0.2	1322 6.1	1935 0.5

APRIL

Day	Time m	Time m	Time m	Time m
1 TH	0133 6.1	0807 0.2	1401 6.0	2014 0.5
2 F	0214 6.1	0841 0.4	1439 5.9	2050 0.6
3 SA	0255 5.9	0913 0.6	1516 5.6	2123 0.8
4 SU	0336 5.7	0942 0.9	1553 5.4	2155 1.0
5 M	0419 5.3	1013 1.2	1632 5.0	2231 1.2
6 TU ◑	0509 4.9	1055 1.5	1720 4.7	2322 1.5
7 W	0615 4.6	1157 1.8	1830 4.4	
8 TH	0053 1.6	0737 4.5	1333 1.9	1958 4.4
9 F	0238 1.5	0900 4.6	1456 1.8	2117 4.6
10 SA	0345 1.3	1003 4.9	1556 1.5	2215 4.9
11 SU	0437 1.1	1050 5.2	1644 1.3	2259 5.2
12 M	0519 0.9	1128 5.4	1725 1.1	2336 5.4
13 TU	0555 0.8	1202 5.5	1801 1.0	
14 W ●	0010 5.5	0629 0.8	1234 5.6	1836 0.9
15 TH	0044 5.6	0702 0.7	1307 5.7	1913 0.8
16 F	0117 5.7	0736 0.7	1340 5.7	1949 0.8
17 SA	0152 5.7	0810 0.7	1413 5.6	2025 0.8
18 SU	0228 5.7	0842 0.9	1448 5.6	2059 0.8
19 M	0307 5.6	0912 1.0	1527 5.4	2136 0.9
20 TU	0352 5.5	0950 1.2	1611 5.2	2222 1.0
21 W ◑	0445 5.3	1042 1.4	1707 5.0	2325 1.1
22 TH	0551 5.1	1155 1.5	1819 4.8	
23 F	0052 1.2	0712 5.0	1325 1.6	1943 4.9
24 SA	0220 1.0	0834 5.2	1444 1.4	2100 5.1
25 SU	0334 0.8	0944 5.4	1550 1.2	2203 5.4
26 M	0440 0.6	1042 5.7	1610 1.0	2257 5.6
27 TU	0534 0.5	1131 5.8	1742 0.8	2344 5.8
28 W ○	0619 0.5	1215 5.9	1828 0.7	
29 TH	0028 5.9	0659 0.5	1257 5.9	1912 0.6
30 F	0112 6.0	0737 0.5	1336 5.8	1953 0.6

Chart Datum: 2·90 metres below Ordnance Datum (Newlyn). HAT is 6·3 metres above Chart Datum; see 0.19

TIME ZONE (UT)
For Summer Time add ONE hour in **non-shaded areas**

SHEERNESS   LAT 51°27'N   LONG 0°45'E
TIMES AND HEIGHTS OF HIGH AND LOW WATERS

Dates in red are **SPRINGS**
Dates in blue are NEAPS

YEAR 2010

MAY

Time	m	Time	m
1 SA 0154 / 0812 / 1414 / 2032	5.9 / 0.6 / 5.7 / 0.7	**16** SU 0135 / 0751 / 1356 / 2016	5.7 / 0.8 / 5.7 / 0.7
2 SU 0236 / 0845 / 1451 / 2107	5.8 / 0.8 / 5.5 / 0.8	**17** M 0217 / 0830 / 1436 / 2059	5.8 / 0.9 / 5.6 / 0.7
3 M 0318 / 0915 / 1527 / 2138	5.5 / 1.1 / 5.3 / 1.0	**18** TU 0301 / 0910 / 1519 / 2145	5.7 / 1.0 / 5.5 / 0.7
4 TU 0400 / 0947 / 1604 / 2211	5.3 / 1.3 / 5.1 / 1.2	**19** W 0350 / 0955 / 1607 / 2235	5.6 / 1.1 / 5.3 / 0.8
5 W 0446 / 1026 / 1649 / 2256	5.0 / 1.5 / 4.8 / 1.3	**20** TH 0445 / 1047 / 1702 / 2335	5.5 / 1.3 / 5.2 / 0.8
6 TH 0541 / 1119 / 1746	4.7 / 1.7 / 4.6	**21** F 0547 / 1149 / 1807	5.3 / 1.4 / 5.1
7 F 0000 / 0645 / 1230 / 1859	1.5 / 4.6 / 1.9 / 4.5	**22** SA 0044 / 0657 / 1300 / 1919	0.9 / 5.2 / 1.4 / 5.1
8 SA 0133 / 0757 / 1355 / 2014	1.5 / 4.6 / 1.8 / 4.6	**23** SU 0156 / 0808 / 1411 / 2030	0.8 / 5.3 / 1.3 / 5.2
9 SU 0246 / 0902 / 1502 / 2118	1.4 / 4.8 / 1.6 / 4.8	**24** M 0304 / 0915 / 1516 / 2134	0.8 / 5.4 / 1.2 / 5.3
10 M 0342 / 0956 / 1556 / 2210	1.2 / 5.0 / 1.4 / 5.0	**25** TU 0407 / 1014 / 1618 / 2231	0.8 / 5.5 / 1.1 / 5.5
11 TU 0430 / 1042 / 1644 / 2255	1.0 / 5.2 / 1.2 / 5.3	**26** W 0502 / 1106 / 1716 / 2323	0.8 / 5.6 / 1.0 / 5.6
12 W 0513 / 1123 / 1727 / 2336	1.0 / 5.4 / 1.0 / 5.4	**27** TH 0550 / 1153 / 1807	0.8 / 5.6 / 0.8
13 TH 0554 / 1202 / 1809	0.9 / 5.6 / 0.9	**28** F 0011 / 0631 / 1237 / 1854	5.7 / 0.8 / 5.6 / 0.7
14 F 0015 / 0632 / 1240 / 1851	5.5 / 0.8 / 5.6 / 0.8	**29** SA 0058 / 0710 / 1317 / 1938	5.7 / 0.8 / 5.6 / 0.7
15 SA 0055 / 0711 / 1318 / 1933	5.6 / 0.8 / 5.7 / 0.7	**30** SU 0141 / 0747 / 1356 / 2018	5.7 / 0.9 / 5.6 / 0.7
		31 M 0223 / 0821 / 1432 / 2054	5.6 / 1.0 / 5.5 / 0.8

JUNE

Time	m	Time	m
1 TU 0303 / 0853 / 1508 / 2126	5.5 / 1.1 / 5.3 / 0.9	**16** W 0257 / 0908 / 1513 / 2149	5.9 / 0.9 / 5.7 / 0.4
2 W 0342 / 0925 / 1543 / 2157	5.3 / 1.3 / 5.2 / 1.1	**17** TH 0346 / 0953 / 1600 / 2237	5.8 / 0.9 / 5.6 / 0.5
3 TH 0423 / 1001 / 1622 / 2234	5.1 / 1.4 / 5.0 / 1.1	**18** F 0438 / 1039 / 1651 / 2327	5.7 / 1.1 / 5.5 / 0.6
4 F 0506 / 1045 / 1708 / 2320	4.9 / 1.5 / 4.9 / 1.3	**19** SA 0533 / 1130 / 1747	5.5 / 1.2 / 5.4
5 SA 0555 / 1137 / 1802	4.8 / 1.7 / 4.7	**20** SU 0021 / 0633 / 1228 / 1850	0.7 / 5.4 / 1.3 / 5.3
6 SU 0017 / 0652 / 1240 / 1906	1.4 / 4.7 / 1.7 / 4.7	**21** M 0122 / 0737 / 1333 / 1958	0.8 / 5.3 / 1.4 / 5.2
7 M 0127 / 0755 / 1353 / 2014	1.4 / 4.7 / 1.7 / 4.7	**22** TU 0227 / 0843 / 1442 / 2106	1.0 / 5.2 / 1.3 / 5.2
8 TU 0238 / 0857 / 1501 / 2116	1.3 / 4.9 / 1.5 / 4.9	**23** W 0331 / 0946 / 1551 / 2211	1.0 / 5.2 / 1.2 / 5.3
9 W 0339 / 0954 / 1600 / 2213	1.2 / 5.1 / 1.3 / 5.1	**24** TH 0432 / 1045 / 1658 / 2310	1.1 / 5.3 / 1.1 / 5.4
10 TH 0432 / 1046 / 1654 / 2304	1.1 / 5.3 / 1.1 / 5.3	**25** F 0525 / 1137 / 1755	1.1 / 5.4 / 1.0
11 F 0521 / 1134 / 1744 / 2352	1.0 / 5.5 / 1.0 / 5.5	**26** SA 0002 / 0610 / 1223 / 1844	5.5 / 1.1 / 5.5 / 0.8
12 SA 0608 / 1218 / 1834	0.9 / 5.6 / 0.8	**27** SU 0049 / 0650 / 1305 / 1928	5.5 / 1.0 / 5.5 / 0.8
13 SU 0038 / 0652 / 1302 / 1922	5.7 / 0.9 / 5.6 / 0.7	**28** M 0131 / 0727 / 1342 / 2007	5.6 / 1.0 / 5.5 / 0.8
14 M 0124 / 0737 / 1345 / 2011	5.8 / 0.8 / 5.7 / 0.5	**29** TU 0210 / 0801 / 1417 / 2041	5.6 / 1.1 / 5.5 / 0.8
15 TU 0210 / 0823 / 1428 / 2100	5.9 / 0.8 / 5.7 / 0.4	**30** W 0246 / 0834 / 1449 / 2112	5.5 / 1.1 / 5.4 / 0.9

JULY

Time	m	Time	m
1 TH 0321 / 0905 / 1522 / 2140	5.4 / 1.1 / 5.4 / 0.9	**16** F 0333 / 0940 / 1545 / 2223	6.0 / 0.8 / 5.9 / 0.3
2 F 0355 / 0939 / 1556 / 2211	5.3 / 1.2 / 5.3 / 1.0	**17** SA 0420 / 1021 / 1630 / 2305	5.9 / 0.9 / 5.8 / 0.5
3 SA 0431 / 1014 / 1632 / 2246	5.2 / 1.3 / 5.2 / 1.1	**18** SU 0509 / 1103 / 1720 / 2349	5.6 / 1.1 / 5.6 / 0.7
4 SU 0511 / 1054 / 1714 / 2326	5.0 / 1.5 / 5.0 / 1.2	**19** M 0602 / 1152 / 1818	5.4 / 1.2 / 5.4
5 M 0556 / 1141 / 1804	4.9 / 1.6 / 4.9	**20** TU 0041 / 0702 / 1254 / 1926	1.0 / 5.1 / 1.4 / 5.1
6 TU 0016 / 0652 / 1242 / 1908	1.4 / 4.8 / 1.7 / 4.8	**21** W 0147 / 0809 / 1412 / 2042	1.2 / 5.0 / 1.5 / 5.0
7 W 0125 / 0800 / 1402 / 2023	1.5 / 4.8 / 1.7 / 4.8	**22** TH 0259 / 0921 / 1534 / 2157	1.4 / 5.0 / 1.4 / 5.1
8 TH 0248 / 0909 / 1520 / 2134	1.4 / 4.9 / 1.5 / 5.0	**23** F 0408 / 1028 / 1650 / 2302	1.4 / 5.1 / 1.2 / 5.3
9 F 0356 / 1013 / 1625 / 2238	1.3 / 5.2 / 1.2 / 5.2	**24** SA 0508 / 1124 / 1750 / 2354	1.3 / 5.3 / 1.0 / 5.4
10 SA 0455 / 1110 / 1724 / 2334	1.1 / 5.4 / 1.0 / 5.5	**25** SU 0555 / 1211 / 1837	1.2 / 5.4 / 0.9
11 SU 0548 / 1201 / 1821	1.0 / 5.6 / 0.8	**26** M 0038 / 0634 / 1251 / 1915	5.5 / 1.2 / 5.5 / 0.8
12 M 0026 / 0638 / 1249 / 1914	5.7 / 0.9 / 5.7 / 0.6	**27** TU 0117 / 0708 / 1325 / 1949	5.6 / 1.1 / 5.6 / 0.8
13 TU 0114 / 0727 / 1334 / 2005	5.9 / 0.8 / 5.8 / 0.4	**28** W 0151 / 0741 / 1357 / 2020	5.6 / 1.0 / 5.6 / 0.8
14 W 0201 / 0814 / 1417 / 2054	6.1 / 0.7 / 5.9 / 0.2	**29** TH 0223 / 0813 / 1427 / 2049	5.6 / 1.0 / 5.6 / 0.8
15 TH 0247 / 0858 / 1501 / 2139	6.1 / 0.7 / 6.0 / 0.2	**30** F 0254 / 0844 / 1457 / 2117	5.5 / 1.0 / 5.6 / 0.8
		31 SA 0325 / 0915 / 1527 / 2145	5.5 / 1.1 / 5.5 / 0.9

AUGUST

Time	m	Time	m
1 SU 0356 / 0945 / 1559 / 2213	5.3 / 1.2 / 5.4 / 1.1	**16** M 0438 / 1034 / 1652 / 2311	5.6 / 1.1 / 5.7 / 0.9
2 M 0430 / 1016 / 1635 / 2242	5.2 / 1.3 / 5.2 / 1.2	**17** TU 0526 / 1118 / 1747 / 2357	5.3 / 1.3 / 5.3 / 1.3
3 TU 0510 / 1053 / 1718 / 2321	5.0 / 1.5 / 5.0 / 1.4	**18** W 0624 / 1217 / 1857	5.0 / 1.5 / 5.0
4 W 0559 / 1145 / 1816	4.9 / 1.6 / 4.9	**19** TH 0105 / 0735 / 1347 / 2021	1.6 / 4.8 / 1.6 / 4.8
5 TH 0021 / 0706 / 1305 / 1935	1.6 / 4.7 / 1.7 / 4.8	**20** F 0230 / 0856 / 1523 / 2144	1.7 / 4.8 / 1.5 / 5.0
6 F 0200 / 0828 / 1446 / 2101	1.6 / 4.8 / 1.6 / 4.9	**21** SA 0348 / 1010 / 1642 / 2249	1.6 / 5.0 / 1.2 / 5.3
7 SA 0327 / 0944 / 1602 / 2216	1.5 / 5.1 / 1.3 / 5.2	**22** SU 0451 / 1107 / 1737 / 2339	1.4 / 5.3 / 1.0 / 5.5
8 SU 0433 / 1049 / 1709 / 2318	1.2 / 5.4 / 0.9 / 5.6	**23** M 0537 / 1151 / 1818	1.3 / 5.4 / 0.9
9 M 0531 / 1143 / 1810	1.0 / 5.7 / 0.7	**24** TU 0019 / 0613 / 1229 / 1852	5.6 / 1.2 / 5.6 / 0.8
10 TU 0011 / 0624 / 1231 / 1903	5.9 / 0.9 / 5.9 / 0.4	**25** W 0055 / 0646 / 1301 / 1922	5.6 / 1.1 / 5.6 / 0.8
11 W 0100 / 0713 / 1316 / 1952	6.1 / 0.8 / 6.0 / 0.2	**26** TH 0125 / 0717 / 1331 / 1951	5.7 / 1.0 / 5.7 / 0.8
12 TH 0145 / 0758 / 1358 / 2037	6.2 / 0.7 / 6.1 / 0.1	**27** F 0154 / 0748 / 1359 / 2020	5.7 / 1.0 / 5.7 / 0.7
13 F 0229 / 0840 / 1440 / 2119	6.2 / 0.7 / 6.2 / 0.1	**28** SA 0223 / 0820 / 1428 / 2049	5.7 / 1.0 / 5.7 / 0.8
14 SA 0312 / 0920 / 1522 / 2158	6.1 / 0.7 / 6.1 / 0.3	**29** SU 0252 / 0851 / 1458 / 2116	5.6 / 1.0 / 5.6 / 0.9
15 SU 0354 / 0957 / 1605 / 2234	5.9 / 0.9 / 5.9 / 0.6	**30** M 0323 / 0918 / 1529 / 2140	5.5 / 1.2 / 5.5 / 1.1
		31 TU 0355 / 0944 / 1604 / 2202	5.3 / 1.2 / 5.4 / 1.3

Chart Datum: 2·90 metres below Ordnance Datum (Newlyn). HAT is 6·3 metres above Chart Datum; see 0.19

TIME ZONE (UT)
For Summer Time add ONE hour in **non-shaded areas**

SHEERNESS LAT 51°27'N LONG 0°45'E
TIMES AND HEIGHTS OF HIGH AND LOW WATERS

Dates in red are **SPRINGS**
Dates in blue are **NEAPS**

YEAR 2010

E England

SEPTEMBER

Time m	Time m
1 0432 5.2 / 1016 1.4 / W 1647 5.2 / ◑ 2237 1.4	**16** 0545 4.9 / 1145 1.6 / TH 1829 4.9
2 0519 5.0 / 1106 1.6 / TH 1743 5.0 / 2338 1.6	**17** 0023 1.8 / 0657 4.6 / F 1324 1.7 / 1955 4.7
3 0624 4.8 / 1227 1.7 / F 1901 4.8	**18** 0158 1.9 / 0824 4.6 / SA 1503 1.6 / 2120 4.9
4 0123 1.8 / 0752 4.7 / SA 1421 1.6 / 2035 4.9	**19** 0319 1.8 / 0941 4.9 / SU 1616 1.3 / 2224 5.2
5 0302 1.6 / 0918 5.0 / SU 1543 1.2 / 2156 5.3	**20** 0421 1.5 / 1039 5.2 / M 1707 1.1 / 2312 5.5
6 0411 1.3 / 1026 5.4 / M 1652 0.8 / 2259 5.7	**21** 0508 1.3 / 1122 5.4 / TU 1746 0.9 / 2351 5.6
7 0511 1.0 / 1120 5.7 / TU 1753 0.6 / 2352 6.0	**22** 0545 1.2 / 1159 5.6 / W 1819 0.9
8 0605 0.9 / 1208 6.0 / W 1845 0.3 / ●	**23** 0024 5.7 / 0617 1.1 / TH 1231 5.7 / ○ 1848 0.8
9 0038 6.2 / 0652 0.7 / TH 1252 6.2 / 1930 0.2	**24** 0054 5.7 / 0649 1.0 / F 1300 5.7 / 1918 0.8
10 0122 6.2 / 0736 0.7 / F 1334 6.3 / 2013 0.2	**25** 0122 5.7 / 0722 0.9 / SA 1330 5.8 / 1948 0.8
11 0204 6.2 / 0817 0.6 / SA 1415 6.3 / 2052 0.3	**26** 0151 5.7 / 0755 0.9 / SU 1400 5.7 / 2018 0.9
12 0245 6.1 / 0856 0.7 / SU 1457 6.2 / 2128 0.5	**27** 0221 5.7 / 0827 1.0 / M 1431 5.7 / 2047 1.0
13 0325 5.9 / 0932 0.9 / M 1540 5.9 / 2200 0.8	**28** 0253 5.6 / 0856 1.1 / TU 1505 5.6 / 2111 1.2
14 0407 5.6 / 1008 1.1 / TU 1626 5.6 / 2234 1.2	**29** 0326 5.4 / 0923 1.2 / W 1542 5.4 / 2136 1.3
15 0451 5.2 / 1048 1.3 / W 1719 5.2 / ◑ 2317 1.5	**30** 0404 5.2 / 0957 1.3 / TH 1628 5.3 / 2215 1.5

OCTOBER

Time m	Time m
1 0452 5.0 / 1051 1.5 / F 1726 5.0 / ◑ 2321 1.7	**16** 0616 4.6 / 1244 1.7 / SA 1917 4.7
2 0557 4.8 / 1213 1.6 / SA 1843 4.9	**17** 0109 2.0 / 0738 4.6 / SU 1422 1.6 / 2037 4.8
3 0059 1.8 / 0723 4.8 / SU 1400 1.4 / 2014 5.0	**18** 0234 1.9 / 0856 4.7 / M 1529 1.4 / 2143 5.0
4 0235 1.6 / 0849 5.0 / M 1521 1.1 / 2133 5.4	**19** 0337 1.7 / 0956 5.0 / TU 1622 1.2 / 2233 5.3
5 0344 1.3 / 0958 5.4 / TU 1630 0.8 / 2235 5.7	**20** 0427 1.4 / 1043 5.3 / W 1704 1.0 / 2313 5.5
6 0445 1.1 / 1053 5.7 / W 1729 0.5 / 2327 6.0	**21** 0508 1.2 / 1121 5.5 / TH 1739 1.0 / 2347 5.6
7 0539 0.9 / 1141 6.0 / TH 1819 0.4 / ●	**22** 0545 1.1 / 1156 5.6 / F 1812 0.9
8 0013 6.1 / 0626 0.8 / F 1226 6.1 / 1903 0.3	**23** 0019 5.7 / 0619 1.0 / SA 1229 5.7 / ○ 1843 0.9
9 0057 6.2 / 0711 0.7 / SA 1309 6.2 / 1944 0.4	**24** 0051 5.7 / 0655 0.9 / SU 1302 5.7 / 1916 0.9
10 0138 6.1 / 0753 0.7 / SU 1352 6.2 / 2022 0.5	**25** 0123 5.7 / 0731 0.9 / M 1335 5.7 / 1949 0.9
11 0218 6.0 / 0833 0.7 / M 1435 6.1 / 2057 0.7	**26** 0155 5.7 / 0806 0.9 / TU 1411 5.7 / 2021 1.0
12 0258 5.8 / 0911 0.9 / TU 1518 5.8 / 2129 1.0	**27** 0229 5.6 / 0841 1.0 / W 1448 5.7 / 2053 1.1
13 0338 5.5 / 0946 1.1 / W 1604 5.5 / 2202 1.3	**28** 0306 5.5 / 0917 1.1 / TH 1530 5.5 / 2127 1.3
14 0419 5.2 / 1100 1.3 / TH 1656 5.1 / ◑ 2242 1.6	**29** 0347 5.3 / 0958 1.2 / F 1619 5.4 / 2212 1.5
15 0509 4.9 / 1115 1.5 / F 1800 4.8 / 2340 1.9	**30** 0437 5.1 / 1053 1.3 / SA 1718 5.2 / ◑ 2315 1.6
	31 0540 4.9 / 1208 1.3 / SU 1831 5.1

NOVEMBER

Time m	Time m
1 0038 1.7 / 0658 4.9 / M 1338 1.2 / 1951 5.2	**16** 0127 2.0 / 0751 4.6 / TU 1427 1.5 / 2041 4.8
2 0202 1.6 / 0818 5.1 / TU 1454 1.0 / 2105 5.4	**17** 0240 1.8 / 0857 4.8 / W 1524 1.4 / 2138 5.0
3 0311 1.4 / 0926 5.4 / W 1600 0.8 / 2207 5.6	**18** 0337 1.6 / 0952 5.0 / TH 1613 1.2 / 2226 5.2
4 0412 1.2 / 1024 5.7 / TH 1659 0.7 / 2300 5.8	**19** 0426 1.3 / 1039 5.3 / F 1656 1.1 / 2307 5.4
5 0509 1.0 / 1115 5.9 / F 1750 0.6 / 2348 5.9	**20** 0510 1.2 / 1121 5.4 / SA 1735 1.0 / 2346 5.6
6 0600 0.8 / 1202 6.0 / SA 1834 0.6 / ●	**21** 0551 1.0 / 1200 5.6 / SU 1812 1.0 / ○
7 0032 5.9 / 0648 0.7 / SU 1248 6.1 / 1915 0.6	**22** 0023 5.6 / 0630 0.9 / M 1239 5.6 / 1849 0.9
8 0114 5.9 / 0733 0.7 / M 1333 6.0 / 1953 0.7	**23** 0100 5.7 / 0711 0.9 / TU 1317 5.7 / 1926 0.9
9 0155 5.8 / 0815 0.7 / TU 1418 5.9 / 2029 0.9	**24** 0137 5.7 / 0753 0.8 / W 1357 5.8 / 2005 1.0
10 0235 5.7 / 0854 0.9 / W 1502 5.7 / 2102 1.2	**25** 0214 5.6 / 0835 0.8 / TH 1439 5.7 / 2043 1.0
11 0314 5.4 / 0930 1.1 / TH 1547 5.4 / 2134 1.4	**26** 0254 5.6 / 0918 0.8 / F 1524 5.7 / 2125 1.1
12 0354 5.2 / 1004 1.2 / F 1634 5.1 / 2211 1.6	**27** 0338 5.4 / 1005 0.9 / SA 1614 5.5 / 2211 1.3
13 0438 5.0 / 1046 1.4 / SA 1726 4.9 / ◑ 2259 1.8	**28** 0428 5.3 / 1056 1.0 / SU 1710 5.4 / ◑ 2306 1.4
14 0532 4.8 / 1144 1.6 / SU 1827 4.7	**29** 0525 5.2 / 1158 1.0 / M 1814 5.2
15 0004 1.9 / 0638 4.6 / M 1312 1.6 / 1935 4.7	**30** 0010 1.5 / 0632 5.1 / TU 1308 1.1 / 1924 5.2

DECEMBER

Time m	Time m
1 0123 1.5 / 0745 5.2 / W 1419 1.0 / 2033 5.3	**16** 0119 1.8 / 0747 4.7 / TH 1411 1.5 / 2032 4.7
2 0233 1.4 / 0854 5.3 / TH 1526 1.0 / 2137 5.4	**17** 0236 1.7 / 0854 4.8 / F 1518 1.4 / 2133 4.9
3 0339 1.3 / 0957 5.5 / F 1627 0.9 / 2235 5.5	**18** 0340 1.5 / 0954 5.0 / SA 1613 1.3 / 2227 5.2
4 0442 1.1 / 1054 5.6 / SA 1722 0.9 / 2326 5.6	**19** 0434 1.3 / 1047 5.2 / SU 1701 1.2 / 2316 5.4
5 0540 0.9 / 1146 5.7 / SU 1809 0.9	**20** 0524 1.1 / 1136 5.4 / M 1746 1.1
6 0013 5.7 / 0632 0.8 / M 1236 5.8 / 1850 0.9	**21** 0000 5.5 / 0611 0.9 / TU 1221 5.6 / ○ 1828 1.0
7 0058 5.7 / 0719 0.7 / TU 1322 5.8 / 1930 0.9	**22** 0043 5.6 / 0658 0.8 / W 1305 5.7 / 1911 0.9
8 0139 5.7 / 0803 0.7 / W 1406 5.7 / 2006 1.0	**23** 0124 5.7 / 0745 0.6 / TH 1348 5.8 / 1954 0.8
9 0218 5.6 / 0843 0.8 / TH 1448 5.6 / 2040 1.1	**24** 0205 5.7 / 0832 0.5 / F 1432 5.9 / 2038 0.9
10 0255 5.5 / 0917 1.0 / F 1529 5.4 / 2111 1.3	**25** 0246 5.7 / 0919 0.5 / SA 1517 5.9 / 2120 0.9
11 0332 5.3 / 0947 1.1 / SA 1608 5.2 / 2144 1.4	**26** 0330 5.7 / 1004 0.6 / SU 1605 5.7 / 2203 1.0
12 0409 5.2 / 1019 1.2 / SU 1650 5.0 / 2223 1.5	**27** 0416 5.6 / 1049 0.7 / M 1655 5.6 / 2248 1.2
13 0451 5.0 / 1058 1.3 / M 1735 4.9 / ◑ 2310 1.7	**28** 0506 5.5 / 1136 0.8 / TU 1750 5.3 / ◑ 2339 1.3
14 0540 4.8 / 1149 1.4 / TU 1828 4.7	**29** 0604 5.3 / 1232 1.0 / W 1852 5.2
15 0007 1.8 / 0639 4.7 / W 1254 1.5 / 1928 4.6	**30** 0041 1.4 / 0711 5.2 / TH 1339 1.1 / 2000 5.1
	31 0155 1.4 / 0824 5.1 / F 1450 1.2 / 2108 5.1

Chart Datum: 2·90 metres below Ordnance Datum (Newlyn). HAT is 6·3 metres above Chart Datum; see 0.19

1.12   RIVER THAMES

Canvey Island to Teddington lock. See 1.13 for Southend and Leigh-on-Sea.

CHARTS AC 5606, 1185,1186, 2151, 3337, 2484, 3319. Imray C1, C2, Y18, 2100 Series. Stanfords 5, 8.

Publications. The Port of London Authority (PLA), London River House, Royal Pier Road, Gravesend, Kent DA12 2BG, ☎ 01474 562200, publish (or download free from www. portoflondon. co.uk) *A Pleasure Users Guide; General Directions; Permanent Notices to Mariners; Port of London River Byelaws; Tide Tables* and a *Port Handbook*.

HARBOURS IN SEA REACH and GRAVESEND REACH

HOLEHAVEN CREEK, Essex, **51°30´·57N 00°33´·16E**. AC 2484, 1186. HW +0140 on Dover; use differences for CORYTON, see 1.13; ML 3·0m; Duration 0610. Shelter is good, but beware swell from passing traffic. Keep to Canvey Is side on ent. Temp ⚓ in lee of Chainrock jetty or call PLA ☎ 01474 562462 for possible mooring. 5ca N of ent an overhead oil pipe crosses chan with 11m clearance, plus 2 FY lts (horiz). 2 FG (vert) on all jetty heads, plus Chainrock SHM buoy Fl G 5s. FW from Lobster Smack pub, P & D from Canvey Village (1M); all other facilities on Canvey Is.

Small craft crossing routes. To clear tanker berths off Holehaven, Coryton and Thames Haven yachts should navigate as follows:
Inward from north: Keep close to SHM buoys & bcns. At W Leigh Middle ensure the fairway is clear, then cross to the S side of Yantlet Channel. Make for E Blyth buoy before turning onto the inward track, so as to clear outward vessels passing close to the PHM buoys. It is safe to pass close S of Mid Blyth, W Blyth and Lower Hope buoys. When safe, cross to the N side in Lower Hope Reach as quickly as possible.

Outward to north, as above in reverse, but cross to the N side between Sea Reach Nos 4 & 5 buoys.

Inward from the south: Keep well south of Yantlet Channel, crossing to the N side in Lower Hope Reach as described above.

> Caution: In Gravesend Reach beware 6 groynes off the N bank, WSW of Coalhouse Pt, which project almost into the fairway. Outer ends marked by SHM beacons, Fl G 2·5s. *No passage exists inshore of the groynes.*
>
> A light, Iso 6s, on Tilbury Cargo Jetty (51°27´·06N 00°20´·95E) is shown when vessels are manoeuvring off Tilbury Dock locks or for a berth in Northfleet Hope. *Proceed with caution.*

GRAVESEND, Kent, **51°26´·61N 00°22´·92E**. AC 1186, 2151. HW +0150 on Dover; ML 3·3m; Duration 0610. Use Tilbury diffs overleaf. ⚓ E of Clubb's Jetty close to S shore, but remote from town. There are 2 ⚓s off **Gravesend SC** ☎ 01474 533974, www.gravesendsailing club.co.uk, opposite Tilbury Power Station. ⚓ nearest club dries; ⚓ downriver in 2m. Larger PLA ⚓s are just upriver, £14/night. **Embankment Marina** ☎ 01474 535700, www.theembankmentmarina.co.uk, Ch 80. Lock into Canal Basin HW −1 to HW Tilbury by arrangement: 1 Apr-31 Oct, 0800-2000; Winter 1000-1600. Lock closes at local HW. Out of hours openings up to HW by arrangement with lock keeper. D, Gaz, Bar, M, Ⓔ, ME, El, ⚒, slip.
Town Tourist info ☎ (01474) 337600, Ⓔ, ME, El, ⚒, P & D, BH (70 ton) at Denton Wharf, R, 🛒.

Thurrock YC 51°28´·28N 00°19´·47E at Grays, ☎ 01375 373720. 1 ⚓, D, P (2M), Bar, R (occas). M-F 1000-1500; Thu 2000-2300.

1.12A   THAMES TIDAL BARRIER

51°29´·91N 00°02´·21E (Span G)

CHARTS AC 5606, 2484 and 3337.

DESCRIPTION Located at Woolwich Reach, it protects London from floods. There are 9 piers between which gates can be rotated upwards from the river bed to form a barrier. The piers are numbered 1-9 from N to S; the spans are lettered A-K from S to N (see diagram). A, H, J & K are not navigable. C-F, with depth 5·8m and 61m wide, are for larger ships. Spans B and G, with 1·25m, are for small craft/yachts which should lower sail and use engine: W-bound via G and E-bound via B (51°29´·73N 00°02´·24E).

LIGHTS AND SIGNALS To the E at Barking Creek (N bank),to the W at Blackwall Stairs (N bank) and Blackwall Pt (S bank), noticeboards and lights indicate:
Fl ⚪ = Barrier is about to close.
Fl ⚫ = Barrier closing; all vessels must stop.
Short textual messages may also be displayed.
On the Barrier piers:
⚫ lts laid out as arrows = span indicated is open to traffic.
⚫ lts in St Andrew's cross layout = barrier or span closed.
3 ⚫ in ▽ layout on spans A, H, J and K = No passage.

SPANS OPEN TO NAVIGATION In reduced visibility, spans open to navigation are marked by high intensity lts and racons (T). Information will be included in routine broadcasts by *London VTS* on VHF Ch **14** at H + 15 and H + 45.

CONTROL AND COMMUNICATIONS The Thames Barrier Navigation Centre controls all traffic in a Zone from Margaret Ness (51°30´·5N 00°05´·56E) to Blackwall Point (51°30´·3N 00°00´·2E), using the callsign *London VTS*, VHF Ch **14**, 22, 16.
Inbound yachts and small craft should call *London VTS* to obtain clearance to proceed through the Barrier when passing Margaret Ness (51°30´·54N 00°05´·50E).
Outbound yachts and small craft should call *London VTS* to obtain clearance to proceed through the Barrier when passing Blackwall Point (51°30´·30N 00°00´·18E).
Non-VHF craft should, if possible, pre-notify the Barrier Control ☎ 020 8855 0315; then observe all visual signals, proceed with caution keeping clear of larger vessels and use spans B or G as appropriate. Call before and after transiting the Barrier.

NAVIGATION Sailing craft should transit the Barrier under power, not sail. When all spans are closed, keep 200m clear to avoid turbulence.

It is dangerous to transit a closed span, as the gate may be semi-raised.

Small craft should not navigate between Thames Refinery Jetty and Gulf Oil Island, unless intending to transit the Barrier.

On N side of river (Spans E and F) a cross-tide component is reported; expect to lay-off a compensating drift angle.

TESTING
The Barrier is completely closed for testing once a month for about 3hrs, LW ±1½. Call ☎ 0208 3054188, and see Reeds Almanac monthly updates, for details. In Sept/Oct an annual closure lasts about 10 hrs, LW to LW; this may affect passage plans.

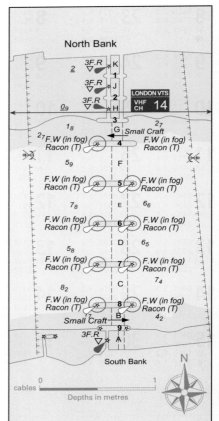

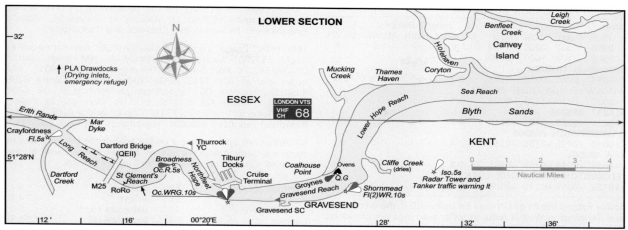

CANVEY ISLAND TO CRAYFORDNESS (AC 1185, 1186, 2484, 2151)

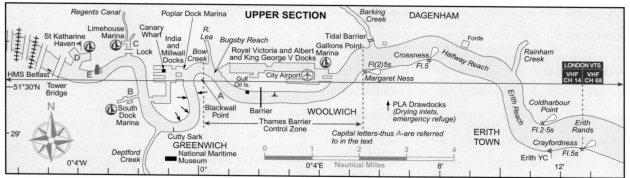

CRAYFORDNESS TO TOWER BRIDGE (AC 2484, 2151, 3337)

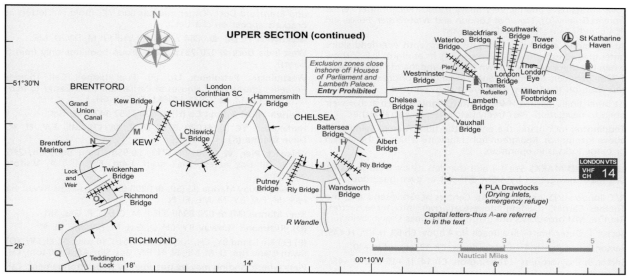

TOWER BRIDGE TO TEDDINGTON (AC 3319)

Tide Boards, showing height of tide above CD, are at Lower Pool (Met Police Boatyard), King's Reach (Temple Stairs), Nine Elms Reach (Cringle Wharf) and Battersea Reach (Plantation Wharf).

TIDES The river is tidal up to Teddington. +0252 Dover; ML 3·6; Duration 0555.

Standard Port LONDON BRIDGE (→)

Times				Height (metres)			
High Water		Low Water		MHWS	MHWN	MLWN	MLWS
0300	0900	0400	1100	7·1	5·9	1·3	0·5
1500	2100	1600	2300				
Differences TILBURY							
−0055	−0040	−0050	−0115	−0·7	−0·5	+0·1	0·0
WOOLWICH (GALLIONS POINT)							
−0020	−0020	−0035	−0045	−0·1	0·0	+0·2	0·0
ALBERT BRIDGE							
+0025	+0020	+0105	+0110	−0·9	−0·8	−0·7	−0·4
HAMMERSMITH BRIDGE							
+0040	+0035	+0205	+0155	−1·4	−1·3	−1·0	−0·5
KEW BRIDGE							
+0055	+0050	+0255	+0235	−1·8	−1·8	−1·2	−0·5
TEDDINGTON (RICHMOND) LOCK							
+0105	+0055	+0325	+0305	−2·2	−2·2	−1·3	−0·5

Above Putney the ht of LW may be below CD if the water flow over Teddington Weir is reduced; prior warnings are broadcast by London VTS. If the Thames Barrier (previous page) is closed, water levels will vary greatly from predictions.

SHELTER Very good in marinas. PLA Drawdocks, arrowed, are drying inlets offering emergency refuge, but subject to wash.

NAVIGATION WPT 51°29′·62N 00°44′·17E, Sea Reach No 4 buoy, 276°/6·8M to abm Holehaven Creek and 37·8M to Tower Bridge. **Speed limits.** Minimise wash. 8kn speed limit applies inshore of Southend-on-sea, at Coryton and Thurrock when gas tankers are berthed, in all creeks and above Wandsworth Bridge.

Keep at least 60m clear of oil/gas jetties at Canvey Island, Coryton, Thames Haven, Thurrock, Purfleet and Dagenham. Pleasure craft should always keep clear of commercial vessels, including tug/barge tows.

Sea Reach, keep well S of the main chan to clear tankers turning abeam Canvey Is and Shellhaven.

Lower Hope Reach, hold the NW bank until Ovens SHM; long groynes extend from the N bank for the next 2M. Tilbury Landing Stage is used by the Gravesend ferry and cruise liners.

Northfleet Hope, beware ships/tugs turning into Tilbury Docks; container berths and a grain terminal are close up-river.

Above **Gravesend** keep to stbd side of channel – do not cut corners.

Above **Cherry Garden Pier** (Wapping), vessels > 40m LOA and tugs/tows always have priority. Very heavy traffic/frequent River Ferries from/to Greenwich, Tower of London and Westminster. Police and PLA launches are always willing to assist.

At **Richmond** a half-tide lock and a weir with overhead sluice gates give access up-river. 3 R discs (3 Ⓡ lts at night) in a ▽ show when the sluice gates are down (closed) and maintaining at least 1·72m between Richmond and Teddington bridges. The half-tide lock, on the Surrey bank, must then be used.

At other times (approx HW ±2) two Ⓨ lights at each arch = weir open to navigation. Pass freely below the 3 central arches.

Teddington lock marks the end of the tidal Thames (semi-tidal above Richmond). Red/green lights indicate which of the launch or barge locks is in operation.

LIGHTS AND MARKS See 1.3 and chartlets. Glare from shore lts can make navigation by night difficult or even hazardous.

R/T *London VTS* operates from Centres at Gravesend and the Thames Barrier, dividing the estuary/river into three sectors. Routine MSI broadcasts are made at the times shown below.

Sector 1: Outer limits – Sea Reach No 4 buoy. Ch **69**, H +15, H +45.

Sector 2: Sea Reach 4 – Crayfordness. Ch **68**, H and H +30.

Sector 3: Crayfordness – Teddington. Ch **14**, H +15 and H +45.

PLA launches *Thames Patrol* Ch 69, 68, 14. Police launches *Thames Police* Ch 14. Do not use tug Channels 8, 10, 13, 36, 72, 77. For marina VHF see overleaf.

EMERGENCY In emergency call *London Coastguard* Ch 16, 67, co-located with London VTS at the Thames Barrier Navigation Control and covering from Canvey Island to Teddington.

Thames Coastguard covers the area to seaward of Canvey Island. The RNLI operates four LB stations at Gravesend, Victoria Embankment (Waterloo Br), Chiswick and Teddington.

TELEPHONE Port of London Authority (PLA): General enquiries 01474 562200. www.portoflondon.co.uk. HM lower district (01474) 562200. Port Controller Gravesend (01474) 560311. HM upper district 020 7743 7912. Thames Barrier Centre 0208 8550315. London CG londoncoastguard@mcga.gov.uk 0208 3127380. Thames CG (01255) 675518. Metropolitan Police, Marine Support Unit 0207 2754421. Tower Bridge 0207 9403984. Richmond lock 0208 9400634; Teddington lock 0208 9408723.

BRIDGES Craft approaching a bridge against the tide give way to those approaching with the tide. All bridges above Tower Bridge are fixed. Clearances (m) above HAT are as follows:

Dartford (QEII)	53	Chelsea	6·1
Tower (closed)	8·1	Albert	4·4
Tower (open)	42	Battersea road	5·0
London	8·4	Battersea rail	5·5
Cannon St	6·6	Wandsworth	5·3
Southwark	6·8	Fulham	6·3
Millennium	8·9	Putney	4·9
Blackfriars rail	6·6	Hammersmith	3·0
Blackfriars road	6·4	Barnes	4·9
Waterloo	8·0	Chiswick	6·1
Charing Cross	6·5	Kew rail	5·1
Westminster	4·9	Kew road	4·7
Lambeth	5·9	Richmond foot	4·7
Vauxhall	5·1	Twickenham	8·5*
Victoria Railway	5·5	Richmond rail	7·9*
		Richmond road	7·9*

* Above maintained water level.

Tower Bridge fog horn sounds a 10s blast every 20s when bascules are open for shipping; standby signal is a bell 30s. A ▽ of R discs (● lts) below a bridge span = this arch closed.

On bridge arches between Tower and Wandsworth bridges high intensity white signal lts are electronically triggered by one or more large vessels approaching a bridge. Iso W 4s means a single large vessel, VQ a second large vessel, nearing the same bridge. Other vessels keep clear of that arch.

FACILITIES Marinas See overleaf for Gallions Point, Poplar Dock, South Dock, Limehouse, St Katharine Haven, Chelsea Harbour and Brentford Dock. Other marinas and YCs (Bold red letters in brackets appear on chartlets):

Greenwich YC (A) ☎ 0844 736 5846; VHF Ch M. FW, ⚓, ME.

West India Dock ☎ 020 7517 5500; group bookings only (min 6 boats).

Westminster Petroleum Ltd (F) (Fuel barge). Call *Thames Refueller* (moored off Houses of Parliament from Easter to mid-Oct) VHF Ch 14, ☎ 07831 110681, D, Gas, CH, L.

Chelsea Yacht & Boat Co (H) ☎ 020 7352 1427, M, Gas;

Hurlingham YC (J) ☎ 020 8788 5547, M, CH, ME, FW, El, ✕; **Dove Marina (K)**.

Chiswick Pier, ☎ 0208 7422713, £0.95m, long pontoon, 2FG (vert). All tide access, max draft 1·4m. FW, ⌁, ⚓. Visitors welcome.

Chiswick Quay Marina (L) (50) ☎ 0208 9948743, Access HW±2 via lock, M, FW, BY, M, ME, El, ✕.

Kew Marina (M) ☎ 020 8940 8364, M, CH, D, P, Gas, SM;

(O), Richmond Slipway BY, CH, D, Gas, M, FW, ME, El, ✕.

(P) Eel Pie Island BY, CH, ⌁, ME, M, Gas, C (6 ton), ✕, El, FW; **(Q) Swan Island Hbr**, D, M, ME, El, ✕, FW, Gas, Slip, AB, C (30 ton), CH.

Piers where landing may be possible, by prior arrangement. Call London River Services ☎ 0207 9412400 for: Greenwich, Tower Millennium, Embankment, Bankside, Festival, Westminster, Millbank, Blackfriars and Waterloo.

(G) Cadogan 0208 7482715, give 24 hrs notice. Chiswick 0208 7422713. Dove 0208 7482715. St Katharine 0207 4880555. Putney 0207 3781211. 0207 9302062 for Kew Pier and Richmond Lndg Stage.

MARINAS ON THE TIDAL THAMES, from seaward to Brentford

GALLIONS POINT MARINA, 51°30'·30N 00°04'·66E in entry basin for Royal Albert Dock. ☎ 020 7476 7054, www.gallionspoint marina.co.uk. Ch M/80, when vessel expected. Access via lock (width 7·6m) HW±5; Locking £5 each way; H24 security, AB £12/yacht, Showers, WC, ♿, Gas, P & D (by arrangement), ME. 2 x ☆s 2FG (vert) on river pier. 8m depth in basin. DLR from N Woolwich to central London, until 0030. Woolwich ferry & foot tunnel 15 mins walk. ✈ (City) is adjacent.

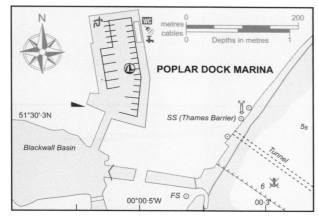

POPLAR DOCK MARINA, 51°30'·07N 00°00'·50W (lock ent). AC 484, 3337. Tides: India & Millwall Docks ent. 4·5M below Tower Bridge. Canary Wharf twr (244m) is conspic 4ca W of marina. Lock (200m x 24m) opens 0700-1700LT at HW for outbound and HW-1 to HW+1 for arrivals, foc, but OT £20. Least width 12·1m into marina. **Marina** ☎ 020 7308 9930. VHF Ch 13 (H24). **Facilities:** Slip, Bar, R, ☕, ♿, ▣, ♿; Dr ☎ 020 7237 1078; Ħ ☎ 020 7955 5000; Police ☎ 252 2836. ⇌, Blackwall DLR, Canary Wharf Tube, ✈ City.

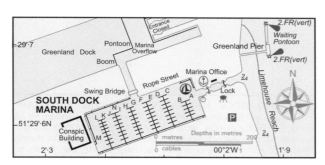

SOUTH DOCK MARINA (B), 51°29'·65N 00°01'·97W. AC 2484, 3337. Tides as for Surrey Dock Greenland Ent. 1·1M above Greenwich, 2·5M below Tower Bridge. Baltic Quay building at SW end of marina is conspic with five arched rooftops. Waiting pontoon at Greenland Pier. Approx access via lock (width 6·4m)

HW-2½ to HW+1½ for 2m draft. **Marina** ☎ 020 7252 2244, (250 + ♥, £15 <15m, £20 >15.5m). VHF Ch **M** 80. **Facilities:** ME, ✗, El, CH, C (20 ton), Bar, R, ☕, ♿, ▣, Dr ☎ 237 1078; Ħ ♿ ☎ 020 7955 5000; Police ☎ 020 7252 2836. ⇌, Surrey Quays and Canada Water tube, ✈ City Airport.

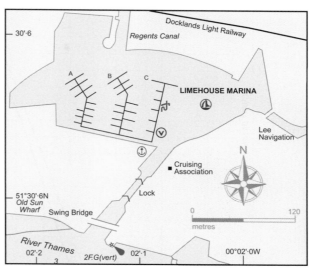

LIMEHOUSE MARINA (C), 51°30'·57N 00°02'·27W. Entry HW±3 via swing bridge/lock (width 8m), 0800-1800LT daily Apr-Sep; 0800-1600 Oct-Mar; other times by prior arrangement (24hrs notice) to BW Lock control ☎ 0207 3089930, beware cross-tide at lock cut, mid flood/ebb. **Marina** ☎ 0207 3089930, www.bwml.co.uk. Waiting pontoon in lock entrance is accessible outside LW±2. Call VHF Ch 80 *Limehouse Marina.* **Facilities:** (90 berths, from £25/craft ♥) H24 security, ♿, ⚓, ♿, ▣, Bar, ⇌, DLR; also entry to Regents Canal and Lee Navigation.

ST KATHARINE HAVEN, (D) 51°30'·36N 00°04'·35W. AC 3337, 3319. HW +0245 on Dover. Tides as London Bridge. Beware of cross tide at mid-flood/ebb. Good shelter under all conditions. Tower Bridge and the Tower of London are uniquely conspic, close up-river. Six Y waiting buoys are close downstream of ent in 0.1–1.9m. Or berth on inshore side of St Katharine Pier, 30m upriver of ent, but limited berthing/shore access, only suitable for shoal draft. Pleasure launches berth on S side of pier.
St Katharine Haven Ch 80 M. Lock (41m x 12·5m with 2 small lifting bridges), access HW –2 to HW +1½, season 0600-2030, winter 0800-1800LT; other times by prior arrangement. R/G tfc lts at ent. Lock is shut Tues and Wed, Nov to Feb.
Facilities: (100 + 50 ♥, usually in Centre Basin or East Dock; give 1 week's notice in season) ☎ 0207 2645312, www.skdocks.co.uk; £25·80/yacht, ✗, ♿, @, Wi-fi, YC, Bar, R, ☕, ⊖, ▣. **Fuel Barge (E)** is 400m downstream of lock ent. ☎ 0207 4811774; VHF Ch 14 *Heiko.* D & Gas, Mon-Fri 0630-1430. W/ends Apr-Oct, HW±2, not open before 0600 & not after 1800.

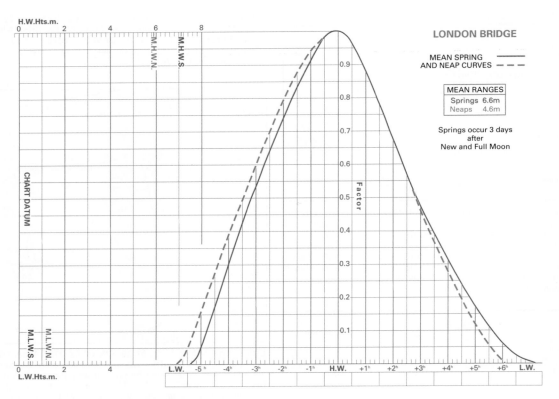

LONDON BRIDGE

MEAN SPRING ——
AND NEAP CURVES - - -

MEAN RANGES
Springs 6.6m
Neaps 4.6m

Springs occur 3 days
after
New and Full Moon

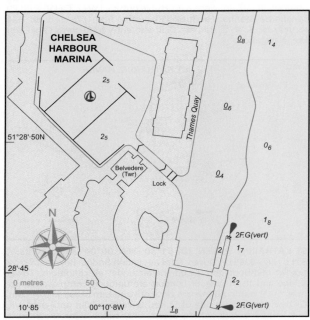

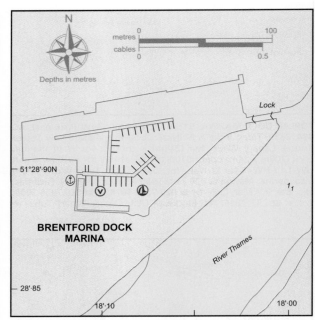

CHELSEA HARBOUR, (I) London, **51°28′·48N 00°10′·82W.** AC 3319. Tides: see Albert Bridge. Good shelter in all conditions, 5M above Tower Bridge, reached via 14 fixed bridges. Battersea railway bridge is 120m upstream. Belvedere Tower (80m high with tide ball) is conspic, next to the lock and bascule bridge. Max sizes for lock: LOA 24m, beam 5·5m, draft 1·8m. Lock opens when 2·5m water above sill; tide gauge outside, access HW np ±30mins/HW sp±1½, R/G tfc lts. Limited waiting berths and shore access on Chelsea Hbr Pier (1·7m) close upriver. **Marina,** 50+10 Ⓥ £15.00. ☎ 0207 225 9100, mobile ☎ 07770 542783. VHF Ch 80. Bar, R, Ⓑ, ▣, showers, 🆆🅲, &, ⚓, 🛒.

BRENTFORD DOCK MARINA (N). 51°28′·92N 00°18′·05W, 1100m beyond Kew bridge. AC 3319. Tides, see Kew Bridge. 60 AB inc Ⓥ, £18·94 for all LOA. ☎ 020 8232 8941, mobile 07970 143 987. No VHF. Access HW±2½ via lock 4·8m x 9·8m (longer LOA during freeflow); 15m waiting pontoon. **Facilities:** El, ME, Bar, R, 🛒, 🔧; Gunnersbury & Ealing tubes. Ent to Grand Union Canal via lock is nearby: M, AB.

TIME ZONE (UT)
For Summer Time add ONE hour in **non-shaded areas**

LONDON BRIDGE LAT 51°30'N LONG 0°05'W
TIMES AND HEIGHTS OF HIGH AND LOW WATERS

Dates in red are **SPRINGS**
Dates in blue are **NEAPS**

YEAR 2010

E England

JANUARY

	Time	m		Time	m
1 F	0141 0827 1400 2041	6.7 0.6 7.1 1.0	**16** SA	0222 0859 1444 2101	6.5 0.8 6.6 1.2
2 SA	0231 0925 1451 2133	6.8 0.4 7.3 1.0	**17** SU	0256 0933 1518 2136	6.6 0.8 6.7 1.1
3 SU	0317 1017 1540 2220	6.9 0.2 7.3 0.8	**18** M	0328 1006 1549 2208	6.6 0.7 6.6 1.1
4 M	0402 1102 1629 2303	7.0 0.1 7.3 0.8	**19** TU	0358 1036 1618 2238	6.6 0.7 6.6 1.1
5 TU	0447 1143 1717 2343	7.0 0.1 7.2 0.9	**20** W	0427 1102 1647 2307	6.6 0.8 6.6 1.2
6 W	0532 1221 1806	6.9 0.2 6.9	**21** TH	0457 1122 1719 2333	6.5 0.8 6.4 1.3
7 TH ☽	0024 0619 1301 1857	1.0 6.7 0.4 6.6	**22** F	0529 1144 1755	6.4 0.9 6.3
8 F	0107 0712 1344 1950	1.2 6.5 0.7 6.4	**23** SA ◑	0003 0607 1217 1837	1.3 6.3 0.9 6.1
9 SA	0157 0812 1434 2051	1.4 6.3 1.0 6.1	**24** SU	0041 0654 1259 1931	1.4 6.1 1.1 5.8
10 SU	0302 0920 1533 2203	1.6 6.1 1.3 5.9	**25** M	0132 0754 1354 2044	1.6 5.9 1.3 5.7
11 M	0421 1029 1645 2314	1.6 6.0 1.4 5.9	**26** TU	0240 0924 1524 2207	1.7 5.9 1.5 5.8
12 TU	0533 1136 1756	1.4 6.1 1.4	**27** W	0444 1044 1705 2326	1.5 6.2 1.4 6.1
13 W	0013 0637 1236 1853	6.0 1.2 6.3 1.3	**28** TH	0559 1152 1821	1.1 6.6 1.2
14 TH	0104 0733 1325 1941	6.2 1.0 6.5 1.2	**29** F	0033 0711 1255 1934	6.4 0.8 6.9 1.0
15 F ●	0146 0820 1407 2023	6.4 0.9 6.6 1.2	**30** SA ○	0129 0823 1350 2037	6.7 0.4 7.2 0.9
			31 SU	0218 0920 1441 2129	7.0 0.1 7.4 0.8

FEBRUARY

	Time	m		Time	m
1 M	0303 1007 1528 2214	7.1 -0.1 7.5 0.7	**16** TU	0306 0945 1524 2152	6.8 0.7 6.8 1.0
2 TU	0347 1049 1613 2254	7.3 -0.1 7.4 0.7	**17** W	0336 1015 1552 2223	6.8 0.6 6.8 1.0
3 W	0428 1125 1657 2329	7.3 0.0 7.2 0.7	**18** TH	0404 1042 1620 2251	6.8 0.6 6.7 1.0
4 TH	0509 1157 1739	7.2 0.2 6.9	**19** F	0432 1059 1650 2315	6.8 0.7 6.6 1.1
5 F ◑	0002 0551 1228 1821	0.9 6.9 0.5 6.4	**20** SA	0504 1118 1724 2340	6.7 0.8 6.4 1.2
6 SA	0036 0636 1301 1906	1.1 6.6 0.8 6.2	**21** SU	0541 1147 1804	6.5 0.9 6.1
7 SU	0113 0728 1343 1956	1.3 6.3 1.2 5.9	**22** M ◑	0014 0624 1226 1853	1.3 6.3 1.0 5.9
8 M	0202 0835 1440 2104	1.6 6.1 1.6 5.6	**23** TU	0102 0722 1319 2005	1.4 6.1 1.3 5.6
9 TU	0324 0952 1558 2239	1.8 5.7 1.8 5.6	**24** W	0207 0851 1452 2134	1.6 5.9 1.7 5.6
10 W	0459 1112 1729 2351	1.5 5.8 1.6 5.8	**25** TH	0415 1020 1643 2305	1.5 6.1 1.5 6.0
11 TH	0615 1221 1832	1.3 6.2 1.4	**26** F	0543 1136 1811	1.1 6.5 1.2
12 F	0044 0714 1311 1921	6.2 1.0 6.5 1.2	**27** SA	0017 0704 1243 1924	6.4 0.6 6.9 1.0
13 SA	0127 0759 1350 2005	6.4 0.8 6.6 1.1	**28** SU ○	0112 0811 1337 2024	6.8 0.2 7.2 0.8
14 SU ●	0203 0838 1424 2044	6.6 0.8 6.7 1.1			
15 M	0235 0913 1455 2119	6.7 0.7 6.8 1.1			

MARCH

	Time	m		Time	m
1 M	0159 0902 1424 2113	7.1 0.0 7.4 0.7	**16** TU	0207 0843 1426 2055	6.7 0.7 6.7 1.0
2 TU	0242 0947 1508 2156	7.3 -0.1 7.4 0.6	**17** W	0238 0917 1455 2130	6.9 0.6 6.8 0.9
3 W	0323 1025 1550 2234	7.4 -0.1 7.4 0.6	**18** TH	0308 0947 1524 2203	6.9 0.6 6.8 0.8
4 TH	0403 1058 1630 2307	7.4 0.1 7.2 0.7	**19** F	0338 1014 1554 2233	7.0 0.6 6.8 0.9
5 F	0443 1125 1708 2335	7.3 0.4 6.9 0.8	**20** SA	0409 1036 1626 2300	6.9 0.7 6.6 1.0
6 SA	0522 1150 1744	7.0 0.7 6.5	**21** SU	0443 1057 1700 2325	6.8 0.8 6.4 1.1
7 SU ◑	0002 0602 1220 1822	1.0 6.6 1.0 6.1	**22** M	0521 1126 1741 2359	6.7 1.0 6.2 1.1
8 M	0034 0650 1258 1908	1.2 6.2 1.4 5.8	**23** TU ◑	0607 1206 1833	6.4 1.2 5.9
9 TU	0118 0754 1355 2010	1.5 5.8 1.8 5.5	**24** W	0046 0708 1305 1944	1.2 6.1 1.5 5.7
10 W	0228 0915 1516 2152	1.8 5.6 2.0 5.4	**25** TH	0154 0837 1443 2112	1.5 6.0 1.7 5.7
11 TH	0419 1042 1659 2317	1.7 5.7 1.8 5.7	**26** F	0358 1002 1630 2245	1.4 6.2 1.6 6.0
12 F	0541 1155 1803	1.3 6.1 1.4	**27** SA	0530 1121 1756 2355	0.9 6.6 1.2 6.5
13 SA	0014 0641 1244 1854	6.1 1.0 6.4 1.2	**28** SU	0647 1225 1904	0.5 7.0 0.9
14 SU	0058 0728 1323 1939	6.4 0.8 6.6 1.1	**29** M	0049 0748 1317 2001	6.9 0.2 7.2 0.8
15 M ●	0134 0808 1356 2019	6.6 0.8 6.7 1.1	**30** TU ○	0135 0837 1402 2050	7.1 0.0 7.3 0.6
			31 W	0217 0919 1443 2132	7.3 0.1 7.3 0.6

APRIL

	Time	m		Time	m
1 TH	0257 0955 1523 2210	7.4 0.2 7.2 0.6	**16** F	0240 0916 1459 2141	7.0 0.7 6.8 0.8
2 F	0337 1024 1601 2241	7.4 0.4 7.1 0.7	**17** SA	0314 0947 1533 2215	7.0 0.7 6.7 0.7
3 SA	0417 1050 1637 2307	7.3 0.6 6.8 0.8	**18** SU	0350 1016 1608 2247	7.0 0.8 6.6 0.8
4 SU	0455 1115 1712 2332	6.9 0.9 6.4 1.0	**19** M	0428 1046 1646 2318	6.9 0.9 6.4 0.8
5 M	0535 1144 1748	6.5 1.2 6.1	**20** TU	0510 1122 1730 2356	6.7 1.1 6.2 0.9
6 TU ◑	0003 0620 1223 1832	1.2 6.1 1.5 5.8	**21** W ◐	0601 1209 1825	6.5 1.3 6.0
7 W	0045 0719 1317 1931	1.4 5.7 1.8 5.5	**22** TH	0045 0708 1314 1935	1.1 6.3 1.5 5.9
8 TH	0146 0836 1432 2056	1.7 5.5 2.0 5.4	**23** F	0155 0827 1434 2056	1.2 6.2 1.6 5.9
9 F	0328 0955 1609 2227	1.7 5.6 1.9 5.6	**24** SA	0344 0945 1613 2221	1.1 6.4 1.5 6.2
10 SA	0448 1111 1722 2330	1.5 6.0 1.5 6.0	**25** SU	0506 1101 1731 2329	0.8 6.6 1.1 6.6
11 SU	0550 1204 1816	1.1 6.3 1.3	**26** M	0617 1203 1835	0.5 6.9 0.9
12 M	0018 0642 1246 1903	6.4 0.9 6.5 1.1	**27** TU	0023 0716 1254 1932	6.9 0.4 7.0 0.8
13 TU	0058 0728 1320 1946	6.6 0.8 6.6 1.0	**28** W ○	0109 0805 1338 2022	7.0 0.6 7.0 0.7
14 W ●	0133 0807 1353 2026	6.8 0.8 6.7 0.9	**29** TH	0152 0846 1419 2106	7.2 0.5 7.0 0.6
15 TH	0207 0843 1426 2104	6.9 0.7 6.8 0.8	**30** F	0233 0921 1459 2144	7.3 0.6 7.0 0.6

Chart Datum: 2·90 metres below Ordnance Datum (Newlyn). HAT is 7·6 metres above Chart Datum; see 0.19

TIME ZONE (UT)
For Summer Time add ONE hour in **non-shaded areas**

LONDON BRIDGE LAT 51°30'N LONG 0°05'W
TIMES AND HEIGHTS OF HIGH AND LOW WATERS

Dates in red are **SPRINGS**
Dates in blue are **NEAPS**

YEAR 2010

MAY

Day	Time m	Time m	Time m	Time m
1 SA	0314 7.3	0951 0.7	1537 6.9	2216 0.7
2 SU	0355 7.1	1019 0.9	1612 6.7	2243 0.8
3 M	0434 6.8	1047 1.1	1647 6.4	2310 1.0
4 TU	0514 6.4	1119 1.3	1722 6.1	2341 1.1
5 W	0556 6.1	1156 1.5	1805 5.9	
6 TH	0019 1.3	0649 5.8	1245 1.8	1859 5.7
7 F	0112 1.5	0753 5.6	1347 1.9	2008 5.6
8 SA	0233 1.6	0900 5.7	1503 1.9	2128 5.6
9 SU	0349 1.4	1008 5.8	1621 1.7	2237 5.9
10 M	0450 1.2	1110 6.1	1724 1.4	2331 6.2
11 TU	0545 1.1	1159 6.3	1818 1.2	
12 W	0017 6.5	0637 1.0	1242 6.5	1908 1.1
13 TH	0058 6.7	0725 0.9	1322 6.6	1955 0.9
14 F	0137 6.9	0809 0.9	1401 6.7	2039 0.8
15 SA	0216 7.0	0849 0.8	1440 6.7	2121 0.7
16 SU	0256 7.1	0927 0.8	1520 6.7	2201 0.6
17 M	0337 7.1	1005 0.9	1600 6.6	2239 0.6
18 TU	0420 7.0	1045 0.9	1642 6.5	2318 0.6
19 W	0508 6.9	1128 1.1	1729 6.4	
20 TH	0000 0.7	0602 6.7	1218 1.2	1823 6.3
21 F	0052 0.8	0706 6.5	1314 1.3	1926 6.2
22 SA	0201 0.9	0814 6.5	1423 1.4	2039 6.2
23 SU	0320 0.8	0924 6.5	1546 1.4	2154 6.4
24 M	0430 0.7	1035 6.6	1700 1.2	2259 6.6
25 TU	0538 0.7	1137 6.7	1804 1.1	2356 6.7
26 W	0640 0.7	1230 6.7	1903 0.9	
27 TH	0046 6.8	0730 0.8	1317 6.7	1955 0.8
28 F	0132 6.9	0813 0.8	1400 6.7	2042 0.7
29 SA	0215 7.0	0850 0.9	1440 6.7	2123 0.7
30 SU	0258 7.0	0925 0.9	1518 6.7	2158 0.7
31 M	0340 6.9	0957 1.0	1555 6.6	2228 0.8

JUNE

Day	Time m	Time m	Time m	Time m
1 TU	0419 6.7	1030 1.1	1629 6.4	2257 0.9
2 W	0457 6.5	1103 1.3	1704 6.3	2328 1.0
3 TH	0536 6.2	1138 1.4	1743 6.1	
4 F	0002 1.1	0618 6.0	1219 1.5	1827 6.0
5 SA	0042 1.2	0709 5.9	1305 1.7	1921 5.8
6 SU	0132 1.3	0805 5.8	1401 1.8	2026 5.7
7 M	0241 1.4	0906 5.8	1510 1.8	2138 5.8
8 TU	0350 1.4	1009 5.9	1628 1.6	2241 6.1
9 W	0451 1.2	1110 6.1	1734 1.3	2335 6.4
10 TH	0550 1.1	1205 6.4	1831 1.1	
11 F	0025 6.6	0645 1.0	1255 6.6	1925 0.9
12 SA	0112 6.9	0739 1.0	1341 6.7	2018 0.7
13 SU	0158 7.0	0829 0.9	1427 6.7	2109 0.6
14 M	0244 7.1	0916 0.9	1511 6.8	2158 0.4
15 TU	0330 7.2	1002 0.8	1555 6.8	2244 0.3
16 W	0417 7.2	1047 0.8	1639 6.8	2328 0.3
17 TH	0506 7.1	1131 0.9	1725 6.7	
18 F	0011 0.3	0558 7.0	1217 1.0	1815 6.6
19 SA	0057 0.4	0654 6.8	1306 1.1	1911 6.6
20 SU	0148 0.6	0752 6.6	1403 1.3	2014 6.5
21 M	0246 0.7	0856 6.5	1512 1.4	2122 6.4
22 TU	0347 0.9	1004 6.3	1625 1.3	2228 6.4
23 W	0454 1.0	1110 6.3	1733 1.2	2330 6.5
24 TH	0601 1.1	1209 6.4	1836 1.0	
25 F	0027 6.5	0658 1.1	1300 6.4	1934 0.9
26 SA	0119 6.7	0746 1.1	1346 6.5	2024 0.8
27 SU	0205 6.8	0829 1.1	1427 6.6	2108 0.7
28 M	0248 6.8	0907 1.1	1504 6.6	2145 0.7
29 TU	0327 6.8	0943 1.1	1540 6.6	2217 0.8
30 W	0404 6.7	1017 1.1	1614 6.6	2248 0.8

JULY

Day	Time m	Time m	Time m	Time m
1 TH	0438 6.6	1050 1.2	1646 6.5	2317 0.8
2 F	0511 6.4	1122 1.2	1719 6.4	2345 0.9
3 SA	0546 6.3	1154 1.3	1754 6.3	
4 SU	0010 1.0	0624 6.1	1227 1.5	1834 6.1
5 M	0042 1.1	0709 5.9	1307 1.6	1923 5.9
6 TU	0123 1.2	0805 5.8	1358 1.7	2028 5.8
7 W	0222 1.4	0912 5.8	1513 1.7	2149 5.9
8 TH	0353 1.4	1024 5.9	1653 1.5	2256 6.2
9 F	0509 1.3	1132 6.2	1759 1.1	2355 6.6
10 SA	0614 1.1	1232 6.5	1900 0.8	
11 SU	0051 6.9	0717 1.0	1325 6.7	2004 0.6
12 M	0143 7.1	0819 0.9	1414 6.8	2104 0.4
13 TU	0233 7.3	0914 0.9	1500 7.0	2157 0.1
14 W	0321 7.4	1003 0.7	1544 7.1	2243 0.0
15 TH	0408 7.4	1047 0.7	1627 7.1	2325 -0.1
16 F	0455 7.3	1128 0.7	1711 7.1	
17 SA	0004 0.0	0542 7.1	1208 0.8	1756 6.9
18 SU	0041 0.2	0631 6.8	1249 1.0	1845 6.8
19 M	0120 0.5	0722 6.5	1334 1.2	1942 6.5
20 TU	0206 0.8	0820 6.2	1431 1.4	2047 6.3
21 W	0302 1.2	0928 6.0	1546 1.5	2156 6.2
22 TH	0411 1.4	1042 6.0	1703 1.4	2307 6.2
23 F	0529 1.4	1149 6.1	1815 1.1	
24 SA	0014 6.4	0634 1.3	1246 6.3	1918 0.9
25 SU	0110 6.6	0727 1.2	1333 6.5	2010 0.7
26 M	0155 6.7	0812 1.1	1412 6.6	2052 0.7
27 TU	0234 6.8	0852 1.1	1448 6.7	2128 0.7
28 W	0310 6.8	0928 1.1	1521 6.7	2200 0.7
29 TH	0343 6.8	1001 1.0	1552 6.8	2230 0.7
30 F	0413 6.7	1033 1.0	1623 6.7	2258 0.7
31 SA	0442 6.6	1103 1.1	1651 6.6	2321 0.8

AUGUST

Day	Time m	Time m	Time m	Time m
1 SU	0510 6.5	1130 1.2	1721 6.5	2338 0.9
2 M	0542 6.3	1155 1.3	1755 6.3	
3 TU	0002 1.0	0619 6.0	1227 1.4	1836 6.1
4 W	0038 1.1	0707 5.8	1311 1.5	1931 5.9
5 TH	0128 1.3	0816 5.6	1412 1.7	2055 5.8
6 F	0246 1.6	0940 5.7	1611 1.6	2220 6.1
7 SA	0433 1.5	1102 6.0	1732 1.1	2329 6.5
8 SU	0551 1.2	1211 6.4	1842 0.8	
9 M	0033 6.9	0704 1.0	1307 6.7	1955 0.4
10 TU	0129 7.2	0811 0.9	1357 7.0	2055 0.1
11 W	0219 7.4	0906 0.8	1442 7.2	2144 -0.1
12 TH	0305 7.5	0953 0.6	1525 7.3	2228 -0.2
13 F	0350 7.5	1036 0.6	1606 7.4	2307 -0.2
14 SA	0434 7.3	1114 0.6	1647 7.3	2341 0.1
15 SU	0517 7.1	1149 0.7	1729 7.1	
16 M	0012 0.4	0600 6.7	1224 0.9	1814 6.8
17 TU	0045 0.7	0645 6.4	1301 1.2	1906 6.5
18 W	0125 1.0	0737 6.0	1348 1.4	2011 6.1
19 TH	0219 1.5	0844 5.7	1502 1.6	2126 5.9
20 F	0332 1.7	1012 5.7	1635 1.5	2245 6.0
21 SA	0506 1.6	1128 5.9	1757 1.2	
22 SU	0001 6.3	0614 1.3	1227 6.3	1900 0.8
23 M	0055 6.6	0706 1.0	1313 6.5	1948 0.7
24 TU	0137 6.8	0752 1.1	1351 6.7	2028 0.6
25 W	0213 6.8	0831 1.0	1424 6.8	2102 0.6
26 TH	0245 6.8	0907 1.0	1455 6.8	2133 0.6
27 F	0314 6.8	0940 1.0	1525 6.9	2203 0.6
28 SA	0342 6.8	1012 0.9	1554 6.9	2230 0.6
29 SU	0409 6.7	1041 0.9	1621 6.8	2251 0.8
30 M	0437 6.6	1107 1.1	1650 6.6	2307 0.9
31 TU	0507 6.4	1129 1.2	1724 6.5	2329 1.0

Chart Datum: 2·90 metres below Ordnance Datum (Newlyn). HAT is 7·6 metres above Chart Datum; see 0.19

TIME ZONE (UT)
For Summer Time add ONE hour in **non-shaded areas**

LONDON BRIDGE   LAT 51°30'N   LONG 0°05'W
TIMES AND HEIGHTS OF HIGH AND LOW WATERS

Dates in red are SPRINGS
Dates in blue are NEAPS

YEAR **2010**

E England

SEPTEMBER

Day	Time	m	Day	Time	m
1 W ☽	0542 / 1157 / 1805	6.1 / 1.3 / 6.3	**16** TH	0046 / 0653 / 1310 / 1937	1.4 / 5.8 / 1.4 / 5.9
2 TH	0003 / 0627 / 1239 / 1856	1.1 / 5.9 / 1.4 / 6.1	**17** F	0139 / 0756 / 1418 / 2054	1.7 / 5.5 / 1.7 / 5.7
3 F	0051 / 0732 / 1337 / 2015	1.4 / 5.6 / 1.5 / 5.9	**18** SA	0254 / 0932 / 1603 / 2218	2.0 / 5.5 / 1.6 / 5.8
4 SA	0208 / 0900 / 1526 / 2149	1.7 / 5.6 / 1.6 / 6.0	**19** SU	0439 / 1056 / 1728 / 2335	1.8 / 5.8 / 1.2 / 6.2
5 SU	0405 / 1033 / 1711 / 2307	1.6 / 5.9 / 1.1 / 6.5	**20** M	0547 / 1156 / 1828	1.4 / 6.2 / 0.9
6 M	0535 / 1148 / 1827	1.3 / 6.4 / 0.7	**21** TU	0028 / 0638 / 1243 / 1914	6.6 / 1.1 / 6.5 / 0.7
7 TU	0014 / 0649 / 1245 / 1938	6.9 / 1.0 / 6.8 / 0.3	**22** W	0109 / 0723 / 1321 / 1954	6.7 / 1.0 / 6.7 / 0.7
8 W ●	0110 / 0754 / 1333 / 2035	7.2 / 0.8 / 7.1 / 0.0	**23** TH ○	0143 / 0804 / 1353 / 2029	6.8 / 1.0 / 6.8 / 0.7
9 TH	0158 / 0848 / 1417 / 2122	7.4 / 0.7 / 7.3 / -0.1	**24** F	0213 / 0840 / 1424 / 2101	6.8 / 1.0 / 6.9 / 0.7
10 F	0243 / 0934 / 1459 / 2204	7.5 / 0.6 / 7.5 / -0.1	**25** SA	0242 / 0914 / 1454 / 2131	6.8 / 0.9 / 6.9 / 0.7
11 SA	0326 / 1016 / 1540 / 2240	7.4 / 0.5 / 7.5 / 0.0	**26** SU	0310 / 0947 / 1523 / 2158	6.8 / 0.8 / 6.9 / 0.7
12 SU	0407 / 1052 / 1621 / 2311	7.3 / 0.6 / 7.4 / 0.3	**27** M	0339 / 1018 / 1553 / 2220	6.8 / 0.9 / 6.9 / 0.8
13 M	0447 / 1125 / 1702 / 2339	7.0 / 0.7 / 7.1 / 0.7	**28** TU	0408 / 1045 / 1625 / 2240	6.6 / 1.0 / 6.8 / 0.9
14 TU	0526 / 1155 / 1744	6.6 / 0.9 / 6.8	**29** W	0440 / 1109 / 1701 / 2305	6.4 / 1.1 / 6.6 / 1.1
15 W ◑	0008 / 0606 / 1227 / 1832	1.0 / 6.2 / 1.2 / 6.3	**30** TH	0516 / 1138 / 1743 / 2340	6.2 / 1.2 / 6.4 / 1.2

OCTOBER

Day	Time	m	Day	Time	m
1 F ☽	0602 / 1220 / 1837	5.9 / 1.2 / 6.2	**16** SA	0104 / 0714 / 1338 / 2016	1.9 / 5.5 / 1.6 / 5.6
2 SA	0030 / 0706 / 1318 / 1956	1.5 / 5.7 / 1.4 / 6.0	**17** SU	0212 / 0837 / 1512 / 2134	2.1 / 5.4 / 1.7 / 5.7
3 SU	0155 / 0830 / 1501 / 2124	1.8 / 5.6 / 1.5 / 6.1	**18** M	0347 / 1007 / 1635 / 2253	2.0 / 5.6 / 1.4 / 6.0
4 M	0341 / 1004 / 1650 / 2243	1.7 / 5.9 / 1.0 / 6.5	**19** TU	0506 / 1113 / 1737 / 2350	1.6 / 6.0 / 1.1 / 6.3
5 TU	0516 / 1120 / 1805 / 2351	1.3 / 6.4 / 0.6 / 6.9	**20** W	0600 / 1202 / 1828	1.3 / 6.3 / 0.9
6 W	0626 / 1217 / 1913	1.0 / 6.8 / 0.3	**21** TH	0032 / 0647 / 1243 / 1911	6.5 / 1.1 / 6.6 / 0.8
7 TH ●	0046 / 0728 / 1306 / 2008	7.2 / 0.8 / 7.1 / 0.1	**22** F	0108 / 0730 / 1318 / 1950	6.6 / 1.0 / 6.7 / 0.8
8 F	0134 / 0822 / 1350 / 2054	7.3 / 0.7 / 7.3 / 0.1	**23** SA ○	0139 / 0809 / 1351 / 2025	6.7 / 0.9 / 6.8 / 0.8
9 SA	0218 / 0910 / 1432 / 2134	7.3 / 0.6 / 7.4 / 0.2	**24** SU	0210 / 0846 / 1423 / 2057	6.8 / 0.9 / 6.9 / 0.8
10 SU	0300 / 0951 / 1514 / 2209	7.3 / 0.6 / 7.5 / 0.4	**25** M	0242 / 0922 / 1456 / 2127	6.8 / 0.8 / 7.0 / 0.8
11 M	0340 / 1028 / 1556 / 2238	7.1 / 0.6 / 7.3 / 0.7	**26** TU	0314 / 0956 / 1530 / 2155	6.7 / 0.8 / 6.9 / 0.9
12 TU	0419 / 1059 / 1637 / 2305	6.8 / 0.7 / 7.0 / 0.9	**27** W	0347 / 1027 / 1606 / 2224	6.6 / 0.8 / 6.9 / 1.0
13 W	0456 / 1127 / 1719 / 2335	6.5 / 0.9 / 6.6 / 1.2	**28** TH	0422 / 1058 / 1646 / 2256	6.4 / 0.9 / 6.8 / 1.1
14 TH ◑	0533 / 1158 / 1806	6.1 / 1.2 / 6.2	**29** F	0501 / 1131 / 1732 / 2337	6.3 / 1.0 / 6.6 / 1.3
15 F	0013 / 0616 / 1238 / 1904	1.5 / 5.8 / 1.4 / 5.8	**30** SA	0550 / 1215 / 1830	6.1 / 1.1 / 6.3
			31 SU	0033 / 0653 / 1313 / 1944	1.5 / 5.9 / 1.2 / 6.2

NOVEMBER

Day	Time	m	Day	Time	m
1 M	0149 / 0808 / 1449 / 2102	1.7 / 5.9 / 1.2 / 6.3	**16** TU	0238 / 0902 / 1529 / 2144	2.0 / 5.5 / 1.5 / 5.7
2 TU	0318 / 0934 / 1622 / 2217	1.6 / 6.1 / 0.9 / 6.5	**17** W	0400 / 1014 / 1631 / 2251	1.9 / 5.8 / 1.3 / 5.9
3 W	0449 / 1049 / 1733 / 2325	1.4 / 6.4 / 0.6 / 6.8	**18** TH	0507 / 1112 / 1727 / 2344	1.6 / 6.1 / 1.2 / 6.2
4 TH	0558 / 1148 / 1840	1.1 / 6.7 / 0.5	**19** F	0601 / 1159 / 1819	1.3 / 6.3 / 1.1
5 F	0021 / 0659 / 1239 / 1935	6.9 / 0.9 / 7.0 / 0.4	**20** SA	0026 / 0650 / 1241 / 1906	6.4 / 1.1 / 6.6 / 1.0
6 SA ●	0110 / 0755 / 1325 / 2022	7.0 / 0.8 / 7.1 / 0.5	**21** SU ○	0105 / 0736 / 1320 / 1948	6.6 / 1.0 / 6.7 / 1.0
7 SU	0154 / 0844 / 1409 / 2103	7.0 / 0.7 / 7.2 / 0.6	**22** M	0143 / 0819 / 1358 / 2027	6.7 / 0.9 / 6.9 / 0.9
8 M	0237 / 0927 / 1453 / 2137	7.0 / 0.6 / 7.3 / 0.7	**23** TU	0221 / 0900 / 1436 / 2104	6.7 / 0.8 / 6.9 / 1.0
9 TU	0318 / 1005 / 1536 / 2208	6.9 / 0.6 / 7.2 / 0.9	**24** W	0259 / 0940 / 1515 / 2140	6.7 / 0.7 / 7.0 / 1.0
10 W	0357 / 1037 / 1619 / 2238	6.7 / 0.8 / 6.9 / 1.1	**25** TH	0336 / 1018 / 1556 / 2218	6.6 / 0.7 / 7.0 / 1.0
11 TH	0433 / 1106 / 1645 / 2310	6.4 / 0.9 / 6.5 / 1.3	**26** F	0415 / 1055 / 1639 / 2300	6.5 / 0.7 / 6.9 / 1.1
12 F	0509 / 1136 / 1743 / 2347	6.2 / 1.1 / 6.2 / 1.6	**27** SA	0457 / 1133 / 1728 / 2345	6.4 / 0.7 / 6.7 / 1.2
13 SA ◑	0549 / 1213 / 1833	5.9 / 1.3 / 5.9	**28** SU ◑	0545 / 1218 / 1825	6.3 / 0.8 / 6.6
14 SU	0031 / 0638 / 1303 / 1932	1.8 / 5.7 / 1.5 / 5.7	**29** M	0037 / 0642 / 1314 / 1929	1.4 / 6.2 / 0.9 / 6.4
15 M	0128 / 0743 / 1414 / 2036	2.0 / 5.5 / 1.6 / 5.6	**30** TU	0137 / 0748 / 1431 / 2038	1.5 / 6.1 / 1.0 / 6.4

DECEMBER

Day	Time	m	Day	Time	m
1 W	0252 / 0904 / 1546 / 2149	1.6 / 6.2 / 0.9 / 6.4	**16** TH	0235 / 0907 / 1523 / 2139	2.0 / 5.6 / 1.5 / 5.7
2 TH	0418 / 1018 / 1655 / 2258	1.5 / 6.3 / 0.9 / 6.5	**17** F	0400 / 1016 / 1628 / 2245	1.9 / 5.8 / 1.5 / 5.9
3 F	0528 / 1120 / 1803 / 2358	1.2 / 6.5 / 0.8 / 6.6	**18** SA	0512 / 1114 / 1728 / 2344	1.6 / 6.1 / 1.3 / 6.2
4 SA	0632 / 1216 / 1902	1.0 / 6.7 / 0.8	**19** SU	0610 / 1205 / 1824	1.2 / 6.4 / 1.2
5 SU ●	0050 / 0730 / 1306 / 1952	6.6 / 0.9 / 6.8 / 0.9	**20** M	0035 / 0704 / 1253 / 1916	6.4 / 1.0 / 6.6 / 1.1
6 M	0137 / 0822 / 1353 / 2035	6.7 / 0.7 / 6.9 / 0.9	**21** TU ○	0122 / 0755 / 1337 / 2005	6.6 / 0.8 / 6.8 / 1.1
7 TU	0220 / 0909 / 1439 / 2113	6.7 / 0.7 / 7.0 / 1.0	**22** W	0206 / 0845 / 1422 / 2051	6.7 / 0.7 / 7.0 / 1.0
8 W	0301 / 0949 / 1523 / 2147	6.7 / 0.7 / 7.0 / 1.1	**23** TH	0249 / 0934 / 1506 / 2136	6.7 / 0.5 / 7.1 / 1.0
9 TH	0340 / 1023 / 1605 / 2220	6.6 / 0.8 / 6.8 / 1.2	**24** F	0330 / 1021 / 1550 / 2220	6.8 / 0.4 / 7.2 / 0.9
10 F	0417 / 1052 / 1644 / 2253	6.5 / 0.9 / 6.5 / 1.3	**25** SA	0411 / 1104 / 1635 / 2304	6.8 / 0.4 / 7.1 / 0.9
11 SA	0451 / 1122 / 1722 / 2327	6.3 / 1.0 / 6.3 / 1.4	**26** SU	0452 / 1144 / 1722 / 2346	6.7 / 0.4 / 7.0 / 1.0
12 SU	0526 / 1153 / 1801	6.2 / 1.1 / 6.1	**27** M	0537 / 1224 / 1813	6.7 / 0.5 / 6.8
13 M ◑	0003 / 0606 / 1229 / 1846	1.5 / 6.0 / 1.2 / 5.9	**28** TU ◑	0030 / 0626 / 1309 / 1908	1.1 / 6.5 / 0.6 / 6.6
14 TU	0044 / 0654 / 1311 / 1938	1.7 / 5.8 / 1.4 / 5.8	**29** W	0120 / 0724 / 1402 / 2009	1.3 / 6.4 / 0.8 / 6.3
15 W	0133 / 0753 / 1410 / 2035	1.9 / 5.7 / 1.5 / 5.7	**30** TH	0220 / 0832 / 1504 / 2116	1.5 / 6.3 / 1.0 / 6.2
			31 F	0340 / 0946 / 1613 / 2229	1.5 / 6.2 / 1.2 / 6.1

Chart Datum: 2·90 metres below Ordnance Datum (Newlyn). HAT is 7·6 metres above Chart Datum; see 0.19

1.13   SOUTHEND-ON-SEA/LEIGH-ON-SEA

Essex 51°31'·07N 00°42'·57E ✿✿✿✿✿

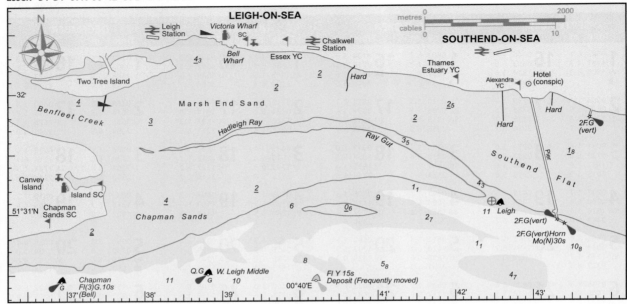

CHARTS AC 5606, 1183, 1185; Imray C1, C2, Y18; Stanfords 5, 8.

TIDES +0125 Dover; ML 3·0; Duration 0610

Standard Port SHEERNESS (←)

Times				Height (metres)			
High Water		Low Water		MHWS	MHWN	MLWN	MLWS
0200	0800	0200	0700	5·8	4·7	1·5	0·6
1400	2000	1400	1900				
Differences SOUTHEND-ON-SEA							
−0005	−0005	−0005	−0005	0·0	0·0	−0·1	−0·1
CORYTON							
+0005	+0010	+0010	+0010	+0·4	+0·3	0·0	0·0

SHELTER The whole area dries soon after half ebb, except Ray Gut (0·4–4·8m) which leads to Leigh Creek and Hadleigh Ray, either side of Two Tree Island, thence to Benfleet Creek where the limit of W navigation is the Tidal Barrier just above Benfleet YC; all are buoyed, but echo-sounder is essential. Craft can take the ground alongside Bell Wharf or Victoria Wharf. It is also possible to secure at the end of Southend Pier to collect stores, FW. NOTE: Southend-on-Sea and Leigh-on-Sea are both part of the lower PLA Area and an 8kn speed limit is enforced in inshore areas.

NAVIGATION WPT 51°31'·07N 00°42'·57E, Leigh SHM buoy, at ent to Ray Gut; this SHM buoy can be left close to port on entering Ray Gut, since there is now more water NE of it than to the SW. Appr from Shoeburyness, keep outside the W Shoebury SHM buoy, Fl G 2·5s.

Beware some 3000 small boat moorings 1M either side of Southend Pier. Speed limit in Canvey Island/Hadleigh Ray areas is 8kn.

LIGHTS AND MARKS Pier lts as on chartlet.

R/T Port Control London: *London VTS* VHF Ch 68 inward from Sea Reach No4, *London VTS* VHF Ch 69 seaward from Sea Reach No4,

TELEPHONE (Code 01702) HM ☎ 215620; HM Leigh-on-Sea 710561; MRCC (01255) 675518; Essex Police Marine Section (01268) 775533; Marinecall 09068 969645; Police 431212; Dr 225500; Ⓗ 348911.

FACILITIES
SOUTHEND-ON-SEA: Southend Pier ☎ 215620, AB (craft not to be unattended), 24hrs free then £10/night <35' LOA, £17/night >35', M, L. **Alexandra YC** ☎ 340363, Bar, FW; **Thorpe Bay YC** ☎ 587563, Bar, L, Slip, R, FW; **Thames Estuary YC** ☎ 345967; **Halfway YC** ☎ 582025, pre-book 1 ⚓, FW; **Town** CH, ACA, Ⓔ, 🛒, R, Bar, ✉, Ⓑ, ≈, ✈.

LEIGH-ON-SEA: Essex YC ☎ 478404, FW, Bar; **Leigh on Sea SC** ☎ 476788, FW, Bar; **Bell Wharf**, AB 24hrs free then £9/night; **Victoria Wharf** AB 24hrs free then £9/night, D, SM, Slip (Two Tree Is HW±2½); **Town:** ME, El, ⚒, C, CH, SM.

CANVEY ISLAND: (Code 01268) **Services:** Slip, M, D, FW, ME, El, ⚒, C, Gas, CH, Access HW±2; **Island YC** ☎ 683729; **Benfleet YC** (on S side of Benfleet Creek on Canvey Island) ☎ 792278, Access HW±2½, M, Slip, FW, D (by day), CH, ME, El, ⚒, C, Bar, 🛒, Ⓓ.

SHOEBURYNESS TO RIVER COLNE

(Charts 1185, 1975) Maplin and Foulness Sands extend nearly 6M NE from Foulness Pt, the extremity being marked by Whitaker bn. On N side of Whitaker chan leading to R. Crouch and R Roach lies Buxey Sand, inshore of which is the Ray Sand chan (dries), a convenient short cut between R. Crouch and R. Blackwater with sufficient rise of tide.

To seaward of Buxey Sand and the Spitway, Gunfleet Sand extends 10M NE, marked by buoys and dries in places. ► *A conspic disued lt tr stands on SE side of Gunfleet Sand, about 6M SSE of the Naze tr, and here the SW-going (flood) stream begins* about HW Sheerness + 0600, and the NE-going stream at about HW Sheerness − 0030, sp rates 2kn. ◄

The Rivers Blackwater and Colne share a common estuary which is approached from the NE via NE Gunfleet lt buoy; thence along Goldmer Gat and the Wallet towards Knoll and Eagle lt buoys. For the Colne turn NNW via Colne Bar buoy towards Inner Bench Hd buoy keeping in mid-chan. For R Blackwater, head WNW for NW Knoll and Bench Hd buoys. From the S or SE, make for the Whitaker ECM buoy, thence through the Spitway, via Swin Spitway and Wallet Spitway buoys to reach Knoll buoy and deeper water.

1.14 RIVER ROACH/HAVENGORE

Essex 51°36'·98N 00°52'·14E (Branklet SPM buoy), R Roach ❀❀❀❁✿✿✿. 51°33'·62N 00°50'·52E, Havengore Bridge ❀❁✿

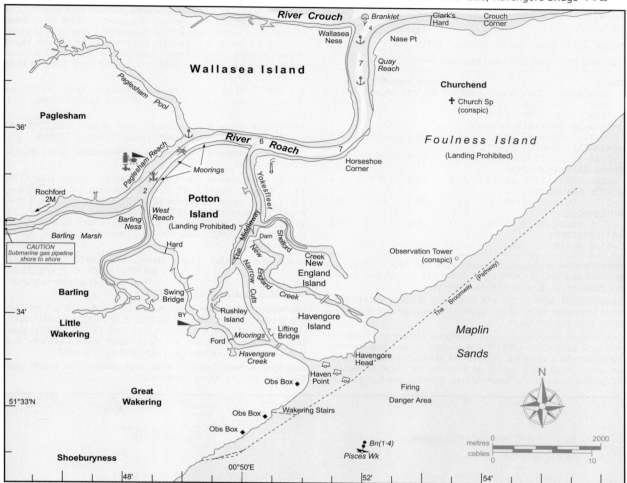

CHARTS AC 5607, 1185, 3750; Imray C1, Y17; Stanfords 5, 4.

TIDES +0110 Dover; ML 2·7; Duration 0615

Standard Port WALTON-ON-THE-NAZE (→)

Times				Height (metres)			
High Water		Low Water		MHWS	MHWN	MLWN	MLWS
0000	0600	0500	1100	4·2	3·4	1·1	0·4
1200	1800	1700	2300				
Differences ROCHFORD							
+0050	+0040	Dries		–0·8	–1·1	Dries	

SHELTER Good. The Roach gives sheltered sailing and access to a network of secluded creeks, including Havengore (the 'backdoor' from the Crouch to the Thames Estuary). No AB available in the area. ⚓s behind sea-walls can be found for all winds at: Quay Reach (often more protected than the Crouch), Paglesham Reach, West Reach, Barling Reach and Yokes Fleet. An ⚓ light is essential due to freighters H24. Speed limit 8kn. Crouch Hbr Authority controls R Roach and Crouch, out to Foulness Pt.

NAVIGATION Normal access H24 to the Roach is from R Crouch (see 1.15 for WPT from seaward); the ent between Branklet SPM buoy and Nase Pt is narrowed by mudbanks. Unlit buoys up-river to Barling Ness, above which few boats go. To exit at Havengore Creek, appr via Middleway and Narrow Cuts to reach the bridge before HW.

Entry via **Havengore Creek** is possible in good weather, with great care and adequate rise of tide (max draft 1·5m at HW sp). Shoeburyness Range is usually active Mon-Fri 0600-1700LT; give 24hrs notice to Range Officer by ☎. Subsequent clearance on VHF by Havengore lifting bridge (☎ HW±2, HJ); no passage unless bridge raised. Least water is over the shifting bar, just inside creek ent. From the S, cross Maplin Sands at HW –1 from S Shoebury SHM buoy, leaving Pisces wreck (conspic, 1M from ent) to port.

LIGHTS AND MARKS Unlit, but night entry to R Roach may be possible.

R/T VHF Ch 72 16 is worked by Range Officer (*Shoe Base*) (HO); Radar Control (*Shoe Radar*) (HO); & Bridge keeper (*Shoe Bridge*) (HW±2 by day). Radar guidance may be available.

TELEPHONE (Code 01702 Southend) Crouch HM ☎ (01621) 783602; Range Officer 383211; Havengore Br 383436; Swing Br to Potton I. ☎ 219491; Marinecall 09068 969645; MRCC (01255) 675518; Dr 218678.

FACILITIES Paglesham (East End) FW, D, slip, El, ME (from BY), ✸, Bar; Gt Wakering: Slip, P, D, FW, ME, El, ✸, C, CH (from BY); at Rochford Wakering YC ☎ 530926, M, L, Bar. Towns Gt Wakering & Rochford; 🛒, R, Bar, ✉ (Great Wakering and Barling); most facilities, Ⓑ and 🚂 in Rochford and Shoeburyness, ✈ (Southend).

1.15 BURNHAM-ON-CROUCH

Essex 51°37'·50N 00°48'·23E (Yacht Hbr) ✿✿✿✿🌢🌢🌢✿✿

CHARTS AC 5607, 1183, 1975, 3750; Imray C1, Y17; Stanfords 1, 19, 5, 4.

TIDES +0115 Dover; ML 2·5; Duration 0610.

Standard Port WALTON-ON-THE-NAZE (→)

Times				Height (metres)			
High Water		Low Water		MHWS	MHWN	MLWN	MLWS
0000	0600	0500	1100	4·2	3·4	1·1	0·4
1200	1800	1700	2300				
Differences WHITAKER BEACON							
+0022	+0024	+0033	+0027	+0·6	+0·5	+0·2	+0·1
HOLLIWELL POINT							
+0034	+0037	+0100	+0037	+1·1	+0·9	+0·3	+0·1
BURNHAM-ON-CROUCH							
+0050	+0035	+0115	+0050	+1·0	+0·8	−0·1	−0·2
NORTH FAMBRIDGE							
+0115	+0050	+0130	+0100	+1·1	+0·8	0·0	−0·1
HULLBRIDGE							
+0115	+0050	+0135	+0105	+1·1	+0·8	0·0	−0·1
BATTLESBRIDGE							
+0120	+0110	Dries		−1·8	−2·0	Dries	

SHELTER River is exposed to most winds. Cliff Reach (off W edge of lower chartlet) is sheltered from SW'lies. ‡ prohib in fairway but possible just E or W of the moorings.

NAVIGATION WPT 51°39'·79N 01°02'·50E, S Buxey SHM lit buoy. Appr from East Swin, or the Wallet via Spitway and N Swallow SWM, into the Whitaker Chan.

Near Sunken Buxey seas can be hazardous with strong wind over tide. Ray Sand Chan (dries 1·7m), usable on the tide by shoal draft boats as a short cut from/to the Blackwater. Shoeburyness Artillery ranges lie E and S of Foulness Pt, clear of fairway. R Crouch is navigable to Battlesbridge, 10M beyond Burnham. No

landing on Foulness (limited access) and Bridgemarsh Is (up-river). Keep N of Wallasea Wetlands (opposite and down-river of Burnham) which are marked with PHM bcns.

LIGHTS AND MARKS There are few landmarks to assist entering, but Whitaker Chan and the river are lit/buoyed to 0·5M W of Essex Marina. From Sunken Buxey NCM lit buoy, the spire of St Mary's ✠ (difficult to identify) leads 233° to Outer Crouch SCM lit buoy; thence steer 240° past Foulness Pt into the river. There is a 2·2M unlit gap between Inner Crouch SWM lit buoy, and Horse Shoal NCM lit buoy.

R/T VHF Ch 80 for: Crouch HM Launch (0900-1700LT, w/e); Essex Marina; Burnham Yacht Harbour; W Wick Marina (1000-1700), also Ch M.

TELEPHONE (Code Maldon 01621) HM 783602; MRCC (01255) 675518; Marinecall 09068 969645; Police 773663; Dr 782054.

FACILITIES There are five marinas or yacht hbrs. Speed limit in moorings is 8kn.

BURNHAM Burnham Yacht Hbr, ☎ 782150, Access H24, (350) £2.10, some 🌢s, Wi-fi, D, ME, El, ⚒, BH (30 ton), BY, CH, 🅿, R, Bar, Slip (£10), 🖢. **Royal Corinthian YC** ☎ 782105, AB, FW, M, L, R, Bar. **Royal Burnham YC** ☎ 782044, FW, L, R, Bar. **Crouch YC** ☎ 782252, L, R, Bar. **Services:** AB, BY, C (15 ton), D, P, FW, ME, El, ⚒, M, Slip, CH, ACA, Gas, SM, Gaz. **Town** 🛒, R, Bar, ✉, 🅑, ⇌, ✈ (Southend).

WALLASEA ISLAND. Essex Marina (400) ☎ (01702) 258531, £2.00, BY, Gas, Bar, C (13 ton), BH (40 ton), CH, D, P, LPG, El, M, ME, R, ⚒, Slip. Ferry to Burnham Town Hard at w/ends in season, ☎ 258870. **Essex YC.** ACA.

FAMBRIDGE Fambridge Yacht Haven (170 + ♥) LOA < 10m: £12/ night; LOA > 10m: £17/night, 🌢s £7/£12, ☎ 740370, Access HW±5, Wi-fi, M, ⚒, ME, BY, BH (25ton), C (5 ton), El, Slip (£6-£15), Gas, Gaz, 🖢, showers, YC, Bar, 🍴. ♥ pontoon (with electricity and water) at former Fambridge Yacht Station, £5/night.

Brandy Hole Yacht Stn (120) ☎ (01702) 230248, L, M, ME, ⚒, Slip, Gas, Gaz, Bar, BY, D, Access HW±4.

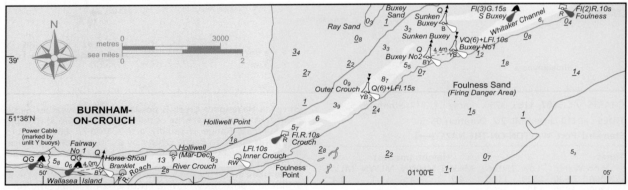

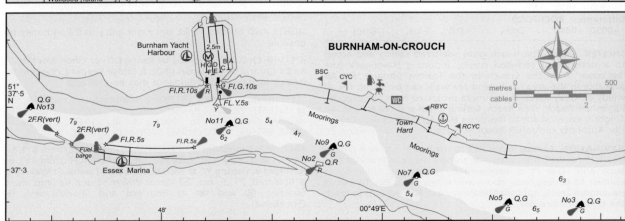

1.16 RIVER BLACKWATER

Essex 51°45'·33N 00°54'·90E ✺✺✺❄❄❄✿✿✿

CHARTS AC 5607, 1183, 1975, 3741; Imray C1, Y17, 2000 Series; Stanfords 5, 6.

TIDES Maldon +0130 Dover; ML 2·8; Duration 0620)

Standard Port WALTON-ON-THE-NAZE (→)

Times				Height (metres)			
High Water		Low Water		MHWS	MHWN	MLWN	MLWS
0000	0600	0500	1100	4·2	3·4	1·1	0·4
1200	1800	1700	2300				
Differences SUNK HEAD							
0000	+0002	−0002	+0002	−0.3	−0.3	−0.1	−0.1
WEST MERSEA							
+0035	+0015	+0055	+0010	+0·9	+0·4	+0·1	+0·1
BRADWELL							
+0035	+0023	+0047	+0004	+1·0	+0·8	+0·2	0·0
OSEA ISLAND							
+0057	+0045	+0050	+0007	+1·1	+0·9	+0·1	0·0
MALDON							
+0107	+0055	No data		−1·3	−1·1	No data	

SHELTER Good, as appropriate to wind. ⚓ restricted by oyster beds and many moorings.

NAVIGATION WPT Knoll NCM, Q, 51°43'·88N 01°05'·07E, 287°/ 6·7M to Nass bn, ECM VQ (3) 5s. Speed limit 8kn W of Osea Is.

WEST MERSEA Avoid oyster beds between Cobmarsh and Packing Marsh Is and in Salcott Chan. ⚓ in Mersea Quarters, access approx HW±1½. There is a pontoon for landing (limited waiting); also pile moorings in Ray Chan.

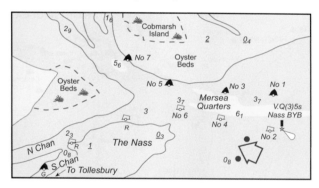

TOLLESBURY FLEET Proceed via S Chan up Woodrolfe Creek. A tide gauge shows depth over marina ent sill (approx 2·4m at MHWS and 1·4m at MHWN). Speed limits: Tollesbury Fleet S Chan 8kn; Woodrolfe Creek upper reaches 4kn.

BRADWELL No dangers, but only suitable for small craft and area gets very crowded; see below under Lts & Marks. Ent has SCM bn Q with tide gauge in Creek; leave to **STBD** on entry. 4 PHM buoys, 3 SHM withies and 2 B/W △ ldg bns mark the chan which doglegs past a SHM buoy to marina ent. Power stn is conspic 7ca NNE.

MALDON From S of Osea Is, 'The Doctor', No 3 SHM buoy on with Blackwater SC lt, Iso G 5s, lead 300° approx up the chan; or No 3 and No 8 buoys in line at 305°.

LIGHTS AND MARKS See chartlets and 1.3.

R/T Bradwell and Tollesbury Marinas Ch **80** M (HO). Blackwater Marina Ch M, 0900-2300. Heybridge Lock Ch 80 HW −2+1. Clark and Carter launch: call CC1.

TELEPHONE Codes: 01621 Maldon. 01206 Colchester/W Mersea. R. Bailiff 875837, Mobile 0860 456802. MRCC (01255) 675518. Marinecall 09068 969645. Police: Colchester 762212; W Mersea 382930. Dr 854118; W Mersea 382015.

FACILITIES **WEST MERSEA** (01206). **W Mersea YC** 382947, Bar, launch service call YC 1. **Town** P, D, FW, ME, El, CH, 🛒, R, Bar, ✉, ⑧, ⚒ (bus to Colchester, Ⓗ ☎ 01206-853535), ✈ (Southend/ Stansted).

TOLLESBURY (01621). **Tollesbury Marina** (220+20 Ⓥ) ☎ 869202, £1·75, marina@woodrolfe.demon.co.uk Access HW±1½, Slip, D, BH (20 ton), Gas, Gaz, LPG, El, ME, ✖, C (5 ton), CH, R, Bar, Wi-fi, 🖸. **Tollesbury Cruising Club** ☎ 869561, Bar, R, M. **Village** P, 🛒, R, Bar, ✉, ⑧ (Tues, Thurs 1000-1430), ⚒ (bus to Witham), ✈ (Southend or Cambridge).

BRADWELL (01621). **Bradwell Marina** (300, some Ⓥ) ☎ 776235, £1·70, short stay £1.00/hr. Slip, D, P, ME, El, ✖, BH (16 ton), CH, R, Bar, Access HW±4½, approx 2m. **Bradwell Quay YC** ☎ 776539, M, FW, Bar, L, Slip. **Town** ✉, ⚒ (bus/taxi to Southminster), ✈ (Southend).

MAYLANDSEA (01621). **Blackwater Marina** (230) ☎ 740264, £10/ craft, Slip, D, ✖, CH, R, Bar; Access HW±2. 150 moorings (£5/craft) in chan. Taxi to Southminster ⚒.

MALDON (01621). **Maldon Quay** Beyond No 8 buoy, the chan which shifts and carries 0·2m, is lit and buoyed. Access near HW; pontoons dry to soft mud. HM/River bailiff ☎ 856487, Mobile 07818 013723; M, P, D, FW, AB < 8m £8, > 8m £10, Slip. **Maldon Little Ship Club** ☎ 854139, Bar. **Services:** Slip, D, ✖, CH, M, ACA, SM, ME, El, Ⓔ. **Town** ✉, ⑧, ⚒ (bus to Chelmsford, Ⓗ ☎ (01245) 440761), ✈ (Southend, Cambridge or Stansted).

HEYBRIDGE BASIN (01621). **Lock** ☎ 853506, opens HW −1 to HW approx. A SHM buoy opposite the lock marks the deep water ent. Access to Chelmer & Blackwater Canal (not navigable). **Blackwater SC** ☎ 853923, L, FW. **Services:** at CRS Marine ☎ 854684, Mobile 07850 543873 (pontoon outside lock), Slip, D, L, M, FW, ME, El, ✖, C. Bus to Heybridge/Maldon.

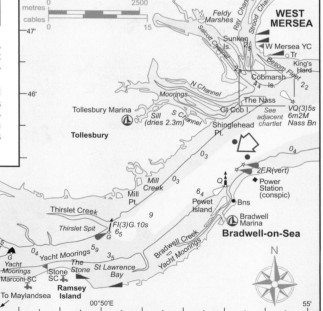

E England

1.17 RIVER COLNE

Essex **51°47'·98N 01°00'·60E** (Brightlingsea) ❀❀⚓⚓⚓❀❀

CHARTS AC 5607, 1183, 1975, 3741; Imray C1, Y17, 2000 Series; Stanfords 5, 6.

TIDES +0050 Dover; ML 2·5; Duration 0615

Standard Port WALTON-ON-THE-NAZE (→)

Times				Height (metres)			
High Water		Low Water		MHWS	MHWN	MLWN	MLWS
0000	0600	0500	1100	4·2	3·4	1·1	0·4
1200	1800	1700	2300				
Differences BRIGHTLINGSEA							
+0025	+0021	+0046	+0004	+0.8	+0.4	+0.1	0.0
COLCHESTER							
+0035	+0025	Dries		0.0	−0.3	Dries	
CLACTON-ON-SEA							
+0012	+0010	+0025	+0008	+0.3	+0.1	+0.1	+0.1

SHELTER Suitable shelter can be found from most winds, but outer hbr is exposed to W'lies. In the creek S of Cindery Island are moorings (as shown) and long pontoons in about 1·5m, with possible AB for Ⓥs. ⚓ prohib in Brightlingsea Hbr, but there are

⚓s to the NW of Mersea Stone Pt and in Pyefleet Chan, E of Pewit Island. R Colne is navigable for 4·5m draft to Wivenhoe, where the river dries; and to The Hythe, Colchester (3m draft).

NAVIGATION WPT Colne Bar By, SHM Fl (2) G 5s, 51°44'·61N 01°02'·57E, 340°/3·6M to Mersea Stone. See also 1.16. Extensive mud and sand banks flank the ent chan. Large coasters use the Brightlingsea chans. The ent to Brightlingsea Creek is narrow at LW and carries about 1m.

A flood barrier 2ca below Wivenhoe church is normally open (30m wide) allowing unrestricted passage; keep to stbd, max speed 5kn. Tfc lts on N pier are 3FR (vert), vis up/downstream. When lit, they indicate the barrier gates are shut; see also LIGHTS AND MARKS.

Speed limits in approaches and up-river: No13–15By(s) = 8kn; No15–18By(s) = no spd limit; No18–34By(s) = 8kn; No 34 – Colchester = 5kn; Brightlingsea Harbour = 4kn.

LIGHTS AND MARKS Well buoyed/lit up to Wivenhoe. Bateman's Tr (conspic) by Westmarsh Pt. Ldg lts/marks 041° for Brightlingsea: both FR 7/10m 4M; dayglo W ☐, R stripes on posts; adjusted to suit the chan. Then Spit SCM lt buoy, and chan lt buoys SHM, PHM, plus NCM bn Q where chan is divided by Cindery Is. Pyefleet Chan and other creeks are unlit.

The flood barrier is marked by 2FR/FG (vert) on both sides and there are bns, QR/QG, up/downstream on the river banks.

R/T *Brightlingsea Harbour Radio* VHF Ch 68.

TELEPHONE HM (Brightlingsea) (01206) 302200, mob 07952 734814; MRCC (01255) 675518; Marinecall 09068 969645; Police (01255) 221312; Dr 302522.

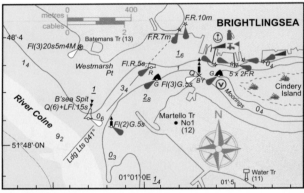

FACILITIES

BRIGHTLINGSEA: Town Hard ☎ (01206) 302200, L, FW, Pontoon moorings £9 up to 26ft, £10 up to 36ft, £11 over 36ft, ⚓ afloat near NCM opposite Town Hard, Slip £8; @ Brightlingsea Wireless 07719 096369 and Colne Community College (HO Term time) **Colne YC** ☎ 302594, L, FW, R, Bar.

Brightlingsea SC Slip, Bar; **Services:** M, L, FW, ME, El, Ⓔ, ✖, CH supply P & D (cans HO), ACA, P & D (cans), Gas, SM, BY, C, Slip. **Town** FW, ME, El, ✖, C (mobile), CH, 🛒, R, Bar, ✉, Ⓑ, ⇌ (bus to Wivenhoe or Colchester), ✈ (Southend or Stansted).

WIVENHOE: Wivenhoe SC. AB (pontoons 10 Ⓥ drying berths), **Village** P, 🛒, Bar, ✉, ⇌.

ROWHEDGE: Quay AB(drying) some Ⓥ.

RIVER COLNE TO HARWICH

(Chart 1975, 1593) 4M SW of the Naze tr at Hollands Haven a conspic radar tr (67m, unlit) is an excellent daymark. From the S, approach Walton and Harwich via the Medusa chan about 1M E of Naze tr. At N end of this chan, 1M off Dovercourt, Pye End buoy marks chan SSW to Walton Backwaters. Harwich and Landguard Pt are close to the N. Making Harwich from the SE beware the drying Cork Sand, which lies N/S.

Sunk Inner SWM buoy, 11M E of The Naze, marks the outer apprs to Harwich, an extensive and well sheltered hbr accessible at all times (chart 2693).

- Harwich, Felixstowe Docks and Ipswich are referred to collectively as the Haven Ports.
- Small craft should give plenty of sea room to shipping manoeuvring to board/disembark Pilots in the Sunk Inner Precautionary Area, see chartlet at 1.6.
- The Harwich DW channel begins 1·5M NNW of Sunk Inner buoy and runs N between Rough and Shipwash shoals, then W past the Cork Sand PHM lt buoy. Constantly used by commercial shipping, approach should be via the recommended track for yachts.

Approaching from NE and 2M off the ent to R. Deben, beware Cutler shoal, with least depth of 1·2m, marked by SHM buoy on E side; Wadgate Ledge and the Platters are about 1·5M ENE of Landguard Point. ▶ *S of Landguard Point the W-going (flood) stream begins at HW Harwich + 0600, and the E-going stream at HW Harwich, sp rates about 1·5kn. Note: HW Harwich is never more than 7 mins after HW Walton; LW times are about 10 mins earlier.* ◀

HARWICH TO ORFORD NESS

(Chart 2052) Shipwash shoal, buoyed and with a drying patch, runs NNE from 9M E of Felixstowe to 4M SSE of Orford Ness. Inshore of this is Shipway Chan, then Bawdsey Bank, buoyed with depths of 2m, on which the sea breaks in E'ly swell.

The Sledway Chan lies between Bawdsey Bank and Whiting Bank (buoyed) which is close SW of Orford Ness, and has depths less than 1m. Hollesley Chan, about 1M wide, runs inshore W and N of this bank. In the SW part of Hollesley B is the ent to Orford Haven and the R Ore/Alde. ▶ *There are overfalls S of Orford Ness on both the ebb and flood streams. 2M E of Orford Ness the SW-going stream begins at HW Harwich +0605, sp rate 2·5kn; the NE-going stream begins at HW Harwich – 0010, sp rate 3kn.* ◀

Note: The direction of local buoyage becomes S to N off Orford Ness (52°05'N).

ORFORD NESS TO GREAT YARMOUTH

(Chart 1543) N of Orford Ness seas break on Aldeburgh Ridge (1.3m), but the coast is clear of offlying dangers past Aldeburgh and Southwold, as far as Benacre Ness, 5M S of Lowestoft. Sizewell power stn is a conspic 3 bldg 1·5M N of Thorpe Ness. Keep 1·5M offshore to avoid fishing floats.

▶ *Lowestoft is best approached from both S and E by the buoyed/lit Stanford chan, passing E of Newcome Sand and SW of Holm Sand; beware possible strong set across hbr ent.* ◀ From the N, approach through Cockle Gatway, Caister Road, Yarmouth Road, passing Great Yarmouth (beware of prohibited area N of harbour entrance); then proceed S through Gorleston, Corton and Lowestoft North Roads (buoyed). ▶ *1M E of hbr ent, the S-going stream begins at HW Dover –0600, and the N-going at HW Dover, sp rates 2·6kn.* ◀

Scroby Sands Wind Farm consists of 30 turbines centred on 52°39'·00N 01°47'·00E. Each turbine is 61m high, with 80m diameter blades and clearance height of 18m and six of the perimeter ones are lit. Vessels to keep well clear and not enter the area.

In the approaches to Great Yarmouth from seaward the banks are continually changing; use the buoyed chans which, from N and S, are those described in the preceding paragraph. But from the E the shortest approach is via Corton ECM lt buoy and the Holm Channel leading into Gorleston Road. ▶ *The sea often breaks on North Scroby, Middle Scroby and Caister Shoal (all of which dry), and there are heavy tide rips over parts of Corton and South Scroby Sands, Middle and South Cross Sands, and Winterton Overfalls.* ◀

▶ *1M NE of ent to Gt Yarmouth the S-going stream begins at HW Dover –0600, and the N-going at HW Dover – 0015, sp rates 2·3kn. Breydon Water (tidal) affects streams in the Haven; after heavy rain the out-going stream at Brush Quay may exceed 5kn.* ◀ About 12M NE of Great Yarmouth lie Newarp Banks, on which the sea breaks in bad weather.

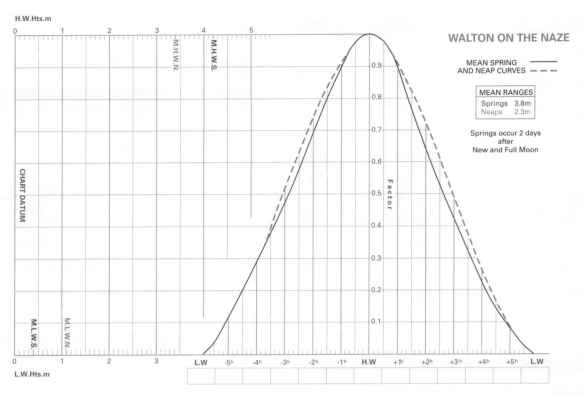

WALTON ON THE NAZE

MEAN SPRING
AND NEAP CURVES

MEAN RANGES	
Springs	3.8m
Neaps	2.3m

Springs occur 2 days
after
New and Full Moon

1.18   WALTON BACKWATERS

Essex **51°54'·57N 01°16'·79E** (No 2 PHM buoy) ✿ ✿ ✿ ◊◊◊◊ ✿ ✿

CHARTS   AC 5607, 2052, 2695; Imray C1, Y16, 2000 Series; Stanfords 5, 6.

TIDES +0030 Dover; ML 2·2; Duration 0615. Walton is a Standard Port. Predictions   are for Walton Pier, ie to seaward. Time differences for Bramble Creek (N of Hamford Water) are +10, –7, –5, +10 mins; height differences are all +0·3m.

SHELTER Good in all weather, but ent not advised if a big sea is running from the NE. Good ‡s in Hamford Water (clear of Oakley Creek) and in N end of Walton Chan, 2ca S of Stone Pt on E side.

NAVIGATION From S, appr via Medusa Chan; from N and E via the Harwich recomended yacht track. WPT Pye End SWM buoy, L Fl 10s, 51°55'·05N 01°17'·89E, 234°/1·1M to Crab Knoll SHM at chan ent. NB this stretch carries only 0·9m. Beware lobster pots off the Naze and Pye Sands and oyster beds in the Backwaters. Buoys may be moved to suit channel changes.
At narrow ent to Walton Chan leave NCM buoy to stbd, and 3 PHM buoys close to port; after a SHM Fl G 10s buoy abeam Stone Pt best water is on E side.

LIGHTS AND MARKS Naze Tr (49m) is conspic 3M S of Pye End buoy. 2M NNE at Felixstowe, cranes and Y flood lts are conspic D/N.

R/T Titchmarsh Marina Ch 80, 0800-2000 in season.

TELEPHONE (Code 01255) HM 851899; MRCC 675518; Marinecall 09068 969645; Police 851212; Ⓗ 421145.

FACILITIES
Titchmarsh Marina 420 inc ♥, £1.60. ☎ 672185. Access HW±5 over sill 1·3m. Pontoons lettered A-H from ent, dredged 1·3m; or on adjacent pontoons in the Twizzle. D, Gas, Gaz, LPG, ME, CH, El, C (10 ton), BH (35 ton), Slip, R, Bar, Wi-fi. **Walton & Frinton YC,** ☎ 675526/678161, R, Bar. **Yacht Basin** (60) run by YC; appr dries. AB (long stay), ⬡, Slip, M, D, C (½ ton), El.
Town P, SM, 🛒, R, Bar, ✉, ⇌, ✈ (Southend/Cambridge/Stansted).

TIME ZONE (UT)
For Summer Time add ONE hour in **non-shaded areas**

WALTON-ON-THE-NAZE LAT 51°51′N LONG 1°17′E
TIMES AND HEIGHTS OF HIGH AND LOW WATERS

Dates in red are SPRINGS
Dates in blue are NEAPS

YEAR **2010**

E England

JANUARY

Time	m	Time	m
1 0540	0.4	**16** 0008	4.0
1146	4.3	0625	0.5
F 1755	0.7	SA 1226	4.0
		1827	0.9
2 0018	4.2	**17** 0041	4.0
0631	0.3	0657	0.5
SA 1236	4.4	SU 1301	4.0
1842	0.7	1857	0.9
3 0106	4.3	**18** 0113	4.1
0720	0.2	0725	0.5
SU 1326	4.5	M 1336	4.0
1928	0.7	1925	0.9
4 0153	4.3	**19** 0146	4.1
0809	0.1	0753	0.5
M 1415	4.4	TU 1410	4.0
2014	0.8	1953	0.9
5 0239	4.3	**20** 0218	4.0
0857	0.1	0822	0.5
TU 1504	4.3	W 1443	3.9
2100	0.9	2024	0.9
6 0324	4.2	**21** 0250	4.0
0945	0.2	0852	0.6
W 1553	4.1	TH 1516	3.8
2148	0.9	2058	1.0
7 0412	4.1	**22** 0322	3.9
1035	0.4	0925	0.6
TH 1644	3.9	F 1552	3.7
◑ 2240	1.0	2138	1.1
8 0504	3.9	**23** 0400	3.8
1128	0.5	1004	0.8
F 1739	3.7	SA 1636	3.6
2339	1.1	◐ 2227	1.2
9 0607	3.8	**24** 0447	3.7
1225	0.8	1056	0.9
SA 1845	3.5	SU 1732	3.5
		2333	1.2
10 0050	1.2	**25** 0549	3.6
0718	3.6	1209	1.0
SU 1336	0.9	M 1841	3.4
2004	3.5		
11 0209	1.1	**26** 0103	1.2
0830	3.6	0711	3.5
M 1452	1.0	TU 1336	1.1
2113	3.6	1959	3.5
12 0320	1.0	**27** 0234	1.0
0933	3.7	0834	3.6
TU 1550	1.1	W 1458	1.0
2207	3.7	2120	3.6
13 0420	0.8	**28** 0338	0.8
1026	3.8	0944	3.9
W 1637	1.0	TH 1602	0.9
2253	3.8	2224	3.9
14 0510	0.7	**29** 0436	0.5
1111	3.9	1043	4.1
TH 1718	1.0	F 1656	0.8
2332	3.9	2317	4.1
15 0551	0.6	**30** 0529	0.3
1149	3.9	1136	4.3
F 1754	0.9	SA 1744	0.7
●		○	
		31 0005	4.3
		0619	0.1
		SU 1225	4.5
		1829	0.7

FEBRUARY

Time	m	Time	m
1 0051	4.4	**16** 0052	4.2
0706	0.0	0657	0.4
M 1312	4.5	TU 1312	4.1
1912	0.6	1903	0.7
2 0135	4.5	**17** 0123	4.2
0751	0.0	0724	0.4
TU 1357	4.5	W 1344	4.1
1953	0.7	1932	0.7
3 0217	4.5	**18** 0153	4.2
0832	0.1	0751	0.4
W 1442	4.4	TH 1414	4.0
2035	0.7	2003	0.8
4 0259	4.4	**19** 0222	4.1
0912	0.2	0820	0.5
TH 1525	4.1	F 1445	3.9
2117	0.8	2035	0.8
5 0341	4.3	**20** 0252	4.0
0952	0.4	0850	0.6
F 1610	3.9	SA 1518	3.8
◑ 2202	0.9	2110	0.9
6 0426	4.0	**21** 0328	4.0
1036	0.7	0926	0.7
SA 1658	3.7	SU 1559	3.7
2254	1.0	2156	1.0
7 0523	3.7	**22** 0413	3.9
1129	1.0	1015	0.9
SU 1756	3.4	M 1651	3.5
		◐ 2258	1.1
8 0000	1.2	**23** 0512	3.7
0638	3.5	1129	1.1
M 1243	1.2	TU 1801	3.4
1921	3.3		
9 0140	1.2	**24** 0029	1.2
0802	3.4	0639	3.5
TU 1423	1.3	W 1315	1.2
2046	3.4	1933	3.4
10 0304	1.1	**25** 0212	1.0
0914	3.5	0818	3.6
W 1529	1.2	TH 1444	1.1
2146	3.6	2105	3.6
11 0410	0.9	**26** 0320	0.7
1010	3.7	0932	3.9
TH 1618	1.1	F 1546	0.9
2233	3.8	2208	3.9
12 0457	0.7	**27** 0420	0.4
1055	3.8	1031	4.1
F 1658	1.0	SA 1638	0.8
2313	3.9	2300	4.1
13 0532	0.6	**28** 0513	0.2
1132	3.9	1121	4.3
SA 1732	0.9	SU 1725	0.7
2348	4.0	○ 2346	4.4
14 0603	0.5		
1206	4.0		
SU 1804	0.8		
●			
15 0020	4.1		
0630	0.4		
M 1240	4.0		
1834	0.8		

MARCH

Time	m	Time	m
1 0601	0.0	**16** 0558	0.5
1207	4.5	1212	4.1
M 1808	0.6	TU 1808	0.7
2 0029	4.5	**17** 0023	4.2
0644	0.0	0625	0.4
TU 1251	4.5	W 1244	4.1
1849	0.6	1838	0.7
3 0111	4.6	**18** 0055	4.2
0724	0.0	0652	0.4
W 1334	4.4	TH 1315	4.1
1930	0.6	1910	0.6
4 0151	4.6	**19** 0125	4.2
0801	0.1	0720	0.4
TH 1414	4.3	F 1346	4.0
2009	0.6	1942	0.7
5 0230	4.5	**20** 0155	4.2
0835	0.3	0749	0.5
F 1454	4.1	SA 1418	4.0
2049	0.7	2015	0.7
6 0309	4.3	**21** 0228	4.1
0910	0.6	0822	0.6
SA 1535	3.9	SU 1452	3.9
2130	0.8	2052	0.8
7 0352	4.0	**22** 0306	4.0
0951	0.8	0901	0.8
SU 1618	3.6	M 1533	3.7
◑ 2217	0.9	2138	0.9
8 0446	3.7	**23** 0353	3.9
1042	1.1	0953	1.0
M 1710	3.4	TU 1626	3.6
2317	1.1	◐ 2241	1.0
9 0602	3.4	**24** 0455	3.7
1155	1.4	1112	1.2
TU 1829	3.2	W 1736	3.4
10 0103	1.2	**25** 0023	1.0
0731	3.3	0630	3.5
W 1346	1.5	TH 1306	1.3
2008	3.3	1918	3.4
11 0236	1.1	**26** 0153	0.8
0847	3.5	0803	3.7
TH 1458	1.3	F 1423	1.1
2113	3.5	2044	3.6
12 0346	0.9	**27** 0300	0.6
0945	3.7	0915	3.9
F 1550	1.2	SA 1523	0.9
2203	3.7	2146	3.9
13 0431	0.7	**28** 0400	0.3
1029	3.8	1013	4.2
SA 1630	1.0	SU 1614	0.8
2244	3.9	2237	4.2
14 0503	0.6	**29** 0453	0.2
1106	3.9	1102	4.3
SU 1704	0.9	M 1701	0.7
2319	4.0	2322	4.4
15 0531	0.5	**30** 0538	0.1
1140	4.0	1146	4.4
M 1737	0.8	TU 1744	0.6
● 2352	4.1	○	
		31 0004	4.5
		0618	0.1
		W 1227	4.4
		1826	0.5

APRIL

Time	m	Time	m
1 0044	4.6	**16** 0025	4.2
0655	0.2	0621	0.5
TH 1307	4.3	F 1248	4.1
1907	0.5	1848	0.6
2 0123	4.5	**17** 0059	4.2
0729	0.3	0651	0.5
F 1346	4.2	SA 1323	4.1
1947	0.5	1923	0.6
3 0202	4.4	**18** 0134	4.2
0802	0.5	0724	0.6
SA 1424	4.1	SU 1358	4.0
2026	0.6	2000	0.6
4 0242	4.2	**19** 0212	4.2
0836	0.7	0802	0.7
SU 1502	3.9	M 1436	3.9
2105	0.7	2042	0.7
5 0325	3.9	**20** 0255	4.2
0915	1.0	0847	0.9
M 1543	3.7	TU 1521	3.7
2148	0.9	2132	0.7
6 0418	3.6	**21** 0347	3.9
1004	1.2	0946	1.1
TU 1633	3.4	W 1616	3.6
◑ 2244	1.0	◐ 2241	0.8
7 0530	3.4	**22** 0457	3.7
1116	1.4	1114	1.2
W 1742	3.3	TH 1730	3.5
8 0018	1.2	**23** 0018	0.8
0651	3.3	0623	3.7
TH 1258	1.5	F 1247	1.2
1916	3.2	1901	3.5
9 0146	1.1	**24** 0131	0.6
0806	3.4	0742	3.8
F 1415	1.4	SA 1356	1.1
2027	3.4	2017	3.7
10 0258	0.9	**25** 0236	0.5
0906	3.6	0852	3.9
SA 1511	1.2	SU 1456	0.9
2121	3.6	2119	4.0
11 0348	0.8	**26** 0336	0.4
0953	3.8	0951	4.1
SU 1555	1.0	M 1549	0.8
2205	3.8	2211	4.2
12 0424	0.7	**27** 0428	0.3
1032	3.9	1040	4.2
M 1632	0.9	TU 1637	0.7
2243	3.9	2257	4.3
13 0454	0.6	**28** 0513	0.3
1107	4.0	1123	4.2
TU 1707	0.8	W 1722	0.6
2318	4.1	○ 2339	4.4
14 0523	0.5	**29** 0553	0.3
1141	4.0	1204	4.2
W 1741	0.7	TH 1807	0.5
● 2351	4.1		
15 0552	0.5	**30** 0019	4.4
1214	4.1	0629	0.4
TH 1815	0.6	F 1243	4.2
		1850	0.5

Chart Datum: 2·16 metres below Ordnance Datum (Newlyn). HAT is 4·6 metres above Chart Datum; see 0.19

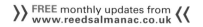

TIME ZONE (UT)
For Summer Time add ONE
hour in **non-shaded areas**

WALTON-ON-THE-NAZE   LAT 51°51'N   LONG 1°17'E

TIMES AND HEIGHTS OF HIGH AND LOW WATERS

Dates in red are **SPRINGS**
Dates in blue are NEAPS

YEAR 2010

MAY

Date	Time	m	Date	Time	m
1 SA	0059 / 0704 / 1321 / 1931	4.4 / 0.6 / 4.1 / 0.5	**16** SU	0040 / 0631 / 1308 / 1912	4.3 / 0.6 / 4.1 / 0.5
2 SU	0140 / 0738 / 1359 / 2009	4.3 / 0.7 / 4.0 / 0.6	**17** M	0122 / 0710 / 1350 / 1955	4.3 / 0.7 / 4.0 / 0.5
3 M	0221 / 0812 / 1437 / 2047	4.1 / 0.9 / 3.9 / 0.7	**18** TU	0207 / 0754 / 1434 / 2043	4.2 / 0.8 / 3.9 / 0.5
4 TU	0305 / 0849 / 1517 / 2127	3.9 / 1.0 / 3.7 / 0.8	**19** W	0256 / 0847 / 1522 / 2140	4.1 / 0.9 / 3.8 / 0.5
5 W	0356 / 0934 / 1605 / 2218	3.6 / 1.2 / 3.6 / 0.9	**20** TH	0354 / 0952 / 1619 / ◑2250	4.0 / 1.1 / 3.8 / 0.6
6 TH	0456 / 1036 / 1704 / ◔2332	3.5 / 1.4 / 3.4 / 1.0	**21** F	0458 / 1106 / 1724	3.9 / 1.1 / 3.7
7 F	0604 / 1202 / 1817	3.4 / 1.5 / 3.3	**22** SA	0000 / 0605 / 1219 / 1836	0.5 / 3.8 / 1.1 / 3.7
8 SA	0048 / 0711 / 1321 / 1930	1.0 / 3.4 / 1.4 / 3.4	**23** SU	0105 / 0715 / 1326 / 1946	0.5 / 3.8 / 1.1 / 3.8
9 SU	0154 / 0814 / 1424 / 2029	1.0 / 3.5 / 1.3 / 3.6	**24** M	0209 / 0825 / 1428 / 2049	0.5 / 3.9 / 1.0 / 3.9
10 M	0250 / 0906 / 1514 / 2119	0.9 / 3.7 / 1.1 / 3.7	**25** TU	0310 / 0927 / 1525 / 2145	0.5 / 3.9 / 0.9 / 4.1
11 TU	0336 / 0951 / 1557 / 2202	0.8 / 3.8 / 0.9 / 3.9	**26** W	0404 / 1019 / 1617 / 2235	0.5 / 4.0 / 0.7 / 4.1
12 W	0415 / 1031 / 1637 / 2242	0.7 / 3.9 / 0.8 / 4.0	**27** TH	0451 / 1105 / 1706 / ○2319	0.6 / 4.0 / 0.6 / 4.2
13 TH	0450 / 1109 / 1715 / 2320	0.7 / 4.0 / 0.7 / 4.1	**28** F	0533 / 1146 / 1754	0.6 / 4.1 / 0.5
14 F	0523 / 1147 / 1753 / ●2359	0.6 / 4.0 / 0.6 / 4.2	**29** SA	0001 / 0613 / 1226 / 1839	4.2 / 0.7 / 4.1 / 0.5
15 SA	0556 / 1227 / 1832	0.6 / 4.1 / 0.6	**30** SU	0043 / 0651 / 1304 / 1922	4.2 / 0.8 / 4.0 / 0.5
			31 M	0124 / 0725 / 1341 / 1959	4.1 / 0.9 / 4.0 / 0.6

JUNE

Date	Time	m	Date	Time	m
1 TU	0206 / 0758 / 1419 / 2034	4.0 / 1.0 / 3.9 / 0.6	**16** W	0206 / 0800 / 1433 / 2046	4.3 / 0.8 / 4.1 / 0.3
2 W	0248 / 0831 / 1458 / 2109	3.9 / 1.0 / 3.8 / 0.7	**17** TH	0256 / 0851 / 1520 / 2139	4.3 / 0.9 / 4.1 / 0.3
3 TH	0333 / 0910 / 1541 / 2151	3.7 / 1.1 / 3.7 / 0.8	**18** F	0348 / 0945 / 1610 / 2235	4.1 / 0.9 / 4.0 / 0.3
4 F	0421 / 0957 / 1629 / ◑2243	3.6 / 1.2 / 3.6 / 0.9	**19** SA	0442 / 1042 / 1705 / ◑2333	4.0 / 1.0 / 4.0 / 0.4
5 SA	0513 / 1057 / 1723 / 2348	3.5 / 1.3 / 3.5 / 0.9	**20** SU	0540 / 1145 / 1807	3.9 / 1.1 / 3.9
6 SU	0609 / 1211 / 1825	3.4 / 1.4 / 3.5	**21** M	0033 / 0643 / 1251 / 1914	0.6 / 3.8 / 1.1 / 3.8
7 M	0052 / 0707 / 1327 / 1928	1.0 / 3.4 / 1.3 / 3.5	**22** TU	0137 / 0755 / 1400 / 2021	0.6 / 3.7 / 1.0 / 3.8
8 TU	0152 / 0806 / 1428 / 2027	1.0 / 3.5 / 1.2 / 3.6	**23** W	0244 / 0904 / 1505 / 2123	0.7 / 3.7 / 0.9 / 3.9
9 W	0247 / 0902 / 1520 / 2119	0.9 / 3.7 / 1.0 / 3.8	**24** TH	0345 / 1002 / 1605 / 2218	0.8 / 3.8 / 0.8 / 4.0
10 TH	0337 / 0953 / 1607 / 2208	0.8 / 3.8 / 0.8 / 3.9	**25** F	0435 / 1051 / 1659 / 2307	0.8 / 3.9 / 0.7 / 4.0
11 F	0421 / 1041 / 1652 / 2255	0.8 / 3.9 / 0.7 / 4.0	**26** SA	0520 / 1134 / 1748 / ○2350	0.9 / 4.0 / 0.6 / 4.1
12 SA	0503 / 1127 / 1737 / ●2341	0.8 / 4.0 / 0.6 / 4.2	**27** SU	0600 / 1214 / 1832	0.8 / 4.0 / 0.5
13 SU	0544 / 1213 / 1822	0.7 / 4.1 / 0.5	**28** M	0031 / 0637 / 1251 / 1910	4.1 / 0.9 / 4.0 / 0.5
14 M	0028 / 0627 / 1300 / 1908	4.3 / 0.7 / 4.1 / 0.4	**29** TU	0110 / 0712 / 1326 / 1944	4.1 / 0.9 / 4.0 / 0.5
15 TU	0117 / 0712 / 1346 / 1956	4.4 / 0.7 / 4.2 / 0.3	**30** W	0149 / 0743 / 1401 / 2015	4.0 / 0.9 / 4.0 / 0.5

JULY

Date	Time	m	Date	Time	m
1 TH	0228 / 0813 / 1437 / 2046	3.9 / 0.9 / 4.0 / 0.6	**16** F	0242 / 0836 / 1503 / 2119	4.4 / 0.7 / 4.4 / 0.2
2 F	0306 / 0845 / 1514 / 2118	3.8 / 1.0 / 3.9 / 0.6	**17** SA	0329 / 0922 / 1548 / 2207	4.2 / 0.8 / 4.3 / 0.3
3 SA	0344 / 0922 / 1552 / 2156	3.7 / 1.1 / 3.8 / 0.7	**18** SU	0417 / 1012 / 1637 / ◑2257	4.0 / 0.9 / 4.1 / 0.5
4 SU	0425 / 1006 / 1635 / ◑2240	3.6 / 1.2 / 3.7 / 0.9	**19** M	0509 / 1107 / 1733 / 2354	3.8 / 1.0 / 3.9 / 0.7
5 M	0511 / 1059 / 1725 / 2336	3.5 / 1.3 / 3.6 / 1.0	**20** TU	0609 / 1213 / 1842	3.6 / 1.1 / 3.8
6 TU	0605 / 1207 / 1826	3.4 / 1.3 / 3.5	**21** W	0101 / 0724 / 1334 / 1956	0.9 / 3.5 / 1.1 / 3.7
7 W	0046 / 0706 / 1334 / 1935	1.0 / 3.5 / 1.3 / 3.5	**22** TH	0221 / 0843 / 1451 / 2106	1.0 / 3.6 / 1.0 / 3.7
8 TH	0158 / 0813 / 1444 / 2041	1.0 / 3.5 / 1.1 / 3.6	**23** F	0327 / 0945 / 1558 / 2206	1.0 / 3.7 / 0.8 / 3.8
9 F	0304 / 0921 / 1540 / 2141	0.9 / 3.7 / 0.9 / 3.8	**24** SA	0420 / 1037 / 1654 / 2255	1.0 / 3.8 / 0.7 / 3.9
10 SA	0401 / 1020 / 1632 / 2237	0.9 / 3.8 / 0.7 / 4.0	**25** SU	0504 / 1120 / 1739 / 2337	1.0 / 3.9 / 0.6 / 4.0
11 SU	0451 / 1112 / 1722 / ●2328	0.8 / 4.0 / 0.5 / 4.2	**26** M	0542 / 1158 / 1817 / ○	0.9 / 4.0 / 0.5
12 M	0538 / 1200 / 1811	0.8 / 4.1 / 0.3	**27** TU	0015 / 0617 / 1233 / 1849	4.0 / 0.9 / 4.1 / 0.5
13 TU	0018 / 0623 / 1248 / 1859	4.4 / 0.7 / 4.3 / 0.2	**28** W	0051 / 0650 / 1306 / 1919	4.1 / 0.8 / 4.1 / 0.5
14 W	0107 / 0707 / 1334 / 1946	4.5 / 0.7 / 4.4 / 0.1	**29** TH	0127 / 0720 / 1339 / 1947	4.0 / 0.8 / 4.1 / 0.5
15 TH	0155 / 0751 / 1419 / 2033	4.5 / 0.7 / 4.4 / 0.1	**30** F	0201 / 0750 / 1411 / 2015	4.0 / 0.8 / 4.1 / 0.5
			31 SA	0235 / 0820 / 1443 / 2043	3.9 / 0.8 / 4.0 / 0.6

AUGUST

Date	Time	m	Date	Time	m
1 SU	0307 / 0853 / 1515 / 2114	3.8 / 0.9 / 3.9 / 0.7	**16** M	0347 / 0941 / 1605 / ◑2215	4.0 / 0.8 / 4.1 / 0.6
2 M	0341 / 0929 / 1550 / 2149	3.7 / 1.0 / 3.8 / 0.8	**17** TU	0435 / 1032 / 1700 / 2308	3.7 / 0.9 / 3.9 / 0.9
3 TU	0421 / 1013 / 1632 / ◑2235	3.6 / 1.1 / 3.7 / 1.0	**18** W	0532 / 1136 / 1812	3.5 / 1.0 / 3.6
4 W	0512 / 1112 / 1729 / 2341	3.5 / 1.2 / 3.6 / 1.1	**19** TH	0022 / 0652 / 1310 / 1933	1.2 / 3.4 / 1.1 / 3.5
5 TH	0616 / 1235 / 1846	3.4 / 1.3 / 3.5	**20** F	0157 / 0820 / 1436 / 2049	1.3 / 3.4 / 1.0 / 3.6
6 F	0113 / 0733 / 1412 / 2010	1.2 / 3.4 / 1.1 / 3.6	**21** SA	0307 / 0924 / 1550 / 2150	1.2 / 3.6 / 0.8 / 3.8
7 SA	0241 / 0856 / 1516 / 2121	1.1 / 3.6 / 0.8 / 3.8	**22** SU	0401 / 1016 / 1643 / 2238	1.1 / 3.8 / 0.7 / 3.9
8 SU	0344 / 1001 / 1613 / 2221	0.9 / 3.8 / 0.6 / 4.0	**23** M	0443 / 1059 / 1721 / 2318	1.0 / 3.9 / 0.5 / 4.0
9 M	0436 / 1055 / 1706 / 2313	0.8 / 4.0 / 0.4 / 4.3	**24** TU	0519 / 1135 / 1753 / ○2353	0.9 / 4.0 / 0.5 / 4.0
10 TU	0523 / 1143 / 1755 / ●	0.7 / 4.2 / 0.2	**25** W	0552 / 1208 / 1821	0.8 / 4.1 / 0.4
11 W	0002 / 0606 / 1229 / 1842	4.4 / 0.6 / 4.4 / 0.1	**26** TH	0026 / 0623 / 1239 / 1847	4.1 / 0.7 / 4.1 / 0.4
12 TH	0049 / 0649 / 1313 / 1926	4.5 / 0.6 / 4.5 / 0.0	**27** F	0059 / 0654 / 1310 / 1914	4.1 / 0.7 / 4.2 / 0.4
13 F	0135 / 0731 / 1356 / 2009	4.5 / 0.6 / 4.5 / 0.1	**28** SA	0131 / 0724 / 1341 / 1940	4.0 / 0.7 / 4.1 / 0.5
14 SA	0219 / 0813 / 1437 / 2049	4.4 / 0.6 / 4.5 / 0.2	**29** SU	0202 / 0755 / 1410 / 2008	4.0 / 0.7 / 4.1 / 0.6
15 SU	0303 / 0856 / 1519 / 2130	4.2 / 0.7 / 4.3 / 0.4	**30** M	0231 / 0826 / 1440 / 2036	3.9 / 0.8 / 4.0 / 0.7
			31 TU	0302 / 0900 / 1513 / 2109	3.8 / 0.8 / 3.9 / 0.8

Chart Datum: 2·16 metres below Ordnance Datum (Newlyn). HAT is 4·6 metres above Chart Datum; see 0.19

TIME ZONE (UT)
For Summer Time add ONE hour in **non-shaded areas**

WALTON-ON-THE-NAZE   LAT 51°51'N   LONG 1°17'E

TIMES AND HEIGHTS OF HIGH AND LOW WATERS

Dates in red are SPRINGS
Dates in blue are NEAPS

YEAR 2010

E England

SEPTEMBER

Time m	Time m
1 0339 3.6 / 0940 1.0 / W 1554 3.8 / ◑ 2152 1.0	**16** 0453 3.4 / 1105 1.0 / TH 1744 3.5 / 2342 1.4
2 0427 3.5 / 1036 1.1 / TH 1649 3.6 / 2257 1.2	**17** 0614 3.3 / 1241 1.1 / F 1908 3.4
3 0532 3.4 / 1156 1.2 / F 1808 3.5	**18** 0123 1.4 / 0746 3.3 / SA 1410 1.0 / 2025 3.5
4 0042 1.3 / 0659 3.3 / SA 1345 1.0 / 1947 3.6	**19** 0238 1.3 / 0853 3.5 / SU 1528 0.8 / 2126 3.7
5 0219 1.2 / 0834 3.5 / SU 1453 0.7 / 2102 3.8	**20** 0333 1.2 / 0946 3.7 / M 1618 0.7 / 2212 3.9
6 0321 1.0 / 0939 3.8 / M 1551 0.5 / 2203 4.1	**21** 0415 1.0 / 1028 3.9 / TU 1652 0.6 / 2250 4.0
7 0413 0.8 / 1032 4.1 / TU 1645 0.3 / 2254 4.3	**22** 0451 0.9 / 1104 4.0 / W 1720 0.5 / 2324 4.0
8 0500 0.7 / 1119 4.3 / W 1734 0.1 / ● 2341 4.4	**23** 0524 0.8 / 1136 4.1 / TH 1747 0.5 / ○ 2356 4.1
9 0543 0.6 / 1203 4.5 / TH 1818 0.0	**24** 0556 0.7 / 1207 4.1 / F 1813 0.5
10 0026 4.5 / 0625 0.5 / F 1246 4.6 / 1900 0.0	**25** 0028 4.1 / 0627 0.7 / SA 1238 4.2 / 1839 0.5
11 0109 4.5 / 0708 0.5 / SA 1328 4.6 / 1939 0.2	**26** 0059 4.1 / 0656 0.6 / SU 1309 4.2 / 1906 0.5
12 0152 4.4 / 0749 0.5 / SU 1408 4.5 / 2016 0.3	**27** 0129 4.0 / 0730 0.7 / M 1339 4.1 / 1933 0.6
13 0233 4.2 / 0831 0.6 / M 1450 4.3 / 2053 0.6	**28** 0200 3.9 / 0803 0.7 / TU 1411 4.0 / 2003 0.7
14 0315 3.9 / 0915 0.7 / TU 1534 4.1 / 2135 0.8	**29** 0232 3.8 / 0837 0.8 / W 1447 4.0 / 2039 0.9
15 0359 3.7 / 1003 0.8 / W 1629 3.8 / ◑ 2227 1.1	**30** 0309 3.7 / 0919 0.9 / TH 1530 3.8 / 2126 1.1

OCTOBER

Time m	Time m
1 0357 3.5 / 1014 0.9 / F 1626 3.7 / ◑ 2233 1.3	**16** 0528 3.3 / 1202 1.0 / SA 1831 3.4
2 0501 3.4 / 1139 1.0 / SA 1749 3.5	**17** 0035 1.5 / 0659 3.3 / SU 1324 1.0 / 1946 3.5
3 0024 1.3 / 0633 3.3 / SU 1320 0.9 / 1925 3.6	**18** 0154 1.4 / 0809 3.4 / M 1440 0.9 / 2048 3.6
4 0152 1.2 / 0807 3.5 / M 1426 0.6 / 2039 3.9	**19** 0254 1.2 / 0904 3.6 / TU 1535 0.8 / 2136 3.8
5 0253 1.0 / 0912 3.8 / TU 1526 0.4 / 2140 4.1	**20** 0340 1.1 / 0949 3.8 / W 1612 0.7 / 2216 3.9
6 0346 0.8 / 1006 4.1 / W 1620 0.2 / 2231 4.3	**21** 0419 0.9 / 1027 3.9 / TH 1642 0.6 / 2251 4.0
7 0434 0.7 / 1053 4.3 / TH 1708 0.1 / ● 2317 4.4	**22** 0454 0.8 / 1102 4.0 / F 1711 0.6 / 2324 4.0
8 0519 0.6 / 1136 4.5 / F 1751 0.1	**23** 0528 0.7 / 1135 4.1 / SA 1739 0.6 / ○ 2356 4.1
9 0001 4.4 / 0603 0.5 / SA 1219 4.5 / 1831 0.2	**24** 0602 0.6 / 1207 4.1 / SU 1807 0.6
10 0043 4.4 / 0646 0.5 / SU 1300 4.5 / 1909 0.3	**25** 0028 4.1 / 0635 0.6 / M 1240 4.2 / 1834 0.6
11 0124 4.3 / 0729 0.5 / M 1341 4.4 / 1946 0.6	**26** 0102 4.1 / 0709 0.6 / TU 1314 4.1 / 1904 0.7
12 0204 4.1 / 0812 0.5 / TU 1423 4.2 / 2022 0.8	**27** 0136 4.0 / 0744 0.6 / W 1351 4.1 / 1939 0.8
13 0244 3.9 / 0854 0.6 / W 1509 4.0 / 2103 1.0	**28** 0212 3.9 / 0823 0.6 / TH 1431 4.0 / 2021 0.9
14 0327 3.7 / 0940 0.8 / TH 1604 3.7 / ◑ 2153 1.2	**29** 0252 3.8 / 0908 0.7 / F 1518 3.9 / 2112 1.1
15 0417 3.5 / 1038 0.9 / F 1714 3.4 / 2303 1.5	**30** 0341 3.6 / 1007 0.8 / SA 1619 3.7 / ◑ 2223 1.3
	31 0446 3.5 / 1135 0.8 / SU 1739 3.6

NOVEMBER

Time m	Time m
1 0001 1.3 / 0611 3.5 / M 1254 0.7 / 1859 3.7	**16** 0055 1.5 / 0710 3.4 / TU 1331 1.0 / 1954 3.5
2 0119 1.2 / 0735 3.6 / TU 1358 0.5 / 2011 3.9	**17** 0203 1.3 / 0811 3.5 / W 1431 0.9 / 2049 3.6
3 0222 1.0 / 0842 3.9 / W 1457 0.4 / 2114 4.0	**18** 0258 1.2 / 0902 3.6 / TH 1521 0.8 / 2135 3.8
4 0318 0.8 / 0938 4.1 / TH 1553 0.3 / 2208 4.2	**19** 0343 1.0 / 0946 3.8 / F 1601 0.8 / 2215 3.9
5 0409 0.7 / 1027 4.2 / F 1642 0.3 / 2255 4.2	**20** 0424 0.8 / 1026 3.9 / SA 1637 0.7 / 2252 4.0
6 0457 0.6 / 1112 4.4 / SA 1726 0.4 / ● 2339 4.3	**21** 0502 0.7 / 1104 4.0 / SU 1709 0.7 / ○ 2329 4.0
7 0544 0.5 / 1155 4.4 / SU 1809 0.4	**22** 0539 0.6 / 1141 4.1 / M 1740 0.7
8 0020 4.3 / 0631 0.4 / M 1238 4.4 / 1848 0.6	**23** 0006 4.1 / 0616 0.6 / TU 1220 4.2 / 1811 0.7
9 0101 4.2 / 0716 0.4 / TU 1321 4.3 / 1926 0.7	**24** 0045 4.1 / 0655 0.5 / W 1300 4.2 / 1847 0.7
10 0141 4.1 / 0759 0.5 / W 1404 4.1 / 2002 0.9	**25** 0125 4.1 / 0735 0.5 / TH 1342 4.2 / 1928 0.8
11 0220 3.9 / 0840 0.6 / TH 1450 3.9 / 2040 1.1	**26** 0206 4.0 / 0818 0.5 / F 1427 4.1 / 2015 0.9
12 0301 3.8 / 0922 0.7 / F 1541 3.7 / 2123 1.2	**27** 0249 3.9 / 0908 0.5 / SA 1519 4.0 / 2110 1.0
13 0347 3.6 / 1011 0.8 / SA 1638 3.5 / ◖ 2221 1.4	**28** 0339 3.8 / 1008 0.5 / SU 1617 3.9 / ◗ 2218 1.2
14 0444 3.4 / 1116 0.9 / SU 1742 3.4 / 2336 1.5	**29** 0437 3.7 / 1117 0.6 / M 1722 3.8 / 2332 1.2
15 0555 3.3 / 1225 1.0 / M 1850 3.4	**30** 0546 3.7 / 1224 0.5 / TU 1830 3.8

DECEMBER

Time m	Time m
1 0043 1.2 / 0701 3.7 / W 1326 0.5 / 1940 3.8	**16** 0056 1.4 / 0703 3.4 / TH 1326 1.0 / 1943 3.4
2 0150 1.1 / 0810 3.8 / TH 1428 0.5 / 2048 3.9	**17** 0207 1.3 / 0807 3.5 / F 1427 1.0 / 2043 3.6
3 0252 0.9 / 0912 4.0 / F 1528 0.6 / 2148 4.0	**18** 0303 1.1 / 0902 3.6 / SA 1521 0.9 / 2136 3.7
4 0349 0.8 / 1006 4.1 / SA 1622 0.6 / 2239 4.0	**19** 0352 0.9 / 0952 3.8 / SU 1607 0.9 / 2223 3.8
5 0443 0.6 / 1055 4.2 / SU 1711 0.6 / ● 2324 4.1	**20** 0437 0.8 / 1038 3.9 / M 1648 0.8 / 2308 4.0
6 0534 0.5 / 1141 4.2 / M 1755 0.7	**21** 0520 0.6 / 1122 4.1 / TU 1726 0.8 / ○ 2351 4.1
7 0006 4.1 / 0622 0.4 / TU 1225 4.2 / 1837 0.8	**22** 0602 0.5 / 1206 4.2 / W 1805 0.9
8 0046 4.1 / 0708 0.4 / W 1307 4.2 / 1915 0.9	**23** 0035 4.2 / 0645 0.4 / TH 1252 4.3 / 1845 0.7
9 0125 4.1 / 0749 0.5 / TH 1350 4.1 / 1949 1.0	**24** 0119 4.2 / 0729 0.3 / F 1338 4.3 / 1929 0.8
10 0203 4.0 / 0826 0.5 / F 1432 3.9 / 2022 1.0	**25** 0203 4.2 / 0814 0.3 / SA 1425 4.3 / 2016 0.8
11 0241 3.9 / 0901 0.6 / SA 1515 3.8 / 2057 1.1	**26** 0247 4.1 / 0902 0.3 / SU 1513 4.2 / 2105 0.9
12 0321 3.8 / 0938 0.7 / SU 1601 3.6 / 2138 1.2	**27** 0332 4.1 / 0953 0.3 / M 1604 4.0 / 2159 1.0
13 0405 3.6 / 1023 0.8 / M 1649 3.5 / ◖ 2230 1.3	**28** 0420 4.0 / 1049 0.4 / TU 1658 3.9 / ◗ 2258 1.1
14 0456 3.5 / 1119 0.9 / TU 1743 3.4 / 2336 1.4	**29** 0517 3.9 / 1149 0.5 / W 1757 3.7
15 0556 3.4 / 1223 1.0 / W 1842 3.4	**30** 0004 1.1 / 0626 3.8 / TH 1252 0.7 / 1906 3.6
	31 0118 1.1 / 0741 3.7 / F 1400 0.8 / 2024 3.6

Chart Datum: 2·16 metres below Ordnance Datum (Newlyn). HAT is 4·6 metres above Chart Datum; see 0.19

1.19 & 20   RIVERS STOUR AND ORWELL

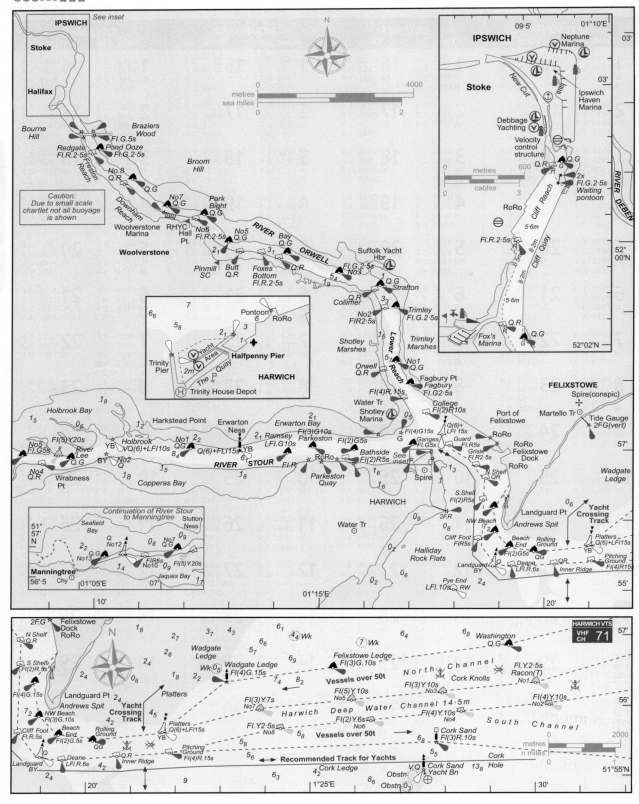

1.19 RIVER STOUR

Essex/Suffolk **51°57'·06N 01°17'·77E** (Guard PHM buoy)

❀❀❀❀⚓⚓⚓❀❀❀

CHARTS AC 5607, 2052, 2693, 1491, 1594; Imray C1, Y16, 2000 Series; Stanfords 5, 6.

TIDES Harwich +0050 Dover; ML 2·1; Duration 0630

Standard Port HARWICH (→)

Times				Height (metres)			
High Water		Low Water		MHWS	MHWN	MLWN	MLWS
0000	0600	0000	0600	4·0	3·4	1·1	0·4
1200	1800	1200	1800				
Differences MISTLEY							
+0032	+0027	–0010	–0012	0·0	0·0	–0·1	–0·1

SHELTER Good at Shotley Marina; access (H24) via chan dredged 2m, outer limits lit, to lock. Enter only on F.G tfc lt. AB also at Halfpenny Pier (H24), Mistley, Manningtree (both dry). No yachts at Parkeston Quay. ⚓s off Wrabness Pt, Holbrook Creek and Stutton Ness.

NAVIGATION WPT Cork Sand Yacht Bn, 51°55'·21N 01°25'·20E.

• Keep clear of commercial shipping/HSS. Outside the hbr, yachts should cross the DW chan at 90° between Rolling Ground and Platters buoys. See 1.4. Stay clear of the DW chan (Y lit SPMs) using Recommended Yacht Track, running S and W of DW chan to beyond Harwich. High Speed Craft operate in this area and may generate large waves causing serious impact on small craft particularly in shallow waters.

• **Caution**: Bkwtr, ESE of Blackman's Hd, covers at HW; marked by PHM lit Bn, only 5ca W of main chan. The Guard Shoal (0·8m), about 2ca S of Guard PHM, lies close to the Recommended Yacht Track. R Stour is well marked; sp limit 8kn. Beware 'The Horse' 4ca NE and drying bank 1½ca NW of Wrabness Pt. From Mistley Quay local knowledge needed for the narrow, tortuous chan to Manningtree.

Special local sound signals
Commercial vessels may use these additional signals:

Four short and rapid blasts followed by one short blast	} =	I am turning short around to stbd.
Four short and rapid blasts followed by two short blasts	} =	I am turning short around to port.
One prolonged blast	=	I am leaving dock, quay or ⚓.

LIGHTS AND MARKS The R Stour to Mistley Quay is lit. At Cattawade, 8M up river, a conspic chy leads 270° through the best water up to Harkstead Pt. Shotley Marina: a Dir lt at lock indicates the dredged chan (2·0m) by Inogen (or Moiré) visual marker lt which is a square, ambered display; a vert B line indicates on the appr centre line 339°. If off the centre line, arrows indicate the direction to steer to regain it.

R/T Harwich VTS Ch **71** 11 14 16 (H24). Yachts should monitor Ch 71 for tfc info, but not transmit. Weather, tidal info and possibly

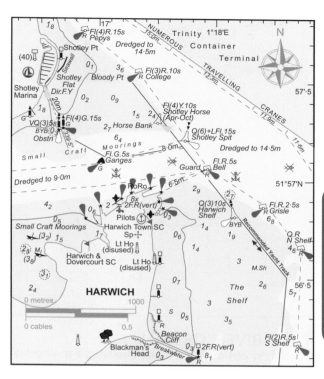

help in poor vis may be available on request. The Hbr Patrol launch listens on Ch 11. Hbr Radar Ch 20. Shotley Marina Ch **80** (lock master).

TELEPHONE (Code 01255) Harwich HM 243030; Hbr Ops 243000; Marinecall 09068 226455; MRCC 675518; Police 0300 3334444; Dr 201299; Ⓗ 201200.

FACILITIES HARWICH Halfpenny Pier Available Apr–Oct, no reservations. Free 0900-1600; overnight: £1·00/m up to 20m, £30 > 20m, max stay 72hrs, FW, showers. **Town** P, D, ME, SM, Gas, El, ⚒, 🍴, R, Bar, ✉, Ⓑ, ⇌, ✈ (Cambridge). **Ferries:** Hook of Holland: 2/day; 6¼ Hrs; Stena (www.stenaline.co.uk); Esbjerg: 3/week; 18 Hrs; DFDS Seaways (dfdsseaways.com).

SHOTLEY (01473) **Shotley Marina** (350, visitors welcome) ☎ 788982 H24, sales@shotleymarina.co.uk, £2.20, access H24 via lock (width 7m); Wi-fi, D(H24), 🅿, ♿, ME, El, Ⓔ, ⚒, BH (40 ton), C, 🍴, BY, CH, SM, Wi-fi, Bar, R, Gas, Gaz, Ferries to Harwich; **Shotley SC** ☎ 787500, Slip, FW, Bar.

WRABNESS: M, FW, 🍴.

MANNINGTREE, AB (drying), FW. **Stour SC** ☎ (01206) 393924, M (drying but free), FW, Bar, showers. **Town** P & D (cans), 🍴, Gas.

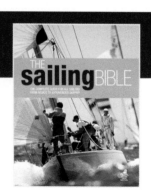

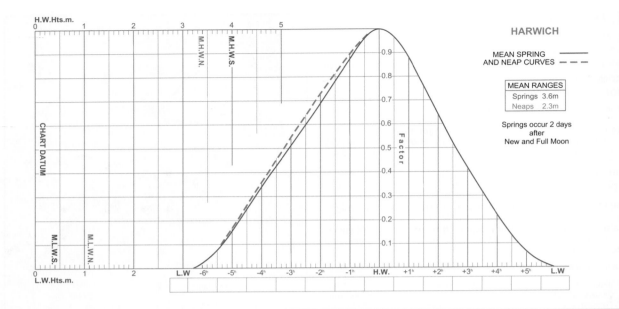

HARWICH

MEAN SPRING AND NEAP CURVES

MEAN RANGES
Springs 3.6m
Neaps 2.3m

Springs occur 2 days after New and Full Moon

1.20   RIVER ORWELL

Suffolk **51°57'·06N 01°17'·77E** (Guard PHM by) ❀❀❀⚓⚓⚓✿✿✿

CHARTS AC 5607, 2052, 2693, 1491; Imray C1,Y16, 2000 Series; Stanfords 5, 6. A *Yachting Guide to Harwich Harbour and its Rivers* has much useful info; it can be obtained free from Harwich Haven Authority, The Quay, Harwich CO12 3HH; ☎ (01255) 243030.

TIDES Pin Mill +0100 Dover; Ipswich +0115 Dover; ML 2·4; Duration 0555

Standard Port HARWICH (→)

Times				Height (metres)			
High Water		Low Water		MHWS	MHWN	MLWN	MLWS
0000	0600	0000	0600	4·0	3·4	1·1	0·4
1200	1800	1200	1800				
Differences IPSWICH							
+0015	+0025	0000	+0010	+0·2	0·0	−0·1	−0·1

SHELTER Good. Ent and river well marked, but many unlit moorings line both banks. ⚓s above Shotley Pt on W side, or off Pinmill. No yacht facilities at Felixstowe. ❿'s (pre-book) at Suffolk Yacht Hbr, Woolverstone Marina, Ipswich Dock (via Prince Philip Lock) and Fox's Marina (Ipswich) all accessible H24 as is Ipswich Haven – call *Ipswich Port Radio* Ch 68 before arrival, then call *Neptune Marina* or *Ipswich Port Marina*.

NAVIGATION Appr/ent from seaward as in 1.19. WPT Shotley Spit SCM buoy, Q (6)+L Fl 15s, 51°57'·21N 01°17'·68E, at river ent.

- Keep clear of the many large ships, ferries from/to Harwich, Felixstowe and Ipswich, especially container ships turning between Trinity container terminal, Shotley Spit and Guard buoys.
- 6kn speed limit in R Orwell. Ipswich Dock ent closed when tide >4.6m above CD. Ipswich New Cut entrance, *Velocity Control Structure is raised from seabed when required with the top of it just below sea level;* 3 FR (vert) = no passage.

LIGHTS AND MARKS Suffolk Yacht Hbr appr marked by four bns and ldg lts: front Iso Y; rear Oc Y 4s.
A14 bridge lts: Centre FY (clearance 38m)
No 9 Pier 2 FR (vert) ⎫ shown up and
No 10 Pier 2 FG (vert) ⎭ down stream.
● and ● tfc lts control ent to Ipswich Dock (H24).
Ipswich New Cut: 3 FR (vert) when closed to navigation.

R/T Call: *Ipswich Port Radio* and *Ipswich Lock Control* VHF Ch 68 (H24). Once above Shotley Pt or anywhere in the area, monitor Ch 68 continuously in fog. Suffolk Yacht Hbr, Woolverstone Marina, Fox's Marina: Ch 80 M. Neptune Marina: Ch M, 80 (0800-1730LT), Ipswich Haven Marina Ch M 80.

TELEPHONE (Code 01473)   Orwell Navigation Service 211066 (also Ipswich HM and Port Radio); MRCC (01255) 675518; Marinecall 09068 226455; Police 613500; ⊞ 712233.

FACILITIES
LEVINGTON Suffolk Yacht Hbr (SYH) Ch 80 (550+❿ £2.19) ☎ 659240, info@syharbour.co.uk, slip (launching £12.50), ⬚,P & D (0815-1750), ME, El, Ⓔ, ✕, C (15 ton), BH (10/60 ton), CH, ⬚, Gas, Gaz, LPG, SM, Wi-fi, ⬚, ⬚, ⬚, Access H24; **Haven Ports YC** ☎ 659658, R, Bar. **Town** ⊠, Ⓑ (Felixstowe), ⇌ (bus to Ipswich), ✈ (Cambridge/Norwich).

PIN MILL King's Boatyard 780258 M (£6.50/night), Slip, L, CH, C (6 ton), ✕, ME, El, FW, Bar, R; **Pin Mill SC** ☎ 780271; Facilities at Ipswich.

WOOLVERSTONE Marina 345+❿, £2.70 (inc electricity). ☎ 780206 (H24), Mob 07803 968209. D (0800-1800), BY, ME, El, Gas, Gaz, ⬚, ⬚, Wi-fi, C (20 ton), SM, CH, Slip, ⬚, R. **Royal Harwich YC** ☎ 780319, AB, R, Bar. **Town** Chelmondiston: ⊠, ⬚.

IPSWICH Fox's Marina 75 + some ❿ £1.98. Ch 80, ☎ 689111. D (0800-1730), BY, Gas, Gaz, BH (44/70 ton), C (7 ton), P, ME, El, Ⓔ, ✕, CH, ACA, SM, Rigger, Wi-fi, ⬚, Bar.

Prince Philip Lock gives H24 access to **Neptune Marina** 150+❿ £2.18, ☎ 215204; and to **Ipswich Haven Marina** 270+❿ ☎ 236644, £2.10. Both are near city centre. Services: D (0800-1700 Neptune; 0800-1900 Haven), ✕, ME, C, BH, BY, El, Ⓔ, Gas, Gaz, ⬚, R, Bar, Wi-fi. **Orwell YC** ☎ 602288, Slip, FW, Bar. **City** ⊠, Ⓑ, P (cans), ⇌, ✈ (Cambridge/Norwich).

HARWICH   LAT 51°57'N   LONG 1°17'E
TIMES AND HEIGHTS OF HIGH AND LOW WATERS

TIME ZONE (UT)
For Summer Time add ONE hour in **non-shaded areas**

Dates in red are SPRINGS
Dates in blue are NEAPS

YEAR 2010

E England

JANUARY

Time	m		Time	m
1 F	0519 0.5 / 1148 4.1 / 1737 0.6		**16** SA	0009 3.8 / 0608 0.6 / 1234 3.7 / 1804 0.9
2 SA	0014 4.0 / 0608 0.3 / 1239 4.2 / 1821 0.6		**17** SU	0044 3.8 / 0640 0.6 / 1308 3.7 / 1836 0.8
3 SU	0101 4.1 / 0656 0.2 / 1328 4.2 / 1905 0.6		**18** M	0113 3.7 / 0708 0.6 / 1337 3.7 / 1907 0.8
4 M	0147 4.1 / 0743 0.1 / 1416 4.1 / 1949 0.7		**19** TU	0141 3.7 / 0737 0.6 / 1406 3.7 / 1940 0.8
5 TU	0233 4.0 / 0831 0.2 / 1505 4.0 / 2035 0.8		**20** W	0212 3.7 / 0810 0.6 / 1440 3.7 / 2014 0.8
6 W	0320 3.9 / 0919 0.3 / 1554 3.9 / 2122 0.9		**21** TH	0246 3.7 / 0844 0.6 / 1518 3.6 / 2051 0.9
7 TH	0408 3.8 / 1012 0.4 / 1646 3.7 / 2214 1.0		**22** F	0324 3.7 / 0922 0.7 / 1601 3.6 / 2132 0.9
8 F	0502 3.7 / 1111 0.6 / 1741 3.5 / 2320 1.1		**23** SA	0407 3.6 / 1004 0.8 / 1651 3.4 / 2221 1.1
9 SA	0603 3.5 / 1219 0.8 / 1843 3.3		**24** SU	0500 3.4 / 1056 0.9 / 1750 3.3 / 2323 1.2
10 SU	0042 1.2 / 0710 3.4 / 1324 0.9 / 1949 3.3		**25** M	0607 3.3 / 1208 1.0 / 1854 3.2
11 M	0156 1.1 / 0819 3.4 / 1424 1.0 / 2054 3.3		**26** TU	0044 1.2 / 0719 3.3 / 1334 1.1 / 2002 3.3
12 TU	0300 1.0 / 0923 3.5 / 1519 1.0 / 2153 3.5		**27** W	0205 1.1 / 0832 3.4 / 1447 1.0 / 2113 3.4
13 W	0357 0.8 / 1020 3.6 / 1608 0.9 / 2244 3.6		**28** TH	0317 0.9 / 0943 3.6 / 1548 0.8 / 2217 3.6
14 TH	0447 0.7 / 1110 3.7 / 1651 0.9 / 2329 3.7		**29** F	0419 0.6 / 1045 3.8 / 1640 0.7 / 2312 3.9
15 F	0531 0.6 / 1154 3.8 / 1730 0.9 ●		**30** SA	0511 0.3 / 1139 4.1 / 1726 0.6 ○
			31 SU	0001 4.0 / 0558 0.1 / 1228 4.2 / 1808 0.5

FEBRUARY

Time	m		Time	m
1 M	0047 4.1 / 0643 0.0 / 1314 4.2 / 1850 0.4		**16** TU	0055 3.7 / 0641 0.5 / 1315 3.7 / 1845 0.7
2 TU	0131 4.2 / 0726 0.0 / 1359 4.2 / 1931 0.5		**17** W	0121 3.7 / 0710 0.5 / 1341 3.7 / 1916 0.7
3 W	0213 4.2 / 0808 0.0 / 1442 4.1 / 2012 0.6		**18** TH	0147 3.8 / 0740 0.5 / 1411 3.7 / 1947 0.7
4 TH	0255 4.1 / 0851 0.2 / 1525 3.9 / 2055 0.7		**19** F	0218 3.8 / 0811 0.5 / 1446 3.7 / 2022 0.7
5 F	0337 3.9 / 0936 0.4 / 1609 3.6 / 2139 0.8 ◗		**20** SA	0252 3.8 / 0845 0.6 / 1526 3.6 / 2101 0.8
6 SA	0424 3.7 / 1027 0.7 / 1656 3.4 / 2233 1.0		**21** SU	0333 3.7 / 0925 0.7 / 1612 3.4 / 2147 0.9
7 SU	0519 3.5 / 1134 0.9 / 1751 3.2		**22** M	0422 3.5 / 1014 0.9 / 1708 3.2 / 2245 1.1 ◗
8 M	0000 1.2 / 0632 3.2 / 1250 1.1 / 1907 3.0		**23** TU	0527 3.3 / 1118 1.1 / 1817 3.1
9 TU	0133 1.1 / 0757 3.2 / 1357 1.2 / 2028 3.1		**24** W	0005 1.1 / 0648 3.2 / 1307 1.2 / 1933 3.1
10 W	0244 1.0 / 0907 3.3 / 1457 1.1 / 2132 3.3		**25** TH	0147 1.0 / 0814 3.3 / 1435 1.1 / 2054 3.3
11 TH	0344 0.8 / 1005 3.5 / 1549 1.0 / 2224 3.5		**26** F	0308 0.8 / 0933 3.5 / 1536 0.9 / 2201 3.6
12 F	0433 0.6 / 1053 3.7 / 1633 0.9 / 2310 3.7		**27** SA	0409 0.4 / 1033 3.8 / 1625 0.7 / 2254 3.9
13 SA	0514 0.5 / 1137 3.8 / 1711 0.8 / 2350 3.8		**28** SU	0458 0.2 / 1124 4.1 / 1709 0.5 / 2342 4.1 ○
14 SU	0548 0.5 / 1215 3.8 / 1744 0.8 ●			
15 M	0025 3.8 / 0615 0.5 / 1249 3.7 / 1814 0.7			

MARCH

Time	m		Time	m
1 M	0542 0.0 / 1210 4.2 / 1750 0.4		**16** TU	0542 0.5 / 1220 3.8 / 1748 0.7
2 TU	0026 4.2 / 0623 -0.1 / 1253 4.2 / 1830 0.4		**17** W	0028 3.7 / 0610 0.5 / 1248 3.7 / 1819 0.6
3 W	0108 4.3 / 0702 -0.1 / 1335 4.2 / 1910 0.4		**18** TH	0055 3.7 / 0640 0.4 / 1314 3.7 / 1851 0.6
4 TH	0148 4.2 / 0741 0.0 / 1415 4.0 / 1949 0.4		**19** F	0122 3.8 / 0711 0.4 / 1343 3.8 / 1924 0.5
5 F	0228 4.2 / 0820 0.2 / 1453 3.9 / 2028 0.5		**20** SA	0153 3.8 / 0742 0.5 / 1418 3.7 / 1959 0.6
6 SA	0308 4.0 / 0900 0.5 / 1532 3.6 / 2109 0.7		**21** SU	0229 3.8 / 0818 0.6 / 1456 3.6 / 2040 0.6
7 SU	0351 3.7 / 0945 0.8 / 1613 3.4 / 2157 0.9 ◗		**22** M	0311 3.7 / 0900 0.7 / 1540 3.4 / 2127 0.8
8 M	0443 3.4 / 1046 1.1 / 1701 3.2 / 2320 1.1		**23** TU	0402 3.5 / 0949 0.9 / 1635 3.2 / 2226 0.9 ◗
9 TU	0554 3.1 / 1215 1.3 / 1810 3.0		**24** W	0509 3.3 / 1053 1.2 / 1748 3.1 / 2349 1.0
10 W	0109 1.1 / 0735 3.1 / 1330 1.3 / 1956 3.0		**25** TH	0634 3.2 / 1254 1.3 / 1913 3.1
11 TH	0221 1.0 / 0845 3.2 / 1432 1.2 / 2103 3.2		**26** F	0138 0.9 / 0803 3.3 / 1418 1.1 / 2033 3.3
12 F	0320 0.8 / 0941 3.5 / 1525 1.0 / 2156 3.5		**27** SA	0254 0.6 / 0917 3.6 / 1516 0.9 / 2137 3.6
13 SA	0407 0.6 / 1029 3.7 / 1608 0.9 / 2242 3.6		**28** SU	0351 0.3 / 1014 3.9 / 1604 0.6 / 2230 3.9
14 SU	0445 0.5 / 1111 3.8 / 1645 0.8 / 2322 3.7		**29** M	0438 0.1 / 1102 4.1 / 1648 0.5 / 2317 4.1
15 M	0515 0.5 / 1149 3.8 / 1717 0.7 / 2357 3.7 ●		**30** TU	0520 0.0 / 1147 4.2 / 1729 0.4 ○
			31 W	0001 4.2 / 0558 0.0 / 1229 4.2 / 1809 0.3

APRIL

Time	m		Time	m
1 TH	0043 4.2 / 0637 0.1 / 1309 4.1 / 1849 0.3		**16** F	0027 3.8 / 0613 0.5 / 1247 3.8 / 1830 0.5
2 F	0123 4.2 / 0714 0.2 / 1347 4.0 / 1928 0.4		**17** SA	0100 3.8 / 0646 0.5 / 1321 3.8 / 1906 0.5
3 SA	0203 4.1 / 0751 0.4 / 1423 3.8 / 2006 0.5		**18** SU	0135 3.9 / 0721 0.5 / 1357 3.8 / 1945 0.5
4 SU	0243 3.9 / 0828 0.6 / 1459 3.6 / 2045 0.6		**19** M	0216 3.8 / 0800 0.6 / 1437 3.7 / 2028 0.6
5 M	0327 3.7 / 0909 0.9 / 1539 3.4 / 2132 0.8		**20** TU	0302 3.7 / 0844 0.8 / 1523 3.5 / 2119 0.6
6 TU	0417 3.4 / 1002 1.2 / 1627 3.2 / 2246 1.0 ◗		**21** W	0358 3.5 / 0936 1.0 / 1620 3.3 / 2221 0.8 ◗
7 W	0521 3.1 / 1130 1.4 / 1729 3.0		**22** TH	0506 3.4 / 1042 1.2 / 1735 3.2 / 2350 0.8
8 TH	0035 1.0 / 0658 3.0 / 1254 1.4 / 1904 3.0		**23** F	0627 3.3 / 1233 1.2 / 1856 3.2
9 F	0145 0.9 / 0812 3.2 / 1358 1.3 / 2022 3.2		**24** SA	0120 0.7 / 0745 3.4 / 1351 1.1 / 2007 3.4
10 SA	0241 0.8 / 0908 3.4 / 1451 1.1 / 2118 3.4		**25** SU	0229 0.5 / 0851 3.6 / 1449 0.9 / 2108 3.6
11 SU	0327 0.7 / 0956 3.6 / 1534 0.9 / 2205 3.5		**26** M	0324 0.3 / 0947 3.8 / 1539 0.7 / 2202 3.8
12 M	0403 0.6 / 1038 3.7 / 1611 0.8 / 2246 3.6		**27** TU	0411 0.2 / 1037 4.0 / 1625 0.5 / 2251 4.0
13 TU	0434 0.5 / 1115 3.8 / 1645 0.7 / 2323 3.7		**28** W	0454 0.2 / 1122 4.0 / 1709 0.4 / 2337 4.1 ○
14 W	0506 0.5 / 1147 3.8 / 1720 0.6 / 2356 3.7 ●		**29** TH	0534 0.2 / 1205 4.0 / 1751 0.4
15 TH	0540 0.5 / 1217 3.8 / 1755 0.5		**30** F	0020 4.1 / 0612 0.3 / 1245 4.0 / 1832 0.4

Chart Datum: 2·02 metres below Ordnance Datum (Newlyn). HAT is 4·4 metres above Chart Datum; see 0.19

TIME ZONE (UT)
For Summer Time add ONE hour in **non-shaded areas**

HARWICH   LAT 51°57'N   LONG 1°17'E
TIMES AND HEIGHTS OF HIGH AND LOW WATERS

Dates in red are **SPRINGS**
Dates in blue are NEAPS

YEAR 2010

MAY

Day	Time	m	Time	m	Time	m	Time	m
1 SA	0102	4.1	0650	0.4	1322	3.9	1912	0.4
2 SU	0143	4.0	0726	0.6	1358	3.8	1950	0.5
3 M	0224	3.8	0803	0.8	1434	3.7	2029	0.6
4 TU	0307	3.6	0841	1.0	1514	3.7	2114	0.8
5 W	0355	3.4	0928	1.2	1601	3.4	2215	0.9
6 TH	0449	3.2	1034	1.3	1658	3.2	2334	1.0
7 F	0556	3.1	1156	1.4	1806	3.1		
8 SA	0045	0.9	0714	3.1	1306	1.3	1919	3.1
9 SU	0141	0.9	0818	3.3	1402	1.2	2023	3.3
10 M	0228	0.8	0910	3.4	1449	1.0	2116	3.4
11 TU	0311	0.7	0954	3.6	1531	0.9	2202	3.5
12 W	0352	0.6	1034	3.7	1612	0.7	2244	3.6
13 TH	0433	0.6	1111	3.8	1653	0.6	2324	3.7
14 F	0512	0.5	1148	3.8	1733	0.5		
15 SA	0003	3.8	0551	0.5	1226	3.9	1813	0.5
16 SU	0043	3.9	0629	0.6	1305	3.8	1855	0.4
17 M	0125	3.9	0708	0.6	1345	3.8	1938	0.4
18 TU	0211	3.9	0750	0.7	1429	3.7	2026	0.4
19 W	0301	3.8	0837	0.8	1518	3.6	2119	0.5
20 TH	0358	3.7	0930	1.0	1617	3.5	2221	0.5
21 F	0502	3.6	1034	1.1	1725	3.4	2337	0.6
22 SA	0611	3.5	1159	1.1	1834	3.4		
23 SU	0052	0.5	0718	3.5	1316	1.1	1938	3.5
24 M	0157	0.6	0821	3.6	1418	0.9	2038	3.6
25 TU	0254	0.4	0919	3.7	1513	0.8	2135	3.8
26 W	0344	0.4	1011	3.8	1604	0.6	2228	3.9
27 TH	0429	0.4	1100	3.9	1652	0.5	2317	3.9
28 F	0512	0.5	1144	3.9	1737	0.5		
29 SA	0004	3.9	0552	0.6	1226	3.9	1820	0.4
30 SU	0048	3.9	0630	0.7	1304	3.8	1902	0.5
31 M	0129	3.8	0707	0.8	1339	3.8	1941	0.5

JUNE

Day	Time	m	Time	m	Time	m	Time	m
1 TU	0209	3.7	0742	0.9	1415	3.7	2017	0.6
2 W	0249	3.6	0819	1.0	1453	3.6	2056	0.7
3 TH	0331	3.5	0901	1.1	1536	3.5	2142	0.7
4 F	0416	3.4	0951	1.2	1626	3.4	2236	0.8
5 SA	0506	3.3	1051	1.2	1722	3.3	2336	0.9
6 SU	0601	3.2	1157	1.3	1821	3.2		
7 M	0035	0.9	0700	3.3	1301	1.2	1921	3.3
8 TU	0132	0.8	0801	3.3	1358	1.1	2020	3.3
9 W	0225	0.8	0859	3.5	1451	1.0	2117	3.5
10 TH	0316	0.7	0915	3.6	1541	0.8	2209	3.6
11 F	0404	0.7	1039	3.7	1629	0.7	2258	3.8
12 SA	0450	0.6	1125	3.8	1716	0.5	2345	3.9
13 SU	0534	0.6	1210	3.9	1802	0.4		
14 M	0031	4.0	0617	0.6	1255	3.8	1847	0.3
15 TU	0119	4.0	0700	0.6	1339	3.9	1934	0.2
16 W	0207	4.0	0744	0.7	1426	3.9	2022	0.2
17 TH	0258	4.0	0830	0.8	1515	3.8	2113	0.3
18 F	0351	3.9	0920	0.8	1607	3.7	2209	0.3
19 SA	0446	3.7	1015	1.0	1704	3.6	2311	0.5
20 SU	0546	3.6	1122	1.0	1806	3.6		
21 M	0018	0.6	0647	3.5	1238	1.1	1908	3.5
22 TU	0124	0.6	0750	3.5	1348	1.0	2012	3.6
23 W	0223	0.7	0851	3.5	1451	0.9	2114	3.6
24 TH	0318	0.7	0949	3.6	1548	0.7	2212	3.7
25 F	0408	0.7	1042	3.7	1640	0.6	2305	3.8
26 SA	0453	0.8	1129	3.8	1728	0.5	2353	3.8
27 SU	0535	0.8	1212	3.8	1812	0.5		
28 M	0037	3.8	0614	0.8	1252	3.8	1852	0.5
29 TU	0118	3.8	0649	0.8	1326	3.8	1928	0.5
30 W	0155	3.7	0723	0.9	1358	3.7	1959	0.5

JULY

Day	Time	m	Time	m	Time	m	Time	m
1 TH	0228	3.6	0757	0.9	1431	3.7	2031	0.6
2 F	0303	3.6	0834	0.9	1509	3.7	2108	0.6
3 SA	0341	3.5	0915	1.0	1551	3.6	2151	0.7
4 SU	0425	3.5	1002	1.1	1639	3.5	2241	0.8
5 M	0515	3.4	1057	1.2	1733	3.4	2340	0.9
6 TU	0610	3.3	1203	1.2	1833	3.3		
7 W	0044	0.9	0709	3.3	1311	1.2	1934	3.3
8 TH	0147	0.9	0812	3.4	1414	1.1	2038	3.4
9 F	0247	0.9	0915	3.5	1514	0.9	2140	3.6
10 SA	0343	0.8	1014	3.7	1611	0.7	2239	3.8
11 SU	0434	0.7	1107	3.8	1703	0.5	2332	4.0
12 M	0521	0.6	1157	4.0	1752	0.3		
13 TU	0021	4.1	0605	0.6	1244	4.0	1838	0.2
14 W	0110	4.2	0648	0.6	1329	4.1	1924	0.1
15 TH	0157	4.2	0731	0.6	1414	4.1	2009	0.1
16 F	0244	4.1	0815	0.6	1459	4.0	2055	0.1
17 SA	0331	4.0	0900	0.7	1545	3.9	2143	0.3
18 SU	0421	3.8	0949	0.8	1636	3.8	2238	0.5
19 M	0514	3.6	1047	1.0	1733	3.6	2342	0.7
20 TU	0613	3.4	1202	1.1	1839	3.5		
21 W	0051	0.9	0719	3.3	1322	1.1	1950	3.4
22 TH	0157	0.9	0828	3.3	1433	1.0	2059	3.5
23 F	0256	1.0	0931	3.5	1537	0.8	2200	3.6
24 SA	0349	0.9	1026	3.6	1631	0.6	2253	3.8
25 SU	0436	0.8	1114	3.8	1718	0.5	2340	3.9
26 M	0518	0.9	1157	3.8	1759	0.5		
27 TU	0023	3.9	0555	0.9	1236	3.9	1835	0.5
28 W	0102	3.8	0629	0.8	1310	3.8	1905	0.5
29 TH	0134	3.7	0700	0.8	1338	3.8	1931	0.5
30 F	0202	3.7	0731	0.8	1406	3.8	2000	0.5
31 SA	0231	3.7	0805	0.8	1437	3.8	2033	0.6

AUGUST

Day	Time	m	Time	m	Time	m	Time	m
1 SU	0305	3.7	0841	0.9	1513	3.7	2109	0.7
2 M	0346	3.6	0921	1.0	1554	3.6	2150	0.8
3 TU	0433	3.5	1007	1.1	1644	3.5	2239	0.9
4 W	0528	3.3	1107	1.2	1747	3.3	2349	1.1
5 TH	0630	3.3	1225	1.3	1856	3.3		
6 F	0114	1.1	0736	3.3	1344	1.2	2007	3.3
7 SA	0225	1.1	0847	3.4	1455	0.9	2120	3.5
8 SU	0326	0.9	0954	3.6	1557	0.7	2224	3.8
9 M	0419	0.8	1050	3.9	1651	0.4	2318	4.1
10 TU	0505	0.6	1140	4.1	1738	0.2		
11 W	0006	4.2	0548	0.6	1226	4.2	1822	0.0
12 TH	0053	4.3	0630	0.5	1310	4.3	1904	0.0
13 F	0137	4.3	0711	0.5	1352	4.3	1946	0.0
14 SA	0221	4.2	0753	0.5	1433	4.2	2028	0.1
15 SU	0304	4.0	0836	0.6	1516	4.1	2113	0.3
16 M	0349	3.8	0922	0.8	1603	3.9	2203	0.6
17 TU	0437	3.5	1015	1.0	1658	3.6	2306	0.9
18 W	0533	3.3	1132	1.1	1810	3.4		
19 TH	0022	1.1	0646	3.2	1303	1.2	1933	3.3
20 F	0132	1.2	0805	3.2	1418	1.0	2044	3.4
21 SA	0234	1.2	0910	3.4	1522	0.8	2144	3.6
22 SU	0329	1.1	1005	3.6	1616	0.7	2235	3.8
23 M	0416	1.0	1052	3.8	1659	0.5	2320	3.9
24 TU	0457	0.9	1135	3.9	1736	0.5		
25 W	0001	3.9	0532	0.8	1213	3.9	1807	0.5
26 TH	0037	3.9	0604	0.8	1245	3.9	1833	0.5
27 F	0107	3.8	0633	0.8	1311	3.8	1858	0.6
28 SA	0131	3.7	0704	0.8	1336	3.8	1927	0.6
29 SU	0157	3.8	0736	0.8	1403	3.8	1957	0.6
30 M	0229	3.8	0810	0.8	1436	3.8	2030	0.7
31 TU	0307	3.7	0847	0.8	1515	3.7	2107	0.8

Chart Datum: 2·02 metres below Ordnance Datum (Newlyn). HAT is 4·4 metres above Chart Datum; see 0.19

TIME ZONE (UT)
For Summer Time add ONE hour in **non-shaded areas**

HARWICH LAT 51°57′N LONG 1°17′E
TIMES AND HEIGHTS OF HIGH AND LOW WATERS

Dates in red are SPRINGS
Dates in blue are NEAPS

YEAR **2010**

E England

SEPTEMBER

#	Time m	#	Time m
1	0351 3.5 / 0931 1.0 / W 1601 3.6 / ☽ 2153 1.0	**16**	0448 3.3 / 1109 1.1 / TH 1741 3.3 / 2351 1.4
2	0445 3.3 / 1026 1.1 / TH 1704 3.4 / 2252 1.2	**17**	0606 3.1 / 1243 1.2 / F 1913 3.2
3	0552 3.2 / 1143 1.2 / F 1823 3.2	**18**	0106 1.4 / 0737 3.2 / SA 1355 1.0 / 2022 3.4
4	0042 1.3 / 0706 3.2 / SA 1322 1.2 / 1944 3.3	**19**	0209 1.3 / 0841 3.4 / SU 1456 0.9 / 2119 3.6
5	0208 1.2 / 0823 3.3 / SU 1439 0.9 / 2104 3.6	**20**	0303 1.2 / 0935 3.6 / M 1547 0.7 / 2208 3.8
6	0309 1.0 / 0932 3.6 / M 1542 0.6 / 2207 3.9	**21**	0350 1.0 / 1022 3.8 / TU 1629 0.6 / 2252 3.9
7	0400 0.8 / 1028 3.9 / TU 1633 0.3 / 2259 4.1	**22**	0430 0.9 / 1104 3.9 / W 1703 0.6 / 2332 4.0
8	0445 0.6 / 1116 4.1 / W 1718 0.1 / ● 2345 4.3	**23**	0504 0.8 / 1142 3.9 / TH 1731 0.6 / ○
9	0527 0.5 / 1201 4.3 / TH 1800 0.0	**24**	0006 3.9 / 0534 0.8 / F 1214 3.8 / 1757 0.6
10	0029 4.3 / 0608 0.4 / F 1244 4.4 / 1839 0.0	**25**	0035 3.8 / 0605 0.7 / SA 1240 3.8 / 1825 0.6
11	0112 4.3 / 0649 0.4 / SA 1325 4.4 / 1919 0.1	**26**	0058 3.8 / 0637 0.7 / SU 1305 3.9 / 1855 0.6
12	0153 4.2 / 0730 0.5 / SU 1406 4.3 / 1959 0.3	**27**	0125 3.8 / 0710 0.7 / M 1335 3.9 / 1926 0.7
13	0233 4.0 / 0812 0.6 / M 1447 4.1 / 2041 0.5	**28**	0157 3.8 / 0744 0.7 / TU 1409 3.9 / 1959 0.7
14	0314 3.8 / 0856 0.7 / TU 1532 3.9 / 2127 0.8	**29**	0233 3.8 / 0823 0.8 / W 1449 3.8 / 2038 0.9
15	0357 3.5 / 0948 1.0 / W 1626 3.6 / ☽ 2227 1.1	**30**	0315 3.6 / 0908 0.9 / TH 1537 3.6 / 2125 1.1

OCTOBER

#	Time m	#	Time m
1	0406 3.4 / 1003 1.0 / F 1639 3.4 / ☽ 2223 1.3	**16**	0516 3.2 / 1213 1.1 / SA 1839 3.2
2	0516 3.2 / 1118 1.1 / SA 1800 3.3	**17**	0031 1.5 / 0652 3.2 / SU 1321 1.0 / 1948 3.3
3	0006 1.4 / 0639 3.2 / SU 1304 1.0 / 1926 3.4	**18**	0136 1.4 / 0801 3.3 / M 1418 0.9 / 2045 3.5
4	0145 1.3 / 0758 3.4 / M 1419 0.8 / 2043 3.6	**19**	0231 1.2 / 0857 3.5 / TU 1507 0.8 / 2135 3.7
5	0245 1.0 / 0904 3.6 / TU 1519 0.5 / 2143 3.9	**20**	0317 1.1 / 0945 3.7 / W 1548 0.7 / 2218 3.9
6	0336 0.8 / 0959 3.9 / W 1609 0.3 / 2234 4.1	**21**	0356 0.9 / 1028 3.8 / TH 1621 0.7 / 2257 3.9
7	0422 0.6 / 1048 4.1 / TH 1653 0.2 / ● 2320 4.3	**22**	0431 0.8 / 1106 3.8 / F 1651 0.7 / 2331 3.9
8	0505 0.5 / 1134 4.3 / F 1734 0.1	**23**	0505 0.8 / 1139 3.8 / SA 1723 0.6 / ○
9	0003 4.3 / 0546 0.4 / SA 1218 4.3 / 1813 0.2	**24**	0000 3.9 / 0539 0.7 / SU 1210 3.8 / 1756 0.7
10	0045 4.2 / 0628 0.4 / SU 1300 4.3 / 1852 0.3	**25**	0028 3.9 / 0614 0.7 / M 1240 3.9 / 1829 0.7
11	0125 4.1 / 0710 0.5 / M 1341 4.2 / 1932 0.5	**26**	0059 3.9 / 0650 0.7 / TU 1314 3.9 / 1902 0.7
12	0203 4.0 / 0751 0.6 / TU 1424 4.1 / 2012 0.7	**27**	0133 3.9 / 0727 0.7 / W 1353 3.9 / 1938 0.8
13	0242 3.8 / 0835 0.7 / W 1509 3.8 / 2054 1.0	**28**	0211 3.8 / 0808 0.7 / TH 1436 3.8 / 2020 0.9
14	0322 3.6 / 0926 0.9 / TH 1601 3.5 / ☾ 2147 1.3	**29**	0253 3.6 / 0855 0.8 / F 1527 3.7 / 2108 1.1
15	0410 3.4 / 1044 1.1 / F 1709 3.3 / 2309 1.5	**30**	0344 3.5 / 0951 0.9 / SA 1629 3.5 / ☾ 2206 1.3
		31	0451 3.3 / 1105 0.9 / SU 1745 3.4 / 2330 1.4

NOVEMBER

#	Time m	#	Time m
1	0615 3.3 / 1238 0.9 / M 1904 3.5	**16**	0044 1.4 / 0659 3.2 / TU 1325 1.0 / 1956 3.3
2	0111 1.3 / 0730 3.4 / TU 1350 0.7 / 2014 3.7	**17**	0144 1.3 / 0803 3.3 / W 1413 0.9 / 2050 3.5
3	0215 1.1 / 0833 3.7 / W 1450 0.5 / 2114 3.9	**18**	0233 1.2 / 0858 3.5 / TH 1456 0.8 / 2136 3.7
4	0308 0.9 / 0930 3.9 / TH 1541 0.4 / 2206 4.0	**19**	0315 1.0 / 0945 3.6 / F 1536 0.8 / 2217 3.8
5	0357 0.7 / 1021 4.0 / F 1626 0.3 / 2254 4.1	**20**	0356 0.9 / 1027 3.7 / SA 1615 0.7 / 2254 3.9
6	0443 0.6 / 1109 4.2 / SA 1709 0.3 / ● 2339 4.2	**21**	0436 0.8 / 1106 3.8 / SU 1654 0.7 / ○ 2329 3.9
7	0528 0.5 / 1155 4.2 / SU 1750 0.4	**22**	0516 0.7 / 1144 3.9 / M 1733 0.7
8	0021 4.1 / 0611 0.5 / M 1240 4.2 / 1829 0.4	**23**	0005 3.9 / 0556 0.6 / TU 1222 3.9 / 1810 0.7
9	0101 4.0 / 0654 0.5 / TU 1323 4.1 / 1908 0.7	**24**	0042 3.9 / 0636 0.6 / W 1302 4.0 / 1847 0.8
10	0139 3.9 / 0737 0.6 / W 1406 4.0 / 1947 0.9	**25**	0120 3.9 / 0718 0.5 / TH 1344 4.0 / 1926 0.8
11	0217 3.8 / 0820 0.7 / TH 1450 3.8 / 2026 1.1	**26**	0200 3.8 / 0801 0.6 / F 1431 3.9 / 2009 0.9
12	0256 3.7 / 0907 0.8 / F 1538 3.6 / 2111 1.3	**27**	0244 3.7 / 0849 0.6 / SA 1522 3.8 / 2057 1.0
13	0342 3.5 / 1005 0.9 / SA 1632 3.4 / ☾ 2210 1.4	**28**	0335 3.6 / 0943 0.6 / SU 1621 3.6 / ☾ 2152 1.1
14	0437 3.3 / 1119 1.0 / SU 1738 3.2 / 2330 1.5	**29**	0436 3.5 / 1048 0.7 / M 1727 3.5 / 2259 1.2
15	0544 3.2 / 1228 1.0 / M 1853 3.2	**30**	0549 3.4 / 1204 0.7 / TU 1836 3.5

DECEMBER

#	Time m	#	Time m
1	0026 1.2 / 0658 3.5 / W 1316 0.7 / 1942 3.6	**16**	0033 1.3 / 0654 3.3 / TH 1309 1.0 / 1934 3.3
2	0139 1.1 / 0803 3.6 / TH 1418 0.6 / 2044 3.7	**17**	0135 1.2 / 0757 3.3 / F 1405 0.9 / 2035 3.4
3	0240 0.9 / 0903 3.7 / F 1513 0.6 / 2140 3.8	**18**	0231 1.1 / 0856 3.4 / SA 1456 0.9 / 2131 3.6
4	0335 0.8 / 0959 3.9 / SA 1602 0.6 / 2232 3.9	**19**	0322 0.9 / 0950 3.6 / SU 1545 0.8 / 2220 3.7
5	0426 0.6 / 1051 4.0 / SU 1648 0.6 / ● 2319 3.9	**20**	0411 0.8 / 1039 3.7 / M 1632 0.8 / 2305 3.8
6	0514 0.5 / 1140 4.0 / M 1731 0.6	**21**	0457 0.6 / 1125 3.8 / TU 1715 0.7 / ○ 2348 3.9
7	0003 4.0 / 0600 0.5 / TU 1227 4.0 / 1811 0.7	**22**	0542 0.5 / 1209 4.0 / W 1757 0.7
8	0045 3.9 / 0644 0.5 / W 1310 4.0 / 1850 0.8	**23**	0031 3.9 / 0626 0.4 / TH 1254 4.0 / 1836 0.7
9	0123 3.9 / 0726 0.5 / TH 1352 3.9 / 1927 0.9	**24**	0113 3.9 / 0710 0.4 / F 1339 4.0 / 1917 0.7
10	0159 3.8 / 0806 0.6 / F 1433 3.7 / 2003 1.0	**25**	0155 3.9 / 0754 0.3 / SA 1425 4.0 / 2000 0.8
11	0236 3.7 / 0843 0.7 / SA 1513 3.6 / 2041 1.1	**26**	0239 3.9 / 0840 0.3 / SU 1514 3.9 / 2045 0.8
12	0316 3.6 / 0923 0.8 / SU 1555 3.5 / 2125 1.2	**27**	0326 3.8 / 0928 0.4 / M 1606 3.8 / 2134 0.9
13	0402 3.5 / 1011 0.9 / M 1641 3.4 / ☾ 2219 1.3	**28**	0418 3.7 / 1022 0.5 / TU 1702 3.6 / ☾ 2229 1.0
14	0454 3.4 / 1108 0.9 / TU 1734 3.3 / 2324 1.3	**29**	0518 3.6 / 1126 0.6 / W 1803 3.5 / 2340 1.1
15	0553 3.3 / 1209 1.0 / W 1832 3.3	**30**	0626 3.5 / 1239 0.7 / TH 1909 3.4
		31	0104 1.1 / 0734 3.5 / F 1348 0.8 / 2015 3.4

Chart Datum: 2·02 metres below Ordnance Datum (Newlyn). HAT is 4·4 metres above Chart Datum; see 0.19

1.21 RIVER DEBEN

Suffolk **51°59'·38N 01°23'·58E** (Felixstowe Ferry) ✿♨♦♦♦✿✿✿

CHARTS AC 5607, 2052, 2693; Imray C1, C28, Y16, 2000 Series; Stan 3, 5, 6.

TIDES Woodbridge Haven +0025 Dover; Woodbridge +0105 Dover; ML 1·9; Duration 0635

Standard Port WALTON-ON-THE-NAZE (◄—)

Times				Height (metres)			
High Water		Low Water		MHWS	MHWN	MLWN	MLWS
0100	0700	0100	0700	4·2	3·4	1·1	0·4
1300	1900	1300	1900				
Differences FELIXSTOWE PIER (51° 57'N 1° 21'E)							
–0005	–0007	–0018	–0020	–0·5	–0·4	0·0	0·0
BAWDSEY							
–0016	–0020	–0030	–0032	–0·8	–0·6	–0·1	–0·1
WOODBRIDGE HAVEN (Entrance)							
0000	–0005	–0020	–0025	–0·5	–0·5	–0·1	+0·1
WOODBRIDGE (Town)							
+0045	+0025	+0025	–0020	–0·2	–0·3	–0·2	0·0

SHELTER Good in Tide Mill Yacht Hbr (TMYH) Woodbridge. ‡s upriver, clear of moorings: N of Horse Sand; off Ramsholt, The Rocks, Waldringfield, The Tips, Methersgate, Kyson Pt and Woodbridge.

NAVIGATION WPT 51°58'·20N 01°23'·85E Woodbridge Haven SWM buoy (off chartlet to the S), thence NNW'ly leaving W Knoll PHM to port to Mid Knoll SHM and then head north upriver to the entrance.

Chartlet depicts the ent at latest survey, but depths can change significantly and the buoyage is adjusted as required. Visit *www.eastcoastrivers.com* for essential info (including sketch chartlet and aerial photos) and call *Odd Times* Ch 08 or telephone HM/Asst HM (see below).

Cross the shifting shingle bar HW–4 to HW depending on draft. Best to enter after half-flood, and leave on the flood. The ent is only 1ca wide and in strong on-shore winds gets dangerously choppy; channel is well buoyed/marked. Keep to the W shore until PHM opposite the SC, then move E of Horse Sand. No commercial traffic. 8kn max speed N of Green Reach.

LIGHTS AND MARKS See 1.3 and chartlets.

R/T Pilotage for river ent, call *Odd Times* Ch 08 or HM on mobile.

TELEPHONE (Code 01394) HM 270106, mob 07803 476621; Asst HM 07860 191768; MRCC (01255) 675518; Marinecall 09068 969645; Police (01473) 613500.

FACILITIES

FELIXSTOWE FERRY (01394) Quay Slip, M, L, FW, ME, El, ✖, CH, ☲, R, Bar; Felixstowe Ferry SC ☎ 272466; BY ☎ 282173, M (200), Gas, Slip £10.

RAMSHOLT HM ☎ 07930 304061. M, FW, Bar.

WALDRINGFIELD AC 2693. Possibly some ⚓ for <11m by prior arrangement with HM or Secretary Waldringfield Fairway Committee, ☎ 01394 276004 or 07810 233445. Craft >11m should anchor at the Rocks (NW of Prettyman's Pt) or upriver at The Tips. Waldringfield SC ☎ 736633, Bar (Wed and Sat evenings only). Services BY, C, Slip.

WOODBRIDGE (01394) **Tide Mill Yacht Hbr**, 200+Ⓥ (max 24m) £2. info@tidemillyachtharbour.co.uk; ☎ 385745. Ent by No 26 PHM buoy. Depth over sill, dries 1·5m, is 1·6m @ MHWN and 2·5m MHWS, with very accurate tide gauge and 6 waiting buoys. D, L, ME, El, ✖, C (18 ton), ⚓, ☲, ◎, FW, Gas/Gaz, ℞, CH, C, M, ACA, Wi-fi; **Woodbridge Cruising Club,** ☎ 386737. **Deben YC. Town** P, D, CH, ☲, R, Bar, ✉, Ⓑ, ⇌, ✈ (Cambridge, Norwich).

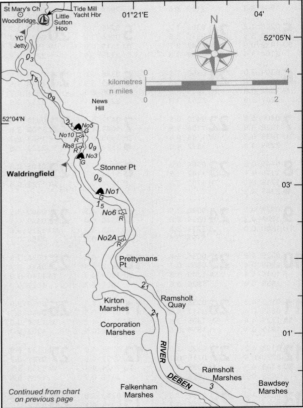

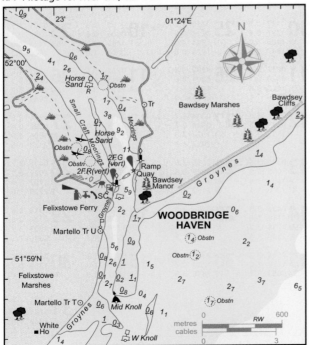

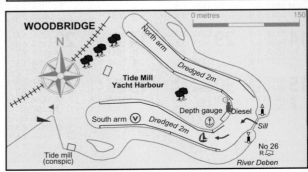

1.22 RIVER ORE/ALDE

Suffolk **52°02'·13N 01°27'·49E** (Ent) ❀♦♦♦✿✿✿

CHARTS AC 5607, 1543, 2052, 2693, 2695; Imray C28, 2000 Series; Stanfords 3, 5, 6.

TIDES Ent. +0015 Dover Slaughden Quay +0155 Dover; ML1·6; Duration 0620

Standard Port WALTON-ON-THE-NAZE (←—)

Times				Height (metres)			
High Water		Low Water		MHWS	MHWN	MLWN	MLWS
0100	0700	0100	0700	4·2	3·4	1·1	0·4
1300	1900	1300	1900				
Differences ORFORD HAVEN BAR							
−0026	−0030	−0036	−0038	−1·0	−0·8	−0·1	0·0
ORFORD QUAY							
+0040	+0040	+0055	+0055	−1·4	−1·1	0·0	+0·2
SLAUGHDEN QUAY							
+0105	+0105	+0125	+0125	−1·3	−0·8	−0·1	+0·2
IKEN CLIFF							
+0130	+0130	+0155	+0155	−1·3	−1·0	0·0	+0·2

SHELTER Good shelter within the river, but the entrance should not be attempted in strong E/ESE onshore winds and rough seas or at night. Good ⚓s as shown and at Iken; also between Martello Tr and Slaughden Quay. Landing on Havergate Island bird sanctuary, is prohib. Visitors' moorings at Orford have small pick-up buoys marked V. Possible use of private mooring via Upson's BY at Slaughden.

NAVIGATION WPT Orford Haven SWM buoy, 52°01'·62N 01°28'·00E, may be moved as required. For latest position call Thames CG ☎ (01255) 675518.

Chartlet is based on surveys carried out in 2009, but depths can change significantly. It is essential to obtain the latest plan of entrance and directions. For regularly updated local information, including chartlet and aerial photos, see *www.eastcoast rivers.com*. For latest info call Small Craft Deliveries: ☎ (01394) 387672, sales@scd-charts.co.uk; or local marinas or chandlers.

- The bar (approx 0·5m) shifts after onshore gales and is dangerous in rough or confused seas. These result from tidal streams offshore running against those within the shingle banks. Sp ebb reaches 6kn.
- Without local info do not enter before half flood or at night. For a first visit, appr at about LW+2½ in settled conditions and at nps.
- Beware Horse Shoal close WNW of N Weir Pt and shoals S & SW of Dove Pt (SW tip of Havergate Island).

R Ore (re-named R Alde between Orford and Slaughden Quay) is navigable up to Snape. The upper reaches are shallow and winding, and marked by withies with red and green topmarks. Shellfish beds on the E bank centred on 52°08'·0N 01°35'·6E.

LIGHTS AND MARKS As chartlet. Ent and river are unlit. Shingle Street, about 2ca S of ent, is identified by Martello tr 'AA', CG Stn, terrace houses and DF aerial. Up-river, Orford Ch and Castle are conspic; also Martello Tr 'CC', 3ca S of Slaughden Quay.

R/T Call *Chantry* on Ch 08.

TELEPHONE (Codes 01394 Orford; 01728 Aldeburgh) Hbr Office 459950; Small Craft Deliveries (pilotage info) 382655; Marinecall 09068 969645; MRCC (01255) 675518; Police (01473) 613500; Orford Dr 450315 (HO); Aldeburgh Dr 452027 (HO).

FACILITIES
ORFORD: Orford Quay AB (1 hour free, any longer by arrangement with Quay Office), M £8/ night (collected by launch 'Chantry'), L, FW, D(cans), C (mobile 5 ton), Orford SC (OSC) visitors may use showers (£6 deposit, key held in Quay Office), R, Bar, Internet (White Lion Hotel Aldeburgh).

Village (¼M) P & D (HO cans), Gas, Gaz, ✉, 🛒, R, Bar, ⇌ (twice daily bus to Woodbridge).

ALDEBURGH: Slaughden Quay L, FW, Slip, BH (20 ton), CH;
Aldeburgh YC (AYC) ☎ 452562, 📶, ✗.

Slaughden SC (SSC). **Services:** M (via Upson's BY if any vacant) £5, ✗, Slip, D, ME, BY, Gas, Gaz, P.
Town (¾M) P, 🛒, R, Bar, ✉, Ⓑ, ⇌ (bus to Wickham Market), ✈ (Norwich).

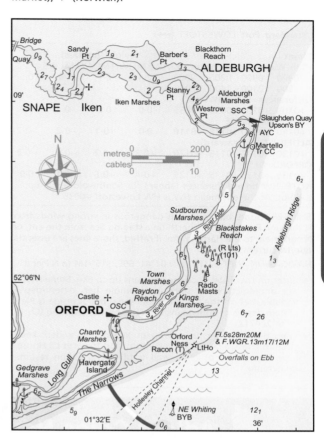

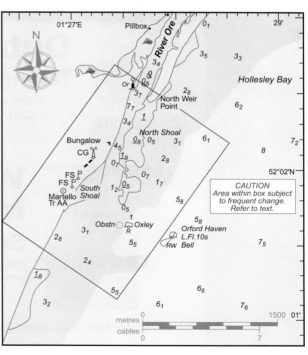

1.23 SOUTHWOLD

Suffolk **52°18'·78N 01°40'·54E** ✿❀✢✢✢✿✿✿

CHARTS AC 5614, 1543, *2695*; Imray C29, C28; Stanfords 3.

TIDES –0105 Dover; ML 1·5; Duration 0620

Standard Port LOWESTOFT (→)

Times				Height (metres)			
High Water		Low Water		MHWS	MHWN	MLWN	MLWS
0300	0900	0200	0800	2·4	2·1	1·0	0·5
1500	2100	1400	2000				
Differences SOUTHWOLD							
+0105	+0105	+0055	+0055	0·0	0·0	–0·1	0·0
MINSMERE SLUICE							
+0110	+0110	+0110	+0110	0·0	–0·1	–0·2	–0·2
ALDEBURGH (seaward)							
+0130	+0130	+0115	+0120	+0·3	+0·2	–0·1	–0·2
ORFORD NESS							
+0135	+0135	+0135	+0125	+0·4	+0·6	–0·1	0·0

NOTE: HW time differences (above) for Southwold apply up the hbr. At the ent mean HW is HW Lowestoft +0035.

SHELTER Good, but the ent is dangerous in strong winds from N through E to S. Visitors berth on a staging 6ca from the ent, on N bank near to the Harbour Inn. If rafted, shore lines are essential due to current.

NAVIGATION WPT 52°18'·09N 01°41'·69E, 315°/1M to N Pier lt.

- Enter on the flood since the ebb runs up to 6kn. Some shoals are unpredictable; a sand and shingle bar, extent/depth variable, lies off the hbr ent and a shoal builds inside N Pier. Obtain details of appr chans from HM before entering (Ch 12 or ☎ 724712).

- Enter between piers in midstream. When chan widens keep close to The Knuckle (2 FG vert), turn stbd towards LB House; keep within 3m of quay wall until it ends, then resume midstream.

- **Caution** Rowing ferry (which has right of way at all times) 3ca and unlit low footbridge 7.5ca upstream of ent.

LIGHTS AND MARKS See 1.3 and chartlet. Walberswick ✠ in line with N Pier lt = 268°. Hbr ent opens on 300°. 3 FR (vert) at N pier = port closed. Lt ho, W ○ tr, in Southwold town, 0·86M NNE of hbr ent.

R/T *Southwold Port Radio* Ch **12** 16 09 (as reqd).

TELEPHONE (Code 01502) HM 724712; MRCC (01493) 851338; Marinecall 09068 969645; Police (01986) 855321; Dr 722326; Ⓗ 723333.

FACILITIES **Hbr** AB 20-30ft £14.50, FW, D (cans) also by bowser 100 litres min, BY, CH, ME, ✕, Slip HW±3 (Hbr dues £5.95), BH (20 ton). **Southwold SC**; **Town** (¾M), Gas, Gaz, Kos, R, ⌕, ✉, Ⓑ, ⇌ (bus to Brampton/Darsham), ✈ (Norwich).

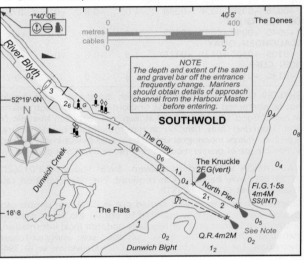

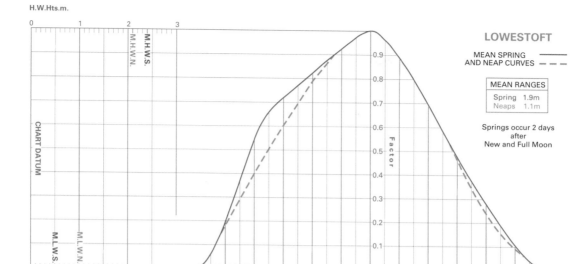

H.W.Hts.m.

LOWESTOFT

MEAN SPRING
AND NEAP CURVES

MEAN RANGES
Spring   1.9m
Neaps   1.1m

Springs occur 2 days
after
New and Full Moon

1.24   LOWESTOFT

Suffolk 52°28'·31N 01°45'·39E ✵✵✵✵⚓⚓⚓✿✿✿

CHARTS AC 5614, 1535, 1543; Imray C28, C29; Stanfords 3.

TIDES –0133 Dover; ML 1·6; Duration 0620

SHELTER Good; accessible H24. Wind over tide, especially on the ebb, can make the entrance lively. Fairway is dredged 4·7m. Yacht Basin in SW corner of Outer Hbr is run by RN&S YC with 2 to 2·5m; no berthing on N side of S Pier. Lowestoft Haven Marina 1·5M upriver with additional 47 berths in Hamilton Dock.

NAVIGATION Call on Ch 14 for permission to enter or leave hbr. Sands continually shift and buoys are moved to suit. Beware shoals and drying areas; do not cross banks in bad weather, nor at mid flood/ebb. Speed limit in harbour is 4 kn.
From S, WPT is E Barnard ECM buoy, Q (3) 10s, 52°25'·15N 01°46'·36E; thence via Stanford Chan E of Newcome Sand QR, Stanford Fl R 2.5s and N Newcome Fl (4) R 15s, all PHM buoys. S Holm SCM, VQ (6)+L Fl 10s, and SW Holm SHM, Fl (2) G 5s, buoys mark the seaward side of this channel.

From E, WPT is Corton ECM buoy, Q (3) 10s Whis, 52°31'·14N 01°51'·37E; then via Holm Chan (buoyed) into Corton Road. Or approach direct to S Holm SCM buoy for Stanford Channel.

From N, appr via Yarmouth, Gorleston and Corton Roads.

Bridge to Inner Hbr (Lake Lothing and Lowestoft CC) lifts at the following times (20 mins notice required): every day at 0300, 0500, 0700, 0945, 1115, 1430, 1600, 1800 (W/Es + BHs only), 1900, 2100 and 2400. Small craft may pass under the bridge (clearance 2.2m) at any time but call on VHF Ch 14. Craft waiting for bridge opening must do so on pontoon at E end of Trawl Dock.

LIGHTS AND MARKS N Newcome PHM lt buoy bears 082°/6ca from hbr ent. Lowestoft lt ho, Fl 15s 37m 23M, is 1M N of hbr ent.

Tfc Sigs: Comply with IPTS (only Nos 2 and 5 are shown) on S pierhead; also get clearance on VHF Ch 14 when entering or leaving, due to restricted vis in appr and ent.

Bridge Sigs (on N bank each side of bridge):
● = bridge operating, keep 150m clear.
● = vessels may pass through bridge channel.

Yacht Basin tfc sigs on E arm (only visible from inside):
3 FR (vert) = no exit; GWG (vert) = proceed on instruction.

R/T *Lowestoft Hbr Control* (ABP) VHF Ch **14** 16 11 (H24). *Lowestoft Haven Marina* Ch **80**, 37. *Oulton Broad YS and Mutford Lock Control* Ch 73, 9, 14. Pilot Ch 14. RN & SYC Ch 14, 80.

TELEPHONE (Code 01502) HM & Bridge Control 572286; Mutford Bridge and Lock 531778 (+Ansafone, checked daily at 0830, 1300 & 1730); Oulton Broad Yacht Stn 574946; MRCC (01493) 851338; Pilot 572286 ext 243; Marinecall 09068 969645; Police (01986) 835100; H 01493 452452.

FACILITIES Royal Norfolk & Suffolk YC ☎ 566726,www.rnsyc.net, £1·95 inc YC facilities, ⚓, Slip, R, Bar, WiFi; **Lowestoft Cruising Club** ☎ 07913 391950, www.lowestoftcruisingclub.co.uk. AB (max 13m) £1.40, ⊕, FW, Slip (emergency only); **Lowestoft Haven Marina** ☎ 580300, www. lowestofthavenmarina.co.uk, 140 AB, £1·95 (+ 47 AB in Hamilton Dock, £2.15). **Services**: @, BH (70 tons), ME, El, ⚒, D, Gas, Gaz, ▢, ⚒, Ⓔ, ACA. **Town** 🛒, R, CH, ACA, Bar, ✉, Ⓑ, 🚆, ✈ (Norwich).

Entry to the Broads: See also 1.25 & www.norfolkbroads.com. Passage to Oulton Broad from Lake Lothing is via two bridges and Mutford Lock (width 5·9m). The lock is available 0800-1200 and 1300-1730 daily; 0800-1200 and 1300-1930 at weekends/ Bank Holidays; 0900-1200 only 1 Nov to 31 Mar. Charge is £10/ day. Booking 24 hours in advance is recommended, ☎ 01502 531778 or Ch 14. Oulton Broad Yacht Station ☎ (01502) 574946. From Oulton Broad, access into the R Waveney is via Oulton Dyke.

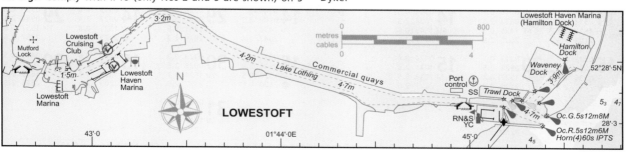

TIME ZONE (UT)
For Summer Time add ONE hour in **non-shaded areas**

LOWESTOFT LAT 52°28'N LONG 1°45'E
TIMES AND HEIGHTS OF HIGH AND LOW WATERS

Dates in red are SPRINGS
Dates in blue are NEAPS

YEAR **2010**

JANUARY

Time	m		Time	m
1 0322	0.7	**16**	0415	0.7
0930	2.5		1027	2.3
F 1538	0.8	SA 1605	1.0
2143	2.6		2213	2.6
2 0416	0.5	**17**	0450	0.7
1022	2.6		1059	2.3
SA 1626	0.8	SU 1633	1.0
2227	2.7		2245	2.6
3 0507	0.4	**18**	0521	0.7
1111	2.6		1128	2.3
SU 1712	0.8	M 1702	1.0
2313	2.8		2319	2.6
4 0556	0.3	**19**	0552	0.7
1200	2.5		1158	2.3
M 1756	0.9	TU 1734	1.0
2358	2.8		2354	2.6
5 0643	0.3	**20**	0623	0.7
1249	2.4		1231	2.2
TU 1838	1.0	W 1809	1.0
6 0045	2.7	**21**	0031	2.5
0730	0.4		0655	0.8
W 1342	2.3	TH 1306	2.2
1921	1.1		1847	1.1
7 0134	2.7	**22**	0109	2.5
0821	0.6		0730	0.9
TH 1447	2.2	F 1346	2.2
◑ 2008	1.2		1929	1.1
8 0229	2.6	**23**	0150	2.4
0919	0.7		0812	0.9
F 1604	2.2	SA 1434	2.1
2107	1.2	◐ 2019	1.2
9 0338	2.4	**24**	0239	2.3
1026	0.9		0906	1.0
SA 1707	2.2	SU 1542	2.1
2236	1.3		2122	1.3
10 0459	2.4	**25**	0344	2.3
1132	1.0		1025	1.1
SU 1805	2.2	M 1710	2.1
2359	1.2		2253	1.2
11 0613	2.3	**26**	0516	2.2
1233	1.1		1145	1.1
M 1901	2.3	TU 1811	2.2
12 0109	1.1	**27**	0013	1.1
0729	2.3		0629	2.3
TU 1329	1.1	W 1246	1.0
1950	2.3		1903	2.3
13 0209	0.9	**28**	0116	0.9
0828	2.3		0733	2.4
W 1419	1.1	TH 1342	1.0
2031	2.4		1952	2.4
14 0257	0.8	**29**	0216	0.7
0913	2.3		0832	2.5
TH 1500	1.1	F 1436	0.9
2108	2.4		2039	2.5
15 0338	0.8	**30**	0313	0.5
0952	2.4		0924	2.5
F 1535	1.1	SA 1527	0.8
● 2141	2.5	○ 2125	2.7
		31	0405	0.3
			1010	2.6
		SU 1614	0.8
			2210	2.8

FEBRUARY

Time	m		Time	m
1 0453	0.2	**16**	0453	0.6
1055	2.6		1058	2.3
M 1657	0.7	TU 1642	0.8
2254	2.8		2255	2.6
2 0537	0.2	**17**	0523	0.6
1139	2.5		1127	2.3
TU 1737	0.8	W 1713	0.8
2339	2.9		2329	2.6
3 0620	0.2	**18**	0552	0.7
1222	2.4		1158	2.3
W 1817	0.8	TH 1746	0.9
4 0024	2.8	**19**	0003	2.5
0702	0.4		0621	0.7
TH 1308	2.3	F 1233	2.3
1856	0.9		1821	0.9
5 0111	2.7	**20**	0040	2.6
0746	0.6		0654	0.8
F 1357	2.2	SA 1310	2.2
◑ 1941	1.0		1901	1.0
6 0204	2.5	**21**	0120	2.4
0836	0.9		0732	0.9
SA 1459	2.1	SU 1354	2.2
2035	1.1		1949	1.1
7 0316	2.3	**22**	0209	2.3
0943	1.1		0822	1.0
SU 1618	2.1	M 1450	2.1
2203	1.2	◐ 2051	1.1
8 0449	2.2	**23**	0316	2.2
1106	1.2		0934	1.2
M 1725	2.1	TU 1611	2.1
2343	1.1		2226	1.1
9 0614	2.2	**24**	0503	2.2
1217	1.3		1119	1.2
TU 1832	2.2	W 1733	2.2
			2355	1.0
10 0058	1.0	**25**	0623	2.3
0732	2.2		1229	1.1
W 1321	1.2	TH 1834	2.3
1930	2.3		
11 0157	0.9	**26**	0101	0.8
0823	2.3		0729	2.4
TH 1410	1.2	F 1329	1.0
2013	2.3		1927	2.4
12 0241	0.8	**27**	0202	0.6
0902	2.3		0824	2.4
F 1448	1.1	SA 1424	0.9
2048	2.4		2016	2.5
13 0319	0.7	**28**	0258	0.4
0935	2.3		0910	2.5
SA 1519	1.0	SU 1512	0.8
2118	2.5	○ 2103	2.7
14 0352	0.6			
1004	2.3			
SU 1546	0.9			
● 2149	2.5			
15 0424	0.6			
1031	2.3			
M 1613	0.9			
2221	2.6			

MARCH

Time	m		Time	m
1 0347	0.2	**16**	0350	0.6
0951	2.5		0959	2.4
M 1556	0.7	TU 1548	0.8
2149	2.8		2154	2.5
2 0431	0.1	**17**	0420	0.6
1032	2.5		1026	2.4
TU 1637	0.6	W 1620	0.8
2233	2.9		2229	2.6
3 0513	0.2	**18**	0451	0.6
1113	2.5		1057	2.4
W 1716	0.6	TH 1653	0.7
2318	2.8		2304	2.5
4 0553	0.3	**19**	0521	0.6
1154	2.4		1129	2.4
TH 1755	0.7	F 1727	0.8
			2339	2.5
5 0003	2.7	**20**	0552	0.7
0631	0.5		1204	2.3
F 1235	2.3	SA 1802	0.8
1834	0.8		
6 0051	2.6	**21**	0016	2.4
0711	0.7		0625	0.8
SA 1317	2.2	SU 1242	2.3
1918	0.9		1842	0.9
7 0145	2.4	**22**	0100	2.4
0754	1.0		0705	0.9
SU 1405	2.2	M 1327	2.2
◑ 2012	1.0		1932	0.9
8 0304	2.2	**23**	0154	2.3
0849	1.2		0756	1.1
M 1510	2.1	TU 1421	2.2
2138	1.1	◐ 2038	1.0
9 0438	2.1	**24**	0309	2.2
1037	1.4		0906	1.2
TU 1633	2.1	W 1532	2.1
2323	1.0		2215	1.0
10 0602	2.2	**25**	0503	2.2
1159	1.4		1056	1.3
W 1744	2.1	TH 1656	2.1
			2339	0.8
11 0032	0.9	**26**	0618	2.3
0715	2.2		1211	1.2
TH 1302	1.3	F 1803	2.3
1851	2.2		
12 0128	0.8	**27**	0043	0.6
0803	2.3		0718	2.4
F 1348	1.2	SA 1311	1.1
1941	2.3		1859	2.4
13 0211	0.8	**28**	0142	0.5
0839	2.3		0807	2.4
SA 1424	1.1	SU 1404	0.9
2016	2.3		1951	2.5
14 0248	0.7	**29**	0236	0.3
0909	2.3		0849	2.5
SU 1453	1.0	M 1451	0.8
2047	2.4		2039	2.7
15 0320	0.6	**30**	0323	0.3
0934	2.3		0928	2.5
M 1520	0.9	TU 1534	0.7
● 2120	2.5	○ 2127	2.8
		31	0406	0.2
			1008	2.6
		W 1615	0.6
			2213	2.8

APRIL

Time	m		Time	m
1 0446	0.3	**16**	0420	0.6
1047	2.5		1029	2.4
TH 1656	0.6	F 1634	0.7
2259	2.7		2241	2.5
2 0524	0.5	**17**	0454	0.7
1126	2.4		1104	2.4
F 1736	0.6	SA 1712	0.7
2346	2.6		2320	2.4
3 0602	0.7	**18**	0529	0.7
1205	2.4		1141	2.4
SA 1817	0.7	SU 1752	0.7
4 0035	2.4	**19**	0002	2.4
0638	0.9		0606	0.9
SU 1245	2.3	M 1221	2.4
1901	0.8		1836	0.7
5 0132	2.3	**20**	0051	2.3
0717	1.1		0649	1.0
M 1328	2.2	TU 1308	2.3
1953	0.9		1930	0.8
6 0253	2.1	**21**	0151	2.2
0803	1.3		0742	1.2
TU 1421	2.2	W 1402	2.2
◑ 2113	1.0	◐ 2038	0.8
7 0417	2.1	**22**	0317	2.2
0918	1.4		0849	1.3
W 1530	2.1	TH 1507	2.2
2250	1.0		2204	0.8
8 0531	2.1	**23**	0456	2.2
1123	1.4		1026	1.3
TH 1646	2.1	F 1622	2.1
2352	0.9		2318	0.7
9 0640	2.2	**24**	0602	2.3
1224	1.4		1143	1.2
F 1751	2.1	SA 1732	2.3
10 0044	0.8	**25**	0019	0.6
0730	2.2		0658	2.3
SA 1311	1.2	SU 1244	1.1
1846	2.2		1830	2.4
11 0129	0.8	**26**	0117	0.5
0807	2.3		0744	2.4
SU 1347	1.1	M 1338	1.0
1931	2.3		1925	2.5
12 0207	0.7	**27**	0209	0.4
0836	2.3		0825	2.4
M 1417	1.0	TU 1427	0.8
2010	2.4		2017	2.6
13 0241	0.7	**28**	0256	0.4
0901	2.3		0904	2.5
TU 1448	0.9	W 1513	0.7
2048	2.4	○ 2108	2.6
14 0313	0.6	**29**	0339	0.4
0927	2.4		0944	2.5
W 1530	0.8	TH 1557	0.6
● 2125	2.5		2157	2.6
15 0346	0.6	**30**	0419	0.5
0957	2.4		1023	2.5
TH 1557	0.7	F 1639	0.5
2203	2.5		2246	2.5

Chart Datum: 1·50 metres below Ordnance Datum (Newlyn). HAT is 2·9 metres above Chart Datum; see 0.19

TIME ZONE (UT)
For Summer Time add ONE hour in **non-shaded areas**

LOWESTOFT LAT 52°28'N LONG 1°45'E
TIMES AND HEIGHTS OF HIGH AND LOW WATERS

Dates in red are SPRINGS
Dates in blue are NEAPS

YEAR 2010

E England

MAY

	Time	m		Time	m
1 SA	0458 1102 1721 2335	0.7 2.5 0.6 2.4	**16** SU	0433 1043 1703 2308	0.7 2.5 0.6 2.4
2 SU	0534 1141 1803	0.8 2.4 0.6	**17** M	0514 1123 1749 2356	0.8 2.5 0.6 2.4
3 M	0025 0609 1219 1847	2.3 1.0 2.4 0.7	**18** TU	0556 1206 1838	0.9 2.4 0.6
4 TU	0120 0645 1300 1936	2.2 1.1 2.3 0.8	**19** W	0049 0642 1254 1932	2.3 1.0 2.4 0.6
5 W	0228 0725 1346 2038	2.1 1.3 2.3 0.9	**20** TH	0150 0732 1347 2034	2.3 1.1 2.4 0.6
6 TH	0342 0814 1441 2201	2.1 1.4 2.2 0.9	**21** F	0311 0831 1445 2145	2.2 1.2 2.4 0.6
7 F	0447 0929 1545 2306	2.1 1.5 2.2 0.9	**22** SA	0436 0945 1552 2252	2.2 1.3 2.4 0.6
8 SA	0548 1125 1655 2357	2.1 1.4 2.2 0.9	**23** SU	0537 1106 1703 2353	2.3 1.2 2.3 0.6
9 SU	0642 1217 1754	2.2 1.3 2.2	**24** M	0631 1212 1806	2.3 1.1 2.4
10 M	0041 0723 1258 1846	0.8 2.2 1.2 2.2	**25** TU	0049 0719 1311 1904	0.6 2.3 1.0 2.4
11 TU	0121 0755 1336 1933	0.8 2.3 1.1 2.3	**26** W	0142 0802 1406 2002	0.6 2.4 0.9 2.5
12 W	0158 0825 1414 2016	0.7 2.3 0.9 2.3	**27** TH	0231 0843 1457 2057	0.6 2.4 0.7 2.5
13 TH	0236 0856 1454 2058	0.7 2.4 0.8 2.4	**28** F	0315 0923 1544 2149	0.7 2.5 0.6 2.5
14 F	0314 0929 1536 2140	0.7 2.4 0.7 2.4	**29** SA	0357 1003 1628 2239	0.8 2.5 0.6 2.4
15 SA	0353 1005 1618 2223	0.7 2.5 0.6 2.4	**30** SU	0435 1043 1711 2326	0.8 2.5 0.6 2.3
			31 M	0511 1120 1752	0.9 2.5 0.6

JUNE

	Time	m		Time	m
1 TU	0012 0543 1157 1832	2.3 1.0 2.5 0.7	**16** W	0548 1154 1834	0.9 2.6 0.4
2 W	0058 0617 1235 1913	2.2 1.1 2.4 0.7	**17** TH	0042 0632 1240 1924	2.4 1.0 2.6 0.4
3 TH	0146 0653 1317 1959	2.1 1.2 2.4 0.8	**18** F	0136 0718 1329 2017	2.3 1.1 2.6 0.5
4 F	0244 0735 1403 2051	2.1 1.3 2.3 0.9	**19** SA	0242 0808 1422 2117	2.2 1.1 2.5 0.6
5 SA	0351 0824 1455 2157	2.1 1.3 2.3 0.9	**20** SU	0402 0907 1524 2222	2.2 1.2 2.5 0.6
6 SU	0450 0925 1556 2300	2.1 1.4 2.2 0.9	**21** M	0506 1025 1638 2325	2.2 1.2 2.4 0.7
7 M	0542 1055 1705 2351	2.1 1.4 2.2 0.9	**22** TU	0602 1144 1748	2.2 1.2 2.4
8 TU	0628 1203 1805	2.2 1.3 2.2	**23** W	0024 0654 1252 1855	0.8 2.3 1.0 2.4
9 W	0036 0710 1255 1858	0.9 2.3 1.1 2.2	**24** TH	0120 0743 1354 2001	0.9 2.4 0.9 2.4
10 TH	0120 0749 1343 1948	0.8 2.3 1.0 2.3	**25** F	0212 0827 1449 2059	0.9 2.4 0.8 2.4
11 F	0203 0826 1430 2037	0.8 2.4 0.9 2.3	**26** SA	0259 0908 1537 2148	0.9 2.5 0.7 2.4
12 SA	0247 0905 1518 2125	0.7 2.4 0.7 2.4	**27** SU	0341 0947 1620 2232	0.9 2.5 0.6 2.4
13 SU	0332 0944 1607 2213	0.8 2.5 0.6 2.3	**28** M	0418 1024 1659 2312	1.0 2.6 0.6 2.3
14 M	0418 1026 1656 2302	0.8 2.6 0.5 2.3	**29** TU	0451 1100 1736 2350	1.0 2.6 0.6 2.3
15 TU	0503 1109 1745 2351	0.8 2.6 0.4 2.4	**30** W	0521 1134 1811	1.0 2.6 0.6

JULY

	Time	m		Time	m
1 TH	0026 0551 1210 1845	2.2 1.0 2.5 0.7	**16** F	0023 0616 1222 1904	2.5 0.9 2.8 0.3
2 F	0101 0624 1248 1920	2.2 1.1 2.5 0.8	**17** SA	0111 0658 1309 1952	2.4 1.0 2.7 0.5
3 SA	0138 0702 1329 1958	2.1 1.0 2.4 0.8	**18** SU	0204 0743 1359 2044	2.3 1.0 2.6 0.6
4 SU	0222 0746 1413 2042	2.1 1.2 2.4 0.9	**19** M	0313 0836 1501 2147	2.2 1.1 2.5 0.8
5 M	0321 0837 1504 2139	2.1 1.3 2.3 1.0	**20** TU	0428 0951 1623 2258	2.2 1.2 2.4 1.0
6 TU	0439 0941 1610 2252	2.1 1.3 2.2 1.0	**21** W	0530 1124 1743	2.2 1.2 2.3
7 W	0537 1110 1727 2355	2.2 1.3 2.2 1.0	**22** TH	0004 0629 1241 1902	1.1 2.3 1.1 2.3
8 TH	0628 1220 1830	2.2 1.2 2.2	**23** F	0107 0726 1349 2010	1.1 2.3 0.9 2.3
9 F	0048 0715 1316 1927	1.0 2.3 1.0 2.3	**24** SA	0203 0813 1442 2059	1.1 2.4 0.8 2.4
10 SA	0138 0759 1410 2023	0.9 2.4 0.9 2.4	**25** SU	0249 0853 1526 2139	1.1 2.5 0.7 2.4
11 SU	0227 0842 1504 2115	0.9 2.5 0.7 2.5	**26** M	0328 0929 1604 2216	1.0 2.6 0.6 2.4
12 M	0317 0925 1557 2204	0.8 2.6 0.5 2.5	**27** TU	0401 1003 1640 2249	1.0 2.6 0.6 2.4
13 TU	0406 1008 1646 2251	0.8 2.7 0.4 2.5	**28** W	0430 1036 1713 2320	1.0 2.6 0.6 2.3
14 W	0452 1052 1734 2337	0.8 2.8 0.3 2.5	**29** TH	0457 1109 1743 2350	1.0 2.6 0.6 2.3
15 TH	0535 1137 1820	0.8 2.8 0.3	**30** F	0526 1143 1813	1.0 2.6 0.7
			31 SA	0020 0557 1219 1842	2.3 1.0 2.6 0.8

AUGUST

	Time	m		Time	m
1 SU	0054 0633 1256 1915	2.3 1.1 2.5 0.8	**16** M	0128 0720 1339 2008	2.3 1.0 2.6 0.8
2 M	0132 0713 1336 1953	2.2 1.1 2.4 0.9	**17** TU	0223 0813 1445 2107	2.3 1.1 2.5 1.0
3 TU	0216 0801 1422 2040	2.2 1.2 2.3 1.0	**18** W	0339 0928 1619 2231	2.2 1.2 2.3 1.2
4 W	0314 0859 1522 2146	2.2 1.3 2.3 1.1	**19** TH	0453 1112 1744 2349	2.2 1.1 2.3 1.3
5 TH	0441 1023 1653 2316	2.2 1.3 2.2 1.2	**20** F	0559 1230 1906	2.3 1.2 2.3
6 F	0547 1151 1810	2.2 1.2 2.3	**21** SA	0057 0703 1336 2004	1.3 2.4 0.9 2.4
7 SA	0022 0642 1255 1915	1.1 2.3 1.0 2.3	**22** SU	0152 0753 1424 2045	1.2 2.4 0.8 2.4
8 SU	0118 0731 1353 2013	1.1 2.4 0.8 2.4	**23** M	0234 0831 1504 2120	1.2 2.5 0.7 2.4
9 M	0211 0818 1449 2103	1.0 2.5 0.6 2.5	**24** TU	0307 0904 1539 2151	1.1 2.6 0.7 2.4
10 TU	0303 0903 1541 2149	0.9 2.7 0.4 2.6	**25** W	0337 0935 1611 2219	1.0 2.6 0.6 2.4
11 W	0350 0947 1629 2232	0.8 2.8 0.2 2.6	**26** TH	0404 1007 1641 2246	0.9 2.7 0.6 2.4
12 TH	0434 1031 1714 2315	0.8 2.9 0.2 2.6	**27** F	0432 1041 1710 2314	0.9 2.7 0.7 2.4
13 F	0516 1116 1757 2357	0.8 2.9 0.2 2.5	**28** SA	0501 1115 1738 2345	0.9 2.7 0.7 2.4
14 SA	0556 1200 1839	0.8 2.9 0.4	**29** SU	0533 1149 1806	0.9 2.6 0.8
15 SU	0041 0636 1247 1921	2.4 0.9 2.8 0.6	**30** M	0018 0607 1225 1837	2.4 1.0 2.5 0.9
			31 TU	0055 0646 1304 1913	2.3 1.1 2.4 1.0

Chart Datum: 1·50 metres below Ordnance Datum (Newlyn). HAT is 2·9 metres above Chart Datum; see 0.19

WGS84 DATUM

TIME ZONE (UT)
For Summer Time add ONE hour in **non-shaded areas**

LOWESTOFT **LAT 52°28′N   LONG 1°45′E**
TIMES AND HEIGHTS OF HIGH AND LOW WATERS

Dates in red are **SPRINGS**
Dates in blue are **NEAPS**

YEAR **2010**

SEPTEMBER

Day	Time	m	Time	m		Day	Time	m	Time	m
1 W ◑	0137 / 0732 / 1351 / 1959	2.3 / 1.1 / 2.4 / 1.1				16 TH	0247 / 0912 / 1613 / 2156	2.3 / 1.1 / 2.3 / 1.4		
2 TH	0229 / 0830 / 1452 / 2100	2.3 / 1.2 / 2.4 / 1.2				17 F	0407 / 1055 / 1733 / 2328	2.3 / 1.1 / 2.3 / 1.4		
3 F	0339 / 0953 / 1634 / 2237	2.2 / 1.2 / 2.2 / 1.3				18 SA	0518 / 1206 / 1849	2.3 / 1.0 / 2.3		
4 SA	0505 / 1129 / 1759 / 2359	2.3 / 1.1 / 2.3 / 1.2				19 SU	0035 / 0623 / 1305 / 1943	1.4 / 2.3 / 0.9 / 2.4		
5 SU	0608 / 1235 / 1904	2.4 / 0.9 / 2.4				20 M	0127 / 0718 / 1352 / 2022	1.3 / 2.4 / 0.8 / 2.4		
6 M	0059 / 0701 / 1334 / 1959	1.2 / 2.5 / 0.7 / 2.6				21 TU	0206 / 0757 / 1431 / 2054	1.2 / 2.5 / 0.8 / 2.4		
7 TU	0153 / 0750 / 1429 / 2045	1.0 / 2.6 / 0.5 / 2.6				22 W	0238 / 0830 / 1505 / 2121	1.1 / 2.6 / 0.7 / 2.4		
8 W ●	0243 / 0837 / 1519 / 2127	0.9 / 2.8 / 0.3 / 2.6				23 TH ○	0307 / 0903 / 1536 / 2146	1.0 / 2.6 / 0.7 / 2.5		
9 TH	0329 / 0923 / 1606 / 2208	0.8 / 2.9 / 0.2 / 2.6				24 F	0335 / 0937 / 1605 / 2212	0.9 / 2.7 / 0.7 / 2.5		
10 F	0412 / 1008 / 1649 / 2249	0.7 / 3.0 / 0.2 / 2.6				25 SA	0405 / 1012 / 1634 / 2241	0.9 / 2.7 / 0.7 / 2.5		
11 SA	0454 / 1054 / 1730 / 2330	0.7 / 3.0 / 0.3 / 2.6				26 SU	0437 / 1047 / 1703 / 2313	0.9 / 2.6 / 0.7 / 2.5		
12 SU	0535 / 1140 / 1810	0.7 / 2.9 / 0.5				27 M	0511 / 1123 / 1734 / 2347	0.9 / 2.6 / 0.8 / 2.5		
13 M	0012 / 0616 / 1229 / 1850	2.5 / 0.8 / 2.7 / 0.7				28 TU	0547 / 1159 / 1806	0.9 / 2.5 / 0.9		
14 TU	0056 / 0702 / 1323 / 1934	2.4 / 0.9 / 2.6 / 1.0				29 W	0024 / 0626 / 1241 / 1843	2.4 / 1.0 / 2.4 / 1.0		
15 W ◑	0145 / 0755 / 1437 / 2026	2.3 / 1.0 / 2.4 / 1.2				30 TH	0107 / 0713 / 1331 / 1931	2.4 / 1.0 / 2.3 / 1.2		

OCTOBER

Day	Time	m				Day	Time	m		
1 F ◑	0159 / 0813 / 1437 / 2032	2.3 / 1.1 / 2.3 / 1.3				16 SA	0312 / 1023 / 1706 / 2249	2.3 / 1.0 / 2.3 / 1.5		
2 SA	0302 / 0937 / 1628 / 2200	2.3 / 1.1 / 2.3 / 1.4				17 SU	0426 / 1129 / 1814 / 2356	2.3 / 1.0 / 2.3 / 1.5		
3 SU	0421 / 1108 / 1747 / 2333	2.3 / 1.0 / 2.4 / 1.3				18 M	0530 / 1223 / 1910	2.3 / 0.9 / 2.3		
4 M	0532 / 1212 / 1847	2.4 / 0.8 / 2.4				19 TU	0047 / 0625 / 1310 / 1950	1.4 / 2.4 / 0.9 / 2.4		
5 TU	0034 / 0629 / 1309 / 1937	1.2 / 2.5 / 0.6 / 2.5				20 W	0128 / 0711 / 1350 / 2021	1.3 / 2.4 / 0.8 / 2.4		
6 W	0128 / 0720 / 1403 / 2021	1.1 / 2.7 / 0.5 / 2.6				21 TH	0202 / 0751 / 1424 / 2047	1.2 / 2.5 / 0.8 / 2.5		
7 TH ●	0218 / 0810 / 1453 / 2102	1.0 / 2.8 / 0.4 / 2.6				22 F	0233 / 0829 / 1456 / 2112	1.1 / 2.5 / 0.8 / 2.5		
8 F	0305 / 0858 / 1539 / 2142	0.7 / 2.9 / 0.3 / 2.7				23 SA ○	0305 / 0907 / 1527 / 2140	1.0 / 2.6 / 0.8 / 2.5		
9 SA	0350 / 0946 / 1621 / 2223	0.7 / 2.9 / 0.4 / 2.6				24 SU	0339 / 0944 / 1600 / 2211	0.9 / 2.6 / 0.8 / 2.6		
10 SU	0433 / 1035 / 1702 / 2304	0.7 / 2.9 / 0.5 / 2.6				25 M	0416 / 1022 / 1633 / 2245	0.8 / 2.6 / 0.8 / 2.6		
11 M	0517 / 1123 / 1742 / 2345	0.7 / 2.8 / 0.7 / 2.6				26 TU	0453 / 1101 / 1707 / 2321	0.8 / 2.5 / 0.9 / 2.5		
12 TU	0600 / 1214 / 1821	0.7 / 2.6 / 0.9				27 W	0533 / 1141 / 1744	0.9 / 2.5 / 1.0		
13 W	0027 / 0646 / 1312 / 1901	2.5 / 0.8 / 2.4 / 1.1				28 TH	0001 / 0616 / 1227 / 1825	2.5 / 0.9 / 2.4 / 1.1		
14 TH ◑	0113 / 0740 / 1427 / 1948	2.4 / 0.9 / 2.3 / 1.3				29 F	0045 / 0706 / 1321 / 1913	2.5 / 0.9 / 2.3 / 1.2		
15 F	0206 / 0852 / 1553 / 2052	2.4 / 0.9 / 2.3 / 1.5				30 SA ◑	0136 / 0807 / 1429 / 2012	2.4 / 0.9 / 2.3 / 1.3		
						31 SU	0236 / 0924 / 1614 / 2126	2.4 / 0.9 / 2.3 / 1.4		

NOVEMBER

Day	Time	m				Day	Time	m		
1 M	0344 / 1042 / 1726 / 2257	2.4 / 0.8 / 2.4 / 1.4				16 TU	0432 / 1137 / 1822 / 2354	2.3 / 1.0 / 2.3 / 1.5		
2 TU	0456 / 1145 / 1823	2.5 / 0.7 / 2.4				17 W	0533 / 1224 / 1907	2.3 / 1.0 / 2.3		
3 W	0003 / 0557 / 1242 / 1912	1.3 / 2.6 / 0.6 / 2.5				18 TH	0040 / 0626 / 1305 / 1941	1.3 / 2.4 / 0.9 / 2.4		
4 TH	0100 / 0653 / 1335 / 1956	1.1 / 2.7 / 0.6 / 2.5				19 F	0120 / 0714 / 1342 / 2010	1.2 / 2.4 / 0.9 / 2.4		
5 F	0153 / 0746 / 1425 / 2037	1.0 / 2.7 / 0.5 / 2.6				20 SA	0158 / 0758 / 1417 / 2039	1.1 / 2.4 / 0.9 / 2.5		
6 SA ●	0243 / 0838 / 1512 / 2118	0.8 / 2.8 / 0.5 / 2.6				21 SU ○	0236 / 0840 / 1453 / 2111	1.0 / 2.5 / 0.8 / 2.5		
7 SU	0331 / 0930 / 1556 / 2159	0.7 / 2.8 / 0.6 / 2.7				22 M	0316 / 0921 / 1531 / 2146	0.9 / 2.5 / 0.8 / 2.6		
8 M	0418 / 1021 / 1637 / 2241	0.7 / 2.7 / 0.7 / 2.6				23 TU	0358 / 1003 / 1610 / 2222	0.9 / 2.5 / 0.8 / 2.6		
9 TU	0503 / 1112 / 1716 / 2322	0.6 / 2.6 / 0.9 / 2.6				24 W	0442 / 1046 / 1650 / 2301	0.8 / 2.5 / 0.9 / 2.6		
10 W	0548 / 1204 / 1755	0.7 / 2.5 / 1.0				25 TH	0526 / 1132 / 1731 / 2343	0.7 / 2.5 / 1.0 / 2.6		
11 TH	0003 / 0633 / 1259 / 1832	2.6 / 0.8 / 2.4 / 1.2				26 F	0613 / 1220 / 1814	0.7 / 2.4 / 1.1		
12 F	0046 / 0723 / 1403 / 1912	2.5 / 0.8 / 2.3 / 1.3				27 SA	0028 / 0703 / 1314 / 1901	2.6 / 0.7 / 2.4 / 1.2		
13 SA ◑	0132 / 0821 / 1518 / 1959	2.4 / 0.9 / 2.2 / 1.5				28 SU ◑	0118 / 0759 / 1416 / 1953	2.5 / 0.7 / 2.3 / 1.3		
14 SU	0224 / 0935 / 1625 / 2100	2.4 / 1.0 / 2.2 / 1.5				29 M	0212 / 0903 / 1542 / 2054	2.5 / 0.7 / 2.3 / 1.3		
15 M	0325 / 1043 / 1726 / 2253	2.3 / 1.0 / 2.2 / 1.5				30 TU	0312 / 1012 / 1657 / 2211	2.5 / 0.7 / 2.3 / 1.3		

DECEMBER

Day	Time	m				Day	Time	m		
1 W	0422 / 1117 / 1755 / 2329	2.5 / 0.7 / 2.3 / 1.3				16 TH	0442 / 1134 / 1809 / 2344	2.3 / 1.1 / 2.2 / 1.4		
2 TH	0531 / 1215 / 1846	2.5 / 0.7 / 2.3				17 F	0546 / 1221 / 1853	2.3 / 1.0 / 2.3		
3 F	0032 / 0631 / 1310 / 1932	1.1 / 2.6 / 0.7 / 2.5				18 SA	0038 / 0641 / 1304 / 1932	1.3 / 2.3 / 1.0 / 2.4		
4 SA	0132 / 0730 / 1402 / 2015	1.0 / 2.6 / 0.7 / 2.5				19 SU	0125 / 0731 / 1345 / 2009	1.1 / 2.3 / 1.0 / 2.4		
5 SU ●	0228 / 0828 / 1450 / 2058	0.9 / 2.6 / 0.8 / 2.6				20 M	0211 / 0819 / 1427 / 2046	1.0 / 2.4 / 0.9 / 2.5		
6 M	0320 / 0924 / 1535 / 2140	0.7 / 2.6 / 0.8 / 2.6				21 TU ○	0257 / 0906 / 1510 / 2124	0.9 / 2.4 / 0.9 / 2.6		
7 TU	0408 / 1015 / 1617 / 2222	0.6 / 2.6 / 0.9 / 2.6				22 W	0345 / 0952 / 1554 / 2204	0.7 / 2.5 / 0.9 / 2.6		
8 W	0454 / 1104 / 1656 / 2303	0.6 / 2.5 / 1.0 / 2.6				23 TH	0433 / 1038 / 1638 / 2246	0.6 / 2.5 / 0.9 / 2.7		
9 TH	0537 / 1151 / 1732 / 2342	0.6 / 2.4 / 1.1 / 2.6				24 F	0520 / 1124 / 1721 / 2329	0.5 / 2.5 / 0.9 / 2.7		
10 F	0619 / 1237 / 1805	0.7 / 2.3 / 1.1				25 SA	0607 / 1210 / 1804	0.5 / 2.5 / 1.0		
11 SA	0020 / 0700 / 1324 / 1839	2.6 / 0.8 / 2.2 / 1.2				26 SU	0013 / 0654 / 1259 / 1847	2.7 / 0.5 / 2.4 / 1.0		
12 SU	0100 / 0743 / 1416 / 1918	2.5 / 0.9 / 2.2 / 1.3				27 M	0059 / 0743 / 1351 / 1933	2.7 / 0.6 / 2.3 / 1.1		
13 M ◑	0144 / 0832 / 1522 / 2003	2.5 / 0.9 / 2.1 / 1.4				28 TU ◑	0149 / 0836 / 1455 / 2024	2.6 / 0.6 / 2.2 / 1.2		
14 TU	0233 / 0931 / 1626 / 2057	2.4 / 1.0 / 2.1 / 1.4				29 W	0244 / 0939 / 1619 / 2129	2.6 / 0.7 / 2.2 / 1.2		
15 W	0331 / 1038 / 1721 / 2217	2.3 / 1.1 / 2.2 / 1.5				30 TH	0354 / 1047 / 1723 / 2257	2.5 / 0.9 / 2.2 / 1.2		
						31 F	0512 / 1151 / 1819	2.5 / 0.9 / 2.3		

Chart Datum: 1·50 metres below Ordnance Datum (Newlyn). HAT is 2·9 metres above Chart Datum; see 0.19

1.25 GREAT YARMOUTH

Norfolk **52°34'·36N 01°44'·39E** ❀❀⚓❀❀

CHARTS AC 5614, 1543, 1535, 1534; Imray C29, C28; Stanfords 3.

TIDES –0210 Dover; ML 1·5; Duration 0620

Standard Port LOWESTOFT (←)

Times				Height (metres)			
High Water		Low Water		MHWS	MHWN	MLWN	MLWS
0300	0900	0200	0800	2·4	2·1	1·0	0·5
1500	2100	1400	2000				

Differences GORLESTON (To be used for Great Yarmouth)
–0035 –0035 –0030 –0030 0·0 0·0 0·0 0·0
CAISTER-ON-SEA
–0120 –0120 –0100 –0100 0·0 –0·1 0·0 0·0
WINTERTON-ON-SEA
–0225 –0215 –0135 –0135 +0·8 +0·5 +0·2 +0·1

- Rise of tide occurs mainly during 3.5 hours after LW. From HW Lowestoft –3 until HW the level is usually within 0·3m of predicted HW. Flood tide runs until about HW +15 and ebb until about LW +25. See also NAVIGATION.

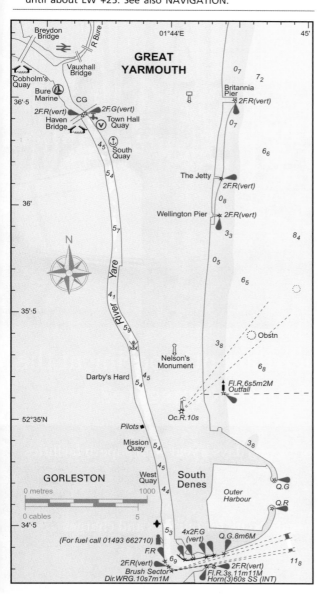

SHELTER Excellent on Town Hall Quay, close S of Haven Bridge; ⚓ prohib in hbr which is a busy commercial port.

NAVIGATION WPT 52°34'·43N 01°45'·56E, 264°/1M to front ldg lt.

- Access is H24, subject to clearance, but small craft must not attempt ent in strong SE winds which cause dangerous seas, especially on the ebb. Except at local slack water, which occurs at HW+1½ and LW+1¾, tidal streams at the ent are strong.
- On the flood, the stream eddies NW past S pier, thence up-river; a QY tidal lt on S pier warns of this D/N. Beware being set onto the N pier.
- Temporary shoaling may occur in the ent during strong E'lies, with depths 1m less than those charted.
- Beware strong tidal streams that sweep through the Haven Bridge. Proceed slowly past Bure Marine.
- Outer harbour is for commercial vessels only.

LIGHTS AND MARKS See 1.3 and chartlet. Note: Tfc Sigs and the tidal QY are co-located with the Main lt on a R brick bldg, W lower half floodlit, at S pier. W sector (252·5°-257·5°) of Brush Sector Light leads to harbour entrance. Ent and bend marked by five x 2 FG and seven x 2FR (all vert).

TRAFFIC SIGNALS Port operations advise on Ch 12, this should always be heeded. **Inbound**: now IALA sigs on S pier: 3 Fl ● = hbr closed; 3F ● = do not proceed; 3 F ● = vessels may proceed, oneway; ● ○ ● = proceed only when told to; **Outbound**: 3 ● (vert) = no vessel to go down river south of LB shed. Haven and Breydon bridges: 3 ● (vert) = passage prohib.

R/T *Yarmouth Radio* Ch **12** (H24). *Breydon Bridge* Ch **12** (OH).

TELEPHONE (Code 01493) HM 335511; MRCC 851338; Marinecall 09068 969645; Police 336200; Breydon Bridge 651275.

FACILITIES Town Hall Quay (50m stretch) AB £15/yacht, then £7 for successive days. **Bure Marine Cobholm** ☎ 656996, H24. (Marina planned 2007). FW, El, ⚓, BH, C, Slip. **Burgh Castle Marina** (top of Breydon Water 5M) (90+10 visitors) ☎ 780331, £16, Slip, D, ⚓, ME, El, ⚒, ▣, Gas, CH, 🛒, R, Bar, Access HW ±4 (1m), diving ACA; **Goodchild Marine Services** (top of Breydon Water 5M) (27+6Ⓥ £12.50) ☎ 782301, D, FW, ME, El, C (32 tons, including mast stepping), ⚓, Access 6ft at LW; **Services**: AB, L, M, ⚒, SM, ACA. **Town** P, D, CH, 🛒, R, Bar, ✉, Ⓑ, ⇌, ✈ (Norwich).

Entry to the Broads: Pass up R Yare at slack LW, under Haven Bridge (1·8m HAT) thence to Breydon Water via Breydon Bridge (4·0m) or to R Bure. Both bridges lift in co-ordination to pass small craft in groups. All br lifts on request to Hbr Office (01493) 335503 during office hrs. Weekend and bank holiday lifts to be requested working afternoon before. Call the Bridge Officer on VHF Ch 12. R Bure has two fixed bridges (2·3m MHWS).

NORFOLK BROADS: The Broads comprise about 120 miles of navigable rivers and lakes in Norfolk and Suffolk. The main rivers (Bure, Yare and Waveney) are tidal, flowing into the sea at Great Yarmouth. The N Broads have a 2·3m headroom limit. Br clearances restrict cruising to R Yare (Great Yarmouth to Norwich, but note that 3M E of Norwich, Postwick viaduct on S bypass has 10·7m HW clearance) and River Waveney (Lowestoft to Beccles). The Broads may be entered also at Lowestoft (1.24). Broads Navigation Authority ☎ (01603) 610734.

Tidal data on the rivers and Broads is based on the time of LW at Yarmouth Yacht Stn (mouth of R Bure), which is LW Gorleston +0100 (see TIDES). Add the differences below to time of LW Yarmouth Yacht Stn to get local LW times:

R Bure		R Waveney		R Yare	
Acle Bridge	+0230	Berney Arms	+0100	Reedham	+0130
Horning	+0300	St Olaves	+0130	Cantley	+0200
Potter Heigham	+0300	Oulton Broad	+0300	Norwich	+0300

LW at Breydon (mouth of R Yare) is LW Yarmouth Yacht Stn +0100. Tide starts to flood on Breydon Water whilst still ebbing from R Bure. Max draft is 1·8m; 2m with care. Tidal range 0·6m to 1·8m.

Licences (compulsory) are obtainable from: The Broads Authority, 18 Colegate, Norwich NR3 1BQ, ☎ 01603-610734; the Info Centre, Yarmouth Yacht Stn or the River Inspectors. *Hamilton's Guide to the Broads* is recommended. www.hamilton publications.com.

Netherlands & Belgium

Delfzijl to Nieuwpoort

Netherlands

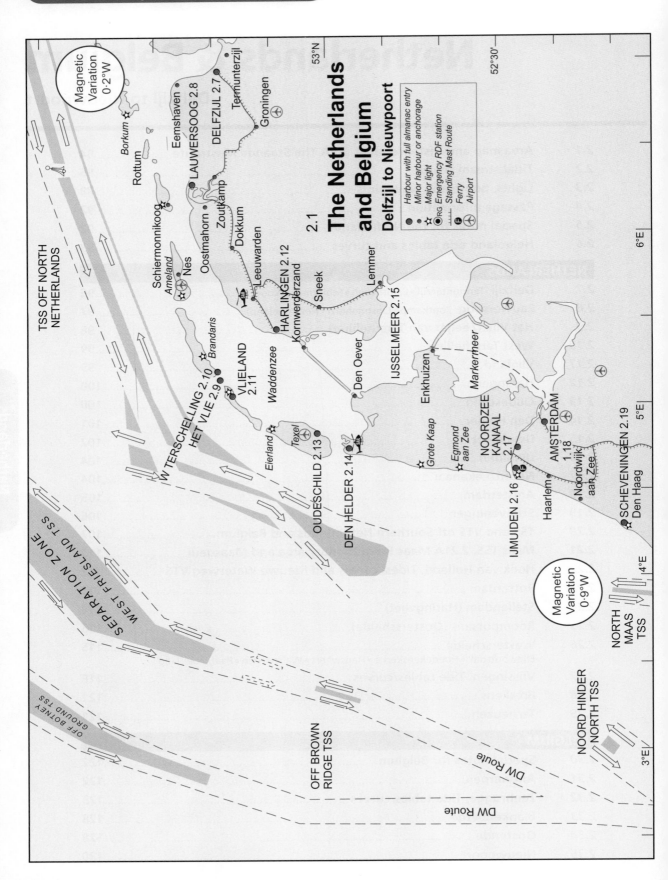

2.1
The Netherlands and Belgium
Delfzijl to Nieuwpoort

Harbour with full almanac entry
Minor harbour or anchorage
Major light
RG Emergency RDF station
Standing Mast Route
Ferry
Airport

Magnetic Variation 0.2°W

Magnetic Variation 0.9°W

TSS OFF NORTH NETHERLANDS

SEPARATION ZONE

WEST FRIESLAND TSS

OFF BROWN RIDGE TSS

OFF BOTNEY GROUND TSS

NOORD HINDER NORTH TSS

NORTH MAAS TSS

DW Route

DW Route

Borkum

Rottum

Eemshaven

LAUWERSOOG 2.8

DELFZIJL 2.7

Termunterzijl

Groningen

Schiermonnikoog

Ameland

Nes

Oostmahorn

Zoutkamp

Dokkum

Leeuwarden

HARLINGEN 2.12

Kornwerderzand

Sneek

Lemmer

IJSSELMEER 2.15

Brandaris

VLIELAND 2.11

W TERSCHELLING 2.10

HET VLIE 2.9

Texel

Eierland

Waddenzee

OUDESCHILD 2.13

DEN HELDER 2.14

Den Oever

Enkhuizen

Markermeer

Grote Kaap

Egmond aan Zee

NOORDZEE KANAAL 2.17

AMSTERDAM 1.18

Haarlem

Noordwijk aan Zee

IJMUIDEN 2.16

SCHEVENINGEN 2.19

Den Haag

53°N

52°30'

6°E

5°E

4°E

3°E

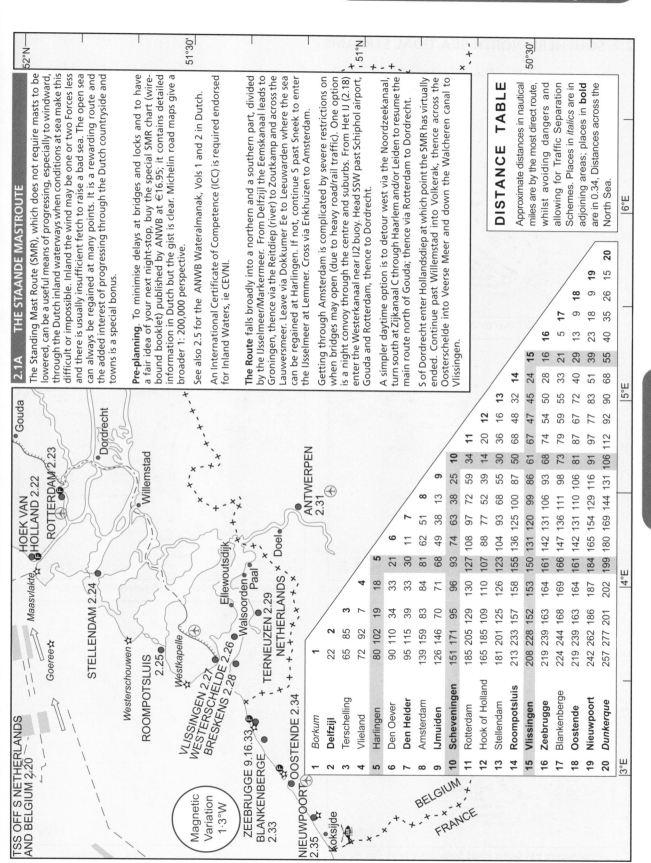

2.1A THE STAANDE MASTROUTE

The Standing Mast Route (SMR), which does not require masts to be lowered, can be a useful means of progressing, especially to windward, through the Dutch inland waterways when conditions at sea make this difficult or impossible. Inland the wind may be one or two Forces less and there is usually insufficient fetch to raise a bad sea. The open sea can always be regained at many points. It is a rewarding route and the added interest of progressing through the Dutch countryside and towns is a special bonus.

Pre-planning. To minimise delays at bridges and locks and to have a fair idea of your next night-stop, buy the special SMR chart (wire-bound booklet) published by ANWB at €16.95; it contains detailed information in Dutch but the gist is clear. Michelin road maps give a broader 1: 200,000 perspective.

See also 2.5 for the ANWB Wateralmanak, Vols 1 and 2 in Dutch.

An International Certificate of Competence (ICC) is required endorsed for Inland Waters, ie CEVNI.

The Route falls broadly into a northern and a southern part, divided by the IJsselmeer/Markermeer. From Delfzijl the Eemskanaal leads to Groningen, thence via the Reitdiep (river) to Zoutkamp and across the Lauwersmeer. Leave via Dokkumer Ee to Leeuwarden where the sea can be regained at Harlingen. If not, continue S past Sneek to enter the IJsselmeer at Lemmer. Cross via Enkhuizen to Amsterdam.

Getting through Amsterdam is complicated by severe restrictions on when bridges may open (due to heavy road/rail traffic). One option is a night convoy through the centre and suburbs. From Het IJ (2.18) enter the Westerkanaal near IJ2 buoy. Head SSW past Schiphol airport, Gouda and Rotterdam, thence to Dordrecht.

A simpler daytime option is to detour west via the Noordzeekanaal, turn south at Zijkanaal C through Haarlem and/or Leiden to resume the main route north of Gouda; thence via Rotterdam to Dordrecht.

S of Dordrecht enter Hollandsdiep at which point the SMR has virtually ended. Continue past Willemstad into Volkerak, thence across the Oosterschelde into Veerse Meer and down the Walcheren canal to Vlissingen.

DISTANCE TABLE

Approximate distances in nautical miles are by the most direct route, whilst avoiding dangers and allowing for Traffic Separation Schemes. Places in *italics* are in adjoining areas; places in **bold** are in 0.34, Distances across the North Sea.

#	Place	1	2	3	4	5	6	7	8	9	10	11	12	13	14	15	16	17	18	19	20
1	*Borkum*	**1**																			
2	**Delfzijl**	22	**2**																		
3	Terschelling	65	85	**3**																	
4	Vlieland	72	92	7	**4**																
5	Harlingen	80	102	19	18	**5**															
6	Den Oever	90	110	34	33	21	**6**														
7	**Den Helder**	95	115	39	33	30	11	**7**													
8	Amsterdam	139	159	83	84	81	62	51	**8**												
9	IJmuiden	126	146	70	71	68	49	38	13	**9**											
10	**Scheveningen**	151	171	95	96	93	74	63	38	25	**10**										
11	Rotterdam	185	205	129	130	127	108	97	72	59	34	**11**									
12	Hook of Holland	165	185	109	110	107	88	77	52	39	14	20	**12**								
13	Stellendam	181	201	125	126	123	104	93	68	55	30	36	16	**13**							
14	**Roompotsluis**	213	233	157	158	155	136	125	100	87	50	68	48	32	**14**						
15	**Vlissingen**	208	228	152	153	150	131	120	99	86	61	67	47	45	24	**15**					
16	Zeebrugge	219	239	163	164	161	142	131	106	93	68	74	54	50	28	16	**16**				
17	Blankenberge	224	244	168	169	166	147	136	111	98	73	79	59	55	33	21	5	**17**			
18	**Oostende**	219	239	163	164	161	142	131	110	106	81	87	67	72	40	29	13	9	**18**		
19	Nieuwpoort	242	262	186	187	184	165	154	129	116	91	97	77	83	51	39	23	18	9	**19**	
20	*Dunkerque*	257	277	201	202	199	180	169	144	131	106	112	92	90	68	55	40	35	26	15	**20**

Netherlands

2.2 SOUTHERN NORTH SEA TIDAL STREAMS

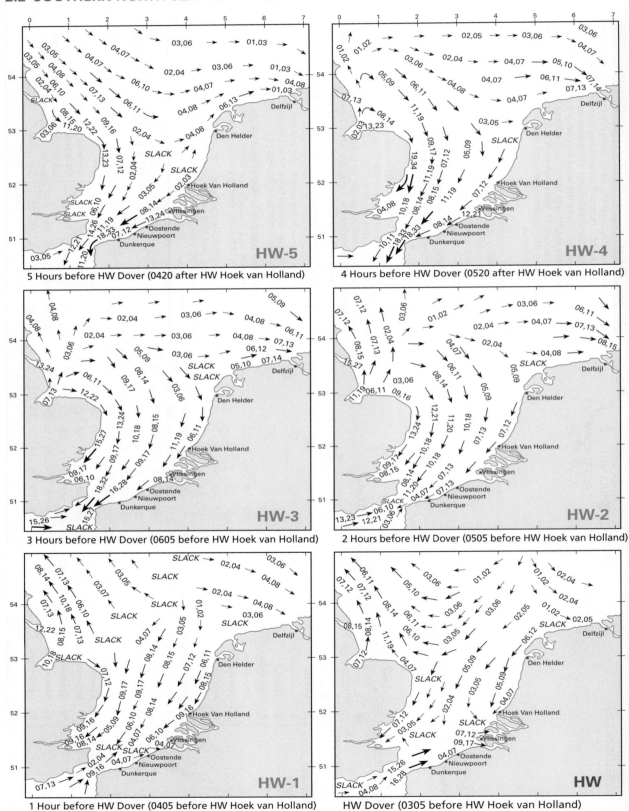

5 Hours before HW Dover (0420 after HW Hoek van Holland) — HW-5

4 Hours before HW Dover (0520 after HW Hoek van Holland) — HW-4

3 Hours before HW Dover (0605 before HW Hoek van Holland) — HW-3

2 Hours before HW Dover (0505 before HW Hoek van Holland) — HW-2

1 Hour before HW Dover (0405 before HW Hoek van Holland) — HW-1

HW Dover (0305 before HW Hoek van Holland) — HW

South-westward 1.2

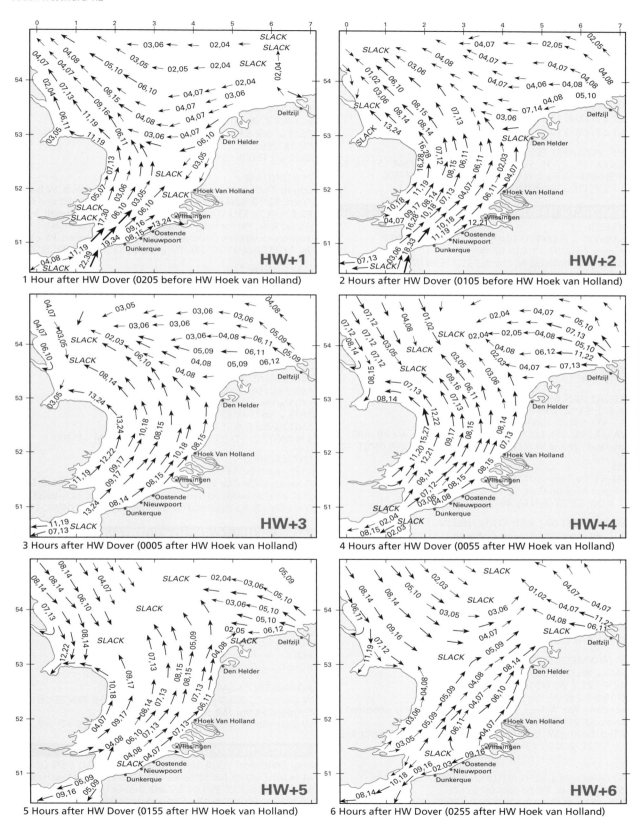

1 Hour after HW Dover (0205 before HW Hoek van Holland)

2 Hours after HW Dover (0105 before HW Hoek van Holland)

3 Hours after HW Dover (0005 after HW Hoek van Holland)

4 Hours after HW Dover (0055 after HW Hoek van Holland)

5 Hours after HW Dover (0155 after HW Hoek van Holland)

6 Hours after HW Dover (0255 after HW Hoek van Holland)

2.3 LIGHTS, BUOYS AND WAYPOINTS

Bold print = light with a nominal range of 15M or more.
CAPITALS = place or feature. *CAPITAL ITALICS* = light-vessel,
light float or Lanby. *Italics* = Fog signal. ***Bold italics*** = Racon.
See 0.2 for Abbreviations.

TSS OFF NORTHERN NETHERLANDS

TERSCHELLING-GERMAN BIGHT TSS
TG1/Ems ⚲ IQ G 13s; 53°43'·33N 06°22'·24E.
TE5 ⚲ Fl (3) G 10s; 53°37'·79N 05°53'·69E.
TE1 ⚲ Fl (3) G 10s; 53°29'·58N 05°11'·31E.

OFF VLIELAND TSS
VL-CENTER ⚲ Fl 5s 12M; ***Racon C, 12-15M;*** 53°26'·93N
04°39'·88E. VL7 ⚲ L Fl G 10s; 53°26'·40N 04°57'·60E.
VL1 ⚲ Fl (2) G 10s; 53°10'·96N 04°35'·31E.

DELFZIJL TO HARLINGEN

DELFZIJL
PS3/BW26 ⚲ Fl (2+1) G 12s; 53°19'·25N 07°00'·32E.
W mole ⚲ FG; 53°19'·01N 07°00'·27E.
Ldg lts 203° both Iso 4s. Front, 53°18'·63N 07°00'·17E.

SCHIERMONNIKOOG AND LAUWERSOOG
WG (Westgat) ⚲ Iso 8s; ***Racon Z;*** 53°32'·00N 05°58'·54E.
WRG ⚲ Q; 53°32'·87N 06°03'·24E.
AM ⚲ VQ; 53°30'·95N 05°44'·72E.
Schiermonnikoog ☆ Fl (4) 20s 43m **28M**; dark R ○ twr. Same
twr: F WR 29m **W15M**, R12M; 210°-W-221°-R-230°. 53°29'·20N
06°08'·79E.
Lauwersoog W mole ⚲ FG 3M; *Horn (2) 30s;* 53°24'·68N
06°12'·00E.

ZEEGAT VAN AMELAND
BR ⚲ Q; 53°30'·66N 05°33'·52E.
TS ⚲ VQ; 53°28'·15N 05°21'·53E.
WA ⚲ 53°28'·35N 05°28'·64E. (Westgat buoys are all unlit).
Ameland , W end ☆ Fl (3) 15s 57m **30M**; 53°26'·89N 05°37'·42E.

NES
VA2-R1 ⚲ VQ(6) + L Fl 10s; 53°25'·71N 05°45'·88E.
Reegeul R3 ⚲ Iso G 4s; 53°25'·80N 05°45'·93E.
R7 ⚲ QG; 53°25'·91N 05°46'·21E.

HET VLIE (ZEEGAT VAN TERSCHELLING)
ZS (Zuider Stortemelk) ⚲ Iso 4s; ***Racon T;*** 53°19'·58N 04°55'·77E.
ZS1 ⚲ VQ G; 53°19'·22N 04°57'·58E.
ZS5 ⚲ L Fl G 8s; 53°18'·53N 05°01'·10E.
ZS11-VS2 ⚲ Q (9) 15s; 53°18'·66N 05°05'·95E.

SCHUITENGAT TO WEST TERSCHELLING
VL 4/SG 1 ⚲ 53°19'·17N 05°10'·45E; buoys are frequently moved.
SG 3 ⚲ 53°19'·38N 05°10'·51E.
SG 19 ⚲ L Fl G 5s; 53°20'·89N 05°12'·42E.
SG 23 ⚲ L Fl G 8s; 53°21'·17N 05°13'·28E.

NOORD MEEP/SLENK TO WEST TERSCHELLING
WM3 ⚲ Iso G 2s; 53°17'·45N 05°12'·28E.
NM 4-S 21 ⚲ VQ (3) 5s; 53°19'·02N 05°15'·47E.
SG 15-S 2 ⚲ Q (9) 15s; 53°20'·44N 05°11'·70E.
Brandaris Twr ☆ Fl 5s 54m **29M**; Y □ twr partly obscured by
dunes; 53°21'·62N 05°12'·86E.
W Terschelling W hbr mole ⚲ FR 5m 5M; R post, W bands; *Horn
15s;* 53°21'·26N 05°13'·09E. E pier hd ⚲ FG 4m 4M.

VLIELAND
VS3 (Vliesloot) ⚲ VQ G; 53°18'·27N 05°06'·25E.
VS14 ⚲ Iso R 4s; 53°17'·58N 05°05'62E.
VS16-VB1 ⚲ Fl (2+1) R 10s; 53°17'·62N 05°05'·19E.
E/W mole hds ⚲ FG and ⚲ FR; 53°17'·68N 05°05'·51E.

Ldg lts 282° ⚲ Iso 4s 10/16m 1M, synch; 53°17'·75N 05°04'·47W
(100m apart); mainly for the ferry terminal at E Vlieland.
E Vlieland (Vuurduin) ☆ Iso 4s 54m **20M**; 53°17'·75N 05°03'·49E.

APPROACHES TO HARLINGEN (selected marks):
VLIESTROOM buoys are frequently moved.
VL1 ⚲ QG; 53°18'·99N 05°08'·82E. VL 2 ⚲ QR; 53°19'·40N
05°09'·19E.
IN 1 ⚲ VQ G; 53°16'·07N 05°09'·70E (Inschot).

BLAUWE SLENK
BS1-IN2 ⚲ VQ (3) 5s; 53°15'·99N 05°10'·32E.
BS13 ⚲ QG; 53°13'·31N 05°17'·13E. BS19 ⚲ VQ G; 53°11'·90N
05°18'·28E.
BS23 ⚲ L Fl G 8s; 53°11'·42N 05°19'·60E.

POLLENDAM
Ldg lts 112°, both Iso 6s 8/19m 13M (H24); B masts, W bands.
Front, 53°10'·52N 05°24'·19E. Use only between P2 and P6.
P2 ⚲ Iso R 2s; 53°11'·47N 05°20'·38E on the training wall, as are
P4, Iso R 8s; P6, Iso R 4s; P8, Iso R 8s; and P10, Iso R 2s.
Yachts should keep outboard of P1 thru 7 SHM buoys. P1 ⚲ Iso G
2s; 53°11'·39N 05°20'·32E. P7 ⚲ VQ G; 53°10'·68N 05°23'·45E.

HARLINGEN
S mole hd ⚲ FG 9m; *Horn (3) 30s;* 53°10'·56N 05°24'·18E.
N mole hd ⚲ FR 9m 4M; R/W pedestal; 53°10'·59N 05°24'·32E.

TEXEL AND THE WADDENZEE

APPROACHES TO EIERLANDSCHE GAT
Eierland ☆ Fl (2) 10s 52m **29M**; R ○ twr; 53°10'·93N 04°51'·31E.
EG ⚲ VQ (9) 10s; 53°13'·36N 04°47'·08E.

MOLENGAT (from the N)
MG ⚲ Mo (A) 8s; 53°03'·91N 04°39'·37E.
MG1 ⚲ Iso G 4s; 53°02'·89N 04°40'·86E.
MG5 ⚲ Iso G 4s; 53°01'·26N 04°41'·74E.
MG13 ⚲ Iso G 8s; 52°59'·16N 04°42'·35E.
S14-MG17 ⚲ VQ (6) + L Fl 10s; 52°58'·50N 04°43'·60E.

OUDESCHILD
T12 ⚲ Iso R 8s; 53°02'·23N 04°51'·52E.
Oudeschild Dir ⚲ Oc 6s; intens 291°; 53°02'·40N 04°50'·94E; leads
291° into hbr between N mole head FG 6m; and S mole head ⚲ FR
6m; *Horn (2) 30s* (sounded 0600-2300); 53°02'·33N 04°51'·17E.

APPROACHES TO KORNWERDERZAND SEALOCK

DOOVE BALG (From Texelstroom eastward)
T23 ⚲ VQ G; 53°03'·60N 04°55'·85E, 066°/3M from Oudeschild.
T29 ⚲ 53°03'·25N 05°00'·05E.
D1 ⚲ Iso G 4s; 53°02'·18N 05°03'·42E.
D21 ⚲ Iso G 8s; 53°03'·55N 05°15'·71E.
BO2-WG1 ⚲ Q (6) + L Fl 10s; 53°05'·00N 05°17'·91E.

BOONTJES (From Harlingen southward)
BO40 ⚲ Iso R 4s; 53°09'·87N 05°23'·29E.
BO28 ⚲ Iso R 8s; 53°07'·81N 05°22'·49E.
BO9/KZ2 ⚲ Q; 53°04'·95N 05°20'·24E.

KORNWERDERZAND SEALOCK
W mole ⚲ FG 9m 7M; *Horn Mo(N) 30s;* 53°04'·78N 05°20'·03E.
E mole ⚲ FR 9m 7M; 53°04'·70N 05°20'·08E.
W mole elbow ⚲ Iso G 6s 6m 7M; 53°04'·61N 05°19'·90E.

APPROACHES TO DEN OEVER SEALOCK

MALZWIN and VISJAGERSGAATJE CHANS TO DEN OEVER
MH4-M1 ⚲ VQ (9) 10s; 52°58'·09N 04°47'·52E, close N Den Helder.
M15 ⚲ QG; 52°59'·39N 04°55'·48E (hence use DYC 1811.3).
VG1-W2 ⚲ Fl (2+1) G 10s; 52°59'·00N 04°56'·85E.
O9 ⚲ Iso G 8s; 52°56'·63N 05°02'·38E.

Plot waypoints on chart before use

DEN OEVER SEALOCK
Ldg lts 131°, both Oc 10s 6m 7M; 127°-137°. Front, 52°56'·32N 05°02'·98E. Rear, 280m from front.
E end of swing bridge, ⚡ Iso WRG 5s 14m 10/7M; 226°-G-231°-W-235°-R-290°-G-327°-W-335°-R-345°; 52°56'·12N 05°02'·52E.

ZEEGAT VAN TEXEL AND DEN HELDER
OFFSHORE MARKS W and SW OF DEN HELDER
NH (Noorderhaaks) ⚓ VQ; 53°00'·24N 04°35'·37E.
MR ⚓ Q (9) 15s; 52°56'·77N 04°33'·82E.
ZH (Zuiderhaaks) ⚓ VQ (6) + L Fl 10s; 52°54'·65N 04°34'·72E.
Vinca G wreck ⚓ Q (9) 15s; *Racon D*; 52°45'·93N 04°12'·31E.

SCHULPENGAT (from the SSW)
Schulpengat Dir ☆ 026·5°, Dir WRG, Al WR, Al WG, **W22M R/G18M**; church spire; 025.1°–FG–025.6°–AlWG–026.3°–FW–026.7°–Al WR–027.4°–F–027.9°; shown H24.
Schilbolsnol ☆ F WRG 27m **W15M**, R12M, G11M; 338°-W-002°-G-035°-W(ldg sector for Schulpengat)-038°-R-051°-W-068°; post; 53°00'·50N 04°45'·70E (on Texel).
SG ⚓ Mo (A) 8s; *Racon Z*; 52°52'·90N 04°37'·90E.
S1 ▲ Iso G 4s; 52°53'·53N 04°38'·82E.
S7 ▲ QG; 52°56'·25N 04°40'·92E. S6A ⚓ QR; 52°56'·52N 04°40'·51E.
S10 ⚓ Iso R 8s; 52°57'·59N 04°41'·57E. S14-MG17 ⚓, see Molengat.
S11 ▲ Iso G 8s; 52°57'·55N 04°43'·25E.
Huisduinen ⚡ F WR 26m W14M, R11M; 070°-W-113°-R-158°-W-208°; □ twr; 52°57'·14N 04°43'·30E (abeam S10 PHM buoy).
Kijkduin ☆ Fl (4) 20s 56m **30M**; vis 360°, except where obsc'd by dunes on Texel; brown twr; 52°57'·33N 04°43'·58E (mainland).

MARSDIEP and DEN HELDER
T1 ▲ Fl (3) G 10s; 52°57'·99N 04°44'·62E.
T3 ▲ Iso G 8s; 52°58'·07N 04°46'·42E.
Den Helder ldg lts 191°, both Oc G 5s 15/24m 14M, synch. Front, vis 161°-221°; B ▽ on bldg; 52°57'·37N 04°47'·08E.
Marinehaven, W bkwtr head ⚡ QG 11m 8M; *Horn 20s*; 52°57'·95N 04°47'·07E (Harssens Island).
W side, ⚡ Fl G 5s 9m 4M (H24); 180°-067°; 52°57'·78N 04°47'·08E.
Yacht hbr (KMYC), ent ⚡ FR & FG; 165m SW of ⚡ Fl G 5s, above.
E side, MH6 ⚓ Iso R 4s; 52°57'·99N 04°47'·41E.
Ent E side, ⚡ QR 9m 4M (H24); 52°57'·77N 04°47'·37E.

DEN HELDER TO AMSTERDAM
Zanddijk Grote Kaap ⚡ Oc WRG 10s 30m W11M, R8M, G8M; 041°-G-088°-W-094°-R-131°; brown twr; 52°52'·86N 04°42'·88E.
Petten ⚓ VQ (9) 10s; 52°47'·33N 04°36'·78E (Power stn outfall).
Egmond-aan-Zee ☆ Iso WR 10s 36m **W18M**, R14M; 010°-W-175°-R-188°; W ○ twr; 52°36'·99N 04°37'·16E.
Wind farm approx 6·4M W of Egmond-aan-Zee is marked by: a Meteomast, Mo (U) 15s 11m 10M; 52°36'·36N 04°23'·41E; and by L Fl Y 15s; Horn Mo (U) 30s on 5 of the peripheral wind turbines.

IJMUIDEN
Baloeran ⚓ Q (9) 15s; 52°29'·21N 04°32'·00E.
IJmuiden ⚓ Mo (A) 8s; *Racon Y, 10M*; 52°28'·45N 04°23'·92E.
Ldg lts 100·5° (FW 5M by day; 090·5°-110·5°). **Front** ☆ F WR 30m **W16M**, R13M; 050°-W-122°-R-145°-W-160°; (Tidal and traffic sigs); dark R ○ twrs; 52°27'·70N 04°34'·47E. **Rear** ☆ Fl 5s 52m **29M**; 019°-199° (FW 5M by day; 090·5°-110·5°); 560m from front.
S bkwtr hd ⚡ Fl G 14m 10M (in fog Fl 3s); *Horn (2) 30s*; W twr, G bands; 52°27'·82N 04°31'·93E.
N bkwtr hd ⚡ FR 15m 10M; 52°28'·05N 04°32'·55E.
IJM 1 ▲ Iso G 4s; 52°27'·75N 04°33'·59E.
S outer chan ⚡ Iso G 6s, 52°27'·75N 04°33'·81E. ⚡ Iso R 6s, 52°27'·84N 04°34'·39E (Forteiland). Kleine Sluis 52°27'·84N 04°35'·43E.

AMSTERDAM
IJ8 ⚓ Iso R 8s (for Sixhaven marina); 52°22'·84N 04°54'·29E.
Oranjesluizen, N lock 52°22'·93N 04°57'·60E (for IJsselmeer).

AMSTERDAM TO ROTTERDAM
Noordwijk-aan-Zee ☆ Oc (3) 20s 32m **18M**; W □ twr; 52°14'·88N 04°26'·02E.

SCHEVENINGEN
Lighthouse ☆ Fl (2) 10s 48m **29M**; 014°-244°; brown twr; 52°06'·23N 04°16'·13E, 5ca E of hbr ent.
Ldg lts 156°, both Iso 4s 18/22m 14M, H24; synch; Gy masts. Front 52°05'·78N 04°15'·60E; rear 100m from front. Intens at night.
SCH ⚓ Iso 4s; 52°07'·76N 04°14'·12E.
KNS ⚓ Q (9)15s; 52°06'·41N 04°15'·32E.
W mole ⚡ FG 12m 9M; G twr, W bands; 52°06'·23N 04°15'·16E.
E mole ⚡, FR 12m 9M; R twr, W bands; 52°06'·24N 04°15'·37E.
Inner ldg lts 131°: both Oc G 5s 8/9m 11M synch; Gy posts. Front 52°05'·81N 04°15'·89E. Rear, 50m from front.

NOORD HINDER N & S TSS and JUNCTION
NHR-N ⚓ L Fl 8s; *Racon K, 10M*; 52°10'·91N 03°04'·76E.
Noord Hinder ⚓ Fl (2) 10s; *Horn (2) 30s*; *Racon T, 12-15M*; 52°00'·10N 02° 51'·11E.
NHR-S ⚓ Fl Y 10s; 51°51'·37N 02°28'·72E.
NHR-SE ▲ Fl G 5s; 51°45'·42N 02°39'·96E.
Birkenfels ⚓ Q (9) 15s; 51°38'·98N 02°31'·75E.
Twin ⚓ Fl (3) Y 9s; 51°32'·00N 02°22'·59E.
Garden City ⚓ Q (9) 15s; 51°29'·20N 02°17'·54E.

APPROACHES TO HOEK VAN HOLLAND
Europlatform ⚓ Mo (U) 15s; W structure, R bands; helicopter platform; *Horn Mo(U) 30s*; 51°59'·89N 03°16'·46E.
Goeree ☆ Fl (4) 20s 32m **28M**; R/W chequered twr on platform; helicopter platform; *Horn (4) 30s*; *Racon T, 12-15M*; 51°55'·42N 03°40'·03E.
Maasvlakte ☆ Fl (5) 20s 67m **28M**, H24; 340°-267°; W twr, B bands; 51°58'·20N 04°00'·84E, 1·5M SSW of Maas ent.
Maas Center ⚓ Iso 4s; *Racon M, 10M*; 52°00'·92N 03°48'·79E.
SB ⚓ Fl(4)Y 10s; *Racon Z*; 51°59·8N 3°54·6E
MO ⚓ Mo (A) 8s; 52°00'·95N 03°58'·07E.
MN3 ▲ Fl (3) G 10s; 52°04'·47N 03°58'·76E.
MN1 ▲ Fl G 5s; 52°02'·07N 04°00'·83E.

HOEK VAN HOLLAND
Maasmond ldg lts 112° (for deep draught vessels): both Iso 4s 30/46m **21M**; 101°-123°, synch; W twr, B bands. **Front**, 51°58'·88N 04°04'·88E (NW end of Splitsingsdam). **Rear**, 0·6M from front.
Indusbank N ⚓ VQ; 52°02'·89N 04°03'·57E.
MVN ⚓ VQ; 51°59'·61N 04°00'·20E.
MV ⚓ Q (9) 15s; 51°57'·45N 03°58'·45E.
Maas 1 ▲ L Fl G 5s; 51°59'·35N 04°01'·68E.
Nieuwe Waterweg ldg lts 107°: both Iso R 6s 29/43m **18M**; 099.5°-114.5°; R twr, W bands. Front, 51°58'·55N 04°07'·52E. Rear, 450m from front.
Nieuwe Noorderdam ⚡ FR 25m 10M (In fog Al Fl WR 6s; 278°-255°); R twr, W bands; 51°59'·67N 04°02'·80E.
Nieuwe Zuiderdam ⚡ FG 25m 10M, 330°-307°; (In fog Al Fl WG 6s); G twr, W bands; 51°59'·14N 04°02'·49E.

ROTTERDAM
Maassluis ⚡ FG 6m; 51°54'·94N 04°14'·81E; and FR.
Vlaardingen ⚡ FG; 51°53'·99N 04°20'·95E; and FR.
Spuihaven, W ent ⚡ FR; 51°53'·98N 04°23'·97E.
Veerhaven, E ent ⚡ FG; 51°54'·42N 04°28'·75E; and FR.
City marina ent, 51°54'·64N 04°29'·76E.

APPROACHES TO HARINGVLIET
Buitenbank , Iso 4s; 51°51'·16N 03°25'·71E.
Hinder ⚓ Q (9) 15s; 51°54'·55N 03°55'·42E.
SH ⚓ VQ (9) 10s; 51°49'·49N 03°45'·79E; also SH-N ⚓ & SH-S ⚓.
Westhoofd ☆ Fl (3) 15s 55m **30M**; R □ tr; 51°48'·79N 03°51'·85E.
Ooster ⚓ Q (9) 15s; 51°47'·90N 03°41'·27E.

Netherlands

SLIJKGAT
SG ⌁ Iso 4s; 51°51'·95N 03°51'·42E.
SG 2 ⌁ Iso R 4s; 51°51'·71N 03°53'·45E.
SG 5 ⌁ Iso G 4s; 51°50'·91N 03°55'·44E.
SG 11 ⌁ Iso G 4s; 51°50'·81N 03°58'·52E.
P1 ⌁ Iso G 4s; 51°51'·27N 04°00'·51E.
P3 ⌁ Iso G 8s; 51°51'·12N 04°01'·45E.
P9 ⌁ Iso G 8s; 51°49'·98N 04°02'·15E.

STELLENDAM
N mole ⌁ FG; *Horn (2) 15s;* 51°49'·88N 04°02'·03E.
Buitenhaven ⌁ Oc 6s; 51°49'·73N 04°01'·75E.

APPROACHES TO OOSTERSCHELDE
OUTER APPROACHES
Schouwenbank ⌁ Mo (A) 8s; *Racon O, 10M;* 51°44'·94N 03°14'·32E.
Middelbank ⌁ Iso 8s; 51°40'·86N 03°18'·20E.
MW ⌁ Q (9) 15s; 51°44'·55N 03°24'·04E (Schouwendiep).
MD 3 ⌁ Fl G 5s; 51°42'·70N 03°26'·98E.
TB (Thornton Bank) ⌁ Q; 51°34'·40N 02°59'·11E.
SW Thornton ⌁ Iso 8s; 51°30'·98N 02°50'·90E.
Rabsbank ⌁ Iso 4s; 51°38'·25N 03°09'·93E.
Westpit ⌁ Iso 8s; 51°33'·65N 03°09'·92E.
ZSB ⌁ VQ (9) 10s; 51°36'·57N 03°15'·62E.
OG1 ⌁ QG; 51°36'·14N 03°20'·08E.

WESTGAT, OUDE ROOMPOT and ROOMPOTSLUIS
West Schouwen ☆ Fl (2+1)15s 57m **30M**; Gy twr, R diagonals on upper part; 51°42'·52N 03°41'·50E, 5·8M N of Roompotsluis.
OG-WG ⌁ VQ (9) 10s; 51°37'·18N 03°23'·82E.
WG1 ⌁ Iso G 8s; 51°38'·00N 03°26'·24E.
WG4 ⌁ L Fl R 8s; 51°38'·62N 03°28'·78E.
WG7 ⌁ Iso G 4s 51°39'·40N 03°32'·67E.
WG-GB (Geul de Banjaard) ⌁ 51°39'·72N 03°32'·69E.
OR1 ⌁ 51°39'·15N 03°33'·59E.
OR5 ⌁ Iso G 8s; 51°38'·71N 03°35'·53E.
OR11 ⌁ Iso G 4s; 51°36'·98N 03°38'·40E.
OR12 ⌁ Iso R 4s; 51°37'·27N 03°39'·25E.
OR-R ⌁ VQ (3) 5s; 51°36'·41N 03°38'·96E.

Roompotsluis ldg lts 073·5°, both Oc G 5s; synch. Front, 51°37'·33N 03°40'·75E. Rear, 280m from front.
N bkwtr ⌁ FR 7m; 51°37'·31N 03°40'·09E.

WESTKAPELLE TO VLISSINGEN
OOSTGAT
Ldg lts 149·5°: Front, Noorderhoofd Oc WRG 10s 20m; W13M, R/G10M; 353°-R-008°-G-029°-W-169°; R ○ twr, W band; 51°32'·40N 03°26'·21E, 0·73M from rear (Westkapelle).
Westkapelle ☆, rear, Fl 3s 49m **28M**; obsc'd by land on certain brgs; ☐ twr, R top; 51°31'·75N 03°26'·83E.
Kaloo ⌁ Iso 8s; 51°35'·55N 03°23'·24E. Chan is well buoyed/lit.
OG5 ⌁ Iso G 8s; 51°33'·95N 03°25'·92E.
OG-GR ⌁ VQ (3) 5s; 51°32'·74N 03°24'·71E.
Molenhoofd ⌁ Oc WRG 6s 10m; 306°-R-329°-W-349°-R-008°-G-034·5°-W-036·5°-G-144°-W-169°-R-198°; W mast R bands; 51°31'·58N 03°26'·05E.
Zoutelande FR 21m 12M; 321°-352°; R ☐ twr; 51°30'·28N 03°28'·41E.
Kaapduinen, ldg lts 130°: both Oc 5s 25/34m 13M; synch; Y ☐ twrs, R bands. Front, 115°-145°; 51°28'·47N 03°30'·99E. Rear, 107·5°-152·5°; 220m from front.
Fort de Nolle ⌁ Oc WRG 9s 11m W6M, R/G4M; 293°-R-309°-W-324·5°-G-336·5°-R-014°-G-064°-R-099·5°-W-110·5°-G-117°-R-130°; W col, R bands; 51°26'·94N 03°33'·12E.
Ldg lts 117°: Front, Leugenaar, Oc R 5s 6m 7M; intens 108°-126°; W&R pile; 51°26'·43N 03°34'·14E.
Rear, Sardijngeul Oc WRG 5s 8m W12M, R9M, G8M; synch;

245°-R-272°-G-282.5°-W-123°-R-147°; R △, W bands on R & W mast; 550m from front; 51°26'·30N 03°34'·56E.

OFFSHORE: W HINDER TSS TO SCHEUR CHANNEL
West Hinder ☆ Fl (4) 30s 23m 13M; *Horn Mo (U) 30s;* **Racon W;** 51°23'·30N 02°26'·27E.
WH Zuid ⌁ Q (6) + L Fl 15s; 51°22'·78N 02°26'·25E.
Oost-Dyck ⌁ Q; 51°21'·38N 02°31'·12E.
Oost-Dyck OD1 ⌁ Q; 51°21'·45N 02°30'·83E.
Bergues N ⌁ Q; 51°19'·96N 02°24'·53E.
Oost-Dyck West ⌁ Q (9) 15s; 51°17'·15N 02°26'·32E.
Oostdyck radar twr; ☆ Mo (U) 15s 15m 12M on 4 corners; *Horn Mo (U) 30s;* **Racon O.** R twr, 3 W bands, with adjacent red twr/helipad; 51°16'·49N 02°26'·83E.
AN ⌁ Fl (4) R 20s; 51°23'·45N 02°36'·92E.
AZ ⌁ Fl (3) G 10s; 51°21'·15N 02°36'·92E.
KB2 ⌁ VQ; 51°21'·04N 02°42'·20E.
KB ⌁ Q; *Racon K;* 51°21'·03N 02°42'·80E.
MBN ⌁ Q; 51°20'·82N 02°46'·19E.
SWA ⌁ Q (9) 15s; 51°22'·28N 02°46'·34E.
VG ⌁ Q ; 51°23'·36N 02°46'·32E, Vaargeul 1.
VG1 ⌁ VQ G; 51°25'·03N 02°49'·04E.
VG2 ⌁ Q (6) + L Fl R 15s; *Racon V;* 51°25'·96N 02°48'·16E.
VG3 ⌁ QG; 51°25'·05N 02°52'·85E.
VG5 ⌁ Fl G 5s; 51°24'·63N 02°57'·90E.
VG7 ⌁ Q ; 51°24'·53N 02°59'·90E.
Goote Bank ⌁ Q (3) 10s; 51°26'·95N 02°52'·72E.
A1 ⌁ Iso 8s; 51°22'·36N 02°53'·33E.
A1bis ⌁ L Fl 10s; 51°21'·68N 02°58'·02E.

WESTERSCHELDE APPROACHES
SCHEUR CHANNEL
S1 ⌁ Fl G 5s; 51°23'·14N 03°00'·12E.
S3 ⌁ Q; 51°24'·30N 03°02'·92E.
MOW 0 ☉ Fl (5) Y 20s; *Racon S, 10M;* 51°23'·67N 03°02'·75E.
S5 ⌁ Fl G 5s; 51°23'·69N 03°05'·92E.
S7 ⌁ Fl G 5s; 51°23'·98N 03°10'·42E.
S9 ⌁ QG; 51°24'·42N 03°14'·99E.
S12 ⌁ Fl (4) R 10s; 51°24'·67N 03°18'·22E.
S-W ⌁ Q; 51°24'·13N 03°18'·22E, here Wielingen chan merges.
S14 ⌁ Fl R 5s; 51°24'·58N 03°19'·67E.

WIELINGEN CHANNEL
BVH ⌁ Q (6) + L Fl R 15s; 51°23'·13N 03°12'·04E.
MOW3 tide gauge ⌁ Fl (5) Y 20s; *Racon H, 10M;* 51°23'·38N 03°11'·92E.
W ⌁ Fl (3) G 15s; 51°23'·27N 03°14'·92E.
W1 ⌁ Fl G 5s; 51°23'·48N 03°18'·22E.
Fort Maisonneuve ⌁ VQ (9) 10s; wreck; 51°24'·20N 03°21'·50E.
W3 ⌁ Iso G 8s; 51°23'·96N 03°21'·49E.
W5 ⌁ Iso G 4s; 51°24'·31N 03°24'·50E.
W7 ⌁ Iso G 8s; 51°24'·60N 03°27'·23E.
W9 ⌁ Iso G 4s; 51°24'·96N 03°30'·43E.
Nieuwe Sluis ⌁ Oc WRG 10s 26m W14M, R11M, G10M; 055°-R-089°-W-093°-G-105°-R-134°-W-136·5°- G-156·5°-W-236·5°-G-243° -W-254°-R-292°-W-055°; B 8-sided twr, W bands; 51°24'·41N 03°31'·29E.
Songa ⌁ QG; 51°25'·16N 03°33'·66E.
W10 ⌁ QR; 51°25'·85N 03°33'·28E.

VLISSINGEN
Koopmanshaven, W mole root, ⌁ Iso WRG 3s 15m W12M, R10M, G9M; 253°-R-277°-W-284°-R-297°- W-306·5°-G-013°-W-024°-G-033°-W-035°-G-039°-W-055°-G-084·5°-R-092°-G-111°-W-114°; R pylon; 51°26'·37N 03°34'·52E.
Sardijngeul Oc WRG 5s; 51°26'·30N 03°34'·56E: see OOSTGAT last 3 lines. E mole head, ⌁ FG 7m; W mast; 51°26'·32N 03°34'·67E.
Buitenhaven ent, W side ⌁ FR 10m 5M; also Iso WRG 4s: W073°-

Plot waypoints on chart before use

324°, G324°-352°, W352°-017°, G017°-042°, W042°-056°, R056°-073°; W post, R bands; tfc sigs; 51°26'·38N 03°36'·06E.
Buitenhaven ent, E side ⚡ FG 7m 4M; 51°26'·41N 03°36'·38E.

Schone Waardin ⚡ Oc WRG 9s 10m W13M, R10M, G9M; 235°-R-271°-W-288°-G-335°-R-341°-G-026°-W-079°-R-091°; R mast, W bands; 51°26'·54N 03°37'·91E (1M E of Buitenhaven ent).

BRESKENS
ARV-VH ⚟ Q; 51°24'·71N 03°33'·89E.
VH2 (Vaarwaterlangs Hoofdplaat) ⚟ 51°24'·34N 03°33'·90E.
Yacht hbr, W mole ⚡ FG 7m; in fog FY; Gy post; 51°24'·03N 03°34'·06E. E mole ⚡ FR 6m; Gy mast; 51°23'·95N 03°34'·09E.

WESTERSCHELDE: TERNEUZEN TO PAAL
TERNEUZEN
Nieuw Neuzenpolder ldg lts 125°, both Oc 5s 6/16m 9/13M; intens 117°-133°; synch. Front, W col, B bands; 51°20'·97N 03°47'·24E. Rear, B & W twr; 365m from front.
Oost Buitenhaven E mole ⚡ FR 5M; 51°20'·56N 03°49'·19E.
Former ferry hbr (W part) & marinas (E part), W mole head ⚡ FG, Gy mast; 51°20'·57N 03°49'·64E. E mole, FR.
W mole ⚡ Oc WRG 5s 15m W9M, R7M, G6M; 090°-R-115°-W-120°-G-130°-W-245°-G-249°-W-279°-R-004°; B & W post; 51°20'·54N 03°49'·58E, close SW of ⚡ FG.

HANSWEERT
W mole ⚡ Oc WRG 10s 9m W9M, R7M, G6M; (in fog FY); 288°-R-311°-G-320°-W-332·5°-G-348·5°-W-042·5°-R-061·5°-W-078°-G-099°-W-114·5°-R-127·5°-W-288°; R twr, W bands; 51°26'·41N 04°00'·53E.

BELGIUM
ZANDVLIET TO ANTWERPEN
ZANDVLIET
Dir ⚡ 118·3°,WRG 20m W4M, R/ G3M; 116·63°-Oc G-117·17°- FG-117·58°-Alt GW-118·63°-F-118·63°-Alt RW-119·18°-FR-119·58°-Oc R-120·13°; 51°20'·61N 04°16'·47E, near Zandvliet locks.

ANTWERPEN
Royerssluis, ldg lts 091°, both FR. Ent FR/FG (for Willemdok ⚓).
No. 109 ⚟ Iso G 8s; 51°13'·88N 04°23'·87E, (off Linkeroever ⚓).
Linkeroever marina ⚟ F WR 9m W3M, R2M; shore-W-283°- R-shore; B ⊙, R lantern; 51°13'·91N 04°23'·70E. Marina ent, FR/FG.

COASTAL MARKS
SWW ⚟ Fl (4) R 20s; 51°21'·95N 03°00'·94E; Wandelaar.
WBN ⚟ QG; 51°21'·50N 03°02'·59E; Wandelaar.
Oostende Bank N ⚟ Q; 51°21'·20N 02°52'·93E.
Wenduine Bank E ⚟ QR; 51°18'·83N 03°01'·64E.
Wenduine Bank W ⚟ Q (9) 15s; 51°17'·23N 02°52'·76E.
Nautica Ena wreck ⚟ Q; 51°18'·08N 02°52'·79E.
Oostendebank E ⚟ Fl (4) R 20s; 51°17'·35N 02°51'·91E.
Oostendebank W ⚟ Q (9)15s; 51°16'·20N 02°44'·74E.
LST 420 ⚟ Q (9)15s; 51°15'·45N 02°40'·61E.
MBN ⚟ Q; 51°20'·82N 02°46'·27E.
Middelkerke Bank ⚟ Fl G 5s; 51°18'·19N 02°42'·75E.
Middelkerke Bank S ⚟ Fl G (9) R 15s; 51°14'·73N 02°41'·89E.
D1 ⚟ Q (3) 10s; 51°13'·95N 02°38'·59E.
BT Ratel ⚟ Fl (4) R 15s; 51°11'·63N 02°27'·92E; Buiten Ratel.

ZEEBRUGGE TO THE FRENCH BORDER
ZEEBRUGGE
A2 ⚟ Iso 8s; 51°22'·41N 03°07'·05E.
Ldg lts 136°, both Oc 5s 22/45m 8M; 131°-141°; H24, synch; W cols, R bands. Front, 51°20'·71N 03°13'·11E. Rear, 890m SE.
SZ ⚟ Q (3) 10s; 51°23'·62N 03°07'·58E (Scheur Channel).
Z ⚟ QG; 51°22'·48N 03°09'·95E.
WZ ⚟ Q (9) 15s; 51°22'·57N 03°10'·72E.

W outer mole ⚡ Oc G 7s 31m 7M; G vert strip lts visible from seaward; 057°-267°; *Horn (3) 30s*; IPTS; 51°21'·74N 03°11'·17E.
E outer mole ⚡ Oc R 7s 31m 7M; R vert strip lts visible from seaward; 087°-281°; *Bell 25s*; 51°21'·78N 03°11'·86E.
Ldg lts 154°: Front, Oc WR 6s 20m 3M, 135°-W-160°-R-169°; W pylon, R bands; 51°20'·33N 03°12'·89E. Rear, Oc 6s 38m 3M, H24, synch; 520m from front.
Leopold II mole ☆ Oc WR 15s 22m, **W20M, R18M**; 068°-W-145°-R-212°-W-296°; IPTS; *Horn (3+1) 90s*; 51°20'·85N 03°12'·17E.
Entrance to Marina and FV hbr 51°19'·88N 03°11'·85E.

BLANKENBERGE
Promenade pier Fl (3) Y 20s, 8m 4M; 51°19'·28N 03°08'·18E.
Lt ho ☆ Fl (2) 8s 30m **20M**; 065°-245°; W twr, B top; 51°18'·75N 03°06'·85E.
Ldg lts 134°, both FR 5/9m 3/10M, R cross (X) topmarks on masts; front 51°18'·70N 03°08'·82E; rear 81m from front.
E pier ⚡ FR 12m 11M; 290°-245°; W ○ twr; *Bell (2) 15s*; 51°18'·91N 03°06'·55E.
W pier ⚡ FG 14m 11M; intens 065°-290°, unintens 290°-335°; W ○ twr; 51°18'·89N 03°06'·42E.
OBST 4 – OBST 14 are eleven ⚟s Q approx 3ca offshore, marking Spoil Ground between Blankenberge and Oostende.

OOSTENDE
Oostendebank East ⚟ Fl (4) R 20s; 51°17'·35N 02°51'·91E.
Wenduinebank West ⚟ Q (9) 15s; 51°17'·23N 02°52'·76E.
Buitenstroombank ⚟ Q; 51°15'·17N 02°51'·71E.
Binnenstroombank ⚟ Q (3) 10s; 51°14'·47N 02°53'·65E.
⚟ Fl (5) Y 20s, Y beacon; 51°14'·83N 02°55'·33E.
Ldg lts 128°: both Iso 4s (triple vert) 21/32m 4M, 051°-201°; X on framework twrs, R/W bands. Front, 51°14'·13N 02°55'·55E.
Oostende lt ho ☆ Fl (3) 10s 65m **27M**; obsc 069·5°-071°; Gy twr, 2 sinusoidal Bu bands; 51°14'·18N 02°55'·84E.
E pier ⚡ and *Horn* have been withdrawn. The E pier has been demolished (2008) and a new pier is being built further east; WIP until 2012 is marked by 1 NCM buoy Q; 2 SPM buoys QY; and 3 PHM buoys QR. IPTS, tidal and storm sigs are shown from sig mast 51°14'·25N 02°55'·44E, plus QY when chan closed for ferry.
W pier ⚡ FG 12m 10M, 057°-327°; *Bell 4s*; W ○ twr 51°14'·31N 02°55'·03E.

NIEUWPOORT
Zuidstroombank ⚟ Fl R 5s; 51°12'·28N 02°47'·37E.
Weststroombank ⚟ Fl (4) R 20s; 51°11'·34N 02°43'·03E.
Wreck 4 ⚟ Q (6) + L Fl 15s; 51°10'·90N 02°405'·03E.
Nieuwpoort Bank ⚟ Q (9) 15s; 51°10'·16N 02°36'·09E.
Oostduinkerke ⚟ Q; 51°09'·15N 02°39'·44E.
Lt ho ☆ Fl (2) R 14s 28m **16M**; R/W twr; 51°09'·27N 02°43'·79E.
E pier ⚡ FR 11m 10M; vis 025°-250° & 307°-347°; W ○ twr; 51°09'·41N 02°43'·08E.
W pier ⚡ FG 11m 9M; vis 025°-250° & 284°-324°; *Bell (2) 10s*; W ○ twr; IPTS from root; 51°09'·35N 02°43'·00E.
⚡ QG 51°08'·65N 02°44'·31E marks the Y-junction where the channel forks stbd for KYCN and port for WSKLM and VVW-N.

WESTDIEP and PASSE DE ZUYDCOOTE
Den Oever wreck 2 ⚟ Q; 51°08'·11N 02°37'·43E.
Wreck 1 ⚟ Q; 51°08'·32N 02°35'·03E (adjacent to ⚟ next line).
Wave recorder ⚟ Fl (5) Y 20s; 51°08'·32N 02°34'·91E.
Trapegeer ⚟ Fl G 10s; 51°08'·41N 02°34'·36E.
E12 ⚟ VQ (6) + L Fl 10s; 51°07'·89N 02°30'·68E.
French waters, for continuity:
CME ⚟ Q (3) 10s; 51°07'·30N 02°30'·00E.
E11 ⚟ Fl G 4s; 51°06'·90N 02°30'·90E.
E10 ⚟ Fl (2) R 6s; 51°06'·30N 02°30'·47E.
E9 ⚟ Fl (2) G 6s; 51°05'·64N 02°29'·68E.
E8 ⚟ Fl (3) R 12s; 51°05'·16N 02°28'·67E.

2.4 PASSAGE INFORMATION

More Passage Information is threaded between harbours in this Area. **Bibliography** *N France and Belgium CC* (NDL/Featherstone). *N Sea Passage Pilot* (Imray/Navin). NP 55 *N Sea (East) Pilot*. NP 28 *Dover Strait Pilot*. *Hafenhandbuch Nordsee* (DSV-Verlag).

CHARTS, PSSA AND TSS

While AC 2182A, 1405/06/08, 1630/31/32/33, 1872 suffice for coastal passages and entry to the main ports, larger scale **Dutch yacht charts** (1800 series) are essential for exploring the cruising grounds along this coast or entering the smaller hbrs. Inland, the ANWB booklet-style chart (€16.95) of the *Staande-Mast Route* (Fixed Mast Route; see 2.1A) is very detailed with copious, but intelligible, notes in Dutch.

From the Ems estuary west to Den Helder a **Particularly Sensitive Sea Area** (PSSA) extends 3M seaward from the West Frisian Islands. Yachts should carefully avoid damaging the maritime environment and marine organisms living in it.

The Terschelling-German Bight TSS, Off Vlieland TSS and Off Texel TSS lie between 5 and 10M to seaward of the West Frisian Islands. Cruising yachts are advised to navigate within this relatively narrow ITZ. Further offshore, and particularly in and near the Off Vlieland TSS, West Friesland TSS and Botney Ground TSS, navigation is further complicated by the many oil and gas fields. For general notes on North Sea oil & gas installations, see Chapter 3 and Area 5.

CROSSING THE NORTH SEA TO THE UK

From ports S of Hoek van Holland make for NHR-SE, where cross the TSS for destinations between Harwich and Great Yarmouth (AC *1406*, *1408*, *1872*, *2449*, 3371). From ports N of Hoek van Holland passages can be more problematic. For example, a route from IJmuiden to the Humber crosses two DW routes, N and NW of Brown Ridge, and then runs into extensive offshore Gas Fields. These might cause you to opt for two shorter legs, stopping a night at Great Yarmouth. Similar thinking might apply if coming out of Den Helder, even if a stop at Great Yarmouth might incur some southing. From east of Den Helder, make ground west via the ITZ before taking departure.

2.5 SPECIAL NOTES: NETHERLANDS

PROVINCES are given in lieu of UK 'counties'.

CHARTS The following types of chart are available from agents. The Chart catalogue (HP7) is downloadable from www.hydro.nl:

- Zeekaarten (equivalent to AC) are issued by the Royal Netherlands Navy Hydrographer and corrected by Notices to Mariners (*Berichten aan Zeevarenden* or *BaZ*).
- 1800 series *voor Kust-en Binnenwateren* (coastal and inland waters) are yacht charts (DYC) issued annually in March by the Hydrographer in 8 folios (1801-1812, excluding 1802/4/6 & 8); about 9 loose double-sided sheets (54 x 38cm) per folio.

TIME ZONE is –0100, but add 1 hr for DST in the summer months.

TIDES HP 33 *Waterstanden & Stromen* (Tide tables and tidal streams in **English** and Dutch, €18.95) is most useful especially if cruising Dutch waters for any length of time. It contains tide tables for 15 Dutch and 2 Belgian coastal ports; and 8 tidal stream atlases, including Westerschelde, Oosterschelde and the Maas.

REGULATIONS Discharge of toilet waste from recreational boats is forbidden in all Dutch waters, including inland waterways, lakes and the Waddenzee.

MARINAS Most marinas are private YCs or Watersport Associations (WSV or WV): *Gemeentelijke (Gem)* = municipal. Marinas with >50 berths must have a pump-out unit ⚓. Sometimes (in Belgium also) berth-holders show a green tally if a berth is free, or a red tally if returning same day, but check with HM. Duty-free fuel (coloured red) is not available for leisure craft and may only be carried in the tank, NOT in cans. A tourist tax of €0.55–€1.82/head/night is often levied. VAT (BTW) is 19%. A useful website with links to other marinas is www.allejachthavens.nl

CUSTOMS Ports of entry are: Delfzijl, Lauwersoog, W Terschelling, Vlieland*, Harlingen, Kornwerderzand, Den Helder, IJmuiden, Scheveningen, Hoek van Holland, Maassluis, Schiedam, Vlaardingen, Rotterdam, Roompot*, Vlissingen and Breskens. *Summer only. Den Oever and Stellendam are *not* Ports of entry.

FERRIES TO THE UK IJmuiden-Newcastle; Hoek van Holland-Harwich; Rotterdam (Europoort)-Hull.

BUOYAGE Buoys are often named by the abbreviations of the banks or chans which they mark (eg VL = Vliestroom). A division buoy has the abbreviations of both chans meeting there, eg VL2-SG2 = as above, plus Schuitengat.

Some minor, tidal channels are marked by withies: SHM bound ↥; PHM unbound ↧. On tidal flats (eg Friesland) where the direction of main flood stream is uncertain, bound withies are on the S side of a chan and unbound on the N side; the banks thus marked are steep-to. In minor chans the buoyage may be moved without notice to accommodate changes.

The SIGNI buoyage system is used in the IJsselmeer, but not in the Eems, Waddenzee and Westerschelde.

SIGNALS When **motor-sailing** yachts must by law hoist a ▼ and when **at anchor** a black ball ●; these laws are rigidly enforced.

IPTS are widely used at coastal ports. Local signals, if any, are given where possible.

Sluicing signals may be shown by day: A blue board, with the word 'SPUIEN' on it; by night 3 ● in a △; sometimes both at once.

Storm warning signals, lts only, are shown by day & night at West Terschelling, Den Helder and IJmuiden.

R/T In emergency call *Den Helder Rescue* Ch 16 for Netherlands CG; or the working channel of a VTS sector or nearest lock or bridge. Monitor TSS info broadcasts and VTS sector channels. Ch 31 is for Dutch marinas. Note: Do not use Ch M in Dutch waters, where it is a salvage frequency. Ch 13 is for commercial ship-ship calling. English is the second language and widely spoken.

TELEPHONE To call UK from the Netherlands, dial 00-44; then the UK area code minus the prefix 0, followed by the number required. To call the Netherlands from UK dial 00-31 then the area code minus the prefix 0 followed by two or three digits, followed by a 7 or 6 digits subscriber no. Mobile phone Nos start 06.

Emergency: Fire, Police, Ambulance, dial 112 (free); Non-emergency 0900 8844 (local tariff).

PUBLIC HOLIDAYS New Year's Day, Easter Sun and Mon, Queen's Birthday (30 April), Liberation Day (5 May), Ascension Day, Whit Mon, Christmas and Boxing Days

BRITISH CONSULS Contact British Consulate-General, Koningslaan 44, 1075 AE Amsterdam; ☎ 020 676 4343. Or British Embassy, Lange Voorhout 10, 2514 ED The Hague; ☎ 070 427 0427.

INLAND WATERWAYS The sealocks at Kornwerderzand, Den Oever (2.15), IJmuiden (2.16), Stellendam (2.24) and Roompotsluis (2.25) are fully covered. The Staandemast (mast-up) route (2.1A) and the IJsselmeer (2.15) are outlined. Lack of space precludes detailed coverage of other harbours in the very extensive and enjoyable inland seas, waterways and canals.

Regulations. All craft must carry a copy of waterway regulations, *Binnenvaartpolitiereglement (BPR)*, as given in Dutch in the annual ANWB *Wateralmanak Vol 1* or available separately. Vol 2, also in Dutch, is essential reading; it gives pictograph details of marinas and the opening hours of bridges and locks.

Qualifications. Craft >15m LOA or capable of more than 20kph (11kn) must be skippered by the holder of an RYA Coastal Skipper's Certificate or higher qualification; *plus* an International Certificate of Competence (ICC) endorsed for Inland waterways, ie CEVNI.

Bridges and locks mostly work VHF Ch 18, 20 or 22, but CEVNI light signals (shown up/down-stream) largely negate the need for R/T. The most commonly seen signals include:
● = Bridge closed (opens on request).
To request bridges to open, call on VHF low power (1 watt), or sound 'K' (−·−).
● over ● = Bridge about to open.
● = Bridge open.

TIME ZONE -0100
Subtract 1 hour for UT
For German Summer Time add
ONE hour in **non-shaded areas**

2.6 HELGOLAND
LAT 54°11'N LONG 7°53'E
TIMES AND HEIGHTS OF HIGH AND LOW WATERS

Dates in red are SPRINGS
Dates in blue are NEAPS

YEAR **2010**

Netherlands

JANUARY

Time	m	Time	m
1 0625 / 1203 / F 1842	0.6 / 3.1 / 0.7	**16** 0024 / 0712 / SA 1248 / 1922	3.3 / 0.7 / 3.1 / 0.7
2 0021 / 0719 / SA 1255 / 1933	3.3 / 0.5 / 3.1 / 0.6	**17** 0058 / 0748 / SU 1322 / 1956	3.3 / 0.6 / 3.0 / 0.6
3 0112 / 0814 / SU 1347 / 2024	3.4 / 0.5 / 3.1 / 0.5	**18** 0131 / 0821 / M 1353 / 2026	3.3 / 0.6 / 3.0 / 0.6
4 0201 / 0903 / M 1435 / 2109	3.4 / 0.4 / 3.0 / 0.5	**19** 0201 / 0850 / TU 1422 / 2052	3.3 / 0.5 / 3.0 / 0.5
5 0246 / 0946 / TU 1519 / 2152	3.4 / 0.4 / 2.9 / 0.5	**20** 0229 / 0918 / W 1450 / 2121	3.2 / 0.6 / 2.9 / 0.6
6 0329 / 1028 / W 1604 / 2237	3.4 / 0.5 / 2.9 / 0.6	**21** 0300 / 0947 / TH 1521 / 2153	3.2 / 0.6 / 2.9 / 0.6
7 0415 / 1112 / TH 1653 / ◑ 2325	3.3 / 0.5 / 2.9 / 0.7	**22** 0332 / 1017 / F 1553 / 2225	3.1 / 0.6 / 2.9 / 0.7
8 0508 / 1159 / F 1746	3.2 / 0.7 / 2.8	**23** 0405 / 1046 / SA 1628 / ◗ 2301	3.0 / 0.7 / 2.8 / 0.8
9 0019 / 0607 / SA 1254 / 1845	0.8 / 3.1 / 0.8 / 2.8	**24** 0446 / 1127 / SU 1716 / 2356	2.9 / 0.8 / 2.8 / 0.9
10 0123 / 0715 / SU 1402 / 1954	0.9 / 3.0 / 1.0 / 2.9	**25** 0546 / 1231 / M 1825	2.9 / 0.9 / 2.8
11 0238 / 0829 / M 1516 / 2104	1.0 / 3.0 / 1.0 / 3.0	**26** 0113 / 0706 / TU 1353 / 1948	0.9 / 2.8 / 0.9 / 2.8
12 0352 / 0940 / TU 1622 / 2207	1.0 / 3.0 / 1.0 / 3.1	**27** 0241 / 0832 / W 1518 / 2110	0.9 / 2.9 / 0.9 / 3.0
13 0456 / 1040 / W 1717 / 2300	0.9 / 3.1 / 0.9 / 3.2	**28** 0404 / 0951 / TH 1634 / 2220	0.8 / 3.0 / 0.8 / 3.1
14 0549 / 1129 / TH 1804 / 2345	0.8 / 3.1 / 0.9 / 3.3	**29** 0516 / 1059 / F 1739 / 2319	0.6 / 3.1 / 0.7 / 3.3
15 0633 / 1211 / F 1845 / ●	0.7 / 3.1 / 0.8	**30** 0617 / 1156 / SA 1834 / ○	0.5 / 3.1 / 0.6
		31 0011 / 0711 / SU 1245 / 1925	3.3 / 0.4 / 3.1 / 0.5

FEBRUARY

Time	m	Time	m
1 0100 / 0803 / M 1333 / 2014	3.4 / 0.3 / 3.1 / 0.4	**16** 0109 / 0758 / TU 1330 / 2004	3.2 / 0.4 / 3.0 / 0.4
2 0148 / 0849 / TU 1418 / 2058	3.4 / 0.3 / 3.1 / 0.3	**17** 0137 / 0825 / W 1356 / 2030	3.2 / 0.4 / 3.0 / 0.4
3 0232 / 0930 / W 1500 / 2137	3.4 / 0.3 / 3.0 / 0.3	**18** 0205 / 0852 / TH 1424 / 2059	3.2 / 0.4 / 2.9 / 0.4
4 0312 / 1006 / TH 1539 / 2215	3.3 / 0.3 / 3.0 / 0.4	**19** 0235 / 0921 / F 1454 / 2131	3.1 / 0.5 / 3.0 / 0.4
5 0353 / 1042 / F 1620 / 2255	3.3 / 0.5 / 2.9 / 0.6	**20** 0308 / 0950 / SA 1524 / 2200	3.1 / 0.5 / 2.9 / 0.5
6 0436 / 1120 / SA 1703 / ◑ 2338	3.2 / 0.7 / 2.9 / 0.7	**21** 0338 / 1014 / SU 1552 / 2228	3.0 / 0.6 / 2.9 / 0.6
7 0525 / 1206 / SU 1755	3.0 / 0.7 / 2.8	**22** 0412 / 1046 / M 1633 / ◗ 2315	2.9 / 0.7 / 2.8 / 0.7
8 0036 / 0629 / M 1311 / 1904	0.8 / 2.9 / 1.0 / 2.8	**23** 0507 / 1147 / TU 1740	2.8 / 0.9 / 2.8
9 0154 / 0748 / TU 1434 / 2026	1.0 / 2.8 / 1.1 / 2.9	**24** 0034 / 0631 / W 1317 / 1912	0.9 / 2.7 / 1.0 / 2.8
10 0322 / 0913 / W 1556 / 2143	1.0 / 2.8 / 1.0 / 3.0	**25** 0214 / 0809 / TH 1455 / 2046	0.8 / 2.8 / 0.9 / 2.9
11 0438 / 1024 / TH 1700 / 2243	0.9 / 2.9 / 0.9 / 3.1	**26** 0348 / 0937 / F 1620 / 2205	0.7 / 2.9 / 0.8 / 3.1
12 0535 / 1115 / F 1749 / 2328	0.8 / 3.0 / 0.8 / 3.2	**27** 0505 / 1048 / SA 1727 / 2305	0.5 / 3.0 / 0.6 / 3.2
13 0618 / 1155 / SA 1829	0.7 / 3.0 / 0.7	**28** 0606 / 1143 / SU 1823 / ○ 2356	0.4 / 3.0 / 0.5 / 3.3
14 0006 / 0656 / SU 1229 / ● 1905	3.2 / 0.6 / 3.0 / 0.5		
15 0039 / 0729 / M 1301 / 1937	3.2 / 0.5 / 3.0 / 0.5		

MARCH

Time	m	Time	m
1 0657 / 1229 / M 1911	0.2 / 3.1 / 0.3	**16** 0011 / 0659 / TU 1231 / 1909	3.1 / 0.4 / 3.0 / 0.4
2 0043 / 0742 / TU 1312 / 1956	3.3 / 0.2 / 3.1 / 0.2	**17** 0041 / 0728 / W 1301 / 1937	3.1 / 0.3 / 3.0 / 0.3
3 0128 / 0825 / W 1353 / 2038	3.3 / 0.2 / 3.1 / 0.2	**18** 0110 / 0756 / TH 1328 / 2007	3.1 / 0.4 / 3.0 / 0.3
4 0211 / 0904 / TH 1433 / 2116	3.3 / 0.3 / 3.1 / 0.2	**19** 0140 / 0824 / F 1357 / 2038	3.1 / 0.4 / 3.0 / 0.3
5 0251 / 0938 / F 1510 / 2151	3.3 / 0.3 / 3.0 / 0.2	**20** 0213 / 0856 / SA 1429 / 2112	3.1 / 0.4 / 3.0 / 0.3
6 0329 / 1011 / SA 1546 / 2226	3.2 / 0.5 / 3.0 / 0.4	**21** 0247 / 0927 / SU 1500 / 2143	3.0 / 0.4 / 3.0 / 0.4
7 0407 / 1044 / SU 1624 / ◗ 2304	3.1 / 0.6 / 2.9 / 0.6	**22** 0322 / 0955 / M 1532 / 2215	3.0 / 0.5 / 3.0 / 0.5
8 0449 / 1123 / M 1711 / 2355	2.9 / 0.8 / 2.8 / 0.7	**23** 0359 / 1029 / TU 1614 / ◗ 2302	2.9 / 0.6 / 2.9 / 0.6
9 0547 / 1224 / TU 1817	2.7 / 1.0 / 2.8	**24** 0453 / 1128 / W 1721	2.7 / 0.8 / 2.8
10 0112 / 0707 / W 1349 / 1943	0.9 / 2.6 / 1.0 / 2.8	**25** 0020 / 0615 / TH 1259 / 1852	0.7 / 2.6 / 0.9 / 2.9
11 0246 / 0838 / TH 1521 / 2110	0.9 / 2.6 / 1.0 / 2.9	**26** 0200 / 0753 / F 1439 / 2027	0.7 / 2.7 / 0.8 / 3.0
12 0411 / 0957 / F 1635 / 2216	0.8 / 2.7 / 0.8 / 3.0	**27** 0334 / 0921 / SA 1604 / 2146	0.6 / 2.8 / 0.7 / 3.1
13 0511 / 1051 / SA 1726 / 2302	0.6 / 2.8 / 0.7 / 3.1	**28** 0447 / 1028 / SU 1708 / 2245	0.4 / 2.9 / 0.5 / 3.2
14 0553 / 1128 / SU 1804 / 2338	0.5 / 2.9 / 0.6 / 3.1	**29** 0544 / 1120 / M 1802 / 2335	0.2 / 3.0 / 0.4 / 3.3
15 0627 / 1200 / M 1838 / ●	0.4 / 3.0 / 0.4	**30** 0632 / 1205 / TU 1850 / ○	0.2 / 3.0 / 0.3
		31 0022 / 0716 / W 1246 / 1934	3.3 / 0.2 / 3.1 / 0.2

APRIL

Time	m	Time	m
1 0106 / 0757 / TH 1325 / 2014	3.3 / 0.2 / 3.1 / 0.2	**16** 0042 / 0726 / F 1300 / 1944	3.1 / 0.4 / 3.1 / 0.3
2 0147 / 0835 / F 1404 / 2052	3.2 / 0.3 / 3.1 / 0.2	**17** 0116 / 0759 / SA 1332 / 2020	3.1 / 0.4 / 3.1 / 0.3
3 0227 / 0910 / SA 1441 / 2127	3.2 / 0.4 / 3.1 / 0.2	**18** 0153 / 0834 / SU 1408 / 2057	3.0 / 0.4 / 3.1 / 0.3
4 0304 / 0942 / SU 1516 / 2202	3.0 / 0.4 / 3.0 / 0.3	**19** 0233 / 0910 / M 1445 / 2135	3.0 / 0.4 / 3.0 / 0.4
5 0341 / 1013 / M 1553 / 2238	2.9 / 0.6 / 2.9 / 0.5	**20** 0314 / 0946 / TU 1525 / 2216	2.9 / 0.5 / 3.0 / 0.4
6 0422 / 1050 / TU 1637 / ◗ 2325	2.7 / 0.8 / 2.9 / 0.6	**21** 0359 / 1029 / W 1613 / ◗ 2308	2.8 / 0.6 / 3.0 / 0.5
7 0514 / 1144 / W 1737	2.6 / 0.9 / 2.8	**22** 0456 / 1129 / TH 1718	2.7 / 0.7 / 3.0
8 0033 / 0626 / TH 1302 / 1857	0.8 / 2.5 / 1.0 / 2.8	**23** 0021 / 0611 / F 1252 / 1841	0.6 / 2.7 / 0.8 / 3.0
9 0200 / 0752 / F 1433 / 2022	0.9 / 2.5 / 0.9 / 2.8	**24** 0150 / 0738 / SA 1423 / 2007	0.6 / 2.7 / 0.7 / 3.0
10 0327 / 0912 / SA 1552 / 2133	0.7 / 2.6 / 0.7 / 2.9	**25** 0314 / 0858 / SU 1541 / 2121	0.5 / 2.8 / 0.6 / 3.1
11 0430 / 1010 / SU 1646 / 2221	0.5 / 2.7 / 0.6 / 3.0	**26** 0420 / 1000 / M 1641 / 2218	0.4 / 2.9 / 0.5 / 3.2
12 0512 / 1049 / M 1725 / 2258	0.4 / 2.8 / 0.5 / 3.0	**27** 0512 / 1050 / TU 1735 / 2310	0.3 / 3.0 / 0.4 / 3.2
13 0547 / 1123 / TU 1801 / 2334	0.4 / 2.9 / 0.4 / 3.1	**28** 0602 / 1137 / W 1826 / ○ 2359	0.3 / 3.1 / 0.3 / 3.2
14 0622 / 1157 / W 1835 / ●	0.3 / 3.0 / 0.4	**29** 0648 / 1221 / TH 1911	0.3 / 3.1 / 0.3
15 0009 / 0654 / TH 1229 / 1909	3.1 / 0.3 / 3.0 / 0.3	**30** 0043 / 0729 / F 1300 / 1951	3.2 / 0.3 / 3.1 / 0.3

Chart Datum: 1·68 metres below Normal Null (German reference level). HAT is 3·0 metres above Chart Datum; see 0.19

TIME ZONE −0100
Subtract 1 hour for UT
For German Summer Time add
ONE hour in **non-shaded areas**

HELGOLAND   LAT 54°11′N LONG 7°53′E
TIMES AND HEIGHTS OF HIGH AND LOW WATERS

Dates in red are SPRINGS
Dates in blue are NEAPS

YEAR 2010

MAY

Day	Time	m	Day	Time	m
1 SA	0124 / 0807 / 1338 / 2029	3.1 / 0.4 / 3.1 / 0.3	16 SU	0056 / 0738 / 1313 / 2007	3.1 / 0.4 / 3.1 / 0.3
2 SU	0202 / 0843 / 1415 / 2106	3.0 / 0.4 / 3.1 / 0.3	17 M	0141 / 0820 / 1355 / 2051	3.0 / 0.4 / 3.1 / 0.3
3 M	0242 / 0916 / 1453 / 2143	2.9 / 0.4 / 3.0 / 0.3	18 TU	0226 / 0901 / 1438 / 2134	3.0 / 0.4 / 3.1 / 0.3
4 TU	0321 / 0949 / 1531 / 2220	2.8 / 0.5 / 3.0 / 0.5	19 W	0311 / 0944 / 1523 / 2222	2.9 / 0.5 / 3.1 / 0.4
5 W	0401 / 1026 / 1612 / 2302	2.7 / 0.7 / 3.0 / 0.6	20 TH	0401 / 1033 / 1615 / 2316	2.8 / 0.6 / 3.1 / 0.4
6 TH	0446 / 1112 / 1702 / 2356 ☽	2.6 / 0.8 / 2.9 / 0.7	21 F	0458 / 1132 / 1717 ☽	2.8 / 0.6 / 3.1
7 F	0544 / 1215 / 1807	2.6 / 0.8 / 2.8	22 SA	0020 / 0605 / 1243 / 1828	0.5 / 2.7 / 0.7 / 3.1
8 SA	0107 / 0655 / 1333 / 1922	0.7 / 2.5 / 0.8 / 2.8	23 SU	0133 / 0718 / 1400 / 1944	0.5 / 2.8 / 0.7 / 3.1
9 SU	0224 / 0809 / 1450 / 2032	0.6 / 2.6 / 0.7 / 2.8	24 M	0245 / 0829 / 1511 / 2052	0.5 / 2.9 / 0.6 / 3.1
10 M	0330 / 0912 / 1551 / 2128	0.5 / 2.8 / 0.6 / 2.9	25 TU	0347 / 0928 / 1611 / 2151	0.5 / 3.0 / 0.5 / 3.1
11 TU	0418 / 1000 / 1637 / 2212	0.4 / 2.8 / 0.5 / 3.0	26 W	0440 / 1020 / 1707 / 2245	0.4 / 3.0 / 0.5 / 3.1
12 W	0459 / 1041 / 1720 / 2254	0.4 / 2.9 / 0.5 / 3.1	27 TH	0532 / 1111 / 1802 / 2337	0.5 / 3.1 / 0.4 / 3.1
13 TH	0540 / 1120 / 1802 / 2336	0.4 / 3.0 / 0.5 / 3.1	28 F	0622 / 1159 / 1851 ○	0.5 / 3.2 / 0.4
14 F ●	0620 / 1157 / 1842	0.4 / 3.1 / 0.4	29 SA	0024 / 0705 / 1240 / 1932	3.1 / 0.4 / 3.2 / 0.4
15 SA	0015 / 0658 / 1234 / 1923	3.1 / 0.4 / 3.1 / 0.4	30 SU	0104 / 0744 / 1318 / 2011	3.0 / 0.5 / 3.2 / 0.3
			31 M	0143 / 0821 / 1356 / 2050	3.0 / 0.5 / 3.2 / 0.3

JUNE

Day	Time	m	Day	Time	m
1 TU	0222 / 0856 / 1434 / 2127	2.9 / 0.5 / 3.1 / 0.4	16 W	0221 / 0857 / 1432 / 2133	3.0 / 0.4 / 3.2 / 0.3
2 W	0301 / 0929 / 1511 / 2203	2.8 / 0.5 / 3.1 / 0.5	17 TH	0307 / 0941 / 1518 / 2220	2.9 / 0.4 / 3.2 / 0.3
3 TH	0339 / 1004 / 1548 / 2239	2.8 / 0.6 / 3.1 / 0.6	18 F	0356 / 1031 / 1609 / 2312	2.9 / 0.5 / 3.2 / 0.4
4 F ☽	0418 / 1043 / 1629 / 2320	2.7 / 0.7 / 3.0 / 0.6	19 SA ☽	0450 / 1126 / 1706	2.8 / 0.5 / 3.2
5 SA	0501 / 1131 / 1717	2.6 / 0.7 / 2.9	20 SU	0006 / 0548 / 1225 / 1808	0.4 / 2.8 / 0.6 / 3.1
6 SU	0011 / 0555 / 1231 / 1817	0.6 / 2.6 / 0.8 / 2.8	21 M	0104 / 0649 / 1329 / 1915	0.5 / 2.8 / 0.6 / 3.1
7 M	0113 / 0658 / 1339 / 1923	0.6 / 2.6 / 0.7 / 2.8	22 TU	0208 / 0754 / 1438 / 2022	0.6 / 2.9 / 0.7 / 3.1
8 TU	0218 / 0804 / 1446 / 2027	0.6 / 2.7 / 0.7 / 2.9	23 W	0313 / 0857 / 1544 / 2126	0.7 / 3.0 / 0.7 / 3.1
9 W	0317 / 0904 / 1545 / 2123	0.5 / 2.8 / 0.6 / 2.9	24 TH	0414 / 0955 / 1645 / 2226	0.7 / 3.1 / 0.6 / 3.1
10 TH	0410 / 0956 / 1639 / 2215	0.5 / 2.9 / 0.6 / 3.0	25 F	0510 / 1050 / 1743 / 2320	0.7 / 3.1 / 0.6 / 3.1
11 F	0501 / 1044 / 1731 / 2306	0.5 / 3.0 / 0.6 / 3.1	26 SA ○	0601 / 1141 / 1834	0.6 / 3.2 / 0.5
12 SA ●	0551 / 1129 / 1820 / 2355	0.5 / 3.1 / 0.5 / 3.1	27 SU	0008 / 0646 / 1225 / 1917	3.0 / 0.6 / 3.2 / 0.4
13 SU	0637 / 1214 / 1909	0.5 / 3.2 / 0.4	28 M	0049 / 0726 / 1303 / 1956	3.0 / 0.5 / 3.2 / 0.4
14 M	0043 / 0725 / 1300 / 1959	3.1 / 0.5 / 3.2 / 0.4	29 TU	0128 / 0804 / 1340 / 2034	3.0 / 0.5 / 3.2 / 0.4
15 TU	0132 / 0812 / 1347 / 2047	3.1 / 0.5 / 3.3 / 0.3	30 W	0204 / 0839 / 1415 / 2108	2.9 / 0.5 / 3.2 / 0.4

JULY

Day	Time	m	Day	Time	m
1 TH	0239 / 0909 / 1448 / 2140	2.9 / 0.5 / 3.2 / 0.5	16 F	0255 / 0933 / 1506 / 2207	3.0 / 0.3 / 3.3 / 0.2
2 F	0312 / 0940 / 1520 / 2212	2.8 / 0.5 / 3.1 / 0.6	17 SA	0340 / 1018 / 1553 / 2252	2.9 / 0.4 / 3.2 / 0.4
3 SA	0346 / 1015 / 1555 / 2245	2.8 / 0.6 / 3.1 / 0.6	18 SU ☽	0428 / 1050 / 1645 / 2338	2.9 / 0.5 / 3.2 / 0.5
4 SU ☽	0421 / 1051 / 1633 / 2320	2.8 / 0.6 / 3.0 / 0.6	19 M	0519 / 1156 / 1740	2.9 / 0.6 / 3.1
5 M	0501 / 1135 / 1718	2.7 / 0.7 / 2.9	20 TU	0027 / 0613 / 1253 / 1842	0.6 / 2.9 / 0.7 / 3.0
6 TU	0006 / 0552 / 1231 / 1817	0.6 / 2.7 / 0.8 / 2.8	21 W	0128 / 0717 / 1403 / 1952	0.8 / 2.9 / 0.8 / 3.0
7 W	0106 / 0656 / 1341 / 1926	0.7 / 2.7 / 0.8 / 2.8	22 TH	0241 / 0828 / 1520 / 2106	0.9 / 3.0 / 0.8 / 3.0
8 TH	0216 / 0807 / 1454 / 2037	0.7 / 2.8 / 0.7 / 2.9	23 F	0353 / 0936 / 1631 / 2213	0.9 / 3.1 / 0.7 / 3.0
9 F	0324 / 0914 / 1602 / 2143	0.7 / 2.9 / 0.7 / 2.9	24 SA	0454 / 1035 / 1729 / 2309	0.8 / 3.2 / 0.7 / 3.0
10 SA	0429 / 1015 / 1706 / 2245	0.6 / 3.0 / 0.6 / 3.0	25 SU	0545 / 1126 / 1819 / 2354	0.8 / 3.2 / 0.6 / 3.0
11 SU ●	0529 / 1109 / 1804 / 2341	0.6 / 3.1 / 0.5 / 3.1	26 M ○	0630 / 1209 / 1901	0.7 / 3.3 / 0.5
12 M	0624 / 1159 / 1858	0.5 / 3.3 / 0.4	27 TU	0034 / 0711 / 1247 / 1939	3.0 / 0.6 / 3.2 / 0.5
13 TU	0033 / 0715 / 1249 / 1951	3.1 / 0.5 / 3.3 / 0.3	28 W	0110 / 0747 / 1321 / 2014	3.0 / 0.5 / 3.2 / 0.5
14 W	0123 / 0804 / 1337 / 2040	3.1 / 0.4 / 3.3 / 0.3	29 TH	0142 / 0819 / 1351 / 2044	3.0 / 0.5 / 3.2 / 0.5
15 TH	0211 / 0850 / 1422 / 2124	3.0 / 0.3 / 3.3 / 0.2	30 F	0211 / 0845 / 1420 / 2111	2.9 / 0.4 / 3.2 / 0.5
			31 SA	0240 / 0913 / 1450 / 2140	2.9 / 0.6 / 3.1 / 0.6

AUGUST

Day	Time	m	Day	Time	m
1 SU	0312 / 0945 / 1523 / 2210	2.9 / 0.5 / 3.1 / 0.6	16 M ◐	0358 / 1039 / 1618 / 2303	3.0 / 0.5 / 3.2 / 0.6
2 M	0344 / 1018 / 1556 / 2238	2.9 / 0.5 / 3.0 / 0.6	17 TU	0443 / 1123 / 1708 / 2348	2.9 / 0.6 / 3.0 / 0.8
3 TU	0417 / 1050 / 1632 / 2311 ◑	2.8 / 0.6 / 2.9 / 0.7	18 W	0534 / 1216 / 1807	2.9 / 0.7 / 2.9
4 W	0457 / 1135 / 1722	2.8 / 0.8 / 2.8	19 TH	0047 / 0637 / 1328 / 1922	0.9 / 2.8 / 0.9 / 2.8
5 TH	0005 / 0556 / 1244 / 1835	0.8 / 2.7 / 0.8 / 2.8	20 F	0206 / 0757 / 1456 / 2046	1.0 / 2.9 / 0.9 / 2.8
6 F	0122 / 0716 / 1410 / 2000	0.8 / 2.7 / 0.8 / 2.8	21 SA	0331 / 0917 / 1617 / 2202	1.0 / 3.0 / 0.8 / 2.9
7 SA	0248 / 0839 / 1534 / 2121	0.8 / 2.8 / 0.7 / 2.9	22 SU	0441 / 1022 / 1717 / 2258	0.9 / 3.1 / 0.7 / 2.9
8 SU	0406 / 0953 / 1648 / 2231	0.7 / 3.0 / 0.6 / 3.0	23 M	0531 / 1110 / 1802 / 2338	0.8 / 3.2 / 0.6 / 3.0
9 M	0514 / 1054 / 1751 / 2330	0.7 / 3.2 / 0.5 / 3.1	24 TU ○	0612 / 1148 / 1839	0.7 / 3.2 / 0.6
10 TU ●	0611 / 1146 / 1846	0.6 / 3.3 / 0.5	25 W	0013 / 0650 / 1223 / 1914	3.0 / 0.5 / 3.2 / 0.5
11 W	0020 / 0702 / 1234 / 1936	3.1 / 0.5 / 3.4 / 0.3	26 TH	0046 / 0723 / 1255 / 1945	3.0 / 0.5 / 3.2 / 0.4
12 TH	0107 / 0750 / 1321 / 2023	3.1 / 0.4 / 3.4 / 0.2	27 F	0115 / 0752 / 1324 / 2013	3.0 / 0.4 / 3.2 / 0.5
13 F	0152 / 0835 / 1405 / 2105	3.1 / 0.3 / 3.3 / 0.2	28 SA	0142 / 0818 / 1352 / 2038	3.0 / 0.4 / 3.2 / 0.5
14 SA	0235 / 0916 / 1448 / 2144	3.0 / 0.3 / 3.3 / 0.3	29 SU	0208 / 0845 / 1421 / 2107	3.0 / 0.4 / 3.1 / 0.5
15 SU	0316 / 0957 / 1532 / 2223	3.0 / 0.4 / 3.2 / 0.4	30 M	0238 / 0917 / 1454 / 2137	3.0 / 0.5 / 3.0 / 0.6
			31 TU	0310 / 0949 / 1527 / 2203	3.0 / 0.6 / 3.0 / 0.7

Chart Datum: 1·68 metres below Normal Null (German reference level). HAT is 3·0 metres above Chart Datum; see 0.19

»» **FREE** monthly updates from ««
www.reedsalmanac.co.uk

WGS84 DATUM

TIME ZONE -0100
Subtract 1 hour for UT
For German Summer Time add
ONE hour in **non-shaded areas**

HELGOLAND   LAT 54°11'N LONG 7°53'E
TIMES AND HEIGHTS OF HIGH AND LOW WATERS

Dates in red are SPRINGS
Dates in blue are NEAPS

YEAR 2010

SEPTEMBER

Time	m		Time	m
1 0341	2.9	**16**	0456	2.9
1018	0.7		1142	0.8
W 1600	2.9	TH 1732	2.7
☽ 2232	0.7			
2 0417	2.8	**17**	0006	1.0
1057	0.8		0559	2.8
TH 1647	2.8	F 1252	0.9
2322	0.9		1848	2.6
3 0515	2.8	**18**	0127	1.1
1205	0.9		0721	2.8
F 1801	2.7	SA 1423	1.0
			2018	2.7
4 0044	1.0	**19**	0259	1.1
0640	2.8		0849	3.0
SA 1339	0.9	SU 1552	0.9
1935	2.7		2140	2.8
5 0221	0.9	**20**	0417	1.0
0813	2.9		1000	3.1
SU 1514	0.8	M 1656	0.7
2105	2.8		2236	2.9
6 0348	0.8	**21**	0509	0.8
0934	3.0		1046	3.1
M 1633	0.6	TU 1735	0.6
2217	2.9		2312	2.9
7 0458	0.7	**22**	0545	0.7
1037	3.2		1119	3.2
TU 1735	0.4	W 1807	0.5
2313	3.0		2342	3.0
8 0554	0.5	**23**	0619	0.6
1128	3.3		1152	3.1
W 1827	0.3	TH 1840	0.5
●		○		
9 0000	3.1	**24**	0014	3.0
0643	0.4		0651	0.5
TH 1215	3.3	F 1225	3.1
1913	0.2		1911	0.5
10 0044	3.1	**25**	0045	3.0
0729	0.3		0722	0.5
F 1300	3.3	SA 1255	3.1
1957	0.3		1939	0.5
11 0126	3.1	**26**	0113	3.0
0813	0.3		0751	0.5
SA 1345	3.3	SU 1325	3.1
2039	0.3		2007	0.5
12 0208	3.1	**27**	0140	3.0
0854	0.3		0821	0.5
SU 1427	3.3	M 1356	3.1
2116	0.4		2037	0.5
13 0248	3.1	**28**	0209	3.0
0933	0.4		0853	0.5
M 1508	3.2	TU 1429	3.0
2152	0.5		2108	0.6
14 0327	3.0	**29**	0242	3.0
1011	0.5		0926	0.5
TU 1550	3.1	W 1505	3.0
2228	0.7		2137	0.7
15 0408	3.0	**30**	0315	3.0
1052	0.6		0958	0.7
W 1636	2.9	TH 1542	2.9
☽ 2310	0.9		2209	0.8

OCTOBER

Time	m		Time	m
1 0355	2.9	**16**	0523	2.9
1039	0.8		1216	0.9
F 1631	2.8	SA 1811	2.6
☽ 2301	1.0			
2 0454	2.9	**17**	0042	1.1
1147	0.9		0639	2.8
SA 1744	2.7	SU 1339	1.0
			1934	2.6
3 0022	1.1	**18**	0211	1.1
0618	2.9		0804	2.9
SU 1320	0.9	M 1506	0.9
1917	2.7		2055	2.7
4 0200	1.0	**19**	0333	1.0
0751	3.0		0917	3.0
M 1456	0.8	TU 1613	0.8
2047	2.8		2155	2.8
5 0328	0.9	**20**	0430	0.8
0913	3.1		1007	3.0
TU 1613	0.6	W 1655	0.6
2157	2.9		2234	2.9
6 0435	0.7	**21**	0507	0.7
1015	3.2		1042	3.1
W 1711	0.4	TH 1726	0.6
2249	3.0		2306	3.0
7 0529	0.5	**22**	0541	0.6
1105	3.3		1117	3.1
TH 1800	0.4	F 1800	0.5
● 2335	3.1		2339	3.1
8 0619	0.4	**23**	0617	0.6
1153	3.3		1153	3.1
F 1846	0.3	SA 1834	0.5
		○		
9 0018	3.1	**24**	0013	3.1
0705	0.4		0651	0.5
SA 1239	3.3	SU 1227	3.1
1929	0.4		1907	0.5
10 0100	3.2	**25**	0045	3.1
0749	0.4		0726	0.5
SU 1323	3.3	M 1300	3.1
2010	0.5		1939	0.6
11 0141	3.2	**26**	0116	3.1
0830	0.4		0801	0.5
M 1405	3.2	TU 1336	3.0
2049	0.5		2013	0.6
12 0221	3.1	**27**	0148	3.1
0910	0.4		0837	0.5
TU 1445	3.1	W 1413	3.0
2124	0.6		2047	0.6
13 0300	3.1	**28**	0223	3.1
0947	0.5		0912	0.6
W 1525	2.9	TH 1452	2.9
2158	0.7		2122	0.7
14 0339	3.0	**29**	0301	3.1
1026	0.6		0950	0.7
TH 1609	2.8	F 1535	2.9
☽ 2237	0.9		2201	0.8
15 0425	2.9	**30**	0346	3.1
1113	0.8		1037	0.8
F 1702	2.6	SA 1626	2.8
2329	1.0		☽ 2254	1.0
		31	0445	3.0
			1142	0.8
		SU 1734	2.7

NOVEMBER

Time	m		Time	m
1 0009	1.0	**16**	0109	1.1
0602	3.0		0701	2.9
M 1305	0.8	TU 1359	0.9
1858	2.8		1948	2.6
2 0138	1.0	**17**	0227	1.0
0728	3.1		0814	2.9
TU 1431	0.8	W 1508	0.8
2021	2.9		2054	2.7
3 0301	0.9	**18**	0332	0.9
0845	3.1		0913	3.0
W 1543	0.6	TH 1559	0.7
2129	3.0		2145	2.9
4 0406	0.7	**19**	0421	0.8
0948	3.2		0959	3.0
TH 1639	0.5	F 1640	0.7
2221	3.0		2226	3.0
5 0501	0.6	**20**	0502	0.7
1041	3.2		1040	3.1
F 1730	0.5	SA 1720	0.7
2308	3.1		2305	3.1
6 0554	0.5	**21**	0544	0.7
1131	3.3		1121	3.1
SA 1819	0.5	SU 1800	0.7
● 2354	3.2	○ 2343	3.1
7 0643	0.5	**22**	0624	0.7
1219	3.2		1201	3.1
SU 1904	0.5	M 1839	0.6
8 0037	3.2	**23**	0020	3.2
0727	0.5		0705	0.6
M 1302	3.2	TU 1241	3.1
1944	0.6		1918	0.7
9 0117	3.2	**24**	0058	3.2
0808	0.5		0747	0.6
TU 1344	3.1	W 1323	3.1
2023	0.6		1958	0.7
10 0158	3.2	**25**	0136	3.2
0849	0.5		0829	0.6
W 1425	3.0	TH 1405	3.0
2100	0.6		2037	0.6
11 0238	3.1	**26**	0215	3.2
0928	0.5		0908	0.6
TH 1505	2.9	F 1446	3.0
2134	0.7		2115	0.7
12 0318	3.1	**27**	0255	3.2
1006	0.6		0950	0.6
F 1547	2.8	SA 1531	2.9
2211	0.8		2159	0.8
13 0359	3.1	**28**	0341	3.2
1048	0.8		1039	0.7
SA 1632	2.7	SU 1622	2.9
☽ 2256	1.0	☽ 2252	0.9
14 0448	3.0	**29**	0437	3.2
1139	0.9		1136	0.7
SU 1728	2.6	M 1723	2.8
2355	1.1		2356	0.9
15 0549	2.9	**30**	0545	3.1
1244	1.0		1243	0.8
M 1835	2.6	TU 1834	2.8

DECEMBER

Time	m		Time	m
1 0111	1.0	**16**	0110	1.0
0700	3.1		0659	2.9
W 1357	0.8	TH 1349	0.9
1948	2.9		1940	2.7
2 0227	0.9	**17**	0222	1.0
0814	3.2		0807	2.9
TH 1507	0.8	F 1453	0.9
2055	3.0		2045	2.8
3 0335	0.8	**18**	0326	0.9
0920	3.2		0909	2.9
F 1608	0.7	SA 1550	0.8
2153	3.1		2142	3.0
4 0435	0.7	**19**	0422	0.8
1018	3.2		1003	3.0
SA 1704	0.7	SU 1642	0.8
2246	3.1		2231	3.1
5 0533	0.7	**20**	0513	0.8
1113	3.2		1053	3.1
SU 1756	0.7	M 1732	0.8
● 2336	3.2		2316	3.2
6 0625	0.6	**21**	0602	0.7
1203	3.2		1141	3.1
M 1843	0.7	TU 1818	0.7
		○		
7 0020	3.2	**22**	0000	3.2
0710	0.6		0649	0.6
TU 1246	3.1	W 1227	3.1
1924	0.7		1904	0.7
8 0100	3.3	**23**	0044	3.3
0751	0.5		0737	0.6
W 1327	3.1	TH 1313	3.1
2003	0.7		1949	0.7
9 0141	3.3	**24**	0128	3.3
0832	0.6		0824	0.5
TH 1408	3.0	F 1359	3.1
2041	0.7		2031	0.6
10 0221	3.2	**25**	0210	3.3
0912	0.6		0906	0.5
F 1448	2.9	SA 1441	3.0
2115	0.7		2111	0.6
11 0258	3.2	**26**	0249	3.3
0948	0.6		0948	0.5
SA 1524	2.9	SU 1524	2.9
2148	0.7		2155	0.6
12 0335	3.2	**27**	0333	3.3
1023	0.8		1033	0.6
SU 1601	2.8	M 1612	2.9
2225	0.9		2244	0.7
13 0413	3.1	**28**	0425	3.3
1100	0.9		1122	0.6
M 1642	2.7	TU 1705	2.9
☽ 2308	1.0	☽ 2338	0.8
14 0458	3.0	**29**	0523	3.2
1145	0.9		1215	0.7
TU 1732	2.7	W 1804	2.9
15 0003	1.0	**30**	0039	0.9
0553	2.9		0628	3.1
W 1242	0.9	TH 1318	0.8
1832	2.7		1910	2.9
		31	0150	0.9
			0740	3.0
		F 1429	0.9
			2021	3.0

Chart Datum: 1·68 metres below Normal Null (German reference level). HAT is 3·0 metres above Chart Datum; see 0.19

Netherlands

2.7 DELFZIJL

Groningen 53°18'·99N 07°00'·45E ✸✸✸◊◊✿✿

CHARTS AC 3631, 3632; DYC 1812.6; Zeekaart 1555; Imray C26; ANWB A

TIDES –0025 Dover; ML 2·1; Duration 0605

Standard Port HELGOLAND (←)

Times				Height (metres)			
High Water		Low Water		MHWS	MHWN	MLWN	MLWS
0200	0700	0200	0800	2·7	2·4	0·5	0·0
1400	1900	1400	2000				
Differences DELFZIJL							
+0020	–0005	–0040	0000	+1·0	+1·0	+0·3	+0·4
EEMSHAVEN							
–0025	–0045	–0115	–0045	+0·5	+0·5	+0·3	+0·4
HUIBERTGAT							
–0150	–0150	–0210	–0210	0·0	0·0	+0·2	+0·3
SCHIERMONNIKOOG							
–0120	–0130	–0240	–0220	+0·2	+0·1	+0·2	+0·3

SHELTER Good in Handelshaven, where at Neptunus Marina a floating jetty acts as a wavebreak.

NAVIGATION From the E or N, WPT 53°38'·96N 06°27'·06E (Riffgat SWM buoy) 121°/4·2M to Nos 11/12 buoys.

From the W, WPT 53°36'·93N 06°19'·39E (Westereems SWM buoy) 091°/8·2M to join Riffgat at Nos 11/12 buoys.

Huibertgat lies parallel to and S of Westereems. It is marked by unlit R/W buoys H1-H5, least depths about 9m but prone to silt.

From Nos 11/12 buoys follow the well marked/lit river channel for approx 25M via Randzelgat or Alte Eems, Dukegat and Ostfriesisches Gatje to enter Zeehavenkanaal abeam Knock lt ho. Beware strong cross tides at the ent (Lat/Long under title).

INLAND ROUTE TO IJSSELMEER See 2.1A and 2.15.

LIGHTS AND MARKS See chartlet and 2.3. From the river, appr ldg lts 203°, both Iso 4s. Hbr ent, FG on W arm and FR on E arm (in fog, FY). Zeehavenkanaal, 2·5M long, has Fl G lts to N and Fl R to S. Entry sigs on both piers: 2 ● = No entry, unless cleared by Hbr office on VHF Ch 14.

R/T All vessels, except leisure craft, must call *Delfzijl Radar* VHF Ch 03 (H24) for VTS, co-ordinated with Ems Traffic. *Port Control* is Ch 66. *Eemskanaal lock* Ch 26. Traffic, weather and tidal info is broadcast every even H+10 on Ch 14 in Dutch and English on request. *Ems Traffic* Ch 15, 18, 20 & 21 (H24) broadcasts every H + 50 weather and tidal info in German, and gale warnings for coastal waters between Die Ems and Die Weser. See also 2.24.

TELEPHONE (Code 0596) Port HM 640400; HM 't Dok 616560; Eemskanaal Sea locks 613293; CG (Police) 613831; ⊜ 0598 696560; Police 112; Ⓗ 644444; Brit Consul (020) 6764343.

FACILITIES Neptunus Yacht Hbr (4·4m, 53°19'·80N 06°55'·86E) ☎ 615004, €0.24 per gross ton, D (not 0900-1700), Bar, M. **Yacht Hbr 't Dok** at N end of the Old Eemskanaal in 4m, AB €0.41, D. Note: Eems (Dutch) = Ems (German). **Ems Canal** L, FW, AB. **Motor Boat Club Abel Tasman** ☎ 616560 Bar, M, D, 🅿, 🛒. **Services:** CH, ACA, DYC Agent, ME, El, Gaz. **Town** P, D, 🍴, R, Bar, Ⓑ, ✉, ⇌, ✈ (Groningen/Eelde). Ferry: 2.21 & .22.

MINOR HARBOUR 1·3M ESE OF DELFZIJL ENTRANCE

TERMUNTERZIJL Groningen, **53°18'·20N 07°02'·21E.** AC 3632; Zeekaart 1555; DYC 1812.6. HW –0025 on Dover (UT); use Differences Delfzijl. Ent (1·3M ESE of Delfzijl ent) is close to BW13 SHM buoy Fl G 5s (53°18'·63N 07°02'·32E); thence chan marked by 7 R and 7 G unlit bns. Yachts berth in Vissershaven (0·9m), stbd of ent, or on pontoons (1m) to port of ent, €0.36. HM ☎ (0596) 601891 (Apr-Sept), VHF Ch 09, FW, ⟍⟍, Bar, R.

COMMERCIAL HARBOUR AT MOUTH OF THE EEMS (EMS)

EEMSHAVEN, Groningen, **53°27'·66N 06°50'·27E.** AC 3631, 3632, Zeekaart 1555, DYC 1812.5/.6. HW –0100 (approx) on Dover. Eemshaven is a modern commercial port, but may be used by

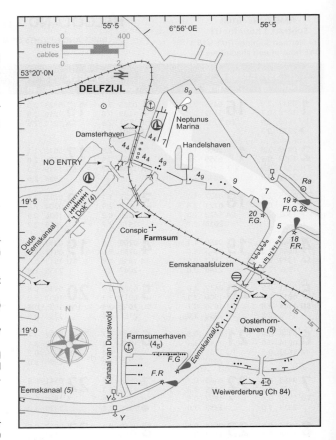

yachts as a port of refuge. Outer appr via Hubertgat (see 2.6) or Westereems; inner appr via Randzelgat or Alte Eems, passing the outer anchorage for merchant ships. From the nearest buoy, A16 PHM Fl R 4s, the hbr ent bears 137°/1·6M. Call *Eemshaven Radar* Ch 01 (H24) for VTS info; and *Eemshaven Port Control* Ch 66 for info and clearance to enter.

There are many wind turbines S, W and NW of the port. A power stn chy (128m high) is conspic 2M ESE of the port; as are white-roofed bldgs at the port. Enter on 175°, ldg lts Iso 4s, between mole hds, FG and FR. Inner ldg lts, both Iso R 4s, leads 195° to S end of port. Here yachts turn 90° stbd into Emmahaven, marked by FG and FR, and berth on floating jetty in SW corner. HM ☎ (Delfzijl Port Authority) (0596) 640400; ⊜ 0598 696560; other ☎ numbers see Delfzijl. No special facilities for yachts, but dues are €0.24 per gross ton.

MINOR HARBOUR IN THE WEST FRISIAN ISLANDS

SCHIERMONNIKOOG, Friesland, **53°28'·07N 06°10'·05E.** AC 3761; Zeekaart 1458; DYC 1812.3. HW –0150 on Dover. See 2.7. WPT 53°32'·00N 05°58'·54E, [WG SWM buoy, Iso 8s, Racon Z], 150°/1·1M to WG1 SHM buoy, VQ G, at the ent to Westgat; buoyed/lit, but in bad weather dangerous due to shoals (3·8m) at seaward end. Follow Westgat chan into Zoutkamperlaag; leave at Z4 & Z6-GVS buoys to enter buoyed Gat van Schiermonnikoog (GVS).

From GVS16-R1 buoy a drying chan, marked by perches/withies, runs 1M N to small yacht hbr (1·3-1·5m). Access HW –2 to +1, with 1·5m max depth at HW in apprs. Picturesque, but very full in high season; not cheap, ie €1.27. A ferry pier is 1·26M E of the yacht hbr. HM VHF Ch 31; ☎ (0519) 51544 (May-Sept). Facilities: FW, AC.

Note: Lt ho Fl (4) 20s, R twr, is conspic 1.35M NNW of yacht hbr. The CG at the lt ho gives radar surveillance of the Terschelling/German Bight TSS out to 48M radius and coordinates local SAR operations. It monitors VHF Ch 00, **05**, 16, 67 and 73 (all H24); ☎ 0519 531247.

THE WEST FRISIAN ISLANDS

This chain of islands stretches from the River Ems estuary W and SSW for some 85M along the Dutch coast to Den Helder (AC 1632, 1633). The islands have similar characteristics – being long, low and narrow, with the major axis parallel to the coast. Texel is the largest and, with Vlieland and Terschelling, lies furthest offshore.

Between the islands, narrow channels (*zeegat* in Dutch, *Seegat* in German) give access to/from the North Sea. Most of these channels are shallow for at least part of their length, and in these shoal areas a dangerous sea builds up in a strong onshore wind against the outgoing (ebb) tide. The Westerems and the Zeegaten van Terschelling and van Texel are safe for yachts in SW–NE winds up to force 8. All the others are unsafe in strong onshore winds.

▶ *The flood stream along this coast is E-going, so it starts to run in through the zeegaten progressively from W to E. Where the tide meets behind each island, as it flows in first at the W end and a little later at the E end, a bank is formed, called a wad (Dutch) or Watt (German).* ◀

These banks between the islands and the coast are major obstacles to E/W progress inside the islands. The chans are narrow and winding, marked by buoys and/or withies (↟ ↡) in the shallower parts, and they mostly dry; so that it is essential to time the tide correctly.

This is an area most suited to shallow-draft yachts, particularly flat bottomed or with bilge keels, centreboards or legs, that can take the ground easily. Whilst the zeegaten are described briefly below, the many channels inside the islands and across the Waddenzee are mentioned only for general orientation.

DELFZIJL TO AMELAND

The Ems estuary (AC 1633, 3631) flows seaward past the SW side of the German island of Borkum. It gives access to **Delfzijl**, **Termunterzijl** and **Emden**. Hubertgat, which runs parallel to and S of the main Westerems chan, is slightly more direct when bound to/from the W, but in both these chans there is a dangerous sea in strong NW winds over the ebb. Hubertgat is now sparsely buoyed and unlit, but is quite acceptable to yachts. ▶ *The E-going (flood) stream begins at HW Helgoland +0530, and the W-going (ebb) stream begins at HW Helgoland –0030, sp rates 1·5kn.* ◀

Friesche Zeegat (DYC 1812.3 & .9), between Schiermonnikoog and Ameland, contains two channels: Westgat marked by 'WG' buoys and Plaatgat marked by 'PL' buoys. In strong winds the sea breaks across the whole estuary. Westgat trends SE past Wierumergronden and N7-FA-1 platform, the S past Het Rif and Engelsmanplaat (a prominent sandbank) into Zoutkamperlaag, the main channel (buoys prefixed 'Z') to **Lauwersoog**. Here locks give access to the Lauwersmeer and inland waterways. Plaatgat is a buoyed but unlit lesser channel which trends SW passing close NW of **Schiermonnikoog** then merging with Westgat at WG14-PL13.

Zeegat van Ameland (DYC 1811.6), between Ameland and Terschelling, is fronted by the sandbank of Bornrif about 3M offshore. The main entrance is also called Westgat, with buoys prefixed by letters 'WA', all unlit except WA12 QR. The channel runs ESE close N of Terschelling, and divides into Boschgat (BG) at the E end of West Terschelling and Borndiep (BB) the wider, deeper channel. This skirts the W end of Ameland and at WA22-WG1 buoy gives access via the Molengat to the small ferry port and yacht hbr at Nes.

▶ *In Westgat the flood stream begins at HW Helgoland +0425, and the ebb stream at HW Helgoland –0150, sp rates 2kn.* ◀ A dangerous sea develops in strong onshore winds.

2.8 LAUWERSOOG

Friesland, **53°24'·68N 06°12'·04E**

CHARTS AC 1632/3; Imray C26; Zeekaart 1458; DYC 1812.3

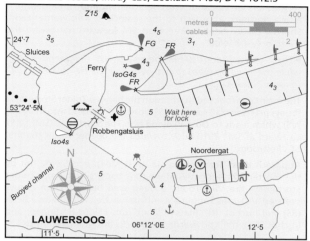

TIDES HW –0150 on Dover; ML 1·7m. See 2.12

SHELTER Outer hbr suffers swell in bad weather; complete shelter in Noordergat Marina.

NAVIGATION See Schiermonnikoog (2.7); continue to Z15 SHM buoy for hbr ent. Await lock on pontoons at W end of FV basin. Lock hrs (LT) **May-Sep**: Mon-Fri 0700-2000 (Sat 1900); Sun 0900-1200, 1400-1830. **Oct-Apr**: Mon-Fri 0700-1800 (Sat 1700); Sun shut. A firing range 1·5m ENE of hbr ent is marked by Fl Y 10s bcns, alternating W/R when the range is active; info broadcasts on Ch 71.

LIGHTS AND MARKS See chartlet and 2.3. Four wind turbines on the N bkwtr are conspic.

R/T Hbr VHF Ch 11; Lock Ch 84; Range broadcast Ch 71.

TELEPHONE (Code 0519) Port HM 349023; Lock 349043; ⊜ 0598 696560.

FACILITIES **Noordergat Marina**, ☎ 349040; (2·4m-2·8m). Ⓥs berth on first pontoon, €1.00. Gaz, BY, D (E end of hbr); P (ferry terminal, W end of hbr), Bar, R, ⟐, YC.
The Staande Mastroute (2.1A, Delfzijl-Harlingen) can be entered from the Lauwersmeer at Dokkum.

OTHER HARBOURS IN THE LAUWERSMEER

ZOUTKAMP, Groningen, **53°20'·38N 06°17'·55E**. AC 2593, Zeekaarten 1458, DYC 1812·4; non-tidal. Appr down the Zoutkamperril (2·6-4·5m); approx 2ca before lock/bridge, Hunzegat marina (1·5-2·1m) is to port. ☎ (0595) 402875, SC, Slip. Beyond the lock (FR lts) and close to port is Oude Binnenhaven marina (2m), €3.63; C, ME, El, ✕, C (20 ton), BH.

Town D, P, SM, Gaz, ✉, R, ⟐, Dr.

OOSTMAHORN, Friesland, **53°22'·94N 06°09'·63E**. AC 2593, Zeekaarten 1458, DYC 1812·4. Non-tidal hbr on W side of Lauwersmeer; lock in as for Lauwersoog. Floating bns with Y flags mark fishing areas. Main hbr with FR and FG lts at ent has marina (2·2-3·0m). VHF Ch 10. HM ☎ (0519) 321445; €0.91, D, P, ⚓, Gaz, R, ⟐, C, BY, BH (15T). Approx 450m to the SSE, next to the Voorm Veerhaven (ferry hbr), is a tiny marina with 1·5-2m.

AMELAND

NES, Friesland, 53°26'·22N 05°46'·53E. AC 2593, Zeekaart 1458, DYC 1811.10 & .2. HW –0055 on Dover; ML 1·6m; Duration 0625. See 2.12. Shelter from all but E/S winds. Appr from WA SWM buoy via Westgat, Borndiep and Molengat to VA2-R1 SCM lt perch, VQ(6) + L Fl 10s. Lts: see 2.3. Beware sandbanks. **Yacht hbr** ('t Leije Gat) HM ☎ (0515) 32159. 140 berths, €0.80. L Fl R 8s and L Fl G 8s piles at ent. Yacht pontoons at N end of hbr (0·8m) beyond ferry terminal; W side dries to soft mud. **Facilities:** Gaz, YC.

TERSCHELLING TO TEXEL AND DEN HELDER

Zeegat Het Vlie, aka Zeegat van Terschelling (AC 112 and DYC 1811.4, .5 and .9), between Terschelling and Vlieland, gives access to the hbrs of **Vlieland, West Terschelling and Harlingen**; it is also a northern approach to the sealock at Kornwerder-zand. Shallow banks extend more than 5M seaward narrowing the ITZ to only 4M wide.

▶*The E-going (flood) stream begins at HW Helgoland +0325, while the W-going (ebb) stream begins at HW Helgoland −0230, sp rates 2·5kn.*◀

The main chan (buoyed/lit) through the banks is Zuider Stortemelk (buoys prefixed 'ZS') running ESE close N of Vlieland into Vliesloot (VS) which leads to **Oost Vlieland** hbr. The Stortemelk (SM) forks eastward at SM1-ZS10 buoy towards the deeper wider channel of Vliestroom.

Approach **West Terschelling** via West Meep and Slenk, **not** by the shorter Schuitengat Zuid which is badly silted. From Zuider Stortemelk the Vliestroom, a deep well buoyed chan (buoys prefixed 'VL'), runs S about 4M until its junction with Blauwe Slenk (BS) and Inschot (IN). Blauwe Slenk runs ESE to **Harlingen**; and Inschot SE to the Kornwerderzand locks into the **IJsselmeer**.

Eierlandsche Gat (DYC 1811.7), between Vlieland and Texel, consists of dangerous shoals between which run very shallow and unmarked chans, only used by fishermen.

Zeegat van Texel (AC 1546) lies between Texel and Den Helder, and gives access to the **Waddenzee**, the tidal part of the former Zuider Zee. Haaksgronden shoals extend 5M seaward. The 3 appr channels are: Molengat from the N along the Texel shore; Westgat unmarked through centre of shoals, where the stream

sets across the chan, is only suitable for passage in good weather and in daylight; and from the SSW the well marked/lit main chan Schulpengat, buoys prefixed 'S'; but strong SW winds cause rough seas against ▶*the SW-going (ebb) stream which begins at HW Helgoland −0330, while the NE-going (flood) stream begins at HW Helgoland +0325, sp rates 1·5kn.*◀

Molengat is marked by 'MG' buoys, but strong winds between W and N raise a bad sea. If approaching from the NW or NE the Molengat is always the best route unless the weather is exceptionally bad.

▶*In Molengat the N-going (ebb) stream begins at HW Helgoland −0145, and the S-going (flood) stream at HW Helgoland +0425, sp rates 1·25kn.*◀

From the N the Schulpengat involves a southerly deviation of approx 15M and leads W of the very dangerous Zuider Haaks which should be avoided in bad weather.

E of **Den Helder** and the Marsdiep, the flood makes in three main directions through the SW Waddenzee:

- to E and SE through Malzwin and Wierbalg to **Den Oever** (where the lock into IJsselmeer is only available during daylight hours on working days); thence NE along the Afsluitdijk, and then N towards Harlingen;

- to NE and E through Texelstroom and Doove Balg towards the Pollen flats; and

- from Texelstroom, NE and N through Scheurrak, Omdraai and Oude Vlie, where it meets the flood stream from Zeegat van Terschelling. The ebb runs in reverse. The **Kornwerderzand** locks (available H24), near NE end of Afsluitdijk, also give access to the IJsselmeer.

2.9 HET VLIE (ZEEGAT VAN TERSCHELLING)

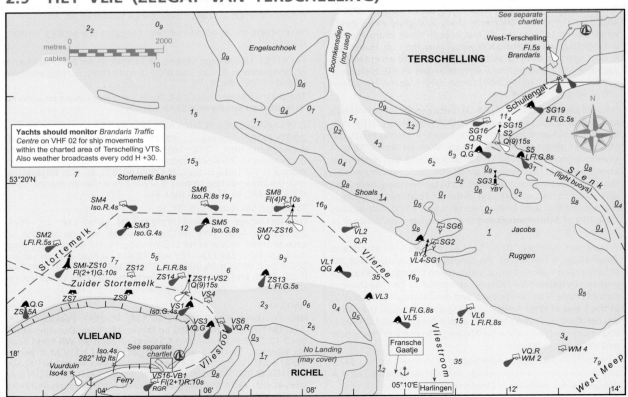

2.10   WEST TERSCHELLING

West Frisian Islands **53°21'·26N 05°13'·13E** ✵✵✵✵◊◊◊❀❀

CHARTS AC 1633, 112; Zeekaart 1456; DYC 1811.4/.5; Imray C25

TIDES –0300 Dover; ML 1·4; Duration No data.

Standard Port HELGOLAND (←)

Times				Height (metres)			
High Water		Low Water		MHWS	MHWN	MLWN	MLWS
0200	0700	0200	0800	2·7	2·4	0·5	0·0
1400	1900	1400	2000				
Differences WEST TERSCHELLING							
–0220	–0250	–0335	–0310	–0·3	–0·2	+0·1	+0·3
VLIELAND-HAVEN							
–0250	–0320	–0355	–0330	–0·3	–0·2	+0·1	+0·4

SHELTER Good in the marina; very crowded in season.

NAVIGATION WPT 53°19'·58N 04°55'·77E (ZS buoy) 099°/6·2M to ZS11-VS2 buoy via Zuider Stortemelk which is well marked/lit. In strong W/NW'lies beware dangerous seas from ZS to ZS5/6 buoys. Stortemelk, the deeper N'ly route, is no shorter and is more exposed. From Vlieree (Vlieland Roads) make for the West Meep Channel; approach HW±2. Call *Brandaris* Ch 02 or 04; see R/T.

West Meep/Slenk is long, but wide, safe and 3·2m deep; hence easier for visitors. Route: WM2, 4 & 6 buoys, NM4–S21 buoy to enter Slenk buoyed/lit chan leading NW into the inner Schuitengat (11m) at SG15/S2 WCM buoy. Expect much commercial traffic and ferries in Slenk.

Note: Schuitengat Zuid, a former approach channel, **is no longer an option for the foreseeable future.**

Ameland can be reached if draft <1.5m by the inshore channels across the Waddenzee (Meep, Noorder Balgen and Oosterom; DYC 1811.4 & .6). Leave at HW –3 to arrive at HW.

LIGHTS AND MARKS Hbr lts as chartlet and 2.3. The square, yellow Brandaris light tower dominates the town and hbr.

R/T *Brandaris* (VTS) Ch 02, 04 broadcasts weather, visibility, nav info, traffic, tidal data at odd H+30 in Dutch; English on request. Yachts must monitor Ch 02. Port HM Ch 12. Marina Ch 31 HO.

TELEPHONE (Code 0562) Port HM 443337 (H24), mobile 0655 192503; CG 442341; ⊖ 442884.

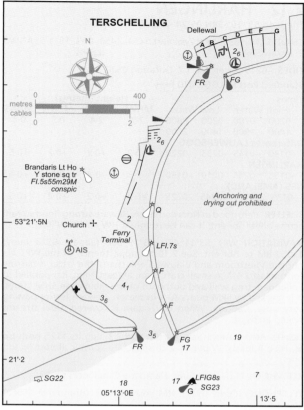

FACILITIES Marina Stichting Passantenhaven ☎ 443337. info@jachthaventerschelling.nl. Notices on pontoons A-G indicate berths by LOA and type of boat (yacht, motor cruiser or traditional craft). 500 AB, €1.63/metre + €0.80/head + €0.55. D at marina ent, @, Wi-Fi, Slip, C, Gaz, ME, SM, Chart agent, ▣, ♿.

Village is an easy walk: CH, 🛒, R, Bar, ✉, P (cans 5km), Ⓑ. ✈ Amsterdam. Ferry to Harlingen, thence ⇌ for Hook-Harwich.

2.11   VLIELAND

WEST FRISIAN ISLANDS
Friesland **53°17'·68N 05°05'·49E** ✵✵✵✵◊◊❀❀

CHARTS AC 1633, 112; Zeekaart 1456; DYC 1811.4/.5; Imray C26

TIDES –0300 Dover; ML 1·4; Duration 0610. See 2.10. The Dutch use Harlingen as a Standard Port.

SHELTER Good in yacht hbr. Two ⚓s, both affected by swell in strong SE-SW'lies near HW: (a) in up to 3m ½M S of the hbr or (b) in 4-9m 1M W of the hbr (beyond the ferry pier). Do not ⚓ in buoyed chan from hbr ent to ferry pier (no AB).

NAVIGATION From ZS buoy (WPT) follow 2.11 Navigation, lines 1-3. At ZS11-VS2 and VS1 buoys turn S into Vliesloot (narrow and in places only 2·5m MLWS). Keep in mid-chan past VS3-VS7 buoys to hbr ent (strong current across); tight berths difficult in SW wind.

LIGHTS AND MARKS A dark red lt ho (W lantern, R top) stands on Vuurduin, 1·2M W of the hbr. Hbr lts as chartlet. Tfc sigs: R Flag or ●● at ent = hbr closed (full). The 282° ldg lts (2.3 & 2.10) lead toward the ferry terminal in E Vlieland.

R/T HM Ch 12. All vessels in Zeegat van Terschelling and N Waddenzee must monitor Ch 02 for *Brandaris Traffic Centre VTS*.

TELEPHONE (Code 0562) HM 451729 (mob 06 201 33086); CG 442341; ⊖ 058 2949488 (Leeuwarden); Police 451312; Dr 451307; Brit Consul (020) 6764343.

FACILITIES Yacht Hbr ☎ 451729. 300 inc ♥s; finger berths on all pontoons in 2m. €0.64 per m² + €1.15 per head; dinghy slip, ▣, ♿, P & D (cans, 10 mins); D at Harlingen. Yacht hbr now complete, no details currently.

Village El, Gaz, 🛒, R, @, ✉, Ⓑ, ✈ (Amsterdam). Ferry as 2.10.

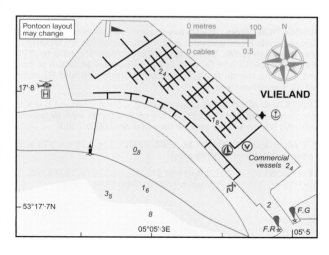

2.12 HARLINGEN

Friesland 53°10'·58N 05°24'·23E ✿✿❀❀❀❀

CHARTS AC 1633, 112; Zeekaart 1454, 1456; DYC 1811·5; ANWB B; Imray C26

TIDES −0210 Dover; ML 1·2; Duration 0520.
Standard Port HELGOLAND (←—)

Times				Height (metres)			
High Water		Low Water		MHWS	MHWN	MLWN	MLWS
0200	0700	0200	0800	2·7	2·4	0·5	0·0
1400	1900	1400	2000				
Differences LAUWERSOOG							
−0130	−0145	−0235	−0220	+0·2	+0·2	+0·2	+0·5
HARLINGEN							
−0155	−0245	−0210	−0130	−0·3	−0·3	0·0	+0·4
NES (AMELAND)							
−0135	−0150	−0245	−0225	+0·2	+0·2	+0·2	+0·5

SHELTER Very good in Noorderhaven. Beware strong flood stream across outer hbr ent; it can be rough at HW in W/NW'lies.

NAVIGATION WPT 53°11'·48N 05°19'·63E [abeam BS23 buoy] 110°/2·8M to hbr ent. See 2.10 for appr, thence to the WPT via buoyed Vliestroom and Blauwe Slenk chans; the latter is narrow for the last 2½M. A small craft chan, at least 1·8m, lies parallel to Pollendam trng wall and outboard of the main chan SHM buoys; it is marked by SPM buoys A–N in season. Beware ferries passing very close. Caution: When Pollendam is covered, tidal streams sweep across it.

LIGHTS AND MARKS See chartlet and 2.3. Ldg lts 112°, both Iso 6s, H24; B masts, W bands. 2 ch spires are conspic almost on ldg line.

R/T VHF Ch 11 (Not on Sun). Harinxma Canal locks Ch 22.

TELEPHONE (Code 0517) HM 492300; CG (Brandaris) (0562)

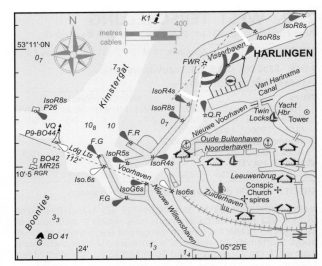

442341; ⊜ 058 2949444; Police 413333; Ⓗ 499999; Brit Consul (020) 6764343.

FACILITIES Lifting bridges across the Oude Buitenhaven and Noorderhaven open in unison 2 x per hr 0600-2200 in season (on request in winter), but are shut at times of boat trains/ferries and at HW springs.
Noorderhaven Yacht Hbr ☎ 415666, El, CH, ME, D, P, SM, Ⓔ, Gaz, Diving/salvage (by arrangement) 🛒, R, Bar, Ⓞ.
Yacht Hbr Van Harinxma Canal ☎ 416898, Ⓞ, C (6 ton); only relevant if going the canal to the lakes.
Town 🛒, R, Bar, ✉, Ⓑ, ⇌, ✈ (Amsterdam). Ferry: See Hoek van Holland.

2.13 OUDESCHILD

Texel, 53°02'·35N 04°51'·18E ✿✿❀❀❀❀❀

CHARTS AC 1631, 1546; Zeekaart 1546, 1454; DYC 1811·3

TIDES −0355 Dover; ML 1·1m; Duration 0625.
Standard Port HELGOLAND (←—)

Times				Height (metres)			
High Water		Low Water		MHWS	MHWN	MLWN	MLWS
0200	0700	0200	0800	2·7	2·4	0·5	0·0
1400	1900	1400	2000				
Differences OUDESCHILD							
−0310	−0420	−0445	−0400	−0·8	−0·7	0·0	+0·3

SHELTER Very good in marina (2·4m) in far NE basin. ⚓ prohib. Visitors are always welcome.

NAVIGATION From Waddenzee appr via Doove Balg and Texelstroom. From seaward, app via Schulpengat or Molengat into Marsdiep (2.14). Thence NE via Texelstroom for 3·5M to WPT 53°02'·26N 04°51'·55E (abeam T12 PHM buoy), 291°/400m to hbr ent, keeping the dir lt Oc 6s, midway between FR and FG mole hd lts. Speed limit 5kn.

LIGHTS AND MARKS See chartlet and 2.3. Dir lt Oc 6s, on G mast, is vis only on brg 291°. FR/FG lts are on R/G masts with W bands. Horn (2) 30s on S mole may be sounded only 0600-2300.

R/T Marina Ch 31. HM Ch 12, 0800-2000LT. See 2.14 for VTS and radar assistance/info on request.

TELEPHONE (Code 0222) Port HM 312710, mobile 06 1502 8380; ⊜ via HM; CG 316270; Police/ambulance 0900 8844 or 112.

FACILITIES **Waddenhaven Texel Marina** 250 berths ☎ 321227. info@waddenhaventexel.nl €2·00, D & P, Slip, Ⓞ, ⚓, &, Bar, R, mini 🛒 in season, bike hire, Gaz, Internet desk, Wi-fi. **YC WSV Texel**, members only. Dry dock (FVs only). **Village** (walking distance), CH, SM, Gaz, 🛒, Ⓑ, ✉, Bar, R. Ferry from 't Horntje to Den Helder. UK ferries from Hook/Rotterdam. ✈ Amsterdam.

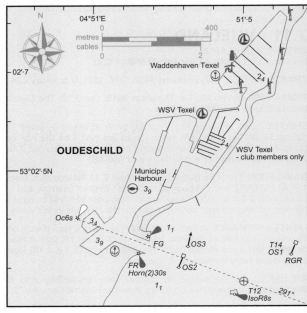

2.14 DEN HELDER

Noord Holland **52°57'·94N 04°47'·24E**

CHARTS AC 1408, 1631, 1546, 126; Zeekaart 1454, 1546; DYC 1811.2, 1801.10; ANWB F; Imray C25; Stanfords 19.

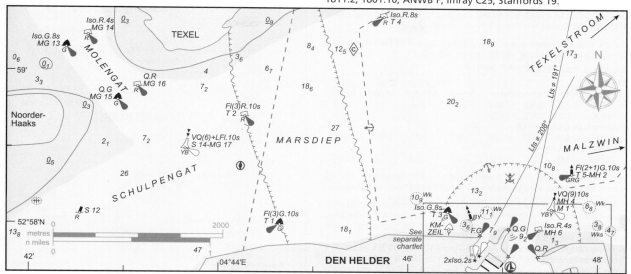

TIDES −0430 Dover; ML 1·1; Duration No data.

Standard Port HELGOLAND (◄—)

Times				Height (metres)			
High Water		Low Water		MHWS	MHWN	MLWN	MLWS
0200	0700	0200	0800	2·7	2·4	0·5	0·0
1400	1900	1400	2000				
Differences DEN HELDER							
−0410	−0520	−0520	−0430	−0·8	−0·7	+0·1	+0·2
K13A PLATFORM (53°13'·0N 03°13'·1E; 58M WNW of Den Helder)							
−0420	−0430	−0520	−0530	−0·9	−0·9	+0·2	+0·3

SHELTER Good in all yacht hbrs (see Facilities). Hbr speed limit 5kn. Den Helder is the main base of the Royal Netherlands Navy which manages the Marinehaven Willemsoord and KMYC.

NAVIGATION Caution: fast ferries to/from Texel, many FVs and offshore service vessels, strong tidal streams across the hbr ent.

Two chans lead into Marsdiep for the hbr ent:

- From the N, Molengat is good except in strong NW winds when seas break heavily. WPT 53°03'·90N 04°39'·37E (MG SWM buoy, Mo (A) 8s) 132°/1.34M to first chan buoys, MG 1/2. Thence to join Marsdiep at S14/MG17 SCM lt buoy.

- From S, the Schulpengat is the main chan, well marked/lit. WPT 52°52'·90N 04°37'·90E [SG (SWM) buoy, Mo (A) 8s, Racon Z] 026·5°/6M towards S14/MG17 SCM lt buoy.

LIGHTS AND MARKS See chartlet and 2.3. Schulpengat: Ldg lts, both Oc 8s, and spire 026·5° on Texel. Kijkduin lt ho, R twr, is conspic 2·3M WSW of hbr. Hbr 191° ldg lts; front B ▲ on bldg; rear B ▼ on B lattice twr. A 60m radar twr is conspic on E side of hbr.

Entry sigs, from Hbr Control twr (W side of ent): ● ● (vert) = No entry/exit, except for the vessel indicated by Hbr Control.

Bridges: Moorman bridge operates H24 7/7, giving access to Nieuwe Diep, Koopvaarder Lock and N Holland Canal.

Van Kinsbergen bridge is operated by HM, 0500-2300 Mon-Fri; 0700-1400 Sat. All bridges are closed 0715-0810, 1200-1215, 1245-1300, Mon-Fri. Also 0830-0910 Mon and 1545-1645 Fri. All LT.

R/T Monitor Ch 62 *Den Helder Traffic* (VTS) in the Schulpengat, Molengat and Marsdiep; info on request. *Port Control* Ch 14 (H24); also remote control of van Kinsbergen bridge. Moorman bridge Ch 18 (H24). *Koopvaarders Lock* Ch 22 (H24), also remote control of Burgemeester Vissersbrug.

TELEPHONE (Code 0223) VTS 657522; Municipal HM 613955, mobile ☎ 0652 97 94 80; Pilot 0255 564500; Emergency 112; Police

655700; Ⓗ 611414; Water Police 616767; Immigration 657515; ⊖ 020 5813614; Brit Consul (020) 6764343.

FACILITIES KMYC is hard to stbd on entering Naval Hbr. ☎ 652645, €1.20 + €0.73/head, D, Bar, R.

In or near Binnenhaven, YCs/marinas (MWV and YC Den Helder) can only be reached via the Rijkshaven, Moorman bridge, Nieuwe Diep and lock:

MWV YC ☎ 624422, €0.54, P (at garage), D, AB.

YC Den Helder ☎ 637444, mobile 0653 78159, €0.73, Ch 31, AB, ME, El, ✗, C, CH, Slip, R, Bar.

YC WSOV ☎ 652173. **YC HWN** ☎ 624422.

Services: CH, SM, Floating dock, Gaz.

Town P, CH, ▦, R, Bar, ✉, Ⓑ, ⇌, ✈ (Amsterdam). Ferry: Hook-Harwich; Rotterdam-Hull.

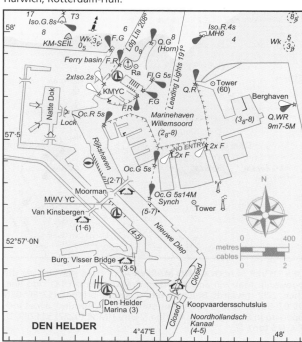

2.15 IJSSELMEER

CHARTS Zeekaart 1351, 1454; In-date DYC 1810, sheets 3-5, are essential to avoid live firing ranges, fishing areas and other hazards; 1810 also has many hbr chartlets.

TIDES The IJsselmeer is non-tidal. Tides seaward of Den Oever and Kornwerderzand locks: −0230 Dover; ML 1·2.

Standard Port HELGOLAND (←)

Times				Height (metres)			
High Water		Low Water		MHWS	MHWN	MLWN	MLWS
0200	0700	0200	0800	2·7	2·4	0·5	0·0
1400	1900	1400	2000				
Differences DEN OEVER							
−0245	−0410	−0400	−0305	−0·7	−0·6	−0·1	+0·3
KORNWERDERZAND							
−0210	−0315	−0300	−0215	−0·5	−0·4	0·0	+0·3

SHELTER Excellent in the marinas, but in the IJsselmeer strong winds can get up very quickly and often raise short, steep seas.

NAVIGATION Enter from sea by Den Oever or Kornwerderzand locks; also from IJmuiden via the Noordzeekanaal (2.17) and Amsterdam. **Speed limits**: 10·5kn in buoyed chans and <250m from shore. Hbr limits vary; see 2.5 for the ANWB *Wateralmanak*.
A firing range, operational Tues to Thurs 1000 - 1900LT, extends S from Breezanddijk (53°01'·0N 05°12'·5E) to 3M NE of Medemblik then NNW to Den Oever (DYC 1811.3 & 1810.3). Call *Schietterrein Breezanddijk* (range control) Ch 71. Firing times are broadcast on VHF Ch 01 by Centrale Meldpost at H +15 on the day of firing, after weather forecasts.

R/T Nav info VHF Ch 01. Sealocks: Kornwerderzand 18; Den Oever 20. Enkhuizen naviduct 22; Lelystad 20; Oranjesluizen 18.

SEALOCKS Standard signals, see 2.5.

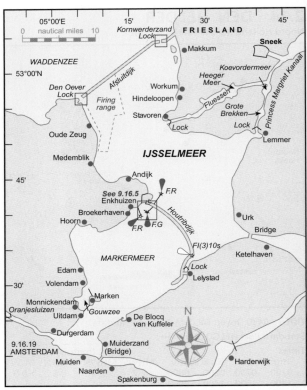

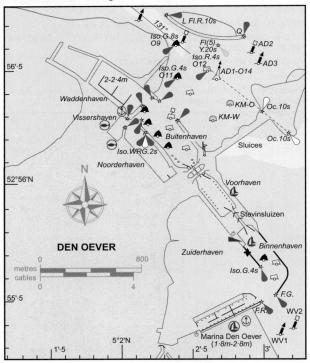

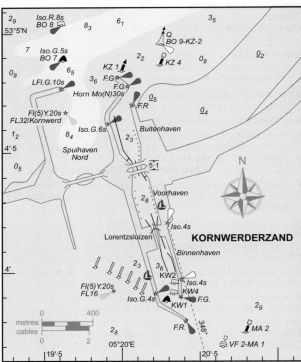

DEN OEVER SEALOCK AND MARINA Appr from seaward via the buoyed/lit Malzwin and Wierbalg chans. Enter on 131° ldg line, then 220° towards Buitenhaven. 2 swing bridges (52°56'·05N 05°02'·50E) and lock open in unison HO. If NW-bound, await lock opening in Binnenhaven. Marina (2-3m) HM ☎ (0227) 511789, D, P, C (15 ton), ▣.

KORNWERDERZAND SEALOCK From seaward approach from the W via Doove Balg; from NW via shallow Inschot chan; or from N via Boontjes. Entrance to Buitenhaven has FR/G and Iso G 6s lts. When two road bridges (53°04'·44N 05°20'·09E) have opened, yachts enter the smaller Lorentz E lock, operates H24. N-bound, follow 348° ldg lts, Iso 4s, to FR/G at ent. Await lock in Binnenhaven (3·6m). HM ☎ (0517) 578170. ▣ 058 2949444.

FACILITIES clockwise from Kornwerderzand. Overnight fees range from approx €0.80 - €1.80/metre LOA. Most berths are bows on to a pontoon, stern lines to piles; there are few ⚓s.

IJSSELMEER EAST

MAKKUM: About 1M SE of Kornwerderzand, MA5 SHM buoy, Iso G4s, marks the buoyed chan. FR/FG lts lead 090·5° into Makkum. To stbd, **Marina Makkum** (2·5-2·8m) ☎ (0515) 232828, P, D, SM, Gaz, 🛒, Bar, R, ◻. 5 other marinas/YCs are further E; BY, ME, C (30 ton), BH (30 ton). **Town** Ⓑ, Dr, 🛒, R.

WORKUM: 5M S of Makkum; FW ldg lts 081° along buoyed chan to **It Soal Marina** (0515) 542937, BY, ME, C, D, P (cans), Gaz, BH.

HINDELOOPEN: WV Hylper Haven HM ☎ (0514) 522009, P, D, ME, EI, ✕. **Old Hbr** D, P, ME, EI, ✕. **Jachthaven Hindeloopen** (500) HM ☎ (0514) 524554, P, D, ◻, BH (30 ton), CH, R, Bar.

STAVOREN: Ent Buitenhaven 048° on Dir lt Iso 4s between FR/G. Marina, €1·00, E of ent in Oudehaven; ☎ (0514) 681216, VHF Ch 74. Or, 1km S, ent Nieuwe Voorhaven (FR/G & Fl 5s Dir lt) then via lock to **Marina Stavoren** (3m) ☎ (0514) 684684, BY, ME, C, P, D, SM, Gaz, BH (20 ton); **Outer Marina** (3·5m) close S of Nieuwe Voorhaven. Also 3 other marinas. **Town** Ⓑ, Dr, 🛒, R, ⇌.

LEMMER: Appr on ldg lts 038°, Iso 8s, to KL5/VL2 By; then ldg lts 083°, Iso 8s, through Lemstergeul. Lastly FG and Iso G 4s lead 065° into town and some 14 marinas. **Gem. Jachthaven** HM ☎ (0514) 563343. **Services:** BY, ME, C, P, D, Gaz, SM. **Town** Ⓑ, Dr, 🛒, R, ✉.

URK: Hbr ent ½M SE of lt ho. Dir lt Iso G 4s to hbr ent, FR/G. Hbr has 4 basins; keep NNW to berth in Nieuwe Haven, Westhaven or Oosthaven (3·3m). HM ☎ (0527) 689970. **Westhaven** P & D (cans), SM; **Oosthaven** ME, EI, ✕, Ⓔ, CH. **Town** EC Tues; Ⓑ, ✉, Dr.

LELYSTAD: Flevo is 2M NNE of lock. (550) ☎ (0320) 279800, BY, ME, C, P, D, Gaz, ◻, BH (50 ton), R, Bar, 🛒. **Deko Marina** is close N of the lock; ☎ (0320) 269000, SM, C, R. **WV Lelystad, Houtribhaven** (560) HM ☎ (0320) 260198, D, CH, ◻, 🛒, R, Bar, BH (20 ton). S of lock **Bataviahaven** (150), Ch 14, HM ☎ 06 511 77049. **Marina Lelystadhaven** ☎ (0320) 260326, R.

MARKERMEER is divided from the IJsselmeer by the Houtribdijk 13M long. Access from sea via IJmuiden, Noordzeekanaal, Amsterdam/Oranjesluizen. Hbrs clockwise from Lelystad to Enkhuizen.

DE BLOCQ VAN KUFFELER: (8·5M SW Lelystad), ☎ 06 2751 2497, R.

MUIDERZAND: Ent 1M N of Hollandsebrug (12·7m cl'nce at SE corner of Markermeer) at buoys IJM5 & IJM7/JH2. **Marina** ☎ (036) 5369151, D, P, C, ME, R, CH.

MUIDEN: Ldg lts Q 181° into **KNZ & RV Marina** (2·6m), W of ent; home of Royal Netherlands YC (150 berths). HM ☎ (0294) 261450, www.knzrv.nl €1·90, D, P (cans), CH, Bar, R. On E bank **Stichting Jachthaven** (70) ☎ (0294) 261223, €1.60, D, P.

DURGERDAM: ½M E of overhead power lines (70m); convenient for Oranjesluizen. Keep strictly in buoyed chan. **WV Durgerdam** Berth to stbd of ent (1·8m). ☎ 06-14750510.

UITDAM Appr from MIJ5 buoy Fl Y 5s via buoyed chan to FR/FG at ent. C (9 ton), P, D, Gaz, 🛒. HM (020) 4031433.

MARKEN (picturesque show piece): Ent Gouwzee from N, abeam Volendam, thence via buoyed chan; Dir FW lt 116° between FR/G at hbr (2·2m). Lt ho, conspic, Oc 8s 16m 9M, on E end of island. HM ☎ (0299) 601253, free on quay, 🛒, R, Ⓑ, P & D (cans).

MONNICKENDAM: Appr as for Marken, then W to MO10 Iso R 8s and 236° ldg lts FR. **Hemmeland Marina** ☎ (0299) 655555, (2·0m), C. **Waterland Marina** ☎ 652000, (2·5m), CH, C (15 ton) www.jachthavenwaterland.nl. **Marina Monnickendam** ☎ 652595, (2·0m), C. **Zeilhoek Marina** ☎ 651463, (2·5m), BY.

VOLENDAM: Fork stbd to old hbr (2·4m). Dir lt Fl 5s 313°. FR/FG at ent. ☎ 06 51337494, ME, C, P, D, Gaz, SM. Fork port via unlit buoyed chan to **Marina Volendam** (2·7m) HM(0299) 320262. C (16t), SM, 🛒, B, R.

EDAM: Appr via unlit chan keeping Iso W 8s between FG /R at narrow ent; beware commercial traffic. **Jachthaven WSV De Zeevang** (2·2m) S side of outer hbr. ☎ (0299) 350174, ME, EI, ✕. Or lock into the Oorgat and via S canal to Nieuwe Haven. **Town** Bar, ◻, ✉, Gaz, Ⓑ.

HOORN: Radio twr (80m) 1·5M ENE of hbr. Iso 4s 15m 10M and FR/G at W Hbr ent. Four options: To port **Grashaven** (700) HM ☎

(0229) 215208, ◻, CH, 🛒, ME, EI, ✕, C. To stbd ⚓ in **Buitenhaven** (1.6m). Ahead & to stbd **WSV Hoorn**, (100) ☎ 213540. Ahead to **Binnenhaven** (2·5m) via narrow lock (open H24) AB, P. **Town** 🛒, CH, ✉, R, Dr, Ⓑ, Gaz, ⇌.

ENKHUIZEN: 036° ldg lts Iso 4s; 230° ldg lts Iso 8s. Yachts transit the Houtribdijk via a 'Naviduct', ie a twin-chambered lock above the road tunnel below (see chartlet), saving long delays for boat & road traffic; call Ch 22. Krabbersgat lock & bridge, the former bottleneck for both road and sea traffic, can still be used by boats with <6m air clearance.

Compagnieshaven (500) HM ☎ (0228) 313353, P, D, CH, BH (12), Gaz; **Buyshaven** (195) ☎ 315660, FW, AC; **Buitenhaven** ☎ 312444. **Town** EC Mon; Market Wed; C, Slip, CH, SM, ME, EI, ✕, Ⓑ, Bar, P & D (cans), Dr, ✉, ⇌.

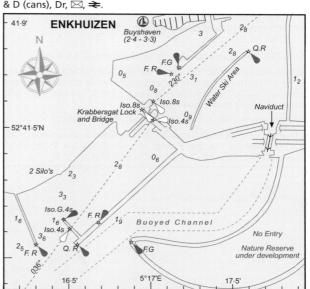

BROEKERHAVEN: Small yacht hbr 1·5M SW of Enkhuizen. Appr from KG15-BR2 buoy. WSV de Broekerhaven ☎ (0228) 518798.

IJSSELMEER WEST

ANDIJK: Visitors use **Stichting Jachthaven Andijk,** the first of 2 marinas; (600) ☎ (0228) 593075, narrow ent with tight turn between FR/G lts. ME, C (20 ton), SM, Gaz, ◻, D, CH.

MEDEMBLIK: Ent on 232°, Dir lt Oc 5s between FR/G. Thence via Oosterhaven (P & D) into Middenhaven (short stay) and via bridge to Westerhaven. **Pekelharinghaven** (120) HM ☎ (0227) 542175; ent is to port by Castle, CH, Bar, R. **Middenhaven** HM ☎ 541686, FW. **Stichting Jachthaven** HM ☎ 541681 in Westerhaven, ◻, C. **Town** Ⓑ, CH, ME, EI, SM, ✕, ✉, Dr, Bar, ◻, R, 🛒. **Regatta Centre** 0·5M S of hbr entr. HM ☎ (0227) 547781, AB 450, C, Slip, CH, R.

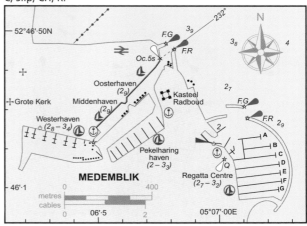

2.16 IJMUIDEN

N Holland 52°27'·94N 04°32'·39E (Hbr ent) SPM ⊗⊗◊◊◊❀❀

CHARTS AC 1631, 124; Zeekaart 1450, 1543, 1035, 1350; DYC 1801.8; Imray C25; Stanfords 19

TIDES +0400 Dover; ML 1·0. Noordzeekanaal level may be above or below sea level

Standard Port VLISSINGEN (→)

Times				Height (metres)			
High Water		Low Water		MHWS	MHWN	MLWN	MLWS
0300	0900	0400	1000	5·0	4·1	1·1	0·5
1500	2100	1600	2200				
Differences IJMUIDEN							
+0145	+0140	+0305	+0325	−2·8	−2·3	−0·7	−0·2
PETTEN (SOUTH) 18M N of IJmuiden							
+0210	+0215	+0345	+0500	−2·9	−2·3	−0·6	−0·2

SHELTER Very good at Seaport (SPM) marina (2·9m-4·8m).

NAVIGATION WPT 52°28'·10N 04°30'·94E, 100°/0·9M to ent. Beware strong tidal streams across hbr ent, scend inside Buitenhaven and commercial tfc – do not impede. Keep a good lookout, especially astern. 3 knots max speed in marina.

Marina access chan is buoyed/lit as per the chartlet.

LOCKS In IJmuiden the 4 locks are North, Middle, South and Small. Yachts normally use the S'most Small lock (Kleine Sluis) which opens H24 on request Ch 22; wait W or E of it.

Lock signals shown W and E from each lock are standard, ie:

- ●
- ● = Lock not in use; no entry. ● = No entry/exit.
- ●
- ● = Prepare to enter/exit. ● = Enter or exit.

Tidal & sluicing sigs may be shown from or near the conspic Hbr Ops Centre (HOC) bldg, near the front 100·5° ldg lt:

Tidal signals: ● over ⓦ = rising tide; ⓦ over ● = falling tide.

Sluicing sigs are a △ of 3 horiz lts and 1 lt at the apex. The sluices are N of the N lock, so unlikely to affect yachts.

LIGHTS AND MARKS Both ldg lt ho's 100·5° for Zuider Buitenkanaal are dark R twrs. The HOC bldg is conspic next to front lt; so are 6 chimneys (138-166m high) 7ca N and ENE of Small lock.

R/T Seaport Marina call *SPM* Ch 74. See also VTS overleaf.

TELEPHONE (Code 0255) Tfc Centre IJmuiden 564500; Hbr Ops 523934; Pilot 564503; ⊖ 020 5813614; CG 537644; Police 0900 8844; ⊞ (023) 5453200; Brit Consul (020) 6764343.

FACILITIES Seaport Marina (SPM) ☎ 560300. www.marinaseaport.nl info@ marinaseaport.nl 600 inc Ⓥ, €2.20 inc shwr & AC. Berth as directed, or on M pontoon in a slot with green tally. D & P, El, Ⓔ, BH (70 ton), CH, Gas, Slip, SM, ✖, ME, Wi-fi, R, Bar, ▣, 🛒. Buses to Amsterdam and Haarlem in summer.

Town Gaz, 🛒, R, Bar, @, ✉, Ⓑ, ⇌ (bus to Beverwijk), ✈ Amsterdam. Ferry: IJmuiden-Newcastle.

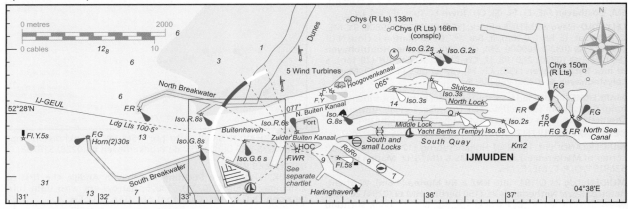

2.17 NOORDZEEKANAAL

VTS Monitor the following VTS stns (H24) in sequence to approach, enter and transit the canal (see diagram opposite):

• *Pilot-VTS IJmuiden*	Ch 07	W of IJM SWM buoy.
• *IJmuiden Port Control*	Ch 61	IJM buoy to locks.
• *IJmuiden Locks*	Ch 22	At the locks
• *Sector Noordzeekanaal*	Ch 03	Locks to km 10·8.
• *Amsterdam Port Control*	Ch 68	Km 10·8 - Amsterdam
• *Sector Schellingwoude*	Ch 60	City centre (04°55'E) to Buiten IJ.

Radar surveillance is available on request Ch 07. Visibility reports are broadcast on all VHF chans every H+00 when vis <1000m.

NAVIGATION Canal speed limit is 9 knots. The 13·5M transit is simple, but there is much commercial traffic. Keep as far to stbd as possible. Keep a good lookout for vessels emerging from dock basins and side canals. The banks and ents to basins and side canals are well lit, so night navigation need be no problem apart from the risk of not being seen by other vessels against shore lights.

FACILITIES There are small marinas at IJmond beyond lifting bridge (Ch 18) in Zijkanaal C, km 10 (S bank); and at Nauerna (Zijkanaal D, km 12) (N bank).

WV IJmond ⊗⊗◊◊◊❀. Ch 31, HM ☎ (023) 5375003. AB €1.10. AC, D, BY, C (20 ton), ▣, Bar, R.

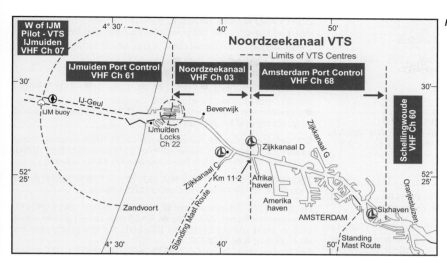

Fig 2.17A Noordzeekanaal VTS

2.18 AMSTERDAM

Noord Holland 52°22'·97N 04°53'·92E   Marinas ✿✿✿♨♨♨✿✿✿

CHARTS AC 124; DYC 1801.8, 1810.2; ANWB G, I

NAVIGATION Het IJ (pronounced eye) is the well lit/buoyed chan through the city centre. From IJ 10/11 to IJ 14/15 buoys yachts must keep out of Het IJ, using a yacht chan between the lateral buoys and RW (N side) or GW (S side) buoys further outboard.

At Oranjesluizen yachts use the most N'ly of 4 locks, marked 'SPORT'; Ch 18, H24. There are waiting piers/jetties either side. The Schellingwoude bridge (9m) opens on the hour and ±20 min, except Mon-Fri 0600-0900 and 1600-1800; VHF Ch 18.

R/T Port Control Ch 68; Info Ch 14. Oranjesluizen Ch 18.

TELEPHONE (Code 020) Port Control (East) 6221515; Port Control (West) 0255 514457; ⊖ 5867511; Emergency 112; Police 0900 8844; Dr 0880 030600; Brit Consul 6764343.

FACILITIES Complete shelter in all yacht hbrs/marinas.

WVDS Sixhaven (52°22'·90N 04°54'·40E, close NE of IJ8 buoy and NE of conspic Central ➔ Stn) is small and popular, so in season is often full and log-jammed 1800-1100. ☎ 6329429. 100 + ♥, max LOA 15m. €1.50 inc AC, Bar (w/e), ◻, 🛒. www.sixhaven.nl WIP, due to end 2012, on adjacent new Metro N-S line detracts only slightly. Free ferries to N bank (ditto for next entry WV Aeolus).

WV Aeolus 52°22'·91N 04°55'·17E. Few ♥ berths and rafting is strictly controlled. ☎ 6360791. Often full in season, no pre-booking, berth as directed. 45 + 8 ♥, €1.10. AC, YC, Bar, 🛒.

Aquadam Twellegea 52°23'·04N 04°56'·63E, ent to Zijkanaal K. ☎ 6320616. €2.50, ⚓, P, C (30 ton). www.aquadam.nl Full BY facilities. Bus to city centre.

WV Zuiderzee 52°22'·95N 04°57'·77E, 140m NE of Oranjesluizen. ☎ 4904222. €1.10, YC.

City All needs; Gaz, Ⓔ, ACA, DYC Agent, Ⓑ, @, Wi-Fi, ✉, ➔, ✈. Amsterdam gives access to the N Holland and Rijn canals.

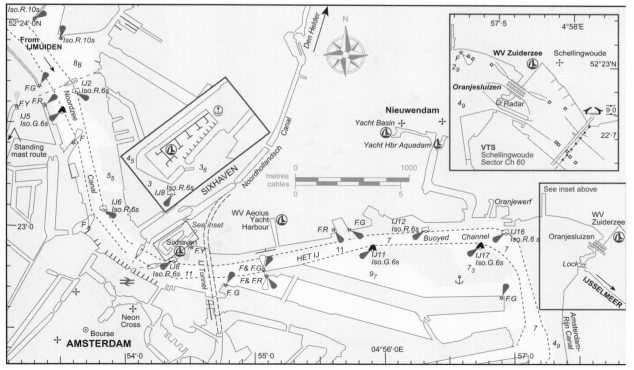

2.19 SCHEVENINGEN

Zuid Holland **52°06'·24N 04°15'·26E** ✲⊛◊◊◊✿✿

CHARTS AC 1630, 122; Zeekaart 1035, 1349, 1350, 1449; DYC 1801.7; ANWB H/J; Imray C25; Stanfords 19

TIDES +0320 Dover; ML 0·9; Duration 0445.

Standard Port VLISSINGEN (→)

Times				Height (metres)			
High Water		Low Water		MHWS	MHWN	MLWN	MLWS
0300	0900	0400	1000	5·0	4·1	1·1	0·5
1500	2100	1600	2200				
Differences SCHEVENINGEN							
+0105	+0100	+0220	+0245	−2·7	−2·2	−0·7	−0·2

SHELTER Very good in marina. Ent difficult in SW-N F6 winds, and dangerous in NW F6-8 which cause scend in outer hbr.

NAVIGATION WPT 52°07'·75N 04°14'·12E (SCH buoy) 156°/1·6M to ent; access H24. Close west of the 156° leading line and 1M from the hbr ent, outfalls are marked by E and W cardinal light buoys and by 2 SPM buoys (off chartlet). The promenade pier, Iso 5s, is 1·2M NE of the hbr ent. Caution: Strong tidal streams set across the ent. Slack water is about HW Scheveningen –2 and +3. Beware large ships and FVs entering/leaving.

LIGHTS AND MARKS Daymarks include: the reddish-brown lt ho (5ca E of hbr ent); twr bldgs in Scheveningen and Den Haag.

Traffic signals (from signal mast, N side of ent to Voorhaven):

● over ○ = No entry. ○ over ● = No exit.
Fl ◐ = One or more large vessels are leaving the port.

Tide sigs (same mast): ● over ○ = tide rising. ○ ● = tide falling.

Shown from SE end of narrow chan between 1st and 2nd Hbrs: ● = vessels must not leave the 2nd Hbr. The chan is generally blind, so go slowly and sound horn.

R/T Call *Traffic Centre Scheveningen* Ch 21 (H24) prior to entry/departure to avoid FVs. Radar (info only) on request Ch 21. When in 2nd Hbr call *Yacht Club Scheveningen* Ch 31 for a berth.

TELEPHONE (Code 070) Port HM 3527701; ⊜ 020 5813614; Police 0900 8844; Dr 3450650; Brit Consul (020) 6764343.

FACILITIES YC Scheveningen ☎ 3520017, mobile 0653 293137. www.jachtclub.com 223 + 100 ♥, €1.66 plus tax €1.27 per adult. Visitors *must* turn to berth/raft bows NE, for fire safety reasons. Wi-Fi, ▣, Bar, R ☎ 3520308.
2nd Harbour Fuel barge GEO (0630-1600), D only. Slip, DYC agent; WIP (2007) on new BY, C, CH, El, ME, ✕, SM.
Town P, ▤, R, Bar, ✉, ⑬, ⇌, ✈ Rotterdam and Amsterdam. The town is effectively merged with Den Haag (The Hague), seat of Dutch government and well worth a visit by bus.

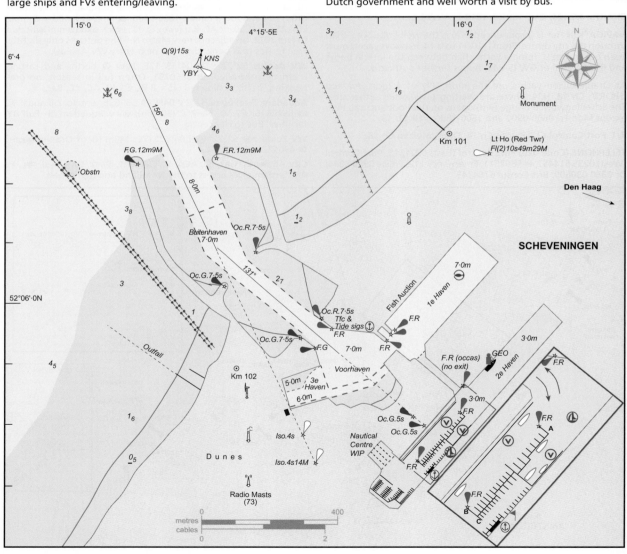

DEN HELDER TO SCHEVENINGEN

South of Den Helder the coast is low, and, like most of the Dutch coast, not readily visible from seaward. Conspic landmarks include: chimneys of nuclear power station 1·5M NNE of Petten; Egmond aan Zee light house; chimneys of steelworks N of IJmuiden; two light houses at IJmuiden; big hotels at Zandvoort; Noordwijk aan Zee light house; and Scheveningen light house and big hotels.

A wind farm centred on 52°36'·2N 04°26'·4E (about 6·7M W of Egmond aan Zee) contains a No Entry area marked by 5 peripheral turbines, each L Fl Y 15s 15m 5M, Horn Mo (U) 30s. A second No Entry wind farm is 8M further W, centred on 52°35'·4N 04°13'·2E and marked by 6 cardinal lt buoys (2W, 2E, 1N, 1S); see AC 1631.

▶3M W of IJmuiden the N-going stream begins at HW Hoek van Holland –0120, and the S-going at HW Hoek van Holland +0430, sp rates about 1·5kn. Off ent to IJmuiden the stream turns about 1h earlier and is stronger, and in heavy weather there may be a dangerous sea.◀ From **IJmuiden** the **Noordzeekanaal** leads east to **Amsterdam** and the **IJsselmeer**.

HOEK VAN HOLLAND TO THE WESTERSCHELDE

Off Hoek van Holland at the ent to Europoort and **Rotterdam** shipping is very dense and fast-moving. Yachts must go up-river via the Nieuwe Waterweg which near Vlaardingen becomes the Nieuwe Maas.

The Slijkgat (lit) is the approach chan to **Stellendam** and entry to the Haringvliet. The Schaar, Schouwenbank, Middelbank and Steenbanken lie parallel to the coast off the approaches to Oosterschelde. From the N, Geul van de Banjaard (partly lit) joins

Westgat and leads to Oude Roompot, which with Roompot (unlit) are the main, well marked channels to the **Roompotsluis**, in S half of the barrage. Here the Oosterschelde (AC 192) is entered.

Rounding Walcheren via the Oostgat, close inshore, Westkapelle lt ho is conspic with two smaller lts nearby: Molenhoofd 5ca WSW and Noorderhoofd 7ca NNW. The Oostgat is the inshore link between Oosterschelde and Westerschelde and also the N approach to the latter.

Deurloo and Spleet are unlit secondary channels parallel to Oostgat and a mile or so to seaward. By day they keep yachts clear of commercial traffic in the Oostgat.

All channels converge between **Vlissingen** and **Breskens**. This bottleneck is declared a Precautionary Area in which yachts have no rights of way over other vessels and therefore must keep an above average lookout, staying clear of all traffic. Vessels <20m must give way to larger craft; and yachts <12m should stay just outside the main buoyed chans.

The main approach chan to the Westerschelde from the W is the Scheur, which yachts may follow just outside the fairway. From **Zeebrugge** and the SW use the Wielingen chan, keeping close to S side of estuary until past **Breskens**.

If proceeding to **Vlissingen**, cross between Songa and SS1 buoys, observing the mini-TSS which runs E/W close off Vlissingen. The tide runs hard in the estuary, causing a bad sea in chans and overfalls on some banks in strong winds.

The passage up-river to **Antwerpen** is best made in one leg, starting from Breskens, Vlissingen or **Terneuzen** in order to get the tidal timing right. More detail in *North France and Belgium Cruising Companion*, NDL/Featherstone.

2.20 TSS AND VTS OFF SOUTHERN NETHERLANDS AND BELGIUM

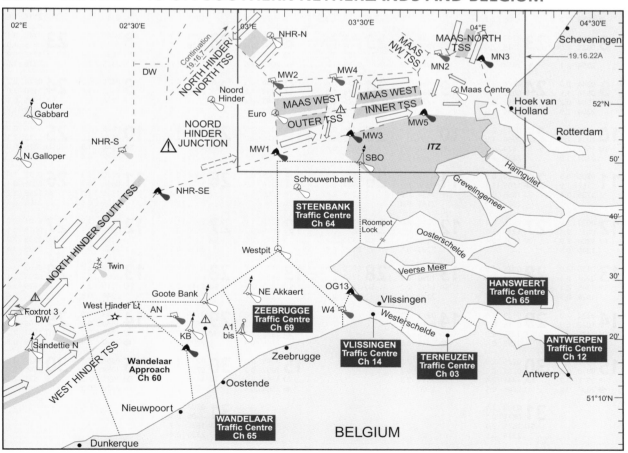

TIME ZONE -0100
Subtract 1 hour for UT
For Dutch Summer Time add
ONE hour in **non-shaded areas**

HOEK VAN HOLLAND   LAT 51°59'N   LONG 4°07'E
TIMES AND HEIGHTS OF HIGH AND LOW WATERS

Dates in red are SPRINGS
Dates in blue are NEAPS

YEAR **2010**

JANUARY

Time	m		Time	m
1 0239	2.1	**16** 0339	2.1
0756	0.3		0833	0.2
F 1457	2.4	SA 1546	2.2
2015	0.5		2104	0.6
2 0325	2.1	**17** 0405	2.1
0836	0.2		0903	0.2
SA 1541	2.4	SU 1619	2.3
2340	0.5		2129	0.6
3 0408	2.1	**18** 0445	2.1
0911	0.2		0934	0.2
SU 1626	2.4	M 1656	2.2
4 0026	0.5	**19** 0000	0.6
0455	2.1		0515	2.1
M 0959	0.1	TU 1016	0.2
1715	2.4		1725	2.2
5 0105	0.5	**20** 0044	0.5
0546	2.1		0545	2.1
TU 1056	0.1	W 1044	0.2
1800	2.4		1800	2.2
6 0150	0.5	**21** 0126	0.5
0635	2.1		0616	2.1
W 1143	0.1	TH 1125	0.1
1859	2.3		1829	2.2
7 0210	0.5	**22** 0140	0.5
0729	2.0		0650	2.0
TH 1254	0.1	F 1204	0.1
◑ 1955	2.2		1905	2.1
8 0205	0.5	**23** 0140	0.5
0825	2.0		0735	2.0
F 1354	0.1	SA 1304	0.2
2054	2.1	◐ 1954	2.1
9 0244	0.5	**24** 0220	0.5
0930	1.9		0836	1.9
SA 1504	0.2	SU 1414	0.2
2204	2.0		2104	2.0
10 0406	0.5	**25** 0315	0.5
1039	1.9		0950	1.9
SU 1615	0.4	M 1524	0.3
2324	1.9		2225	1.9
11 0505	0.5	**26** 0420	0.5
1156	1.9		1105	1.9
M 1735	0.4	TU 1656	0.4
			2334	1.9
12 0033	1.9	**27** 0525	0.4
0825	0.4		1215	2.0
TU 1300	2.0	W 1806	0.4
1840	0.5			
13 0136	2.0	**28** 0045	1.9
0924	0.4		0614	0.4
W 1345	2.1	TH 1305	2.1
1924	0.5		2120	0.4
14 0230	2.0	**29** 0139	2.0
1020	0.3		0656	0.3
TH 1435	2.1	F 1355	2.2
2004	0.5		2155	0.4
15 0310	2.1	**30** 0225	2.0
0810	0.3		0731	0.2
F 1515	2.2	SA 1441	2.4
● 2034	0.6	○ 2246	0.5
		31 0308	2.1
			0815	0.1
		SU 1525	2.4
			2314	0.5

FEBRUARY

Time	m		Time	m
1 0355	2.1	**16** 0416	2.1
0851	0.1		0909	0.2
M 1606	2.5	TU 1626	2.3
			2335	0.5
2 0005	0.5	**17** 0445	2.2
0435	2.2		0934	0.2
TU 0935	0.0	W 1656	2.2
1656	2.4			
3 0044	0.5	**18** 0025	0.4
0521	2.2		0511	2.1
W 1025	0.0	TH 1015	0.2
1737	2.4		1725	2.2
4 0125	0.5	**19** 0105	0.4
0606	2.2		0539	2.1
TH 1119	0.1	F 1045	0.1
1828	2.3		1758	2.2
5 0150	0.5	**20** 0135	0.4
0656	2.1		0616	2.1
F 1234	0.1	SA 1125	0.1
1926	2.1		1836	2.2
6 0127	0.4	**21** 0000	0.3
0750	2.1		0651	2.1
SA 1344	0.1	SU 1209	0.1
◑ 2014	2.0		1915	2.1
7 0226	0.4	**22** 0034	0.3
0850	2.0		0739	2.0
SU 1455	0.2	M 1350	0.2
2129	1.8	◐ 2019	1.9
8 0336	0.4	**23** 0225	0.4
1016	1.8		0906	1.9
M 1605	0.4	TU 1505	0.3
2316	1.7		2155	1.7
9 0456	0.4	**24** 0334	0.4
1135	1.8		1046	1.8
TU 1724	0.4	W 1625	0.4
			2315	1.7
10 0026	1.8	**25** 0444	0.4
0550	0.3		1156	1.9
W 1250	1.9	TH 1950	0.4
1830	0.5			
11 0125	1.9	**26** 0029	1.8
0926	0.3		0544	0.3
TH 1334	2.0	F 1255	2.1
2145	0.4		2106	0.4
12 0216	2.0	**27** 0125	1.9
1010	0.2		0625	0.2
F 1419	2.1	SA 1339	2.2
2225	0.5		2135	0.4
13 0249	2.0	**28** 0205	2.0
1056	0.2		0710	0.1
SA 1455	2.2	SU 1420	2.3
2257	0.5	○ 2225	0.4
14 0314	2.1			
0814	0.2			
SU 1526	2.2			
● 2045	0.5			
15 0345	2.1			
0834	0.2			
M 1555	2.2			
2300	0.5			

MARCH

Time	m		Time	m
1 0251	2.1	**16** 0316	2.1
0745	0.1		0815	0.2
M 1505	2.4	TU 1521	2.2
2254	0.5		2237	0.4
2 0331	2.2	**17** 0339	2.1
0830	0.0		0839	0.2
TU 1547	2.4	W 1556	2.2
2350	0.4		2315	0.4
3 0416	2.2	**18** 0411	2.2
0911	0.0		1155	0.2
W 1633	2.4	TH 1625	2.2
4 0035	0.4	**19** 0016	0.3
0456	2.2		0441	2.2
TH 1005	0.1	F 1235	0.2
1715	2.3		1655	2.2
5 0125	0.4	**20** 0035	0.3
0537	2.2		0515	2.2
F 1055	0.1	SA 1015	0.2
1801	2.1		1729	2.2
6 0210	0.4	**21** 0120	0.3
0625	2.2		0548	2.2
SA 1230	0.2	SU 1059	0.2
1844	2.0		1807	2.1
7 0040	0.3	**22** 0000	0.2
0715	2.1		0625	2.2
SU 1335	0.2	M 1144	0.2
◑ 1935	1.8		1851	2.0
8 0135	0.3	**23** 0004	0.2
0804	1.9		0718	2.1
M 1424	0.3	TU 1416	0.2
2050	1.6	◐ 1956	1.8
9 0300	0.3	**24** 0216	0.2
0935	1.8		0830	1.9
TU 1545	0.4	W 1504	0.3
2235	1.5		2124	1.6
10 0436	0.3	**25** 0315	0.3
1126	1.7		1015	1.8
W 1705	0.4	TH 1615	0.4
2359	1.6		2255	1.6
11 0525	0.2	**26** 0414	0.3
1236	1.9		1131	1.9
TH 1805	0.4	F 1934	0.4
12 0059	1.8	**27** 0015	1.7
0615	0.2		0520	0.2
F 1313	2.0	SA 1235	2.1
2125	0.4		2035	0.3
13 0150	1.9	**28** 0101	1.8
0934	0.2		0559	0.2
SA 1355	2.1	SU 1315	2.2
2205	0.4		2114	0.4
14 0226	2.0	**29** 0145	1.9
1025	0.2		0645	0.1
SU 1426	2.1	M 1412	2.3
2246	0.4		2200	0.4
15 0249	2.0	**30** 0227	2.1
1037	0.2		0725	0.1
M 1456	2.2	TU 1446	2.3
● 2300	0.4	○ 2246	0.4
		31 0307	2.2
			0806	0.1
		W 1525	2.3
			2330	0.4

APRIL

Time	m		Time	m
1 0347	2.2	**16** 0338	2.2
0849	0.1		1125	0.2
TH 1609	2.2	F 1557	2.2
			2355	0.3
2 0026	0.3	**17** 0415	2.2
0431	2.3		1210	0.2
F 1244	0.2	SA 1631	2.1
1652	2.1		2140	0.3
3 0105	0.3	**18** 0448	2.2
0510	2.2		1256	0.2
SA 1325	2.0	SU 1712	2.1
1738	2.0		2226	0.2
4 0156	0.2	**19** 0527	2.2
0555	2.2		1304	0.2
SU 1330	0.3	M 1751	2.0
1822	1.9		2316	0.3
5 0000	0.2	**20** 0612	2.2
0646	2.1		1356	0.3
M 1320	0.3	TU 1839	1.8
1909	1.8			
6 0105	0.2	**21** 0020	0.2
0734	1.9		0705	2.1
TU 1426	0.3	W 1405	0.3
◑ 2004	1.6	◑ 1945	1.7
7 0240	0.2	**22** 0134	0.1
0906	1.7		0819	2.0
W 1455	0.4	TH 1455	0.4
2130	1.5		2115	1.6
8 0405	0.2	**23** 0245	0.1
1034	1.7		0956	1.9
TH 1635	0.4	F 1756	0.3
2325	1.5		2236	1.6
9 0455	0.2	**24** 0344	0.2
1145	1.8		1110	2.0
F 1744	0.4	SA 1905	0.3
			2339	1.7
10 0026	1.7	**25** 0740	0.2
0555	0.2		1210	2.1
SA 1246	1.9	SU 2026	0.4
2024	0.4			
11 0110	1.8	**26** 0035	1.8
0634	0.2		0846	0.1
SU 1325	2.0	M 1258	2.2
2125	0.3		2106	0.3
12 0146	1.9	**27** 0121	0.1
0917	0.2		0619	0.1
M 1356	2.1	TU 1338	2.2
2155	0.3		2135	0.4
13 0209	2.0	**28** 0202	2.1
1006	0.2		0705	0.1
TU 1419	2.1	W 1425	2.2
2246	0.3	○ 2204	0.4
14 0235	2.0	**29** 0245	2.2
1030	0.2		0749	0.1
W 1449	2.2	TH 1507	2.2
● 2240	0.2		2009	0.4
15 0308	2.1	**30** 0327	2.2
1054	0.2		0840	0.2
TH 1525	2.2	F 1551	2.1
2310	0.3			

Chart Datum is 0·84 metres below NAP Datum. HAT is 2·4 metres above Chart Datum; see 0.19

TIME ZONE -0100
Subtract 1 hour for UT
For Dutch Summer Time add
ONE hour in **non-shaded areas**

HOEK VAN HOLLAND
LAT 51°59'N LONG 4°07'E

TIMES AND HEIGHTS OF HIGH AND LOW WATERS

Dates in red are SPRINGS
Dates in blue are NEAPS

YEAR **2010**

MAY

Day	Time	m		Day	Time	m
1 SA	0005	0.2		16 SU	0350	2.2
	0411	2.2			1150	0.3
	1215	0.3			1615	2.1
	1636	2.0			2130	0.2
2 SU	0045	0.2		17 M	0431	2.2
	0455	2.2			1236	0.3
	1316	0.3			1656	2.0
	1719	1.9			2205	0.2
3 M	0135	0.1		18 TU	0515	2.2
	0535	2.1			1316	0.3
	1350	0.3			1741	1.9
	1759	1.8			2305	0.1
4 TU	0200	0.1		19 W	0601	2.2
	0626	2.0			1345	0.3
	1310	0.4			1835	1.8
	1844	1.7				
5 W	0034	0.1		20 TH	0004	0.1
	0713	1.9			0659	2.1
	1345	0.4			1440	0.3
	1946	1.7			1956	1.7
6 TH	0150	0.1		21 F	0120	0.0
	0820	1.8			0815	2.1
	1500	0.4			1600	0.4
	◑ 2035	1.6			◑ 2106	1.7
7 F	0325	0.1		22 SA	0225	0.1
	0925	1.7			0929	2.0
	1605	0.4			1730	0.4
	2145	1.5			2206	1.7
8 SA	0445	0.1		23 SU	0315	0.1
	1055	1.8			1040	2.1
	1710	0.4			1835	0.4
	2330	1.6			2305	1.8
9 SU	0524	0.1		24 M	0420	0.1
	1156	1.9			1139	2.1
	1755	0.4			1950	0.3
10 M	0026	1.7		25 TU	0005	1.9
	0620	0.2			0805	0.2
	1236	2.0			1236	2.1
	2027	0.3			2040	0.3
11 TU	0056	1.8		26 W	0057	2.0
	0820	0.2			0609	0.2
	1316	2.0			1326	2.1
	2125	0.3			2125	0.4
12 W	0130	1.9		27 TH	0145	2.0
	0925	0.2			0654	0.3
	1346	2.1			1411	2.1
	2155	0.3			1924	0.3
13 TH	0201	2.0		28 F	0228	2.1
	0725	0.3			0750	0.3
	1419	2.2			1458	2.1
	2245	0.3			○ 2005	0.3
14 F	0238	2.1		29 SA	0315	2.2
	0755	0.3			0834	0.4
	● 1455	2.2			1545	2.1
	● 2310	0.3			2050	0.2
15 SA	0315	2.2		30 SU	0357	2.2
	1114	0.3			1205	0.4
	1535	2.1			1625	2.0
	2334	0.3				
				31 M	0036	0.1
					0434	2.2
					1256	0.4
					1704	1.9

JUNE

Day	Time	m		Day	Time	m
1 TU	0110	0.1		16 W	0506	2.3
	0521	2.1			1300	0.3
	1336	0.4			1739	1.9
	1745	1.9			2245	0.1
2 W	0140	0.1		17 TH	0555	2.2
	0603	2.1			1356	0.4
	1330	0.5			1829	1.9
	1825	1.8			2345	0.0
3 TH	0000	0.1		18 F	0648	2.2
	0656	2.0			1425	0.4
	1330	0.5			1924	1.8
	1916	1.8				
4 F	0054	0.1		19 SA	0055	0.0
	0746	1.9			0755	2.2
	1430	0.5			1520	0.4
	◑ 2006	1.7			◑ 2024	1.8
5 SA	0220	0.1		20 SU	0154	0.0
	0845	1.9			0905	2.1
	1517	0.4			1650	0.4
	2055	1.7			2135	1.8
6 SU	0400	0.1		21 M	0306	0.1
	0940	1.8			1005	2.0
	1615	0.4			1757	0.4
	2155	1.7			2240	1.8
7 M	0445	0.2		22 TU	0405	0.2
	1034	1.9			1111	2.0
	1705	0.4			1855	0.4
	2306	1.7			2339	1.9
8 TU	0540	0.2		23 W	0515	0.2
	1133	1.9			1215	2.0
	1745	0.4			2010	0.4
9 W	0006	1.8		24 TH	0039	2.0
	0617	0.3			0609	0.3
	1230	2.0			1315	2.0
	1830	0.3			1834	0.3
10 TH	0045	1.9		25 F	0135	2.0
	0625	0.3			0716	0.4
	1311	2.1			1405	2.0
	1855	0.3			1919	0.3
11 F	0129	2.0		26 SA	0225	2.1
	0655	0.3			0745	0.4
	1355	2.1			1456	2.0
	1930	0.3			○ 2006	0.2
12 SA	0215	2.1		27 SU	0305	2.1
	0739	0.3			0834	0.5
	1435	2.1			1533	2.0
	● 2000	0.3			2035	0.2
13 SU	0256	2.2		28 M	0345	2.2
	0815	0.4			0904	0.5
	1519	2.1			1613	2.0
	2036	0.2			2114	0.1
14 M	0338	2.3		29 TU	0425	2.2
	1135	0.4			1230	0.5
	1606	2.0			1649	2.0
	2116	0.2			2144	0.1
15 TU	0418	2.3		30 W	0505	2.2
	1215	0.4			1315	0.5
	1649	2.0			1730	2.0
	2155	0.1			2224	0.1

JULY

Day	Time	m		Day	Time	m
1 TH	0546	2.1		16 F	0537	2.3
	1320	0.5			1336	0.4
	1759	1.9			1809	2.0
	2320	0.1			2315	0.0
2 F	0626	2.1		17 SA	0629	2.3
	1317	0.5			1410	0.5
	1833	1.9			1854	2.0
	2355	0.1				
3 SA	0654	2.0		18 SU	0019	0.1
	1350	0.5			0726	2.2
	1915	1.9			1430	0.5
					◑ 1956	2.0
4 SU	0044	0.1		19 M	0140	0.1
	0745	2.0			0830	2.1
	1420	0.4			1424	0.4
	◑ 2010	1.8			2056	1.9
5 M	0144	0.2		20 TU	0234	0.1
	0835	1.9			0924	2.0
	1445	0.4			1515	0.4
	2105	1.8			2206	1.9
6 TU	0235	0.2		21 W	0350	0.2
	0945	1.9			1043	1.9
	1600	0.4			1624	0.4
	2204	1.8			2320	1.9
7 W	0344	0.3		22 TH	0504	0.3
	1046	1.9			1210	1.9
	1710	0.4			1735	0.4
	2316	1.8				
8 TH	0520	0.3		23 F	0024	1.9
	1145	1.9			0604	0.4
	1800	0.4			1310	1.9
					1825	0.3
9 F	0016	1.9		24 SA	0124	2.0
	0610	0.3			0654	0.5
	1246	2.0			1406	2.0
	1824	0.3			1905	0.3
10 SA	0108	2.0		25 SU	0213	2.1
	0644	0.4			0734	0.5
	1336	2.0			1445	2.0
	1854	0.3			1950	0.2
11 SU	0152	2.1		26 M	0254	2.2
	0724	0.4			0805	0.6
	1418	2.0			1523	2.0
	● 1935	0.2			○ 2014	0.2
12 M	0237	2.2		27 TU	0328	2.2
	0806	0.4			0844	0.6
	1506	2.0			1554	2.1
	2015	0.2			2044	0.2
13 TU	0321	2.3		28 W	0405	2.2
	1120	0.5			0904	0.6
	1548	2.0			1629	2.1
	2056	0.1			2126	0.1
14 W	0405	2.4		29 TH	0446	2.2
	1154	0.5			1220	0.6
	1636	2.0			1659	2.1
	2135	0.1			2200	0.1
15 TH	0447	2.4		30 F	0515	2.2
	1245	0.4			1237	0.5
	1721	2.0			1729	2.1
	2221	0.0			2236	0.2
				31 SA	0545	2.1
					1307	0.5
					1759	2.0
					2309	0.2

AUGUST

Day	Time	m		Day	Time	m
1 SU	0615	2.1		16 M	0651	2.2
	1340	0.5			1330	0.5
	1829	2.0			1920	2.1
	2349	0.2			◑	
2 M	0649	2.1		17 TU	0115	0.2
	1330	0.5			0749	2.0
	1904	2.0			1354	0.4
					2013	2.0
3 TU	0035	0.2		18 W	0225	0.3
	0729	2.0			0855	1.9
	1400	0.4			1444	0.4
	◑ 1953	1.9			2136	1.9
4 W	0206	0.2		19 TH	0325	0.4
	0835	1.9			1024	1.7
	1456	0.4			1614	0.4
	2115	1.8			2306	1.9
5 TH	0254	0.3		20 F	0444	0.5
	0955	1.9			1155	1.8
	1600	0.4			1714	0.4
	2236	1.8				
6 F	0430	0.4		21 SA	0026	2.0
	1105	1.8			0710	0.5
	1720	0.4			1306	1.9
	2345	1.9			1809	0.3
7 SA	0550	0.4		22 SU	0114	2.1
	1219	1.9			0946	0.5
	1754	0.4			1344	2.0
					2156	0.3
8 SU	0045	2.0		23 M	0205	2.2
	0624	0.4			1015	0.5
	1319	1.9			1425	2.1
	1833	0.3			2225	0.3
9 M	0138	2.2		24 TU	0234	2.2
	0937	0.5			1054	0.6
	1405	2.0			1506	2.1
	1915	0.2			○ 2006	0.3
10 TU	0221	2.3		25 W	0309	2.2
	1026	0.5			0815	0.6
	1449	2.1			1536	2.1
	● 1949	0.2			2025	0.2
11 W	0302	2.4		26 TH	0339	2.3
	1106	0.5			0844	0.6
	1529	2.1			1559	2.2
	2030	0.1			2055	0.2
12 TH	0345	2.5		27 F	0415	2.3
	1140	0.5			0915	0.6
	1610	2.1			1629	2.2
	2112	0.1			2126	0.2
13 F	0429	2.4		28 SA	0438	2.3
	1225	0.5			1205	0.5
	1656	2.2			1655	2.2
	2155	0.1			2155	0.3
14 SA	0515	2.4		29 SU	0509	2.2
	1305	0.5			1250	0.5
	1738	2.2			1726	2.1
	2245	0.1			2230	0.3
15 SU	0601	2.3		30 M	0537	2.2
	1347	0.5			1050	0.5
	1825	2.2			1755	2.2
	2349	0.2			2305	0.2
				31 TU	0611	2.2
					1114	0.5
					1825	2.2
					2344	0.2

Chart Datum is 0·84 metres below NAP Datum. HAT is 2·4 metres above Chart Datum; see 0.19

Netherlands

TIME ZONE -0100
Subtract 1 hour for UT
For Dutch Summer Time add
ONE hour in **non-shaded areas**

HOEK VAN HOLLAND LAT 51°59'N LONG 4°07'E
TIMES AND HEIGHTS OF HIGH AND LOW WATERS

Dates in red are SPRINGS
Dates in blue are NEAPS

YEAR 2010

SEPTEMBER

	Time	m		Time	m
1 W ◐	0655 1204 1909	2.1 0.4 2.1	**16** TH	0205 0814 1415 2105	0.4 1.8 0.4 1.9
2 TH	0044 0738 1400 2009	0.3 2.0 0.4 2.0	**17** F	0326 0955 1606 2256	0.5 1.6 0.4 1.8
3 F	0235 0916 1515 2206	0.4 1.8 0.4 1.9	**18** SA	0450 1136 1705	0.6 1.7 0.4
4 SA	0404 1040 1624 2326	0.5 1.7 0.4 1.9	**19** SU	0006 0710 1235 1745	2.0 0.6 1.9 0.3
5 SU	0610 1154 1724	0.5 1.8 0.4	**20** M	0055 0905 1326 2125	2.1 0.5 2.0 0.3
6 M	0024 0835 1254 1805	2.1 0.5 1.9 0.3	**21** TU	0134 0956 1405 2210	2.2 0.5 2.1 0.3
7 TU	0118 0930 1341 1848	2.3 0.5 2.0 0.2	**22** W	0209 1036 1436 1945	2.2 0.5 2.1 0.3
8 W ●	0159 0955 1426 1926	2.4 0.5 2.1 0.2	**23** TH ○	0239 1055 1459 1954	2.3 0.6 2.2 0.3
9 TH	0241 0749 1505 2002	2.5 0.6 2.2 0.1	**24** F	0309 0815 1526 2026	2.3 0.6 2.2 0.3
10 F	0323 0825 1547 2045	2.5 0.6 2.3 0.1	**25** SA	0339 0845 1556 2049	2.3 0.5 2.3 0.3
11 SA	0406 0910 1629 2129	2.5 0.6 2.3 0.2	**26** SU	0409 0915 1625 2126	2.3 0.5 2.3 0.4
12 SU	0449 0955 1712 2225	2.4 0.5 2.3 0.3	**27** M	0439 0956 1656 2200	2.3 0.5 2.3 0.3
13 M	0536 1045 1756 2324	2.2 0.5 2.3 0.3	**28** TU	0512 1013 1726 2240	2.2 0.4 2.3 0.3
14 TU	0621 1144 1846	2.1 0.5 2.2	**29** W	0547 1106 1805 2320	2.2 0.4 2.3 0.4
15 W ◑	0116 0715 1305 1945	0.4 1.9 0.4 2.1	**30** TH	0625 1145 1848	2.1 0.3 2.2

OCTOBER

	Time	m		Time	m
1 F ◑	0030 0718 1257 1946	0.4 2.0 0.4 2.1	**16** SA	0245 0904 1530 2210	0.6 1.6 0.4 1.9
2 SA	0225 0834 1434 2135	0.5 1.8 0.4 1.9	**17** SU	0430 1106 1634 2336	0.7 1.7 0.3 1.9
3 SU	0350 1015 1545 2300	0.6 1.7 0.4 2.0	**18** M	0630 1206 1724	0.6 1.8 0.3
4 M	0647 1136 1645	0.6 1.8 0.4	**19** TU	0019 0804 1250 1814	2.1 0.5 1.9 0.3
5 TU	0005 0814 1231 1735	2.2 0.5 1.9 0.3	**20** W	0106 0854 1324 2110	2.2 0.5 2.0 0.4
6 W	0055 0916 1317 1820	2.3 0.5 2.0 0.3	**21** TH	0139 0955 1354 2137	2.2 0.5 2.1 0.4
7 TH ●	0135 0935 1358 1859	2.4 0.6 2.2 0.2	**22** F	0210 1015 1425 1934	2.2 0.5 2.2 0.4
8 F	0217 0726 1441 1939	2.5 0.6 2.3 0.2	**23** SA ○	0235 0754 1455 1954	2.3 0.5 2.2 0.4
9 SA	0300 0805 1525 2025	2.5 0.5 2.3 0.2	**24** SU	0305 0825 1525 2029	2.3 0.5 2.3 0.4
10 SU	0346 0846 1605 2109	2.4 0.5 2.4 0.3	**25** M	0338 0855 1557 2106	2.3 0.5 2.3 0.4
11 M	0427 0929 1647 2159	2.3 0.5 2.4 0.4	**26** TU	0416 0925 1631 2139	2.3 0.4 2.3 0.4
12 TU	0516 1026 1731 2305	2.2 0.6 2.3 0.5	**27** W	0450 0954 1705 2214	2.3 0.4 2.3 0.5
13 W	0555 1125 1819	2.0 0.6 2.2	**28** TH	0530 1045 1748 2309	2.1 0.4 2.3 0.5
14 TH ◑	0040 0649 1234 1915	0.5 1.9 0.3 2.1	**29** F	0609 1134 1835	2.0 0.3 2.2
15 F	0146 0750 1335 2035	0.6 1.8 0.3 1.9	**30** SA ◑	0150 0706 1250 1935	0.5 1.9 0.3 2.1
			31 SU	0230 0824 1355 2115	0.6 1.8 0.3 2.0

NOVEMBER

	Time	m		Time	m
1 M	0504 0950 1510 2235	0.6 1.7 0.3 2.1	**16** TU	0440 1116 1704 2345	0.6 1.7 0.3 2.0
2 TU	0634 1105 1605 2336	0.6 1.8 0.3 2.2	**17** W	0700 1206 1800	0.6 1.8 0.4
3 W	0745 1206 2010	0.5 1.9 0.3	**18** TH	0026 0815 1246 1920	2.0 0.5 1.9 0.4
4 TH	0030 0856 1255 1756	2.3 0.5 2.1 0.3	**19** F	0055 0910 1315 2050	2.1 0.5 2.0 0.4
5 F	0116 0926 1338 1846	2.3 0.6 2.2 0.3	**20** SA	0136 0944 1349 1914	2.2 0.5 2.1 0.5
6 SA ●	0157 0705 1422 1928	2.4 0.5 2.3 0.3	**21** SU ○	0205 0745 1426 1945	2.2 0.4 2.2 0.5
7 SU	0242 0749 1506 2009	2.3 0.5 2.4 0.4	**22** M	0241 0804 1500 2020	2.3 0.5 2.3 0.5
8 M	0329 0835 1547 2054	2.3 0.4 2.4 0.5	**23** TU	0319 0840 1536 2049	2.3 0.4 2.3 0.5
9 TU	0415 0920 1631 2354	2.2 0.4 2.4 0.5	**24** W	0355 0916 1615	2.2 0.4 2.4
10 W	0055 0455 1005 1718	0.5 2.1 0.3 2.3	**25** TH	0438 0945 1655	2.1 0.3 2.3
11 TH	0140 0546 1055 1806	0.6 2.0 0.2 2.2	**26** F	0034 0517 1035 1736	0.5 2.1 0.3 2.3
12 F	0007 0624 1154 1900	0.6 1.9 0.2 2.1	**27** SA	0136 0605 1130 1825	0.5 2.0 0.2 2.3
13 SA ◑	0110 0715 1304 2006	0.6 1.8 0.3 2.0	**28** SU ◑	0205 0740 1230 1924	0.5 1.9 0.2 2.2
14 SU	0214 0815 1440 2105	0.7 1.7 0.3 1.9	**29** M	0250 0815 1334 2045	0.6 1.8 0.2 2.1
15 M	0325 0925 1555 2224	0.7 1.7 0.3 1.9	**30** TU	0427 0914 1435 2206	0.6 1.8 0.2 2.1

DECEMBER

	Time	m		Time	m
1 W	0610 1036 1546 2306	0.6 1.9 0.3 2.1	**16** TH	0435 1034 1730 2326	0.6 1.8 0.4 1.9
2 TH	0725 1136 1646	0.6 1.9 0.3	**17** F	0540 1146 1820	0.5 1.8 0.4
3 F	0006 0826 1225 1739	2.2 0.5 1.9 0.4	**18** SA	0016 0624 1236 1920	2.0 0.5 1.9 0.4
4 SA	0058 0857 1318 1834	2.2 0.5 2.1 0.4	**19** SU	0059 0654 1314 1905	2.1 0.5 2.0 0.5
5 SU ●	0148 0705 1406 1925	2.2 0.5 2.2 0.4	**20** M	0145 0715 1359 1934	2.1 0.4 2.2 0.5
6 M	0236 0745 1451 2004	2.2 0.4 2.3 0.5	**21** TU ○	0225 0743 1439 2003	2.2 0.4 2.3 0.5
7 TU	0318 0825 1535 2054	2.2 0.3 2.3 0.6	**22** W	0300 0826 1518 2034	2.2 0.3 2.3 0.5
8 W	0405 0904 1618	2.1 0.3 2.3	**23** TH	0345 0855 1601 2334	2.2 0.3 2.4 0.5
9 TH	0036 0444 0956 1705	0.6 2.1 0.2 2.3	**24** F	0429 0936 1646	2.1 0.2 2.4
10 F	0105 0535 1034 1745	0.6 2.1 0.2 2.2	**25** SA	0030 0516 1020 1729	0.5 2.1 0.2 2.4
11 SA	0155 0615 1130 1836	0.6 2.0 0.2 2.2	**26** SU	0126 0554 1110 1817	0.5 2.0 0.1 2.3
12 SU	0030 0649 1215 1919	0.6 2.0 0.2 2.1	**27** M	0206 0649 1159 1915	0.5 2.0 0.1 2.3
13 M ◑	0130 0740 1320 2015	0.6 1.9 0.3 2.0	**28** TU ◑	0230 0745 1304 2020	0.6 2.0 0.2 2.2
14 TU	0230 0824 1440 2116	0.6 1.8 0.3 1.9	**29** W	0235 0844 1420 2126	0.6 1.9 0.2 2.1
15 W	0340 0924 1624 2216	0.6 1.8 0.3 1.9	**30** TH	0314 0956 1525 2236	0.6 1.9 0.2 2.0
			31 F	0405 1106 1624 2340	0.6 1.9 0.2 2.0

Chart Datum is 0.84 metres below NAP Datum. HAT is 2.4 metres above Chart Datum; see 0.19

》》 FREE monthly updates from 《《
www.reedsalmanac.co.uk

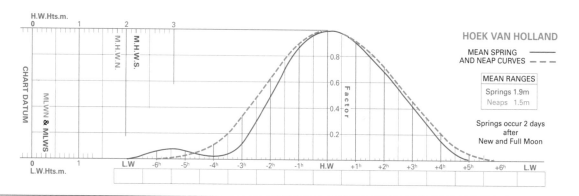

HOEK VAN HOLLAND

MEAN SPRING ——————
AND NEAP CURVES – – – –

MEAN RANGES
Springs 1.9m
Neaps 1.5m

Springs occur 2 days
after
New and Full Moon

2.21 MAAS TSS

Large ships bound up-Channel for Europoort route via the Dover Strait and the Noord Hinder South TSS to Noord Hinder Junction (a large pentagon roughly centred on 52°N 02°51'·1E). Here ships enter the MAAS TRAFFIC SEPARATION SCHEME.

Maas West Outer TSS starts some 33M offshore and funnels large ships 083°/27M via the TSS lanes or Eurogeul (DW route dredged 24·5m) towards a second pentagon 'Maas Precautionary Area' clear of Maas West Inner TSS and 10M offshore. When abeam Maas Centre SWM buoy, ships enter the Maasgeul (Maas narrows) and track inbound 5·5M on the 112° leading lights to the Maasmond (Maas mouth, ie the harbour entrance).

Yachts should avoid the whole complex by using the ITZ and/or crossing the Maasgeul via the recommended track (see 2.22). Knowing the above is to be aware of what you are avoiding.

HOEK VAN HOLLAND TO THE SOUTH EAST UK

Yachts out of Rotterdam/Hoek van Holland bound for the southern Thames Estuary should route 254°/52M from MV-N buoy to NHR-SE buoy, passing MW5, Goeree tower, MW3 and MW1 buoys. Cross the Noord Hinder South TSS between NHR-SE and NHR-S buoys. Thence depending on destination, set course 242°/44M to Outer Tongue for the River Thames; or 228°/46M to NE Goodwin for Ramsgate or points south.

If bound for the River Orwell or adjacent rivers, it may be best to pass north (rather than south) of the large and busy Sunk Outer and Inner Precautionary Areas and their associated TSS. From NHR-S buoy route via West Gabbard, North Inner Gabbard, S Shipwash and Rough buoys to pick up the recommended yacht track at Cork Sand Yacht beacon; it is a less direct route than going south via Galloper, but it avoids the worst of the commercial traffic.

2.21A MAAS TSS, PRECAUTIONARY AREA AND MAASGEUL

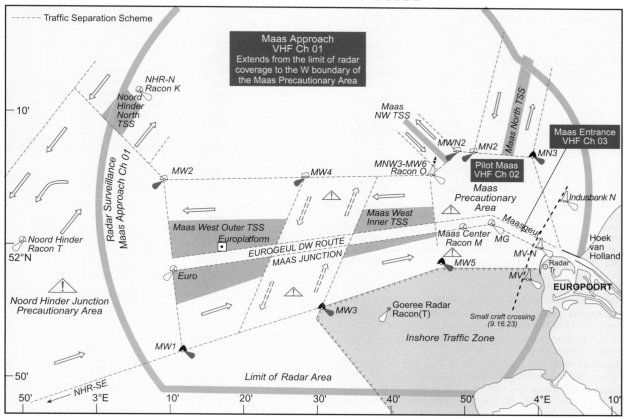

2.22 HOEK VAN HOLLAND AND NIEUWE WATERWEG VTS

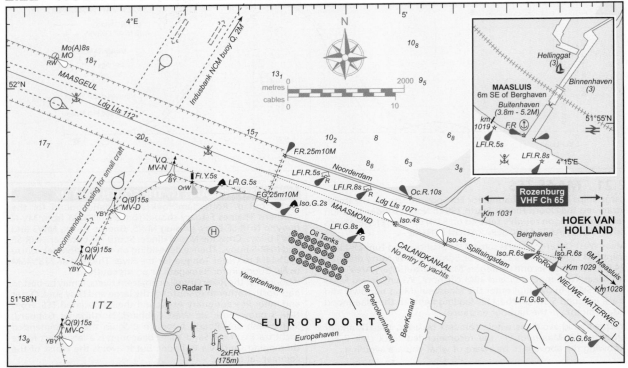

CROSSING THE MAASGEUL To cross the entrance (ie seaward of the bkwtrs), coasting yachts should advise *Maas Ent* Ch 03 of position/course/speed, then monitor Ch 03. Cross on the recommended track, 046° (226°) under power; see chartlet. Beware strong cross tides. Keep a keen lookout for fast moving merchantmen; Rules 18 d (ii) and 28.

HOEK VAN HOLLAND

CHARTS AC 122, 132; Zeekaart 1540, 1349, 1350, 1449; DYC 1801.6, 1801.7; Imray C30, Y5; Stanfords 19

TIDES +0251 Dover; ML 0·9; Duration 0505. HOEK VAN HOLLAND is a Standard Port (◄—), but has no Secondary ports; see also 2.23. Double LWs occur, more obviously at sp; in effect a LW stand. The 1st LW is about 5½ hrs after HW and the 2nd LW about 4¼ hrs before the next HW. Predictions are for the *lower* LW. Prolonged NW gales can raise levels by up to 3m.

SHELTER Entry safe, but in strong on-shore winds heavy seas/swell develop. The first adequate shelter is 6M up river at Maassluis (3m). Complete shelter 10-19M further E at Rotterdam.

NAVIGATION From N, WPT 52°02'·89N 04°03'·57E (Indusbank NCM lt buoy, Q), 190°/3·2M to Noorderdam lt, FR. From S, WPT 51°59'·61N 04°00'·20E (MV-N buoy), 101°/3·0M to ent to Nieuwe Waterweg. *Yachts must on no account enter the Calandkanaal or Europoort. Stay in the Nieuwe Waterweg.*

LIGHTS AND MARKS See chartlet and 2.3 for details. Outer ldg lts 112° to ent; then 107° Red (ie keep to port) ldg lts into Nieuwe Waterweg, both R trs, W bands.

Hbr patrol vessels show a Fl Bu lt; additionally a Fl R lt = 'Stop'.

TELEPHONE (Code 010) Port Authority (HCC) 2522400; ⊖ 2442266; Police 4141414; ⊞ 4112800; Brit Consul (020) 6764343.

FACILITIES Berghaven is currently closed to yachts but a marina is under consideration.

Hoek van Holland ⊠, Ⓑ, ⇌, 🛒, R, Bar, P, D, ✈ (Rotterdam). Ferries: Hook-Harwich; Rotterdam (Vlaardingen)-Hull.

Maassluis Marina ☎ 593 1285. Ent/lock/bridge Ch 80, marina Ch 68. CH, El, FW, BY, ME, ⚒. See tidal differences 2.23 and chartlet inset above.

NIEUWE WATERWEG VTS

Arrival procedure for yachts First report to *Maas Approach* or *Pilot Maas*, depending on distance offshore (or *Maas Ent* if within 4M of hbr ent), stating name/type of vessel, position and destination. Obey any instructions, monitoring the relevant Radar Ch's (limits as shown by W □ signboards on the river banks; Km signs are similar).

Rules for yachts in Nieuwe Waterweg/Nieuwe Maas: Monitor VTS channels (see below); transmit only in emergency or if obliged to deviate from the usual traffic flow. Keep to extreme stbd limit of buoyed line, avoiding debris between buoys and bank. No tacking/beating; no ⚓. Engine ready for instant start. Able to motor at 3·24kn (6km/hr). Hoist a radar reflector, esp in poor vis or at night. Cross chan quickly at 90°. All docks are prohib to yachts, except to access a marina. *Keep a good lookout, especially astern.*

The 3 **Traffic Centres (TC)** oversee their Radar surveillance stations and sub-sectors *(italics)*, on dedicated VHF chans below:

- **TC Hoek van Holland (VCH)** Ch 11. (See diagram above)

Maas Approach	Ch 01	38 – 11M W of Hoek;
Pilot Maas	Ch 02	11 – 4M W of Hoek;
Maas Entrance	Ch 03	4M – km 1031.

  English is the primary language on Ch 01, 02 and 03.

Rozenburg	Ch 65	km 1031 – 1028;
Maassluis	Ch 80	km 1028 – 1017.

- **Botlek Information & Tracking system** Ch 14.

Botlek	Ch 61	km 1017 – 1011;
Eemhaven	Ch 63	km 1011 – 1007.

- **TC Rotterdam (VCR)** Ch 11.

Waalhaven	Ch 60	km 1007 – 1003·5;
Maasbruggen	Ch 81	km 1003·5 – 998;
Brienenoord	Ch 21	km 998 – 993.

Harbour Coordination Centre (HCC) administers and controls Rotterdam port, Ch 19 (H24).

MSI broadcasts by TCs Ch 11 and on request by Radar stns.

Nieuwe Waterweg VTS and Nieuwe Maas into central Rotterdam continued

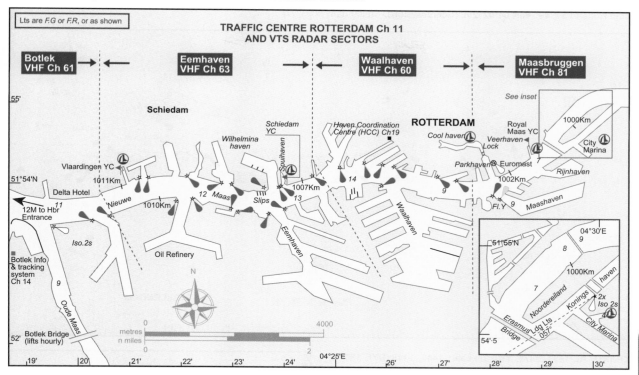

2.23 ROTTERDAM

Zuid Holland **51°54′·00N 04°28′·00E** (610m S of Euromast)
❋❋❋❋♦♦♦✿✿✿

CHARTS AC 122, 132, 133; Zeekaart 1540/1/2; DYC 1809.4, 1809.5; Stanfords 19

TIDES +0414 Dover; ML 0·9; Duration 0440.
Standard Port VLISSINGEN (→)

Times				Height (metres)			
High Water		Low Water		MHWS	MHWN	MLWN	MLWS
0300	0900	0400	1000	5·0	4·1	1·1	0·5
1500	2100	1600	2200				
Differences EUROPLATFORM (30M W of Hoek van Holland)							
+0005	−0005	−0030	−0055	−2·7	−2·2	−0·6	−0·1
MAASSLUIS (Km 1019)							
+0155	+0115	+0100	+0310	−2·9	−2·3	−0·8	−0·2
VLAARDINGEN (Km 1011)							
+0150	+0120	+0130	+0330	−2·9	−2·3	−0·8	−0·2

NOTE: Double LWs occur. Maaslus and Vlaardingen are referenced to Vlissingen, in UK ATT as above. The Dutch HP33 *Tidal heights and streams in Dutch coastal waters* shows the time differences below, relative to HW and the first LW at Hoek van Holland:

HOEK VAN HOLLAND	HW	1st LW
Maaslus	+0102	+0308
Vlaardingen	+0103	+0333
Rotterdam	+0111	+0341

SHELTER Good in the yacht hbrs where visitors are welcome (see Facilities). There is always a considerable chop/swell in the river due to constant heavy traffic to/from Europoort and Rotterdam.

NAVIGATION See 2.22 for WPTs (to enter Nieuwe Waterweg) and Yacht Rules. From the hbr ent to the conspic Euromast (51°54′·33N 04°28′·00E) is about 18M (33km). 6M W of the Euromast, the very busy Oude Maas joins at km 1013, giving access to Dordrecht and the Delta network of canals/lakes.

R/T See chartlet above for VTS in central Rotterdam. In emergency call Rotterdam Tfc Centre Ch 11. See Facilities for VHF Chans at locks/bridges. English is the second language.

TELEPHONE (Code 010) Hbr Coordination Centre (HCC) 2522400, also Emergency; ☎ 2442266; Police 4141414; ☒ 4112800; Brit Consul (020) 6764343.

FACILITIES Marinas/yacht harbours from seaward:

Vlaardingen YC, 51°53′·98N 04°20′·93E, 400m E of Delta Hotel. Berth in Buitenhaven (3·6-4·4m) or lock (Ch 20) into Oude Haven (2·7m). HM ☎ 4346786, M, BY, ME, SM, P, D, Gaz, ⛽.

Spuihaven, 51°54′·00N 04°24′·00E, immediately E of the ent to Wilhelmina Haven. No lock/bridge to transit. Schiedam YC ☎ 4267765, AB (1·6-2·8m), D, ME, El, ✗, CH, ⛽.

Coolhaven Yacht Hbr, 51°54′·12N 04°28′·00E; next to Euromast 185m. Access through Parkhaven via lock (Ch 22) ☎ 4738614, AB (2·7m), M, P, D, ME, El, ✗, C, Slip, CH, 🛒, R, Bar.

Veerhaven. 51°54′·39N 04°28′·76E, 5ca E of Euromast. ☎ 4365446. www.veerhavenrotterdam.nl info@veerhavenrotterdam.nl Centre for traditional sea-going vessels. Ⓥ welcome, €1.50. AB (3·9m), ME, El, SM, CH, 🛒 350m N, Water taxi to S bank. **Royal Maas YC** ☎ 4137681, (clubhouse, members only).

City Marina, 51°54′·64N 04°29′·76E. Go under Erasmus bridge (Ch 18) via lifting section at SE end which only opens 1000, 1100, 1400 & 1500LT or on request Ch 18 1900-0700 (11m clearance under fixed span). Ldg lts 056·7°, both Iso 2s; then 2nd ent to stbd, via lifting bridge. ☎ (0187) 4854096, Mob 0622 215761, www.citymarinarotterdam.nl info@citymarinarotterdam.nl 130 AB +40 Ⓥ in 4m. €1.75/m/night for 2 nights; €1.50 3rd-7th nights; €1.25 7 nights. YC, Water taxi to N bank, @, Wi-Fi, 🛒.

WSV IJsselmonde, 51°54′·24N 04°33′·34E, on S bank at km 994, 800m E of Brienenoordbrug, Ch 20 (off chartlet). ☎ 482833, AB (1·3-2·1m).

City all facilities, ACA, DYC Agent. Ferry: Rotterdam (Vlaardingen) –Hull; Hook–Harwich.

2.24 STELLENDAM (for Haringvliet)

Zuid Holland 51°49'·46N 04°02'·29E (Goereesesluis). Stellendam ⚙⚙◊◊✿

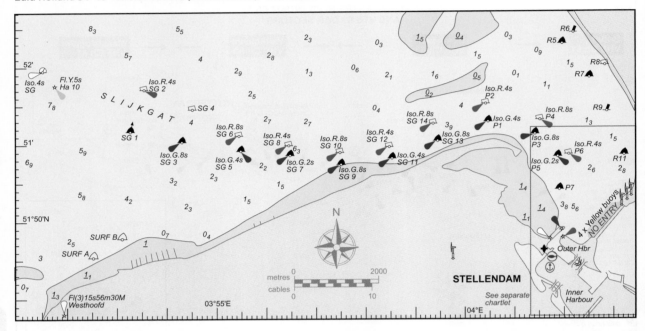

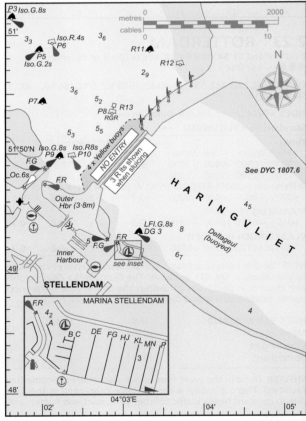

CHARTS AC 1631, 3371, 110; Zeekaart 1447, 1448; DYC 1801.6, 1807.6; Imray C30; Stanfords 19

TIDES +0300 Dover; ML 1·2; Duration 0510.

Standard Port VLISSINGEN (⟶)

Times				Height (metres)			
High Water		Low Water		MHWS	MHWN	MLWN	MLWS
0300	0900	0400	1000	5·0	4·1	1·1	0·5
1500	2100	1600	2200				
Differences HARINGVLIETSLUIZEN							
+0015	+0015	+0015	−0020	−2·0	−1·9	−0·7	+0·2

NOTE: Double LWs occur. The rise after the 1st LW is called the Agger. Water levels on this coast are much affected by weather. Prolonged NW gales can raise levels by up to 3m.

SHELTER Good in marina. The entrance to the Slijkgat can be rough in strong W/NW winds and with wind against tide.

NAVIGATION WPT 51°51'·95N 03°51'·42E (SG SWM buoy, Iso 4s), 112°/2·6M to SG5/6 chan buoys. Thence 3·3M via the well buoyed/lit Slijkgat chan to SG13 and P1 SHM buoys. Follow P1 to P9 SHM buoys SSE for 2·2M to the Buitenhaven, avoiding the no-entry sluicing area, marked by 4 SPM buoys.

Access is via a lock which operates 24/7 and has recessed bollards. 2 bridges lift in sequence to minimise road tfc delays. Note: the W bridge has 14m vertical clearance when down (with digital clearance gauge outside), the E bridge only 5·4m.

LIGHTS AND MARKS Haringvlietsluizen: 3 ● in △ are shown from pier heads on dam when sluicing in progress.

R/T *Goereese Sluis* Ch 20 for bridges and lock. Marina Ch 31.

TELEPHONE (Code 0187) Lock 497350; Stellendam Port HM 491000; ⊖ Rotterdam (010) 4298088 or Vlissingen (0118) 484600; Emergencies 112; Brit Consul (020) 6764343.

FACILITIES Marina ☎ 493769. www.marinastellendam.nl info@marinastellendam.nl 200 AB inc ▼, €2.00 inc tourist tax & shower. Berth as directed in 3m; all pontoons have fingers. D&P, SM, ME, CH, ▣, C (20 ton), Bar, R ☎ 492344, bike hire.

Town (4½ km) 🛒, R, Bar, ✉. ✈ (Rotterdam). Bus to Vlissingen & Spijkenisse. Ferry: Hoek of Holland-Harwich; Rotterdam-Hull.

2.25 ROOMPOTSLUIS (for Oosterschelde)

Zeeland **51°37'·11N 03°41'·08E** Roompot Lock

CHARTS AC 1630, 110; Zeekaart 1448; DYCs 1805.8, 1801.5; Imray C30; Stanfords 1, 19

TIDES +0230 Dover.

Standard Port VLISSINGEN (→)

Times				Height (metres)			
High Water		Low Water		MHWS	MHWN	MLWN	MLWS
0300	0900	0400	1000	5·0	4·1	1·1	0·5
1500	2100	1600	2200				
Differences ROOMPOT BUITEN							
−0015	+0005	+0005	−0020	−1·3	−1·1	−0·4	−0·1

SHELTER An approach in strong W/NW winds is not advised. The Buitenhaven's inner part is sheltered.

NAVIGATION WPT 51°39'·35N 03°33'·65E (abeam OR1 SHM buoy), 122°/4·2M via Oude Roompot chan to the 073·5° ldg line, both Oc G 5s, into the Buitenhaven. The flood sets E from HW Vlissingen −3 to +1. See 2.4 for the several offshore banks.

Alternatively Roompot chan, buoyed but unlit, is further south and closer inshore.

Keep clear of the buoyed areas, W and E of the storm-surge barrier, which are very dangerous due to strong tidal streams and many obstructions.

Roompotsluis lock (☎ 0111 659265). Lock hrs: Mon, Thu 0001-2200; Tue, Sun 0600-2359; Wed 0001-2359; Fri, Sat 0600-2200. Waiting pontoons are W and E of the lock with intercom phones to the lock-keeper. Customs can be cleared at the lock in season.

The fixed bridge has 18·2m least clearance. At LW clearance is approx 21m. Check with tide gauges or lock-keeper if in doubt. Small bollards, fixed at vertical

intervals, are recessed into the lock walls. Ent to/exit from the lock is controlled by R/G traffic lights.

LIGHTS AND MARKS See 2.3 and chartlet.

R/T Lock *Roompotsluis* Ch 18. Roompot Marina Ch 31. Monitor Ch 68 which broadcasts local forecasts at H+15.

FACILITIES Roompot Marina ⚓✷✷◊◊◊✿✿ Good shelter, 1·5M SE of lock. ☎ (0113) 374125, marina@roompot.nl. 50 + 80 ⊻, €2·00, D, P, Slip, Gas, Gaz, ◻, ⬜, Bar, R, Ⓑ. Dr ☎ 372565; ⊖ 0118 484600.

Or follow G3-G17 buoys into **Betonhaven** about 1M NE of the lock. ⚓ in 3-6m, good holding in sticky black mud, or AB on a pontoon (Roompot marina II). €0·85, plus €0·90 tourist tax, for 3 days max stay; no FW, no AC. Easy walk to the Delta Expo.

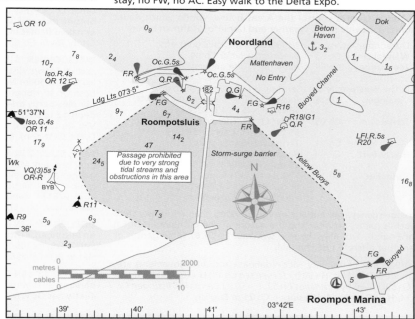

2.26 WESTERSCHELDE

Zeeland mostly, but Belgium for the last 12M to Antwerpen

CHARTS AC 1874, 120, 139; Zeekaart 1443; DYC 1803; Imray C30

TIDES +0200 Dover; ML Hansweert 2·7, Westkapelle 2·0, Bath 2·8; Duration 0555.

Standard Port VLISSINGEN (→)

Times				Height (metres)			
High Water		Low Water		MHWS	MHWN	MLWN	MLWS
0300	0900	0400	1000	5·0	4·1	1·1	0·5
1500	2100	1600	2200				
Differences WESTKAPELLE (8M NW of Vlissingen)							
−0025	−0015	−0010	−0025	−0·6	−0·6	−0·2	−0·1
HANSWEERT							
+0100	+0050	+0040	+0100	+0·6	+0·7	0·0	0·0
BATH							
+0125	+0115	+0115	+0140	+1·1	+1·0	+0·1	+0·1

SHELTER In strong winds a bad sea can be met in the estuary mouth. Conditions become easier further up-river. See Facilities.

NAVIGATION Westerschelde is the waterway to Antwerpen (and via canal to Gent), very full of ships and barges, especially in the last 15M. The main channel winds through a mass of well marked sand-banks. It is essential to work the tides, which average 2½kn, more at springs. Best timing is most easily achieved by starting from Vlissingen, Breskens or Terneuzen. Yachts should keep to the edge of main chan. Use alternative chans with caution; Vaarwater langs Hoofdplat and de Paulinerploder/Thomaesgeul/

Springergeul are buoyed shortcuts popular with yachtsmen, but note that channels shift regularly.

Commercial Shipping: Yachts should keep just outside the busy shipping chans, ie Wielingen from the SW, Scheur from the W, and Oostgat from the NW.

Be aware of large ship anchorages: Wielingen Noord and Zuid, either side of the fairway, as defined by buoys W6-Trawl-WN6 and W9-Songa. Further E, Flushing Roads anchorage is defined by Songa, SS1, SS5 and ARV-VH buoys. Ocean-going ships often manoeuvre off Vlissingen to transfer pilots.

S of Vlissingen (see Breskens) an E-W TSS (part of a Precautionary area) is best avoided by yachts which should cross the fairway via the recommended N-S track between Buitenhaven and ARV3 SPM lt buoy. Fast ferries, which have right of way, ply half-hourly from Vlissingen Buitenhaven to Breskens. *Keep a sharp lookout.*

Recommended small craft routes: **From the SW** there are few dangers. After Zeebrugge, keep S of the Wielingen chan buoys (W1-9). Off Breskens avoid fast ferries to/from Vlissingen; continue E to SS1 buoy, then cross to Vlissingen on a N'ly track.

From the W, keep clear of the Scheur chan by crossing to the S of Wielingen as soon as practicable.

From the N, the narrow, busy Oostgat can be used with caution, keeping just outside the SW edge of the buoyed/lit chan.

Three lesser, unlit day-only N'ly routes which avoid Oostgat are:

- From Kaloo or DR1 buoys, follow the Geul van de Rassen, Deurloo and Spleet chans to SP4 buoy. Thence E via WN6 buoy.

- Or continue down the Deurloo from DL5 buoy to join Oostgat at OG19 buoy; thence cross to the Vlissingen shore as and when traffic in Oostgat permits.
- Another route, slightly further offshore, is to skirt the NW side of Kaloo bank to Botkil-W buoy, thence SE via Geul van de Walvischstaart (PHM buoys only) to Trawl SCM buoy.

LIGHTS AND MARKS The apprs are well lit by lighthouses: on the S shore at Nieuwe Sluis, and on the N shore at Westkapelle; see 2.3. The main fairways are, for the most part, defined by ldg lts and by the W sectors of the many Dir lts.

SCHELDEMOND VTS covers from the North Sea outer approaches up-river to Antwerpen; see the diagram below and 2.20. Yachts should monitor at all times the VHF Ch for the area in which they are, so as to be aware of other shipping and to be contactable if required. Do not transmit, unless called.

7 **Traffic Centres** control the Areas below, within which Radar stations provide radar, weather and hbr info, as shown below:

Outer approaches: (*Traffic Centre* is the callsign prefix)		
Wandelaar	Ch 65	*Zeebrugge Radar Ch 04.*
Zeebrugge	Ch 69	*Radar* as in line above.
Steenbank	Ch 64	*Radar* also on Ch 64.
In the Westerschelde: (*Centrale* is the callsign prefix)		
Vlissingen	Ch 14	*Radar Ch 21.* Vlissingen to E2A/PvN SPR buoys (51°24'N 03°44'E).
Terneuzen	Ch 03	*Radar Ch 03.* Thence to Nos 32/35 buoys (51°23'N 03°57'E).
	Ch 11	Terneuzen-Gent Canal.
Hansweert	Ch 65	*Radar Ch 65.* Thence to Nos 46/55 buoys (51°24'N 04°02'E).
Zandvliet	Ch 12	Thence to Antwerpen. *Radar Waarde* 19; *Saeftinge* 21; *Zandvliet* 04; *Kruisschans* 66.

In **emergency**, call initially on the working channel in use; state yacht's name, position and the nature of the problem, in Dutch or English. You may then be switched to Ch **67 (Emergency)** or another discrete VHF channel.

Broadcasts of visibility, Met, tidal data and ship movements are made in Dutch at: H +00 by *Terneuzen* Ch 11; H +10 by *Zeebrugge* Ch 69; H +30 by *Zandvliet* Ch 12; H +50 by *Centrale Vlissingen* Ch 14; **H +55 by Radar Vlissingen Ch 21 in English.**

FACILITIES Some minor hbrs from Terneuzen to Antwerpen (38M) are listed below. They may be useful in emergency or offer shelter, but most dry. Yachts usually go non-stop to Antwerpen.

ELLEWOUTSDIJK, 51°23'·10N 03°49'·05E. DYC 1803.2. HW +2 and +0·3m on Vlissingen; ML 2·6m. Small, unlit hbr, 27 AB, voluntary donation. Access HW ±3; 1·5m at MLWS. Strong cross eddy on ebb. HM ☎ (0113) 548431/06 251154766. C (10 ton), Gaz, @, YC.

HOEDEKENSKERKE, 51°25'·11N 03°54'·90E. DYC 1803.3. Disused ferry hbr (dries) abeam MG13 SHM buoy. Access HW–2½ to +3 for 1m draft. €1.00/m (min €8.00/night) inc AC, FW. **YC WV Hoedekenskerke ☎** (0113) 639278, mob 0653 794069. 33 + 6 Ⓥ, Gaz, FW, SM, Shwrs at campsite 400m. **Town** ✉, Ⓑ, ⇌ (Goes).

HANSWEERT, 51°26'·37N 04°00'·66E. DYC 1803.3. Tidal differences above. Temporary stop, but it is the busy ent to Zuid Beveland canal. Lt Oc WRG 10s, R lattice tr, W band, at ent. Waiting berths outside lock on E side. Ⓥ berths in inner hbr, W side; **no smoking or naked flames in, or near lock. Services:** ME, BY, P, D, C (17 ton), CH, R. **Town** ✉, Ⓑ, ⇌ (Kruiningen-Yerseke).

WALSOORDEN, 51°22'·93N 04°02'·10E. DYC 1803.3. HW is +0110 and +0·7m on Vlissingen; ML 2·6m. Prone to swell. SHM buoy 57, Iso G 8s, is 500m N of ent where 16 silos are conspic. Ldg lts 220° both Oc 3s. Hbr ent FG & FR. Unmarked stone pier just outside E hbr pier, partly dries at LW. Yacht basin dead ahead on ent to hbr, depths 2 to 2·8m. 4/5 AB, €0.30/m, max stay H24. *Zandvliet Radio* VHF Ch 12. WSV d'Ouwe Haven ☎ (0114) 682925, FW, Slip, Gas, P, D, BY, C (16 ton), ME, El, 🚿. **Town** R, Bar, ✉.

PAAL, 51°21'·25N 04°06'·65E. DYC 1803.3. HW +0120 and +0·8m on Vlissingen; ML 2·7m. Appr HW±2 via No. 63 SHM buoy and tide gauge, across drying Speelmansgat. Unlit, drying yacht hbr on S bank at river mouth, ent marked by withy. HM ☎ (0114) 314974, 0611 028174. *Zandvliet Radio* Ch 12. **Jachthaven** 150 AB, Shwr €0.50, Gaz, ME, El, 🛒, R, @ in YC. P&D (cans) 10 mins walk.

DOEL, 51°18'·67N 04°16'·11E. DYC 1803.5. HW +0100 and +0·7m on Vlissingen. Customs base. Small drying hbr on W bank; no entry LW±2. Ldg lts 185·5°: front Fl WR 3s on N pier hd; rear Fl 3s, synch. HM ☎ (03) 6652585; **YC de Noord ☎** 7733669, R, Bar, FW.

LILLO, 51°18'·16N 04°17'·30E. DYC 1803.5. 1M SE of Doel on opp bank; small drying hbr for shoal-draft only; HW±3. Customs base. T-jetty has Oc WRG 10s. HM (035) 686456; **YC Scaldis.**

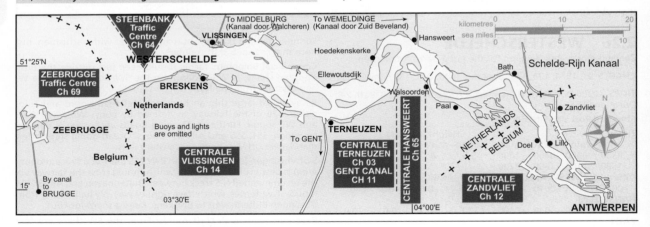

2.27 VLISSINGEN (FLUSHING)

Zeeland 51°26'·31N 03°34'·61E Koopmanshaven 🌸🌸❄❄🏠🏠🏪🏪

CHARTS AC 1872, 1874, 120; Zeekaart 1442, 1443, 1533; DYC 1803.8, 1801.3; Imray C30; Stanfords 1, 19.

TIDES +0215 Dover; ML 2·3; Duration 0555. Note: Vlissingen is a Standard Port (→).

SHELTER Very good in both yacht hbrs.

NAVIGATION WPT 51°25'·16N 03°33'·66E (Songa SHM buoy, QG), 027°/1·29M to Koopmanshaven ent. Study 2.26.

LIGHTS AND MARKS From NW, Oostgat 117° ldg lts: Front RW pile; rear Sardijngeul, Oc WRG 5s, R/W banded mast, R △. Note: Conspic radar twr (close NW of Koopmanshaven) shows a Fl Y lt to warn when ships are approaching in the blind NW arc from Oostgat-Sardijngeul. A conspic, floodlit R/W metal framework tr (50m) near de Ruyter Marina indicates the appr. Buitenhaven traffic signals from mole W side of ent: R flag or extra ● near FR on W mole hd = No entry.

R/T Michiel de Ruyter and Schelde Marinas: nil VHF; use mobile. Sealock Ch 18, canal bridges Ch 22. See also 2.26.

Continued opposite

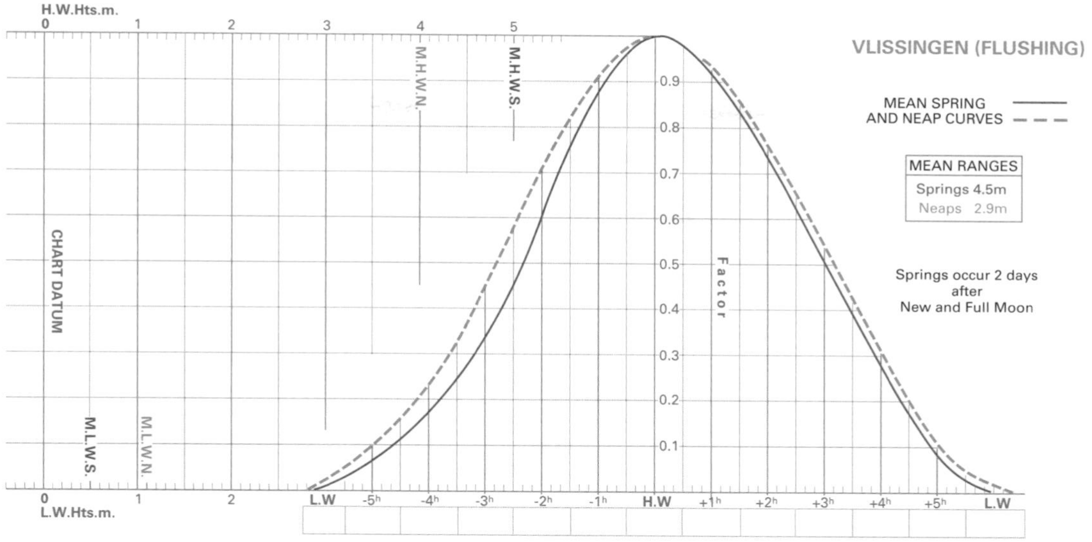
H.W.Hts.m.
0
1
2
3
4
5
M.H.W.N.
M.H.W.S.
CHART DATUM
M.L.W.S.
M.L.W.N.
0
1
2
L.W.Hts.m.
0.9
0.8
0.7
0.6
0.5
0.4
0.3
0.2
0.1
Factor
L.W -5h -4h -3h -2h -1h H.W +1h +2h +3h +4h +5h L.W
VLISSINGEN (FLUSHING)
MEAN SPRING AND NEAP CURVES
MEAN RANGES
Springs 4.5m
Neaps 2.9m
Springs occur 2 days after New and Full Moon

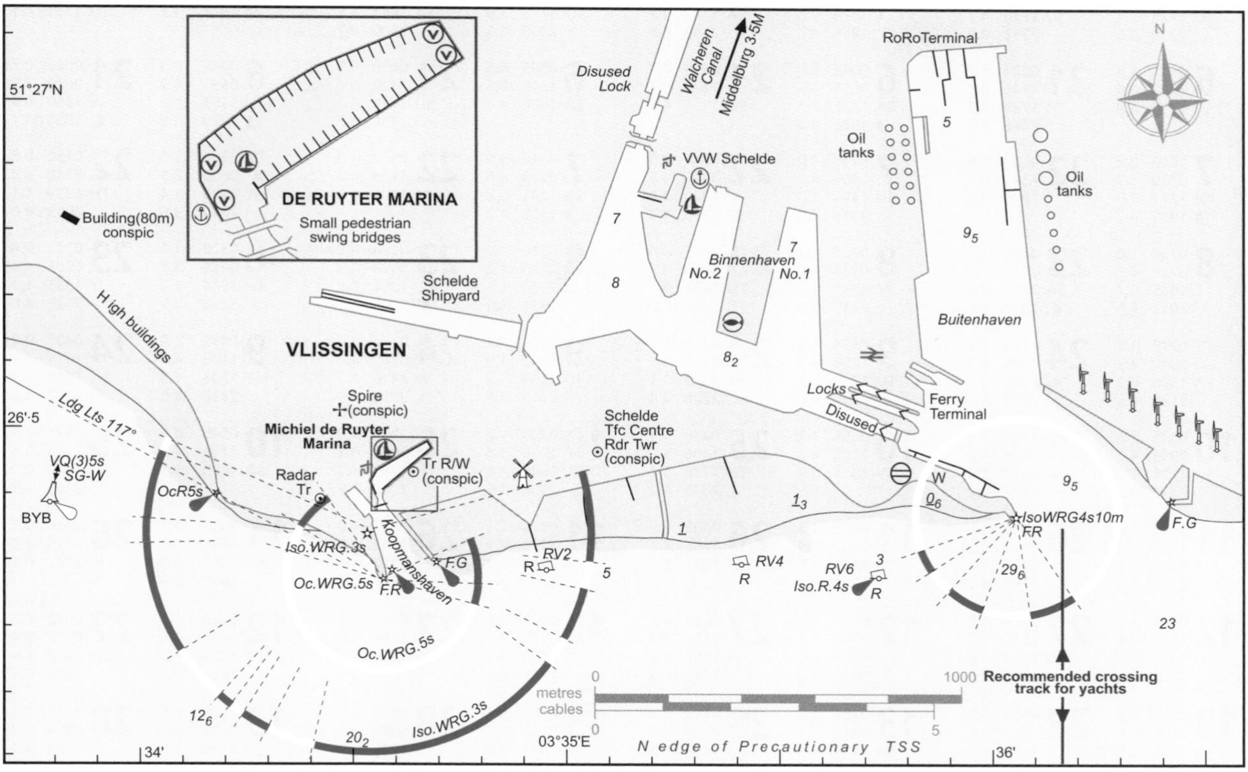
DE RUYTER MARINA
Small pedestrian swing bridges
51°27'N
26'·5
Building(80m) conspic
High buildings
Ldg Lts 117°
VQ(3)5s SG-W
BYB
OcR5s
Radar Tr
Iso.WRG.3s
Oc.WRG.5s
F.R
F.G
Koopmanshaven
Oc.WRG.5s
Iso.WRG.3s
Spire (conspic)
Michiel de Ruyter Marina
Tr R/W (conspic)
VLISSINGEN
Schelde Shipyard
Disused Lock
Walcheren Canal
Middelburg 3.5M
VVW Schelde
Binnenhaven No.2
No.1
Schelde Tfc Centre Rdr Twr (conspic)
Locks
Disused
Ferry Terminal
RoRoTerminal
Oil tanks
Oil tanks
Buitenhaven
IsoWRG4s10m FR
F.G
RV2 R
RV4 R
RV6 Iso.R.4s R
Recommended crossing track for yachts
metres 0 1000
cables 0 5
03°35'E
34'
36'
N edge of Precautionary TSS

TELEPHONE (Code 0118) Port HM 0115 647400; Buitenhaven lock 412372; ⊖ 484600; Schelde Traffic Coordination Centre 424790; Police 0900-8844; Dr 412233; Brit Consul (020) 6764343.

FACILITIES

Michiel de Ruyter Marina (2·9m) ☎ 414498, Mob 06 5353 7181, 📠 4146505. *Pre-booking in season is strongly advised.* 100 + 40 Ⓥ, €2.00. Bar, R, 🗟, Wi-Fi, @. info@montparnasse.nl www.montparnasse.nl

Ent is 6m narrow, over a sill with 1·0m water at MLWS. Access approx HW ±4; check depth gauge on outer wall. 2 small footbridges (R/G tfc lts) are swiftly swung open by HM 0800-2000LT. They stay open 2000–0800LT, but only for yachts to leave; ●● (vert) tfc lts prohibit arrival from sea, because the marina is not lit. Storm barrier is open 1/4-1/11. Pilot boats use the adjacent inlet at high speed with scant regard for safety.

VVW Schelde (3-4·3m) ☎ 465912. www.vvwschelde.nl 90 + 50 Ⓥ, €1.50 + €0.54 tax/head. AC €1.00/4kWh. 500m by road from ferry. D, Bar, R, 🗟, ⛴, Slip (12 ton max), @, bike hire, Wi-Fi.

At ent to the Buitenhaven beware ferries; keep to port, pass S of the ferry terminal for the most N'ly and smallest sealock, which operates H24. Waiting possible on piles to SE.

Town D&P (cans), CH, 🛒, R, Bar, ✉, Ⓑ, ⇌, ✈ (Antwerpen). Foot ferry to Breskens; road tunnel to Terneuzen. At Middelburg: BY, ME, ⚒, SM.

Vlissingen tides

TIME ZONE -0100
Subtract 1 hour for UT
For Dutch Summer Time add
ONE hour in **non-shaded areas**

VLISSINGEN LAT 51°27'N LONG 3°36'E
TIMES AND HEIGHTS OF HIGH AND LOW WATERS

Dates in **red** are **SPRINGS**
Dates in **blue** are **NEAPS**

YEAR **2010**

JANUARY

Day	Time m	Time m	Time m	Time m
1 F	0152 4.9	0815 0.6	1413 5.1	2036 0.7
16 SA	0246 4.7	0902 0.6	1501 4.8	2106 1.0
2 SA	0236 5.0	0905 0.4	1456 5.2	2122 0.7
17 SU	0316 4.8	0938 0.6	1535 4.8	2138 0.9
3 SU	0322 5.0	0955 0.3	1545 5.2	2208 0.7
18 M	0347 4.8	1009 0.5	1606 4.8	2216 0.9
4 M	0408 5.0	1046 0.3	1630 5.2	2256 0.8
19 TU	0420 4.8	1045 0.6	1637 4.8	2246 0.9
5 TU	0456 4.9	1136 0.3	1721 5.1	2339 0.8
20 W	0452 4.8	1116 0.6	1710 4.7	2312 0.9
6 W	0547 4.8	1220 0.4	1816 4.9	
21 TH	0521 4.7	1146 0.7	1739 4.6	2346 1.0
7 TH	0030 0.9	0639 4.7	1311 0.5	1915 4.7
22 F	0558 4.6	1221 0.7	1820 4.5	
8 F	0126 1.0	0738 4.5	1405 0.7	2016 4.5
23 SA	0026 1.0	0635 4.5	1300 0.8	1910 4.4
9 SA	0219 1.2	0840 4.3	1506 0.9	2125 4.3
24 SU	0116 1.1	0735 4.3	1356 0.9	2014 4.2
10 SU	0335 1.2	0956 4.2	1625 1.0	2240 4.2
25 M	0220 1.2	0856 4.2	1510 1.0	2136 4.1
11 M	0506 1.2	1110 4.2	1740 1.1	2345 4.3
26 TU	0350 1.2	1010 4.2	1625 1.1	2249 4.2
12 TU	0610 1.1	1215 4.4	1836 1.1	
27 W	0511 1.1	1126 4.3	1746 1.0	2358 4.4
13 W	0045 4.4	0706 0.9	1316 4.5	1920 1.0
28 TH	0616 0.9	1221 4.6	1839 0.9	
14 TH	0136 4.5	0750 0.8	1356 4.7	1956 1.0
29 F	0051 4.6	0716 0.7	1310 4.9	1935 0.7
15 F	0211 4.6	0826 0.7	1429 4.7	2029 1.0
30 SA	0137 4.8	0805 0.5	1356 5.1	2019 0.7
31 SU	0221 5.0	0853 0.3	1442 5.2	2105 0.6

FEBRUARY

Day	Time m	Time m	Time m	Time m
1 M	0305 5.1	0940 0.2	1526 5.3	2150 0.6
16 TU	0322 4.9	0948 0.4	1537 4.9	2151 0.8
2 TU	0349 5.1	1027 0.1	1612 5.3	2232 0.6
17 W	0351 4.9	1020 0.4	1607 4.9	2220 0.8
3 W	0435 5.1	1110 0.2	1656 5.1	2316 0.7
18 TH	0421 4.9	1050 0.5	1637 4.8	2251 0.8
4 TH	0519 5.0	1151 0.3	1745 4.9	
19 F	0452 4.8	1121 0.5	1707 4.8	2315 0.8
5 F	0002 0.7	0607 4.8	1236 0.5	1835 4.7
20 SA	0523 4.8	1146 0.6	1742 4.7	2356 0.8
6 SA	0046 0.9	0659 4.6	1325 0.7	1938 4.4
21 SU	0559 4.7	1225 0.7	1826 4.5	
7 SU	0139 1.0	0806 4.3	1426 1.0	2046 4.0
22 M	0046 0.9	0649 4.5	1320 0.9	1930 4.2
8 M	0253 1.2	0926 4.0	1535 1.2	2216 3.9
23 TU	0146 1.0	0810 4.2	1436 1.1	2055 4.0
9 TU	0424 1.2	1056 4.0	1716 1.3	2336 4.0
24 W	0316 1.2	0939 4.1	1559 1.1	2228 4.0
10 W	0556 1.1	1205 4.2	1815 1.2	
25 TH	0446 1.1	1106 4.2	1726 1.1	2339 4.2
11 TH	0029 4.2	0655 0.9	1255 4.5	1906 1.1
26 F	0605 0.9	1206 4.6	1825 0.9	
12 F	0118 4.5	0740 0.7	1339 4.6	1946 1.0
27 SA	0035 4.5	0706 0.6	1258 4.9	1915 0.8
13 SA	0156 4.6	0816 0.7	1411 4.7	2016 1.0
28 SU	0119 4.8	0749 0.4	1339 5.1	2006 0.6
14 SU	0222 4.7	0845 0.6	1439 4.8	2045 0.9
15 M	0251 4.8	0916 0.5	1507 4.9	2116 0.8

MARCH

Day	Time m	Time m	Time m	Time m
1 M	0201 5.0	0836 0.2	1421 5.2	2048 0.6
16 TU	0221 4.8	0846 0.5	1439 4.9	2049 0.7
2 TU	0243 5.1	0920 0.1	1505 5.3	2129 0.5
17 W	0249 4.9	0918 0.4	1507 5.0	2125 0.6
3 W	0326 5.2	1003 0.1	1548 5.2	2212 0.5
18 TH	0321 5.0	0952 0.4	1537 5.0	2156 0.6
4 TH	0406 5.2	1045 0.2	1632 5.1	2256 0.6
19 F	0350 5.0	1026 0.5	1608 4.9	2231 0.6
5 F	0450 5.1	1125 0.3	1716 4.9	2336 0.6
20 SA	0423 4.9	1052 0.5	1641 4.8	2300 0.7
6 SA	0536 4.9	1205 0.5	1806 4.6	
21 SU	0455 4.9	1129 0.6	1717 4.7	2338 0.7
7 SU	0016 0.8	0625 4.6	1245 0.8	1855 4.2
22 M	0537 4.8	1208 0.7	1806 4.5	
8 M	0110 1.0	0725 4.2	1356 1.1	1953 3.9
23 TU	0026 0.8	0628 4.5	1254 0.9	1905 4.1
9 TU	0224 1.2	0845 3.9	1503 1.3	2146 3.6
24 W	0124 0.9	0745 4.2	1416 1.1	2036 3.9
10 W	0355 1.2	1036 3.8	1646 1.4	2305 3.8
25 TH	0255 1.0	0922 4.1	1546 1.2	2206 3.9
11 TH	0526 1.1	1139 4.1	1744 1.1	2315 4.1
26 F	0423 1.0	1045 4.3	1717 1.1	2315 4.1
12 F	0008 4.1	0630 0.9	1231 4.4	1846 1.1
27 SA	0556 0.7	1148 4.6	1815 0.9	
13 SA	0056 4.4	0712 0.7	1311 4.6	1920 1.0
28 SU	0011 4.5	0645 0.5	1235 4.9	1906 0.8
14 SU	0125 4.5	0745 0.6	1341 4.7	1945 0.9
29 M	0055 4.7	0736 0.3	1316 5.0	1945 0.6
15 M	0156 4.7	0816 0.6	1412 4.8	2015 0.8
30 TU	0136 4.9	0815 0.2	1400 5.2	2028 0.5
31 W	0220 5.1	0858 0.2	1443 5.2	2110 0.5

APRIL

Day	Time m	Time m	Time m	Time m
1 TH	0301 5.2	0938 0.2	1525 5.1	2152 0.4
16 F	0251 5.0	0919 0.4	1512 5.0	2136 0.6
2 F	0346 5.2	1018 0.3	1606 5.0	2232 0.5
17 SA	0325 5.0	0955 0.5	1546 4.9	2210 0.6
3 SA	0426 5.0	1055 0.5	1650 4.7	2316 0.6
18 SU	0401 5.0	1036 0.5	1623 4.8	2250 0.6
4 SU	0511 4.8	1136 0.7	1735 4.5	2355 0.7
19 M	0439 4.9	1112 0.6	1702 4.6	2336 0.6
5 M	0600 4.5	1216 0.9	1826 4.2	
20 TU	0526 4.8	1155 0.8	1751 4.4	
6 TU	0046 0.9	0651 4.2	1305 1.2	1920 3.9
21 W	0026 0.7	0619 4.5	1250 0.9	1855 4.1
7 W	0206 1.0	0805 3.9	1435 1.4	2040 3.6
22 TH	0136 0.8	0742 4.3	1359 1.1	2019 4.0
8 TH	0320 1.1	0956 3.8	1544 1.4	2236 3.7
23 F	0243 0.8	0905 4.3	1535 1.2	2139 4.0
9 F	0435 1.0	1106 4.0	1706 1.3	2330 4.0
24 SA	0405 0.8	1019 4.4	1656 1.1	2252 4.2
10 SA	0545 0.9	1155 4.3	1805 1.1	
25 SU	0525 0.6	1126 4.6	1749 0.9	2345 4.4
11 SU	0016 4.2	0636 0.7	1235 4.5	1845 0.9
26 M	0626 0.5	1216 4.8	1842 0.8	
12 M	0050 4.4	0709 0.6	1306 4.6	1916 0.8
27 TU	0032 4.7	0712 0.4	1258 4.9	1925 0.6
13 TU	0120 4.6	0739 0.6	1336 4.8	1948 0.7
28 W	0116 4.8	0756 0.3	1342 5.0	2008 0.5
14 W	0147 4.8	0809 0.5	1405 4.9	2019 0.6
29 TH	0159 5.0	0836 0.3	1425 5.0	2050 0.4
15 TH	0216 4.9	0846 0.4	1436 5.0	2055 0.6
30 F	0242 5.1	0916 0.4	1507 4.9	2132 0.4

Chart Datum is 2·32 metres below NAP Datum. HAT is 5·2 metres above Chart Datum; see 0.19

>> **FREE** monthly updates from <<
www.reedsalmanac.co.uk

TIME ZONE -0100
Subtract 1 hour for UT
For Dutch Summer Time add
ONE hour in **non-shaded areas**

VLISSINGEN   LAT 51°27'N   LONG 3°36'E
TIMES AND HEIGHTS OF HIGH AND LOW WATERS

Dates in red are **SPRINGS**
Dates in blue are **NEAPS**

YEAR **2010**

MAY

Day	Time	m	Day	Time	m
1 SA	0325 / 0956 / 1551 / 2215	5.0 / 0.5 / 4.8 / 0.4	16 SU	0305 / 0935 / 1526 / 2158	5.0 / 0.5 / 4.8 / 0.5
2 SU	0408 / 1036 / 1635 / 2255	4.9 / 0.7 / 4.6 / 0.5	17 M	0345 / 1015 / 1609 / 2242	5.0 / 0.6 / 4.7 / 0.5
3 M	0455 / 1110 / 1715 / 2335	4.7 / 0.8 / 4.4 / 0.6	18 TU	0429 / 1100 / 1655 / 2330	4.8 / 0.7 / 4.6 / 0.5
4 TU	0539 / 1150 / 1755	4.5 / 1.0 / 4.2	19 W	0517 / 1145 / 1749	4.8 / 0.8 / 4.4
5 W	0025 / 0630 / 1234 / 1845	0.8 / 4.2 / 1.0 / 4.0	20 TH	0026 / 0619 / 1246 / 1856	0.5 / 4.6 / 0.9 / 4.2
6 TH	0124 / 0736 / 1355 / 1945	0.9 / 4.0 / 1.3 / 3.8	21 F	0126 / 0736 / 1350 / 2006	0.8 / 4.5 / 1.0 / 4.2
7 F	0246 / 0840 / 1511 / 2110	1.0 / 3.9 / 1.3 / 3.7	22 SA	0236 / 0845 / 1454 / 2116	0.6 / 4.5 / 1.1 / 4.2
8 SA	0339 / 1006 / 1605 / 2230	1.0 / 3.9 / 1.2 / 3.9	23 SU	0346 / 0955 / 1604 / 2220	0.6 / 4.5 / 1.1 / 4.3
9 SU	0445 / 1106 / 1705 / 2322	0.9 / 4.1 / 1.1 / 4.1	24 M	0500 / 1056 / 1726 / 2317	0.6 / 4.6 / 1.0 / 4.4
10 M	0534 / 1145 / 1755	0.8 / 4.4 / 1.0	25 TU	0601 / 1148 / 1821	0.5 / 4.7 / 0.8
11 TU	0001 / 0628 / 1225 / 1836	4.3 / 0.7 / 4.6 / 0.9	26 W	0011 / 0648 / 1238 / 1905	4.6 / 0.5 / 4.8 / 0.7
12 W	0037 / 0700 / 1259 / 1916	4.5 / 0.6 / 4.7 / 0.7	27 TH	0057 / 0732 / 1325 / 1950	4.7 / 0.5 / 4.8 / 0.6
13 TH	0116 / 0736 / 1333 / 1952	4.7 / 0.6 / 4.9 / 0.6	28 F	0146 / 0816 / 1410 / 2036	4.8 / 0.5 / 4.8 / 0.5
14 F	0146 / 0816 / 1411 / 2032	4.9 / 0.5 / 4.9 / 0.6	29 SA	0228 / 0851 / 1455 / 2115	4.9 / 0.6 / 4.8 / 0.4
15 SA	0226 / 0856 / 1446 / 2115	5.0 / 0.5 / 4.9 / 0.5	30 SU	0315 / 0936 / 1537 / 2158	4.9 / 0.7 / 4.7 / 0.4
			31 M	0357 / 1010 / 1620 / 2240	4.8 / 0.8 / 4.6 / 0.5

JUNE

Day	Time	m	Day	Time	m
1 TU	0439 / 1048 / 1656 / 2320	4.7 / 0.9 / 4.5 / 0.6	16 W	0422 / 1049 / 1648 / 2326	5.0 / 0.7 / 4.7 / 0.3
2 W	0525 / 1126 / 1738	4.6 / 1.0 / 4.4	17 TH	0512 / 1140 / 1741	4.9 / 0.8 / 4.6
3 TH	0006 / 0605 / 1216 / 1820	0.7 / 4.4 / 1.1 / 4.2	18 F	0015 / 0609 / 1229 / 1835	0.3 / 4.8 / 0.9 / 4.5
4 F	0045 / 0652 / 1306 / 1911	0.8 / 4.2 / 1.2 / 4.1	19 SA	0116 / 0711 / 1325 / 1935	0.4 / 4.7 / 0.9 / 4.4
5 SA	0150 / 0751 / 1415 / 2005	0.8 / 4.1 / 1.3 / 4.0	20 SU	0210 / 0816 / 1425 / 2039	0.5 / 4.6 / 1.0 / 4.4
6 SU	0256 / 0845 / 1516 / 2104	0.9 / 4.0 / 1.2 / 4.0	21 M	0316 / 0926 / 1535 / 2146	0.6 / 4.5 / 1.0 / 4.3
7 M	0346 / 0956 / 1616 / 2215	0.9 / 4.1 / 1.2 / 4.0	22 TU	0420 / 1031 / 1655 / 2256	0.7 / 4.4 / 1.0 / 4.4
8 TU	0434 / 1056 / 1705 / 2316	0.9 / 4.3 / 1.1 / 4.0	23 W	0530 / 1131 / 1755 / 2356	0.7 / 4.5 / 0.9 / 4.5
9 W	0535 / 1145 / 1756 / 2359	0.8 / 4.5 / 0.9 / 4.4	24 TH	0626 / 1225 / 1850	0.7 / 4.6 / 0.8
10 TH	0620 / 1225 / 1839	0.7 / 4.6 / 0.8	25 F	0049 / 0712 / 1319 / 1941	4.6 / 0.7 / 4.6 / 0.6
11 F	0045 / 0706 / 1307 / 1928	4.6 / 0.7 / 4.8 / 0.7	26 SA	0138 / 0756 / 1405 / 2022	4.7 / 0.8 / 4.7 / 0.6
12 SA	0125 / 0748 / 1349 / 2016	4.8 / 0.6 / 4.8 / 0.6	27 SU	0225 / 0836 / 1445 / 2106	4.8 / 0.8 / 4.7 / 0.5
13 SU	0206 / 0832 / 1432 / 2100	4.8 / 0.6 / 4.9 / 0.5	28 M	0306 / 0909 / 1526 / 2146	4.8 / 0.9 / 4.7 / 0.5
14 M	0250 / 0915 / 1515 / 2148	5.0 / 0.6 / 4.8 / 0.4	29 TU	0345 / 0948 / 1558 / 2226	4.8 / 0.9 / 4.7 / 0.5
15 TU	0335 / 1001 / 1601 / 2238	5.0 / 0.6 / 4.8 / 0.3	30 W	0418 / 1025 / 1636 / 2254	4.8 / 0.9 / 4.7 / 0.5

JULY

Day	Time	m	Day	Time	m
1 TH	0458 / 1059 / 1712 / 2340	4.7 / 1.0 / 4.6 / 0.6	16 F	0456 / 1122 / 1721	5.1 / 0.7 / 4.9
2 F	0536 / 1141 / 1751	4.6 / 1.0 / 4.5	17 SA	0000 / 0547 / 1208 / 1811	0.2 / 5.0 / 0.8 / 4.8
3 SA	0016 / 0611 / 1216 / 1830	0.7 / 4.4 / 1.1 / 4.4	18 SU	0048 / 0641 / 1255 / 1905	0.3 / 4.8 / 0.9 / 4.6
4 SU	0045 / 0701 / 1256 / 1915	0.8 / 4.3 / 1.1 / 4.2	19 M	0136 / 0746 / 1355 / 2011	0.5 / 4.6 / 1.0 / 4.5
5 M	0135 / 0750 / 1344 / 2012	0.9 / 4.2 / 1.2 / 4.1	20 TU	0236 / 0848 / 1459 / 2116	0.7 / 4.4 / 1.1 / 4.3
6 TU	0246 / 0844 / 1455 / 2115	0.9 / 4.2 / 1.2 / 4.1	21 W	0346 / 1006 / 1620 / 2236	0.9 / 4.2 / 1.1 / 4.2
7 W	0335 / 0955 / 1616 / 2227	1.0 / 4.2 / 1.2 / 4.1	22 TH	0506 / 1118 / 1746 / 2345	1.0 / 4.3 / 1.0 / 4.4
8 TH	0446 / 1059 / 1715 / 2326	1.0 / 4.3 / 1.1 / 4.3	23 F	0610 / 1219 / 1839	1.0 / 4.4 / 0.8
9 F	0546 / 1200 / 1816	0.9 / 4.5 / 0.9	24 SA	0045 / 0700 / 1311 / 1929	4.6 / 1.0 / 4.6 / 0.7
10 SA	0022 / 0640 / 1249 / 1905	4.6 / 0.8 / 4.6 / 0.7	25 SU	0140 / 0742 / 1355 / 2012	4.7 / 1.0 / 4.7 / 0.6
11 SU	0109 / 0725 / 1335 / 2001	4.8 / 0.7 / 4.8 / 0.6	26 M	0215 / 0820 / 1431 / 2049	4.8 / 1.0 / 4.7 / 0.6
12 M	0156 / 0816 / 1419 / 2048	5.0 / 0.7 / 4.9 / 0.5	27 TU	0251 / 0856 / 1506 / 2126	4.8 / 1.0 / 4.8 / 0.5
13 TU	0236 / 0902 / 1502 / 2136	5.1 / 0.6 / 4.9 / 0.3	28 W	0325 / 0928 / 1535 / 2159	4.9 / 0.9 / 4.8 / 0.5
14 W	0322 / 0948 / 1546 / 2226	5.2 / 0.7 / 4.9 / 0.2	29 TH	0356 / 1002 / 1607 / 2235	4.9 / 0.9 / 4.8 / 0.5
15 TH	0408 / 1035 / 1632 / 2312	5.2 / 0.7 / 4.9 / 0.2	30 F	0427 / 1035 / 1642 / 2310	4.8 / 0.9 / 4.8 / 0.6
			31 SA	0459 / 1106 / 1711 / 2338	4.7 / 1.0 / 4.7 / 0.7

AUGUST

Day	Time	m	Day	Time	m
1 SU	0528 / 1136 / 1745	4.6 / 1.0 / 4.6	16 M	0015 / 0608 / 1225 / 1835	0.4 / 4.8 / 0.8 / 4.7
2 M	0006 / 0606 / 1206 / 1819	0.7 / 4.5 / 1.0 / 4.5	17 TU	0059 / 0710 / 1320 / 1932	0.7 / 4.5 / 1.0 / 4.5
3 TU	0034 / 0645 / 1250 / 1905	0.8 / 4.4 / 1.1 / 4.3	18 W	0155 / 0816 / 1425 / 2050	0.9 / 4.2 / 1.1 / 4.2
4 W	0130 / 0750 / 1344 / 2026	0.9 / 4.2 / 1.2 / 4.1	19 TH	0305 / 0935 / 1554 / 2220	1.2 / 4.0 / 1.2 / 4.1
5 TH	0235 / 0906 / 1520 / 2146	1.1 / 4.1 / 1.3 / 4.1	20 F	0445 / 1106 / 1736 / 2340	1.2 / 4.1 / 1.1 / 4.3
6 F	0406 / 1026 / 1639 / 2300	1.1 / 4.1 / 1.2 / 4.2	21 SA	0555 / 1205 / 1825	1.2 / 4.3 / 0.9
7 SA	0526 / 1135 / 1755	1.1 / 4.3 / 1.0	22 SU	0041 / 0644 / 1300 / 1914	4.6 / 1.2 / 4.5 / 0.7
8 SU	0001 / 0626 / 1231 / 1852	4.5 / 0.9 / 4.5 / 0.7	23 M	0125 / 0730 / 1335 / 2000	4.7 / 1.0 / 4.7 / 0.6
9 M	0052 / 0712 / 1317 / 1946	4.8 / 0.8 / 4.8 / 0.5	24 TU	0200 / 0800 / 1416 / 2029	4.8 / 1.0 / 4.8 / 0.6
10 TU	0137 / 0800 / 1400 / 2032	5.1 / 0.7 / 4.9 / 0.3	25 W	0230 / 0830 / 1439 / 2102	4.9 / 1.0 / 4.8 / 0.6
11 W	0220 / 0845 / 1443 / 2118	5.2 / 0.7 / 5.1 / 0.2	26 TH	0255 / 0902 / 1508 / 2136	4.9 / 0.9 / 4.9 / 0.5
12 TH	0303 / 0930 / 1526 / 2206	5.3 / 0.6 / 5.1 / 0.2	27 F	0326 / 0935 / 1535 / 2205	4.9 / 0.9 / 5.0 / 0.6
13 F	0346 / 1016 / 1608 / 2248	5.3 / 0.6 / 5.1 / 0.2	28 SA	0355 / 1008 / 1607 / 2235	4.9 / 0.9 / 4.9 / 0.6
14 SA	0431 / 1058 / 1655 / 2332	5.2 / 0.7 / 5.1 / 0.3	29 SU	0426 / 1036 / 1636 / 2259	4.8 / 0.9 / 4.9 / 0.7
15 SU	0519 / 1142 / 1741	5.0 / 0.7 / 4.9	30 M	0451 / 1106 / 1707 / 2330	4.8 / 0.9 / 4.8 / 0.8
			31 TU	0522 / 1137 / 1740	4.7 / 0.9 / 4.7

Chart Datum is 2·32 metres below NAP Datum. HAT is 5·2 metres above Chart Datum; see 0.19

Netherlands

TIME ZONE -0100
Subtract 1 hour for UT
For Dutch Summer Time add
ONE hour in **non-shaded areas**

VLISSINGEN LAT 51°27'N LONG 3°36'E
TIMES AND HEIGHTS OF HIGH AND LOW WATERS

Dates in red are **SPRINGS**
Dates in blue are NEAPS

YEAR 2010

SEPTEMBER

Day	Time / m	Time / m	Time / m	Time / m
1 W ◑	0007 0.8	0601 4.6	1215 1.0	1826 4.5
2 TH	0056 1.0	0655 4.3	1315 1.1	1926 4.2
3 F	0206 1.2	0814 4.0	1434 1.3	2111 4.1
4 SA	0330 1.3	0949 4.0	1621 1.2	2236 4.2
5 SU	0455 1.2	1112 4.2	1736 1.0	2346 4.5
6 M	0605 1.2	1212 4.5	1841 0.7	
7 TU	0032 4.9	0655 0.9	1256 4.8	1928 0.5
8 W ●	0117 5.1	0740 0.8	1336 5.0	2012 0.3
9 TH	0156 5.3	0825 0.7	1418 5.2	2055 0.2
10 F	0240 5.4	0908 0.6	1500 5.3	2137 0.2
11 SA	0323 5.3	0950 0.6	1543 5.3	2223 0.3
12 SU	0406 5.2	1033 0.7	1626 5.2	2306 0.4
13 M	0452 5.0	1115 0.7	1712 5.0	2341 0.6
14 TU	0541 4.7	1200 0.8	1806 4.7	
15 W ◑	0026 0.9	0636 4.4	1244 1.0	1859 4.4
16 TH	0125 1.2	0736 4.1	1355 1.2	2014 4.1
17 F	0240 1.4	0910 3.8	1536 1.2	2155 4.0
18 SA	0405 1.5	1040 3.9	1706 1.1	2315 4.2
19 SU	0536 1.3	1145 4.2	1810 0.9	
20 M	0015 4.5	0623 1.2	1235 4.5	1855 0.8
21 TU	0055 4.7	0705 1.1	1316 4.7	1936 0.7
22 W	0132 4.8	0735 1.0	1346 4.8	2006 0.7
23 TH ○	0156 4.9	0805 0.9	1407 4.9	2036 0.6
24 F	0226 4.9	0836 0.9	1436 5.0	2106 0.6
25 SA	0256 5.0	0905 0.8	1506 5.0	2132 0.6
26 SU	0326 5.0	0935 0.8	1535 5.0	2206 0.7
27 M	0350 4.9	1011 0.8	1605 5.0	2232 0.7
28 TU	0425 4.9	1041 0.9	1636 4.9	2306 0.8
29 W	0457 4.8	1116 0.9	1713 4.9	2335 0.9
30 TH	0537 4.6	1156 0.9	1800 4.7	

OCTOBER

Day	Time / m	Time / m	Time / m	Time / m
1 F ◑	0028 1.1	0630 4.3	1256 1.1	1906 4.3
2 SA	0136 1.3	0756 4.0	1426 1.2	2046 4.2
3 SU	0305 1.4	0929 4.0	1545 1.2	2205 4.3
4 M	0429 1.3	1045 4.2	1709 1.0	2315 4.6
5 TU	0545 1.1	1145 4.5	1821 0.7	
6 W	0008 4.9	0636 0.9	1229 4.8	1908 0.5
7 TH ●	0056 5.1	0721 0.8	1313 5.0	1950 0.4
8 F	0136 5.3	0803 0.7	1356 5.2	2032 0.3
9 SA	0216 5.3	0846 0.6	1436 5.3	2116 0.4
10 SU	0300 5.2	0928 0.6	1519 5.3	2155 0.5
11 M	0345 5.1	1012 0.6	1605 5.2	2235 0.6
12 TU	0429 4.9	1056 0.7	1649 5.0	2316 0.8
13 W	0516 4.7	1138 0.8	1735 4.7	2356 1.1
14 TH ◑	0605 4.3	1225 1.0	1836 4.4	
15 F	0056 1.3	0659 4.1	1335 1.1	1945 4.1
16 SA	0205 1.5	0826 3.8	1506 1.2	2114 4.0
17 SU	0336 1.6	0954 3.8	1620 1.2	2240 4.1
18 M	0444 1.5	1105 4.1	1736 1.0	2338 4.4
19 TU	0543 1.3	1155 4.3	1819 0.9	
20 W	0019 4.6	0635 1.1	1235 4.5	1900 0.8
21 TH	0052 4.7	0706 1.0	1305 4.7	1925 0.8
22 F	0125 4.8	0736 1.0	1336 4.8	1956 0.7
23 SA ○	0155 4.9	0806 0.9	1402 4.9	2031 0.7
24 SU	0222 5.0	0838 0.8	1436 5.0	2100 0.7
25 M	0256 5.0	0916 0.8	1506 5.1	2136 0.7
26 TU	0325 5.0	0945 0.8	1542 5.0	2211 0.8
27 W	0403 4.9	1026 0.8	1618 5.0	2246 0.9
28 TH	0437 4.7	1106 0.8	1658 4.9	2327 1.0
29 F	0526 4.5	1150 0.9	1747 4.7	
30 SA	0016 1.1	0619 4.3	1256 1.0	1856 4.4
31 SU	0120 1.3	0746 4.1	1406 1.0	2026 4.3

NOVEMBER

Day	Time / m	Time / m	Time / m	Time / m
1 M	0235 1.4	0858 4.1	1525 1.0	2140 4.4
2 TU	0353 1.3	1012 4.2	1646 0.9	2245 4.6
3 W	0516 1.2	1116 4.5	1756 0.7	2345 4.8
4 TH	0610 1.0	1205 4.7	1842 0.6	
5 F	0031 5.0	0658 0.9	1246 4.9	1929 0.5
6 SA ●	0115 5.1	0745 0.7	1335 5.1	2008 0.5
7 SU	0159 5.1	0825 0.6	1418 5.2	2052 0.5
8 M	0243 5.1	0910 0.6	1503 5.2	2132 0.7
9 TU	0328 5.0	0956 0.6	1547 5.1	2212 0.8
10 W	0412 4.8	1035 0.7	1632 4.9	2249 1.0
11 TH	0457 4.6	1115 0.8	1721 4.7	2330 1.2
12 F	0541 4.4	1206 0.9	1812 4.5	
13 SA ◑	0016 1.3	0636 4.2	1305 1.0	1910 4.2
14 SU	0120 1.5	0726 4.0	1417 1.1	2026 4.0
15 M	0246 1.6	0834 3.8	1526 1.2	2140 4.0
16 TU	0346 1.5	1006 3.9	1625 1.1	2245 4.1
17 W	0450 1.4	1101 4.1	1731 1.0	2336 4.3
18 TH	0547 1.3	1148 4.3	1815 1.0	
19 F	0016 4.5	0626 1.1	1225 4.5	1851 0.9
20 SA	0048 4.7	0700 1.0	1258 4.7	1925 0.8
21 SU ○	0121 4.8	0735 0.9	1335 4.9	1958 0.8
22 M	0157 4.9	0812 0.8	1411 5.0	2032 0.7
23 TU	0233 4.9	0852 0.7	1446 5.0	2109 0.8
24 W	0312 4.9	0936 0.7	1526 5.0	2152 0.8
25 TH	0347 4.8	1015 0.7	1606 5.0	2236 0.9
26 F	0431 4.7	1102 0.7	1652 4.9	2321 1.0
27 SA	0517 4.6	1149 0.7	1745 4.8	
28 SU ◑	0008 1.1	0615 4.4	1250 0.7	1850 4.6
29 M	0105 1.2	0722 4.3	1355 0.8	2000 4.5
30 TU	0216 1.3	0830 4.2	1506 0.9	2110 4.5

DECEMBER

Day	Time / m	Time / m	Time / m	Time / m
1 W	0326 1.3	0938 4.3	1604 0.9	2216 4.5
2 TH	0435 1.2	1042 4.4	1720 0.8	2318 4.6
3 F	0546 1.1	1140 4.6	1818 0.8	
4 SA	0011 4.7	0641 0.9	1231 4.8	1906 0.7
5 SU ●	0101 4.8	0728 0.8	1321 4.9	1950 0.7
6 M	0147 4.9	0812 0.7	1406 5.0	2029 0.7
7 TU	0236 4.9	0858 0.6	1452 5.0	2112 0.8
8 W	0317 4.9	0940 0.6	1537 5.0	2152 0.9
9 TH	0359 4.8	1019 0.6	1618 4.9	2228 1.0
10 F	0442 4.7	1106 0.6	1706 4.8	2308 1.1
11 SA	0519 4.6	1146 0.7	1746 4.6	2351 1.2
12 SU	0606 4.4	1225 0.8	1832 4.4	
13 M ◑	0036 1.3	0646 4.3	1315 1.0	1926 4.2
14 TU	0136 1.4	0735 4.1	1416 1.1	2020 4.1
15 W	0246 1.5	0840 4.0	1515 1.1	2126 4.0
16 TH	0346 1.4	0956 4.0	1615 1.2	2230 4.1
17 F	0446 1.3	1052 4.1	1716 1.1	2326 4.3
18 SA	0535 1.2	1146 4.3	1806 1.0	
19 SU	0011 4.5	0628 1.1	1229 4.5	1850 0.9
20 M	0058 4.6	0710 0.9	1312 4.7	1930 0.8
21 TU ○	0138 4.8	0755 0.8	1352 4.9	2016 0.8
22 W	0215 4.9	0841 0.7	1433 5.0	2056 0.8
23 TH	0256 4.9	0923 0.5	1515 5.1	2135 0.8
24 F	0339 4.9	1012 0.5	1556 5.1	2226 0.8
25 SA	0422 4.8	1055 0.4	1646 5.0	2308 0.9
26 SU	0509 4.7	1148 0.4	1735 4.9	2356 0.9
27 M	0602 4.6	1241 0.5	1828 4.8	
28 TU ◑	0048 1.0	0658 4.5	1330 0.6	1931 4.6
29 W	0145 1.1	0801 4.4	1426 0.7	2038 4.5
30 TH	0250 1.2	0906 4.3	1530 0.9	2145 4.4
31 F	0354 1.2	1016 4.3	1656 1.0	2255 4.3

Chart Datum is 2·32 metres below NAP Datum. HAT is 5·2 metres above Chart Datum; see 0.19

2.28 BRESKENS

Zeeland **51°24'·00N 03°34'·08E** ❀❀❀◊◊◊✿✿✿

CHARTS AC 1874, 1872, 120; Zeekaart 120, 101; DYC 1801.4, 1803.2; Imray C30; Stanfords 1, 19

TIDES +0210 Dover; ML no data; Duration 0600.

Standard Port VLISSINGEN (←) Use Vlissingen data.

SHELTER Good in all winds except N/NW. In fine weather ⚓ off Plaat van Breskens or in peaceful Vaarwater langs Hoofdplaat; no ⚓ in commercial/fishing hbr.

NAVIGATION WPT 51°24'·71N 03°33'·90E [ARV-VH NCM buoy, Q], 170°/7ca to hbr ent. Beware fast ferries and strong tides across the ent. Do not confuse the ent with the ferry port ent, 0·7M WNW, where yachts are prohib.

LIGHTS AND MARKS Large bldg/silo on centre pier in hbr and three apartment blocks (30m) SE of marina are conspic. See chartlet and 2.3 for lights. Nieuwe Sluis lt ho, 28m B/W banded 8-sided twr, is 1·8M W of marina.

R/T Marina Ch 31.

TELEPHONE (Code 0117); ⊖ (0118) 484600; Police 0900 8844; Dr 381566/389284, at night/weekends (0115) 643000; Ⓗ (0117) 459000; British Consul (020) 6764343.

FACILITIES Marina jachthavenbreskens@zonnet.nl ☎ 381902, 06 3087873. www.marinabreskens.nl 580 AB inc Ⓥ, €1.70 + €1.05 tourist tax. Enter marina between two wavebreak barges; access H24, 5m at ent. Berth on 1st pontoon where HM assigns a berth via an intercom ☎, ▣, ⚓, SM, CH, D & P (fuel berth in FV hbr), Gaz, ACA, BY, C (30T), BH (70T), El, Ⓔ, ME, ✗, Slip, ▣, Wi-Fi. **YC Breskens** ☎ 383278, Bar, R (book early), @.

Town ▦, R, Bar, ✉, Ⓑ, Gas, ✈ (Oostende, Antwerp or Brussels). Pedestrian & bike ferry or car tunnel to Vlissingen for ⇌.

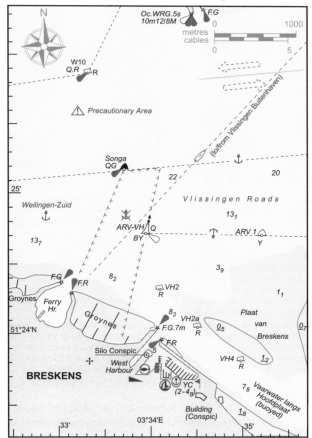

2.29 TERNEUZEN

Zeeland **51°20'·58N 03°49'·69E** ❀❀❀◊◊◊✿✿

CHARTS AC 120; Zeekaart 1443; DYC 1803.2; Imray C30

TIDES +0230 Dover; ML 2·5; Duration 0555.

Standard Port VLISSINGEN (←)

Times				Height (metres)			
High Water		Low Water		MHWS	MHWN	MLWN	MLWS
0300	0900	0400	1000	5·0	4·1	1·1	0·5
1500	2100	1600	2200				
Differences TERNEUZEN							
+0020	+0020	+0020	+0030	+0·3	+0·4	0·0	+0·1

SHELTER Very good except in strong N'lies. Exposed ⚓ on N side of fairway between buoys WPT4, WPT6, PvT-ZE & ZE5.

NAVIGATION WPT 51°20'·82N 03°47'·96E [25B SHM buoy], 101°/1M hugging S bank to hbr ent. The fairway is only 500m wide; big ships pass very close; good lookout E/W when leaving. Very busy traffic from/to the locks; call *Centrale-Terneuzen* Ch 03. If S-bound via Gent Canal transit the E lock to berth in Zijkanaal A.

LIGHTS AND MARKS Dow Chemical works and storage tanks are conspic 2M W of hbr. Lt Oc WRG 5s, B/W post, on W mole is a conspic mark for the Veerhaven.

When entry to E Buitenhaven is prohib, a second ● is shown below FR on E mole. For E lock: ● = no entry; ●● (vert) = get ready; ● = go. No yachts in W Buitenhaven, Middle and W locks.

R/T No marina VHF. Call *Port Control* Ch 11 (H24) for locks and Gent canal; also info broadcasts every H+00. East lock Ch 18.

TELEPHONE (Code 0115) Port HM 612161; ⊖ (0118) 484600; Police 0900 8844; Ⓗ 688000; Dr 616262; Brit Consul (020) 6764343.

FACILITIES Two marinas in SE corner of former Veerhaven: **WV Honte Marina** where vacant Ⓥ berths more likely. ☎ 697089, mobile 0651 168987. www.zealand-seaports.com 130 AB €1.40. AC (230v) €1.25, C (6 ton), Wi-Fi, ▣.
WV Neusen Marina is close ESE (and in Zijkanaal A) ☎ 696331; 100 AB, €0.30/m²; ⚓, Bar, Wi-Fi. Boatyards (full services): **Aricom** www.aricom.nl ☎ 614577, €1.00/m. ME, El, C (50 ton), ✗, Gaz. **Vermeulen's Yachtwerf** ☎ 612716. AB, €0.75, C (50 ton).
Town P, D, CH, ▦, R, Bar, ✉, Ⓑ, ✈ (Antwerpen). Foot ferry Breskens to Vlissingen. Cars by Schelde tunnel Terneuzen-Ellewoutsdijk.

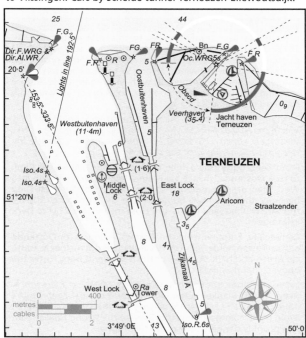

2.30 SPECIAL NOTES FOR BELGIUM

PROVINCES are given in lieu of UK 'counties'.

LANGUAGES Flemish, ie Dutch as spoken in Flanders, is the 1st language along the coast and N of Brussels. English is also widely spoken. French, the 2nd language, is spoken in and S of Brussels.

CURRENCY is the Euro €. VAT (BTW/TVA) is 21%.

CHARTS 'Vlaamse Banken' issued by the Hydrografische Dienst der Kust are most widely used. Dutch yacht charts (DYC 1800 series) cover all Belgian ports. Imray C30 is also popular.

TIME ZONE is –0100, which is allowed for in tidal predictions but no provision is made for daylight saving schemes.

HARBOURS Ports of entry are Nieuwpoort, Oostende and Zeebrugge; plus Blankenberge, early April - late Sep. Berths and moorings are administered by local YCs and municipal authorities. Red diesel fuel, where available, is duty free.

SIGNALS At Nieuwpoort, Oostende and Zeebrugge IPTS are used, and small craft wind warnings (also at Blankenberge). They apply only to craft <6m LOA and indicate onshore wind >F3; offshore wind >F4. Day, 2 ▼s, points together; night, Fl Bu lt.

TELEPHONE To call UK from Belgium, dial 00 44 then the UK area code minus the prefix 0, followed by the number called. To call Belgium from UK, dial 00 32 then the code and 6 digit number.

Emergency: ☎ 101 Police; ☎ 100 Fire, Ambulance and Marine. ☎ 112 (EU emergency number) is also operational.

BRITISH CONSULS Contact British Embassy, Brussels (consular) 02 287 6211 or consularsection.brussels@fco.gov.uk.

MRCC Oostende coordinates SAR operations (7.20). If no contact, call Oostende Radio VHF Ch 16 or ☎ 100. For medical advice call Radiomédical Oostende on Ch 16.

PUBLIC HOLIDAYS New Year's Day, Easter Mon, Labour Day (1 May), Ascension Day, Whit Mon, National Day (21 July), Feast of the Assumption (15 Aug), All Saints' Day (1 Nov), Armistice Day (11 Nov), King's Birthday (15 Nov), Christmas Day.

RULES A ▼ when motor-sailing and a black ball ● at ⚓ are strictly enforced. Navigation within 200m of shore (MLWS) is prohib.

INLAND WATERWAYS At www.mobilit.fgov.be download CEVNI-based regulations in French or Dutch. Licence plates (*Immatriculatieplaat*) are required on Belgian waterways. Helmsman's Competence criteria are as for the Netherlands.

THE BELGIAN COAST

Long shoals lie roughly parallel to this 36M long coast (AC 1872). Mostly the deeper, buoyed channels run within 3M of shore, where the outer shoals can give some protection from strong W or SW winds. Strong W to NE winds can create dangerous conditions especially with wind against tide. Before reaching shoal water get a good fix, so as to correctly identify the required channel.

▶*Off the Belgian coast the E-going stream begins at HW Vlissingen –0320 (HW Dover –0120), and the W-going at HW Vlissingen +0240 (HW Dover +0440), sp rates 2kn. Mostly the streams run parallel with the coast.*◀

From **Zeebrugge** stay a mile offshore inside Wenduine Bank to pass **Oostende**, thence via Kleine Rede or Grote Reede into West Diep off **Nieuwpoort**. At the French border West Diep becomes the narrower, buoyed Passe de Zuydcoote. Thence the very well buoyed route runs close inshore for 25M to Dyck PHM buoy.

Conversely, E-bound from the Thames, if bound for Oostende or the Westerschelde, identify W Hinder lt. From further N, route via NHR-S and NHR-SE buoys or the N Hinder lt buoy. Enter the buoyed channels at Dyck.

Leave Oostende about ▶*HW Vlissingen –0300 on a fair tide*◀. Keep 2M off **Blankenberge**, and 1M or more off Zeebrugge's huge claw-like breakwaters, staying S of the Scheur channel to avoid much commercial traffic. Beware the strong tidal stream and possibly dangerous seas off Zeebrugge.

2.31 ANTWERPEN

Belgium, Antwerpen **51°13'·66N 04°23'·79E** ❄☀⚓⚓❁❁❁

CHARTS AC 139; Zeekaart 1443; DYC 1803.5

TIDES +0342 Dover; ML 2·9; Duration 0605.
Standard Port VLISSINGEN (←)

Times				Height (metres)			
High Water		Low Water		MHWS	MHWN	MLWN	MLWS
0300	0900	0400	1000	5·0	4·1	1·1	0·5
1500	2100	1600	2200				
Differences ANTWERPEN							
+0128	+0116	+0121	+0144	+1·2	+1·0	+0·1	+0·1

SHELTER Excellent in both marinas. ⚓ in the river is not advised.

NAVIGATION For Westerschelde see 2.26. Best to check off the buoys coming up-river. There is a gap of 1·4M between No 116 PHM buoy and No 107 SHM buoy, where the river bends 90° onto S, abeam Royersluis and the waiting pontoon (see above). No 109 SHM buoy is 250m NE of Linkeroever Marina ent.

R/T Royersluis Ch 22. Access bridges Ch 62. Willemdok Ch 23. Linkeroever Ch 09 (HW±1). Antwerp Port Ops Ch 74 (H24). VTS, Zandvliet Centre Ch 12; Radar Ch 04, 66.

TELEPHONE (Code 03); ☎ 2292004; Police 5460730; ⊞ 2852000 (W Bank), 234111 (E Bank).

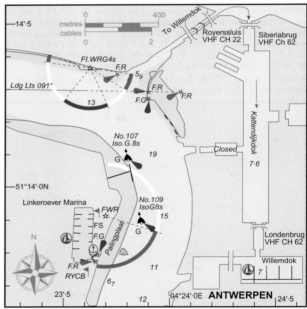

FACILITIES from seaward: **Willemdok Marina** 51°13'·78N 04°24'·43E. ☎ 2315066, Mobile 0495 535455. www.jachthaven-antwerpen.be jaw@pandora.be Wait on inshore side of T-shaped ferry pontoon S of No. 107 buoy. H24 access via Royersluis, or from canals/docks. Siberia and Londen bridges open 0630, 0830, 1000, 1130, 1245, 1415, 1515, 1615*, 1730, 1845, 2015, 2145, 2245LT.*Sat/Sun/Public hols. To enter the Dock areas and marina, pre-arrange an FD number via ☎, e-mail or fax to Willemdok (0500-2300). 200 + ♥, €1·50, €8·00 week. D, 🛒, 🗑, El, Wi-fi.

Linkeroever Marina (W bank); Lat/Long under title. Access by gate HW ±1, 0800–2200 (1800 in winter). Y waiting buoy is off the ent. ☎ 2190895, Mobile 0475 643957. www.jachthaven-antwerpen.be jachthaven_linkeroever@skynet.be 200+♥, €1·50, €8·00 week. D, Gaz, El, ✂, C (1·5 ton), BH (38 ton), CH, Slip, R, 🛒, Wi-fi.

Royal YC van België ☎ 2195231. www.rycb.be rycb@rycb.be. Bar, R, M, BY, D, P, CH, Slip .

Kon. Liberty YC ☎ 2191147. **Services:** ME, BH, ACA, DYC Agent.

City centre is ¾M from Linkeroever via St. Annatunnel (pedestrian), 51°13'·22N. All facilities, @, ➾, ✈.

2.32   ZEEBRUGGE

Belgium, West Flanders 51°21'·83N 03°11'·39E ❄❄❄♨♨♨❀❀

CHARTS AC 2449, 3371, 1872, 1874; Zeekaart 1441; DYC 1801.3, 1803; Imray C30; Stanfords 1, 19

TIDES +0110 Dover; ML 2·4; Duration 0535. Note: Zeebrugge is a Standard Port (⟶).

SHELTER Very good in the marina, access H24.

NAVIGATION WPT 51°22'·48N 03°09'·95E [Z SHM buoy, QG], 129°/1·1M to ent (lat/long under title). Lts on outer bkwtr heads show high-vis strip lts to seaward. Beware strong currents in hbr apprs (up to 4kn at HW −1). Caution on ent/dep due to limited vis; give all jetties a wide berth. A busy commercial, naval and fishing port and a ferry terminal. An inner WPT 51°20'·85N 03°12'·29E off Leopold II Dam head is useful to avoid getting 'lost' inside the vast outer hbr, especially in poor vis; see chartlet.

LIGHTS AND MARKS Big ship ldg marks (hard to see by day) & lts (as chartlet) lead in sequence to Vissershaven and the marina:

- 136°: Both W cols, R bands.
- 154°: Front, W pylon, R bands; rear, W bldg, R bands.
- 220°: Both W cols, B bands. • 193°: Both W cols, R bands.

IPTS are shown from W outer bkwtr and Leopold II Dam. Extra sigs: 3 Fl Y lts (vert) + IPTS No 2 or 5 = LNG tanker entering/leaving. No exit/entry without specific permission.

R/T Port Control Ch 71 (H24). Marina, nil VHF. Sealock Ch 68.

TELEPHONE (Code 050) Port HM 543241; Port Control 546867; Lock Mr 543231; CG 545072; Sea Saving Service 544007; ⊖ 54.54.55; Police 544148; Dr 544590; Brit Consul (02) 2179000.

FACILITIES **Marina** ☎ 544903, mob 0496 789053. havenmeester@rbsc.be www.rbsc.be 100 + 100 ❦, €2.19. Slip, ⚒, CH, D, ME, EI, ▣.

Royal Belgian SC (VZW) info@rbsc.be Bar, R (Alberta) ☎ 544197.

Town P, D, ⚒, Gaz, ☷, R, Bar, ⊠, Ⓑ. ⇌ 15 mins to Brugge. Tram service to Oostende for ✈. Ferries to Hull and Rosyth (Edinburgh).

BRUGGE Masted yachts can transit Zeebrugge's eastern sealock to go 6M S via the Boudewijnkanaal (Ch 68) & 2 lifting bridges to Brugge docks. Thence unmasted boats can go clockwise on the Oostende-Gent Canal (Ch 18) to **Flandria Marina** (S of city): ☎ 380866, mob 0477 384456. www.yachtclubflandria.be 10 mins walk to city centre; close to ⇌ (a visit by train is quick and easy).

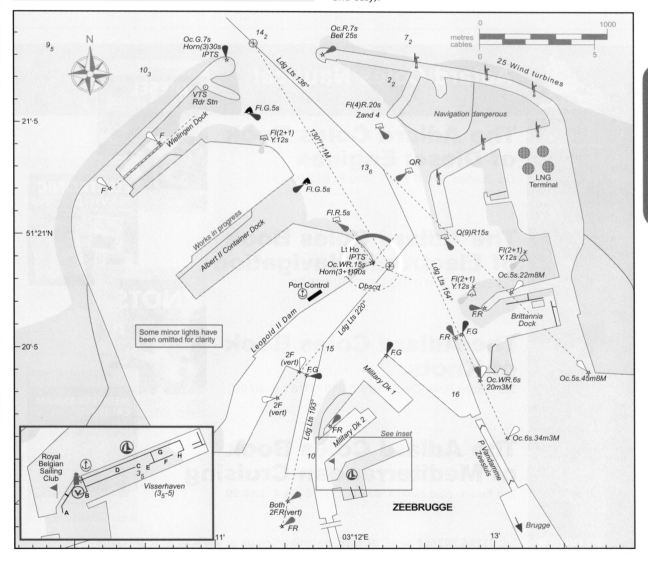

Belgium

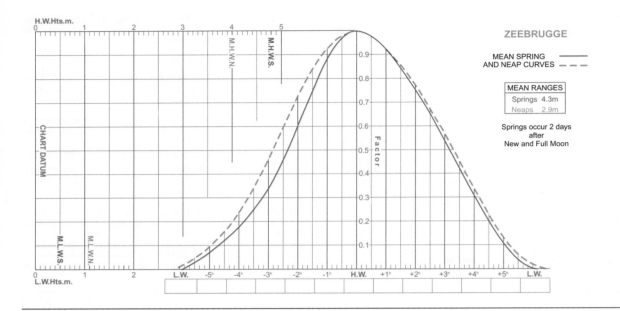

ZEEBRUGGE

MEAN SPRING ————
AND NEAP CURVES – – – –

MEAN RANGES
Springs 4.3m
Neaps 2.9m

Springs occur 2 days
after
New and Full Moon

TIME ZONE -0100
Subtract 1 hour for UT
For Dutch Summer Time add
ONE hour in **non-shaded areas**

ZEEBRUGGE   LAT 51°21'N   LONG 3°12'E
TIMES AND HEIGHTS OF HIGH AND LOW WATERS

Dates in red are **SPRINGS**
Dates in blue are **NEAPS**

YEAR 2010

Belgium

JANUARY

Time	m	Time	m
1 0126 0747 F 1346 2005	4.5 0.3 4.7 0.4	**16** 0212 0836 SA 1430 2039	4.3 0.3 4.4 0.7
2 0210 0834 SA 1432 2052	4.5 0.2 4.8 0.4	**17** 0245 0908 SU 1502 2108	4.3 0.3 4.4 0.7
3 0254 0922 SU 1518 2139	4.6 0.1 4.8 0.4	**18** 0315 0938 M 1533 2137	4.3 0.3 4.4 0.7
4 0339 1010 M 1606 2226	4.5 0.0 4.7 0.5	**19** 0345 1008 TU 1603 2208	4.3 0.4 4.4 0.7
5 0426 1059 TU 1656 2314	4.5 0.1 4.6 0.6	**20** 0415 1038 W 1635 2240	4.3 0.4 4.3 0.7
6 0515 1149 W 1749	4.5 0.2 4.4	**21** 0447 1110 TH 1710 2315	4.3 0.5 4.3 0.7
7 0003 0609 TH 1241 ◐ 1847	0.7 4.3 0.3 4.2	**22** 0525 1146 F 1752 2355	4.2 0.6 4.2 0.8
8 0056 0707 F 1338 1949	0.9 4.1 0.5 4.0	**23** 0611 1230 SA 1842 ◑	4.1 0.7 4.1
9 0158 0812 SA 1443 2058	1.0 3.9 0.7 3.8	**24** 0045 0707 SU 1333 1946	1.0 4.0 0.8 3.9
10 0315 0925 SU 1556 2215	1.1 3.8 0.8 3.8	**25** 0200 0819 M 1503 2107	1.1 3.8 0.9 3.7
11 0442 1044 M 1710 2325	1.1 3.8 0.9 3.9	**26** 0341 0941 TU 1615 2226	1.1 3.8 0.9 3.8
12 0551 1150 TU 1811	0.9 4.0 0.8	**27** 0453 1055 W 1717 2332	0.9 3.9 0.8 3.9
13 0019 0642 W 1239 1858	0.8 4.2 0.6 0.7	**28** 0554 1157 TH 1814	0.7 4.2 0.6
14 0101 0725 TH 1320 1937	4.2 0.5 4.3 0.7	**29** 0026 0648 F 1248 1905	4.2 0.4 4.5 0.5
15 0138 0802 F 1356 ● 2010	4.3 0.4 4.4 0.7	**30** 0111 0737 SA 1334 ○ 1952	4.4 0.2 4.7 0.4
		31 0154 0822 SU 1417 2037	4.5 0.0 4.8 0.4

FEBRUARY

Time	m	Time	m
1 0236 0907 M 1501 2121	4.6 -0.1 4.8 0.3	**16** 0247 0910 TU 1505 2111	4.4 0.2 4.4 0.5
2 0319 0952 TU 1546 2205	4.7 -0.1 4.8 0.4	**17** 0315 0939 W 1533 2142	4.4 0.2 4.5 0.5
3 0403 1036 W 1632 2249	4.7 -0.1 4.7 0.4	**18** 0345 1009 TH 1605 2215	4.5 0.3 4.5 0.5
4 0449 1121 TH 1720 2333	4.6 0.0 4.5 0.6	**19** 0418 1041 F 1640 2249	4.5 0.3 4.5 0.5
5 0537 1208 F 1810	4.4 0.3 4.2	**20** 0455 1115 SA 1719 2326	4.5 0.4 4.4 0.6
6 0019 0628 SA 1259 ◐ 1907	0.7 4.2 0.5 3.9	**21** 0538 1156 SU 1805	4.4 0.5 4.2
7 0115 0730 SU 1406 2018	1.0 3.9 0.8 3.6	**22** 0011 0630 M 1251 ◐ 1904	0.7 4.1 0.7 3.8
8 0242 0851 M 1526 2144	1.1 3.6 1.0 3.5	**23** 0116 0741 TU 1426 2032	1.0 3.8 1.0 3.6
9 0414 1023 TU 1645 2303	1.1 3.6 1.0 3.6	**24** 0316 0915 W 1552 2204	1.0 3.7 1.0 3.6
10 0528 1135 W 1753 2359	0.9 3.8 0.9 3.9	**25** 0433 1038 TH 1659 2314	0.9 3.9 0.8 3.8
11 0625 1225 TH 1844	0.6 4.1 0.5	**26** 0538 1142 F 1759	0.6 4.2 0.7
12 0044 0709 F 1305 1922	4.1 0.4 4.2 0.7	**27** 0007 0633 SA 1233 1850	4.1 0.3 4.5 0.5
13 0119 0745 SA 1338 1951	4.2 0.3 4.3 0.7	**28** 0052 0720 SU 1316 ○ 1935	4.4 0.1 4.7 0.4
14 0151 0818 SU 1408 ● 2016	4.3 0.3 4.4 0.6		
15 0220 0843 M 1437 2042	4.3 0.3 4.4 0.6		

MARCH

Time	m	Time	m
1 0133 0804 M 1358 2018	4.6 -0.1 4.8 0.3	**16** 0149 0810 TU 1407 2012	4.3 0.3 4.4 0.5
2 0214 0846 TU 1440 2100	4.7 -0.2 4.8 0.3	**17** 0216 0837 W 1434 2043	4.4 0.2 4.5 0.4
3 0256 0928 W 1522 2141	4.8 -0.2 4.8 0.2	**18** 0245 0908 TH 1504 2117	4.5 0.2 4.5 0.3
4 0339 1011 TH 1606 2223	4.8 -0.1 4.7 0.3	**19** 0317 0942 F 1537 2152	4.6 0.2 4.5 0.3
5 0422 1053 F 1651 2304	4.7 0.0 4.4 0.4	**20** 0352 1016 SA 1614 2228	4.6 0.2 4.5 0.3
6 0507 1136 SA 1737 2346	4.5 0.3 4.2 0.6	**21** 0431 1053 SU 1654 2306	4.6 0.3 4.4 0.5
7 0555 1223 SU 1829 ◑	4.2 0.6 3.8	**22** 0515 1135 M 1740 2353	4.4 0.5 4.1 0.6
8 0038 0653 M 1330 1940	0.8 3.8 1.0 3.5	**23** 0607 1231 TU 1840 ◐	4.1 0.8 3.8
9 0216 0818 TU 1457 2110	1.1 3.5 1.2 3.3	**24** 0103 0720 W 1406 2012	0.9 3.8 1.0 3.5
10 0342 0955 W 1613 2232	1.0 3.5 1.2 3.5	**25** 0257 0859 TH 1530 2142	0.9 3.7 0.9 3.6
11 0455 1108 TH 1724 2332	0.9 3.7 1.0 3.7	**26** 0411 1020 F 1638 2250	0.7 3.9 0.9 3.8
12 0556 1200 F 1819	0.6 4.0 0.8	**27** 0515 1122 SA 1739 2344	0.5 4.2 0.7 4.1
13 0017 0642 SA 1239 1857	4.0 0.4 4.2 0.7	**28** 0612 1212 SU 1831	0.2 4.4 0.6
14 0052 0718 SU 1312 1923	4.1 0.3 4.6 0.7	**29** 0029 0659 M 1255 1915	4.3 0.1 4.6 0.4
15 0122 0745 M 1340 ● 1946	4.2 0.3 4.3 0.6	**30** 0110 0741 TU 1336 ○ 1956	4.5 0.0 4.7 0.3
		31 0151 0823 W 1417 2037	4.7 -0.1 4.7 0.2

APRIL

Time	m	Time	m
1 0233 0904 TH 1459 2118	4.8 -0.1 4.7 0.2	**16** 0217 0840 F 1438 2055	4.5 0.1 4.5 0.2
2 0315 0945 F 1542 2158	4.7 0.0 4.5 0.2	**17** 0253 0918 SA 1514 2133	4.6 0.1 4.5 0.2
3 0359 1026 SA 1625 2239	4.6 0.2 4.4 0.3	**18** 0332 0956 SU 1553 2213	4.6 0.2 4.5 0.3
4 0443 1106 SU 1709 2321	4.4 0.4 4.1 0.4	**19** 0413 1037 M 1636 2256	4.5 0.4 4.2 0.4
5 0529 1150 M 1759	4.1 0.7 3.8	**20** 0500 1123 TU 1725 2348	4.4 0.6 4.0 0.6
6 0012 0625 TU 1255 ◑ 1905	0.8 3.8 1.0 3.5	**21** 0556 1224 W 1829 ◐	4.1 0.8 3.7
7 0152 0746 W 1425 2031	1.0 3.5 1.2 3.3	**22** 0108 0713 TH 1350 1957	0.7 3.9 1.0 3.6
8 0307 0914 TH 1534 2148	1.0 3.4 1.2 3.4	**23** 0235 0841 F 1505 2116	0.7 3.8 1.0 3.6
9 0412 1027 F 1639 2250	0.9 3.6 1.1 3.6	**24** 0343 0955 SA 1611 2221	0.6 4.0 0.9 3.8
10 0512 1121 SA 1737 2338	0.7 3.8 0.9 3.8	**25** 0447 1057 SU 1713 2317	0.4 4.2 0.7 4.1
11 0601 1203 SU 1817	0.5 4.0 0.8	**26** 0545 1149 M 1808	0.3 4.3 0.6
12 0015 0637 M 1237 1845	4.0 0.5 4.2 0.7	**27** 0004 0635 TU 1233 1854	4.3 0.2 4.4 0.5
13 0046 0705 TU 1306 1911	4.1 0.4 4.3 0.6	**28** 0048 0718 W 1315 ○ 1936	4.4 0.1 4.5 0.4
14 0115 0733 W 1335 ● 1942	4.3 0.3 4.4 0.4	**29** 0130 0800 TH 1357 2017	4.6 0.1 4.5 0.2
15 0145 0805 TH 1405 2017	4.4 0.2 4.5 0.3	**30** 0213 0841 F 1439 2058	4.6 0.1 4.5 0.2

Chart Datum is 0·23 metres below TAW Datum. HAT is 5·6 metres above Chart Datum; see 0.19

Zeebrugge tides

TIME ZONE -0100
Subtract 1 hour for UT
For Dutch Summer Time add
ONE hour in **non-shaded areas**

ZEEBRUGGE LAT 51°21'N LONG 3°12'E
TIMES AND HEIGHTS OF HIGH AND LOW WATERS

Dates in red are **SPRINGS**
Dates in blue are NEAPS

YEAR 2010

MAY

#	Time	m	#	Time	m
1 SA	0256 0921 1521 2139	4.6 0.2 4.4 0.2	**16** SU	0235 0857 1458 2119	4.6 0.2 4.4 0.2
2 SU	0339 1001 1604 2220	4.5 0.4 4.3 0.3	**17** M	0317 0940 1540 2204	4.6 0.3 4.3 0.3
3 M	0423 1040 1647 2303	4.3 0.6 4.1 0.4	**18** TU	0402 1026 1626 2253	4.5 0.5 4.2 0.3
4 TU	0509 1122 1733 2356	4.1 0.8 3.8 0.7	**19** W	0452 1116 1718 2350	4.3 0.6 4.0 0.4
5 W	0600 1215 1830	3.8 1.1 3.6	**20** TH	0551 1217 1821	4.2 0.8 3.9
6 TH ☽	0120 0707 1343 1943	0.8 3.6 1.2 3.4	**21** F ☽	0059 0702 1326 1934	0.5 4.0 0.9 3.8
7 F	0227 0824 1449 2055	0.9 3.5 1.2 3.4	**22** SA	0208 0817 1433 2044	0.5 4.0 0.9 3.8
8 SA	0325 0932 1547 2156	0.9 3.5 1.2 3.5	**23** SU	0311 0925 1538 2149	0.4 4.0 0.9 3.9
9 SU	0418 1029 1639 2247	0.8 3.7 1.0 3.6	**24** M	0414 1028 1644 2248	0.4 4.1 0.8 4.0
10 M	0506 1116 1724 2330	0.7 4.0 0.9 3.8	**25** TU	0516 1125 1745 2342	0.4 4.2 0.7 4.2
11 TU	0546 1155 1801	0.6 4.0 0.7	**26** W	0611 1215 1836	0.3 4.2 0.6
12 W	0007 0622 1230 1837	4.0 0.5 4.2 0.6	**27** TH	0030 0658 1300 1920	4.3 0.3 4.3 0.4
13 TH	0041 0658 1304 1915	4.2 0.4 4.3 0.4	**28** F ○	0115 0741 1342 2002	4.4 0.4 4.3 0.3
14 F ●	0117 0736 1340 1955	4.4 0.3 4.3 0.3	**29** SA	0159 0821 1423 2043	4.5 0.4 4.3 0.3
15 SA	0155 0816 1418 2036	4.5 0.2 4.4 0.2	**30** SU	0241 0901 1505 2124	4.5 0.4 4.3 0.2
			31 M	0324 0939 1545 2206	4.4 0.5 4.2 0.3

JUNE

#	Time	m	#	Time	m
1 TU	0405 1017 1626 2248	4.3 0.7 4.1 0.4	**16** W	0353 1015 1616 2247	4.6 0.5 4.3 0.2
2 W	0447 1054 1707 2334	4.1 0.8 3.9 0.5	**17** TH	0444 1106 1706 2341	4.5 0.6 4.2 0.2
3 TH	0531 1134 1750	4.0 1.0 3.8	**18** F	0539 1159 1802	4.4 0.7 4.1
4 F ☽	0031 0620 1225 1842	0.7 3.8 1.1 3.6	**19** SA ☽	0037 0640 1256 1904	0.3 4.2 0.8 4.0
5 SA	0134 0721 1341 1946	0.8 3.7 1.2 3.5	**20** SU	0136 0745 1356 2008	0.3 4.1 0.9 4.0
6 SU	0230 0825 1446 2049	0.9 3.6 1.2 3.5	**21** M	0237 0850 1502 2114	0.4 3.9 0.9 3.9
7 M	0322 0925 1542 2146	0.8 3.7 1.1 3.6	**22** TU	0341 0958 1614 2221	0.5 3.9 0.9 3.9
8 TU	0411 1020 1633 2239	0.8 3.8 1.0 3.7	**23** W	0449 1104 1726 2326	0.6 4.0 0.8 4.0
9 W	0458 1110 1721 2327	0.8 3.9 0.8 3.9	**24** TH	0551 1201 1823	0.6 4.1 0.6
10 TH	0543 1156 1807	0.6 4.1 0.6	**25** F	0020 0643 1249 1910	4.2 0.6 4.2 0.5
11 F	0012 0628 1239 1852	4.1 0.4 4.2 0.5	**26** SA ○	0107 0727 1341 1952	4.3 0.6 4.2 0.4
12 SA ●	0055 0711 1320 1937	4.3 0.3 4.3 0.3	**27** SU	0148 0806 1409 2032	4.4 0.6 4.3 0.3
13 SU	0138 0756 1402 2022	4.5 0.3 4.4 0.2	**28** M	0228 0843 1448 2111	4.4 0.6 4.3 0.2
14 M	0222 0841 1445 2109	4.6 0.3 4.4 0.2	**29** TH	0307 0919 1525 2149	4.4 0.6 4.2 0.3
15 TU	0306 0927 1529 2157	4.6 0.4 4.4 0.1	**30** W	0345 0952 1601 2226	4.3 0.7 4.2 0.3

JULY

#	Time	m	#	Time	m
1 TH	0421 1025 1635 2301	4.2 0.7 4.1 0.4	**16** F	0427 1047 1646 2320	4.7 0.5 4.5 0.0
2 F	0457 1058 1710 2336	4.2 0.8 4.1 0.6	**17** SA	0517 1134 1736	4.5 0.7 4.4
3 SA	0533 1134 1747	4.1 0.9 4.0	**18** SU ☽	0009 0611 1224 1831	0.1 4.4 0.7 4.3
4 SU	0014 0615 1216 1832	0.7 4.0 1.0 3.9	**19** M	0102 0710 1318 1931	0.3 4.2 0.7 4.1
5 M	0103 0706 1310 1929	0.8 3.9 1.1 3.8	**20** TU	0202 0814 1426 2040	0.5 3.9 1.0 3.9
6 TU	0211 0811 1432 2038	0.8 3.8 1.1 3.7	**21** W	0311 0928 1549 2159	0.7 3.8 1.0 3.8
7 W	0318 0922 1547 2148	0.8 3.8 1.0 3.7	**22** TH	0426 1046 1710 2315	0.8 3.8 0.7 4.0
8 TH	0417 1028 1648 2252	0.8 3.8 0.9 3.9	**23** F	0535 1149 1812	0.8 4.0 0.6
9 F	0512 1127 1743 2348	0.7 4.0 0.7 4.1	**24** SA	0013 0631 1237 1900	4.1 0.7 4.1 0.5
10 SA	0603 1218 1834	0.5 4.2 0.5	**25** SU	0057 0714 1316 1941	4.3 0.7 4.3 0.3
11 SU ●	0038 0652 1304 1923	4.4 0.4 4.3 0.3	**26** M ○	0136 0751 1353 2017	4.4 0.7 4.3 0.3
12 M	0124 0739 1347 2010	4.6 0.4 4.5 0.1	**27** TU	0212 0824 1427 2052	4.4 0.6 4.4 0.3
13 TU	0209 0826 1430 2057	4.7 0.4 4.5 0.0	**28** W	0246 0854 1500 2124	4.5 0.6 4.4 0.2
14 W	0253 0912 1514 2144	4.8 0.4 4.6 0.0	**29** TH	0319 0924 1531 2155	4.5 0.6 4.4 0.3
15 TH	0339 1000 1559 2232	4.7 0.4 4.5 0.0	**30** F	0351 0955 1602 2225	4.5 0.6 4.4 0.4
			31 SA	0422 1026 1633 2255	4.4 0.6 4.4 0.4

AUGUST

#	Time	m	#	Time	m
1 SU	0454 1059 1707 2327	4.3 0.7 4.3 0.5	**16** M ☽	0540 1152 1759	4.4 0.6 4.4
2 M	0531 1135 1748	4.2 0.7 4.3	**17** TU	0029 0634 1244 1857	0.4 4.2 0.8 4.1
3 TU ☽	0006 0615 1219 1837	0.6 4.0 0.8 4.1	**18** W	0128 0740 1357 2010	0.7 3.9 1.0 3.9
4 W	0057 0710 1318 1942	0.8 4.0 1.0 3.9	**19** TH	0245 0901 1529 2140	0.9 3.7 1.0 3.8
5 TH	0221 0827 1505 2105	0.9 3.8 1.1 3.8	**20** F	0404 1026 1649 2302	1.0 3.7 0.9 3.9
6 F	0344 0953 1622 2225	0.9 3.8 0.9 3.9	**21** SA	0517 1131 1753 2359	0.9 3.9 0.6 4.2
7 SA	0447 1103 1724 2330	0.8 3.9 0.7 4.2	**22** SU	0615 1219 1843	0.8 4.2 0.4
8 SU	0544 1159 1818	0.6 4.2 0.5	**23** M	0042 0658 1257 1922	4.4 0.7 4.3 0.3
9 M	0023 0635 1246 1908	4.5 0.5 4.4 0.2	**24** TU ○	0118 0732 1331 1956	4.5 0.7 4.4 0.3
10 TU ●	0108 0723 1328 1954	4.7 0.4 4.6 0.1	**25** W	0150 0800 1402 2025	4.5 0.6 4.5 0.3
11 W	0152 0809 1410 2039	4.8 0.4 4.7 -0.1	**26** TH	0220 0826 1431 2053	4.5 0.6 4.5 0.3
12 TH	0235 0854 1453 2124	4.9 0.3 4.8 -0.1	**27** F	0250 0855 1500 2122	4.5 0.5 4.5 0.3
13 F	0319 0938 1536 2209	4.9 0.3 4.8 -0.1	**28** SA	0319 0925 1529 2152	4.6 0.5 4.6 0.3
14 SA	0404 1023 1616 2254	4.8 0.4 4.8 0.2	**29** SU	0348 0957 1601 2222	4.6 0.5 4.6 0.4
15 SU	0451 1107 1709 2340	4.7 0.4 4.6 0.2	**30** M	0421 1030 1636 2255	4.6 0.5 4.6 0.4
			31 TU	0457 1106 1716 2333	4.5 0.6 4.5 0.5

Chart Datum is 0·23 metres below TAW Datum. HAT is 5·6 metres above Chart Datum; see 0.19

TIME ZONE -0100
Subtract 1 hour for UT
For Dutch Summer Time add
ONE hour in non-shaded areas

ZEEBRUGGE   LAT 51°21'N   LONG 3°12'E
TIMES AND HEIGHTS OF HIGH AND LOW WATERS

Dates in red are SPRINGS
Dates in blue are NEAPS

YEAR 2010

SEPTEMBER

Time	m		Time	m
1 0540	4.3	**16**	0058	0.9
1147	0.7		0709	3.8
W 1803	4.3	TH	1336	1.0
☽			1945	3.8
2 0020	0.7	**17**	0222	1.1
0632	4.1		0834	3.6
TH 1242	0.9	F	1507	1.0
1905	4.1		2118	3.7
3 0138	1.0	**18**	0339	1.2
0749	3.8		0958	3.6
F 1436	1.1	SA	1620	0.9
2035	3.9		2238	3.9
4 0319	1.0	**19**	0451	1.1
0927	3.7		1104	3.9
SA 1600	0.9	SU	1725	0.7
2204	4.0		2335	4.1
5 0426	0.9	**20**	0551	0.9
1041	3.9		1153	4.1
SU 1704	0.7	M	1817	0.5
2311	4.2			
6 0525	0.7	**21**	0018	4.3
1137	4.2		0635	0.8
M 1800	0.4	TU	1232	4.3
			1856	0.4
7 0004	4.5	**22**	0053	4.5
0618	0.6		0706	0.7
TU 1224	4.5	W	1304	4.4
1849	0.2		1927	0.4
8 0049	4.8	**23**	0123	4.5
0705	0.5		0731	0.6
W 1306	4.7	TH	1333	4.5
● 1934	0.0	○	1953	0.3
9 0131	4.9	**24**	0152	4.5
0749	0.4		0756	0.6
TH 1348	4.9	F	1401	4.6
2018	-0.1		2020	0.3
10 0213	5.0	**25**	0219	4.6
0832	0.3		0826	0.5
F 1430	5.0	SA	1430	4.6
2101	-0.1		2050	0.3
11 0256	5.0	**26**	0248	4.6
0915	0.3		0859	0.4
SA 1513	5.0	SU	1500	4.7
2145	-0.1		2122	0.3
12 0340	4.9	**27**	0320	4.7
0958	0.3		0933	0.4
SU 1557	4.9	M	1534	4.7
2228	0.1		2156	0.3
13 0425	4.7	**28**	0354	4.6
1041	0.4		1008	0.4
M 1643	4.7	TU	1611	4.7
2312	0.3		2231	0.4
14 0512	4.4	**29**	0431	4.5
1125	0.5		1045	0.5
TU 1732	4.5	W	1652	4.6
2359	0.6		2310	0.6
15 0604	4.1	**30**	0514	4.3
1216	0.8		1128	0.7
W 1828	4.1	TH	1740	4.4
☾				

OCTOBER

Time	m		Time	m
1 0000	0.8	**16**	0155	1.2
0608	4.0		0801	3.6
F 1226	0.9	SA	1438	1.0
☽ 1844	4.1		2045	3.7
2 0119	1.1	**17**	0307	1.3
0727	3.8		0920	3.6
SA 1419	1.0	SU	1545	0.9
2018	3.9		2200	3.8
3 0256	1.1	**18**	0414	1.2
0904	3.7		1026	3.8
SU 1537	0.8	M	1647	0.8
2143	4.0		2259	4.0
4 0403	1.0	**19**	0514	1.0
1015	3.9		1118	4.0
M 1640	0.6	TU	1740	0.6
2248	4.3		2345	4.2
5 0503	0.8	**20**	0601	0.9
1112	4.2		1159	4.2
TU 1737	0.4	W	1821	0.6
2341	4.6			
6 0557	0.6	**21**	0021	4.3
1200	4.5		0633	0.8
W 1827	0.4	TH	1232	4.3
			1851	0.5
7 0027	4.8	**22**	0053	4.4
0645	0.5		0659	0.7
TH 1243	4.7	F	1302	4.4
● 1912	0.1		1918	0.4
8 0109	4.9	**23**	0122	4.5
0729	0.4		0727	0.6
F 1325	4.9	SA	1332	4.5
1955	0.0	○	1948	0.4
9 0151	4.9	**24**	0151	4.6
0811	0.3		0800	0.4
SA 1408	5.0	SU	1402	4.6
2038	0.0		2021	0.3
10 0234	4.9	**25**	0222	4.6
0854	0.2		0836	0.4
SU 1451	5.0	M	1436	4.7
2121	0.1		2057	0.3
11 0318	4.8	**26**	0256	4.6
0937	0.3		0913	0.4
M 1536	4.9	TU	1513	4.7
2203	0.2		2134	0.4
12 0403	4.6	**27**	0333	4.6
1020	0.3		0952	0.4
TU 1622	4.7	W	1552	4.7
2246	0.4		2213	0.5
13 0449	4.4	**28**	0413	4.4
1104	0.5		1033	0.5
W 1710	4.4	TH	1636	4.6
2332	0.7		2257	0.7
14 0539	4.1	**29**	0459	4.3
1157	0.7		1120	0.6
TH 1806	4.1	F	1727	4.4
☾			2350	0.9
15 0031	1.0	**30**	0555	4.0
0642	3.8		1226	0.8
F 1319	0.9	SA	1834	4.1
1920	3.8			
		31	0106	1.1
			0713	3.8
		SU	1358	0.8
			2000	4.0

NOVEMBER

Time	m		Time	m
1 0229	1.1	**16**	0327	1.3
0837	3.8		0934	3.6
M 1509	0.7	TU	1559	0.9
2117	4.1		2210	3.8
2 0335	1.0	**17**	0424	1.2
0945	4.0		1030	3.8
TU 1611	0.6	W	1651	0.8
2222	4.3		2301	4.0
3 0437	0.9	**18**	0514	1.1
1044	4.2		1117	3.9
W 1710	0.4	TH	1735	0.8
2317	4.5		2344	4.1
4 0535	0.7	**19**	0553	0.9
1135	4.4		1156	4.1
TH 1804	0.3	F	1811	0.7
5 0006	4.6	**20**	0021	4.3
0626	0.6		0627	0.8
F 1222	4.6	SA	1232	4.3
1851	0.2		1845	0.6
6 0050	4.7	**21**	0055	4.4
0711	0.5		0702	0.6
SA 1307	4.8	SU	1306	4.4
● 1935	0.2	○	1920	0.5
7 0134	4.7	**22**	0128	4.5
0754	0.4		0739	0.4
SU 1351	4.8	M	1341	4.6
2018	0.2		1957	0.4
8 0217	4.7	**23**	0203	4.5
0837	0.3		0819	0.4
M 1435	4.9	TU	1418	4.7
2100	0.3		2037	0.4
9 0301	4.6	**24**	0240	4.5
0920	0.3		0859	0.3
TU 1520	4.8	W	1458	4.7
2142	0.4		2118	0.4
10 0345	4.5	**25**	0319	4.5
1004	0.3		0942	0.4
W 1605	4.6	TH	1541	4.6
2224	0.6		2201	0.6
11 0430	4.3	**26**	0402	4.4
1049	0.4		1028	0.4
TH 1653	4.4	F	1627	4.5
2309	0.8		2248	0.7
12 0518	4.1	**27**	0450	4.2
1142	0.6		1120	0.5
F 1744	4.1	SA	1720	4.4
2359	1.1		2342	0.9
13 0612	3.9	**28**	0545	4.1
1253	0.8		1223	0.6
SA 1847	3.9	SU	1823	4.2
☽		☽		
14 0115	1.3	**29**	0047	1.0
0719	3.7		0653	4.0
SU 1402	0.9	M	1331	0.6
2000	3.7		1936	4.1
15 0226	1.3	**30**	0156	1.0
0830	3.6		0805	3.9
M 1503	0.9	TU	1436	0.6
2109	3.7		2046	4.1

DECEMBER

Time	m		Time	m
1 0302	1.0	**16**	0327	1.3
0912	4.0		0929	3.6
W 1539	0.6	TH	1558	1.0
2152	4.1		2206	3.7
2 0407	1.0	**17**	0423	1.2
1015	4.1		1026	3.7
TH 1643	0.5	F	1647	0.9
2253	4.2		2300	3.9
3 0513	0.9	**18**	0513	1.0
1113	4.2		1117	3.9
F 1743	0.5	SA	1732	0.8
2349	4.3		2348	4.0
4 0611	0.7	**19**	0559	0.8
1207	4.4		1203	4.1
SA 1835	0.5	SU	1815	0.7
5 0038	4.4	**20**	0030	4.2
0700	0.5		0641	0.6
SU 1255	4.5	M	1245	4.3
● 1921	0.4		1857	0.5
6 0122	4.5	**21**	0109	4.4
0744	0.4		0723	0.5
M 1340	4.6	TU	1325	4.5
2003	0.4	○	1939	0.5
7 0205	4.5	**22**	0148	4.5
0827	0.3		0805	0.3
TU 1424	4.7	W	1405	4.6
2044	0.5		2021	0.4
8 0247	4.5	**23**	0227	4.5
0909	0.3		0849	0.2
W 1507	4.7	TH	1447	4.7
2125	0.6		2105	0.4
9 0329	4.5	**24**	0308	4.5
0952	0.3		0935	0.2
TH 1550	4.6	F	1531	4.7
2205	0.7		2151	0.5
10 0411	4.4	**25**	0351	4.4
1036	0.4		1022	0.2
F 1633	4.4	SA	1617	4.6
2245	0.8		2238	0.6
11 0453	4.2	**26**	0438	4.4
1122	0.5		1112	0.3
SA 1718	4.2	SU	1707	4.5
2326	1.0		2328	0.7
12 0537	4.0	**27**	0529	4.3
1213	0.7		1205	0.3
SU 1806	4.0	M	1803	4.4
13 0012	1.2	**28**	0021	0.8
0626	3.8		0626	4.2
M 1312	0.9	TU	1301	0.4
☽ 1901	3.8	☽	1906	4.2
14 0116	1.3	**29**	0119	0.9
0724	3.7		0729	4.1
TU 1410	1.0	W	1401	0.5
2004	3.7		2012	4.0
15 0226	1.3	**30**	0224	1.0
0827	3.6		0836	4.0
W 1505	1.0	TH	1506	0.6
2107	3.7		2120	3.9
		31	0338	1.0
			0947	3.9
		F	1617	0.7
			2232	3.9

Chart Datum is 0·23 metres below TAW Datum. HAT is 5·6 metres above Chart Datum; see 0.19

Belgium

2.33 BLANKENBERGE

Belgium, West Flanders **51°18'·90N 03°06'·48E** ✣✲⚓⚓⚓🏳🏳

CHARTS AC 2449, 1872, 1874; DYC 1801.3; Imray C30; Stan 1, 19

TIDES +0130 Dover; ML 2·5; Duration 0535.
Standard Port VLISSINGEN (←)

Times		Height (metres)			
High Water	Low Water	MHWS	MHWN	MLWN	MLWS
All times	**All times**	**5·0**	**4·1**	**1·1**	**0·5**
Differences BLANKENBERGE					
–0040	–0040	–0·3	0·0	+0·3	+0·2

SHELTER Good, but entry is dangerous in NW'lies F6 and above.

NAVIGATION WPT 51°19'·60N 03°05'·31E, 134°/1M to pierheads. Caution: 4 unlit Y SPM buoys and one Fl (4) Y 20s lie E and W of hbr ent about 400m offshore. Beware strong tides (& fishing lines) across ent. Access HW ±2 but up to ±4 in season, when it is said to be dredged 2·5m; out of season it silts between piers and dries at LW. Do not try to ent/exit LW±1½, especially at springs. Oct-end May, only ent/exit HW±1, unless depths have been pre-checked. Call dredger Ch 10 for clearance to pass.

LIGHTS AND MARKS Conspic high-rise blocks E of lt ho, W twr B

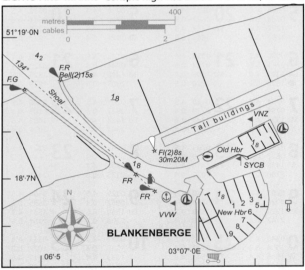

top. Ldg lts 134°, both FR, (Red X on front mast) show the best water. FG on W pier is more visible than FR (E pier). A water twr is conspic on E side of new Hbr. See also 2.3 and chartlet.

R/T VNZ, SYCB and VVW marinas Ch 23. *Blankenberge Rescue* Ch 08; or relay via Zeebrugge Traffic Centre Ch 69. Dredger Ch 10.

TELEPHONE (Code 050) Call VNZ, SYCB or VVW below; ⊖ 544223; Police 429842; Dr 333668; ⊞ 413701; Brit Consul (02) 2179000.

FACILITIES A Port of Entry, with Customs early Apr–late Sept.

Keep to port, past the FV hbr, for the old Yacht Hbr (1·8m); VNZ pontoons are on N side and SYCB to the E. Or turn 90° stbd into new Hbr/marina (2·5m); 12 pontoons, run by VNZ, SYCB & VVW.

Fees (same for all berths): **Beam** <3m €15; <3·5m €22; <4m €29; <4·25m €33; <4·50m €36; <5·00m €45.

VNZ (YC Vrije Noordzeezeilers) ☎ 425292, mobile 0497 565565. www.vnzblankenberge.be vnz@skynet.be Bar, R.

SYCB (Scarphout YC) www.scarphout.be scarphout@skynet.be ☎ 411420, mobile 0476 971692. C (10/2½ ton), Slip, Bar, R, ♿.

VVW (Marina) www.vvwblankenberge.be ☎ 417536, mobile 0495 527536 info@vvwblankenberge.be. ⚓, Bar, 🚿, Slip, P, D (hose, duty free), ME, ✕, Ⓔ, El, SM, CH, C (20 ton).

Town Gaz, R, Bar, ✉, Ⓑ, ≋, ✈ Ostend.

2.34 OOSTENDE

Belgium, West Flanders **51°14'·35N 02°55'·09E** ✣✲✲⚓⚓⚓🏳🏳🏳

CHARTS AC 2449, 1872, 1874, 1873; SHOM 7214; Navi 1010; DYC 1801.2; Imray C30; Stanfords 1, 19, 20

TIDES +0120 Dover; ML 2·79; Duration 0530.
Standard Port ZEEBRUGGE (←)

Times				Height (metres)			
High Water		Low Water		MHWS	MHWN	MLWN	MLWS
0300	0900	0300	0900	4·8	4·0	1·1	0·5
1500	2100	1500	2100				
Differences OOSTENDE							
–0019	–0019	–0008	–0008	+0·4	+0·3	+0·2	+0·1

SHELTER Wash can enter RNSYC (2·2m). Very good in Mercator Marina (5·0m). RYCO (2·7m) may be exposed in strong W/NW'lies. Locals sceptical about the effectiveness of new wavebreaks.

NAVIGATION WPT 51°14'·97N 02°53'·83E, 128°/1M to ent. Avoid the offshore banks esp in bad weather: From the NE stay to seaward of Wenduinebank, except in calm weather. From the NW keep S of W Hinder TSS and approach from MBN buoy. From the SW appr via West Diep and Kleine Rede, inside Stroombank. Major WIP 2008-12: demolish E pier and build new one further E. Note size of Montgomerydok entrance reduced as a result of works.

LIGHTS AND MARKS Europa Centrum bldg (105m; twice as high as other bldgs) is conspic 4ca SSW of ent. W lt ho, 5ca ESE of the ent, is conspic with 2 sinusoidal blue bands. 128° ldg marks are lattice masts with R/W bands and X topmarks. See chartlet and 2.3 for lt details.

IPTS from E pier, plus QY = hbr closed, ferry moving. At blind exit from Montgomerydok, QY lts = no exit, ferry/ship moving.

R/T Port Control Ch 09 (H24); Mercator lock/Marina Ch 14 (lock hrs); Weather Ch 27 at 0820 & 1720 UT (English and Dutch). Demey lock (VHF 10) gives access to Oostende-Brugge canal.

TELEPHONE (Code 059) HM 321687; Mercator lock 705762; ⊖ 242070; Police 701111; ⊞ 552000; Brit Consul (02) 2876232.

FACILITIES from seaward: **Royal North Sea YC** (RNSYC), ☎ 430694 HM 505912. www.rnsyc.be robert@rnsyc.be No VHF. 150+50 Ⓥ, much rafting, €1.92 inc AC & shwr (M/Cruisers + 25%). Limited D, Grid, 🚿, Wi-fi, ME, CH, ✕, El, SM, R, Bar.
Mercator lock Must pre-call Ch 14 for lock-in time and berth. Waiting pontoon N of lock. No freeflow. R/G tfc lts. Hrs (times in brackets are Fri-Sun & public hols): May/Jun 0800-2000 (2100); Jul/Aug 0700-2200, 7/7; Sep 0800-1800 (2000). Oct–Apr, see web.
Mercator Marina ☎ 705762.www.mercatormarina.be 300+50 Ⓥ, €2.05 inc AC; must pay cash/card before entering lock outbound.
Royal YC Oostende (RYCO) ☎ 321452. ryco@skynet.be www.ryco. be No VHF. 160 + 35 Ⓥ, €2.30 inc AC & shwr. Slip (10 ton), Grid, C (½ ton), Wi-Fi, R, Bar.
Town All needs, ≋, ✈. Ferry, ☎ 340260 (no foot pax) to Ramsgate.

CROSSING THE NORTH SEA FROM BELGIUM

(AC *1406*, *323*) There are so many permutations that it is better to try to apply just four broad principles:

- Avoid the N Hinder-Maas and W Hinder-Sandettie complexes.
- Cross TSS at their narrowest parts, ie between NHR-SE and Fairy W; and SW of Sandettie.
- Plan to cross the many offshore ridges at their extremities, zigzagging as necessary to achieve this.
- If bound for Dover or down-Channel use the coastal passage W to Dyck, then via MPC to SW Goodwin buoy. Or route via Sandettie to NE Goodwin buoy and into the southern Thames Estuary.

From the Scheur chan off Zeebrugge a fairly direct course via Track Ferry and S Galloper leads into the N Thames Estuary or towards the Suffolk ports. Avoid shoals, particularly in rough weather when the sea-state and under-keel clearance may be crucial problems. See 0.34 for distances across the North Sea.

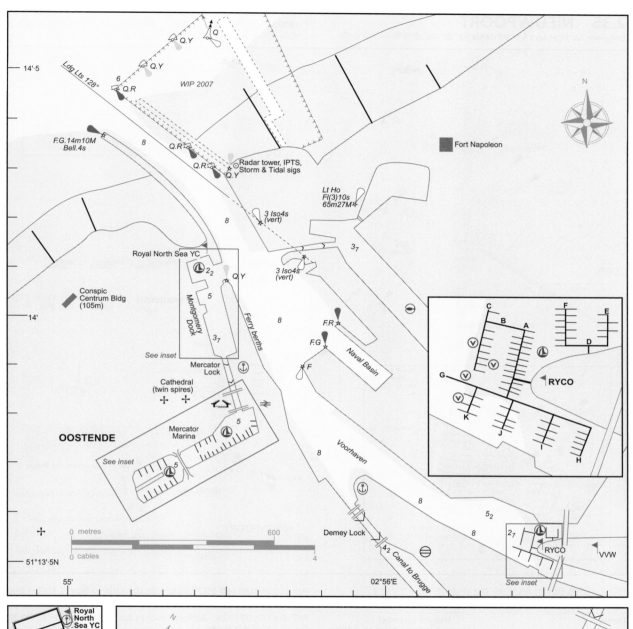

Ldg Lts 128°

WIP 2007

Q
Q.Y
Q.Y
Q.R
6
Q.R

14'·5

Fort Napoleon

N

F.G.14m10M
Bell.4s

8

Q.R
Q.R
Q.Y

Radar tower, IPTS, Storm & Tidal sigs

Lt Ho
Fl(3)10s
65m27M

8

3 Iso4s
(vert)

3₇

Royal North Sea YC

2₂

Q.Y

3 Iso4s
(vert)

Conspic
Centrum Bldg
(105m)

5

14'

Montgomery Dock

3₇

8

F.R

Naval Basin

See inset

F.G

Mercator
Lock

F

Cathedral
(twin spires)

Mercator
Marina

OOSTENDE

5

See inset

5

Voorhaven

8

8

0   metres   600

8

Demey Lock

4₂ Canal to Brugge

0 cables   4

51°13'·5N

5₂

2₇

RYCO

VVW

55'   02°56'E

See inset

Inset (top right)

C
B   A
F
E
D
V
V
V
G   RYCO
V
K
J
I
H

Belgium

Inset (bottom left)

Royal
North
Sea YC

Waiting
pontoon

Q.Y

Montgomery Dock

Dredged to 2·7m

Waiting
pontoon

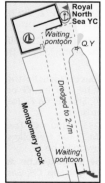

Inset (bottom right) — MERCATOR MARINA

N

MERCATOR MARINA

F
E   D   C   B

Mercator STS

49–1

106–102
97–101

1–27
G   A

Swing
bridge

40–1

96–51

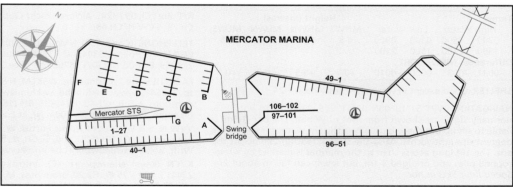

2.35 NIEUWPOORT

Belgium, W Flanders 51°09'·38N 02°43'·04 ❀❀❀♨♨♨✿✿✿

CHARTS AC 2449, 1872, 1873; Belgian 101, D11; DYC 1801.2; SHOM 7214; Navicarte 1010; Imray C30; Stanfords 1, 20

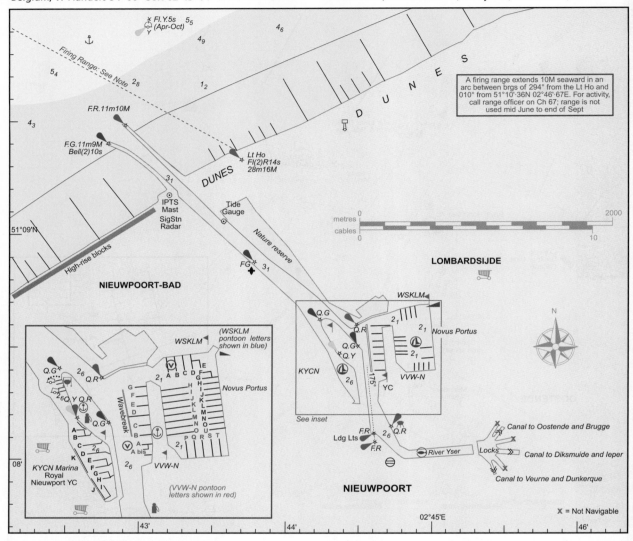

TIDES +0105 Dover; ML 2·96; Duration 0515.

Standard Port ZEEBRUGGE (←)

Times				Height (metres)			
High Water		Low Water		MHWS	MHWN	MLWN	MLWS
0300	0900	0300	0900	4·8	4·0	1·1	0·5
1500	2100	1500	2100				
Differences NIEUWPOORT							
−0031	−0031	−0010	−0010	+0·7	+0·5	+0·3	+0·1

SHELTER Good except in strong NW'lies. Access H24.

NAVIGATION WPT 51°10'·08N 02°41'·90E, 134°/1M to ent. IPTS, normally Sig 4, are shown from root of W pier. The bar (1·5m) is liable to silt up but there is usually sufficient water for all but the deepest draught yachts. At sp the stream reaches 2kn across the ent. The 1M long access chan to the marinas is marked by white-topped piles and dredged 3·1m, but levels can fall to about 2m. *Speed limit 5kts in hbr.*

LIGHTS AND MARKS The high-rise blocks W of the entrance are in stark contrast to the sand dunes and flatlands to the E. The lt ho is a conspic 28m R twr, W bands; see chartlet and 2.3. The central, pyramidal white HM bldg at VVW-N is conspic.

An illuminated red STOP sign near the ents to Novus Portus and KYCN indicates to departing vessels that the fairway is not clear.

R/T Port Ch 09 (H24). *Airforce Yacht Club* (WSKLM): Ch 72. KYCN: Ch 23. VVW-N: Ch 08.

TELEPHONE (Code 058) HM/Pilots 233000; Canal locks 233050; CG/Marine Police 233045; ⊖ 233451; Duty Free Store 233433; Dr 233089; Brit Consul (02) 2876232; Police 234246.

FACILITIES The 3 marinas are: **WSKLM**, N & E sides of Novus Portus. ☎ 233641, www.wsklum.be wsklum@wsklm.be 370 inc Ⓥ on pontoons A & B, €1.40. H24, CH, BH (16 ton), Slip, ▣, Wi-Fi, Ice, bike hire, R, Bar; Okay 🛒 800m NE at Lombardsijde.

VVW-N, S & W sides of Novus Portus. ☎ 235232, 1000 + Ⓥ, fees not given. El, Ⓔ, BH (50t), Slip, ▣, CH, ♂, ✕, SM, R, Bar, free bikes, Wi-fi. www.vvwnieuwpoort.be info@vvwnieuwpoort.be

KYCN (Royal Nieuwport YC). info@kycn.be www.kycn.be ☎ 234413. 420 + 75 Ⓥ, €2.20, often busy. M, C (12 ton), Slip, CH, Gas, ME, El, ✕, 🛒, D, ▣, R, Bar, Wi-Fi.

Fuel is only available at KYCN and S of VVW-N on the E bank of the river, see inset. The river accesses the N Belgian canals.

Town P, D, Gaz, 🛒, R, Bar, ✉, Ⓑ, ⇌, ✈ (Oostende).

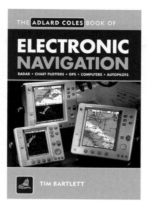

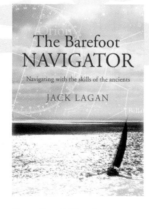

DISTANCE TABLE

Approximate distances in nautical miles are by the most direct route, whilst avoiding dangers and allowing for Traffic Separation Schemes. Places in *italics* are in adjoining areas; places in **bold** are in 0.34. Distances across the North Sea.

	1	2	3	4	5	6	7	8	9	10	11	12	13	14	15	16	17	18	19	20
1. *Great Yarmouth*	**1**																			
2. Blakeney	44	**2**																		
3. **King's Lynn**	85	42	**3**																	
4. Boston	83	39	34	**4**																
5. Humber Lt Buoy	82	45	55	54	**5**															
6. **Grimsby**	99	54	61	58	17	**6**														
7. Hull	113	68	75	72	31	14	**7**													
8. Bridlington	114	79	87	83	35	44	58	**8**												
9. Scarborough	130	96	105	98	50	59	81	20	**9**											
10. Whitby	143	101	121	114	66	75	88	35	16	**10**										
11. River Tees (ent)	166	122	138	135	87	96	118	56	37	21	**11**									
12. **Hartlepool**	169	126	140	137	89	98	122	58	39	24	4	**12**								
13. Seaham	175	137	151	145	100	106	133	66	47	33	15	11	**13**							
14. Sunderland	180	142	156	149	105	110	138	70	51	36	20	16	5	**14**						
15. Tynemouth	183	149	163	154	112	115	145	75	56	41	27	23	12	7	**15**					
16. Blyth	190	156	171	162	120	123	153	83	64	49	35	31	20	15	8	**16**				
17. Amble	203	170	185	176	126	143	157	102	81	65	46	42	32	27	21	14	**17**			
18. Holy Island	225	191	196	198	148	166	180	126	104	88	68	65	54	50	44	37	22	**18**		
19. **Berwick-on-Tweed**	232	200	205	205	157	166	189	126	107	91	82	78	67	61	55	47	31	9	**19**	
20. Eyemouth	240	208	213	213	165	174	197	134	115	99	90	86	75	69	63	55	39	17	8	**20**

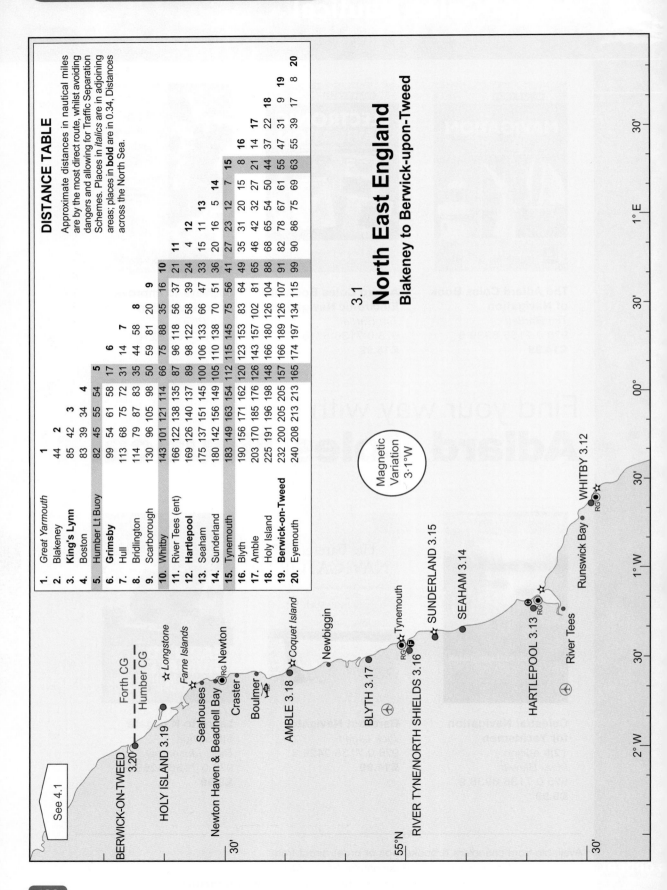

3.1 North East England
Blakeney to Berwick-upon-Tweed

Magnetic Variation 3·1°W

See 4.1

BERWICK-ON-TWEED 3.20
Forth CG
Humber CG
Longstone
Farne Islands
HOLY ISLAND 3.19
Seahouses
Newton Haven & Beadnell Bay — RG Newton
Craster
Boulmer
AMBLE 3.18
Coquet Island
Newbiggin
Tynemouth
BLYTH 3.17
RIVER TYNE/NORTH SHIELDS 3.16
SUNDERLAND 3.15
SEAHAM 3.14
HARTLEPOOL 3.13
River Tees
Runswick Bay
WHITBY 3.12

55°N
2°W — 1°W — 30' — 0° — 30' — 1°E — 30'

Northward 4.2   Southward 1.2

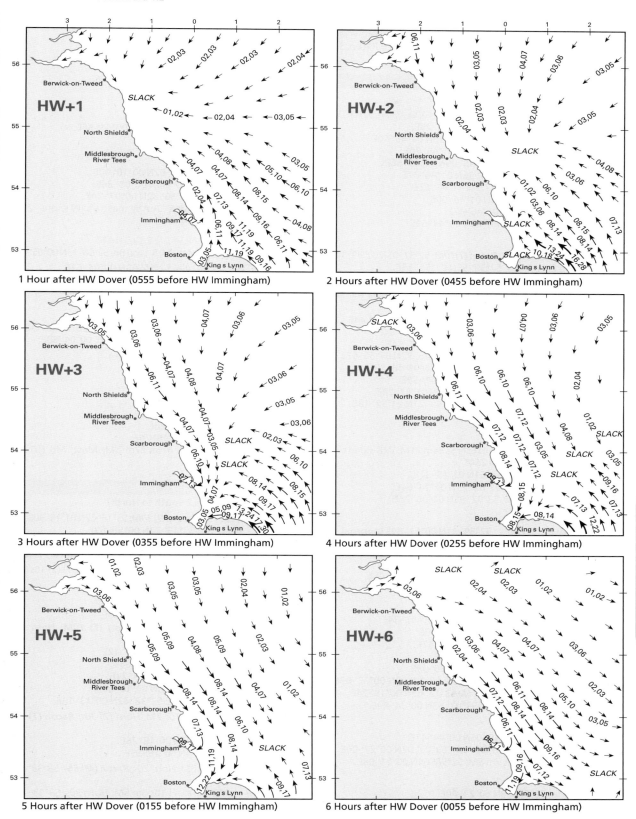

1 Hour after HW Dover (0555 before HW Immingham)

2 Hours after HW Dover (0455 before HW Immingham)

3 Hours after HW Dover (0355 before HW Immingham)

4 Hours after HW Dover (0255 before HW Immingham)

5 Hours after HW Dover (0155 before HW Immingham)

6 Hours after HW Dover (0055 before HW Immingham)

NE England

3.3 LIGHTS, BUOYS AND WAYPOINTS

Bold print = light with a nominal range of 15M or more. CAPITALS = place or feature. *CAPITAL ITALICS* = light-vessel, light float or Lanby. *Italics* = Fog signal. ***Bold italics*** = Racon. See 0.2 for Abbreviations.

GREAT YARMOUTH TO THE WASH
(Direction of buoyage ⟳ South to North)

YARMOUTH and CAISTER ROADS/COCKLE GATEWAY
SW Scroby ▲ Fl G 2·5s; 52°35'·82N 01°46'·26E.
Scroby Elbow ▲ Fl (2) G 5s; *Bell*; 52°37'·35N 01°46'·10E.
Yarmouth Outfall ⚓ Q R; 52°37'·58N 01°45'·70E.
Mid Caister ⚓ Fl (2) R 5s; *Bell*; 52°38'·99N 01°45'·66E.
NW Scroby ▲ Fl (3) G 10s; 52°40'·36N 01°46'·31E.
N Caister ⚓ Fl (3) R 10s; 52°40'·77N 01°45'·65E.
Hemsby ⚓ Fl R 2·5s; 52°41'·80N 01°46'·00E.
N Scroby ⚐ VQ; 52°41'·39N 01°46'·47E.
Cockle ⚐ VQ (3) 5s; *Bell*; 52°44'·03N 01°43'·59E.

OFFSHORE ROUTE
Cross Sand ⚐ L Fl 10s 6m 5M; ***Racon (T)10M***; 52°37'·03N 01°59'·14E.
E Cross Sand ⚓ Fl (4) R 15s; 52°38'·55N 01°53'·55E.
NE Cross Sand ⚐ VQ (3) 5s; 52°44'·22N 01°53'·80E.
Smith's Knoll ⚐ Q (6) + L Fl 15s 7M; ***Racon (T) 10M***; 52°43'·52N 02°17'·89E.
S Winterton Ridge ⚐ Q (6) + L Fl 15s; 52°47'·21N 02°03'·44E.
E Hammond Knoll ⚐ Q (3) 10s; 52°52'·32N 01°58'·64E.
Hammond Knoll ⚐ Q (9) 15s; 52°49'·68N 01°57'·54E.
Newarp ⚐ L Fl 10s 7M; ***Racon (O) 10M***; 52°48'·37N 01°55'·69E.
S Haisbro ⚐ Q (6) + L Fl 15s; *Bell*; 52°50'·82N 01°48'·29E.
Mid Haisbro ▲ Fl (2) G 5s; 52°54'·22N 01°41'·59E.
N Haisbro ⚐ Q; ***Racon (T) 10M***; 53°00'·22N 01°32'·29E.
Happisburgh ☆ Fl (3) 30s 41m 14M; 52°49'·21N 01°32'·18E.

(Direction of buoyage ⟳ East to West)

CROMER
Cromer ☆ 52°55'·45N 01°19'·01E; Fl 5s 84m **21M**; W 8-sided twr; vis: 102°-307° H24; ***Racon (O) 25M***.
Tayjack Wk ⚓ Fl R 2·5s; 52°57'·61N 01°15'·37E.
E Sheringham ⚐ Q (3) 10s; 53°02'·21N 01°14'·84E.
W Sheringham ⚐ Q (9) 15s; 53°02'·95N 01°06'·72E.

BLAKENEY
Blakeney Fairway (SWM) ⚓; 52°59'·31N 00°57'·83E (approx).
Blakeney Overfalls ⚓ Fl (2) R 5s; *Bell*; 53°03'·01N 01°01'·37E.

WELLS-NEXT-THE-SEA/BRANCASTER STAITHE
Wells Leading Buoy ⚓ Fl(2) R 5s; 52°59'·80N 00°50'·49E.
Bridgirdle ⚓ Fl R 2·5s; 53°01'·73N 00°43'·95E.

APPROACHES TO THE WASH
S Race ⚐ Q (6) + L Fl 15s; *Bell*; 53°07'·81N 00°57'·34E.
E Docking ⚓ Fl R 2·5s; 53°09'·82N 00°50'·39E.
N Race ▲ Fl G 5s; *Bell.*; 53°14'·98N 00°43'·87E.
N Docking ⚐ Q; 53°14'·82N 00°41'·49E.
Scott Patch ⚐ VQ (3) 5s; 53°11'·12N 00°36'·39E.
S Inner Dowsing ⚐ Q (6) + L Fl 15s; *Bell*; 53°12'·12N 00°33'·69E.
Boygrift Tower ⚐ Fl (2) 10s 12m 5M; 53°17'·63N 00°19'·24E.
Burnham Flats ⚐ Q (9) 15s; *Bell*; 53°07'·53N 00°34'·89E.

THE WASH
West Ridge ⚐ Q (9) 15s; 53°19'·06N 00°44'·47E.
N Well ⚐ L Fl 10s; *Bell*; ***Racon (T) 10M***; 53°03'·02N 00°27'·90E.
Roaring Middle ⚐ L Fl 10s 7m 8M; 52°58'·64N 00°21'·08E.

CORK HOLE/KING'S LYNN
Sunk ⚐ Q (9) 15s; 52°56'·29N 00°23'·40E.
Seal Sand ⚐ Q; *Bell*; 52°56'·00N 00°20'·00E.

WISBECH CHANNEL/RIVER NENE
Beacons are moved as required.
Masts on W side of River Nene to Wisbech carry FG Lts and those on E side QR or FR Lts.

FREEMAN CHANNEL
Boston Roads ⚓ L Fl 10s; 52°57'·66N 00°16'·04E.
Boston No. 1 ▲ Fl G 3s; 52°57'·88N 00°15'·16E.
Alpha ⚓ Fl R 3s; 52°57'·65N 00°14'·99E.
No. 3 ▲ Fl G 6s; 52°58'·08N 00°14'·07E.
No. 5 ▲ Fl G 3s; 52°58'·51N 00°12'·72E.
Freeman Inner ⚐ Q (9) 15s; 52°58'·59N 00°11'·36E.
Delta ⚓ Fl R 6s; 52°58'·38N 00°11'·25E.

BOSTON LOWER ROAD
Boston No. 7 ▲ Fl G 3s; 52°58'·62N 00°10'·00E.
Boston No. 9 ▲ Fl G 3s; 52°57'·58N 00°08'·36E.
Black Buoy ⚓ Fl (2) R 6s; 52°56'·82N 00°07'·74E.
Tabs Head ⚐ Q WG 4m 1M; R ☐ on W mast; vis: W shore - 251°- G - shore; 52°56'·00N 00°04'·91E.

BOSTON, NEW CUT AND RIVER WITHAM
Ent N side, Dollypeg ⚐ QG 4m 1M; B △ on Bn; 52°56'·13N 00°05'·03E.
New Cut ⚐ Fl G 3s; △ on pile; 52°55'·98N 00°04'·67E.
New Cut Ldg Lts 240°. Front, No. 1, F 5m 5M; 52°55'·85N 00°04'·40E. Rear, 90m from front, F 8m 5M.

WELLAND CUT/RIVER WELLAND
SE side ⚐ Iso R 2s; NW side Iso G 2s. Lts QR (to port) and QG (to stbd) mark the chan upstream; 52°55'·72E 00°04'·68E.

(Direction of buoyage ⟳ North to South)

BOSTON DEEP/WAINFLEET ROADS
Scullridge ▲; 52°59'·76N 00°13'·86E.
Friskney ▲; 53°00'·59N 00°16'·76E.
Long Sand ▲; 53°01'·27N 00°18'·30E.
Pompey ▲; 53°02'·19N 00°19'·26E.
Swatchway ▲; 53°03'·81N 00°19'·70E.
Off Ingoldmells Point ⚐ Fl Y 5s 22m 5M; Mast; *Mo (U) 30s*; 53°12'·49N 00°25'·85E.

THE WASH TO THE RIVER HUMBER
(Direction of buoyage ⟳ South to North)
Dudgeon ⚐ Q (9) 15s 7M; ***Racon (O) 10M***; 53°16'·62N 01°16'·90E.
E Dudgeon ⚐ Q (3) 10s; 53°19'·72N 00°58'·69E.
Mid Outer Dowsing ▲ Fl (3) G 10s; 53°24'·82N 01°07'·79E.
N Outer Dowsing ⚐ Q; 53°33'·52N 00°59'·59E; ***Racon (T) 10M***.
B.1D Platform Dowsing ⚐ 53°33'·68N 00°52'·63E; Fl (2) 10s 28m **22M**; Morse (U) R 15s 28m 3M; *Horn (2) 60s*.

RIVER HUMBER APPROACHES
W Ridge ⚐ Q (9) 15s; 53°19'·04N 00°44'·50E.
Inner Dowsing ⚐ Q (3) 10s 7M, ***Racon (T) 10M***; *Horn 60s*; 53°19'·10N 00°34'·80E.
Protector ⚓ Fl R 2·5s; 53°24'·84N 00°25'·12E.
DZ No. 4 ⚓ Fl Y 5s; 53°27'·15N 00°19'·06E.
DZ No. 3 ⚓ Fl Y 2·5s 53°29'·30N 00°19'·21E.
Rosse Spit ⚓ Fl (2) R 5s 53°30'·56N 00°16'·60E.
Haile Sand No. 2 ⚓ Fl (3) R 10s; 53°32'·42N 00°13'·18E.
Humber ⚐ G lt float L Fl 10s 7M; *Horn (2) 30s*; ***Racon (T) 7M***; 53°38'·70N 00°21'·24E.
N Binks ▲ Fl G 4s; 53°36'·01N 00°18'·28E.
S Binks ▲ Fl G 2s 53°34'·74N 00°16'·55E.
SPURN ⚐ Q (3) 10s 10m 8M; *Horn 20s*; ***Racon (M) 5M***; 53°33'·56N 00°14'·20E.
SE CHEQUER ⚐ VQ (6) + L Fl 10s 6m 6M; *Horn 30s* 53°33'·38N 00°12'·55E.

Chequer No. 3 ⚓ Q (6) + L Fl 15s; 53°33'·07N 00°10'·63E.
No 2B ⚓ Fl R 4s; 53°32'·33N 00°09'·10E.
Tetney ⚓ 2 VQ Y (vert); *Horn Mo (A)60s*; QY on 290m floating hose; 53°32'·35N 00°06'·76E.

RIVER HUMBER/GRIMSBY/HULL
Binks No. 3A ⚓ Fl G 4s; 53°33'·92N 00°07'·43E.
Spurn Pt ⚓ Fl G 3s 11m 5M; 53°34'·37N 00°06'·47E.
BULL ⚓ VQ 8m 6M; *Horn (2) 20s*; 53°33'·54N 00°05'·70E.
Bull Sand ⚓ Q R ; 53°34'·45N 00°03'·69E.
North Fort ⚓ Q; 53°33'·80N 00°04'·19E.
South Fort ⚓ Q (6) + L Fl 15s; 53°33'·65N 00°03'·96E.
Haile Sand Fort ⚓ Fl R 5s 21m 3M; 53°32'·07N 00°01'·99E.
Haile Chan No. 4 ⚓ Fl R 4s; 53°33'·64N 00°02'·84E.
Middle No. 7 ⚓ VQ (6) + L Fl 10s; *Horn 20s*; 53°35'·80N 00°01'·50E.
Grimsby Royal Dock ent E side ⚓ Fl (2) R 6s 10m 8M; Dn; 53°35'·08N 00°04'·04W.
Killingholme Lts in line 292°. Front, Iso R 2s 10m 14M. 53°38'·78N 00°12'·96W. Rear, 219m from front, F WRG 22m 3M; vis: 289·5°-G-290·5°-G/W-291·5°-W-292·5°-R/W-293·5° (H24).

RIVER HUMBER TO WHITBY
Canada & Giorgios Wreck ⚓ VQ (3) 5s; 53°42'·37N 00°07'·16E.

BRIDLINGTON
SW Smithic ⚓ Q (9) 15s; 54°02'·41N 00°09'·21W.
N Pier Hd ⚓ Fl 2s 12m 9M; *Horn 60s*; (Tidal Lts) Fl R or Fl G; 54°04'·77N 00°11'·19W.
N Smithic ⚓ VQ; *Bell*; 54°06'·22N 00°03'·90W.
Flamborough Hd ☆ 54°06'·98N 00°04'·96W; Fl (4) 15s 65m **24M**; W ○ twr; *Horn (2) 90s* .

FILEY/SCARBOROUGH/WHITBY
Filey Brigg ⚓ Q (3) 10s; *Bell*; 54°12'·74N 00°14'·60W.
Scarborough E Pier Hd ⚓ QG 8m 3M; 54°16'·88N 00°23'·36W.
Scarborough Pier ⚓ Iso 5s 17m 9M; W ○ twr; vis: 219°- 039° (tide sigs); *Dia 60s*; 54°16'·91N 00°23'·40W.
Whitby ⚓ Q; *Bell*; 54°30'·33N 00°36'·58W.
Whitby High ☆ 54°28'·67N 00°34'·10W; Ling Hill Fl WR 5s 73m **18M**, R16M; W 8-sided twr and dwellings; vis: 128°-R-143°-W- 319°.

WHITBY TO THE RIVER TYNE
RUNSWICK/REDCAR
Salt Scar ⚓ 54°38'·12N 01°00'·12W VQ; *Bell*.
Luff Way Ldg Lts 197°. Front, on Esplanade, FR 8m 7M; vis: 182°-212°; 54°37'·10N 01°03'·71W. Rear, 115m from front, FR 12m 7M; vis: 182°-212°.
High Stone. Lade Way Ldg Lts 247°. Front, Oc R 2·5s 9m 7M; 54°37'·15N 01°03'·92W. Rear, 43m from front, Oc R 2·5s 11m 7M; vis: 232°-262°.

TEES APPROACHES/HARTLEPOOL
Tees Fairway ⚓ Iso 4s 8m 8M; *Racon (B) unknown range*; *Horn (1) 5s*; 54°40'·94N 01°06'·48W .
Bkwtr Hd S Gare ☆ 54°38'·85N 01°08'·27W; Fl WR 12s 16m **W20M, R17M**; W ○ twr; vis: 020°-W-274°-R-357°; Sig Stn; *Horn 30s*.
Ldg Lts 210·1° Front, FR 18m 13M; 54°37'·22N 01°10'·20W. **Rear,** 560m from front, FR 20m **16M**.
Longscar ⚓ Q (3) 10s; *Bell*; 54°40'·86N 01°09'·89W.
The Heugh ☆ 54°41'·79N 01°10'·56W; Fl (2) 10s 19m**19M** ; W twr.

Hartlepool Marina Lock Dir Lt 308° Dir Fl WRG2s 6m 3M; vis: 305·5°-G-307°-W-309°-R-310·5°; 54°41'·45N 01°11'·92W.

SEAHAM/SUNDERLAND
Seaham N Pier Hd ⚓ Fl G 10s 12m 5M; W col, B bands; *Dia 30s*; 54°50'·26N 01°19'·26W.
Sunderland Roker Pier Hd ☆ 54°55'·28N 01°21'·15W; Fl 5s 25m **23M**; W □ twr, 3 R bands and cupola: vis: 211°- 357°; *Siren 20s*.
Old N Pier Hd ⚓ QG 12m 8M; metal column; *Horn 10s*; 54°55'·13N 01°21'·61W.
DZ ⚓ 54°57'·04N 01°18'·90W and ⚓ 54°58'·61N 01°19'·90W; both Fl Y 2·5s.

TYNE ENTRANCE/NORTH SHIELDS
Ent North Pier Hd ☆ 55°00'·88N 01°24'·18W; Fl (3) 10s 26m **26M**; Gy □ twr, W lantern; *Horn 10s* .
Herd Groyne Hd Ldg Lt 249°, Oc RG 10s 13m, R11M, G11M; R pile structure, R&W lantern; vis: 224°-G-246·5°, 251·5°-R-277°; FR (unintens) 080°-224°. Same structure Dir Oc 10s 14m **19M**; vis: 246·5°-W-251·5°; *Bell (1) 5s*; 55°00'·49N 01°25'·44W.

RIVER TYNE TO BERWICK-UPON-TWEED
CULLERCOATS and BLYTH
Cullercoats Ldg Lts 256°. Front, FR 27m 3M; 55°02'·06N 01°25'·91W. Rear, 38m from front, FR 35m 3M.
Blyth Ldg Lts 324°. Front ⚓ F Bu 11m 10M; 55°07'·42N 01°29'·82W. Rear ⚓, 180m from front, F Bu 17m 10M. Both Or ○ on twr.
Blyth Fairway ⚓ Fl G 3s; *Bell*;55°06'·59N 01°28'·60W.
Blyth E Pier Hd ☆ 55°06'·98N 01°29'·21W; Fl (4) 10s 19m **21M**, W twr; same structure FR 13m 13M, vis:152°-249°; *Horn (3) 30s*.

COQUET ISLAND, AMBLE and WARKWORTH
Coquet ☆ 55°20'·03N 01°32'·39W; Fl (3) WR 20s 25m **W19M, R15M**; W□ twr, turreted parapet, lower half Gy; vis: 330°-R-140°-W-163°-R-180°-W-330°; sector boundaries are indeterminate and may appear as Alt WR; *Horn 30s*.
Amble N Pier Head ⚓ Fl G 6s 12m 6M; 55°20'·39N 01°34'·25W.

SEAHOUSES, BAMBURGH and FARNE ISLANDS
N Sunderland ⚓ Fl R 2·5s; 55°34'·62N 01°37'·12W.
Bamburgh Black Rocks Point ☆ 55°36'·99N 01°43'·45W; Oc(2) WRG 8s 12m **W14M**, R11M, G11M; W bldg; vis: 122°-G-165°-W-175°-R-191°-W- 238°-R- 275°-W- 289°-G-300°.
Inner Farne ⚓ Fl (2) WR 15s 27m W10M, R7M; W ○ twr; vis: 119°-R - 280° - W -119°; 55°36'·92N 01°39'·35W.
Longstone ☆ **W side** 55°38'·62N 01°36'·65W; Fl 20s 23m **24M**; R twr, W band; *Horn (2) 60s*.
Swedman ⚓ Fl G 2·5s; 55°37'·65N 01°41'·63W.

HOLY ISLAND
Ridge ⚓ Q (3) 10s; 55°39'·70N 01°45'·97W.
Plough Rock ⚓ Q (9) 15s; 55°40'·24N 01°46'·00W.
Old Law E Bn ⚓ (Guile Pt) Oc WRG 6s 9m 4M; vis: 180·5°-G-258·5°-W-261·5°-R-shore.
Heugh ⚓ Oc WRG 6s 24m 5M; vis: 135°-G-308°-W-311-R- shore; 55°40'·09N 01°47'·99W.
Plough Seat ⚓ QR; 55°40'·37N 01°44'·97W.
Goldstone ⚓ QG; 55°40'·25N 01°43'·64W.

BERWICK-UPON-TWEED
Bkwtr Hd ⚓ Fl 5s 15m 6M; vis: 201°-009°, (obscured 155°-201°); W ○ twr, R cupola and base; FG (same twr) 8m 1M; vis 009°-G-155°; 55°45'·88N 01°59'·06W.

3.4 PASSAGE INFORMATION

For directions and pilotage refer to *Tidal Havens of the Wash and Humber* (Imray/Irving) which carefully documents the hbrs of this little-frequented cruising ground. N from R Humber see the Royal Northumberland YC's Sailing Directions, Humber to Rattray Head. The Admiralty *North Sea (West) Pilot* covers the whole coast. *North Sea Passage Pilot* (Imray/Navin) goes as far N as Cromer and across to Den Helder. Admiralty Leisure Folio 5614 covers the area Orford Ness to Whitby.

More Passage Information is threaded between the harbours of this Area.

NORTH SEA PASSAGES

See 0.34 for distances across the North Sea. There is further Passage Information in this Area for crossings to the Netherlands and German Bight, in Area 2 for Belgium and the Netherlands, and in Area 4 for Norway and the Baltic.

OIL AND GAS INSTALLATIONS

Any craft going offshore in the N Sea is likely to encounter oil or gas installations. These are shown on Admiralty charts, where scale permits; the position of mobile rigs is updated in weekly NMs. Safety zones of radius 500m are established round all permanent platforms, mobile exploration rigs, and tanker loading moorings, as described in the Annual Summary of Admiralty Notices to Mariners No 20. Some of these platforms are close together or inter-linked. Unauthorised vessels, including yachts, must not enter these zones except in emergency or due to stress of weather.

Platforms show a main lt, Fl Mo (U) 15s 15M. In addition secondary lts, Fl Mo (U) R 15s 2M, synchronised with the main lt, may mark projections at each corner of the platform if not marked by a W lt. The fog signal is Horn Mo (U) 30s. See the Admiralty List of Lights and Fog Signals, Vol A.

3.5 BLAKENEY

Norfolk **52°59'·19N 00°57'·90E** (ent shifts)   ✵⚓⚓✿✿✿ ⌂

CHARTS AC 1190, 108; Imray C28; Stanfords 19, 3.

TIDES –0445 Dover; ML Cromer 2·8; Duration 0530; Zone 0 (UT)

Standard Port IMMINGHAM (→)

Times				Height (metres)			
High Water		Low Water		MHWS	MHWN	MLWN	MLWS
0100	0700	0100	0700	7·3	5·8	2·6	0·9
1300	1900	1300	1900				
Differences BLAKENEY BAR (approx 52°59'N 00°59'E)							
+0035	+0025	+0030	+0040	−1·6	−1·3	No data	
BLAKENEY (approx 52°57'N 01°01'E)							
+0115	+0055	No data		−3·9	−3·8	No data	
CROMER							
+0050	+0030	+0050	+0130	−2·1	−1·7	−0·5	−0·1

SHELTER Very good. Entry, sp HW ±2, nps HW ±1½. No access in fresh on-shore winds when conditions at the ent deteriorate very quickly, especially on the ebb. Moorings in The Pit area dry out.

NAVIGATION WPT 53°00'·00N 00°58'·20E, approx 225°/1M to Fairway RW buoy which is moved as required.

- Hjordis lit IDM buoy marks large dangerous wreck, close E of entrance.
- The bar is shallow, shifts often and the channel is marked by unlit SHM and PHM buoys, relaid each spring.
- Strangers are best advised to follow local boats in. Beware mussel lays, drying, off Blakeney Spit. Speed limit 8kn.

LIGHTS AND MARKS Conspic marks: Blakeney and Langham churches; a chimney on the house on Blakeney Point neck; TV mast (R lts) approx 2M S of entrance.

R/T None.

TELEPHONE (Code 01263) MRCC (01493) 851338; Marinecall 09068 969645; Dr 740314.

FACILITIES Quay AB (Free), Slip, M, D, FW, C (15 ton); **Services:** CH (Stratton Long) ☎ 740362, AB, BY, M, P & D (cans), FW, ME, El, ✕, SM, Gaz, AC. **Village** 🛒, R, Bar, ✉, Ⓑ, ⇌ (Sheringham), ✈ (Norwich).

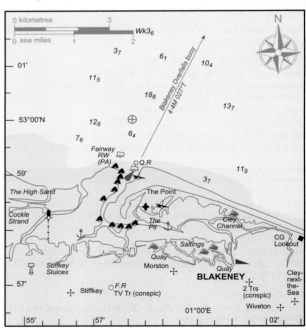

NORTH NORFOLK COAST

(Charts 1503, 108) The coast of N Norfolk is unfriendly in bad weather, with no hbr accessible when there is any N in the wind. The hbrs all dry, and seas soon build up in the entrances or over the bars, some of which are dangerous even in a moderate breeze and an ebb tide. But in settled weather and moderate offshore winds it is a peaceful area to explore, particularly for boats which can take the ground. At Blakeney and Wells chans shift almost every year, so local knowledge is essential and may best be acquired in advance from the HM, or possibly by following a friendly FV of suitable draft.

Haisborough Sand (buoyed) lies parallel to and 8M off the Norfolk coast at Happisburgh lt ho, with depths of less than 1m in many places, and drying 0·4m near the mid-point. The shoal is steep-to, on its NE side in particular, and there are tidal eddies. Even a moderate sea or swell breaks on the shallower parts. There are dangerous wks near the S end. Haisborough Tail and Hammond Knoll (with wk depth 1.6m) lie to the E of S end of Haisborough Sand. Newarp lt F is 5M SE. Similar banks lie parallel to and up to 60M off the coast.

▶ *The streams follow the generally NW/SE direction of the coast and offshore chans. But in the outer chans the stream is somewhat rotatory: when changing from SE-going to NW-going it sets SW, and when changing from NW-going to SE-going it sets NE, across the shoals. Close S of Haisborough Sand the SE-going stream begins at HW Immingham −0030; the NW-going at HW Immingham +0515, sp rates up to 2·5kn. It is possible to carry a fair tide from Gt Yarmouth to the Wash.* ◀

▶ *If proceeding direct from Cromer to the Humber, pass S of Sheringham Shoal (buoyed) where the ESE-going stream begins at HW Immingham −0225, and the WNW-going at +0430.* ◀ Proceed to NE of Blakeney Overfalls and Docking Shoal, and to SW of Race Bank, so as to fetch Inner Dowsing lt tr (lt, fog sig). Thence pass E of Protector Overfalls, and steer for Rosse Spit buoy at SE ent to R Humber.

THE WASH

(Charts 108,1200) The Wash is formed by the estuaries of the rivers Great Ouse, Nene, Welland and Witham; it is an area of shifting sands, most of which dry. Important features are the strong tidal streams, the low-lying shore, and the often poor vis. Watch the echo sounder carefully, because buoys may have been moved to accommodate changes in the channel.
▶ *Near North Well, the in-going stream begins at HW Immingham −0430, and the out-going at HW Immingham +0130, sp rates about 2kn. The in-going stream is usually stronger than the out-going, but its duration is less. Prolonged NE winds cause an in-going current, which can increase the rate and duration of the in-going stream and raise the water level at the head of the estuary. Do not attempt entry to the rivers too early on the flood, which runs hard in the rivers.* ◀

North Well SWM lt buoy and Roaring Middle lt F are the keys to entering the Wash from N or E. But from the E it is also possible to appr via a shallow route N of Stiffkey Overfalls and Bridgirdle PHM buoy; thence via Sledway and Woolpack PHM lt buoy to North Well and into Lynn Deeps. Near north end of Lynn Deeps there are overfalls over Lynn Knock at sp tides. Approach King's Lynn via the buoyed/lit Bulldog chan. For R Nene (Wisbech) follow the Wisbech Chan. Boston and R Welland are reached via Freeman Chan, westward from Roaring Middle; or via Boston Deep, all lit.

The NW shore of The Wash is fronted by mudflats extending 2–3M offshore and drying more than 4m; a bombing range is marked by Y bns and buoys. Wainfleet Swatchway should only be used in good vis; the buoyed chan shifts constantly, and several shoals (charted depths unreliable) off Gibraltar Pt obstruct access to Boston Deep. In an emergency Wainfleet offers good shelter (dries).

3.6 WELLS-NEXT-THE-SEA

Norfolk **52°59'·30N 00°49'·75E** (ent shifts) ✿✿✿✿✿✿✿✿✿

CHARTS AC 1190, 108; Imray C28, Y9; Stanfords 19, 3.

TIDES −0445 Dover; ML 1·2 Duration 0540

Standard Port IMMINGHAM (→)

Times				Height (metres)			
High Water		Low Water		MHWS	MHWN	MLWN	MLWS
0100	0700	0100	0700	7·3	5·8	2·6	0·9
1300	1900	1300	1900				

Differences WELLS BAR (approx 52°59'N 00°49'E)
+0020 +0020 +0020 +0020 −1·3 −1·0 No data
WELLS-NEXT-THE-SEA (approx 52°58'N 00°51'E)
+0035 +0045 +0340 +0310 −3·8 −3·8 Not below CD
NOTE: LW time differences at Wells are for the end of a LW stand which lasts about 4 hrs at sp and about 5 hrs at nps.

SHELTER Good, but ent difficult in strong on-shore winds (N'lies) for small craft. Max draft 3m at sp. Access from HW−2 to HW+2, but best on the flood. Quay berths mostly dry, pontoon berths at W end of Town Quay.

NAVIGATION WPT Wells Leading Buoy, 52°59'·80N 00°50'·49E. Ent varies in depth and position; buoys are altered to suit. Initially keep to W side of chan to counter E-going tide at HW−2; and to E side of chan from No 12 PHM lt buoy to Quay.

Obtain HM's advice, Hbr Launch often available to escort visitors into hbr & up to Quay. Spd limits: No 6 buoy to Quay 8kn; above this 5kn. See www.wellsharbour.co.uk for latest harbour chart.

LIGHTS AND MARKS As plan. Temp buoys may be laid when chan changes. A pine plantation is conspic W of hbr ent; ditto white LB ho with R roof.

R/T Call *'Wells Harbour'* Ch 12 16 before entering, listens HW−2 to HW+2 and when vessels expected.

TELEPHONE (Code 01328 Fakenham) HM 711646, mob 07775 507284, DHM mob 07881824912; MRCC (01493) 851338; Marinecall 09068 969645; Police (01493) 336200; Dr 710741; Ⓗ 710097.

FACILITIES **Main Quay** AB (£13/yacht), ⚓ drying (£12/craft), ⚓ (£5/craft), ⚡, Showers, 🚾, ☉, FW, ME, El, ✕, BH (7·5 ton), C (25 ton mobile), CH, 🛒, R, Bar; **E Quay** Slips (£6/craft/day), M, L; **Wells SC** ☎ 710622, Slip, Bar; **Services:** Ⓔ, ACA, SM, LB. **Town:** P(cans) & D (Hbr fueling stn HW-2 to HW+3; supply up to 500 galls), Gas, ☉, 🛒, R, Bar, ✉, Ⓑ, ⇌ (bus to Norwich/King's Lynn), ✈ (Norwich).

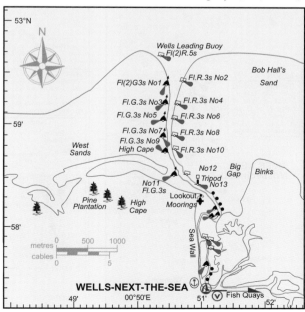

3.7 KING'S LYNN AND WISBECH

Norfolk 52°49'·72N 00°21'·14E (W Stones Bn) ✿✿✿✿✿

CHARTS AC 1190, 108, 1200, 5614. Imray Y9

TIDES –0443 Dover, +0030 Immingham; ML 3·6; Duration 0340;

Standard Port IMMINGHAM (→)

Times				Height (metres)			
High Water		Low Water		MHWS	MHWN	MLWN	MLWS
0100	0700	0100	0700	7·3	5·8	2·6	0·9
1300	1900	1300	1900				
Differences KING'S LYNN							
+0030	+0030	+0305	+0140	–0·5	–0·8	–0·8	+0·1
OUTER WESTMARK KNOCK							
+0010	+0015	+0040	+0020	–0·2	–0·5	–0·6	–0·4
WISBECH CUT							
+0020	+0010	+0120	+0055	–0·3	–0·7	–0·4	No data
WISBECH							
+0055	+0040	Dries		–0·2	–0·6	Dries	
BURNHAM OVERY STAITHE							
+0045	+0055	No data		–5·0	–4·9	No data	
HUNSTANTON							
+0010	+0020	+0105	+0025	+0·1	–0·2	–0·1	0·0
WEST STONES							
+0025	+0025	+0115	+0040	–0·3	–0·4	–0·3	+0·2

SHELTER Port is well sheltered; entry only recommended HW–3. A busy commercial and fishing port with limited facilities. River moorings available from local clubs; keep clear of FV moorings.

NAVIGATION WPT Sunk WCM 52° 56'.29N 00° 23'.40E follow Bulldog chan buoyed/lit apprs to King's Lynn. From there to Denver Sluice (ent to inland routes) 6 bridges span river, min cl 9·15m less ht of tide at King's Lynn above Dock sill. Allow 1½H for passage. The sand banks regularly shift and extend several miles into the Wash; buoyage is altered accordingly. Contact HM a

week beforehand for latest info or see www.portauthority kingslynn.fsnet.co.uk.

LIGHTS AND MARKS See 3.3 and chartlet.

R/T Call: Kings Lynn Hbr Radio Ch **14** 11 (M-F: 0800-1730 LT. Other times: HW –4 to HW+1.) (ABP) Ch **14** 16 11 (HW–2½ to HW).

TELEPHONE HM ☎ 01553 773411 **Docks** ☎ 01553 691555.

FACILITIES AB £42 (9m LOA/48 hrs), FW, C (32 ton); **Services:** CH, ✂, ME, El, Ⓔ, D. **Town** P, D, 🛒, R, Bar, ✉, Ⓑ, ≈, ✈ (Norwich). **Note:** 24M up the Great Ouse river, Ely Marina ☎ (01353) 664622, Slip, M, P, D, FW, ME, El, ✂, C (10 ton), CH. Lock half-way at Denver Sluice ☎ (01366) 382340/VHF Ch 73, and low bridges beyond.

WISBECH Cambridgeshire 52°40'·02N 00°09'·55E ✿✿✿✿✿

SHELTER Excellent shelter in river with Wisbech Yacht Harbour pontoon berths and shower/toilet facilities immediately below Freedom Bridge in Wisbech town. Vessels of 4·8m draft can reach Wisbech at sp (3·4m at nps), but depths vary. Ent to inland waterways above Wisbech to Peterborough, Oundle, Northampton. Mast lift out service available.

NAVIGATION WPT Roaring Middle NCM Lt Flt 52° 58'.64N 00° 21'.08E 220°/7M to Wisbech No 1 SHM Fl G 5s. Monitor Ch 09 and call HM when you reach Holbeach RAF No 4 ECM to check commercial traffic and opening of Cross Keys Sw Br in river. Red flags and lights shown when Firing Range in use. Ent to R Nene from The Wash well marked with lit buoys/bns from Wisbech No 1 Fl G 5s. Best ent HW–3. ⚓s for waiting at Holbeach RAF No 4 ECM. Cross Keys Sw Br in river opens by request given notice. Waiting pontoon 0.5M downstream from bridge thence 6M to Wisbech with FG lts to stbd. Call HM and Cross Keys Sw Br HW±3. 24H prior notice of visit recommended. Departure best at HW, unless draught >3m; if so, aim to clear Kerr NCM by HW+3. For local pilotage notes ☎ Hbr Office or visit www.fenland.gov.uk.

LIGHTS AND MARKS See 3.3 and chartlet.

R/T HM Wisbech Harbour Ch **09**.

TELEPHONE Code (01945) HM 588059 (Hbr Office 24H); Cross Keys Swing Bridge 01406 350364; MRCC (01493) 851338;Marinecall 09068 969645; Police (01354) 652561; Dr 582133; Ⓗ 585781.

FACILITIES **Yacht Hbr** (102AB + 15Ⓥ), £0.90, min charge £5, FW, ⚡, El. D (barge). **Town** P (cans), CH, Bar, R, 🛒, Gas.

ADJACENT HARBOURS
BURNHAM OVERY STAITHE, Norfolk, 52°58'·95N 00°46'·55E ✿✿✿✿✿. AC 1190, 108. HW –0420 on Dover. See 3.7. Small drying hbr; ent chan has 0·3m MLWS. ⚓ off the Staithe only suitable in good weather. No lts. Scolt Hd is conspic to W and Gun Hill to E; Scolt Hd Island is conspic 3M long sandbank which affords some shelter. Chan varies constantly and buoys are moved to suit. Local knowledge advisable. Facilities: (01328) **Burnham Overy Staithe SC** ☎ 738348, M, L; **Services:** CH, M, ME, ✂, Slip, FW; **Burnham Market** EC Wed; Bar, P and D (cans), R, 🛒.

BRANCASTER STAITHE, Norfolk, 52°59'·02N 00°37'·65E ✿✿✿✿✿. AC 1190, 108. HW –0425 on Dover; as Burnham. Small drying hbr, dangerous to enter except by day in settled weather. Spd limit 6kn. Appr from due N. Conspic golf club house with lt, Fl 5s 8m 3M, is 0·5M S of chan ent and Fairway buoy. Beware wk shown on chart. Sandbanks shift; buoys changed to suit. Scolt Hd conspic to E. Local knowledge or Pilot advised. Possible ⚓ in The Hole. HM ☎ (01485) 210638. Facilities: **Brancaster Staithe SC** ☎ 210249, R, Bar; **Services:** BY, CH, El, FW, P & D (cans), ME, R, ✂, Bar, 🛒.

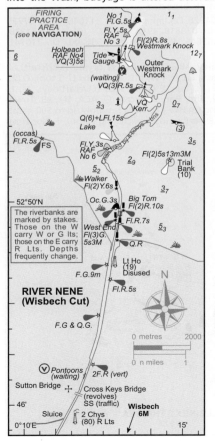

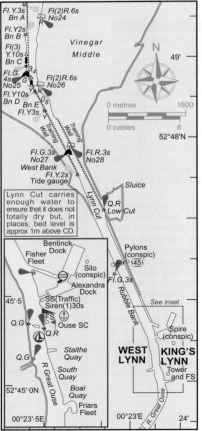

3.8 BOSTON

Lincs **52°56'·00N 00°04'·92E** (Tabs Head bn) ❀❀♨♨❀❀

CHARTS AC 108, 1200, 5614; Imray Y9.

TIDES –0415 Dover; ML 3·3; Duration Flood 0500, Ebb 0700

Standard Port IMMINGHAM (→)

Times				Height (metres)			
High Water		Low Water		MHWS	MHWN	MLWN	MLWS
0100	0700	0100	0700	7·3	5·8	2·6	0·9
1300	1900	1300	1900				
Differences BOSTON							
0000	+0010	+0140	+0050	−0·5	−1·0	−0·9	−0·5
TABS HEAD (WELLAND RIVER)							
0000	+0005	+0125	+0020	+0·2	−0·2	−0·2	−0·2
SKEGNESS							
+0010	+0015	+0030	+0020	−0·4	−0·5	−0·1	0·0
INNER DOWSING LIGHT TOWER							
0000	0000	+0010	+0010	−0·9	−0·7	−0·1	+0·3

SHELTER Very good. Except in emergency berthing in the Dock is prohib wthout HM permission. Yachts secure just above Dock ent and see HM. The port is administered by Port of Boston Ltd.

Yachts capable of lowering masts can pass through the Grand Sluice (**24 hrs notice required**) into fresh water. Sluice dimensions 16m x 9m and opens twice a tide at approx HW±2 . It leads into the R Witham Navigation which goes 31M to Lincoln. Marina is to stbd immediately beyond the sluice. British Waterways have 50 moorings, with FW and ⅅ beyond Grand Sluice.

NAVIGATION WPT Boston Rds SWM lt buoy, 52°57'·63N 00°16'·03E, 280°/0·7M to Freeman Chan ent. Thence Bar Chan is well marked, but liable to change. SW of Clay Hole a new chan has formed which dries 0·6m at entr; it is marked by SHM lt buoys Nos 11N, 13N, and 15. Tabs Head marks the ent to the river; it should be passed not earlier than HW–3 to enable the Grand Sluice to be reached before the start of the ebb. Beware rocky bottom within 100m of the Sluice. On reaching Boston

Dock, masts should be lowered to negotiate swing bridge (cannot always be opened) and three fixed bridges. Chan through town is un-navigable at LW.

LIGHTS AND MARKS St Boltoph's ch tr (the Boston Stump) is conspic from afar. New Cut and R Witham are marked by bns with topmarks. FW lts mark ldg lines: three pairs going upstream and six pairs going downstream.

R/T All vessels between No 9 buoy and Grand Sluice must listen Ch 12. Call: *Boston Port Control* VHF Ch 12 (Mon-Fri 0800-1700 LT & HW –2½ to HW +1½). Ch 11 used by dock staff as required. *Grand Sluice* Ch 74.

TELEPHONE (Code 01205) HM 362328; Dock office 365571; Grand Sluice Control 364864 (not always manned but has answerphone) mob 07712 010920; MRCC (01493) 851338; Marinecall 09068 969645; Police 366222; ⊞ 364801.

FACILITIES **Boston Marina** (48 + some ♥) ☎ 364420, £5 per night any size inc ⅅ, access HW±2; FW, D, CH, ACA, C in dock, see HM (emergency); **Grand Sluice** showers and toilets; **BWB** moorings: 1st night free, then £5·00. **Services:** El, ME, ✕, Gas. **Town** Thurs; 🛒, R, Bar, ✉, ⓑ, ⇌, ✈ (Humberside).

ADJACENT HARBOURS

RIVER WELLAND, Lincolnshire, **52°56'·00N 00°04'·92E** (Tabs Head bn). AC 1190, 1200. At Welland Cut HW –0440 on Dover; ML 0·3m; Duration 0520. See 3.8. At Tabs Head bn HW ±3, ent Welland Cut which is defined by training walls and lt bns. Beware sp flood of up to 5kn. Berth 6M up at **Fosdyke Yacht Haven** ☎ 01205 260240. (50 + 6♥ 2m depth); ⅅ, Showers, ☒, D, FW, ME, BH (50 ton – only one between R. Humber & Lowestoft), R, ⌂.

WAINFLEET, Lincolnshire, **53°04'·79N 00°19'·89E** (chan ent). AC 108. Skegness HW +0500 on Dover. See 3.8 (Skegness). ML 4·0m; Duration 0600. Shelter good, but emergency only. Drying channel starts close S of Gibraltar Point. Channel through saltings marked by posts with radar reflectors and lateral topmarks. Enter HW ±1½. No lts. Facilities: M, AB (larger boats at fishing jetties, smaller at YC), FW at Field Study Centre on stbd side of ent. All shore facilities at Skegness (3½ miles).

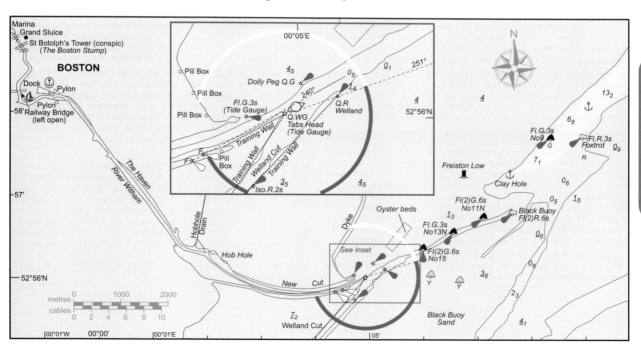

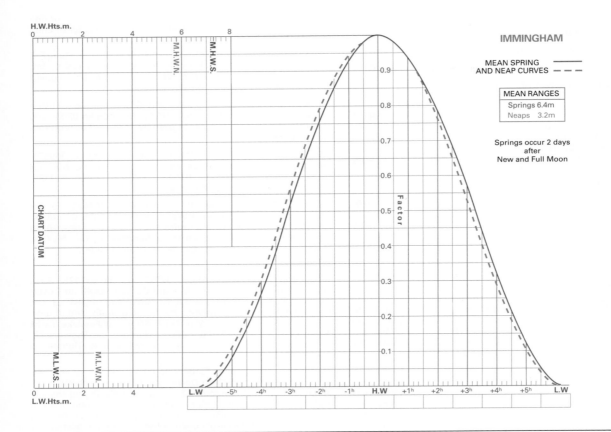

H.W.Hts.m.

IMMINGHAM

MEAN SPRING ———
AND NEAP CURVES − − −

MEAN RANGES
Springs 6.4m
Neaps 3.2m

Springs occur 2 days
after
New and Full Moon

THE WASH TO THE RIVER HUMBER

(Charts 108, 107) Inner Dowsing is a narrow N/S sandbank with a least depth of 1·2m, 8M offshore between Skegness and Mablethorpe. There are overfalls off the W side of the bank at the N end. Inner Dowsing lt float (fog sig) is 1M NE of the bank.

In the outer approaches to The Wash and R. Humber there are many offlying banks, but few of them are of direct danger to yachts. The sea however breaks on some of them in bad weather, when they should be avoided. Fishing vessels may be encountered, and there are many oil/gas installations offshore.

RIVER HUMBER

(Charts 109, 1188, 3497) The Humber is formed by the Ouse and the Trent, which meet 13M above Kingston-upon-Hull. The river is commercially important and gives access to these rivers and inland waterways; it also drains most of Yorkshire and the Midlands. Where the Humber estuary reaches the sea between Northcoates Pt and Spurn Hd it is 4M wide. A VTS scheme is in operation to regulate commercial shipping in the Humber, Ouse and Trent and provide full radar surveillance. Yachts are advised to monitor the appropriate Humber VTS frequency.

Approaching from the S, a yacht should make good Rosse Spit and then Haile Sand No 2, both PHM lt buoys, before altering westward leading SW of Bull Ch.

If bound to/from the N, avoid The Binks, a shoal (dries 1·6m in places) extending 3M E from Spurn Hd, with a rough sea when wind is against tide. Depths offshore are irregular and subject to frequent change; it would be best to round the S Binks SPM buoy, unless in calm conditions and with local knowledge.

Haile Sand and Bull Sand Forts are both conspic to the SW of Spurn Head; beyond them it is advisable to keep just outside one of the buoyed chans, since shoals are liable to change. Hawke Chan (later Sunk) is the main dredged chan to the N. Haile Chan favours the S side and Grimsby. Bull Chan takes a middle course before merging with Haile Chan. There are good yachting facilities at Grimsby and Hull. ‡ inside Spurn Head.

▶ Streams are strong, even fierce at sp; local info suggests that they are stronger than shown in Tidal Streams based upon NP 251 (Admiralty Tidal Stream Atlas). 5ca S of Spurn Hd the flood sets NW from about HW Immingham −0520, sp rate 3·5kn; the ebb sets SE from about HW Immingham, sp rate 4kn. The worst seas are experienced in NW gales against a strong flood tide. 10M E of Spurn Hd the tidal streams are not affected by the river; relative to HW Immingham, the S-going stream begins at −0455, and the N-going at +0130. Nearer the entrance the direction of the S-going stream becomes more W'ly, and that of the N-going stream more E'ly. ◀

TIME ZONE (UT)
For Summer Time add ONE hour in **non-shaded areas**

IMMINGHAM   LAT 53°38'N   LONG 0°11'W
TIMES AND HEIGHTS OF HIGH AND LOW WATERS

Dates in red are SPRINGS
Dates in blue are NEAPS

YEAR 2010

JANUARY

Day	Time m	Time m	Time m	Time m	Day	Time m	Time m	Time m	Time m
1 F	0558 7.1	1213 1.3	1814 7.3		16 SA	0043 1.4	0642 6.6	1245 1.7	1840 7.0
2 SA	0049 0.8	0649 7.3	1301 1.2	1857 7.5	17 SU	0118 1.4	0713 6.6	1319 1.7	1913 7.0
3 SU	0138 0.6	0737 7.3	1346 1.2	1941 7.6	18 M	0150 1.4	0743 6.6	1348 1.7	1944 7.0
4 M	0225 0.6	0824 7.2	1430 1.3	2025 7.5	19 TU	0219 1.5	0812 6.6	1416 1.7	2014 6.9
5 TU	0312 0.7	0911 7.0	1513 1.5	2111 7.4	20 W	0245 1.6	0841 6.5	1445 1.8	2044 6.8
6 W	0359 0.9	1001 6.7	1558 1.7	2201 7.1	21 TH	0312 1.7	0913 6.3	1515 2.0	2116 6.6
7 TH	0447 1.3	1054 6.4	1647 2.1	2258 6.7	22 F	0343 1.8	0948 6.2	1551 2.2	2156 6.4
8 F	0539 1.7	1152 6.1	1743 2.4		23 SA	0421 2.0	1031 5.9	1637 2.4	2245 6.2
9 SA	0002 6.3	0637 2.1	1253 5.9	1851 2.6	24 SU	0514 2.3	1126 5.7	1742 2.6	2348 6.0
10 SU	0113 6.1	0743 2.3	1357 5.8	2014 2.6	25 M	0625 2.5	1244 5.6	1903 2.7	
11 M	0227 6.0	0850 2.4	1500 6.0	2128 2.4	26 TU	0112 5.9	0745 2.5	1416 5.7	2025 2.5
12 TU	0338 6.0	0949 2.3	1557 6.2	2227 2.1	27 W	0246 6.0	0903 2.3	1528 6.1	2143 2.1
13 W	0438 6.2	1040 2.1	1645 6.5	2317 1.8	28 TH	0400 6.4	1011 2.0	1625 6.6	2250 1.5
14 TH	0527 6.4	1126 2.0	1727 6.7		29 F	0501 6.8	1110 1.6	1716 7.0	2348 1.0
15 F	0002 1.6	0607 6.5	1208 1.8	1805 6.9 ●	30 SA	0554 7.1	1202 1.2	1802 7.4	
					31 SU	0040 0.6	0642 7.4	1250 1.0	1845 7.7

FEBRUARY

Day	Time m	Time m	Time m	Time m	Day	Time m	Time m	Time m	Time m
1 M	0127 0.3	0726 7.5	1333 0.9	1927 7.8	16 TU	0129 1.2	0717 6.7	1330 1.5	1921 7.1
2 TU	0211 0.2	0807 7.4	1415 0.9	2009 7.8	17 W	0157 1.3	0744 6.7	1356 1.5	1949 7.0
3 W	0252 0.4	0847 7.2	1454 1.1	2050 7.6	18 TH	0221 1.4	0811 6.7	1422 1.5	2017 7.0
4 TH	0332 0.8	0927 6.9	1532 1.4	2134 7.2	19 F	0244 1.5	0839 6.6	1449 1.7	2048 6.8
5 F	0411 1.3	1009 6.5	1610 1.8	2223 6.7	20 SA	0308 1.6	0910 6.4	1520 1.8	2124 6.6
6 SA	0453 1.9	1059 6.1	1655 2.3	2323 6.1	21 SU	0341 1.9	0949 6.1	1602 2.1	2211 6.3
7 SU	0543 2.4	1201 5.7	1754 2.7		22 M	0429 2.2	1041 5.8	1704 2.5	2314 5.9
8 M	0040 5.7	0653 2.8	1315 5.5	1935 2.9	23 TU	0542 2.6	1154 5.6	1832 2.6	
9 TU	0207 5.5	0822 2.9	1428 5.6	2115 2.6	24 W	0047 5.7	0716 2.7	1344 5.6	2005 2.5
10 W	0327 5.7	0932 2.6	1533 6.0	2214 2.2	25 TH	0240 5.9	0845 2.5	1507 6.0	2132 2.0
11 TH	0430 6.0	1024 2.3	1625 6.3	2302 1.8	26 F	0354 6.3	0958 2.0	1607 6.6	2239 1.3
12 F	0516 6.3	1109 2.0	1708 6.6	2344 1.5	27 SA	0452 6.8	1056 1.5	1658 7.1	2334 0.8
13 SA	0552 6.5	1150 1.8	1745 6.8		28 SU	0542 7.2	1146 1.0	1744 7.5 ○	
14 SU	0022 1.4	0622 6.6	1228 1.5	1819 7.0 ●					
15 M	0058 1.3	0650 6.7	1301 1.5	1850 7.0					

MARCH

Day	Time m	Time m	Time m	Time m	Day	Time m	Time m	Time m	Time m
1 M	0022 0.4	0625 7.4	1232 0.8	1827 7.8	16 TU	0028 1.2	0620 6.7	1236 1.4	1823 7.0
2 TU	0107 0.1	0705 7.5	1315 0.7	1908 7.9	17 W	0101 1.2	0648 6.8	1306 1.4	1854 7.1
3 W	0148 0.2	0742 7.5	1354 0.7	1948 7.8	18 TH	0129 1.2	0715 6.8	1334 1.3	1924 7.1
4 TH	0226 0.4	0817 7.3	1431 0.9	2028 7.6	19 F	0155 1.3	0743 6.8	1401 1.4	1954 7.0
5 F	0301 0.8	0852 7.0	1505 1.2	2108 7.1	20 SA	0218 1.4	0811 6.7	1430 1.5	2026 6.9
6 SA	0335 1.4	0928 6.5	1539 1.7	2153 6.5	21 SU	0245 1.6	0843 6.6	1503 1.6	2105 6.6
7 SU	0409 2.0	1009 6.1	1618 2.2	2249 5.9	22 M	0319 1.9	0923 6.3	1547 1.9	2154 6.2
8 M	0454 2.6	1107 5.6	1713 2.6		23 TU	0409 2.3	1015 5.9	1652 2.3	2303 5.8
9 TU	0014 5.4	0559 3.0	1234 5.4	1842 2.9	24 W	0523 2.7	1131 5.6	1821 2.4	
10 W	0147 5.3	0748 3.1	1357 5.5	2054 2.7	25 TH	0052 5.6	0659 2.8	1321 5.7	1954 2.2
11 TH	0306 5.5	0909 2.8	1505 5.8	2150 2.2	26 F	0232 5.9	0828 2.5	1443 6.1	2115 1.7
12 F	0407 5.9	1001 2.4	1558 6.2	2235 1.8	27 SA	0340 6.4	0938 2.0	1543 6.6	2218 1.1
13 SA	0450 6.2	1045 2.0	1641 6.5	2315 1.5	28 SU	0434 6.8	1034 1.5	1634 7.1	2310 0.7
14 SU	0524 6.5	1125 1.7	1717 6.8	2353 1.3	29 M	0521 7.2	1124 1.1	1721 7.5	2358 0.4
15 M	0554 6.6	1202 1.5	1751 6.9 ●		30 TU	0602 7.3	1210 0.8	1806 7.7 ○	
					31 W	0041 0.3	0640 7.4	1253 0.7	1848 7.7

APRIL

Day	Time m	Time m	Time m	Time m	Day	Time m	Time m	Time m	Time m
1 TH	0122 0.4	0715 7.4	1332 0.7	1928 7.6	16 F	0100 1.2	0648 6.9	1312 1.2	1902 7.0
2 F	0158 0.6	0749 7.2	1409 0.9	2008 7.3	17 SA	0130 1.3	0719 6.9	1345 1.2	1937 7.0
3 SA	0231 1.1	0822 7.0	1442 1.2	2047 6.9	18 SU	0200 1.4	0751 6.9	1419 1.3	2015 6.8
4 SU	0303 1.6	0855 6.6	1515 1.6	2130 6.3	19 M	0232 1.6	0827 6.7	1459 1.5	2100 6.5
5 M	0336 2.1	0933 6.2	1553 2.1	2224 5.8	20 TU	0312 1.9	0911 6.4	1549 1.8	2155 6.2
6 TU	0419 2.6	1024 5.8	1647 2.5	2347 5.3	21 W	0405 2.3	1007 6.1	1657 1.9	2311 5.8
7 W	0520 3.0	1150 5.5	1806 2.8		22 TH	0518 2.6	1124 5.9	1817 2.0	
8 TH	0116 5.3	0651 3.2	1318 5.5	2007 2.6	23 F	0051 5.8	0643 2.6	1258 6.0	1937 1.8
9 F	0229 5.5	0828 2.9	1427 5.7	2109 2.3	24 SA	0211 6.1	0804 2.4	1413 6.3	2049 1.5
10 SA	0327 5.8	0925 2.5	1521 6.1	2155 1.9	25 SU	0314 6.4	0910 2.0	1514 6.7	2148 1.1
11 SU	0412 6.1	1010 2.1	1604 6.4	2236 1.6	26 M	0407 6.7	1007 1.6	1608 7.0	2241 0.9
12 M	0447 6.4	1051 1.8	1641 6.6	2315 1.4	27 TU	0454 7.0	1058 1.2	1658 7.2	2329 0.7
13 TU	0518 6.6	1129 1.6	1717 6.8	2352 1.3	28 W	0535 7.1	1146 1.0	1745 7.3 ○	
14 W	0547 6.7	1205 1.4	1752 6.9 ●		29 TH	0014 0.7	0613 7.2	1231 0.9	1829 7.3
15 TH	0027 1.2	0617 6.8	1239 1.3	1827 7.0	30 F	0055 0.8	0650 7.2	1313 0.9	1912 7.2

NE England

Chart Datum: 3·90 metres below Ordnance Datum (Newlyn). HAT is 8·0 metres above Chart Datum; see 0.19

TIME ZONE (UT)
For Summer Time add ONE hour in **non-shaded areas**

IMMINGHAM LAT 53°38'N LONG 0°11'W
TIMES AND HEIGHTS OF HIGH AND LOW WATERS

Dates in red are **SPRINGS**
Dates in blue are **NEAPS**

YEAR 2010

MAY

Day	Time m	Time m	Time m	Time m		Day	Time m	Time m	Time m	Time m
1 SA	0132 1.0	0724 7.1	1351 1.0	1952 7.0		16 SU	0110 1.3	0702 7.0	1334 1.1	1929 7.0
2 SU	0206 1.3	0758 6.9	1425 1.3	2032 6.6		17 M	0147 1.4	0740 7.0	1416 1.1	2013 6.8
3 M	0239 1.7	0832 6.7	1500 1.6	2114 6.2		18 TU	0227 1.5	0821 6.9	1502 1.2	2103 6.6
4 TU	0312 2.1	0909 6.3	1538 2.0	2203 5.8		19 W	0312 1.8	0908 6.7	1556 1.4	2201 6.3
5 W	0353 2.5	0956 6.0	1629 2.3	2309 5.5		20 TH	0405 2.1	1005 6.5	1658 1.5	2314 6.1
6 TH	0447 2.8	1103 5.7	1733 2.5	◗		21 F	0510 2.3	1115 6.3	1805 1.6	
7 F	0027 5.3	0556 3.0	1223 5.6	1846 2.5		22 SA	0030 6.1	0621 2.3	1231 6.3	1913 1.5
8 SA	0136 5.4	0715 2.9	1332 5.7	1959 2.3		23 SU	0139 6.2	0733 2.2	1341 6.4	2018 1.4
9 SU	0234 5.7	0825 2.7	1429 5.9	2057 2.1		24 M	0241 6.3	0839 2.0	1445 6.6	2117 1.3
10 M	0322 5.9	0920 2.3	1517 6.1	2146 1.8		25 TU	0336 6.5	0940 1.8	1543 6.7	2211 1.3
11 TU	0402 6.2	1007 2.0	1600 6.4	2230 1.6		26 W	0425 6.7	1035 1.5	1638 6.8	2302 1.2
12 W	0438 6.4	1050 1.8	1642 6.6	2313 1.5		27 TH	0509 6.8	1126 1.3	1729 6.9	○ 2348 1.2
13 TH	0514 6.6	1132 1.5	1723 6.8	2353 1.3		28 F	0550 6.9	1214 1.2	1817 6.9	
14 F	0550 6.8	1213 1.3	1805 6.9	●		29 SA	0031 1.3	0628 7.0	1258 1.1	1900 6.8
15 SA	0032 1.3	0626 6.9	1254 1.2	1846 7.0		30 SU	0111 1.4	0705 7.0	1338 1.2	1941 6.7
						31 M	0147 1.5	0740 6.9	1415 1.3	2020 6.5

JUNE

Day	Time m	Time m	Time m	Time m		Day	Time m	Time m	Time m	Time m
1 TU	0220 1.8	0815 6.7	1450 1.5	2057 6.2		16 W	0223 1.3	0816 7.2	1503 0.8	2102 6.9
2 W	0254 2.0	0851 6.5	1526 1.8	2137 6.0		17 TH	0308 1.5	0904 7.1	1553 0.9	2156 6.7
3 TH	0331 2.3	0932 6.3	1608 2.0	2224 5.7		18 F	0358 1.7	0956 6.9	1647 1.1	2256 6.4
4 F	0415 2.5	1021 6.0	1657 2.2	◗ 2320 5.6		19 SA	0452 1.9	1056 6.7	1744 1.3	◗ 2358 6.3
5 SA	0508 2.7	1121 5.8	1752 2.3			20 SU	0553 2.1	1202 6.5	1844 1.5	
6 SU	0022 5.5	0609 2.8	1226 5.8	1851 2.3		21 M	0101 6.1	0659 2.2	1310 6.4	1946 1.7
7 M	0124 5.6	0713 2.7	1328 5.8	1951 2.2		22 TU	0203 6.1	0809 2.2	1418 6.3	2048 1.8
8 TU	0221 5.8	0817 2.5	1426 6.0	2050 2.1		23 W	0303 6.2	0917 2.1	1524 6.3	2146 1.8
9 W	0313 6.0	0917 2.3	1520 6.2	2145 1.9		24 TH	0358 6.4	1018 1.8	1626 6.4	2240 1.7
10 TH	0400 6.3	1011 2.0	1611 6.4	2236 1.7		25 F	0446 6.5	1112 1.6	1722 6.5	2329 1.7
11 F	0445 6.5	1103 1.6	1701 6.7	2325 1.5		26 SA	0530 6.7	1202 1.4	1810 6.6	○
12 SA	0527 6.8	1152 1.3	1750 6.9	●		27 SU	0013 1.6	0610 6.9	1247 1.3	1851 6.6
13 SU	0011 1.4	0609 7.0	1241 1.1	1838 7.0		28 M	0054 1.6	0648 6.9	1328 1.3	1929 6.6
14 M	0056 1.3	0651 7.1	1328 0.9	1925 7.1		29 TU	0131 1.6	0724 6.9	1404 1.3	2003 6.5
15 TU	0139 1.3	0733 7.2	1415 0.8	2012 7.0		30 W	0204 1.7	0758 6.9	1437 1.4	2035 6.4

JULY

Day	Time m	Time m	Time m	Time m		Day	Time m	Time m	Time m	Time m
1 TH	0236 1.8	0832 6.7	1508 1.6	2107 6.2		16 F	0257 1.2	0851 7.5	1538 0.6	2136 6.9
2 F	0308 2.0	0906 6.5	1541 1.8	2142 6.1		17 SA	0340 1.4	0938 7.2	1625 1.0	2226 6.6
3 SA	0343 2.2	0944 6.3	1618 1.9	2223 5.9		18 SU	0427 1.7	1031 6.9	1714 1.4	◗ 2320 6.3
4 SU	0424 2.4	1028 6.1	1701 2.1	◗ 2312 5.8		19 M	0519 2.1	1132 6.5	1809 1.8	
5 M	0514 2.5	1121 5.9	1754 2.3			20 TU	0020 2.4	0622 2.4	1242 6.1	1913 2.2
6 TU	0012 5.6	0614 2.7	1226 5.8	1854 2.3		21 W	0126 5.9	0741 2.5	1358 6.0	2023 2.3
7 W	0123 5.7	0722 2.6	1337 5.8	2000 2.3		22 TH	0232 5.9	0902 2.4	1514 6.0	2128 2.3
8 TH	0230 5.8	0831 2.5	1447 6.0	2106 2.2		23 F	0334 6.1	1008 2.1	1624 6.1	2224 2.1
9 F	0329 6.1	0939 2.1	1550 6.3	2208 1.9		24 SA	0427 6.4	1102 1.7	1718 6.3	2313 1.9
10 SA	0422 6.5	1042 1.7	1648 6.6	2304 1.7		25 SU	0513 6.6	1150 1.5	1802 6.5	2357 1.8
11 SU	0510 6.8	1139 1.3	1742 6.9	● 2356 1.4		26 M	0553 6.9	1232 1.3	1838 6.6	○
12 M	0556 7.1	1232 0.9	1832 7.1			27 TU	0037 1.6	0629 7.0	1311 1.2	1910 6.6
13 TU	0044 1.2	0639 7.4	1321 0.6	1919 7.3		28 W	0114 1.6	0704 7.0	1346 1.2	1939 6.6
14 W	0130 1.1	0723 7.5	1408 0.4	2005 7.3		29 TH	0146 1.6	0736 7.0	1416 1.3	2007 6.6
15 TH	0213 1.1	0806 7.6	1453 0.4	2050 7.2		30 F	0215 1.7	0807 6.9	1444 1.4	2035 6.5
						31 SA	0242 1.8	0838 6.8	1510 1.6	2104 6.4

AUGUST

Day	Time m	Time m	Time m	Time m		Day	Time m	Time m	Time m	Time m
1 SU	0311 1.9	0909 6.6	1537 1.8	2137 6.2		16 M	0357 1.6	1004 6.9	1637 1.6	◗ 2238 6.3
2 M	0343 2.1	0944 6.4	1610 2.0	2216 6.0		17 TU	0443 2.1	1103 6.3	1727 2.2	2338 5.9
3 TU	0425 2.4	1029 6.1	1656 2.3	2307 5.7		18 W	0543 2.5	1218 5.9	1836 2.7	
4 W	0523 2.6	1128 5.9	1801 2.5			19 TH	0050 5.7	0719 2.8	1343 5.7	2002 2.8
5 TH	0021 5.6	0638 2.7	1253 5.7	1919 2.6		20 F	0205 5.7	0854 2.5	1507 5.8	2113 2.6
6 F	0153 5.7	0758 2.6	1426 5.9	2038 2.4		21 SA	0312 6.0	0956 2.1	1616 6.1	2208 2.3
7 SA	0305 6.0	0918 2.2	1539 6.2	2149 2.1		22 SU	0407 6.4	1045 1.8	1704 6.3	2254 2.0
8 SU	0403 6.5	1029 1.7	1640 6.6	2249 1.7		23 M	0451 6.7	1129 1.5	1742 6.6	2336 1.8
9 M	0453 6.9	1127 1.1	1733 7.0	2341 1.4		24 TU	0530 6.9	1209 1.3	1814 6.7	○
10 TU	0539 7.3	1219 0.6	1821 7.3	●		25 W	0015 1.6	0605 7.1	1242 1.2	1842 6.8
11 W	0029 1.1	0623 7.6	1307 0.3	1905 7.5		26 TH	0051 1.5	0638 7.1	1319 1.2	1909 6.8
12 TH	0114 0.9	0706 7.8	1351 0.2	1947 7.5		27 F	0122 1.5	0710 7.1	1348 1.3	1935 6.8
13 F	0157 0.8	0748 7.9	1433 0.3	2027 7.4		28 SA	0150 1.5	0740 7.0	1414 1.4	2002 6.7
14 SA	0237 0.9	0831 7.7	1514 0.6	2107 7.1		29 SU	0215 1.6	0808 6.9	1437 1.5	2028 6.6
15 SU	0317 1.2	0915 7.4	1554 1.1	2149 6.7		30 M	0241 1.8	0837 6.8	1459 1.7	2058 6.4
						31 TU	0310 2.0	0910 6.5	1527 1.9	2133 6.2

Chart Datum: 3·90 metres below Ordnance Datum (Newlyn). HAT is 8·0 metres above Chart Datum; see 0.19

TIME ZONE (UT)
For Summer Time add ONE hour in **non-shaded areas**

IMMINGHAM   LAT 53°38'N   LONG 0°11'W
TIMES AND HEIGHTS OF HIGH AND LOW WATERS

Dates in red are SPRINGS
Dates in blue are NEAPS

YEAR 2010

SEPTEMBER

Time	m	Time	m
1 0348	2.2	**16** 0507	2.6
0953	6.2	1158	5.6
W 1609	2.3	TH 1751	3.0
☾ 2220	5.9		
2 0446	2.5	**17** 0016	5.6
1052	5.9	0655	2.9
TH 1716	2.7	F 1326	5.5
2330	5.6	1935	3.1
3 0608	2.7	**18** 0136	5.7
1226	5.6	0834	2.6
F 1847	2.8	SA 1446	5.7
		2050	2.9
4 0119	5.6	**19** 0244	6.0
0737	2.6	0932	2.2
SA 1415	5.8	SU 1550	6.0
2017	2.6	2143	2.5
5 0241	6.0	**20** 0339	6.4
0904	2.1	1017	1.8
SU 1528	6.3	M 1635	6.4
2132	2.2	2228	2.1
6 0341	6.6	**21** 0423	6.7
1013	1.5	1058	1.5
M 1626	6.8	TU 1711	6.6
2231	1.7	2308	1.8
7 0431	7.1	**22** 0501	6.9
1109	0.9	1136	1.3
TU 1716	7.2	W 1742	6.8
2322	1.3	2347	1.6
8 0518	7.5	**23** 0536	7.0
1158	0.5	1212	1.2
W 1802	7.4	TH 1810	6.9
●		○	
9 0009	1.0	**24** 0022	1.5
0601	7.8	0608	7.1
TH 1244	0.2	F 1246	1.2
1842	7.6	1836	6.9
10 0053	0.8	**25** 0054	1.5
0644	8.0	0640	7.1
F 1327	0.2	SA 1316	1.3
1921	7.6	1903	6.9
11 0135	0.7	**26** 0122	1.5
0727	8.0	0712	7.1
SA 1407	0.4	SU 1342	1.4
1958	7.5	1930	6.9
12 0214	0.9	**27** 0149	1.5
0808	7.7	0742	7.0
SU 1444	0.8	M 1406	1.5
2035	7.2	1958	6.8
13 0252	1.2	**28** 0217	1.7
0851	7.3	0812	6.8
M 1520	1.3	TU 1430	1.7
2113	6.8	2027	6.6
14 0329	1.6	**29** 0248	1.8
0938	6.8	0847	6.6
TU 1558	1.9	W 1501	2.0
2157	6.3	2103	6.4
15 0410	2.1	**30** 0328	2.1
1037	6.1	0933	6.2
W 1643	2.5	TH 1544	2.4
☽ 2255	5.9	2151	6.1

OCTOBER

Time	m	Time	m
1 0427	2.4	**16** 0607	2.8
1037	5.9	1255	5.5
F 1651	2.7	SA 1840	3.3
☽ 2301	5.8		
2 0551	2.6	**17** 0058	5.7
1220	5.7	0752	2.7
SA 1822	2.9	SU 1407	5.6
		2009	3.0
3 0047	5.8	**18** 0206	5.9
0720	2.4	0852	2.3
SU 1400	5.9	M 1507	5.9
1954	2.7	2107	2.6
4 0212	6.2	**19** 0302	6.3
0843	1.9	0938	2.0
M 1509	6.4	TU 1555	6.3
2108	2.2	2153	2.2
5 0313	6.7	**20** 0348	6.5
0948	1.4	1019	1.7
TU 1604	6.8	W 1633	6.5
2206	1.8	2235	1.9
6 0405	7.2	**21** 0426	6.8
1042	0.9	1057	1.5
W 1653	7.2	TH 1705	6.7
2257	1.3	2313	1.7
7 0452	7.5	**22** 0502	6.9
1131	0.6	1135	1.4
TH 1736	7.4	F 1735	6.9
● 2344	1.0	2349	1.6
8 0538	7.8	**23** 0537	7.0
1216	0.4	1210	1.4
F 1816	7.5	SA 1804	7.0
		○	
9 0029	0.8	**24** 0024	1.5
0622	7.9	0612	7.1
SA 1259	0.5	SU 1243	1.4
1854	7.5	1834	7.0
10 0112	0.8	**25** 0056	1.5
0706	7.8	0647	7.1
SU 1338	0.7	M 1312	1.4
1930	7.4	1904	7.0
11 0152	0.9	**26** 0128	1.5
0748	7.5	0722	7.0
M 1415	1.0	TU 1341	1.6
2006	7.2	1935	6.9
12 0229	1.2	**27** 0201	1.5
0831	7.1	0758	6.9
TU 1449	1.5	W 1412	1.7
2042	6.9	2008	6.8
13 0305	1.6	**28** 0237	1.7
0917	6.6	0838	6.6
W 1524	2.1	TH 1448	2.0
2122	6.4	2047	6.6
14 0345	2.1	**29** 0322	1.9
1014	6.0	0928	6.3
TH 1605	2.6	F 1534	2.3
☽ 2215	6.3	2137	6.3
15 0440	2.5	**30** 0423	2.1
1133	5.6	1035	6.0
F 1705	3.1	SA 1637	2.7
2335	5.7	☽ 2245	6.1
		31 0539	2.2
		1209	5.9
		SU 1759	2.8

NOVEMBER

Time	m	Time	m
1 0015	6.1	**16** 0112	5.9
0659	2.1	0743	2.5
M 1333	6.1	TU 1413	5.8
1923	2.6	2007	2.9
2 0137	6.3	**17** 0211	6.0
0813	1.8	0841	2.3
TU 1439	6.4	W 1505	6.0
2035	2.3	2105	2.5
3 0240	6.7	**18** 0302	6.2
0916	1.4	0929	2.0
W 1535	6.4	TH 1548	6.3
2136	1.9	2152	2.2
4 0336	7.0	**19** 0346	6.5
1011	1.1	1013	1.8
TH 1624	7.0	F 1625	6.5
2230	1.5	2235	2.0
5 0428	7.3	**20** 0428	6.7
1101	0.9	1055	1.7
F 1709	7.2	SA 1700	6.7
2320	1.2	2316	1.7
6 0517	7.5	**21** 0508	6.8
1148	0.8	1134	1.6
SA 1750	7.4	SU 1735	6.9
●		○ 2355	1.5
7 0007	1.0	**22** 0549	6.9
0604	7.5	1212	1.5
SU 1232	0.9	M 1811	7.0
1829	7.4		
8 0052	1.0	**23** 0034	1.4
0650	7.4	0629	7.0
M 1312	1.1	TU 1248	1.5
1906	7.3	1845	7.1
9 0133	1.1	**24** 0113	1.3
0734	7.2	0709	7.0
TU 1350	1.3	W 1324	1.5
1943	7.2	1920	7.1
10 0212	1.3	**25** 0153	1.3
0816	6.9	0751	6.9
W 1424	1.7	TH 1401	1.6
2019	6.9	1958	7.0
11 0249	1.6	**26** 0235	1.4
0900	6.5	0836	6.7
TH 1458	2.1	F 1441	1.8
2057	6.6	2040	6.9
12 0328	2.0	**27** 0322	1.6
0950	6.1	0927	6.5
F 1537	2.5	SA 1528	2.1
2143	6.3	2129	6.7
13 0415	2.3	**28** 0418	1.7
1054	5.7	1029	6.3
SA 1627	2.9	SU 1625	2.3
☽ 2246	6.0	☽ 2230	6.5
14 0517	2.6	**29** 0523	1.8
1206	5.5	1143	6.1
SU 1733	3.1	M 1733	2.5
		2343	6.4
15 0002	5.8	**30** 0631	1.8
0630	2.6	1255	6.1
M 1313	5.6	TU 1848	2.5
1852	3.1		

DECEMBER

Time	m	Time	m
1 0058	6.4	**16** 0105	5.8
0739	1.8	0725	2.5
W 1401	6.3	TH 1401	5.7
2000	2.3	1952	2.8
2 0207	6.6	**17** 0208	5.9
0843	1.6	0827	2.4
TH 1501	6.5	F 1457	6.0
2107	2.1	2056	2.6
3 0310	6.7	**18** 0304	6.1
0941	1.5	0924	2.2
F 1555	6.7	SA 1546	6.2
2206	1.8	2153	2.2
4 0408	6.9	**19** 0356	6.4
1035	1.4	1016	1.9
SA 1643	6.9	SU 1630	6.5
2301	1.5	2244	1.9
5 0503	7.0	**20** 0445	6.6
1124	1.3	1103	1.7
SU 1728	7.1	M 1712	6.8
● 2351	1.3	2333	1.6
6 0554	7.1	**21** 0532	6.8
1210	1.3	1148	1.6
M 1809	7.2	TU 1752	7.0
		○	
7 0038	1.2	**22** 0019	1.3
0640	7.1	0617	7.0
TU 1252	1.4	W 1231	1.5
1848	7.2	1831	7.2
8 0122	1.2	**23** 0104	1.1
0723	7.0	0701	7.1
W 1330	1.5	TH 1313	1.4
1925	7.2	1910	7.3
9 0201	1.3	**24** 0148	1.0
0804	6.8	0745	7.1
TH 1405	1.7	F 1354	1.4
2001	7.0	1950	7.3
10 0237	1.5	**25** 0233	1.0
0843	6.5	0830	7.0
F 1438	2.0	SA 1436	1.5
2037	6.8	2032	7.3
11 0312	1.7	**26** 0318	1.1
0922	6.2	0917	6.8
SA 1513	2.2	SU 1520	1.7
2115	6.6	2118	7.1
12 0349	2.0	**27** 0406	1.2
1004	6.0	1009	6.6
SU 1552	2.5	M 1608	1.9
2200	6.3	2211	6.9
13 0433	2.2	**28** 0459	1.5
1055	5.7	1108	6.3
M 1640	2.7	TU 1704	2.2
☽ 2255	6.0	☽ 2313	6.6
14 0525	2.4	**29** 0558	1.7
1155	5.6	1213	6.1
TU 1739	2.9	W 1809	2.4
2359	5.9		
15 0624	2.5	**30** 0023	6.4
1259	5.6	0703	1.9
W 1845	2.9	TH 1320	6.1
		1924	2.4
		31 0137	6.3
		0811	2.0
		F 1426	6.1
		2041	2.3

NE England

Chart Datum: 3·90 metres below Ordnance Datum (Newlyn). HAT is 8·0 metres above Chart Datum; see 0.19

3.9 RIVER HUMBER

S bank: NE and N Lincolnshire
N bank: E Riding of Yorks and City of Kingston-upon-Hull
Hull marina: **53°44'·24N 00°20'·15W** ✲⊛♦♦♦♦✿✿✿

CHARTS AC 1190, 109, 3497, 1188, 5614; Imray C29; ABP (local)

TIDES −0510 Immingham, −0452 Hull, Dover; ML 4·1; Duration 0555

Standard Port IMMINGHAM (←)

Times				Height (metres)			
High Water		Low Water		MHWS	MHWN	MLWN	MLWS
0100	0700	0100	0700	7·3	5·8	2·6	0·9
1300	1900	1300	1900				
Differences BULL SAND FORT							
−0020	−0030	−0035	−0015	−0·4	−0·3	+0·1	+0·2
GRIMSBY							
−0012	−0012	−0015	−0015	−0·2	−0·1	0·0	+0·2
HULL (ALBERT DOCK)							
+0019	+0019	+0033	+0027	+0·3	+0·1	−0·1	−0·2
HUMBER BRIDGE							
+0027	+0022	+0049	+0039	−0·1	−0·4	−0·7	−0·6
BURTON STATHER (R Trent)*							
+0105	+0045	+0335	+0305	−2·1	−2·3	−2·3	Dries
KEADBY (R Trent)*							
+0135	+0120	+0425	+0410	−2·5	−2·8	Dries	
BLACKTOFT (R Ouse)†							
+0100	+0055	+0325	+0255	−1·6	−1·8	−2·2	−1·1
GOOLE (R Ouse)†							
+0130	+0115	+0355	+0350	−1·6	−2·1	−1·9	−0·6

NOTE: Daily predictions for Immingham are given above.

* Normal river level at Burton Stather is about 0·1m below CD, and at Keadby 0·1m to 0·2m below CD.
† Heights of LW can increase by up to 0·3m at Blacktoft and 0·6m at Goole when river in spate. HW hts are little affected.

SHELTER R Humber is the estuary of R Ouse and R Trent. The estuary has strong tidal streams: a strong NW'ly against a spring flood of 3-4kn causes a short steep sea, as does a SE'ly over the ebb stream. Off Hull Marina it can be very choppy with fresh winds over spring tidal streams.

Anchorages. ⚓ inside Spurn Hd only with winds from NE to ESE. ⚓ close off Haile Sand Fort only in fair weather. Immingham should be used by yachts only in emergency. If unable to reach Hull on the tide, in S to W winds there is a good ⚓ off the SW bank 8ca above N Killingholme Oil jetty, well out of main chan. In N'lies ⚓ off Hawkin's Pt, N of S9 buoy.

Marinas at Hull, S Ferriby and the docks at Goole are all entered by lock access HW±3, and Grimsby also by lock HW±2. S Ferriby should not be attempted without up-to-date ABP charts for the ever-changing buoyed chan above Hull. Waiting pontoon at S Ferriby outside the Hope & Anchor pub.

Do not attempt entry to Winteringham (HW±½ MHWS with draft 1.5m) or Brough Havens (HW±1) without contacting Humber Yawl Club for details of approach channel and mooring availability. Both dry to soft mud. Winteringham is prone to bad silting, but is dredged.

NAVIGATION Note TSS on chartlet 2.1 and on AC 109.
From S, WPT 53°30'·50N 00°16'·50E, 1ca SW of Rosse Spit PHM buoy, Fl (2) R 5s. Thence make Haile Sand No 2, then via No 2B, Tetney monobuoy and No 2C into Haile Chan.

From N, WPT 53°34'·74N 00°16'·55E, S Binks SHM buoy, Fl G 2s. Thence passing N of Spurn Lt Float, SE Chequer and Chequer No 3 to make Binks 3A; then enter the estuary to the S of Spurn Hd outside Bull Chan. Best arrival at LW. Sp tides are fierce: 4·4kn ebb off Spurn Head and Immingham. There is a big ship ⚓ S of Spurn Hd. Keep clear of large commercial vessels using Hawke (8·4m) and Sunk (8·8m) Chans; these are marked by S1-S9 SHM buoys, all Fl G 1·5s (S8 is a SHM bn, Fl G 1·5s with tide gauge); and by P2-P9 PHM buoys, all Fl R 1·5s. Foul Holm Chan off Immingham is recommend for small craft.

For **Grimsby,** the lock into Fish Docks is 255°/1·35M from Lower Burcom No 6 Lt Float, Fl R 4s.

Off **Kingston-upon-Hull** a tidal eddy and streams can be rotatory, ie the flood makes W up Hull Roads for ¾hr whilst the ebb is already running down-river over Skitter Sand on the opposite bank (reaches 2½kn at sp). Humber Bridge (conspic) has 29m clearance.

LIGHTS AND MARKS The Humber is well buoyed/lit. At Grimsby a conspic tr (94m with 'minaret' on top) is 300m W of Fish Dock lock. IPTS control entry to Grimsby, Immingham, Killingholme, Hull and Goole.

R/T Advise *VTS Humber* on Ch 14 (or ☎ 01482 212191) posn and intentions on appr from seaward of Clee Ness lt float; listen on Ch 14 or 12 when W of the float up to Gainsborough (R Trent) and Goole (R Ouse). Weather, nav & tidal information is broadcast on Ch 12/14 every odd H+03; more detailed info, including height of tide, is available on request.

Other VHF stns: *Grimsby Docks Radio* Ch **74** (H24) 18 79 call *Humber Cruising* for marina staff or *Fishdock Island* for lock keeper. *Immingham Docks Radio* Ch 19 68 (H24). R Hull Port Ops Service call *Drypool Radio* Ch 22 (Mon-Fri HW−2 to HW+1; Sat 0900-1100 LT). *Hull Marina* Ch M **80** (H24); *Albert Dock Radio* Ch 09. *Ferriby Sluice* (Lock) Ch 74. Humber YC, Ch M (if racing). *Goole Docks Radio* Ch 14 (H24) 09 19. Boothferry Bridge Ch 09 (H24). Selby Railway and Toll Bridges Ch 09. Br Waterways locks Ch 74. *Brough and Winteringham Havens, Humber Yawl Club* Ch M.

TELEPHONE (Codes: Grimsby 01472; Hull 01482) Humber HM 01482 327171 controls whole estuary/river, see www.humber.com

GRIMSBY Port Director 327171; MRCC (01262) 672317; Marinecall 09068 969644; Police (01482) 881111.

HULL Marina ☎ 609960; lock 330508; MRCC (01262) 672317; ⊖ 782107; Marinecall 09068 969644; Police 26111; Dr contact Humber VTS 212191.

FACILITIES

TETNEY HAVEN N Lincs. Humber Mouth YC ☎ (01472) 812063, drying moorings. **GRIMSBY** (01472; NE Lincs) **Grimsby and Cleethorpes YC** ☎ 356678 (tel for berthing, enter via ABP Royal Dock), Bar, R, M, FW, ⊠. **Fish Docks** entered by lock 300m E of conspic tr. Access HW±3(£10 locking fee for ❶), with R/G tfc lts, but enter free of charge HW±2 after authorisation by *Fish Dock Island,* Ch **74**, when both gates open for free flow. In No 2 Fish Dock is: **Meridian Quay Marina** (run by Humber Cruising Association), call *Fish Dock Island* Ch 74) ☎ (01472) 268424, www.hca grimsby.co.uk, 200 berths + 30 ❶ AB, £1.45 inc ⚡, D, BH (35ton), bar, ⊠, Wi-fi. **Town** all facilities, ACA.

HULL (01482; Kingston-upon-Hull) **Hull Marina** ☎ 609960, (312 + 20 ❶ £1.94), access HW±3 via lock (width 8·5m) 150m to the E. Beware no shelter from adverse weather/sea conditions (from W through S to E) when waiting outside lock in river, but waiting pontoon, dries, in basin. Marina office open 0900-1700 daily; D, P, CH, Gas, ⊖, ♿, ⛟, ME, El, ✗, BH (50 ton), C (2 ton), ⊠, SM, ACA, ▦, Wi-fi. **City** All facilities. **Ferries:** Rotterdam and Zeebrugge; daily; 10 Hrs; P&O (www.poferries.com).

SOUTH FERRIBY N Lincs. **South Ferriby Marina** (100+20 ❶ £15/ yacht/60hrs inc lock fee) VHF 80, ☎ (01652) 635620; access HW±3, D, P (cans), ME, El, ✗, C (30 ton), CH, Gas, Gaz, ⛟. **Village** ▦, Bar. S Ferriby Sluice VHF 74: 0730-1600, or ☎ 01652 635219.

BROUGH HAVEN E Riding of Yorkshire, **Humber Yawl Club** ☎ (01482) 667224, Slip, FW, Bar, limited AB; entry HW±1½.

WINTERINGHAM HAVEN N Lincs (belongs to Humber Yawl Club) ☎ (01724) 734452; access HW±1. BH (10 ton), ✉.

GOOLE BOATHOUSE (☎ 01405 763985) and **VIKING MARINA** (☎ 01405 765737) are both situated off the Aire and Calder Canal. Access via the commercial lock for Goole Docks (Ch 14). Limited ❶ £5.00 (Goole Boathouse) or £6.00 (Viking Marina) any size, D, FW, Gas, El. Other facilities include Dry Dk, Slip, CH, ♿. Take the flood up the River Humber, follow the buoyed channel past Hull, Brough and when approaching Trent Falls Apex alter course to stbd and follow the River Ouse to Goole.

NABURN (R Ouse, 4M S of York and 80M above Spurn Pt). **Naburn Marina** (300+50 ❶ £1.00) ☎ (01904) 621021; CH, P, D, FW, showers, ▦, ⛟, ⚡ (£2.00), ✗, ME, BH (16 ton), R.

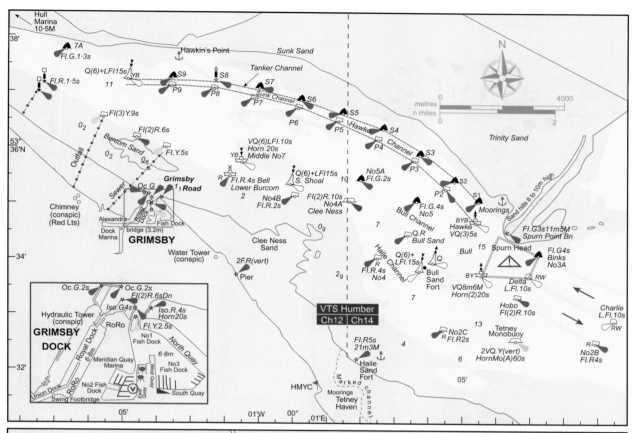

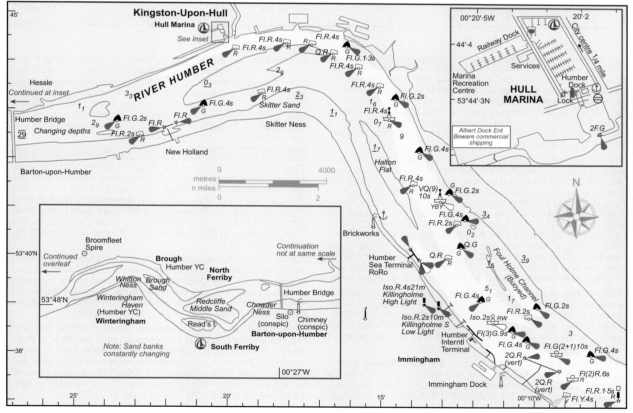

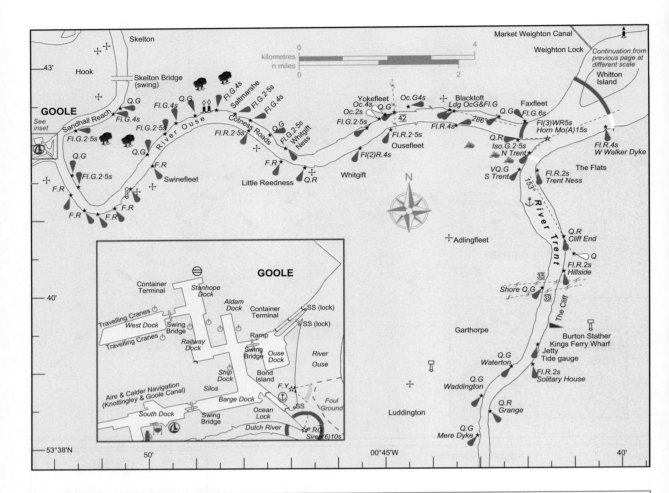

RIVER HUMBER TO HARTLEPOOL

(Charts 107, 121, 129, 134) Air gunnery and bombing practice is carried out 3M off Cowden, 17M S of Bridlington. The range is marked by 6 SPM buoys; 3 seaward ones Fl Y 10s, the 3 inner ones Fl Y 2s or 5s. Bridlington Bay (chart 1882) is clear of dangers apart from Smithic Shoals (marked by N and S cardinal lt buoys), about 3M off Bridlington, seas break on these shoals in strong N or E winds even at HW.

Flamborough Head (lt, fog sig, RG) is a steep, W cliff with conspic lt ho on summit. The lt may be obsc by cliffs when close inshore. An old lt ho, also conspic, is 2½ca WNW. ▶ *Tides run hard around the Head which, in strong winds against a sp tide, is best avoided by 2M.* ◀ From here the coast runs NW, with no offshore dangers until Filey Brigg where rky ledges extend 5ca ESE, marked by an ECM lt buoy. There is anch in Filey B in N or offshore winds. NW of Filey Brigg beware Old Horse Rks and foul ground 5ca offshore; maintain this offing past Scarborough to Whitby High lt. Off Whitby beware Whitby Rk and The Scar (dry in places) to E of hbr, and Upgang Rks (dry in places) 1M to WNW; swell breaks heavily on all these rocks.

From Whitby to Hartlepool there are no dangers more than 1M offshore. Runswick B (AC 1612), 5M NW of Whitby, provides anch in winds from S and W but is dangerous in onshore winds. 2½M further NW the little hbr of Staithes is more suitable for yachts which can take the ground, but only in good weather and offshore winds.

Redcliff, dark red and 205m high, is a conspic feature of this coast which, along to Hunt Cliff, is prone to landslides and is fringed with rky ledges which dry for about 3ca off. There is a conspic radio mast 4ca SSE of Redcliff. Off Redcar and Coatham

beware Salt Scar and West Scar, drying rky ledges lying 1– 8ca offshore. Other ledges lie close SE and S of Salt Scar which has NCM lt buoy. Between R. Tees and Hartlepool beware Long Scar, detached rky ledge (dries 2m) with extremity marked by ECM lt buoy. Tees and Hartlepool Bays are exposed to strong E/SE winds. The R. Tees and Middlesbrough are highly industrialised. At Hartlepool there is a centre specialising in the maintenance and restoration of Tall Ships.

HARTLEPOOL TO COQUET ISLAND

(Charts 134, 152, 156) From The Heugh an offing of 1M clears all dangers until past Seaham and approaching Sunderland (2.40), where White Stones, rky shoals with depth 1·8m, lie 1·75M SSE of Roker Pier lt ho, and Hendon Rk, depth 0·9m, lies 1·25M SE of the lt ho. 1M N of Sunderland is Whitburn Steel, a rky ledge with less than 2m over it; a dangerous wreck (buoyed) lies 1ca SE of it. A firing range at Souter Pt is marked by R flags (R lts) when active.

The coast N of Tynemouth is foul, and on passage to Blyth it should be given an offing of 1M. St Mary's Island (with disused conspic lt ho) is 3·5M N of Tynemouth, joined to the mainland by a causeway. The tiny drying harbour of Seaton Sluice, 1M NW of St Mary's Island, is accessible only in offshore winds via a narrow entrance.

Proceeding N from Blyth, keep well seaward of The Sow and Pigs rks, and set course to clear Newbiggin Pt and Beacon Pt by about 1M. Newbiggin church spire is prominent from N and S, and NW of Beacon Pt are conspic chys of aluminium smelter and power stn. 2M NNW of Beacon Pt is Snab Pt where rks extend 3ca seaward. Further offshore Cresswell Skeres, rky patches with depth 3m, lie about 1·5M NNE of Snab Pt.

3.10 BRIDLINGTON

E Riding of Yorkshire **54°04'·78N 00°11'·21W** ❀❀⚓⚓⚓✿✿

CHARTS AC 1191, 1190, 129, 121, 1882, *5614*; Imray C29.

TIDES +0553 Dover; ML 3·6; Duration 0610

Standard Port RIVER TEES (→)

Times				Height (metres)			
High Water		Low Water		MHWS	MHWN	MLWN	MLWS
0000	0600	0000	0600	5·5	4·3	2·0	0·9
1200	1800	1200	1800				
Differences BRIDLINGTON							
+0100	+0050	+0055	+0050	+0·6	+0·4	+0·3	+0·2
FILEY BAY							
+0042	+0042	+0047	+0034	+0·3	+0·6	+0·4	+0·1

SHELTER Good, except in E, SE and S winds. Hbr dries completely to soft black mud; access HW±3 (for draft of 2·7m). Visitors normally berth on S pier or near HM's Office. A marina is planned but agreement not yet reached.

NAVIGATION WPT SW Smithic WCM, Q (9) 15s, 54°02'·41N 00°09'·21W, 333°/2·6M to ent. Close-in appr is with N pier hd lt on brg 002° to keep W of drying patch (The Canch). Beware bar, 1m at MLWN, could dry out at MLWS.

LIGHTS AND MARKS Hbr is 4M WSW of Flamborough Hd lt, Fl (4) 15s 65m 24M. Y racing marks are laid in the Bay, Apr-Oct. Tidal sigs, by day from S pier: R flag = >2·7m in hbr; No flag = < 2·7m. At night from N pier: Fl ● = >2·7m in hbr; Fl ● = < 2·7m.

R/T Call on VHF Ch 16, then Ch **12**, 67 for working.

TELEPHONE (Code 01262) HM 670148/9, mobile 0860 275150; MRCC 672317; Marinecall 09068 969644; Police (01482) 881111; Ⓗ 673451.

FACILITIES **S Pier** FW, AB £2·80 /sq m/week or £15/yacht <3days, D (tank/hose ☎ 500227), C (5 ton), BH (70 ton), Slip; M, see HM; **Royal Yorks YC** ☎ 672041, L, FW, R, Bar. **Town** P (cans), CH, ME, El, 🛒, R, Bar, ✉, Ⓑ, ⇌, ✈ (Humberside).

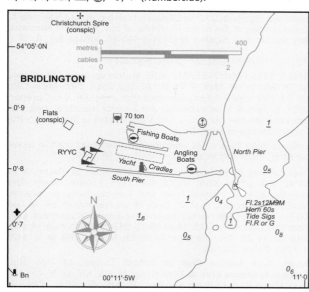

ADJACENT ANCHORAGE (7M SE of Scarborough)

FILEY, N Yorkshire, 54°12'·80N 00°16'·20W, AC 1882, 129. HW +0532 on Dover; ML 3·5m; Duration 0605. See 3.10. Good ⚓ in winds from S to NNE in 4 – 5m on hard sand. Lt on cliff above CG Stn, G metal column, FR 31m 1M vis 272°-308°. Filey Brigg, a natural bkwtr, is marked by ECM buoy, Q(3)10s, Bell. Beware Old Horse Rks, 2M WNW of Filey Brigg, foul ground extending ½M offshore. An unmarked Historic Wreck (see 0.31) lies at 54°11'·51N 00°13'·48W. Facilities: 🛒, R, Bar, L, Ⓗ ☎ (01723) 68111, ✉, Ⓑ, ⇌.

3.11 SCARBOROUGH

N. Yorkshire **54°16'·88N 00°23'·36W** ❀❀⚓⚓⚓✿✿✿

CHARTS AC 1191, 129, 1612, 5614; Imray C29.

TIDES +0527 Dover; ML 3·5; Duration 0615

Standard Port RIVER TEES (→)

Times				Height (metres)			
High Water		Low Water		MHWS	MHWN	MLWN	MLWS
0000	0600	0000	0600	5·5	4·3	2·0	0·9
1200	1800	1200	1800				
Differences SCARBOROUGH							
+0040	+0040	+0030	+0030	+0·2	+0·3	+0·3	0·0

SHELTER Good in E Hbr, access HW±3 via narrow (10m) ent by E pier, but not in strong E/SE'lies. 5 ❶ pontoon berths, (max LOA 10.3m, draft 1.8m), in the SW corner of E Hbr, just below lt ho; 4 ❶ drying AB on Old Pier just N of the drawbridge; ❶ AB on SE side of pontoons in Old Harbour, dredged to 2m. In winter months access to East Hbr is via the drawbridge only.

NAVIGATION WPT 54°16'·50N 00°22'·00W, 302°/0.83M to E pier lt. Appr from the E to avoid Ramsdale Scar, rky shoal 0·9m. Keep careful watch for salmon nets E & SE of ent. Beware rks extending approx 20m SW of E pier head. Give Castle Headland close N of hbr a wide berth due to coastal defences.

LIGHTS AND MARKS Lt ho (conspic), Iso 5s, Dia 60s, on Vincent Pier is shown by night or B ● by day when there is more than 3·7m over bar in entrance. Other lts as shown on chartlet.

R/T Call *Scarborough Port Control* VHF Ch **12** 16 (H24). Watchkeeper will offer guidance to approaching visitors.

TELEPHONE (Code 01723) HM (HO) ☎ 373530; www.scarboroughbc.gov.uk; Port Control 373877; CG 372323; MRCC (01262) 672317; Marinecall 09068 969644; Police 500300; Ⓗ 368111.

FACILITIES **East Harbour** AB £10/night, pontoon berth £23/night <10m LOA, M, FW, ⬚, D, C (4 ton), Slip; **Scarborough YC** ☎ 373821, AB, Slip, M*, FW, ME, El, 🖳; **Services** ME, El, 🔧, CH, P & D (cans), Ⓔ. **Town** P, D, Slip (£11·50) 🛒, R, Bar, ✉, Ⓑ, ⇌, ✈ (Humberside).

3.12 WHITBY

N. Yorkshire 54°29'·65N 00°36'·78W 🌸❄💧💧💧🏵🏵🏵

CHARTS AC 129, 134, 1612, 5614; Imray C29, C24.

TIDES +0500 Dover; ML 3·3; Duration 0605
Standard Port RIVER TEES (→)

Times				Height (metres)			
High Water		Low Water		MHWS	MHWN	MLWN	MLWS
0000	0600	0000	0600	5·5	4·3	2·0	0·9
1200	1800	1200	1800				
Differences WHITBY							
+0015	+0030	+0020	+0005	+0·1	0·0	−0·1	−0·1

SHELTER Good, except in lower hbr in strong NW to NE winds.
NAVIGATION WPT 54°30'·21N 00°36'96W, 169°/0·57M to ent. The harbour can be entered safely under most conditions except during N-NE gales when the approach is dangerous due to breaking seas and entry should not be attempted.

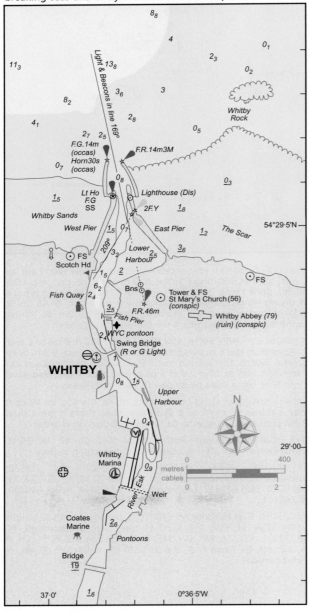

- From the SE beware Whitby Rk; leave Whitby NCM lit buoy to port.
- Beware strong set to E from HW –2 to HW, when nearing piers.

Vessels >37m LOA must embark pilot; via HM.

Access HW±4 for approx 2m draft. Bridge opens on request HW±2 every H and H+30. Additional openings at w/e and BH: May-Sep 0930 and1730; Aug 1300 (irrespective of tides). FG lts = open; FR lts = shut. Wait on pontoon at Fish Pier if necessary. If alongside Fish Quay or FVs, craft must not be left unattended.

LIGHTS AND MARKS See 3.3 and chartlet. Ruins of Whitby Abbey are to the E of the entrance. Whitby High Lt ho (white 8-sided tower) is 2M ESE of harbour entrance.

Leading lines for entering hbr:
FR lt and 2 bns (W △ and W ○ with B stripe), seen between the outer pierheads (FR and FG), lead 169° into hbr. Maintain this line until bns on E pier (two FY lts) are abeam. Thence keep these same bns in transit astern bearing 209°.

R/T Hbr and Marina VHF Ch 11 16 12 (H24). Whitby Bridge Ch 11 16 06 (listens on Ch 16 HW–2 to HW+2).

TELEPHONE (Code 01947) HM/Watchkeepers ☎ 602354/602272, www.yorkshireports.co.uk; MRCC (01262) 672317; Marinecall 09068 969644/453; Police (01653) 692424; Dr 820888.

FACILITIES Whitby Marina (dredged 1.5m) is 2ca beyond swing bridge; visitor berths at seaward end of long pontoon. ☎ 600165. 240+10 **Ⓥ**, £1.82; D (cans), Slip, ME, El, ⚒, C, CH, BH, ACA, SM, Gas, Gaz. **Whitby YC** ☎ 07786 289393, M, L, Bar.

Fish Quay D (in commercial quantities only, ☎ 602255), C (1 ton).
Town All domestic facilities, R, Bar, ≈, ✈ (Teesside).

ADJACENT ANCHORAGE (5M WNW of Whitby)

RUNSWICK BAY, N. Yorkshire, 54°32'·11N 00°44'·20W. AC 1612. HW +0505 on Dover: Differences on R Tees are approx as Whitby; ML 3·1m; Duration 0605. Good shelter in all winds from SSE thru W to NW. Enter bay at 225° keeping clear of many rks at base of cliffs. Two W posts (2FY by night when required by lifeboat) 18m apart are ldg marks 270° to LB ho and can be used to lead into ⚓. Good holding in 6m to 9m in middle of bay. Facilities: **Runswick Bay Rescue Boat Station** ☎ (01947) 840965. **Village** Bar, R, 🛒.

ADJACENT PORT (3M SSE of Hartlepool)

RIVER TEES / MIDDLESBROUGH, Middlesbrough / Stockton, 54°38'·94N 01°08'·48W. 🌸❄💧🏵. AC 152, 2567, 2566; Imray C29; OS 93. HW +0450 Dover; Standard Port (→). ML 3·1; Duration 0605. R. Tees & Middlesbrough are a major industrial area. 5M upriver from the hbr ent a Tall Ships Centre is planned in the former Middlesbrough Dock.

Entry to River Tees is not recommended for small craft in heavy weather, especially in strong winds from NE to SE.

Tees Fairway SWM buoy, Iso 4s 9m 8M, Horn 5s, Racon, is at 54°40'·93N 01°06'·38W, 030°/2·4M from S Gare bkwtr. The channel is well buoyed from the Fairway buoy to beyond Middlesbrough. Ldg lts 210°, both FR on framework trs. At Old CG stn a Q lt, or 3 ● (vert), = no entry without HM's consent. Call: *Tees Port Control* VHF Ch 14 22 16 12 (H24). Monitor Ch 14; also info Ch 14 22. *Tees Barrage Radio* Ch M (37). HM ☎ (01642) 277201; Police 248184.

South Gare Marine Club ☎ 491039 (occas), M, FW, Slip; **Castlegate Marine Club** ☎ 583299 Slip, M, FW, ME, El, ⚒, CH, 🛒; **Tees Motor Boat Club** M; **Services**: El, ME, Ⓔ, ACA. **City** All domestic facilities, ≈, ✈. Hartlepool marina (3.13) lies 3M to the NNW with all yacht facilities.

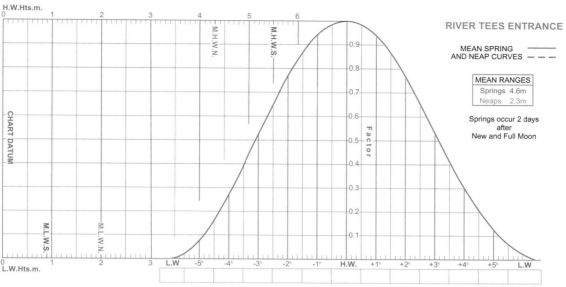

RIVER TEES ENTRANCE

MEAN SPRING AND NEAP CURVES

MEAN RANGES
Springs 4.6m
Neaps 2.3m

Springs occur 2 days after New and Full Moon

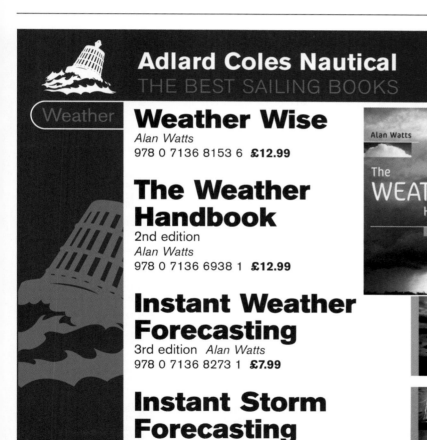

NE England

RIVER TEES   LAT 54°38'N   LONG 0°09'W
TIMES AND HEIGHTS OF HIGH AND LOW WATERS

TIME ZONE (UT)
For Summer Time add ONE hour in **non-shaded areas**

Dates in red are **SPRINGS**
Dates in blue are NEAPS

YEAR 2010

JANUARY

Time	m	Time	m
1 0333 / 0952 / F 1552 / 2223	5.3 / 1.1 / 5.5 / 0.6	**16** 0420 / 1022 / SA 1621 / 2250	4.9 / 1.4 / 5.2 / 1.1
2 0424 / 1040 / SA 1638 / 2312	5.5 / 1.0 / 5.6 / 0.4	**17** 0454 / 1053 / SU 1652 / 2322	5.0 / 1.4 / 5.2 / 1.0
3 0513 / 1126 / SU 1724	5.5 / 1.0 / 5.7	**18** 0526 / 1125 / M 1723 / 2352	5.0 / 1.4 / 5.2 / 1.1
4 0000 / 0602 / M 1212 / 1810	0.3 / 5.4 / 1.1 / 5.7	**19** 0557 / 1156 / TU 1757	4.9 / 1.4 / 5.2
5 0047 / 0651 / TU 1258 / 1858	0.4 / 5.3 / 1.2 / 5.5	**20** 0023 / 0630 / W 1229 / 1831	1.2 / 4.9 / 1.5 / 5.1
6 0135 / 0742 / W 1344 / 1949	0.6 / 5.1 / 1.5 / 5.3	**21** 0055 / 0707 / TH 1304 / 1909	1.3 / 4.7 / 1.7 / 4.9
7 0224 / 0835 / TH 1436 / ◑ 2045	1.0 / 4.8 / 1.7 / 5.0	**22** 0132 / 0748 / F 1344 / 1953	1.4 / 4.6 / 1.8 / 4.8
8 0320 / 0933 / F 1537 / 2148	1.3 / 4.6 / 2.0 / 4.7	**23** 0214 / 0837 / SA 1432 / ◐ 2045	1.6 / 4.4 / 2.0 / 4.6
9 0423 / 1036 / SA 1650 / 2300	1.7 / 4.4 / 2.1 / 4.5	**24** 0307 / 0935 / SU 1536 / 2150	1.8 / 4.3 / 2.2 / 4.4
10 0536 / 1146 / SU 1813	1.9 / 4.4 / 2.1	**25** 0417 / 1042 / M 1658 / 2305	2.0 / 4.2 / 2.1 / 4.4
11 0017 / 0648 / M 1255 / 1924	4.4 / 1.9 / 4.5 / 1.9	**26** 0537 / 1153 / TU 1819	2.0 / 4.3 / 1.9
12 0128 / 0747 / TU 1351 / 2019	4.5 / 1.8 / 4.6 / 1.6	**27** 0022 / 0653 / W 1300 / 1930	4.5 / 1.8 / 4.6 / 1.5
13 0222 / 0833 / W 1437 / 2104	4.6 / 1.7 / 4.8 / 1.4	**28** 0132 / 0758 / TH 1359 / 2031	4.8 / 1.5 / 4.9 / 1.1
14 0306 / 0913 / TH 1515 / 2142	4.8 / 1.6 / 5.0 / 1.2	**29** 0231 / 0853 / F 1451 / 2125	5.1 / 1.3 / 5.3 / 0.7
15 0345 / 0948 / F 1549 / ● 2217	4.9 / 1.5 / 5.1 / 1.1	**30** 0324 / 0943 / SA 1538 / ○ 2214	5.3 / 1.0 / 5.6 / 0.3
		31 0412 / 1029 / SU 1623 / 2300	5.5 / 0.8 / 5.8 / 0.1

FEBRUARY

Time	m	Time	m
1 0458 / 1112 / M 1708 / 2344	5.6 / 0.7 / 5.9 / 0.1	**16** 0459 / 1101 / TU 1658 / 2324	5.1 / 1.1 / 5.3 / 0.9
2 0543 / 1154 / TU 1751	5.6 / 0.8 / 5.9	**17** 0527 / 1131 / W 1728 / 2352	5.1 / 1.2 / 5.3 / 1.0
3 0026 / 0627 / W 1234 / 1835	0.2 / 5.4 / 0.9 / 5.7	**18** 0557 / 1201 / TH 1800	5.0 / 1.2 / 5.2
4 0108 / 0711 / TH 1315 / 1921	0.5 / 5.2 / 1.2 / 5.4	**19** 0023 / 0630 / F 1234 / 1835	1.1 / 4.9 / 1.4 / 5.1
5 0151 / 0757 / F 1358 / ◐ 2012	0.9 / 4.8 / 1.5 / 5.0	**20** 0058 / 0707 / SA 1310 / 1917	1.3 / 4.7 / 1.5 / 4.9
6 0238 / 0849 / SA 1452 / 2113	1.4 / 4.5 / 1.8 / 4.6	**21** 0137 / 0752 / SU 1354 / 2009	1.5 / 4.5 / 1.8 / 4.6
7 0336 / 0950 / SU 1606 / 2227	1.9 / 4.2 / 2.1 / 4.3	**22** 0226 / 0849 / M 1455 / ◑ 2117	1.8 / 4.3 / 2.0 / 4.4
8 0455 / 1104 / M 1747 / 2354	2.2 / 4.1 / 2.2 / 4.1	**23** 0336 / 1002 / TU 1624 / 2240	2.1 / 4.2 / 2.1 / 4.2
9 0626 / 1227 / TU 1913	2.2 / 4.2 / 2.0	**24** 0510 / 1123 / W 1759	2.1 / 4.2 / 1.9
10 0115 / 0731 / W 1334 / 2009	4.3 / 2.1 / 4.4 / 1.7	**25** 0005 / 0638 / TH 1240 / 1918	4.4 / 1.9 / 4.5 / 1.4
11 0211 / 0818 / TH 1421 / 2051	4.5 / 1.9 / 4.7 / 1.4	**26** 0121 / 0746 / F 1342 / 2019	4.7 / 1.6 / 4.9 / 0.9
12 0252 / 0856 / F 1459 / 2126	4.7 / 1.6 / 4.9 / 1.2	**27** 0219 / 0839 / SA 1434 / 2110	5.1 / 1.2 / 5.3 / 0.5
13 0328 / 0930 / SA 1532 / 2158	4.8 / 1.4 / 5.1 / 1.0	**28** 0308 / 0926 / SU 1520 / ○ 2156	5.4 / 0.9 / 5.7 / 0.2
14 0400 / 1002 / SU 1602 / ● 2228	5.0 / 1.3 / 5.2 / 0.9		
15 0430 / 1032 / M 1630 / 2257	5.0 / 1.2 / 5.3 / 0.9		

MARCH

Time	m	Time	m
1 0353 / 1009 / M 1603 / 2239	5.6 / 0.7 / 5.9 / 0.0	**16** 0400 / 1005 / TU 1603 / 2226	5.1 / 1.1 / 5.2 / 0.8
2 0436 / 1050 / TU 1645 / 2320	5.6 / 0.6 / 5.9 / 0.0	**17** 0427 / 1035 / W 1630 / 2254	5.1 / 1.0 / 5.3 / 0.8
3 0517 / 1130 / W 1727 / 2359	5.6 / 0.6 / 5.9 / 0.2	**18** 0455 / 1105 / TH 1700 / 2323	5.1 / 1.0 / 5.3 / 0.9
4 0558 / 1207 / TH 1810	5.4 / 0.8 / 5.7	**19** 0526 / 1136 / F 1733 / 2355	5.1 / 1.0 / 5.2 / 1.0
5 0037 / 0638 / F 1246 / 1854	0.6 / 5.2 / 1.0 / 5.3	**20** 0559 / 1210 / SA 1811	5.0 / 1.2 / 5.1
6 0116 / 0720 / SA 1326 / 1943	1.1 / 4.8 / 1.3 / 4.9	**21** 0030 / 0636 / SU 1248 / 1855	1.2 / 4.8 / 1.3 / 4.9
7 0158 / 0806 / SU 1415 / ◑ 2042	1.6 / 4.5 / 1.7 / 4.4	**22** 0110 / 0720 / M 1334 / 1951	1.5 / 4.6 / 1.6 / 4.6
8 0250 / 0905 / M 1528 / 2157	2.1 / 4.2 / 2.1 / 4.1	**23** 0200 / 0819 / TU 1438 / ◑ 2102	1.9 / 4.3 / 1.8 / 4.3
9 0412 / 1022 / TU 1715 / 2328	2.4 / 4.0 / 2.2 / 4.0	**24** 0312 / 0935 / W 1610 / 2227	2.1 / 4.1 / 1.9 / 4.2
10 0553 / 1151 / W 1848	2.4 / 4.1 / 2.0	**25** 0453 / 1059 / TH 1744 / 2353	2.2 / 4.3 / 1.6 / 4.4
11 0051 / 0704 / TH 1304 / 1943	4.1 / 2.2 / 4.3 / 1.7	**26** 0621 / 1218 / F 1900	1.9 / 4.6 / 1.2
12 0146 / 0752 / F 1353 / 2024	4.4 / 1.9 / 4.6 / 1.4	**27** 0105 / 0725 / SA 1321 / 1958	4.7 / 1.6 / 5.0 / 0.8
13 0226 / 0830 / SA 1432 / 2058	4.6 / 1.6 / 4.8 / 1.2	**28** 0200 / 0816 / SU 1412 / 2047	5.0 / 1.2 / 5.3 / 0.4
14 0301 / 0904 / SU 1505 / 2129	4.8 / 1.4 / 5.0 / 1.0	**29** 0246 / 0902 / M 1457 / 2132	5.3 / 0.9 / 5.6 / 0.2
15 0332 / 0935 / M 1535 / ● 2159	5.0 / 1.2 / 5.2 / 0.9	**30** 0329 / 0945 / TU 1540 / ○ 2214	5.5 / 0.6 / 5.8 / 0.1
		31 0410 / 1026 / W 1622 / 2254	5.5 / 0.5 / 5.8 / 0.2

APRIL

Time	m	Time	m
1 0449 / 1105 / TH 1704 / 2332	5.5 / 0.6 / 5.7 / 0.5	**16** 0427 / 1041 / F 1637 / 2257	5.2 / 0.9 / 5.2 / 0.9
2 0528 / 1143 / F 1747	5.3 / 0.7 / 5.4	**17** 0500 / 1116 / SA 1715 / 2333	5.1 / 0.9 / 5.2 / 1.0
3 0008 / 0606 / SA 1222 / 1832	0.8 / 5.1 / 0.9 / 5.1	**18** 0536 / 1154 / SU 1758	5.0 / 1.0 / 5.0
4 0046 / 0646 / SU 1303 / 1920	1.2 / 4.9 / 1.3 / 4.7	**19** 0011 / 0616 / M 1238 / 1848	1.2 / 4.9 / 1.2 / 4.8
5 0124 / 0730 / M 1351 / 2017	1.7 / 4.6 / 1.6 / 4.3	**20** 0055 / 0704 / TU 1330 / 1947	1.5 / 4.7 / 1.4 / 4.6
6 0212 / 0824 / TU 1458 / ◑ 2128	2.1 / 4.3 / 1.9 / 4.0	**21** 0149 / 0804 / W 1437 / ◑ 2057	1.8 / 4.5 / 1.5 / 4.4
7 0327 / 0937 / W 1630 / 2250	2.4 / 4.1 / 2.1 / 3.9	**22** 0304 / 0918 / TH 1601 / 2216	2.1 / 4.4 / 1.6 / 4.3
8 0503 / 1103 / TH 1759	2.5 / 4.1 / 1.9	**23** 0435 / 1038 / F 1722 / 2333	2.1 / 4.5 / 1.4 / 4.5
9 0008 / 0619 / F 1218 / 1859	4.0 / 2.3 / 4.2 / 1.7	**24** 0553 / 1152 / SA 1832	1.9 / 4.7 / 1.1
10 0106 / 0712 / SA 1312 / 1943	4.3 / 2.0 / 4.5 / 1.5	**25** 0040 / 0656 / SU 1255 / 1930	4.7 / 1.6 / 5.0 / 0.8
11 0149 / 0754 / SU 1354 / 2020	4.5 / 1.7 / 4.8 / 1.2	**26** 0135 / 0749 / M 1348 / 2021	5.0 / 1.2 / 5.2 / 0.6
12 0225 / 0830 / M 1430 / 2054	4.7 / 1.4 / 4.9 / 1.0	**27** 0222 / 0837 / TU 1435 / 2106	5.2 / 1.0 / 5.4 / 0.5
13 0257 / 0903 / TU 1502 / 2124	4.9 / 1.2 / 5.0 / 0.9	**28** 0304 / 0921 / W 1519 / ○ 2149	5.3 / 0.8 / 5.5 / 0.5
14 0327 / 0935 / W 1532 / ● 2154	5.0 / 1.0 / 5.2 / 0.8	**29** 0345 / 1003 / TH 1603 / 2229	5.3 / 0.7 / 5.5 / 0.6
15 0356 / 1008 / TH 1603 / 2224	5.1 / 0.9 / 5.2 / 0.8	**30** 0423 / 1044 / F 1646 / 2307	5.3 / 0.7 / 5.4 / 0.8

Chart Datum: 2·85 metres below Ordnance Datum (Newlyn). HAT is 6·1 metres above Chart Datum; see 0.19

FREE monthly updates from
www.reedsalmanac.co.uk

TIME ZONE (UT)
For Summer Time add ONE hour in **non-shaded areas**

RIVER TEES LAT 54°38'N LONG 0°09'W
TIMES AND HEIGHTS OF HIGH AND LOW WATERS

Dates in red are SPRINGS
Dates in blue are NEAPS

YEAR 2010

MAY

Day	Time	m	Day	Time	m
1 SA	0501 / 1124 / 1730 / 2344	5.2 / 0.8 / 5.2 / 1.1	16 SU	0442 / 1103 / 1706 / 2319	5.2 / 0.8 / 5.2 / 1.1
2 SU	0540 / 1204 / 1815	5.1 / 1.0 / 4.9	17 M	0523 / 1148 / 1755	5.1 / 0.8 / 5.1
3 M	0021 / 0619 / 1247 / 1901	1.4 / 4.9 / 1.2 / 4.6	18 TU	0003 / 0607 / 1237 / 1847	1.3 / 5.1 / 0.9 / 4.9
4 TU	0059 / 0702 / 1334 / 1953	1.7 / 4.7 / 1.5 / 4.4	19 W	0051 / 0657 / 1332 / 1944	1.5 / 4.9 / 1.1 / 4.7
5 W	0144 / 0752 / 1430 / 2053	2.0 / 4.5 / 1.7 / 4.1	20 TH	0147 / 0755 / 1435 / 2049	1.7 / 4.8 / 1.2 / 4.6
6 TH	0245 / 0853 / 1540 / 2202	2.3 / 4.3 / 1.9 / 4.0	21 F	0255 / 0902 / 1544 / 2157	1.9 / 4.7 / 1.2 / 4.5
7 F	0403 / 1006 / 1653 / 2310	2.4 / 4.2 / 1.9 / 4.1	22 SA	0409 / 1013 / 1653 / 2306	1.9 / 4.7 / 1.2 / 4.5
8 SA	0518 / 1118 / 1758	2.3 / 4.2 / 1.8	23 SU	0519 / 1123 / 1800	1.8 / 4.8 / 1.1
9 SU	0011 / 0618 / 1218 / 1850	4.2 / 2.1 / 4.4 / 1.6	24 M	0010 / 0624 / 1228 / 1901	4.7 / 1.6 / 4.9 / 1.0
10 M	0101 / 0707 / 1307 / 1934	4.4 / 1.8 / 4.6 / 1.4	25 TU	0108 / 0722 / 1326 / 1955	4.8 / 1.4 / 5.1 / 0.9
11 TU	0142 / 0750 / 1349 / 2013	4.6 / 1.6 / 4.7 / 1.2	26 W	0158 / 0815 / 1417 / 2043	5.0 / 1.2 / 5.2 / 0.9
12 W	0218 / 0828 / 1427 / 2048	4.8 / 1.3 / 4.9 / 1.1	27 TH	0243 / 0902 / 1505 / 2127	5.1 / 1.0 / 5.2 / 0.9
13 TH	0253 / 0905 / 1504 / 2123	5.0 / 1.1 / 5.1 / 1.0	28 F	0325 / 0947 / 1550 / 2208	5.1 / 0.9 / 5.2 / 1.0
14 F	0327 / 0943 / 1541 / 2200	5.1 / 1.0 / 5.2 / 0.9	29 SA	0404 / 1029 / 1634 / 2247	5.2 / 0.9 / 5.1 / 1.1
15 SA	0403 / 1022 / 1622 / 2238	5.2 / 0.9 / 5.2 / 1.0	30 SU	0441 / 1110 / 1717 / 2325	5.1 / 0.9 / 5.0 / 1.3
			31 M	0519 / 1151 / 1759	5.1 / 1.0 / 4.9

JUNE

Day	Time	m	Day	Time	m
1 TU	0001 / 0557 / 1231 / 1842	1.5 / 5.0 / 1.2 / 4.7	16 W	0000 / 0559 / 1235 / 1841	1.1 / 5.4 / 0.6 / 5.2
2 W	0039 / 0638 / 1313 / 1926	1.6 / 4.9 / 1.4 / 4.5	17 TH	0048 / 0648 / 1326 / 1934	1.3 / 5.3 / 0.7 / 5.0
3 TH	0118 / 0722 / 1358 / 2014	1.8 / 4.7 / 1.6 / 4.3	18 F	0139 / 0742 / 1420 / 2030	1.4 / 5.2 / 0.9 / 4.8
4 F	0205 / 0812 / 1448 / 2107	2.0 / 4.5 / 1.8 / 4.2	19 SA	0235 / 0841 / 1519 / 2130	1.6 / 5.0 / 1.1 / 4.7
5 SA	0303 / 0909 / 1545 / 2206	2.2 / 4.4 / 1.8 / 4.2	20 SU	0338 / 0946 / 1621 / 2233	1.6 / 4.8 / 1.2 / 4.5
6 SU	0409 / 1012 / 1646 / 2305	2.2 / 4.3 / 1.9 / 4.2	21 M	0445 / 1054 / 1728 / 2338	1.8 / 4.7 / 1.4 / 4.5
7 M	0514 / 1115 / 1746	2.2 / 4.3 / 1.8	22 TU	0555 / 1204 / 1835	1.8 / 4.7 / 1.4
8 TU	0001 / 0613 / 1214 / 1840	4.3 / 2.0 / 4.4 / 1.6	23 W	0042 / 0702 / 1311 / 1935	4.6 / 1.6 / 4.8 / 1.4
9 W	0053 / 0705 / 1306 / 1929	4.5 / 1.8 / 4.6 / 1.5	24 TH	0139 / 0801 / 1408 / 2027	4.7 / 1.4 / 4.9 / 1.4
10 M	0139 / 0753 / 1355 / 2015	4.7 / 1.6 / 4.8 / 1.3	25 F	0228 / 0852 / 1458 / 2112	4.9 / 1.2 / 4.9 / 1.3
11 F	0222 / 0839 / 1441 / 2059	4.9 / 1.2 / 5.0 / 1.2	26 SA	0311 / 0937 / 1543 / 2153	5.0 / 1.1 / 5.0 / 1.3
12 SA	0304 / 0924 / 1526 / 2143	5.0 / 1.0 / 5.1 / 1.1	27 SU	0350 / 1018 / 1624 / 2231	5.1 / 1.0 / 5.0 / 1.3
13 SU	0346 / 1010 / 1613 / 2228	5.2 / 0.8 / 5.2 / 1.0	28 M	0426 / 1057 / 1703 / 2307	5.1 / 0.8 / 5.0 / 1.3
14 M	0429 / 1057 / 1701 / 2313	5.3 / 0.7 / 5.3 / 1.0	29 TU	0501 / 1134 / 1740 / 2341	5.1 / 1.0 / 4.9 / 1.4
15 TU	0513 / 1145 / 1750	5.4 / 0.6 / 5.3	30 W	0536 / 1210 / 1817	5.1 / 1.1 / 4.8

JULY

Day	Time	m	Day	Time	m
1 TH	0015 / 0613 / 1245 / 1854	1.5 / 5.0 / 1.2 / 4.7	16 F	0034 / 0632 / 1309 / 1913	1.0 / 5.6 / 0.5 / 5.2
2 F	0050 / 0651 / 1321 / 1933	1.6 / 4.9 / 1.4 / 4.6	17 SA	0119 / 0721 / 1357 / 2004	1.2 / 5.4 / 0.7 / 5.0
3 SA	0128 / 0734 / 1400 / 2017	1.8 / 4.8 / 1.6 / 4.5	18 SU	0208 / 0815 / 1449 / 2058	1.4 / 5.2 / 1.1 / 4.7
4 SU	0211 / 0821 / 1445 / 2107	1.9 / 4.6 / 1.7 / 4.3	19 M	0304 / 0917 / 1548 / 2159	1.7 / 4.9 / 1.5 / 4.5
5 M	0304 / 0915 / 1540 / 2203	2.1 / 4.4 / 1.9 / 4.2	20 TU	0412 / 1027 / 1657 / 2306	1.9 / 4.6 / 1.7 / 4.4
6 TU	0410 / 1017 / 1644 / 2304	2.2 / 4.3 / 1.9 / 4.2	21 W	0532 / 1146 / 1814	1.9 / 4.5 / 1.8
7 W	0519 / 1123 / 1750	2.1 / 4.4 / 1.9	22 TH	0020 / 0652 / 1303 / 1922	4.4 / 1.8 / 4.5 / 1.8
8 TH	0005 / 0624 / 1229 / 1853	4.3 / 1.9 / 4.5 / 1.7	23 F	0126 / 0756 / 1404 / 2016	4.6 / 1.6 / 4.7 / 1.7
9 F	0104 / 0724 / 1329 / 1950	4.5 / 1.6 / 4.7 / 1.5	24 SA	0218 / 0846 / 1451 / 2100	4.8 / 1.3 / 4.8 / 1.6
10 SA	0157 / 0819 / 1423 / 2043	4.8 / 1.3 / 5.0 / 1.3	25 SU	0301 / 0928 / 1532 / 2138	5.0 / 1.2 / 4.9 / 1.4
11 SU	0245 / 0911 / 1512 / 2132	5.1 / 0.9 / 5.2 / 1.1	26 M	0337 / 1005 / 1609 / 2213	5.1 / 1.0 / 5.0 / 1.4
12 M	0331 / 1000 / 1603 / 2219	5.3 / 0.6 / 5.4 / 1.0	27 TU	0410 / 1039 / 1643 / 2246	5.2 / 1.0 / 5.0 / 1.3
13 TU	0416 / 1049 / 1651 / 2305	5.5 / 0.4 / 5.5 / 0.9	28 W	0441 / 1111 / 1715 / 2317	5.2 / 1.0 / 5.0 / 1.3
14 W	0501 / 1136 / 1738 / 2350	5.7 / 0.3 / 5.5 / 0.9	29 TH	0512 / 1142 / 1747 / 2347	5.2 / 1.0 / 5.0 / 1.3
15 TH	0546 / 1222 / 1826	5.7 / 0.3 / 5.4	30 F	0545 / 1212 / 1819	5.2 / 1.1 / 4.9
			31 SA	0019 / 0618 / 1243 / 1853	1.4 / 5.1 / 1.3 / 4.8

AUGUST

Day	Time	m	Day	Time	m
1 SU	0052 / 0656 / 1318 / 1932	1.6 / 4.9 / 1.4 / 4.7	16 M	0138 / 0748 / 1416 / 2023	1.3 / 5.2 / 1.3 / 4.7
2 M	0129 / 0737 / 1358 / 2018	1.7 / 4.8 / 1.7 / 4.5	17 TU	0230 / 0849 / 1513 / 2123	1.6 / 4.8 / 1.8 / 4.4
3 TU	0214 / 0827 / 1448 / 2112	1.9 / 4.6 / 1.9 / 4.3	18 W	0341 / 1003 / 1628 / 2235	2.0 / 4.4 / 2.1 / 4.2
4 W	0313 / 0929 / 1553 / 2216	2.1 / 4.4 / 2.1 / 4.2	19 TH	0515 / 1132 / 1757 / 2358	2.1 / 4.3 / 2.2 / 4.3
5 TH	0432 / 1043 / 1711 / 2326	2.2 / 4.3 / 2.1 / 4.3	20 F	0645 / 1255 / 1909	1.9 / 4.4 / 2.1
6 F	0554 / 1200 / 1828	2.0 / 4.4 / 1.9	21 SA	0111 / 0747 / 1353 / 2001	4.5 / 1.6 / 4.6 / 1.9
7 SA	0035 / 0704 / 1311 / 1933	4.5 / 1.6 / 4.7 / 1.7	22 SU	0202 / 0833 / 1436 / 2042	4.8 / 1.4 / 4.7 / 1.7
8 SU	0136 / 0805 / 1409 / 2029	4.8 / 1.2 / 5.0 / 1.4	23 M	0243 / 0910 / 1513 / 2117	5.0 / 1.2 / 5.0 / 1.5
9 M	0227 / 0858 / 1500 / 2118	5.2 / 0.8 / 5.3 / 1.1	24 TU	0317 / 0943 / 1546 / 2149	5.2 / 1.0 / 5.1 / 1.3
10 TU	0314 / 0947 / 1547 / 2204	5.5 / 0.4 / 5.5 / 0.8	25 W	0348 / 1013 / 1616 / 2219	5.3 / 1.0 / 5.1 / 1.2
11 W	0358 / 1034 / 1633 / 2248	5.8 / 0.2 / 5.7 / 0.7	26 TH	0416 / 1042 / 1645 / 2249	5.3 / 0.9 / 5.2 / 1.2
12 TH	0442 / 1118 / 1717 / 2331	5.9 / 0.1 / 5.7 / 0.7	27 F	0445 / 1110 / 1713 / 2318	5.3 / 1.0 / 5.1 / 1.2
13 F	0525 / 1201 / 1802	6.0 / 0.2 / 5.6	28 SA	0514 / 1138 / 1743 / 2348	5.3 / 1.1 / 5.1 / 1.3
14 SA	0012 / 0609 / 1246 / 1846	0.8 / 5.8 / 0.4 / 5.4	29 SU	0546 / 1208 / 1816	5.2 / 1.2 / 5.0
15 SU	0053 / 0656 / 1328 / 1933	1.0 / 5.6 / 0.8 / 5.1	30 M	0020 / 0620 / 1242 / 1853	1.4 / 5.1 / 1.4 / 4.8
			31 TU	0056 / 0700 / 1320 / 1936	1.6 / 4.9 / 1.6 / 4.6

Chart Datum: 2·85 metres below Ordnance Datum (Newlyn). HAT is 6·1 metres above Chart Datum; see 0.19

RIVER TEES   LAT 54°38'N   LONG 0°09'W
TIMES AND HEIGHTS OF HIGH AND LOW WATERS

TIME ZONE (UT)
For Summer Time add ONE hour in **non-shaded areas**

Dates in red are **SPRINGS**
Dates in blue are NEAPS

YEAR 2010

SEPTEMBER

Day	Time m	Day	Time m
1 W	0137 1.8 / 0750 4.6 / 1407 1.9 / ☽ 2029 4.4	**16** TH	0314 2.0 / 0940 4.3 / 1556 2.4 / 2201 4.2
2 TH	0234 2.0 / 0855 4.4 / 1513 2.2 / 2137 4.2	**17** F	0455 2.1 / 1112 4.2 / 1730 2.4 / 2328 4.2
3 F	0358 2.1 / 1015 4.3 / 1643 2.3 / 2255 4.3	**18** SA	0625 1.9 / 1234 4.3 / 1843 2.3
4 SA	0532 2.0 / 1140 4.4 / 1810 2.1	**19** SU	0042 4.5 / 0723 1.7 / 1329 4.5 / 1934 2.0
5 SU	0010 4.5 / 0649 1.6 / 1254 4.7 / 1917 1.7	**20** M	0134 4.7 / 0806 1.4 / 1410 4.8 / 2014 1.7
6 M	0114 4.9 / 0749 1.1 / 1352 5.1 / 2010 1.4	**21** TU	0214 5.0 / 0841 1.2 / 1445 5.0 / 2048 1.5
7 TU	0206 5.3 / 0840 0.6 / 1441 5.4 / 2058 1.0	**22** W	0249 5.1 / 0912 1.1 / 1517 5.1 / 2120 1.3
8 W	0252 5.7 / 0927 0.3 / ● 1526 5.6 / 2143 0.8	**23** TH	0319 5.3 / 0942 1.0 / 1546 5.2 / ○ 2151 1.2
9 TH	0336 5.9 / 1011 0.1 / 1609 5.8 / 2225 0.6	**24** F	0348 5.3 / 1010 1.0 / 1613 5.2 / 2220 1.1
10 F	0418 6.0 / 1054 0.1 / 1652 5.8 / 2306 0.6	**25** SA	0416 5.3 / 1037 1.0 / 1641 5.2 / 2250 1.1
11 SA	0501 6.0 / 1135 0.2 / 1734 5.6 / 2347 0.7	**26** SU	0445 5.3 / 1105 1.0 / 1710 5.2 / 2321 1.2
12 SU	0546 5.8 / 1216 0.5 / 1817 5.4	**27** M	0517 5.2 / 1137 1.2 / 1744 5.1 / 2354 1.3
13 M	0027 0.9 / 0632 5.5 / 1258 1.0 / 1900 5.1	**28** TU	0553 5.1 / 1211 1.4 / 1820 4.9
14 TU	0111 1.3 / 0723 5.1 / 1343 1.5 / 1948 4.7	**29** W	0031 1.5 / 0635 4.9 / 1254 1.7 / 1903 4.7
15 W	0202 1.6 / 0824 4.6 / 1438 2.0 / ☽ 2047 4.4	**30** TH	0115 1.7 / 0728 4.6 / 1338 2.0 / 1957 4.5

OCTOBER

Day	Time m	Day	Time m
1 F	0214 1.9 / 0835 4.4 / 1445 2.3 / ☽ 2107 4.3	**16** SA	0415 2.1 / 1035 4.1 / 1645 2.5 / 2242 4.3
2 SA	0340 2.0 / 0956 4.3 / 1621 2.3 / 2227 4.4	**17** SU	0541 2.0 / 1152 4.2 / 1800 2.4 / 2356 4.4
3 SU	0513 1.8 / 1121 4.4 / 1747 2.1 / 2343 4.6	**18** M	0642 1.8 / 1250 4.5 / 1855 2.1
4 M	0627 1.4 / 1234 4.8 / 1853 1.8	**19** TU	0052 4.6 / 0726 1.5 / 1334 4.7 / 1938 1.8
5 TU	0048 5.0 / 0726 1.0 / 1331 5.1 / 1946 1.4	**20** W	0137 4.8 / 0804 1.4 / 1411 4.9 / 2015 1.6
6 W	0141 5.4 / 0816 0.6 / 1418 5.4 / 2034 1.0	**21** TH	0214 5.0 / 0837 1.2 / 1443 5.1 / 2049 1.4
7 TH	0228 5.7 / 0902 0.3 / 1502 5.6 / ● 2118 0.8	**22** F	0248 5.1 / 0909 1.1 / 1513 5.2 / 2122 1.2
8 F	0312 5.9 / 0946 0.2 / 1544 5.7 / 2201 0.6	**23** SA	0319 5.2 / 0938 1.0 / 1542 5.3 / ○ 2153 1.1
9 SA	0356 5.9 / 1028 0.3 / 1625 5.7 / 2243 0.6	**24** SU	0350 5.3 / 1007 1.0 / 1612 5.3 / 2226 1.1
10 SU	0440 5.9 / 1109 0.5 / 1707 5.6 / 2324 0.7	**25** M	0421 5.3 / 1038 1.1 / 1644 5.3 / 2300 1.1
11 M	0525 5.6 / 1149 0.8 / 1748 5.4	**26** TU	0457 5.2 / 1113 1.2 / 1719 5.2 / 2337 1.2
12 TU	0006 0.9 / 0612 5.3 / 1230 1.2 / 1830 5.1	**27** W	0538 5.1 / 1150 1.4 / 1758 5.0
13 W	0051 1.2 / 0703 4.9 / 1313 1.7 / 1916 4.8	**28** TH	0018 1.3 / 0624 4.9 / 1232 1.7 / 1843 4.9
14 TH	0141 1.6 / 0802 4.5 / 1404 2.1 / ☽ 2011 4.5	**29** F	0106 1.5 / 0719 4.7 / 1322 2.0 / 1937 4.7
15 F	0248 1.9 / 0913 4.2 / 1517 2.4 / 2121 4.3	**30** SA	0207 1.7 / 0825 4.5 / 1428 2.2 / ☽ 2044 4.6
		31 SU	0325 1.7 / 0940 4.4 / 1556 2.3 / 2159 4.6

NOVEMBER

Day	Time m	Day	Time m
1 M	0446 1.6 / 1057 4.5 / 1716 2.1 / 2313 4.7	**16** TU	0541 1.9 / 1155 4.3 / 1802 2.3 / 2357 4.5
2 TU	0557 1.3 / 1206 4.8 / 1822 1.8	**17** W	0636 1.8 / 1246 4.5 / 1854 2.0
3 W	0018 5.0 / 0657 1.0 / 1304 5.1 / 1918 1.5	**18** TH	0050 4.6 / 0720 1.6 / 1329 4.7 / 1937 1.8
4 TH	0115 5.3 / 0750 0.8 / 1353 5.3 / 2009 1.2	**19** F	0135 4.8 / 0759 1.4 / 1407 4.9 / 2017 1.5
5 F	0206 5.5 / 0838 0.6 / 1438 5.5 / 2056 0.9	**20** SA	0215 4.9 / 0835 1.3 / 1441 5.1 / 2054 1.3
6 SA	0253 5.6 / 0922 0.6 / 1521 5.5 / ● 2141 0.8	**21** SU	0252 5.1 / 0908 1.2 / 1514 5.2 / ○ 2130 1.2
7 SU	0339 5.6 / 1005 0.7 / 1602 5.5 / 2225 0.8	**22** M	0329 5.1 / 0943 1.2 / 1549 5.3 / 2208 1.1
8 M	0424 5.6 / 1047 0.9 / 1643 5.5 / 2308 0.8	**23** TU	0406 5.2 / 1019 1.2 / 1625 5.3 / 2247 1.0
9 TU	0510 5.4 / 1127 1.1 / 1724 5.4 / 2351 1.0	**24** W	0447 5.2 / 1058 1.3 / 1704 5.3 / 2328 1.0
10 W	0557 5.1 / 1207 1.4 / 1805 5.2	**25** TH	0531 5.1 / 1139 1.4 / 1745 5.2
11 TH	0035 1.2 / 0646 4.9 / 1248 1.7 / 1849 5.0	**26** F	0013 1.1 / 0619 5.0 / 1224 1.6 / 1831 5.1
12 F	0123 1.5 / 0738 4.6 / 1334 2.1 / 1937 4.7	**27** SA	0103 1.2 / 0713 4.9 / 1314 1.8 / 1923 5.0
13 SA	0217 1.7 / 0838 4.3 / 1431 2.3 / ☽ 2036 4.5	**28** SU	0200 1.3 / 0813 4.7 / 1414 2.0 / ☽ 2023 4.9
14 SU	0322 1.9 / 0945 4.2 / 1543 2.5 / 2145 4.4	**29** M	0304 1.4 / 0918 4.6 / 1526 2.1 / 2130 4.8
15 M	0434 2.0 / 1053 4.2 / 1658 2.4 / 2255 4.4	**30** TU	0413 1.4 / 1027 4.6 / 1639 2.0 / 2240 4.8

DECEMBER

Day	Time m	Day	Time m
1 W	0521 1.3 / 1133 4.7 / 1748 1.9 / 2348 4.9	**16** TH	0527 2.0 / 1145 4.3 / 1758 2.2 / 2356 4.4
2 TH	0626 1.2 / 1235 4.9 / 1852 1.6	**17** F	0627 1.9 / 1239 4.5 / 1855 2.0
3 F	0051 5.1 / 0725 1.1 / 1330 5.1 / 1949 1.4	**18** SA	0052 4.5 / 0718 1.7 / 1327 4.7 / 1944 1.7
4 SA	0149 5.2 / 0817 1.0 / 1419 5.2 / 2041 1.2	**19** SU	0143 4.7 / 0803 1.5 / 1410 4.9 / 2029 1.5
5 SU	0241 5.3 / 0904 1.0 / 1504 5.3 / ● 2129 1.0	**20** M	0229 4.9 / 0845 1.3 / 1451 5.1 / 2112 1.2
6 M	0330 5.3 / 0948 1.1 / 1546 5.4 / 2214 0.9	**21** TU	0312 5.1 / 0926 1.3 / 1531 5.3 / ○ 2155 1.0
7 TU	0416 5.3 / 1030 1.1 / 1626 5.4 / 2257 0.9	**22** W	0355 5.2 / 1008 1.2 / 1611 5.4 / 2238 0.8
8 W	0500 5.2 / 1110 1.3 / 1705 5.3 / 2338 1.0	**23** TH	0439 5.3 / 1050 1.2 / 1652 5.5 / 2323 0.7
9 TH	0544 5.0 / 1148 1.5 / 1744 5.3	**24** F	0525 5.3 / 1133 1.2 / 1734 5.5
10 F	0019 1.1 / 0626 4.9 / 1226 1.7 / 1824 5.1	**25** SA	0008 0.7 / 0611 5.2 / 1218 1.3 / 1819 5.5
11 SA	0059 1.3 / 0710 4.7 / 1304 1.9 / 1906 4.9	**26** SU	0055 0.7 / 0701 5.1 / 1304 1.4 / 1907 5.4
12 SU	0141 1.5 / 0756 4.5 / 1346 2.1 / 1953 4.7	**27** M	0144 0.9 / 0753 5.0 / 1354 1.6 / 2000 5.2
13 M	0227 1.7 / 0847 4.3 / 1438 2.3 / ☽ 2047 4.5	**28** TU	0238 1.1 / 0850 4.8 / 1453 1.8 / ☽ 2101 5.0
14 TU	0321 1.9 / 0945 4.3 / 1542 2.4 / 2148 4.4	**29** W	0339 1.3 / 0952 4.6 / 1600 1.9 / 2209 4.8
15 W	0423 2.0 / 1045 4.2 / 1652 2.4 / 2253 4.3	**30** TH	0446 1.5 / 1059 4.6 / 1715 2.0 / 2321 4.7
		31 F	0558 1.6 / 1207 4.6 / 1831 1.8

Chart Datum: 2·85 metres below Ordnance Datum (Newlyn). HAT is 6·1metres above Chart Datum; see 0.19

3.13 HARTLEPOOL

Hartlepool **54°41′·26N 01°11′·90W** (West Hbr ent) 🌸🌸🌸🌸🌸🌸🌸🌸

CHARTS AC 152, 2567, 2566; Imray C24.

TIDES +0437 Dover; ML 3·0; Duration 0600

Standard Port RIVER TEES (←—)

Times				Height (metres)			
High Water		Low Water		MHWS	MHWN	MLWN	MLWS
0000	0600	0000	0600	5·5	4·3	2·0	0·9
1200	1800	1200	1800				
Differences HARTLEPOOL							
−0004	−0004	−0006	−0006	−0·1	−0·1	−0·2	−0·1
MIDDLESBROUGH							
0000	+0002	0000	−0003	+0·1	+0·2	+0·1	−0·1

SHELTER Excellent in marina (5m). Strong E/SE winds raise broken water and swell in the bay, making ent channel hazardous, but possible. In such conditions, ask marina's advice.

NAVIGATION WPT 54°40′·86N 01°09′·90W, Longscar ECM buoy, 295°/1·06M to W Hbr ent. (For Victoria Hbr, 308°/0·65M to Nos 1/ 2 buoys.) From S, beware Longscar Rks, 4ca WSW of WPT. Note: Tees Fairway SWM buoy, (54°40′·94N 01°06′·47W) is 2M E of Longscar ECM buoy and may assist the initial landfall. Speed limit 4kn in W Hbr and Marina.

LIGHTS AND MARKS Steetly Works chimney, 1·4M NW of marina ent, and St Hilda's Church tower on The Heugh, are both prominent. Dir lt Fl WRG leads 308° to marina lock, between W Hbr outer piers, Oc R and Oc G, and inner piers, FR and FG; bright street lts on S pier.

Lock sigs: ● = Proceed; ● = Wait; ● ● = Lock closed.

Dir lt, Iso WRG, leads 325° via lit buoyed chan to Victoria Hbr.

R/T Marina Ch **M**, 80. *Tees Port Control* info Ch 14, 22 (H24). *Hartlepool Dock Radio* Ch 12, only for ship docking.

TELEPHONE (Code 01429) MRCC 01262 672317; Tees Port Authority (01642) 277205; Marinecall 09068 969643; ⊖ (0191) 257 9441; Police 221151; Dr 272679.

FACILITIES

Hartlepool Marina Access HW±3 via chan dredged to CD and lock (max beam 8.5m) H24, over tidal cill 0.8m below CD. ☎ 865744, www.hartlepool-marina.com, 500+100 **Ⓥ**, £2. D (H24), LPG, BY, El, ME, CH, SM, 🔧, 🔲, ♿, ⚓, BH (40 and 300 tons), Wi-fi, C (13 tons), Gas, Gaz.

Victoria Hbr (commercial dock, not normally for yachts), access H24. Call *Tees Port Control* Ch 14 for short-stay.

Tees & Hartlepool YC ☎ 233423, Bar, Slip.

Town P (cans), 🛒 (H24), R, Bar, ✉, Ⓑ, 🚉, ✈ (Teesside).

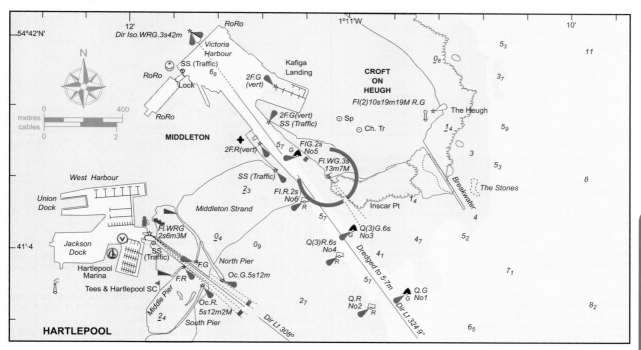

HARTLEPOOL TO SOUTHERN NETHERLANDS

(Charts 2182A, 1191, 1190, 1503, 1408, 1610, 3371, 110) From abeam Whitby the passage can, theoretically, be made on one direct course, but this would conflict with oil/gas activities and platforms including Rough and Amethyst fields off Humber, Hewett off Cromer and very extensive fields further offshore. Commercial, oil-rig support and fishing vessels may be met S of Flamborough Hd and particularly off NE Norfolk where it is advisable to follow an inshore track.

After passing Flamborough Hd, Dowsing B1D, Dudgeon lt buoy and Newarp lt F, either:

Proceed SE'ly to take departure from the Outer Gabbard; thence cross N Hinder South TSS at right angles before heading for Roompotsluis via Middelbank and subsequent buoyed chan.

Or set course ESE from the vicinity of Cross Sand lt buoy and Smith's Knoll, so as to cross the N/S deep-water traffic routes to the E. Thence alter SE towards Hoek van Holland, keeping N of Maas Approaches TSS.

HARTLEPOOL TO THE GERMAN BIGHT

(Charts 2182A, 1191, 266, 1405) Taking departure eastward from abeam Whitby High lt, skirt the SW Patch off Dogger Bank, keeping clear S of Gordon Gas Field and then N of German Bight W Approach TSS. Thence head for the Elbe or Helgoland; the latter may also serve as a convenient haven in order to adjust the passage for Elbe tides and streams, without greatly increasing passage distance. ▶ *Tidal streams are less than 1kn away from the coast and run E/W along much of the route.* ◀

3.14 SEAHAM

Durham 54°50′·24N 01°19′·28W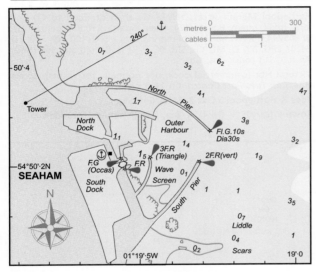

CHARTS AC 152, 1627; Imray C24.

TIDES +0435 Dover; ML 3·0; Duration 0600

Standard Port RIVER TEES (←)

Times				Height (metres)			
High Water		Low Water		MHWS	MHWN	MLWN	MLWS
0000	0600	0000	0600	5·5	4·3	2·0	0·9
1200	1800	1200	1800				
Differences SEAHAM							
−0015	−0015	−0015	−0015	−0·3	−0·2	0·0	−0·2

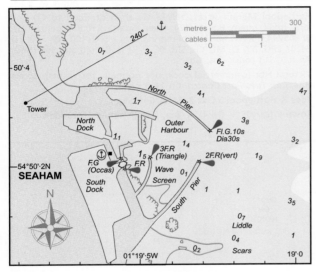

SHELTER Prior to arrival visiting yachts should confirm with HM availability/suitability of berth. Small craft normally berth in North Dock, which dries and is under development. Shelter is variable and dock can be subject to considerable swell. South Dock is not usually available to non-commercial vessels. Speed limit 5kn. Or ⚓ 2½ca offshore with clock tower in transit 240° with St John's church tower.

NAVIGATION WPT 54°50′·36N 01°18′·60W (off chartlet), 256°/ 0·40M to N breakwater lighthouse. Shoals and rocks to S of S breakwater (Liddle Scars). Entrance should not be attempted in strong on-shore winds.

LIGHTS AND MARKS No leading lights, but harbour is easily identified by lighthouse (W with B bands) on N pier, Fl G 10s 12m 5M, Dia 30s (sounded HW–2½ to +1½). FS at NE corner of S dock on with N lighthouse leads in 256° clear of Tangle Rocks. 3FR lts on wave screen are in form of a △.

Traffic sigs at S Dock: ● = Vessels enter: ● = Vessels leave.

R/T VHF Ch 12 16 06 0800–1700 (Mon-Fri).

TELEPHONE (Code 0191) HM 07786 565205; Admin Office 5161700; MRCC 01262 672317; Marinecall 09068 969643; Police 0345 6060365; Dr 5812332.

FACILITIES S Dock (Seaham Hbr Dock Co) ☎ 516 1700, AB £5 but normally no charge for the odd night, L, FW, C (40 ton), AB; **N Dock** M. **Town** (½M) P, D, FW, ME, El, CH (5M), 🛒, R, Bar, ✉, Ⓑ, ⇌, ✈ (Teesside or Newcastle).

3.15 SUNDERLAND

Tyne and Wear 54°55′·23N 01°21′·15W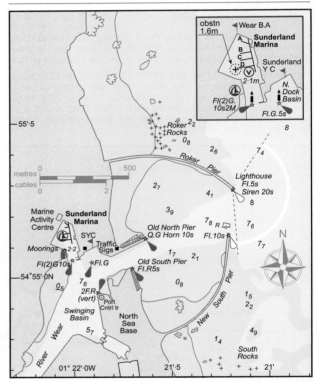

CHARTS AC 152, 1627; Imray C24.

TIDES +0430 Dover; ML 2·9; Duration 0600; Zone 0 (UT)

Standard Port RIVER TEES (←)

Times				Height (metres)			
High Water		Low Water		MHWS	MHWN	MLWN	MLWS
0000	0600	0000	0600	5·5	4·3	2·0	0·9
1200	1800	1200	1800				
Differences SUNDERLAND							
−0017	−0017	−0016	−0016	−0·3	−0·1	0·0	−0·1

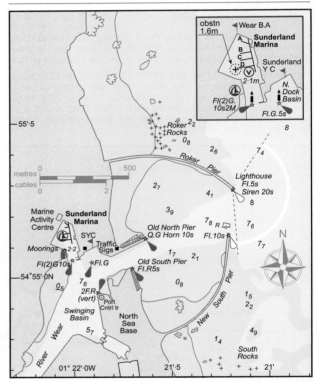

SHELTER Very good, but strong E'lies cause heavy swell in ent and outer hbr. Marina is protected by a fixed breakwater; access H24.

NAVIGATION WPT 54°55′·21N 01°20′·10W, 278°/0·61M to Roker Pier lt. Beware wreck at Whitburn Steel about 1M N of ent, and Hendon Rk (0·9m), 1·2M SE of hbr ent.

Appr to marina ent is marked by SHM dolphin, Fl G 5s, and E jetty, Fl (2) G 10s. Close (4m) SSW of end of pontoon D, beware substantial obst'n (1·6m) in surrounding depth 2·1m, see chartlet.

LIGHTS AND MARKS 3 Fl ● at Pilot Stn (Old N Pier) = danger in harbour; no entry/departure.

R/T Sunderland Marina Ch M, 80. Port VHF Ch 14 (H24); tide and visibility reports on request.

TELEPHONE (Code 0191) HM 567 2626 (HO), 567 0161 (OT); MRCC 01262 672317; ✆ (0191) 257 9441; Marinecall 09068 969643; Police 454 7555; Ⓗ 565 6256.

FACILITIES **Sunderland Marina** 120 pontoon berths in 2·1m, max LOA 13m; and 110 moorings. ☎ 5144721. Ⓥ (if available) £2.05/m; M £10/craft, ⚓, D (H24), Slip, FW, ⚓.
Sunderland YC ☎ 567 5133, FW, AB, Bar, Slip (dinghy).
Wear Boating Association ☎ 567 5313, AB. **Town** P (cans), Gas, Gaz, CH, El, ME, SM, 🛒, R, Bar, ✉, 🖾, Ⓑ, ⇌, ✈ (Newcastle).

3.16 R TYNE/NORTH SHIELDS

Tyne and Wear 55°00'·89N 01°24'·10W ❄❄⚓⚓⚓❀❀

CHARTS AC 152, 1191, 1934; Imray C24.

TIDES +0430 Dover; ML 3·0; Duration 0604

Standard Port NORTH SHIELDS (→)

Times				Height (metres)			
High Water		Low Water		MHWS	MHWN	MLWN	MLWS
0200	0800	0100	0800	5·0	3·9	1·8	0·7
1400	2000	1300	2000				
Differences NEWCASTLE-UPON-TYNE							
+0003	+0003	+0008	+0008	+0·3	+0·2	+0·1	+0·1

SHELTER Good in all weather. Access H24, but in strong E and NE winds appr may be difficult for smaller craft due to much backwash off the piers. Confused seas can build at the ent in severe weather, and a large steep swell can break dangerously when meeting an ebb tide up to half a mile inside the harbour. In emergency or as a refuge yachts may berth on Fish Quay; contact HM.

NAVIGATION WPT 55°01'·01N 01°22'·32W, 258°/1·1M to hbr ent. From S, no dangers. From N, beware Bellhues Rk (approx 1M N of hbr and ¾M off shore); give N pier a wide berth. Dredged chan in Lower Hbr is buoyed. 6kn speed limit in the river west of Herd Groyne Lt Ho.

Proceed up/down river under power keeping to the starboard side. Tacking across the channel is not permitted. The 7 bridges at Newcastle have least clearance above HAT of 23m, or 3·7m when Millennium Bridge is closed.

LIGHTS AND MARKS See 3.3 and chartlet.

R/T *Tyne VTS* Ch **12**, 11 (H24). Royal Quays marina Ch 80. St Peter's Marina Ch **80** M.

TELEPHONE (Code 0191) HM 2570407; Tyne VTS 2572080; MRCC 01262 672317; Marinecall 09068 969643; Met 2326453; Police 2146555; Doctor via Tyne VTS; Ⓗ (Tynemouth) 2596660; Ⓗ (Newcastle) 2325131.

FACILITIES Notes: A conservancy fee (£10) may be levied by the Port Authority on all visiting craft. Craft waiting to enter the marinas should do so outside the fairway.

Royal Quays Marina 54°59'·79N 01°26'·84W, in former Albert Edward Dock, is 2M upriver from pierheads. ☎ 2728282; 302 berths inc Ⓥ, 7·9m depth; £2·15. S lock (42.5m x 7·5m) departures H and H+30; arrivals H+15 and H+45, or on request at quiet times. H24. Waiting pontoon outside lock. BY, BH (30 ton), D, P (H24), FW, ⬚, Bar, El, Gas, Gaz, 🛒, Wi-fi. **St Peter's Marina** 54°57'·94N 01°34'·35W, 8M upriver, and 1M E of city. ☎ 2654472; 140 + 20 Ⓥ, £2.27. Access approx HW±3½ over sill, 0·8m below CD, which retains 2·5m within. Tfc lts at ent. D&P on pontoon outside ent in 2m, ⬚. **Services.** Slip, ME, ✖, C, ACA, Ⓔ. **Millennium Bridge** in city centre, limited pontoon berthing; pre-book ☎ 2211363.

City. All amenities, ⇌ (Newcastle/S Shields), ✈ (Newcastle). **Ferries:** Ijmuiden; daily; 16 hrs; DFDS (www.dfdsseaways.co.uk).

ADJACENT HARBOUR
CULLERCOATS, Tyne & Wear, **55°02'·08N 01°25'·81W.** AC 1191. +0430 Dover. Tides as 3.16. Small drying hbr 1·6M N of R Tyne ent. Appr on ldg line 256°, two bns (FR lts), between drying rks. An occas fair weather ⚓ or dry against S pier. Facilities at Tynemouth.

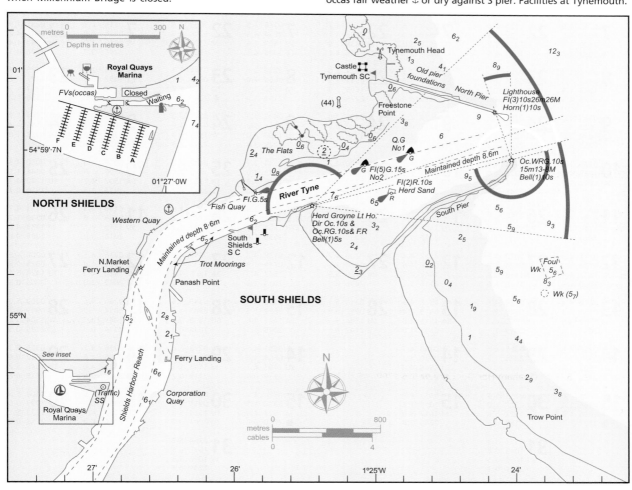

TIME ZONE (UT)
For Summer Time add ONE hour in **non-shaded areas**

RIVER TYNE/NORTH SHIELDS LAT 55°01′N LONG 1°26′W
TIMES AND HEIGHTS OF HIGH AND LOW WATERS

Dates in red are SPRINGS
Dates in blue are NEAPS

YEAR 2010

JANUARY

Day	Time	m		Day	Time	m
1 F	0320 / 0939 / 1536 / 2210	5.1 / 1.0 / 5.2 / 0.6		**16** SA	0408 / 1008 / 1608 / 2239	4.7 / 1.3 / 4.9 / 1.0
2 SA	0409 / 1026 / 1620 / 2259	5.2 / 1.0 / 5.3 / 0.4		**17** SU	0441 / 1039 / 1639 / 2310	4.7 / 1.3 / 5.0 / 1.0
3 SU	0458 / 1111 / 1705 / 2347	5.2 / 1.0 / 5.4 / 0.4		**18** M	0512 / 1109 / 1710 / 2340	4.7 / 1.3 / 5.0 / 1.0
4 M	0546 / 1156 / 1752	5.2 / 1.1 / 5.3		**19** TU	0544 / 1140 / 1743	4.6 / 1.3 / 4.9
5 TU	0035 / 0636 / 1241 / 1841	0.5 / 5.0 / 1.2 / 5.2		**20** W	0012 / 0616 / 1212 / 1816	1.1 / 4.5 / 1.4 / 4.8
6 W	0124 / 0727 / 1328 / 1934	0.7 / 4.7 / 1.4 / 5.0		**21** TH	0045 / 0651 / 1245 / 1852	1.2 / 4.4 / 1.6 / 4.7
7 TH	0215 / 0822 / 1420 / 2033	1.0 / 4.5 / 1.6 / 4.8		**22** F	0121 / 0729 / 1323 / 1933	1.4 / 4.3 / 1.7 / 4.5
8 F	0311 / 0921 / 1523 / 2139	1.3 / 4.3 / 1.9 / 4.5		**23** SA	0201 / 0815 / 1410 / 2024	1.6 / 4.2 / 1.9 / 4.3
9 SA	0415 / 1026 / 1640 / 2253	1.6 / 4.2 / 2.0 / 4.3		**24** SU	0253 / 0912 / 1515 / 2128	1.8 / 4.0 / 2.1 / 4.2
10 SU	0525 / 1135 / 1802	1.8 / 4.2 / 1.9		**25** M	0404 / 1023 / 1641 / 2248	1.9 / 4.0 / 2.1 / 4.1
11 M	0009 / 0635 / 1242 / 1914	4.3 / 1.8 / 4.3 / 1.8		**26** TU	0527 / 1142 / 1807	1.9 / 4.1 / 1.9
12 TU	0117 / 0734 / 1337 / 2010	4.3 / 1.8 / 4.4 / 1.6		**27** W	0012 / 0644 / 1253 / 1920	4.2 / 1.7 / 4.3 / 1.5
13 W	0212 / 0821 / 1423 / 2054	4.4 / 1.7 / 4.6 / 1.4		**28** TH	0124 / 0748 / 1349 / 2019	4.5 / 1.5 / 4.7 / 1.1
14 TH	0256 / 0901 / 1502 / 2133	4.6 / 1.5 / 4.8 / 1.2		**29** F	0221 / 0841 / 1438 / 2111	4.8 / 1.2 / 5.0 / 0.7
15 F	0334 / 0936 / 1536 / 2207	4.6 / 1.4 / 4.9 / 1.1		**30** SA	0311 / 0929 / 1522 / 2159	5.1 / 1.0 / 5.3 / 0.3
				31 SU	0357 / 1013 / 1606 / 2246	5.3 / 0.8 / 5.5 / 0.1

FEBRUARY

Day	Time	m		Day	Time	m
1 M	0442 / 1056 / 1649 / 2330	5.3 / 0.7 / 5.6 / 0.1		**16** TU	0446 / 1047 / 1646 / 2314	4.8 / 1.1 / 5.0 / 0.8
2 TU	0526 / 1137 / 1733	5.2 / 0.8 / 5.5		**17** W	0514 / 1116 / 1716 / 2343	4.7 / 1.1 / 5.0 / 0.9
3 W	0014 / 0610 / 1217 / 1818	0.3 / 5.1 / 0.9 / 5.4		**18** TH	0544 / 1145 / 1747	4.7 / 1.2 / 4.9
4 TH	0057 / 0655 / 1259 / 1906	0.6 / 4.8 / 1.1 / 5.1		**19** F	0013 / 0614 / 1217 / 1821	1.0 / 4.6 / 1.3 / 4.8
5 F	0140 / 0743 / 1344 / 2000	1.0 / 4.5 / 1.4 / 4.7		**20** SA	0044 / 0649 / 1251 / 1900	1.2 / 4.4 / 1.4 / 4.6
6 SA	0229 / 0837 / 1440 / 2104	1.4 / 4.3 / 1.8 / 4.3		**21** SU	0120 / 0731 / 1335 / 1950	1.4 / 4.3 / 1.7 / 4.4
7 SU	0328 / 0940 / 1558 / 2221	1.8 / 4.0 / 2.0 / 4.1		**22** M	0208 / 0826 / 1438 / 2056	1.7 / 4.1 / 1.9 / 4.1
8 M	0445 / 1056 / 1737 / 2350	2.1 / 3.9 / 2.0 / 4.0		**23** TU	0321 / 0941 / 1609 / 2226	2.0 / 3.9 / 2.0 / 4.0
9 TU	0613 / 1217 / 1904	2.1 / 4.0 / 1.9		**24** W	0501 / 1112 / 1748	2.0 / 4.0 / 1.8
10 W	0106 / 0721 / 1321 / 2000	4.1 / 2.0 / 4.2 / 1.6		**25** TH	0000 / 0630 / 1232 / 1906	4.2 / 1.8 / 4.3 / 1.4
11 TH	0202 / 0809 / 1409 / 2042	4.3 / 1.8 / 4.5 / 1.4		**26** F	0113 / 0735 / 1332 / 2005	4.5 / 1.5 / 4.6 / 0.9
12 F	0243 / 0846 / 1447 / 2116	4.4 / 1.6 / 4.7 / 1.2		**27** SA	0208 / 0826 / 1420 / 2056	4.8 / 1.2 / 5.0 / 0.5
13 SA	0318 / 0919 / 1519 / 2147	4.6 / 1.4 / 4.8 / 1.0		**28** SU	0255 / 0912 / 1504 / 2142	5.1 / 0.9 / 5.3 / 0.2
14 SU	0348 / 0950 / 1548 / 2217	4.7 / 1.2 / 4.9 / 0.9				
15 M	0417 / 1019 / 1617 / 2246	4.7 / 1.1 / 5.0 / 0.8				

MARCH

Day	Time	m		Day	Time	m
1 M	0338 / 0954 / 1546 / 2226	5.3 / 0.7 / 5.5 / 0.0		**16** TU	0348 / 0954 / 1550 / 2216	4.8 / 1.0 / 5.0 / 0.7
2 TU	0420 / 1034 / 1628 / 2307	5.3 / 0.6 / 5.6 / 0.1		**17** W	0416 / 1023 / 1619 / 2245	4.8 / 0.9 / 5.0 / 0.7
3 W	0500 / 1114 / 1710 / 2347	5.2 / 0.6 / 5.5 / 0.3		**18** TH	0444 / 1052 / 1649 / 2314	4.8 / 0.9 / 5.0 / 0.8
4 TH	0541 / 1152 / 1755	5.1 / 0.7 / 5.3		**19** F	0513 / 1122 / 1722 / 2344	4.8 / 1.0 / 4.9 / 1.0
5 F	0026 / 0622 / 1232 / 1841	0.6 / 4.8 / 1.0 / 5.0		**20** SA	0545 / 1155 / 1758	4.7 / 1.1 / 4.8
6 SA	0105 / 0705 / 1315 / 1933	1.1 / 4.6 / 1.3 / 4.6		**21** SU	0015 / 0620 / 1233 / 1841	1.2 / 4.5 / 1.3 / 4.6
7 SU	0148 / 0754 / 1407 / 2034	1.5 / 4.3 / 1.6 / 4.2		**22** M	0053 / 0704 / 1320 / 1935	1.4 / 4.4 / 1.5 / 4.3
8 M	0242 / 0855 / 1520 / 2151	2.0 / 4.0 / 1.9 / 3.9		**23** TU	0144 / 0800 / 1426 / 2046	1.7 / 4.1 / 1.7 / 4.1
9 TU	0402 / 1014 / 1706 / 2323	2.3 / 3.8 / 2.0 / 3.8		**24** W	0302 / 0918 / 1557 / 2218	2.0 / 4.0 / 1.7 / 4.0
10 W	0544 / 1143 / 1840	2.3 / 3.9 / 1.9		**25** TH	0445 / 1049 / 1732 / 2347	2.0 / 4.0 / 1.5 / 4.2
11 TH	0044 / 0657 / 1254 / 1935	3.9 / 2.1 / 4.1 / 1.6		**26** F	0612 / 1209 / 1847	1.8 / 4.3 / 1.2
12 F	0139 / 0745 / 1343 / 2015	4.2 / 1.8 / 4.3 / 1.3		**27** SA	0056 / 0715 / 1309 / 1945	4.5 / 1.5 / 4.7 / 0.8
13 SA	0218 / 0822 / 1421 / 2048	4.4 / 1.6 / 4.6 / 1.1		**28** SU	0149 / 0805 / 1358 / 2034	4.8 / 1.1 / 5.0 / 0.4
14 SU	0251 / 0854 / 1453 / 2119	4.5 / 1.3 / 4.7 / 0.9		**29** M	0233 / 0849 / 1441 / 2119	5.0 / 0.8 / 5.3 / 0.2
15 M	0320 / 0924 / 1522 / 2148	4.7 / 1.1 / 4.9 / 0.8		**30** TU	0314 / 0931 / 1524 / 2201	5.2 / 0.6 / 5.4 / 0.2
				31 W	0354 / 1012 / 1606 / 2241	5.2 / 0.5 / 5.5 / 0.3

APRIL

Day	Time	m		Day	Time	m
1 TH	0433 / 1051 / 1649 / 2319	5.2 / 0.6 / 5.3 / 0.5		**16** F	0415 / 1030 / 1627 / 2248	4.8 / 0.9 / 4.9 / 0.9
2 F	0512 / 1131 / 1734 / 2356	5.0 / 0.7 / 5.1 / 0.8		**17** SA	0447 / 1105 / 1704 / 2321	4.8 / 0.9 / 4.9 / 1.0
3 SA	0552 / 1210 / 1821	4.8 / 0.9 / 4.8		**18** SU	0523 / 1143 / 1746 / 2358	4.8 / 0.9 / 4.7 / 1.2
4 SU	0033 / 0633 / 1253 / 1911	1.2 / 4.6 / 1.2 / 4.4		**19** M	0603 / 1226 / 1835	4.6 / 1.1 / 4.6
5 M	0113 / 0719 / 1342 / 2009	1.6 / 4.3 / 1.5 / 4.1		**20** TU	0042 / 0650 / 1320 / 1933	1.5 / 4.5 / 1.2 / 4.3
6 TU	0203 / 0816 / 1448 / 2119	2.0 / 4.0 / 1.8 / 3.8		**21** W	0139 / 0749 / 1427 / 2046	1.7 / 4.3 / 1.4 / 4.2
7 W	0316 / 0928 / 1619 / 2241	2.3 / 3.9 / 1.9 / 3.7		**22** TH	0255 / 0904 / 1549 / 2208	1.9 / 4.2 / 1.4 / 4.1
8 TH	0454 / 1052 / 1751	2.3 / 3.8 / 1.8		**23** F	0426 / 1027 / 1711 / 2326	1.9 / 4.2 / 1.3 / 4.2
9 F	0001 / 0613 / 1208 / 1851	3.8 / 2.1 / 4.0 / 1.6		**24** SA	0544 / 1141 / 1821	1.7 / 4.4 / 1.0
10 SA	0059 / 0706 / 1302 / 1934	4.0 / 1.9 / 4.2 / 1.4		**25** SU	0030 / 0646 / 1242 / 1918	4.5 / 1.5 / 4.5 / 0.7
11 SU	0140 / 0746 / 1343 / 2010	4.3 / 1.6 / 4.4 / 1.2		**26** M	0123 / 0739 / 1333 / 2008	4.7 / 1.2 / 4.9 / 0.6
12 M	0215 / 0821 / 1418 / 2042	4.5 / 1.4 / 4.6 / 1.0		**27** TU	0208 / 0825 / 1420 / 2053	4.9 / 0.9 / 5.1 / 0.5
13 TU	0246 / 0854 / 1449 / 2114	4.6 / 1.2 / 4.7 / 0.9		**28** W	0250 / 0909 / 1504 / 2135	5.0 / 0.7 / 5.2 / 0.5
14 W	0316 / 0925 / 1520 / 2144	4.7 / 1.0 / 4.9 / 0.9		**29** TH	0329 / 0952 / 1548 / 2215	5.1 / 0.6 / 5.2 / 0.6
15 TH	0345 / 0957 / 1553 / 2216	4.8 / 0.9 / 4.9 / 0.8		**30** F	0408 / 1033 / 1633 / 2253	5.0 / 0.6 / 5.1 / 0.8

Chart Datum: 2·60 metres below Ordnance Datum (Newlyn). HAT is 5·7 metres above Chart Datum; see 0.19

RIVER TYNE/NORTH SHIELDS   LAT 55°01'N LONG 1°26'W
TIMES AND HEIGHTS OF HIGH AND LOW WATERS

TIME ZONE (UT)
For Summer Time add ONE hour in **non-shaded areas**

Dates in red are SPRINGS
Dates in blue are NEAPS

YEAR 2010

MAY

Time	m	Time	m
1 0447 1114 SA 1718 2330	4.9 0.7 4.9 1.1	**16** 0428 1054 SU 1654 2308	4.9 0.8 4.9 1.0
2 0527 1154 SU 1804	4.8 0.9 4.6	**17** 0508 1138 M 1741 2352	4.9 0.8 4.8 1.2
3 0006 0607 M 1236 1851	1.4 4.6 1.1 4.3	**18** 0553 1226 TU 1833	4.8 0.8 4.6
4 0046 0651 TU 1321 1944	1.7 4.4 1.4 4.1	**19** 0040 0643 W 1321 1932	1.4 4.7 0.9 4.5
5 0131 0742 W 1416 2043	1.9 4.2 1.6 3.9	**20** 0136 0741 TH 1423 2038	1.6 4.5 1.0 4.3
6 0230 0843 TH 1524 2149	2.1 4.0 1.7 3.8	**21** 0242 0848 F 1533 2148	1.7 4.4 1.1 4.3
7 0348 0953 F 1639 2258	2.2 3.9 1.8 3.8	**22** 0357 1000 SA 1643 2257	1.8 4.4 1.1 4.3
8 0507 1103 SA 1746	2.1 3.9 1.7	**23** 0510 1110 SU 1750	1.7 4.5 1.0
9 0000 0610 SU 1205 1839	3.9 2.0 4.1 1.5	**24** 0000 0614 M 1215 1849	4.4 1.5 4.6 0.9
10 0051 0700 M 1255 1922	4.1 1.7 4.3 1.3	**25** 0056 0713 TU 1311 1942	4.6 1.3 4.7 0.9
11 0132 0741 TU 1337 2001	4.3 1.5 4.4 1.2	**26** 0144 0805 W 1403 2030	4.7 1.1 4.8 0.9
12 0208 0820 W 1415 2038	4.5 1.3 4.6 1.0	**27** 0228 0852 TH 1451 2113	4.8 0.9 4.9 0.9
13 0242 0857 TH 1452 2114	4.7 1.1 4.7 0.9	**28** 0310 0937 F 1537 2154	4.8 0.8 4.9 1.0
14 0316 0934 F 1530 2150	4.8 0.9 4.8 0.9	**29** 0349 1020 SA 1621 2232	4.9 0.8 4.8 1.1
15 0351 1013 SA 1611 2228	4.9 0.8 4.9 0.9	**30** 0428 1100 SU 1705 2309	4.9 0.8 4.7 1.2
		31 0507 1139 M 1747 2344	4.8 0.9 4.5 1.4

JUNE

Time	m	Time	m
1 0546 1218 TU 1830	4.7 1.1 4.4	**16** 0544 1223 W 1827	5.0 0.5 4.8
2 0021 0626 W 1258 1914	1.6 4.6 1.2 4.2	**17** 0033 0632 TH 1314 1920	1.2 5.0 0.6 4.7
3 0102 0710 TH 1342 2002	1.7 4.4 1.4 4.0	**18** 0123 0726 F 1409 2018	1.3 4.9 0.8 4.5
4 0148 0800 F 1433 2055	1.9 4.2 1.5 3.9	**19** 0219 0826 SA 1508 2119	1.5 4.7 0.9 4.4
5 0245 0856 SA 1531 2153	2.0 4.1 1.7 3.9	**20** 0323 0931 SU 1611 2223	1.6 4.6 1.1 4.3
6 0352 0957 SU 1634 2253	2.1 4.0 1.7 3.9	**21** 0433 1040 M 1717 2328	1.7 4.5 1.2 4.3
7 0501 1109 M 1735 2352	2.0 4.0 1.6 4.0	**22** 0545 1151 TU 1823	1.6 4.5 1.3
8 0604 1159 TU 1830	1.9 4.1 1.5	**23** 0030 0652 W 1257 1921	4.4 1.5 4.5 1.3
9 0044 0657 W 1254 1919	4.2 1.7 4.3 1.4	**24** 0125 0752 TH 1354 2013	4.5 1.3 4.6 1.3
10 0130 0746 TH 1343 2005	4.4 1.4 4.5 1.2	**25** 0213 0843 F 1445 2058	4.6 1.1 4.6 1.2
11 0212 0831 F 1429 2049	4.6 1.2 4.6 1.1	**26** 0256 0929 SA 1530 2138	4.8 1.0 4.7 1.2
12 0252 0915 SA 1514 2132	4.8 0.9 4.8 1.0	**27** 0336 1009 SU 1611 2215	4.8 0.9 4.7 1.2
13 0333 1000 SU 1600 2216	4.9 0.7 4.9 1.0	**28** 0413 1047 M 1650 2250	4.9 0.9 4.7 1.2
14 0414 1046 M 1647 2301	5.0 0.6 4.8 1.0	**29** 0448 1122 TU 1726 2323	4.9 0.9 4.6 1.3
15 0457 1134 TU 1736 2346	5.0 0.5 4.9 1.0	**30** 0524 1156 W 1803 2356	4.8 1.0 4.5 1.4

JULY

Time	m	Time	m
1 0600 1231 TH 1840	4.7 1.1 4.4	**16** 0017 0615 F 1257 1858	0.9 5.3 0.4 4.9
2 0031 0638 F 1308 1919	1.5 4.6 1.2 4.2	**17** 0102 0705 SA 1345 1949	1.1 5.1 0.6 4.6
3 0109 0719 SA 1348 2003	1.6 4.5 1.4 4.1	**18** 0151 0800 SU 1437 2046	1.3 4.9 1.0 4.4
4 0153 0804 SU 1434 2052	1.8 4.3 1.5 4.0	**19** 0248 0903 M 1537 2148	1.5 4.6 1.3 4.2
5 0245 0857 M 1528 2148	1.9 4.2 1.7 3.9	**20** 0359 1014 TU 1646 2257	1.7 4.4 1.6 4.2
6 0351 0958 TU 1632 2251	2.0 4.1 1.8 4.0	**21** 0521 1133 W 1800	1.8 4.2 1.7
7 0505 1105 W 1740 2356	2.0 4.1 1.7 4.1	**22** 0008 0642 TH 1249 1908	4.2 1.7 4.3 1.7
8 0615 1214 TH 1843	1.8 4.2 1.6	**23** 0111 0747 F 1350 2002	4.4 1.4 4.4 1.6
9 0055 0716 F 1318 1940	4.3 1.6 4.4 1.4	**24** 0203 0837 SA 1439 2046	4.5 1.2 4.5 1.5
10 0147 0811 SA 1412 2031	4.5 1.2 4.6 1.2	**25** 0245 0919 SU 1520 2124	4.7 1.1 4.6 1.3
11 0233 0901 SU 1454 2119	4.8 0.9 4.9 1.0	**26** 0322 0955 M 1556 2157	4.8 0.9 4.7 1.2
12 0317 0949 M 1549 2205	5.0 0.6 5.1 0.9	**27** 0355 1028 TU 1629 2229	4.9 0.8 4.7 1.2
13 0400 1036 TU 1635 2249	5.2 0.3 5.2 0.8	**28** 0427 1059 W 1701 2300	5.0 0.8 4.7 1.2
14 0443 1123 W 1722 2333	5.3 0.2 5.2 0.8	**29** 0459 1129 TH 1732 2330	5.0 0.8 4.6 1.2
15 0528 1209 TH 1810	5.4 0.2 5.0	**30** 0531 1200 F 1804	4.9 0.9 4.6
		31 0001 0604 SA 1232 1838	1.3 4.8 1.1 4.4

AUGUST

Time	m	Time	m
1 0034 0640 SU 1306 1915	1.4 4.7 1.3 4.3	**16** 0123 0734 M 1404 2010	1.2 4.9 1.2 4.4
2 0111 0720 M 1344 1957	1.6 4.5 1.5 4.2	**17** 0217 0837 TU 1501 2112	1.5 4.5 1.6 4.2
3 0155 0807 TU 1432 2050	1.8 4.3 1.7 4.0	**18** 0330 0953 W 1615 2226	1.8 4.2 1.9 4.1
4 0254 0907 W 1536 2157	2.0 4.1 1.9 4.0	**19** 0504 1119 TH 1742 2346	1.9 4.0 2.0 4.1
5 0415 1023 TH 1657 2313	2.0 4.0 1.9	**20** 0635 1240 F 1857	1.9 4.1 1.9
6 0541 1147 F 1817	1.9 4.1 1.8	**21** 0056 0738 SA 1341 1949	4.3 1.5 4.3 1.8
7 0026 0655 SA 1301 1922	4.2 1.6 4.4 1.6	**22** 0148 0824 SU 1425 2030	4.5 1.3 4.5 1.6
8 0126 0755 SU 1358 2016	4.5 1.2 4.7 1.3	**23** 0228 0901 M 1501 2104	4.7 1.1 4.6 1.4
9 0215 0846 M 1447 2104	4.9 0.7 5.0 1.0	**24** 0302 0933 TU 1533 2135	4.9 0.9 4.7 1.2
10 0259 0934 TU 1533 2148	5.2 0.4 5.2 0.8	**25** 0333 1002 W 1602 2205	5.0 0.8 4.8 1.1
11 0341 1020 W 1617 2231	5.4 0.1 5.3 0.6	**26** 0402 1031 TH 1631 2234	5.0 0.8 4.8 1.1
12 0424 1105 TH 1700 2313	5.6 0.0 5.3 0.6	**27** 0431 1059 F 1700 2302	5.1 0.8 4.8 1.1
13 0507 1148 F 1744 2354	5.6 0.1 5.2 0.7	**28** 0501 1129 SA 1729 2332	5.0 0.9 4.7 1.2
14 0553 1231 SA 1829	5.5 0.4 5.0	**29** 0533 1157 SU 1800	4.9 1.0 4.6
15 0036 0641 SU 1316 1917	0.9 5.2 0.7 4.7	**30** 0003 0607 M 1228 1834	1.3 4.8 1.2 4.5
		31 0038 0645 TU 1303 1914	1.5 4.7 1.5 4.3

Chart Datum: 2·60 metres below Ordnance Datum (Newlyn). HAT is 5·7 metres above Chart Datum; see 0.19

NE England

TIME ZONE (UT)	RIVER TYNE/NORTH SHIELDS	Dates in red are SPRINGS
For Summer Time add ONE hour in non-shaded areas	LAT 55°01'N LONG 1°26'W	Dates in blue are NEAPS

TIMES AND HEIGHTS OF HIGH AND LOW WATERS

YEAR 2010

SEPTEMBER

Time	m		Time	m
1 0120	1.7	**16**	0305	1.8
0732	4.4		0931	4.0
W 1347	1.7	TH	1542	2.2
☽ 2005	4.2		2152	4.0
2 0219	1.9	**17**	0444	1.9
0834	4.1		1059	3.9
TH 1453	2.0	F	1718	2.3
2114	4.0		2318	4.1
3 0343	2.0	**18**	0616	1.8
0958	4.0		1221	4.1
F 1627	2.1	SA	1835	2.1
2240	4.0			
4 0518	1.8	**19**	0030	4.2
1130	4.1		0715	1.6
SA 1758	1.9	SU	1318	4.3
			1925	1.9
5 0001	4.3	**20**	0123	4.5
0636	1.5		0757	1.3
SU 1245	4.4	M	1400	4.5
1905	1.6		2004	1.6
6 0104	4.6	**21**	0202	4.7
0736	1.0		0831	1.1
M 1341	4.8	TU	1434	4.6
1958	1.3		2037	1.4
7 0153	5.0	**22**	0235	4.9
0827	0.6		0902	1.0
TU 1428	5.1	W	1504	4.8
2044	1.0		2108	1.2
8 0237	5.3	**23**	0305	5.0
0914	0.3		0931	0.9
W 1511	5.3	TH	1532	4.9
● 2127	0.7	○	2138	1.1
9 0319	5.6	**24**	0334	5.1
0958	0.1		0959	0.8
TH 1553	5.4	F	1600	4.9
2208	0.6		2207	1.0
10 0401	5.7	**25**	0403	5.1
1041	0.0		1027	0.8
F 1634	5.4	SA	1628	4.9
2249	0.6		2236	1.0
11 0444	5.7	**26**	0434	5.0
1122	0.2		1056	0.9
SA 1716	5.3	SU	1657	4.9
2330	0.7		2307	1.1
12 0530	5.5	**27**	0506	4.9
1203	0.5		1126	1.1
SU 1759	5.0	M	1728	4.8
			2339	1.2
13 0012	0.9	**28**	0542	4.8
0618	5.2		1157	1.3
M 1245	1.0	TU	1803	4.6
1843	4.8			
14 0058	1.2	**29**	0016	1.4
0711	4.8		0622	4.6
TU 1330	1.4	W	1233	1.5
1934	4.5		1843	4.5
15 0152	1.5	**30**	0101	1.6
0815	4.4		0713	4.4
W 1425	1.9	TH	1319	1.8
☾ 2036	4.2		1936	4.3

OCTOBER

Time	m		Time	m
1 0202	1.8	**16**	0405	1.9
0819	4.2		1022	3.9
F 1429	2.1	SA	1633	2.4
☽ 2047	4.1		2232	4.1
2 0326	1.8	**17**	0532	1.9
0944	4.1		1140	4.0
SA 1605	2.2	SU	1752	2.2
2214	4.1		2347	4.2
3 0458	1.7	**18**	0634	1.7
1112	4.2		1239	4.2
SU 1735	2.0	M	1848	2.0
2334	4.4			
4 0614	1.3	**19**	0043	4.4
1223	4.5		0718	1.5
M 1842	1.7	TU	1323	4.4
			1929	1.7
5 0037	4.7	**20**	0126	4.6
0713	0.9		0754	1.3
TU 1319	4.8	W	1359	4.6
1934	1.3		2005	1.5
6 0128	5.1	**21**	0202	4.7
0803	0.6		0826	1.1
W 1405	5.1	TH	1431	4.7
2020	1.0		2038	1.3
7 0213	5.4	**22**	0234	4.9
0849	0.3		0857	1.0
TH 1447	5.3	F	1501	4.9
● 2103	0.8		2110	1.2
8 0256	5.6	**23**	0306	5.0
0933	0.2		0927	1.0
F 1527	5.4	SA	1530	4.9
2146	0.6	○	2141	1.1
9 0339	5.6	**24**	0338	5.0
1015	0.3		0958	1.0
SA 1608	5.4	SU	1600	5.0
2228	0.6		2214	1.1
10 0424	5.6	**25**	0411	5.0
1056	0.5		1029	1.0
SU 1648	5.3	M	1630	5.0
2310	0.7		2248	1.1
11 0510	5.3	**26**	0446	4.9
1135	0.8		1101	1.2
M 1730	5.1	TU	1704	4.9
2353	0.9		2324	1.1
12 0559	5.0	**27**	0526	4.8
1216	1.2		1136	1.3
TU 1814	4.8	W	1741	4.8
13 0039	1.2	**28**	0006	1.3
0652	4.6		0611	4.7
W 1259	1.7	TH	1217	1.6
1902	4.6		1825	4.6
14 0131	1.5	**29**	0055	1.4
0753	4.3		0704	4.5
TH 1350	2.0	F	1308	1.8
☾ 2000	4.3		1919	4.5
15 0238	1.8	**30**	0156	1.5
0903	4.0		0811	4.3
F 1501	2.3	SA	1415	2.0
2112	4.1	☽	2027	4.3
		31	0312	1.6
			0929	4.2
		SU	1541	2.1
			2146	4.3

NOVEMBER

Time	m		Time	m
1 0433	1.5	**16**	0528	1.8
1047	4.3		1142	4.1
M 1704	2.0	TU	1751	2.2
2302	4.5		2348	4.2
2 0544	1.2	**17**	0624	1.7
1155	4.5		1235	4.2
TU 1811	1.7	W	1844	1.9
3 0007	4.8	**18**	0040	4.4
0645	1.0		0708	1.5
W 1252	4.8	TH	1318	4.4
1906	1.4		1927	1.7
4 0102	5.0	**19**	0124	4.5
0737	0.8		0747	1.4
TH 1340	5.0	F	1356	4.6
1956	1.1		2006	1.5
5 0151	5.2	**20**	0203	4.7
0825	0.6		0823	1.3
F 1423	5.2	SA	1430	4.8
2043	0.9		2043	1.3
6 0238	5.4	**21**	0240	4.8
0909	0.6		0858	1.2
SA 1505	5.3	SU	1503	4.9
● 2128	0.8		2119	1.2
7 0323	5.4	**22**	0317	4.9
0952	0.7		0933	1.1
SU 1545	5.3	M	1536	5.0
2212	0.7		2156	1.1
8 0410	5.3	**23**	0354	5.0
1033	0.9		1009	1.1
M 1626	5.2	TU	1611	5.0
2255	0.8		2235	1.0
9 0457	5.1	**24**	0435	5.0
1112	1.1		1047	1.2
TU 1707	5.1	W	1648	5.0
2338	1.0		2317	1.0
10 0545	4.9	**25**	0518	4.9
1151	1.4		1127	1.3
W 1750	4.9	TH	1729	5.0
11 0022	1.2	**26**	0002	1.0
0634	4.6		0605	4.8
TH 1232	1.7	F	1211	1.5
1835	4.7		1814	4.9
12 0110	1.4	**27**	0052	1.1
0727	4.3		0658	4.6
F 1317	2.0	SA	1301	1.7
1925	4.4		1906	4.7
13 0204	1.7	**28**	0148	1.2
0825	4.1		0758	4.5
SA 1412	2.2	SU	1359	1.8
☽ 2025	4.2	☽	2007	4.6
14 0308	1.8	**29**	0252	1.3
0930	4.0		0906	4.4
SU 1525	2.3	M	1509	1.9
2134	4.1		2116	4.6
15 0421	1.9	**30**	0402	1.3
1038	3.9		1015	4.4
M 1644	2.3	TU	1625	1.9
2244	4.1		2228	4.6

DECEMBER

Time	m		Time	m
1 0511	1.3	**16**	0516	1.9
1123	4.5		1134	4.0
W 1736	1.8	TH	1746	2.1
2337	4.7		2344	4.2
2 0615	1.2	**17**	0616	1.8
1223	4.6		1231	4.2
TH 1840	1.6	F	1845	1.9
3 0040	4.8	**18**	0042	4.3
0713	1.1		0707	1.7
F 1317	4.8	SA	1319	4.4
1937	1.3		1935	1.7
4 0136	5.0	**19**	0133	4.5
0805	1.0		0753	1.5
SA 1405	4.9	SU	1402	4.6
2029	1.1		2019	1.5
5 0228	5.1	**20**	0218	4.6
0851	0.9		0835	1.4
SU 1448	5.1	M	1440	4.8
● 2117	1.0		2101	1.2
6 0316	5.1	**21**	0301	4.8
0935	1.1		0916	1.2
M 1530	5.1	TU	1518	5.0
2202	0.9	○	2143	1.0
7 0402	5.0	**22**	0343	5.0
1015	1.1		0956	1.1
TU 1610	5.1	W	1556	5.1
2245	0.9		2226	0.8
8 0446	4.9	**23**	0425	5.0
1054	1.3		1038	1.1
W 1650	5.1	TH	1636	5.2
2326	1.0		2310	0.7
9 0530	4.8	**24**	0510	5.0
1131	1.4		1120	1.1
TH 1729	5.0	F	1717	5.2
			2355	0.7
10 0005	1.1	**25**	0556	5.0
0612	4.6		1203	1.2
F 1207	1.6	SA	1802	5.1
1809	4.8			
11 0045	1.3	**26**	0042	0.7
0656	4.4		0644	4.8
SA 1245	1.8	SU	1248	1.4
1852	4.6		1850	5.1
12 0126	1.5	**27**	0132	0.9
0742	4.2		0737	4.7
SU 1327	2.0	M	1338	1.5
1939	4.5		1944	4.9
13 0213	1.7	**28**	0227	1.1
0833	4.1		0836	4.5
M 1419	2.1	TU	1435	1.7
☽ 2033	4.3	☽	2046	4.7
14 0308	1.8	**29**	0328	1.3
0930	4.0		0940	4.4
TU 1523	2.2	W	1545	1.8
2134	4.2		2156	4.6
15 0411	1.9	**30**	0436	1.3
1032	4.0		1048	4.3
W 1637	2.3	TH	1703	1.8
2239	4.1		2311	4.5
		31	0547	1.5
			1156	4.4
		F	1819	1.7

Chart Datum: 2·60 metres below Ordnance Datum (Newlyn). HAT is 5·7 metres above Chart Datum; see 0.19

》 FREE monthly updates from 《
www.reedsalmanac.co.uk

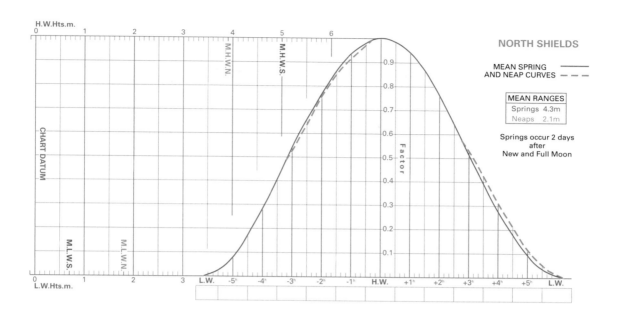

NORTH SHIELDS

MEAN SPRING — AND NEAP CURVES ---

MEAN RANGES
Springs 4.3m
Neaps 2.1m

Springs occur 2 days after New and Full Moon

3.17 BLYTH

Northumberland **55°06'·98N 01° 29'·27W** ✿✿✿♨♨♨♨

CHARTS AC 152, 156, 1626; Imray C24.

TIDES +0430 Dover; ML 2·8; Duration 0558

Standard Port NORTH SHIELDS (←)

Times				Height (metres)			
High Water		Low Water		MHWS	MHWN	MLWN	MLWS
0200	0800	0100	0800	5·0	3·9	1·8	0·7
1400	2000	1300	2000				
Differences BLYTH							
+0005	−0007	−0001	+0009	0·0	0·0	−0·1	+0·1

SHELTER Very good. Access H24 but at LW in strong SE winds, seas break across ent.

NAVIGATION WPT Fairway SHM buoy, Fl G 3s, Bell, 55°06'·58N 01°28'·60W, 320°/0·53M to E pier lt. From N, beware The Pigs, The Sow and Seaton Sea Rks and 2 wind turbines on North Spit (1·2M N of hbr ent) centred on 55°08'·16N 01°29'·41W. No dangers from S. See RNYC Sailing Directions, £28·75 inc P&P, from RNYC, House Yacht Tyne, S Hbr, Blyth NE24 3PB (see website below).

LIGHTS AND MARKS 9 wind turbines are conspic on E pier also Blyth E Pier Hd, W twr on S end. Outer ldg lts 324°, Or ◇ on framework trs. Inner ldg lts 338°, front W 6-sided tr; rear W △ on mast. See chartlet and 3.3 for lt details.

R/T Call: *Blyth Hbr Control* Ch **12** 11 (H24) for clearance to enter or depart.

TELEPHONE (Code 01670) Port HM 352678; MRCC 01262 672317; Marinecall 09068 969643; Police (01661) 872555.

FACILITIES R **Northumberland YC** ☎ 353636, www.rnyc.org.uk hon.sec@rnyc.org.uk In SE part of South Hbr, E side of Middle Jetty, Ⓥ berth on N side of RNYC pontoons in 4·4m least depth. 75 AB £1.50, D (cans), C (1½ ton for trailer sailers), BH (20 ton),ME (www.millermarine.co.uk), Bar. **South Hbr** ☎ 352678, FW, C (50 ton). **Town** @ Town Library (HO), P (cans), D (07836 677730), 🛒, R, Bar, ✉, Ⓑ, Gas, Gaz, bus to Newcastle ⇌, ✈.

ADJACENT ANCHORAGE
NEWBIGGIN, Northumberland, **55°10'·75N 01°30'·10W.** AC 156. Tides approx as for Blyth, 3·5M to the S. Temp, fair weather

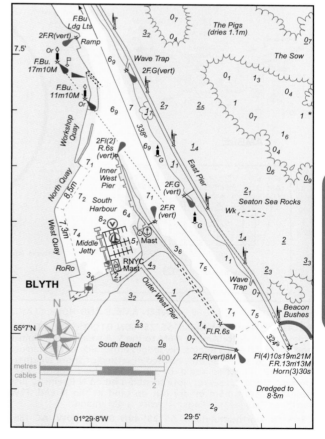

⚓ in about 4m in centre of the bay, off the the conspic sculptures on the breakwater; sheltered from SW to N winds. Caution: offlying rky ledges to N and S. Conspic church on N side of bay; bkwtr lt Fl G 10s 4M. Facilities: **SC** (dinghies). **Town** 🛒, R, Bar.

NE England

3.18 AMBLE

Northumberland 55°20'·37N 01°34'·25W ✺✺✺✺✺

CHARTS AC 156, 1627; Imray C24.

TIDES +0412 Dover; ML 3·1; Duration 0606

Standard Port NORTH SHIELDS (◄──)

Times				Height (metres)			
High Water		Low Water		MHWS	MHWN	MLWN	MLWS
0200	0800	0100	0800	5·0	3·9	1·8	0·7
1400	2000	1300	2000				
Differences AMBLE							
–0013	–0013	–0016	–0020	0·0	0·0	+0·1	+0·1
COQUET ISLAND							
–0010	–0010	–0020	–0020	+0·1	+0·1	0·0	+0·1

SHELTER The Hbr (alias Warkworth Hbr) is safe in all winds. But ent is dangerous in strong N to E winds or in swell, when heavy seas break on Pan Bush shoal and on the bar at hbr ent, where least depth is 0·8m. ⚓ in Coquet Road or NNE of North Pier.

NAVIGATION WPT 55°21'·00N 01°33'·10W, 225° to hbr ent, 0·9M. Ent recommended from NE, passing N and W of Pan Bush. The S-going stream sets strongly across ent. Once inside the N bkwtr, beware drying banks to stbd, ie on N side of channel;

keep close (15m) to S quays. 4kn speed limit in hbr.

- In NE'ly gales broken water can extend to Coquet Island, keep E of island and go to Blyth where appr/ent may be safer.
- Coquet Chan (min depth 0·3m) is not buoyed and is only advised with caution, by day, in good vis/weather, slight sea state and with adequate rise of tide, ie HW−2.

LIGHTS AND MARKS Coquet Island lt ho, (conspic) W☐tr, turreted parapet, lower half grey. Sector boundaries are indeterminate and may appear as Al WR. Horn 30s. See chartlet and 3.3.

R/T *Amble Marina* Ch 80 (7/7, 0900-1700). HM Ch 16, works Ch 14 (Mon-Fri 0900-1700 LT). Coquet YC Ch M (occas).

TELEPHONE (Code 01665) HM ☎ 710306; MRCC (01262) 672317; local CG 710575; Police (01661) 872555; Marinecall 09068 969643; Ⓗ (01670) 521212.

FACILITIES Amble Marina is about 5ca from hbr ent. Tidal gauge shows depth over sill; access approx HW±4 between PHM buoy and ECM bn, both unlit. Pontoons are 'A' to 'F' from sill; ♥ berth on 'B' initially. 200+40 ♥, £2·20. ☎ 712168, marina@amble.co.uk, BY, C, D, BH (50 ton), ME, El, ⚒, Ⓔ, SM, R, Bar, 🛒, CH, ⊠, ♿, Gas, Gaz. **Hbr** D, AB. **Coquet YC** ☎ 711179 Slip, Bar, M, FW, L.

Town 🛒, R, Bar, ✉, ≈ (Alnmouth), ✈ (Newcastle).

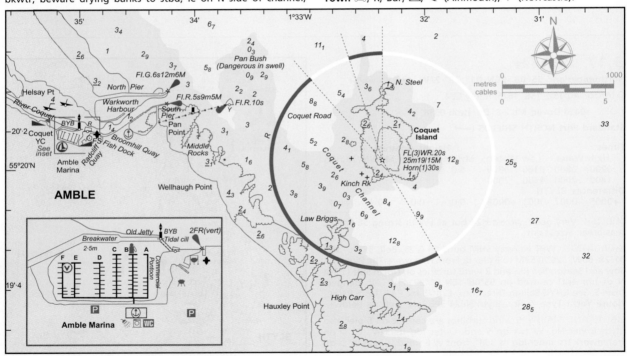

HBRS AND ANCHORAGES BETWEEN AMBLE AND HOLY ISLAND

BOULMER, Northumberland, 55°25'·00N 01°33'·90W. AC 156. Tides approx as for Amble, 4·6M to the S. A small haven almost enclosed by N and S Rheins, rky ledges either side of the narrow (30m) ent, Marmouth; only advised in settled offshore weather. 2 FW bns (lit when req'd by LB or FVs) lead approx 257° through the ent, leaving close to stbd a bn on N Rheins. ⚓ just inside in about 1·5m or dry out on sand at the N end. Few facilities: Pub, ✉ in village. Alnwick is 4M inland.

CRASTER, Northumberland, 55°28'·40N 01°35'·30W. AC 156. Tidal differences: interpolate between Amble (3.18) and N Sunderland (3.19). Strictly a fair weather ⚓ in offshore winds, 1M S of the conspic Dunstanburgh Castle (ru). The ent, 40m wide, is N of Muckle Carr and S of Little Carr which partly covers and has a bn on its S end. ⚓ in about 3·5m just inshore of these 2 rocky outcrops; or berth at the E pier on rk/sand inside the tiny drying hbr. Facilities: 🛒, R, Bar.

NEWTON HAVEN and BEADNELL BAY, Northumberland, 55°30'·90N 01° 36'·70W. AC 156. HW +0342 on Dover; Tidal differences: interpolate between Amble (3.18) and N Sunderland (3.19). ML 2·6m; Duration 0625. A safe ⚓ in winds from NNW to SE via S but susceptible to swell. Ent to S of Newton PHM buoy and Newton Pt. Beware Fills Rks. ⚓ between Fills Rks and Low Newton by the Sea in 4/5m. A very attractive ⚓ with no lts, marks or facilities except a pub. Further ⚓ S of Beadnell Pt (1M N of Newton Pt) in 4–6m; small, fishing hbr whose wall is newly rebuilt; Beadnell SC. Village 0·5M.

SEAHOUSES (North Sunderland), Northumberland, 55°35'·04N 01°38'·91W. AC 1612. HW +0340 on Dover; ML No data; Duration 0618. See 3.19. Good shelter except in on-shore winds when swell makes outer hbr berths (0·7m) very uncomfortable and dangerous. Access HW±3. Inner hbr has excellent berths but usually full of FVs. Beware The Tumblers (rks) to the W of ent and rks protruding NE from bkwtr hd Fl R 2·5s 6m; NW pier hd

FG 11m 3M; vis 159°-294°, on W tr; traffic sigs; Siren 90s when vessels expected. Good facilities. When it is dangerous to enter, a ● is shown over the FG lt (or R flag over a Bu flag) on NW pier hd.

FARNE ISLANDS, Northumberland, 55°37′·15N 01°39′·37W. AC 160, 156, 111. HW +0345 on Dover; ML 2·6m; Duration 0630. See 3.19. The islands are a NT nature reserve in a beautiful area; they should only be attempted in good weather. Landing is only allowed on Farne Is, Staple Is and Longstone. In the inner group, ⚓ in The Kettle on the NE side of Inner Farne; near the Bridges (connecting Knocks Reef to West Wideopen); or to the S of West Wideopen. In the outer group, ⚓ in Pinnacle Haven (between Staple Is/Brownsman). Beware turbulence over Knivestone and Whirl Rks and eddy S of Longstone during NW tidal streams. Lts and marks: Black Rocks Pt, Oc (2) WRG 8s 12m 14/11M;122°-G-165°-W-175°-R-191°-W-238°-R-275°-W-289°-G-300°. Bamburgh Castle is conspic 6ca to the SE. Farne Is lt ho at SW Pt, Fl (2) WR 15s

27m 8/6M; W ○ tr; 119°-R-280°-W-119°. Longstone Fl 20s 23m 24M, R tr with W band (conspic), RC, horn (2) 60s. Caution: reefs extend about 7ca seaward. No facilities.

NATIONAL NATURE RESERVE (Holy Island) A National Nature Reserve (NNR) extends from Budle Bay (55°37′N 01°45′W, close to Black Rocks Point lt ho) along the coast to Cheswick Black Rocks, 3M SE of Berwick-upon-Tweed. The NNR extends seaward from the HW shoreline to the drying line; it includes Holy Island and the adjacent islets.

Visiting craft are asked to respect two constraints:

- Landing is prohibited on the small island of Black Law (55°39′·68N 01°47′·50W) from April to August inclusive.

- Boats should not be landed or recovered anywhere in the NNR except at the designated and buoyed watersports zone on the SE side of Budle Bay.

COQUET ISLAND TO FARNE ISLANDS

(Chart 156) Coquet Is (lt, fog sig) lies about 5ca offshore at SE end of Alnmouth B, and nearly 1M NNE of Hauxley Pt, off which dangerous rks extend 6ca offshore, drying 1·9m. On passage, normally pass 1M E of Coquet Is in the W sector of the lt. Coquet chan may be used in good vis by day; but it is only 2ca wide, not buoyed, has least depth of 0·9m near the centre. ▶*The stream runs strongly: S-going from HW Tyne – 0515 and N-going from HW Tyne + 0045.* ◀ In S or W winds, there are good anchs in Coquet Road, W and NW of the Island.

Amble (Warkworth) Hbr ent is about 1M W of Coquet Is, and 1·5M SE of Warkworth Castle (conspic). 4ca NE and ENE of ent is Pan Bush, rky shoal with least depth of 0·9m on which dangerous seas can build in any swell. The bar has varying depths, down to less than 1m. The entrance is dangerous in strong winds from N/E when broken water may extend to Coquet Is. Once inside, the hbr is safe.

Between Coquet Is and the Farne Is, 19M to N, keep at least 1M offshore to avoid various dangers. To seaward, Craster Skeres lie 5M E of Castle Pt, and Dicky Shad and Newton Skere lie 1·75M and 4·5M E of Beadnell Pt; these are three rky banks on which the sea breaks heavily in bad weather.

FARNE ISLANDS

(Charts 111, 160) The coast between N Sunderland Pt (Snook) and Holy Island, 8M NW, has fine hill (Cheviots) scenery fronted by dunes and sandy beaches. The Farne Is and offlying shoals extend 4·5M offshore, and are a mini-cruising ground well worth visiting in good weather. The islands are a bird sanctuary, owned and operated by the National Trust, with large colonies of sea birds and grey seals. The R Northumberland YC's Sailing Directions (see 3.17) are useful; AC 111 is essential.

Inner Sound separates the islands from the mainland. In good conditions it is a better N/S route than keeping outside the whole group; but the stream runs at 3kn at sp, and with strong wind against tide there is rough water. If course is set outside Farne Is, pass 1M E of Longstone (lt, fog sig) to clear Crumstone

Rk 1M to S, and Knivestone (dries 3·6m) and Whirl Rks (depth 0·6m) respectively 5 and 6ca NE of Longstone lt ho. The sea breaks on these rks.

The islands, rks and shoals are divided by Staple Sound, running NW/SE, into an inner and outer group. The former comprises Inner Farne, W and E Wideopens and Knock's Reef. Inner Farne (lt) is the innermost Is; close NE there is anch called The Kettle, sheltered except from NW, but anch out of stream close to The Bridges connecting Knock's Reef and W Wideopen. 1M NW of Inner Farne Is and separated by Farne Sound, which runs NE/SW, lies the Megstone, a rk 5m high. Beware Swedman reef (dries 0·5m), marked by SHM buoy 4ca WSW of Megstone.

The outer group of Islands comprises Staple and Brownsman Islands, N and S Wamses, the Harcars and Longstone. There is occas anch between Staple and Brownsman Is. ▶ *Piper Gut and Crafords Gut may be negotiated in calm weather and near HW, stemming the S-going stream.* ◀

HOLY ISLAND TO BERWICK

(Charts 1612, 111, 160) ▶ *Near the Farne Is and Holy Is the SE-going stream begins at HW Tyne –0430, and the NW-going at HW Tyne +0130. Sp rates are about 2.5kn in Inner Sound, 4kn in Staple Sound and about 3.5kn 1M NE of Longstone, decreasing to seaward. There is an eddy S of Longstone on NW-going stream.* ◀

Holy Is (or Lindisfarne) lies 6M WNW of Longstone, and is linked to mainland by a causeway covered at HW. There is a good anch on S side (chart 1612) with conspic daymarks and dir lts. The castle and a W obelisk at Emmanuel Head are also conspic. ▶ *The stream runs strongly in and out of hbr, W-going from HW Tyne + 0510, and E-going from HW Tyne –0045. E of Holy Is, Goldstone chan runs N/S between Goldstone Rk (dries) SHM buoy on E side and Plough Seat Reef and Plough Rk (both dry) on W side, with PHM buoy.* ◀

Berwick Bay has some offlying shoals. Berwick-upon-Tweed is easily visible against the low shoreline, which rises again to high cliffs further north. The hbr entrance is restricted by a shallow bar, dangerous in onshore winds.

3.19 HOLY ISLAND

Northumberland 55°39′·57N 01°46′·81W ❋❋⚓❁❁❁

TIDES +0344 Dover; ML No data; Duration 0630

Standard Port NORTH SHIELDS (←)

Times				Height (metres)			
High Water		Low Water		MHWS	MHWN	MLWN	MLWS
0200	0800	0100	0800	5·0	3·9	1·8	0·7
1400	2000	1300	2000				
Differences HOLY ISLAND							
–0043	–0039	–0105	–0110	–0·2	–0·2	–0·3	–0·1
NORTH SUNDERLAND (Seahouses)							
–0048	–0044	–0058	–0102	–0·2	–0·2	–0·2	0·0

CHARTS AC 111, 1612; Imray C24.

SHELTER Good S of The Heugh in 3-6m, but ⚓ is uncomfortable in fresh W/SW winds esp at sp flood, and foul in places; trip-line advised. Better shelter in The Ouse on sand/mud if able to dry out; but not in S/SE winds. For detailed information for trailer sailers see www.dca.uk.com.

NAVIGATION WPT 55°39′·76N 01°44′·88W, 260°/1·55M to Old Law E bn. From N identify Emmanuel Hd, conspic W △ bn, then appr via Goldstone Chan leaving Plough Seat PHM buoy to stbd. From S, clear Farne Is thence to WPT. Outer ldg bns lead 260° close past Ridge ECM and Triton SHM buoys. Possible overfalls in chan across bar (1·6m) with sp ebb up to 4kn. Inner ldg marks lead 310° to ⚓. Inshore route, round Castle Pt via Hole Mouth and The Yares, may be more sheltered, but is not for strangers.

Continued overleaf

NE England

HOLY ISLAND *continued*

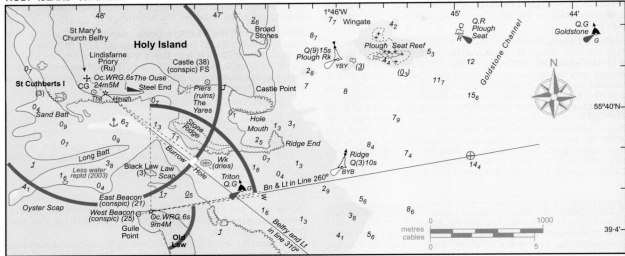

LIGHTS AND MARKS See 3.3 and chartlet. Outer leading marks/lts are Old Law beacons (conspic), 2 reddish obelisks 21/25m on 260°; E beacon has directional light, Oc WRG 6s. Inner leading marks/lights are The Heugh tower, B △, on with St Mary's church belfry 310°. The Heugh has directional light, Oc WRG 6s. Directional lights Oc WRG are aligned on 263° and 309·5° respectively.

R/T None.

TELEPHONE (Code 01289)   HM 389248; MRCC 01262 672317; Marinecall 09068 969643.

FACILITIES Limited. FW on village green, Slip (contact HM prior to launching) £2/day or £5/week, R, Bar, limited 🛒, P & D from Beal (5M); bus (occas) to Berwick. Note Lindisfarne is ancient name; Benedictine Abbey (ruins) and Castle (NT) are worth visiting. Causeway to mainland, covers at HW, is useable by vehicles approx HW+3½ to HW-2.

3.20   BERWICK-UPON-TWEED

Northumberland 55°45'·87N 01°59'·05W ❀❀❀⚓⚓❀❀

CHARTS AC 111, 160, 1612; Imray C24.

TIDES +0348 Dover; ML 2·5; Duration 0620

Standard Port NORTH SHIELDS (←)

Times				Height (metres)			
High Water		Low Water		MHWS	MHWN	MLWN	MLWS
0200	0800	0100	0800	5·0	3·9	1·8	0·7
1400	2000	1300	2000				
Differences	BERWICK-UPON-TWEED						
−0053	−0053	−0109	−0109	−0·3	−0·1	−0·5	−0·1

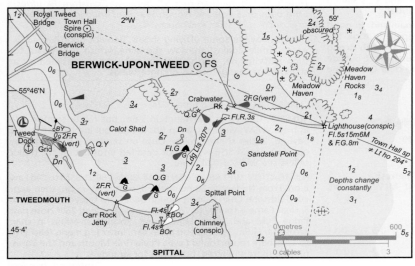

SHELTER Good shelter or ⚓ except in strong E/SE winds. AB may be available in Tweed Dock (no dock gates) which is primarily used by commercial shipping. If possible contact HM beforehand to avoid disappointment. Alternative temporary AB possible at W end of Fish Jetty (1·2m).

NAVIGATION WPT 55°45'·62N 01°58'·0W, 294°/0·65M to breakwater lighthouse.

- On-shore winds and ebb tides cause very confused seas over the bar (0·6m). Access HW±4 at springs. From HW−2 to HW+1 strong flood tide sets S across the entrance; keep well up to breakwater.
- The sands at the mouth of the Tweed shift so frequently that local knowledge is essential to enter the harbour.

Town Hall Spire and Lt ho in line at 294°. Keep close to breakwater to avoid Sandstell Point. When past PHM buoy and S of Crabwater Rk, keep Spittal Bns (Or ▽ on B Or Bn) in line brg 207°; best water may be further W. Berwick Bridge (first/lowest) has about 3m clearance.

LIGHTS AND MARKS See 3.3 and chartlet.

R/T HM VHF Ch 12 16 (0800-1700).

TELEPHONE (Code 01289) HM 307404; MRCC 01333 450666; Marinecall 09068 969643/236; Police 01661 872555; Dr 307484.

FACILITIES **Tweed Dock** ☎ 307404, AB £8.00, M, P(cans), D(cans), FW, Showers, ME, El, ✕, C (Mobile 3 ton), Slip, SM. **Town** P, 🛒, R, Bar, ✉, Ⓑ, ⇌ and ✈ (Newcastle or Edinburgh).

East Scotland

Eyemouth to Shetland Islands

SE Scotland

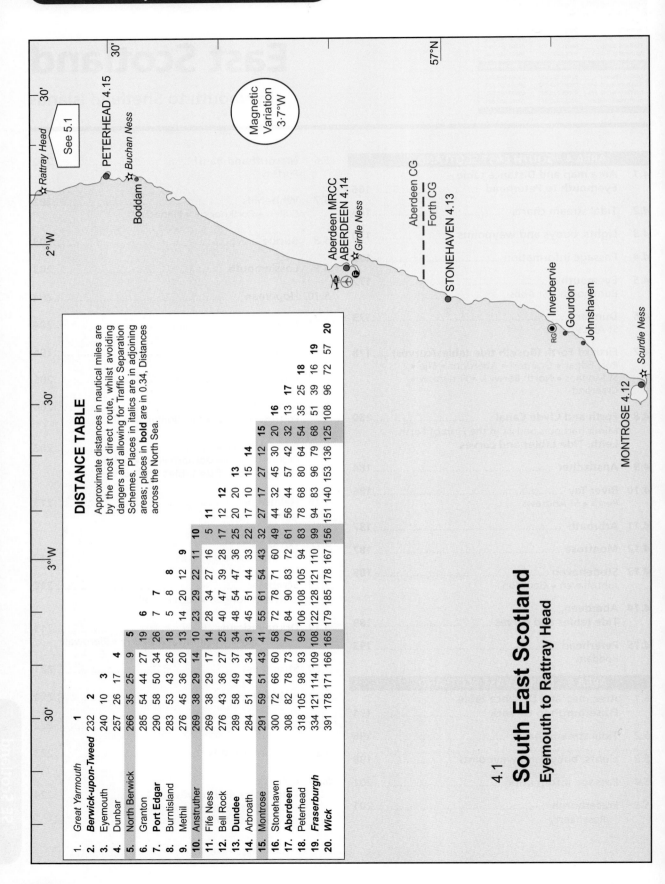

DISTANCE TABLE

Approximate distances in nautical miles are by the most direct route, whilst avoiding dangers and allowing for Traffic Separation Schemes. Places in italics are in adjoining areas; places in **bold** are in 0.34. Distances across the North Sea.

	1	2	3	4	5	6	7	8	9	10	11	12	13	14	15	16	17	18	19	20
1. *Great Yarmouth*	**1**																			
2. **Berwick-upon-Tweed**	232	**2**																		
3. Eyemouth	240	10	**3**																	
4. Dunbar	257	26	17	**4**																
5. North Berwick	266	35	25	9	**5**															
6. Granton	285	54	44	27	19	**6**														
7. **Port Edgar**	290	58	50	34	26	7	**7**													
8. Burntisland	283	53	43	26	18	5	8	**8**												
9. Methil	276	45	36	20	13	14	20	12	**9**											
10. Anstruther	269	38	29	14	10	23	29	22	11	**10**										
11. Fife Ness	269	38	29	17	14	28	34	27	16	5	**11**									
12. Bell Rock	276	43	36	27	25	40	47	39	28	17	12	**12**								
13. **Dundee**	289	58	49	37	34	48	54	47	36	25	20	20	**13**							
14. Arbroath	284	51	44	34	31	45	51	44	33	22	15	10	15	**14**						
15. Montrose	291	59	51	43	41	55	61	54	43	32	17	27	12	15	**15**					
16. Stonehaven	300	72	66	58	60	72	71	60	49	44	32	45	30	20	16	**16**				
17. **Aberdeen**	308	82	78	73	70	84	90	83	72	61	56	44	57	42	32	13	**17**			
18. Peterhead	318	105	98	93	95	106	108	105	94	83	78	68	80	64	54	35	25	**18**		
19. *Fraserburgh*	334	121	114	109	108	122	128	121	110	99	94	83	96	79	68	51	39	16	**19**	
20. *Wick*	391	178	171	166	165	179	185	178	167	156	151	140	153	136	125	108	96	72	57	**20**

Map labels:

Rattray Head · See 5.1 · PETERHEAD 4.15 · Buchan Ness · Boddam · Magnetic Variation 3·7°W · Aberdeen MRCC · ABERDEEN 4.14 · Girdle Ness · Aberdeen CG · Forth CG · STONEHAVEN 4.13 · Inverbervie · Gourdon · Johnshaven · Scurdie Ness · MONTROSE 4.12

30' · 30' · 2°W · 3°W · 30' · 30' · 57°N

4.1 South East Scotland
Eyemouth to Rattray Head

2.2 Scotland

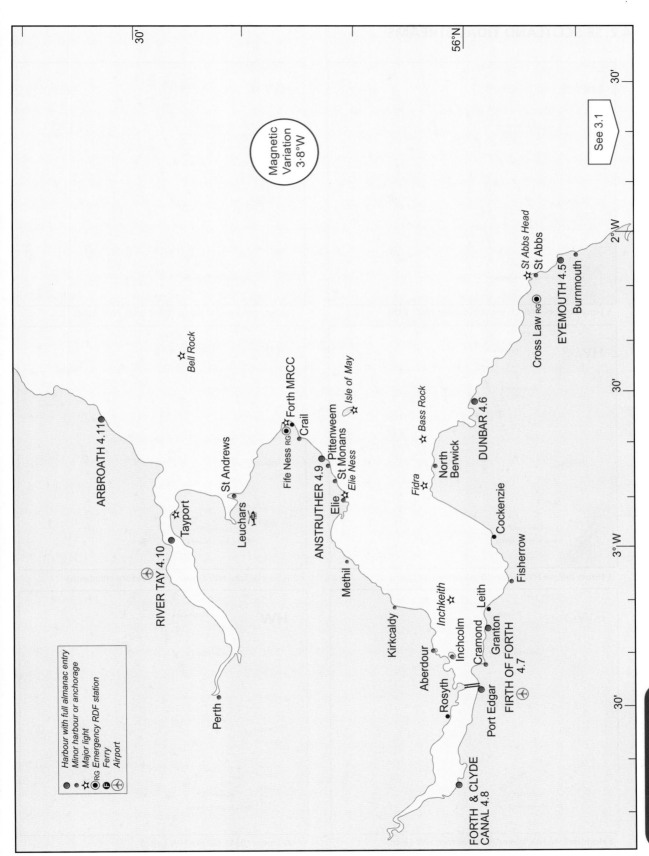

30'

56°N

30'

See 3.1

Magnetic
Variation
3·8°W

2°W

St Abbs Head
St Abbs

Cross Law RG

EYEMOUTH 4.5
Burnmouth

Bell Rock

Forth MRCC
Crail

Fife Ness RG

Isle of May

DUNBAR 4.6

St Andrews

Bass Rock

Pittenweem
St Monans
Elie Ness

ANSTRUTHER 4.9

Elie

Fidra

North
Berwick

Leuchars

ARBROATH 4.11

Tayport

RIVER TAY 4.10

Cockenzie

Methil

Fisherrow

Kirkcaldy

Inchkeith

Perth

Aberdour

Inchcolm

Leith

Cramond
Granton

Rosyth

Port Edgar

FIRTH OF FORTH
4.7

FORTH & CLYDE
CANAL 4.8

Harbour with full almanac entry
Minor harbour or anchorage
Major light
RG Emergency RDF station
Ferry
Airport

30'

3°W

30'

3°W

167

SE Scotland

4.2 SE SCOTLAND TIDAL STREAMS

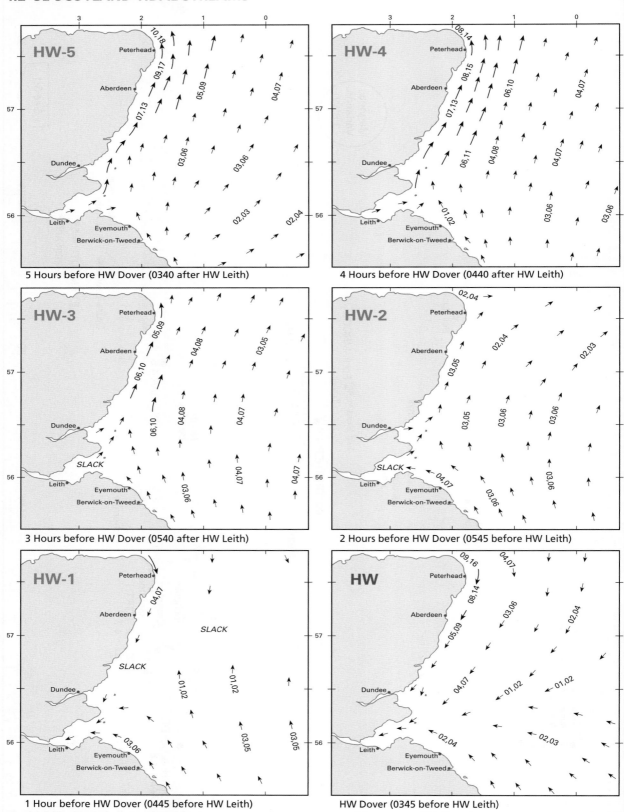

5 Hours before HW Dover (0340 after HW Leith)

4 Hours before HW Dover (0440 after HW Leith)

3 Hours before HW Dover (0540 after HW Leith)

2 Hours before HW Dover (0545 before HW Leith)

1 Hour before HW Dover (0445 before HW Leith)

HW Dover (0345 before HW Leith)

Northward 5.2   Southward 3.2

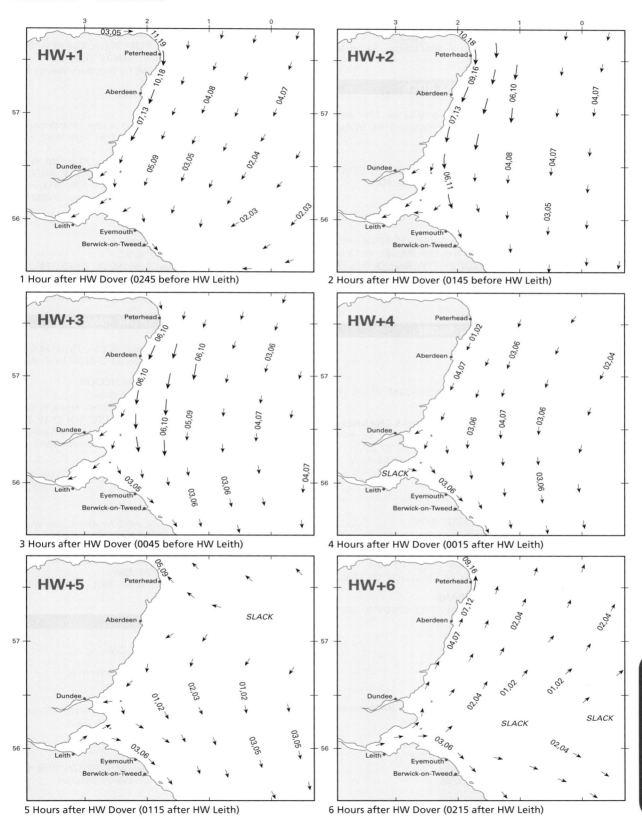

1 Hour after HW Dover (0245 before HW Leith)

2 Hours after HW Dover (0145 before HW Leith)

3 Hours after HW Dover (0045 before HW Leith)

4 Hours after HW Dover (0015 after HW Leith)

5 Hours after HW Dover (0115 after HW Leith)

6 Hours after HW Dover (0215 after HW Leith)

SE Scotland

4.3 LIGHTS, BUOYS AND WAYPOINTS

Bold print = light with a nominal range of 15M or more. CAPITALS = place or feature. *CAPITAL ITALICS* = light-vessel, light float or Lanby. *Italics* = Fog signal. ***Bold italics*** = Racon. See 0.2 for Abbreviations.

BERWICK-UPON-TWEED TO BASS ROCK
BURNMOUTH
Ldg lts 241°. Front, FR 29m 4M; 55°50'·53N 02°04'·25W. Rear, 45m from front, FR 35m 4M. Both on W posts (unclear by day).

EYEMOUTH
Blind Buss ↓ Q; 55°52'·80N 02°05'·25E.
Ldg Lts 174°. Front, W Bkwtr Hd ⚓, FG 9m 6M; 55°52'·47N 02°05'·29W. Rear, elbow 55m from front, FG 10m 6M.

ST ABBS to DUNBAR and BASS ROCK
St Abbs Hd ☆ 55°54'·96N 02°08'·29W; Fl 10s 68m **26M**; W twr; ***Racon (T) 18M***.
Barns Ness Tower (Lt ho disused 36m); 55°59'·22N 02°26'·76W .
Bayswell Hill Ldg Lts 198°. Front, Oc G 6s 15m 3M; W △ on Or col; 188° -G(intens)-208°; 56°00'·25N 02°31'·21W. Rear, Oc G 6s 22m 3M; ▽ on Or col; synch with front, 188°-G(intens)-208°.
Bass Rock, S side, ☆ Fl (3) 20s 46m 10M; W twr; vis: 241°-107°; 56°04'·61N 02°38'·48W.

FIRTH OF FORTH AND SOUTH SHORE
(Direction of buoyage East to West)

NORTH BERWICK
Outfall ↓ Fl Y; 56°04'·29N 02°40'·89W.
Fidra ☆ 56°04'·39N 02°47'·13W; Fl (4) 30s 34m **24M**; W twr; obsc by Bass Rock, Craig Leith and Lamb Island.

PORT SETON, COCKENZIE, FISHERROW and S CHANNEL
Port Seton, E Pier Hd ⚓ Iso WR 4s 10m W9M, R6M; vis: shore - R - 105°- W - 225°- R - shore; *Bell (occas);* 55°58'·40N 02°57'·23W.
Fisherrow E Pier Hd ⚓ Oc 6s 5m 6M; 55°56'·79N 03°04'·11W.
Narrow Deep ≈ Fl (2) R 10s; 56°01'·46N 03°04'·59W.
Herwit ▲ Fl (3) G 10s; 56°01'·05N 03°06'·52W.
North Craig ↓ Q (3) 10s 56°01'·02N 03°03'·52W.
Craigh Waugh ↓ Fl (2) 10s;56°00'·26N 03°04'·47W.
Diffuser Hds (Outer) ↓ 55°59'·81N 03°07'·84W.

LEITH and GRANTON
Leith Approach ≈ Fl R 3s; 55°59'·95N 03°11'·51W .
East Bkwtr Hd ⚓ Iso R 4s 7m 9M; 55°59'·48N 03°10'·94W.
GrantonE Pier Head ⚓ Fl R 2s 5m 6M; 55°59'·28N 03°13'·27W.

NORTH CHANNEL and MIDDLE BANK
Inchkeith Fairway ≈ Iso 2s; ***Racon (T) 5M***; 56°03'·49N 03°00'·10W.
No. 1 ▲ Fl G 9s; 56°03'·22N 03°03'·71W.
No. 2 ≈ Fl R 9s; 56°02'·90N 03°03'·72W.
No. 3 ▲ Fl G 6s; 56°03'·22N 03°06'·10W.
No. 4 ≈ Fl R 6s; 56°02'·89N 03°06'·11W.
No. 5 ▲ Fl G 3s; 56°03'·18N 03°07'·88W.
No. 6 ≈ Fl R 3s; 56°03'·05N 03°08'·44W.
No. 8 ≈ Fl R 9s 56°02'·95N 03°09'·62W.
Inchkeith ☆ 56°02'·01N 03°08'·17W; Fl 15s 67m **22M**; stone twr.
Pallas Rock ↓ VQ (9) 10s 56°01'·50N 03°09'·30W.
East Gunnet ↓ Q (3) 10s; 56°01'·41N 03°10'·38W.
West Gunnet ↓ Q (9) 15s 56°01'·34N 03°11'·06W.
No. 7 ▲ QG; ***Racon (T) 5M***; 56°02'·80N 03°10'·97W.
No. 9 ▲ Fl G 6s; 56°02'·32N 03°13'·48W.
No. 10 ≈ Fl R 6s; 56°02'·07N 03°13'·32W.

No. 11 ▲ Fl G 3s 56°02'·08N 03°15'·26W.
No. 12 ≈ Fl R 3s; 56°01'·78N 03°15'·15W.
No. 13 ▲ Fl G 9s; 56°01'·77N 03°16'·94W.
No. 14 ≈ Fl R 9s; 56°01'·52N 03°16'·82W.
Oxcars ☆ Fl (2) WR 7s 16m W13M, R12M; W twr; R band; vis: 072°-W-087°- R-196°-W-313°-R-072°; 56°01'·36N 03°16'·84W.
Inchcolm E Pt ☆ Fl (3) 15s 20m 10M; Gy twr; part obsc by land 075°-145·5°; 56°01'·72N 03°17'·83W.
No. 15 ▲ Fl G 6s; 56°01'·39N 03°18'·95W.

MORTIMER'S DEEP
Hawkcraig Point Ldg Lts 292°. Front, Iso 5s 12m 14M; W twr; vis: 282°-302°; 56°03'·03N 03°17'·07W. Rear, 96m from front, Iso 5s 16m 14M; W twr; vis: 282°-302°.
Inchcolm S Lts in line 066°. Front, 84m from rear, Q 7m 7M; W twr; vis: 062·5°-082·5°; 56°01'·78N 03°18'·28W. Common Rear, Iso 5s 11m 7M; W twr; vis: 062·5°-082·5°; 56°01'·80N 03°18'·13W. N Lts in line 076·7°. Front, 80m from rear, Q 7m 7M; W twr; vis: 062·5°-082·5°.

APPROACHES TO FORTH BRIDGES
No. 17 ▲ Fl G 3s; 56°01'·23N 03°19'·84W.
No. 16 ≈ Fl R 3s; 56°00'·87N 03°19'·60W.
No. 19 ▲ Fl G 9s; 56°00'·71N 03°22'·47W.
Beamer Rk ⚓ Fl 3s 6m 9M; W twr, R top; 56°00'·28N 03°24'·74W.

PORT EDGAR
W Bkwtr Hd ⚓ Fl R 4s 4m 8M; 55°59'·86N 03°24'·78W. W blockhouse.

FIRTH OF FORTH – NORTH SHORE (INWARD)
BURNTISLAND
W Pier Outer Hd ⚓ Fl (2) R 6s 7m; W twr; 56°03'·22N 03°14'·26W.
E Pier Outer Hd ⚓ Fl (2) G 6s 7m 5M; 56°03'·24N 03°14'·17W.

ABERDOUR, BRAEFOOT BAY and INCHCOLM
Hawkcraig Pt ⚓ (see **MORTIMER'S DEEP** above).
Braefoot Bay Terminal, W Jetty. Ldg Lts 247·3°. **Front**, Fl 3s 6m **15M**; W △ on E dolphin; vis: 237·2°-257·2°; 56°02'·16N 03°18'·71W; 4 dolphins with 2 FG (vert). **Rear**, 88m from front, Fl 3s 12m **15M**; W ▽ on appr gangway; vis: 237·2°-257·2°; synch with front.

INVERKEITHING BAY
St David's ↓ Fl G 5s 3m 7M; Or □, on pile; 56°01'·37N 03°22'·29W.
Channel ▲ QG; 56°01'·43N 03°23'·02W.

HM NAVAL BASE, ROSYTH
Main Chan Dir lt 323·5°. Bn 'A' Oc WRG 7m 4M; R □ on W post with R bands; vis: 318°-G-321°-321°-W-326°-R-328° (H24); 56°01'·19N 03°25'·61W.
Dir lt 115°, Bn 'C' Oc WRG 6s 7m 4M; W ▽ on W Bn; vis: 110°- R -113° W -116·5° - G -120°; 56°00'·61N 03°24'·25W.
S Arm Jetty Hd ⚓ L Fl (2) WR 12s 5m W9M; R6M; vis: 010°-W-280°-R-010°; 56°01'·09N 03°26'·58W.

RIVER FORTH
ROSYTH to GRANGEMOUTH
Dhu Craig ▲ Fl G 5s; 56°00'·74N 03°27'·23W.
Blackness ≈ QR; 56°01'·06N 03°30'·30W.
Tancred Bank ≈ Fl (2) R 10s; 56°01'·58N 03°31'·91W.
Dods Bank ≈ Fl R 3s; 56°02'·03N 03°34'·07W.
Bo'ness ≈ Fl R 10s; 56°02'·23N 03°35'·38W.
Torry ⚓Fl G 10s 5m 7M; G ○ structure; 56°02'·46N 03°35'·28W.
Bo'ness Bcns ⚓ 2 QR 3m 2M; 56°01'·85N 03°36'·22W.
Bo'ness Hbr ↓; 56°01'·26N 03°36'·46W.

GRANGEMOUTH
Grangemouth App No. 1 ↓ Fl (3) 10s 4m 6M;56°02'·12N 03°38'·10W.
Hen & Chickens ▲ Fl (3) G 10s; 56°02'·35N 03°38'·08W.

FIRTH OF FORTH – NORTH SHORE (OUTWARD)

KIRKCALDY and METHIL
Kirkaldy E. Pier Hd ≴Fl WG 10s 12m 8M; vis: 156°-G-336°-W-156°; 56°06'·78N 03°08'·90W.
Methil Outer Pier Hd ≴ Oc G 6s 8m 5M; W twr; vis: 280°-100°; 56°10'·76N 03°00'·48W

ELIE and ST MONANS
Elie Ness ☆ 56°11'·04N 02°48'·77W; Fl 6s 15m **18M**; W twr.

St Monans Bkwtr Hd ≴ Oc WRG 6s 5m W7M, R4M, G4M; vis: 282°-G-355°-W-026°-R-038°; 56°12'·20N 02°45'·94W.

PITTENWEEM and ANSTRUTHER EASTER
Pittenweem, Ldg Lts 037° Middle Pier Hd. Front, FR 4m 5M. Rear, FR 8m 5M. Both Gy Cols, Or stripes; 56°12'·69N 02°43'·69W.
Pittenweem, E Bkwtr Hd ≴ Fl (2) RG 5s 9m R9M, G6M; vis: 265°-R-345°-G-055°; *Horn 90s (occas);* 56°12'·63N 02°43'·74W.
Anstruther, Ldg Lts 019°. Front FG 7m 4M; 56°13'·28N 02°41'·76W. Rear, 38m from front, FG 11m 4M, (both W masts).

MAY I, CRAIL, ST ANDREWS and FIFE NESS to MONTROSE
Isle of May ☆ 56°11'·12N 02°33'·46W(Summit); Fl (2) 15s 73m **22M**; □ twr on stone dwelling.
Crail, Ldg Lts 295°. Front, FR 24m 6M (not lit when hbr closed); 56°15'·46N 02°37'·84W. Rear, 30m from front, FR 30m 6M.
Fife Ness ☆ 56°16'·74N 02°35'·19W; Iso WR 10s 12m **W21M, R20M**; W bldg; vis: 143°-W-197°-R-217°-W-023°.
N Carr ⌁ Q (3) 10s 3m 5M; 56°18'·05N 02°32'·94W.
Bell Rk ☆ 56°26'·08N 02°23'·21W; Fl 5s 28m **18M**; *Racon (M) 18M.*
St Andrews N Bkwtr Bn ≴Fl G 3M 56°20'·36N 02°46'·77W.

RIVER TAY, TAYPORT, DUNDEE and PERTH
Tay Fairway ⌁ L Fl 10s; *Bell;* 56°28'·30N 02°36'·60W.
Middle ⌁ Fl G 3s; 56°27'·93N 02°38'·26W.
Middle ⌁ Fl (2) R 6s 56°27'·65N 02°38'·23W.
Abertay N ⌁ Q (3) 10s; *Racon (T) 8M;* 56°27'·39N 02°40'·36W.
Abertay S (Elbow) ⌁ Fl R 6s 56°27'·13N 02°39'·83W.
Tayport High Lt Ho ☆ 56°27'·17N 02°53'·96W; Dir lt 269°; Iso WRG3s 24m **W22M, R17M, G16M**; W twr; vis: 267°-G-268°-W-270°-R-271°.

ARBROATH
Ldg lts 299·2°. Front , FR 7m 5M; W col; 56°33'·29N 02°35'·16W.
Rear, 50m from front, FR 13m 5M; W col.

MONTROSE
Scurdie Ness ☆ 56°42'·10N 02°26'·24W; Fl (3) 20s 38m **23M**; W twr; *Racon (T) 14-16M.*

Outer Ldg Lts 271·5°; Front, FR 11m 5M; W twin pillars, R bands; 56°42'·21N 02°27'·41W; Rear, 272m from front, FR 18m 5M; W twr, R cupola.

Inner Ldg Lts 265°; Front FG 21m 5M; Rear FG 33m 5M.

MONTROSE TO RATTRAY HEAD

JOHNSHAVEN and GOURDON HARBOUR
Johnshaven, Ldg Lts 316°. Front,FR 5m; 56°47'·62N 02°20'·26W . Rear, 85m from front, FG 20m; shows R when unsafe to enter hbr.
Gourdon Hbr, Ldg Lts 358°. Front, FR 5m 5M; W twr; shows G when unsafe to enter; *Siren (2) 60s* (occas); 56°49'·69N 02°17'·24W. Rear, 120m from front, FR 30m 5M; W twr.
Todhead Lighthouse (disused), white tower, 13m.

STONEHAVEN to GIRDLE NESS
Outer Pier Hd ≴ Iso WRG 4s 7m W11M, R7M, G8M; vis: 214°-G-246°-W-268°-R-280°; 56°57'·59N 02°12'·00W.

Girdle Ness ☆ Fl (2) 20s 56m **22M**; obsc by Greg Ness when brg more than about 020°; *Racon (G) 25M*; 57°08'·34N 02°02'·91W.

ABERDEEN
Fairway ⌁ Mo (A) 5s; *Racon (T) 7M*; 57°09'·31N 02°01'·95W.
Torry Ldg lts 235·7°. Front, FR or G 14m 5M; R when ent safe, FG when dangerous to navigation; vis: 195°-279°; 57°08'·37N 02°04'·51W. Rear, 205m from front, FR 19m 5M; W twr; vis: 195°-279°.
S Bkwtr Hd ≴ Fl (3) R 8s 23m 7M; 57°08'·69N 02°03'·34W.
N Pier Hd ≴ Oc WR 6s 11m 9M; W twr; vis: 145°-W-055°-R-145°; 57°08'·74N 02°03'·69W. In fog FY 10m (same twr) vis: 136°-336°; *Bell (3) 12s.*

PETERHEAD and RATTRAY HEAD
Buchan Ness ☆ Fl 5s 40m **28M**; W twr, R bands; *Racon (O) 14-16M;* 57°28'·23N 01°46'·51W.
Kirktown Ldg lts 314°. Front, FR 13m 8M; R mast, Or △ on R mast; 57°30'·22N 01°47'·21W. Rear, 91m from front, FR 17m 8M.
S Bkwtr Hd ≴ Fl (2) R 12s 24m 7M; 57°29'·79N 01°46'·54W.
N Bkwtr Hd ≴Iso RG 6s 19m 11M; W tripod; vis: 171°-R-236°-G-171°; *Horn 30s;* 57°29'·84N 01°46'·32W .
Rattray Hd ☆ 57°36'·61N 01°49'·03W; Fl (3) 30s 28m **24M**; W twr; *Racon (M) 15M.*

SE Scotland

4.4 PASSAGE INFORMATION

For these waters refer to the Admiralty *North Sea (West) Pilot*; R Northumberland YC's *Sailing Directions Humber to Rattray Head*, and the *Forth Yacht Clubs Association Pilot Handbook*, which covers the Firth of Forth in detail.

A 'Rover Ticket', £30 from Aberdeenshire and Moray Councils allows berthing (subject to availability) for one week from the date of arrival at the first harbour. Scheme includes, Johnshaven, Gourdon, Stonehaven, Rosehearty, Banff, Portsoy, Cullen, Portknockie, Findochty, Hopeman and Burghead. More Passage Information is threaded between the harbours of this Area.

BERWICK-UPON-TWEED TO BASS ROCK

(AC 160,175) From Berwick-upon-Tweed to the Firth of Forth there is no good hbr which can be approached with safety in strong onshore winds. So, if on passage with strong winds from N or E, plan accordingly and keep well to seaward. In late spring and early summer fog (haar) is likely in onshore winds.

The coast N from Berwick is rocky with cliffs rising in height to Burnmouth, then diminishing gradually to Eyemouth. Keep 5ca offshore to clear outlying rks. Burnmouth, although small, has more alongside space than Eyemouth, which is a crowded fishing hbr. 2·1M NW is St Abbs Hbr, with temp anchorage in offshore winds in Coldingham B close to the S.

St Abbs Hd (lt) is a bold, steep headland, 92m high, with no offlying dangers. ▶ *The stream runs strongly round the Hd, causing turbulence with wind against tide; this can be largely avoided by keeping close inshore. The ESE-going stream begins at HW Leith –0345, and the WNW-going at HW Leith +0240.* ◀ There is a good anch in Pettico Wick, on NW side of Hd, in S winds, but dangerous if the wind shifts onshore. There are no off-lying dangers between St Abbs Hd and Fast Castle Hd, 3M WNW. Between Fast Castle Hd and Barns Ness, about 8M NW, is the attractive little hbr of Cove; but it dries and should only be approached in ideal conditions.

Torness Power Station (conspic, lt on bkwtr) is 1·75M SE of Barns Ness (lt) which lies 2·5M ESE of Dunbar and is fringed with rks; tidal streams as for St Abb's Hd. Conspic chys are 7½ca WSW inland of Barns Ness. Between here and Dunbar keep at least 2½ca offshore to clear rky patches. Sicar Rk (7·9m depth) lies about 1·25M ENE of Dunbar, and sea breaks on it in inshore gales.

The direct course from Dunbar to Bass Rk (lt) is clear of all dangers; inshore of this line beware Wildfire Rks (dry) on NW side of Bellhaven B. In offshore winds there is anch in Scoughall Road. Great Carr is ledge of rks, nearly covering at HW, 1M ESE of Gin Hd, with Carr bn (stone tr surmounted by cross) at its N end. Drying ledges of rks extend 1M SE of Great Carr, up to 3ca offshore. Keep at least 5ca off Carr bn in strong onshore winds. Tantallon Castle (ruins) is on cliff edge 1M W of Great Car. Bass Rk (lt) lies 1·25M NNE of Gin Hd, and is a sheer, conspic rk (115m) with no offlying dangers; landing difficult due to swell.

4.5 EYEMOUTH

Borders 55°52'·52N 02°05'·29W ❀❀♨♨♨♙♙♙

CHARTS AC 160, 1612; Imray C24.

TIDES +0330 Dover; ML No data; Duration 0610

Standard Port LEITH (⟶)

Times				Height (metres)			
High Water		Low Water		MHWS	MHWN	MLWN	MLWS
0300	0900	0300	0900	5·6	4·4	2·0	0·8
1500	2100	1500	2100				
Differences EYEMOUTH							
–0005	+0007	+0012	+0008	–0.4	–0.3	0.0	+0.1

SHELTER Good in all weathers except uncomfortable surge in N over F5. Busy FV hbr which encourages yachtsman to visit. Berth as directed by HM. The options are:
- Middle Quay (100m pontoon), depth 0.9m bottom soft mud.
- On the W wall of the N-pointing jetty by the LB;
- On W wall of the centre jetty W of Gunsgreen House (conspic).
- ⚓ in bay only in offshore winds.

NAVIGATION WPT 55°52'·80N 02°05'·34W, 174°/3ca to E bkwtr lt.
- Entry should not be attempted in strong N to E winds. F.R (occas) lt ● or R flag = unsafe to enter indicates unsafe to enter bay or hbr.
- Caution, the entrance is 17m wide and is maintained to 2m depth with soundings taken monthly due to frequent sand movement and silting.
- Appr can be made N or S of Hurkars; from the N, beware Blind Buss 1·2m, marked by NCM lit buoy about 200m ENE of WPT.
- From the S, approach on 250° midway between Hurkars and Hettle Scar (no ldg marks).
- Approaching vessels are advised to contact HM for latest information.

LIGHTS AND MARKS St. Abbs Hd lt ho Fl 10s 68m 26M is 3M NW. Ldg lts 174° both FG 9/10m 6M, orange columns on W pier.

R/T VHF Ch 16 **12** (HO). Advisable to listen to VHF Ch 6 for FVs entering/leaving port.

TELEPHONE (Code 01890) HM 750223, Mobile 07885 742505; MRCC (01333) 450666; Marinecall 09068 969642; Police 750217; Dr 750599, Ⓗ (0131) 536 1000.

FACILITIES Hbr AB (quay) £12/yacht, AB (pontoon) £17/yacht (any LOA +7 days for the price of 5), FW, D (in Gunsgreen Basin),

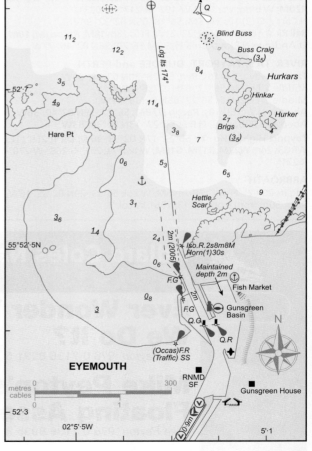

Slip, BY, ME, ✹, El, C (12 ton mobile), Ⓔ. See www.eyemouthharbour.org.

Town LB, P, CH, ⌨, R, Bar, ✉, ▣, Gas, Gaz, Ⓑ, Wi-fi at public library. ⇌ (bus to Berwick-on-Tweed and Edinburgh), ✈ (Edinburgh).

ADJACENT HARBOURS

BURNMOUTH, Borders, **55°50´·61N 02°04´·10W**. AC 160. HW +0315 on Dover, −0025 on Leith; Duration 0615. Use Eyemouth tides 4.5. From S beware Quarry Shoal Rks; and E & W Carrs from N. 2 W posts (unclear by day, FR 29/35m 4M) 45m apart, lead 253° to close N of the hbr; as hbr mouth opens, enter on about 185° with outer hbr ent in line with 2FG (vert). Min depth at ent at LWS is 0·6m. Shelter is good especially in inner hbr (dries). With on-shore winds, swell makes outer hbr uncomfortable. HM (018907) 81283 (home). Facilities: AB £7 (all LOA), FW, limited 🛒.

ST ABBS, Borders, **55°54´·10N 02°07´·74W**. AC 175. HW +0330 on Dover, −0017 on Leith; HW −0·6m on Leith; Duration 0605. Ldg line (about 228°) S face of Maw Carr on village hall (conspic R roof) leads SW until the hbr ent opens to port and the 2nd ldg line (about 167°) can be seen 2FR 4/8m 1M, or Y LB ho visible thru' ent. On E side of ent chan, beware Hog's Nose and on W side the Maw Carr. Shelter good. In strong on-shore winds outer hbr suffers from waves breaking over E pier. Inner hbr (dries) is best but often full of FVs. Access HW±3. HM (0775 1136758) directs visitors. Facilities: AB £10 (all LOA), Slip (launching £10), FW, 🔌, at quay, R, ✉, 🛒, more facilities & bar at Coldingham.

4.6 DUNBAR

East Lothian **56°00´·39N 02°31´·09W** ❀⊛♓♓❀❀❀

CHARTS AC 175, 734; Imray C23, C27.

TIDES +0330 Dover; ML 3·0; Duration 0600

Standard Port LEITH (→)

Times				Height (metres)			
High Water		Low Water		MHWS	MHWN	MLWN	MLWS
0300	0900	0300	0900	5·6	4·4	2·0	0·8
1500	2100	1500	2100				
Differences DUNBAR							
−0005	+0003	+0003	−0003	−0·3	−0·3	0·0	+0·1
FIDRA							
−0001	0000	−0002	+0001	−0·2	−0·2	0·0	0·0

SHELTER Outer (Victoria) Hbr is subject to surge in strong NW to NE winds. N side dries; berth below castle and contact HM. Keep steps clear. Inner (Old or Cromwell) Hbr dries and is safe in strong onshore conditions; entry is through a bridge, lifted on request to HM.

NAVIGATION WPT 56°00´·60N 02°31´·49W, 132°/3ca to hbr ent, preferable entry in marginal conditions.

- Entry is dangerous in heavy on-shore swell with no access in strong winds from NW to E.
- Beware Wallace's Head Rock, Half Ebb Rock (2₁m), 1½ca from ent. and Outer Buss 4ca E of ent.
- Min depth at ent 0·5m, but may be much less in abnormal circumstances.
- Keep to port on entry to avoid rockfall off castle.

LIGHTS AND MARKS Church and Castle ruin both conspic. From NE, ldg lts, Oc G 6s 15/22m 3M, synch, intens 188°-208°, 2 W △ on Or cols, lead 198° through the outer rks to the Roads; thence narrow ent opens with QR brg 132°. From NW, appr on brg 132° between bns on Wallaces Head and Half Ebb Rk.

R/T None.

TELEPHONE (Code 01368) HM 865404, Mobile 07958754858;

DUNBAR

MRCC (01333) 450666; Police 862718; Dr 863704; Ⓗ (0131) 536 1000.

FACILITIES **Quay** AB £10 (£15 over 12m LOA), Slip, FW, D (quayside), P (cans); **N Wall** M, AB; **Inner Hbr** Slip, AB; **Services** ME, Gas, Gaz. **Town** LB, P, 🏧, 🛒, R, Bar, ✉, Ⓑ, ⇌, ✈ Edinburgh.

ADJACENT HARBOUR

NORTH BERWICK, East Lothian, **56°03´·74N 02°43´·04W**. AC 734. Fidra HW +0344 on Dover; ML 3·0m; Duration 0625. See 4.6 Fidra. Shelter good with winds from S to W but dangerous with on-shore winds. Ent is 8m wide. Hbr dries. From E or W, from position 0·25M S of Craigleith, steer S for Plattock Rks, thence SSW 40m off bkwtr before turning 180° port into hbr. Bkwtr lt F WR 7m 3M, R to seaward, W over hbr; not lit when bad weather closes hbr. Beware Maiden Rks (bn) 100m NW of this lt.
Facilities: AB £5.70, P & D (cans), FW on pier, CH, Wi-fi at public library. HM ☎ (01620) 893333, Mob 0776 467373. **East Lothian YC** ☎ (01620) 892698, M, 🚿s, Bar. **Town** 🛒, Gas, Ⓑ, ✉, ⇌ and bus Edinburgh.

FIRTH OF FORTH – SOUTH SHORE

(Chart 734, 735) Westward of Bass Rk, Craigleith (51m), Lamb Is (24m) and Fidra (31m) lie 5ca or more offshore, while the coast is generally foul. Craigleith is steep-to, and temporary anchorage can be found on SE and SW sides; if passing inshore of it keep well to N side of chan. N Berwick hbr (dries) lies S of Craigleith, but is unsafe in onshore winds. Between Craigleith and Lamb Is, beware drying rks up to 3ca from land. Lamb Is is 1·5M WNW of N Berwick and has a rky ledge extending 2½ca SW. Fidra Is (lt) is a bird reserve, nearly connected to the shore by rky ledges, and should be passed to the N; passage and anchorage on S side are tricky. Anchor on E or W sides, depending on wind, in good weather.

In the bay between Fidra and Edinburgh some shelter can be found in SE winds in Aberlady Bay and Gosford Bay. The best anchorage is SW of Craigielaw Pt. Port Seton is a drying fishing harbour 7½ca E of the conspic chys of Cockenzie Power

Station; the E side of the hbr can be entered HW ±3, but not advisable in strong onshore winds. Cockenzie (dries) is close to power station; beware Corsik Rk 400m to E. Access HW ±2·5, but no attractions except boatyard.

There are no dangers on the direct course from Fidra to Inchkeith (lt), which stands between the buoyed deep water chans. Rks extend 7½ca SE from Inchkeith, and 5ca off the W side where there is a small hbr below the lt ho; landing is forbidden without permission. N Craig and Craig Waugh (least depth 0·2m) are buoyed shoals 2·5M SE from Inchkeith lt ho.

▶*In N Chan, close to Inchkeith the W-going (flood) stream begins about HW Leith −0530, and the E-going at HW Leith +0030, sp rates about 1kn. The streams gather strength towards the Forth bridges, where they reach 2·25kn and there may be turbulence.*◀

Leith is wholly commercial; Granton has yacht moorings in the E hbr; Port Edgar is a major yacht hbr close W of Forth Road

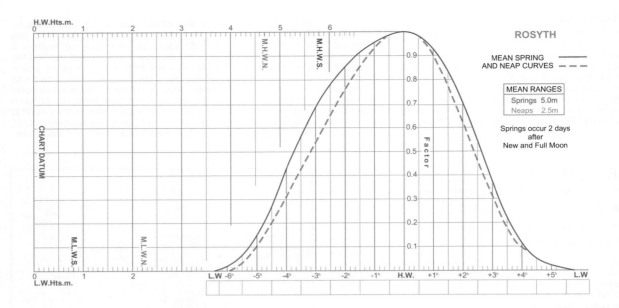

ROSYTH

MEAN SPRING
AND NEAP CURVES

MEAN RANGES	
Springs	5.0m
Neaps	2.5m

Springs occur 2 days
after
New and Full Moon

Bridge. Hound Point oil terminal is an artificial 'island-jetty' almost in mid-stream, connected to the shore by underwater pipeline (no ⚓). Yachts may pass the terminal on either side at least 30m off keeping well clear of manoeuvring ships.

▶ *Tidal streams are quite weak in the outer part of the Firth. Apart from the stream of the Tay, which attains 5kn in most places, the coastwise tidal streams between Fife Ness and Arbroath are weak.*

Northbound. *Leave before HW (Dover +0400) to be at N Carr at Dover +0600. Bound from Forth to Tay aim to arrive at Abertay By at LW slack (Dover –0200).*

Southbound. *Leave before LW (Dover -0200) to be at Bass Rk at HW Dover. Similar timings if bound from Tay to Forth, leave late in ebb to pick up early flood off St Andrews to N Carr and into Forth.*◀

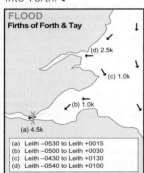

FLOOD
Firths of Forth & Tay

(a)	Leith −0530 to Leith +0015
(b)	Leith −0500 to Leith +0030
(c)	Leith −0430 to Leith +0130
(d)	Leith −0540 to Leith +0100

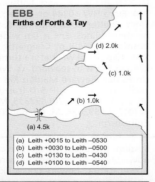

EBB
Firths of Forth & Tay

(a)	Leith +0015 to Leith −0530
(b)	Leith +0030 to Leith −0500
(c)	Leith +0130 to Leith −0430
(d)	Leith +0100 to Leith −0540

RIVER FORTH TO KINCARDINE

(AC 736, 737, 738) The main shipping chan under the N span of the rail bridge is busy with commercial traffic for Grangemouth and Rosyth. W of Beamer Rk the Firth widens as far as Bo'ness (small drying hbr) on the S shore where the chan narrows between drying mudbanks. Charlestown (N bank) dries, but is a secure hbr. Grangemouth is industrially conspicuous. Beware of gas carriers, tankers and other cargo vessels; there are no facilities for yachts. Few yachts go beyond Kincardine swing bridge, clearance 9m, which is no longer opened.

FIRTH OF FORTH – NORTH SHORE

(AC 734, 190) From Burntisland the N shore of Firth of Forth leads E to Kinghorn Ness. 1M SSW of Kinghorn Ness Blae Rk (SHM lt buoy) has least depth of 4·1m, and seas break on it in E gales.

▶ *Rost Bank lies halfway between Kinghorn Ness and Inchkeith, with tide rips at sp tides or in strong winds.* ◀

From Kinghorn Ness to Kirkcaldy, drying rks lie up to 3ca offshore. Kirkcaldy Hbr is effectively closed, but yachts can enter inner dock near HW by arrangement; ent is dangerous in strong E'lies, when seas break a long way out.

Between Kirkcaldy and Methil the only dangers more than 2ca offshore are The Rockheads, extending 4ca SE of Dysart, and marked by 2 SHM buoys. Largo B is anch, well sheltered from N and E, but avoid gaspipes near E side. Close SW of Elie, beware W Vows (dries) and E Vows (dries, bn). There is anch close W of Elie Ness (4.7). Ox Rk (dries 2m) lies 5ca ENE of Elie Ness, and 2½ca offshore; otherwise there are no dangers more than 2ca offshore past St Monance, Pittenweem and Anstruther, but in bad weather the sea breaks on Shield Rk 4ca off Pittenweem. From Anstruther to Crail and on to Fife Ness keep 3ca offshore to clear Caiplie Rk and other dangers.

May Island (lt) lies about 5M S of Fife Ness; its shores are bold except at NW end where rks extend 1ca off. Anch near N end at E or W Tarbert, on lee side according to winds; in good weather it is possible to land. Lt ho boats use Kirkhaven, close SE of lt ho.

FORTH TO NORWAY AND BALTIC

(AC 2182B, 2182C) Heading ENE'ly from the Firth of Forth the main hazards result from offshore industrial activities and their associated traffic. Particularly in summer months oil/gas exploration, movement of drilling rigs and pipe laying create potentially hazardous situations for small craft. Rig movements and many of the more intense activities are published in Notices to Mariners, but even so it is wise to avoid the gas and oil fields where possible and never to approach within 500m of installations. There are TSS to be avoided off the S and SW coast of Norway. Strong currents and steep seas may be experienced in the approaches to the Skagerrak.

ROSYTH LAT 56°01'N LONG 3°27'W
TIMES AND HEIGHTS OF HIGH AND LOW WATERS

TIME ZONE (UT)
For Summer Time add ONE hour in **non-shaded areas**

Dates in red are SPRINGS
Dates in blue are NEAPS

YEAR 2010

JANUARY

Time	m		Time	m
1 0234	5.8		**16** 0317	5.3
0823	1.2		0829	1.4
F 1501	5.9		SA 1535	5.5
2108	0.7		2048	1.1
2 0325	5.9		**17** 0352	5.3
0913	1.1		0905	1.2
SA 1549	6.0		SU 1607	5.5
2159	0.5		2123	1.0
3 0415	6.0		**18** 0427	5.3
0958	1.0		0938	1.2
SU 1639	6.0		M 1639	5.4
2246	0.4		2156	1.0
4 0506	5.9		**19** 0503	5.3
1040	1.1		1007	1.3
M 1729	6.0		TU 1715	5.3
2327	0.5		2224	1.1
5 0556	5.8		**20** 0542	5.2
1119	1.2		1031	1.4
TU 1818	5.8		W 1754	5.2
			2250	1.2
6 0001	0.7		**21** 0623	5.1
0646	5.6		1058	1.5
W 1201	1.4		TH 1834	5.1
1908	5.6		2320	1.3
7 0038	1.0		**22** 0705	4.9
0737	5.3		1133	1.7
TH 1248	1.7		F 1916	4.9
(2000	5.3		2357	1.5
8 0125	1.4		**23** 0750	4.8
0832	5.0		1215	1.9
F 1344	2.0		SA 2003	4.8
2058	5.1		(	
9 0228	1.8		**24** 0043	1.8
0933	4.8		0839	4.6
SA 1457	2.2		SU 1310	2.2
2205	4.9		2058	4.7
10 0429	2.0		**25** 0142	2.1
1040	4.7		0938	4.6
SU 1716	2.2		M 1615	2.3
2313	4.8		2204	4.7
11 0555	2.0		**26** 0449	2.2
1145	4.8		1045	4.7
M 1836	2.0		TU 1717	2.0
			2315	4.8
12 0016	4.9		**27** 0546	1.9
0651	1.9		1152	4.9
TU 1246	5.0		W 1815	1.6
1932	1.7			
13 0113	5.0		**28** 0022	5.1
0734	1.8		0639	1.6
W 1338	5.2		TH 1255	5.3
2016	1.5		1914	1.2
14 0201	5.1		**29** 0122	5.5
0807	1.7		0735	1.3
TH 1423	5.3		F 1351	5.6
2051	1.4		2015	0.7
15 0241	5.2		**30** 0217	5.8
0759	1.5		0828	1.0
F 1501	5.4		SA 1443	5.9
● 2106	1.3		○ 2108	0.4
			31 0307	6.0
			0916	0.8
			SU 1532	6.1
			2153	0.1

FEBRUARY

Time	m		Time	m
1 0356	6.1		**16** 0401	5.4
0958	0.7		0918	1.0
M 1621	6.2		TU 1619	5.5
2232	0.1		2134	0.8
2 0445	6.1		**17** 0437	5.4
1035	0.7		0948	1.0
TU 1709	6.2		W 1653	5.5
2305	0.2		2200	0.9
3 0533	5.9		**18** 0514	5.3
1107	0.8		1010	1.1
W 1755	6.0		TH 1730	5.4
2331	0.5		2222	1.0
4 0619	5.7		**19** 0554	5.2
1135	1.1		1032	1.2
TH 1841	5.7		F 1808	5.2
			2249	1.1
5 0000	1.0		**20** 0634	5.1
0706	5.3		1102	1.4
F 1211	1.5		SA 1848	5.1
(1929	5.3		2323	1.4
6 0041	1.5		**21** 0717	4.9
0755	5.0		1141	1.6
SA 1300	1.9		SU 1933	4.9
2022	4.9			
7 0139	2.0		**22** 0007	1.7
0852	4.6		0805	4.7
SU 1415	2.3		M 1233	2.0
2130	4.6		(2027	4.7
8 0306	2.4		**23** 0104	2.1
1004	4.5		0902	4.5
M 1712	2.4		TU 1348	2.2
2247	4.5		2133	4.6
9 0540	2.4		**24** 0429	2.3
1118	4.6		1011	4.6
TU 1833	2.0		W 1703	1.9
2357	4.6		2250	4.7
10 0639	2.2		**25** 0531	2.0
1223	4.8		1125	4.8
W 1925	1.7		TH 1804	1.5
11 0055	4.8		**26** 0002	5.1
0721	1.9		0626	1.6
TH 1318	5.1		F 1232	5.2
2006	1.5		1905	1.0
12 0143	5.0		**27** 0105	5.4
0754	1.7		0721	1.2
F 1402	5.3		SA 1331	5.6
2039	1.3		2003	0.5
13 0221	5.2		**28** 0158	5.8
0730	1.5		0813	0.9
SA 1439	5.4		SU 1423	6.0
2057	1.2		○ 2051	0.2
14 0255	5.3			
0805	1.2			
SU 1513	5.5			
2026	1.0			
15 0328	5.4			
0843	1.0			
M 1545	5.5			
2102	0.8			

MARCH

Time	m		Time	m
1 0247	6.0		**16** 0301	5.4
0858	0.6		0818	0.9
M 1512	6.2		TU 1520	5.5
2131	0.0		2036	0.8
2 0334	6.1		**17** 0335	5.5
0939	0.5		0854	0.8
TU 1559	6.3		W 1554	5.5
2207	0.0		2108	0.7
3 0420	6.1		**18** 0410	5.5
1016	0.5		0925	0.9
W 1645	6.2		TH 1630	5.5
2237	0.2		2134	0.8
4 0506	5.9		**19** 0448	5.4
1047	0.7		0948	1.0
TH 1730	6.0		F 1707	5.4
2301	0.6		2157	0.9
5 0550	5.6		**20** 0527	5.3
1111	1.0		1010	1.1
F 1815	5.7		SA 1746	5.3
2326	1.1		2224	1.1
6 0635	5.3		**21** 0608	5.1
1137	1.4		1040	1.2
SA 1900	5.2		SU 1827	5.1
			2259	1.4
7 0001	1.6		**22** 0652	4.9
0719	4.9		1121	1.5
SU 1219	1.8		M 1913	4.9
(1950	4.8		2344	1.7
8 0055	2.2		**23** 0741	4.7
0811	4.6		1216	1.8
M 1347	2.2		TU 2007	4.7
2057	4.4		(	
9 0231	2.6		**24** 0045	2.2
0926	4.3		0838	4.6
TU 1659	2.4		W 1536	2.0
2221	4.3		2114	4.6
10 0514	2.6		**25** 0406	2.3
1050	4.4		0949	4.6
W 1811	2.0		TH 1646	1.7
2334	4.4		2232	4.7
11 0614	2.3		**26** 0511	1.9
1156	4.6		1104	4.9
TH 1859	1.7		F 1748	1.2
			2346	5.1
12 0032	4.7		**27** 0607	1.5
0655	2.0		1211	5.2
F 1250	4.9		SA 1848	0.8
1937	1.5			
13 0119	4.9		**28** 0046	5.4
0725	1.7		0701	1.1
SA 1334	5.2		SU 1309	5.6
2008	1.3		1941	0.4
14 0156	5.2		**29** 0139	5.7
0703	1.4		0751	0.8
SU 1412	5.3		M 1402	5.9
1926	1.1		2027	0.2
15 0229	5.3		**30** 0227	5.9
0739	1.1		0837	0.6
M 1446	5.5		TU 1451	6.1
● 2000	0.9		○ 2106	0.1
			31 0312	6.0
			0918	0.4
			W 1538	6.1
			2140	0.2

APRIL

Time	m		Time	m
1 0357	5.9		**16** 0345	5.5
0955	0.5		0902	0.8
TH 1623	6.0		F 1608	5.5
2210	0.5		2108	0.8
2 0441	5.8		**17** 0424	5.5
1027	0.7		0929	0.9
F 1708	5.8		SA 1647	5.5
2234	0.8		2135	0.9
3 0524	5.5		**18** 0505	5.4
1050	1.0		0956	1.0
SA 1752	5.5		SU 1729	5.4
2255	1.3		2207	1.1
4 0606	5.2		**19** 0549	5.2
1108	1.3		1031	1.2
SU 1836	5.1		M 1813	5.2
2323	1.7		2246	1.4
5 0648	4.9		**20** 0635	5.0
1146	1.7		1108	1.4
M 1924	4.7		TU 1901	5.0
			2337	1.8
6 0004	2.2		**21** 0725	4.8
0734	4.6		1222	1.6
TU 1318	2.1		W 1956	4.8
(2023	4.4		●	
7 0150	2.6		**22** 0050	2.2
0840	4.4		0824	4.7
W 1501	2.2		TH 1512	1.7
2147	4.2		2102	4.7
8 0329	2.6		**23** 0334	2.2
1013	4.4		0935	4.8
TH 1726	2.1		F 1624	1.4
2300	4.4		2217	4.8
9 0523	2.4		**24** 0444	1.9
1119	4.5		1047	5.0
F 1814	1.8		SA 1727	1.1
2358	4.6		2326	5.1
10 0606	2.1		**25** 0543	1.5
1212	4.8		1150	5.3
SA 1852	1.6		SU 1824	0.8
11 0044	4.9		**26** 0024	5.4
0604	1.7		0638	1.2
SU 1257	5.0		M 1247	5.6
1915	1.4		1916	0.6
12 0123	5.1		**27** 0117	5.6
0634	1.4		0730	0.9
M 1337	5.2		TU 1341	5.7
1856	1.2		2002	0.5
13 0158	5.3		**28** 0206	5.7
0712	1.2		0817	0.7
TU 1415	5.4		W 1431	5.8
1932	1.0		○ 2042	0.5
14 0233	5.4		**29** 0252	5.8
0751	0.9		0859	0.6
W 1452	5.5		TH 1519	5.8
● 2008	0.8		2116	0.6
15 0308	5.5		**30** 0337	5.7
0829	0.8		0937	0.7
TH 1529	5.5		F 1605	5.8
2040	0.8		2146	0.8

SE Scotland

Chart Datum: 2·95 metres below Ordnance Datum (Newlyn). HAT is 6·4 metres above Chart Datum; see 0.19

ROSYTH LAT 56°01'N LONG 3°27'W
TIMES AND HEIGHTS OF HIGH AND LOW WATERS

TIME ZONE (UT)
For Summer Time add ONE hour in **non-shaded areas**

Dates in red are **SPRINGS**
Dates in blue are NEAPS

YEAR 2010

MAY

Day	Time	m	Day	Time	m
1 SA	0420 / 1010 / 1649 / 2210	5.6 / 0.8 / 5.6 / 1.1	16 SU	0405 / 0918 / 1631 / 2123	5.5 / 0.8 / 5.6 / 1.0
2 SU	0501 / 1034 / 1732 / 2230	5.4 / 1.0 / 5.3 / 1.4	17 M	0449 / 0953 / 1716 / 2201	5.5 / 0.9 / 5.5 / 1.2
3 M	0542 / 1051 / 1815 / 2257	5.2 / 1.3 / 5.1 / 1.7	18 TU	0535 / 1036 / 1803 / 2247	5.3 / 1.0 / 5.4 / 1.4
4 TU	0622 / 1126 / 1859 / 2333	4.9 / 1.6 / 4.8 / 2.0	19 W	0624 / 1131 / 1853 / 2343	5.2 / 1.1 / 5.2 / 1.7
5 W	0705 / 1222 / 1948	4.7 / 1.9 / 4.5	20 TH	0717 / 1251 / 1948	5.1 / 1.3 / 5.0
6 TH	0028 / 0757 / 1408 / 2050	2.3 / 4.5 / 2.0 / 4.3	21 F	0056 / 0815 / 1436 / 2049	1.9 / 5.0 / 1.3 / 4.9
7 F	0231 / 0913 / 1529 / 2206	2.5 / 4.4 / 2.1 / 4.3	22 SA	0235 / 0920 / 1551 / 2156	2.0 / 5.0 / 1.3 / 4.9
8 SA	0348 / 1027 / 1637 / 2307	2.4 / 4.5 / 1.9 / 4.5	23 SU	0405 / 1026 / 1658 / 2301	1.8 / 5.1 / 1.2 / 5.1
9 SU	0445 / 1123 / 1721 / 2357	2.1 / 4.7 / 1.7 / 4.7	24 M	0515 / 1127 / 1759	1.6 / 5.3 / 1.1
10 M	0527 / 1212 / 1753	1.8 / 4.9 / 1.5	25 TU	0000 / 0617 / 1225 / 1853	5.2 / 1.4 / 5.4 / 1.0
11 TU	0041 / 0605 / 1257 / 1827	5.0 / 1.6 / 5.1 / 1.3	26 W	0056 / 0713 / 1321 / 1941	5.4 / 1.2 / 5.5 / 1.0
12 W	0122 / 0645 / 1341 / 1903	5.2 / 1.3 / 5.3 / 1.2	27 TH	0147 / 0803 / 1414 / 2021	5.5 / 1.0 / 5.6 / 1.0
13 TH	0202 / 0725 / 1423 / 1940	5.4 / 1.1 / 5.4 / 1.0	28 F	0235 / 0846 / 1503 / 2056	5.5 / 0.9 / 5.6 / 1.0
14 F	0242 / 0806 / 1505 / 2015	5.5 / 0.9 / 5.5 / 1.0	29 SA	0320 / 0925 / 1548 / 2125	5.5 / 0.9 / 5.5 / 1.1
15 SA	0323 / 0843 / 1547 / 2049	5.5 / 0.8 / 5.6 / 1.0	30 SU	0402 / 0957 / 1631 / 2149	5.4 / 0.9 / 5.4 / 1.2
			31 M	0443 / 1020 / 1712 / 2212	5.3 / 1.0 / 5.3 / 1.4

JUNE

Day	Time	m	Day	Time	m
1 TU	0521 / 1038 / 1752 / 2239	5.2 / 1.2 / 5.1 / 1.6	16 W	0524 / 1108 / 1752 / 2253	5.6 / 0.7 / 5.6 / 1.2
2 W	0600 / 1108 / 1832 / 2311	5.0 / 1.4 / 4.9 / 1.8	17 TH	0614 / 1158 / 1842 / 2344	5.6 / 0.8 / 5.5 / 1.4
3 TH	0640 / 1145 / 1913 / 2350	4.9 / 1.6 / 4.7 / 2.0	18 F	0706 / 1246 / 1933	5.5 / 0.9 / 5.3
4 F	0726 / 1232 / 1959	4.7 / 1.8 / 4.6	19 SA	0039 / 0759 / 1340 / 2028	1.6 / 5.3 / 1.1 / 5.1
5 SA	0041 / 0817 / 1345 / 2052	2.2 / 4.6 / 2.0 / 4.5	20 SU	0141 / 0858 / 1451 / 2129	1.7 / 5.2 / 1.4 / 5.0
6 SU	0236 / 0918 / 1533 / 2154	2.3 / 4.6 / 2.0 / 4.5	21 M	0256 / 1000 / 1620 / 2232	1.9 / 5.1 / 1.5 / 4.9
7 M	0356 / 1022 / 1633 / 2256	2.2 / 4.6 / 1.9 / 4.6	22 TU	0444 / 1103 / 1734 / 2335	1.9 / 5.1 / 1.5 / 5.0
8 TU	0451 / 1120 / 1720 / 2352	2.0 / 4.8 / 1.8 / 4.8	23 W	0605 / 1205 / 1835	1.7 / 5.2 / 1.5
9 W	0538 / 1214 / 1802	1.8 / 5.0 / 1.6	24 TH	0034 / 0707 / 1304 / 1925	5.1 / 1.5 / 5.2 / 1.4
10 TH	0043 / 0622 / 1306 / 1841	5.0 / 1.5 / 5.2 / 1.4	25 F	0130 / 0800 / 1358 / 2006	5.3 / 1.3 / 5.3 / 1.4
11 F	0131 / 0706 / 1355 / 1920	5.2 / 1.2 / 5.4 / 1.3	26 SA	0220 / 0844 / 1447 / 2040	5.4 / 1.1 / 5.4 / 1.3
12 SA	0217 / 0753 / 1442 / 2001	5.4 / 1.2 / 5.5 / 1.1	27 SU	0305 / 0920 / 1530 / 2103	5.4 / 1.0 / 5.4 / 1.3
13 SU	0302 / 0840 / 1528 / 2042	5.6 / 0.8 / 5.7 / 1.0	28 M	0345 / 0947 / 1610 / 2125	5.4 / 1.0 / 5.3 / 1.2
14 M	0348 / 0928 / 1615 / 2123	5.6 / 0.7 / 5.7 / 1.0	29 TU	0423 / 0957 / 1648 / 2153	5.4 / 1.0 / 5.3 / 1.3
15 TU	0435 / 1017 / 1703 / 2206	5.7 / 0.6 / 5.7 / 1.1	30 W	0459 / 1018 / 1724 / 2221	5.3 / 1.0 / 5.2 / 1.3

JULY

Day	Time	m	Day	Time	m
1 TH	0535 / 1045 / 1801 / 2248	5.2 / 1.2 / 5.1 / 1.5	16 F	0557 / 1146 / 1822 / 2332	5.9 / 0.4 / 5.7 / 1.1
2 F	0613 / 1114 / 1840 / 2319	5.1 / 1.3 / 4.9 / 1.6	17 SA	0646 / 1220 / 1910	5.8 / 0.7 / 5.5
3 SA	0655 / 1146 / 1921 / 2356	4.9 / 1.5 / 4.8 / 1.8	18 SU	0016 / 0736 / 1300 / 2001	1.3 / 5.5 / 1.1 / 5.2
4 SU	0739 / 1224 / 2006	4.8 / 1.7 / 4.7	19 M	0107 / 0831 / 1354 / 2058	1.6 / 5.3 / 1.5 / 4.9
5 M	0041 / 0828 / 1312 / 2057	2.1 / 4.7 / 1.9 / 4.6	20 TU	0212 / 0933 / 1517 / 2203	1.6 / 5.0 / 1.9 / 4.8
6 TU	0140 / 0925 / 1415 / 2155	2.2 / 4.6 / 2.1 / 4.6	21 W	0414 / 1042 / 1713 / 2311	2.1 / 4.9 / 2.0 / 4.8
7 W	0419 / 1028 / 1653 / 2300	2.2 / 4.7 / 2.0 / 4.7	22 TH	0605 / 1148 / 1823	1.9 / 4.9 / 1.9
8 TH	0516 / 1133 / 1742	2.0 / 4.8 / 1.8	23 F	0016 / 0708 / 1250 / 1914	4.9 / 1.6 / 5.0 / 1.8
9 F	0003 / 0606 / 1233 / 1828	4.9 / 1.6 / 5.1 / 1.6	24 SA	0114 / 0759 / 1344 / 1955	5.1 / 1.4 / 5.2 / 1.6
10 SA	0100 / 0657 / 1328 / 1914	5.1 / 1.3 / 5.3 / 1.4	25 SU	0204 / 0840 / 1430 / 2025	5.3 / 1.2 / 5.3 / 1.5
11 SU	0152 / 0752 / 1419 / 2002	5.4 / 1.0 / 5.6 / 1.2	26 M	0247 / 0912 / 1510 / 2028	5.4 / 1.1 / 5.3 / 1.3
12 M	0241 / 0848 / 1508 / 2049	5.7 / 0.7 / 5.8 / 1.0	27 TU	0324 / 0932 / 1545 / 2055	5.5 / 1.0 / 5.4 / 1.2
13 TU	0329 / 0940 / 1556 / 2133	5.9 / 0.4 / 5.9 / 0.9	28 W	0358 / 0922 / 1619 / 2129	5.5 / 0.9 / 5.3 / 1.1
14 W	0418 / 1027 / 1645 / 2214	6.0 / 0.3 / 6.0 / 0.8	29 TH	0432 / 0951 / 1653 / 2159	5.4 / 0.9 / 5.3 / 1.1
15 TH	0507 / 1109 / 1734 / 2253	6.0 / 0.3 / 5.9 / 0.9	30 F	0506 / 1018 / 1729 / 2224	5.4 / 1.0 / 5.2 / 1.3
			31 SA	0543 / 1041 / 1807 / 2249	5.3 / 1.0 / 5.1 / 1.4

AUGUST

Day	Time	m	Day	Time	m
1 SU	0623 / 1108 / 1847 / 2319	5.1 / 1.3 / 5.0 / 1.6	16 M	0709 / 1228 / 1931	5.6 / 1.3 / 5.2
2 M	0704 / 1141 / 1929 / 2357	5.0 / 1.5 / 4.8 / 1.8	17 TU	0037 / 0802 / 1323 / 2025	1.7 / 5.2 / 1.8 / 4.8
3 TU	0749 / 1222 / 2014	4.8 / 1.8 / 4.7	18 W	0146 / 0907 / 1442 / 2134	2.1 / 4.8 / 2.2 / 4.6
4 W	0045 / 0839 / 1315 / 2107	2.1 / 4.7 / 2.1 / 4.6	19 TH	0424 / 1023 / 1700 / 2251	2.3 / 4.7 / 2.3 / 4.6
5 TH	0152 / 0942 / 1629 / 2213	2.3 / 4.6 / 2.3 / 4.6	20 F	0604 / 1135 / 1810 / 2359	2.0 / 4.7 / 2.2 / 4.8
6 F	0458 / 1054 / 1754 / 2324	2.1 / 4.7 / 2.0 / 4.8	21 SA	0700 / 1237 / 1859	1.6 / 4.9 / 1.9
7 SA	0552 / 1203 / 1814	1.7 / 5.0 / 1.7	22 SU	0056 / 0745 / 1329 / 1937	5.1 / 1.4 / 5.1 / 1.7
8 SU	0030 / 0647 / 1304 / 1903	5.1 / 1.2 / 5.4 / 1.4	23 M	0144 / 0822 / 1411 / 2001	5.3 / 1.2 / 5.3 / 1.5
9 M	0127 / 0745 / 1357 / 1954	5.5 / 0.8 / 5.7 / 1.1	24 TU	0224 / 0851 / 1446 / 1948	5.5 / 1.1 / 5.4 / 1.3
10 TU	0218 / 0840 / 1446 / 2043	5.8 / 0.4 / 6.0 / 0.8	25 W	0259 / 0820 / 1518 / 2024	5.5 / 1.0 / 5.4 / 1.1
11 W	0307 / 0928 / 1534 / 2127	6.1 / 0.1 / 6.1 / 0.6	26 TH	0331 / 0848 / 1549 / 2101	5.6 / 0.9 / 5.5 / 1.0
12 TH	0355 / 1010 / 1622 / 2206	6.2 / 0.0 / 6.1 / 0.6	27 F	0403 / 0920 / 1622 / 2133	5.5 / 0.8 / 5.4 / 1.0
13 F	0444 / 1048 / 1709 / 2241	6.3 / 0.1 / 6.1 / 0.7	28 SA	0437 / 0948 / 1657 / 2158	5.5 / 0.9 / 5.3 / 1.1
14 SA	0532 / 1121 / 1756 / 2313	6.1 / 0.4 / 5.9 / 0.9	29 SU	0513 / 1009 / 1735 / 2220	5.4 / 1.1 / 5.3 / 1.3
15 SU	0620 / 1150 / 1843 / 2350	5.9 / 0.8 / 5.6 / 1.3	30 M	0551 / 1033 / 1814 / 2247	5.3 / 1.2 / 5.1 / 1.5
			31 TU	0632 / 1105 / 1855 / 2323	5.1 / 1.5 / 4.9 / 1.7

Chart Datum: 2·95 metres below Ordnance Datum (Newlyn). HAT is 6·4 metres above Chart Datum; see 0.19

TIME ZONE (UT)
For Summer Time add ONE hour in **non-shaded areas**

ROSYTH   LAT 56°01'N   LONG 3°27'W
TIMES AND HEIGHTS OF HIGH AND LOW WATERS

Dates in red are SPRINGS
Dates in blue are NEAPS

YEAR **2010**

SEPTEMBER

Time	m		Time	m
1 0715	4.9	**16** 0128		2.1
1146	1.8	0841		4.7
W 1939	4.8	TH 1416		2.5
◗		2104		4.5
2 0010	2.0	**17** 0424		2.1
0805	4.7	1003		4.5
TH 1239	2.2	F 1636		2.6
2030	4.6	2229		4.6
3 0116	2.3	**18** 0545		2.0
0907	4.6	1117		4.6
F 1606	2.4	SA 1746		2.3
2135	4.6	2337		4.8
4 0439	2.0	**19** 0636		1.7
1023	4.7	1217		4.9
SA 1704	2.1	SU 1832		2.1
2251	4.8			
5 0536	1.5	**20** 0032		5.1
1139	5.0	0717		1.4
SU 1755	1.8	M 1306		5.1
		1908		1.8
6 0002	5.2	**21** 0117		5.3
0632	1.1	0752		1.3
M 1242	5.4	TU 1345		5.3
1844	1.4	1844		1.6
7 0101	5.6	**22** 0155		5.5
0728	0.6	0817		1.2
TU 1335	5.8	W 1419		5.4
1935	1.0	1916		1.3
8 0153	6.0	**23** 0229		5.5
0820	0.3	0740		1.0
W 1423	6.1	TH 1449		5.5
● 2024	0.7	○ 1954		1.1
9 0242	6.2	**24** 0302		5.6
0906	0.0	0815		0.9
TH 1510	6.2	F 1520		5.6
2108	0.5	2032		1.0
10 0330	6.4	**25** 0335		5.6
0946	0.0	0849		0.9
F 1556	6.2	SA 1553		5.5
2148	0.5	2105		1.0
11 0418	6.3	**26** 0409		5.6
1021	0.2	0916		0.9
SA 1642	6.1	SU 1628		5.5
2222	0.6	2132		1.1
12 0506	6.2	**27** 0446		5.5
1052	0.5	0939		1.1
SU 1728	5.8	M 1705		5.4
2251	0.9	2155		1.2
13 0554	5.9	**28** 0525		5.3
1121	1.0	1005		1.3
M 1814	5.5	TU 1745		5.2
2323	1.3	2223		1.4
14 0642	5.5	**29** 0606		5.2
1157	1.6	1038		1.5
TU 1901	5.1	W 1827		5.0
		2300		1.6
15 0010	1.7	**30** 0651		5.0
0735	5.0	1120		1.9
W 1255	2.1	TH 1912		4.8
◗ 1952	4.8	2350		1.9

OCTOBER

Time	m		Time	m
1 0742	4.8	**16** 0250		2.3
1217	2.3	0932		4.5
F 2004	4.7	SA 1516		2.6
◗		2156		4.5
2 0309	2.2	**17** 0506		2.1
0843	4.7	1045		4.6
SA 1539	2.4	SU 1702		2.5
2108	4.7	2303		4.7
3 0418	1.8	**18** 0556		1.8
0959	4.8	1143		4.8
SU 1641	2.1	M 1751		2.2
2225	4.9	2357		4.9
4 0517	1.4	**19** 0637		1.6
1117	5.1	1231		5.0
M 1733	1.7	TU 1820		1.9
2337	5.2			
5 0612	1.0	**20** 0041		5.2
1219	5.5	0710		1.5
TU 1823	1.3	W 1312		5.2
		1813		1.6
6 0036	5.6	**21** 0121		5.3
0706	0.6	0637		1.3
W 1312	5.8	TH 1347		5.4
1913	1.0	1847		1.4
7 0129	6.0	**22** 0157		5.5
0756	0.4	0708		1.2
TH 1400	6.1	F 1419		5.5
● 2003	0.7	1926		1.1
8 0218	6.2	**23** 0233		5.6
0841	0.2	0744		1.0
F 1447	6.2	SA 1452		5.6
2048	0.6	○ 2004		1.0
9 0307	6.3	**24** 0308		5.6
0921	0.3	0818		1.0
SA 1532	6.1	SU 1527		5.6
2128	0.6	2039		1.0
10 0355	6.2	**25** 0345		5.6
0956	0.5	0848		1.1
SU 1618	6.0	M 1603		5.6
2203	0.7	2110		1.1
11 0443	6.0	**26** 0424		5.5
1027	0.9	0915		1.2
M 1703	5.7	TU 1642		5.4
2229	1.0	2137		1.2
12 0531	5.7	**27** 0505		5.4
1052	1.3	0944		1.3
TU 1747	5.4	W 1722		5.3
2256	1.3	2209		1.3
13 0619	5.3	**28** 0548		5.3
1124	1.8	1021		1.6
W 1832	5.1	TH 1806		5.1
2341	1.7	2250		1.5
14 0710	5.0	**29** 0635		5.1
1219	2.2	1107		1.9
TH 1920	4.8	F 1853		5.0
◗		2346		1.7
15 0102	2.1	**30** 0727		4.9
0812	4.6	1211		2.2
F 1343	2.6	SA 1946		4.8
2026	4.6	◗		
		31 0236		1.9
		0827		4.8
		SU 1502		2.3
		2050		4.8

NOVEMBER

Time	m		Time	m
1 0350	1.6	**16** 0440		2.1
0940	4.9	1053		4.6
M 1610	2.1	TU 1629		2.3
2204	5.0	2307		4.7
2 0451	1.3	**17** 0530		1.9
1052	5.1	1145		4.8
TU 1707	1.8	W 1710		2.1
2313	5.3	2357		4.9
3 0548	1.1	**18** 0546		1.8
1154	5.4	1230		5.1
W 1800	1.4	TH 1745		1.8
4 0012	5.6	**19** 0041		5.1
0642	0.8	0607		1.6
TH 1248	5.7	F 1310		5.3
1853	1.2	1821		1.5
5 0107	5.8	**20** 0123		5.3
0733	0.7	0640		1.4
F 1339	5.9	SA 1348		5.4
1946	0.9	1900		1.3
6 0159	6.0	**21** 0204		5.5
0819	0.6	0716		1.3
SA 1427	6.0	SU 1426		5.5
● 2033	0.8	○ 1940		1.2
7 0249	6.0	**22** 0244		5.6
0859	0.7	0752		1.2
SU 1513	5.9	M 1504		5.6
2115	0.8	2019		1.1
8 0337	6.0	**23** 0324		5.6
0935	0.9	0826		1.2
M 1558	5.8	TU 1544		5.6
2151	0.9	2055		1.0
9 0424	5.8	**24** 0406		5.6
1006	1.2	0900		1.2
TU 1642	5.6	W 1624		5.6
2214	1.1	2130		1.0
10 0511	5.6	**25** 0449		5.5
1027	1.5	0936		1.3
W 1724	5.4	TH 1707		5.5
2235	1.3	2208		1.1
11 0557	5.3	**26** 0535		5.4
1053	1.8	1017		1.5
TH 1806	5.2	F 1752		5.3
2314	1.6	2253		1.2
12 0644	5.0	**27** 0623		5.3
1133	2.1	1107		1.7
F 1848	4.9	SA 1841		5.2
		2352		1.4
13 0009	1.9	**28** 0716		5.2
0735	4.7	1211		2.0
SA 1242	2.4	SU 1934		5.1
◗ 1936	4.7	◗		
14 0137	2.1	**29** 0116		1.5
0837	4.5	0812		5.1
SU 1412	2.6	M 1346		2.1
2047	4.6	2034		5.1
15 0308	2.2	**30** 0306		1.5
0950	4.5	0917		5.0
M 1528	2.5	TU 1523		2.0
2208	4.6	2141		5.1

DECEMBER

Time	m		Time	m
1 0417	1.4	**16** 0412		2.1
1024	5.1	1037		4.6
W 1634	1.9	TH 1632		2.3
2248	5.2	2258		4.7
2 0521	1.3	**17** 0504		2.0
1126	5.3	1137		4.8
TH 1738	1.7	F 1719		2.0
2350	5.4	2355		4.9
3 0621	1.2	**18** 0545		1.8
1225	5.5	1229		5.0
F 1841	1.4	SA 1802		1.8
4 0048	5.6	**19** 0047		5.1
0715	1.1	0621		1.7
SA 1320	5.6	SU 1317		5.3
1938	1.2	1843		1.5
5 0143	5.7	**20** 0135		5.3
0803	1.1	0659		1.5
SU 1411	5.7	M 1401		5.4
● 2028	1.1	1926		1.3
6 0235	5.7	**21** 0220		5.5
0844	1.1	0738		1.3
M 1458	5.7	TU 1444		5.6
2111	1.0	○ 2010		1.0
7 0322	5.7	**22** 0304		5.6
0920	1.2	0818		1.2
TU 1543	5.7	W 1526		5.7
2147	1.0	2053		0.9
8 0407	5.6	**23** 0348		5.7
0949	1.3	0858		1.2
W 1624	5.6	TH 1610		5.7
2209	1.1	2134		0.8
9 0451	5.5	**24** 0434		5.7
1008	1.4	0938		1.2
TH 1704	5.4	F 1654		5.7
2219	1.2	2216		0.8
10 0533	5.3	**25** 0521		5.7
1031	1.6	1021		1.2
F 1741	5.3	SA 1741		5.7
2250	1.4	2259		0.8
11 0614	5.1	**26** 0610		5.6
1100	1.8	1107		1.4
SA 1818	5.1	SU 1829		5.6
2327	1.6	2347		1.0
12 0655	4.9	**27** 0700		5.4
1137	2.0	1200		1.6
SU 1859	4.9	M 1919		5.4
13 0010	1.8	**28** 0041		1.2
0739	4.7	0752		5.2
M 1224	2.3	TU 1300		1.8
◗ 1946	4.7	◗ 2013		5.3
14 0104	2.0	**29** 0143		1.4
0830	4.6	0849		5.1
TU 1358	2.5	W 1411		2.0
2042	4.6	2115		5.1
15 0258	2.2	**30** 0309		1.7
0930	4.5	0953		5.0
W 1533	2.4	TH 1544		2.0
2150	4.6	2222		5.0
		31 0452		1.7
		1059		5.0
		F 1725		1.9
		2329		5.1

Chart Datum: 2·95 metres below Ordnance Datum (Newlyn). HAT is 6·4 metres above Chart Datum; see 0.19

4.7 FIRTH OF FORTH
E and W Lothian/City of Edinburgh/Fife

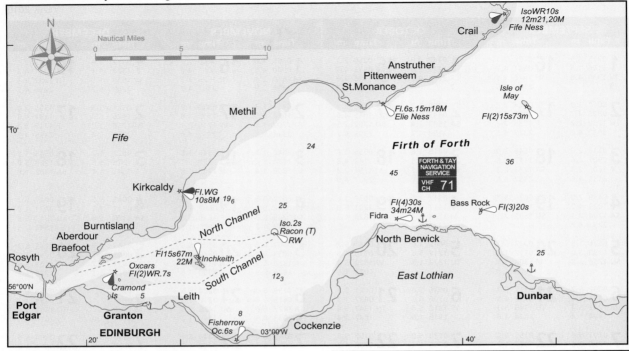

CHARTS AC 734, 735, 736, 737, 741; Imray C23, C27.

TIDES +0350 (Granton) Dover; ML 3·3; Duration 0620

Standard Port LEITH (→)

Times				Height (metres)			
High Water		Low Water		MHWS	MHWN	MLWN	MLWS
0300	0900	0300	0900	5·6	4·4	2·0	0·8
1500	2100	1500	2100				
Differences COCKENZIE							
−0007	−0015	−0013	−0005	−0·2	0·0	No data	

GRANTON: Same as LEITH

SHELTER Granton mostly dries but is open to violent swell in N'lies. Pontoons on E side of Middle Pier in about 2m and RFYC welcomes visitors. Pilot launches berth at seaward end. W hbr is planned for development as a marina. Port Edgar Marina offers good shelter, except for a surge at LW esp in E winds, but prone to silting. Caution: strong tidal streams. Do not enter E of wavebreak; 3kn sp limit. Leith is purely commercial. Rosyth should only be used in emergency. Forth Navigation Service controls the Firth of Forth, Granton Hbr and all commercial impounded docks.

NAVIGATION WPT Granton 56°00′·00N 03°13′·31W, 180°/0·72M to ent. WPT Port Edgar 56°N 03°24′·3W, 244°/3ca to W bkwtr.

- Beware Hound Pt terminal; Forth Railway and Road Bridges; vessels bound to/from Rosyth and Grangemouth especially in local fog (haar). 12kn speed limit W of Forth Rly Bridge.
- On N shore, no vessel may enter Mortimer's Deep (Braefoot gas terminal) without approval from Forth Navigation Service.
- Protected chan runs from Nos 13 & 14 buoys (NNW of Oxcars) under the bridges (N of Inch Garvie and Beamer Rk), to Rosyth. When activated (occas) via Forth Ports plc, other vessels must clear the chan for Rosyth traffic.

LIGHTS AND MARKS See 4.3 and chartlets. Granton: R flag with W diagonal cross (or ● lt) on signal mast at middle pier hd = Entry prohib.

R/T Call *Forth Navigation* (at Grangemouth) Ch **71** (calling and short messages, H24) 16; **20** 12 will be requested if necessary. Traffic, nav and weather info available on request. Leith Hbr

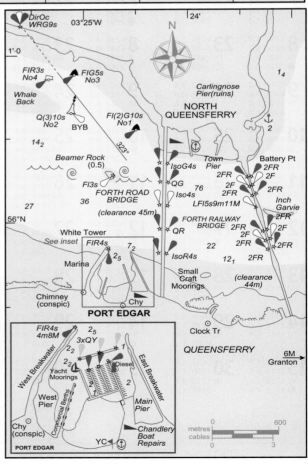

Radio Ch 12. Granton marina, call *Boswell* Ch M. Port Edgar Marina Ch M **80** (Apr-Sept 0900-1930; Oct-Mar 0900-1630 LT). Rosyth Dockyard, call *QHM* Ch 74 13 73 (Mon-Fri: 0730-1700). Grangemouth Docks Ch 14 (H24).

TELEPHONE (Code 0131) Forth Navigation Service 5558700; QHM Rosyth (01383) 425050; MRCC (01333) 450666; Weather (0141) 2483451; Marinecall 09068 969642; Police (S Queensferry) 3311798; Ⓗ Edinburgh Royal Infirmary 2292477; Flag Officer Scotland/Northern Ireland (01436) 674321 ext 3206, for Naval activities off N and E Scotland; Forth Yacht Clubs Ass'n 5523452.

FACILITIES

GRANTON Extensive development of the W hbr is proposed. HM via Leith, ☎ 555 8866, Access HW±3½, FW, Slip; **Royal Forth YC** ☎ 552 3006, Slip, M, L, FW, C (5 ton), D, El, Bar; **Forth Corinthian YC** ☎ 552 5939, Slip, M, L, Bar; **Services:** Gas, Gaz, ✕, CH, ME. **Town** D, P, ☒, R, Bar, ✉, Ⓑ, ⇌, ✈ (Buses to Edinburgh).

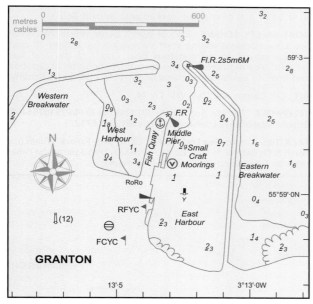

ROSYTH Dockyard and ferry port; no facilities for yachts except in emergency. **Ferries:** Zeebrugge; 3/week; 17 Hrs; Superfast (www.superfast.com).

Standard Port ROSYTH (⟵)

Times				Height (metres)			
High Water		Low Water		MHWS	MHWN	MLWN	MLWS
0300	1000	0300	0900	5·8	4·7	2·2	0·8
1500	2200	1500	2100				
Differences GRANGEMOUTH							
+0015	+0010	−0050	−0045	0·0	−0·1	−0·2	−0·2
KINCARDINE							
+0015	+0030	−0030	−0030	0·0	−0·2	−0·5	−0·3

SOUTH QUEENSFERRY Standard Port Rosyth (⟵)
Port Edgar Marina (301+8 visitors) ☎ 331 3330, admin.PE@ edinburghleisure.co.uk, £1.90, Access H24, Wi-fi, M, Slip, CH, ME, D, C (5 ton) on N end of main pier, El, Ⓔ, ME, ✕, SM, Gas, Gaz, FW, R; Port Edgar YC, Bar. **Town** P, ☒, R, Bar, ✉, Ⓑ, ⇌ (Dalmeny), ✈ Edinburgh.

GRANGEMOUTH: Standard Port Rosyth (⟵). HM ☎ 01324 498566 (H24); Port Office ☎ 498597 (HO). VHF Ch 14 16. Commercial port.

FIRTH OF FORTH

MINOR HARBOURS AND ANCHORAGES ON THE S SHORE

FISHERROW, East Lothian, **55°56′·79N 03°04′·09W.** AC 734, 735. HW +0345 on Dover, −0005 on Leith; HW −0·1m on Leith; ML 3·0m; Duration 0620. Shelter good except in NW winds. Mainly a pleasure craft hbr, dries 5ca offshore. Appr dangerous in on-shore winds. Access HW±2. High-rise block (38m) is conspic 9ca W of hbr. E pier lt, Oc 6s 5m 6M on metal framework tr. Berth on E pier. HM ☎ (0131) 665 5900; **Fisherrow YC** FW.

Town ☒, P & D from garage, R, Bar, Ⓑ, ✉, SM.

CRAMOND, City of Edinburgh, **55°59′·80N 03°17′·49W.** AC 736. Tides as Leith (see 4.7). Cramond Island, approx 1M offshore, is connected to the S shore of the Firth by a drying causeway. A chan, marked by 7 SHM posts, leads W of Cramond Island to Cramond hbr at the mouth of R Almond, conspic white houses. Access HW±2; AB free or ‡ off the Is. Seek local advice from: **Cramond Boat Club** ☎ (0131) 336 1356, FW, M, Bar. **Village** ☒, R, Pub, Bus.

MINOR HARBOURS AND ANCHORAGES ON THE N SHORE

INCHCOLM, Fife, **56°01′·85N 03°17′·89W.** AC 736. Tides see 4.7. Best ‡ in 4m, N of abbey (conspic); appr from NW or ESE, to land at pier close E (small fee). Meadulse Rks (dry) on N side. Ends of island foul. At SE end, lt Fl (3) 15s, obsc 075°-145°. No facilities. ☎ 0131-244 3101. Keep clear of large ships under way in Mortimer's Deep.

ABERDOUR, Fife, **56°03′·00N 03°17′·49W.** AC 735, 736. HW +0345 on Dover; +0005 on Leith; HW 0·5m on Leith; ML 3·3m; Duration 0630. See 4.7. Good shelter except in SE winds when a swell occurs. The ‡ between The Little Craigs and the disused pier is good but exposed to winds from E to SW. Temp berths £2 are available in hbr (dries) alongside the quay wall. Beware Little Craigs (dries 2·2m) and outfall 2ca N marked by bn. There are no lts/ marks. Facilities: FW (tap on pier), P, R, ☒, Bar in village; **Aberdour BC** ☎ (01592) 202827.

ELIE, Fife, **56°11′·20N 02°49′·29W.** AC 734. HW +0325 on Dover, −0015 on Leith; HW −0·1m on Leith; ML 3·0m; Duration 0620; Elie B provides good shelter from N winds for small craft but local knowledge is needed. Hbr dries; 3 short term waiting buoys available. Beware ledge off end of pier which dries. From E beware Ox Rk (dries 1m) 5M ENE of Elie Ness; from W beware rks off Chapel Ness, W Vows, E Vows (surmounted by cage bn) and Thill Rk, marked by PHM Fl(4)R.10s buoy. Lt: Elie Ness Fl 6s 15m 18M, W tr. HM (01333) 330051; AB (3) drying £5, M, ☒, FW, CH, SC, Slip. Police 592100. Dr ☎ 330302; **Services:** P & D (tanker), Gas, Gaz. El. In Elie & Earlsferry: R, ☒, Bar, ✉, Ⓑ.

ST MONANS, Fife, **56°12′·25 N 02°45′·94W.** AC 734. HW +0335 on Dover, −0020 on Leith; HW −0·1m on Leith; ML 3·0m; Duration 0620. Shelter good except in strong SE to SW winds when scend occurs in the hbr (dries). Berth alongside E pier until contact with HM. From NE keep at least 2½ca from coast. Bkwtr hd Oc WRG 6s 5m 7/4M; E pier hd 2 FG (vert) 6m 4M. W pier hd 2 FR (vert) 6m 4M. **Facilities** HM ☎ 07836 703014 if no reply, 01333 310836 (Anstruther HM assists); AB £15.29 then £10.37 thereafter, FW, ☒, El; **Services:** Gas, P & D (tanker), AC. Police ☎ (01333) 592100. **Village** R, Bar, ☒, ✉, Ⓑ.

4.8 FORTH AND CLYDE CANAL

Lowland Carron River Ent. **51°02'·30N 03°41·46W** ❀♨♨♨❀❀

These notes are for the convenience of those entering the canal at Grangemouth.

CHARTS AC 737, 741; Imray C27; BWS *Skipper's Guide* Forth & Clyde and Union Canal essential. Obtain from British Waterways Scotland, Lowland Canals, Rosebank House, Camelon, Main Street, Falkirk. FK1 4DS. ☎ (01324) 671217 or www.scottish canals.co.uk

TIDES Carron River +0325 Dover, 0030 Leith.

SHELTER Carron Sea Lock operates HW–4 to HW+1½, 0800-2000 and daylight hours. Temporary berthing at Grangemouth YC or at nearby Refuge Posts. Temporary anchorages close WNW of Carron PHM and close SSW of Carron Bn SHM dependent on depth.

NAVIGATION Carron River entrance approached from Grangemouth Roads via Small Craft Recommended Tracks close N of Ship Manoeuvring Area.

- Canal passage has to be booked in advance, call *Carron Sea Lock* VHF Ch74, ☎ (01324)483034/07810 0794468.
- The canal is about 30M long with 39 locks. Allow a minimum of 21 hours underway for a passage to Bowling Sea Lock. Transit of the canal can be achieved in 2 days by reaching the Summit Pound at Lock 20 Wyndford on the first day.
- Canal can take vessels 20m LOA, 6m beam, 1.8m draft (add 0.1m/4inches to draft for freshwater), mast height 3.0m. Masts should be unstepped before passing through Kerse

Bridge which is equipped with air draft gauges calibrated for the canal dimensions.

- Mast craneage at Port Edgar or BWS mast crane pontoon near Grangemouth YC.
- Vessels should have a reliable engine and be capable of a minimum speed through the water of 4kn against adverse conditions. Ebb tide attains rates of up to 6kn in Carron River after heavy rainfall. 4mph speed limit throughout the canal.
- Access via Falkirk Wheel to Union Canal and Edinburgh, refer to BWS *Skipper's Guide.*

LOCKS Carron Sea Lock and Bowling Sea Lock are operated by BW Staff. At other locks BW Staff available to assist. 5 day passage licence costs £5/m and £4/m return including access to the Falkirk Wheel, Union Canal and Edinburgh.

LIGHTS AND MARKS Carron River channel is marked by lighted By PHM & Bn SHM and unlit By(s) PHM & SHM. Bkwtr/Training Bank to W & N of channel marked with Bn(s) & Bol(s).

BOAT SAFETY SCHEME BWS *Skipper's Guide* refers. At Carron Sea Lock transient/visiting craft staying no more than 28 days will be subject to a Dangerous Boat Check of gas and fuel systems. Also required to complete a boat condition declaration and provide evidence of insurance for £1M third party liability.

R/T Call *Carron Sea Lock* VHF Ch **74**.

TELEPHONE Carron Sea Lock (01324) 483034/07810794468. British Waterways Lowlands Canals (01324) 671271.

FACILITIES Carron Sea Lock ⚓ ,P,⬛, 🚾, ⚓, Slip. **Falkirk Wheel (on Forth & Clyde)** FW, P, D, ⬛, 🚾, ⚓. For details throughout the canal refer to BWB *Skipper's Guide* (using maps).

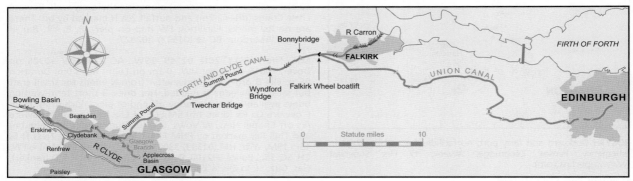

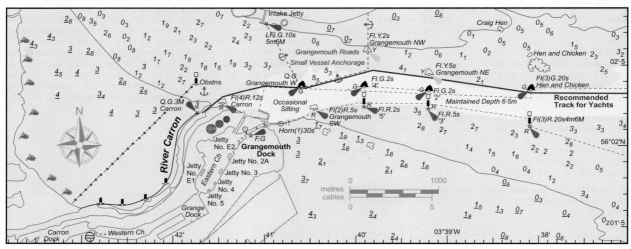

LEITH LAT 55°59′N LONG 3°11′W
TIMES AND HEIGHTS OF HIGH AND LOW WATERS

TIME ZONE (UT)
For Summer Time add ONE hour in **non-shaded areas**

Dates in red are **SPRINGS**
Dates in blue are **NEAPS**

YEAR **2010**

JANUARY

Time	m	Time	m
1 0228	5.6	**16** 0318	5.2
0830	1.1	0847	1.3
F 1448	5.7	SA 1524	5.3
2104	0.6	2124	1.1
2 0316	5.8	**17** 0350	5.2
0920	1.0	0919	1.3
SA 1532	5.8	SU 1555	5.3
2155	0.4	2151	1.0
3 0403	5.8	**18** 0422	5.2
1007	0.9	0950	1.2
SU 1618	5.9	M 1627	5.3
2244	0.3	2219	1.0
4 0450	5.8	**19** 0455	5.1
1052	1.0	1021	1.3
M 1705	5.8	TU 1659	5.2
2331	0.4	2247	1.1
5 0539	5.6	**20** 0529	5.0
1135	1.2	1048	1.4
TU 1755	5.7	W 1733	5.1
		2314	1.3
6 0017	0.7	**21** 0606	4.9
0631	5.3	1114	1.6
W 1217	1.4	TH 1808	5.0
1849	5.4	2342	1.4
7 0103	1.0	**22** 0645	4.7
0726	5.0	1143	1.9
TH 1301	1.7	F 1848	4.8
◑ 1951	5.2		
8 0153	1.4	**23** 0016	1.6
0827	4.8	0729	4.6
F 1400	2.0	SA 1226	2.0
2058	4.9	◐ 1935	4.7
9 0257	1.8	**24** 0105	1.9
0931	4.6	0824	4.4
SA 1519	2.1	SU 1335	2.2
2205	4.7	2037	4.5
10 0414	2.0	**25** 0219	2.1
1036	4.6	0933	4.4
SU 1644	2.1	M 1520	2.2
2314	4.7	2159	4.5
11 0526	2.0	**26** 0408	2.1
1143	4.6	1048	4.5
M 1801	1.9	TU 1658	2.0
		2319	4.6
12 0021	4.7	**27** 0537	1.9
0624	1.9	1159	4.7
TU 1245	4.8	W 1810	1.7
1902	1.7		
13 0119	4.9	**28** 0029	5.0
0707	1.8	0639	1.6
W 1334	5.0	TH 1259	5.1
1947	1.5	1911	1.2
14 0205	5.0	**29** 0127	5.3
0742	1.6	0733	1.3
TH 1415	5.1	F 1348	5.4
2024	1.3	2007	0.7
15 0244	5.1	**30** 0216	5.6
0815	1.5	0822	1.0
F 1451	5.2	SA 1433	5.7
● 2056	1.1	○ 2057	0.3
		31 0302	5.8
		0908	0.7
		SU 1517	6.0
		2144	0.1

FEBRUARY

Time	m	Time	m
1 0346	5.9	**16** 0356	5.2
0952	0.6	0933	1.0
M 1601	6.1	TU 1604	5.4
2229	0.0	2159	0.8
2 0431	5.8	**17** 0427	5.2
1034	0.7	1001	1.0
TU 1646	6.0	W 1634	5.3
2311	0.2	2223	0.9
3 0516	5.6	**18** 0459	5.1
1111	0.9	1023	1.1
W 1733	5.8	TH 1705	5.2
2349	0.5	2242	1.1
4 0603	5.3	**19** 0533	5.0
1144	1.1	1041	1.3
TH 1823	5.5	F 1739	5.1
		2301	1.2
5 0024	1.0	**20** 0609	4.9
0652	5.0	1107	1.5
F 1216	1.5	SA 1818	5.0
◑ 1918	5.1	2330	1.5
6 0058	1.5	**21** 0651	4.7
0747	4.7	1145	1.7
SA 1303	1.8	SU 1905	4.7
2022	4.7		
7 0149	2.0	**22** 0013	1.8
0849	4.4	0741	4.5
SU 1426	2.2	M 1245	2.0
2132	4.5	◐ 2005	4.5
8 0324	2.3	**23** 0126	2.1
0958	4.3	0849	4.3
M 1627	2.2	TU 1438	2.2
2249	4.4	2128	4.4
9 0503	2.3	**24** 0349	2.3
1115	4.4	1017	4.4
TU 1805	2.0	W 1645	2.0
		2258	4.5
10 0009	4.5	**25** 0526	2.0
0612	2.2	1137	4.6
W 1230	4.6	TH 1803	1.5
1902	1.7		
11 0110	4.7	**26** 0014	4.9
0656	1.9	0627	1.6
TH 1322	4.8	F 1240	5.0
1942	1.5	1902	1.0
12 0153	4.9	**27** 0111	5.3
0729	1.7	0718	1.2
F 1401	5.0	SA 1330	5.5
2013	1.2	1955	0.5
13 0228	5.1	**28** 0159	5.6
0759	1.4	0804	0.8
SA 1435	5.2	SU 1414	5.8
2040	1.1	○ 2041	0.2
14 0259	5.2		
0830	1.2		
SU 1505	5.3		
● 2105	0.9		
15 0327	5.2		
0902	1.1		
M 1534	5.4		
2132	0.8		

MARCH

Time	m	Time	m
1 0242	5.8	**16** 0259	5.2
0849	0.6	0839	1.0
M 1456	6.0	TU 1507	5.4
2125	-0.1	2105	0.8
2 0324	5.9	**17** 0328	5.3
0931	0.4	0911	0.9
TU 1540	6.1	W 1537	5.4
2207	0.0	2133	0.8
3 0407	5.8	**18** 0358	5.3
1011	0.5	0939	0.9
W 1624	6.0	TH 1608	5.4
2245	0.2	2156	0.9
4 0450	5.6	**19** 0430	5.2
1047	0.7	1001	1.0
TH 1710	5.8	F 1641	5.3
2319	0.6	2212	1.0
5 0534	5.3	**20** 0504	5.1
1115	1.0	1019	1.1
F 1758	5.4	SA 1718	5.2
2346	1.1	2231	1.2
6 0619	5.0	**21** 0541	5.0
1141	1.3	1046	1.3
SA 1851	5.0	SU 1759	5.0
		2302	1.5
7 0011	1.6	**22** 0623	4.8
0709	4.7	1127	1.5
SU 1224	1.8	M 1849	4.8
◑ 1951	4.6	2348	1.8
8 0058	2.1	**23** 0714	4.5
0809	4.4	1235	1.8
M 1338	2.1	TU 1951	4.5
2058	4.3	◐	
9 0231	2.5	**24** 0114	2.2
0918	4.2	0823	4.4
TU 1614	2.2	W 1441	2.0
2216	4.2	2113	4.4
10 0434	2.5	**25** 0343	2.3
1038	4.2	0955	4.4
W 1747	2.0	TH 1635	1.7
2345	4.3	2241	4.6
11 0544	2.2	**26** 0506	2.0
1200	4.4	1116	4.7
TH 1839	1.7	F 1746	1.3
		2354	4.9
12 0047	4.6	**27** 0604	1.6
0629	1.9	1216	5.1
F 1255	4.7	SA 1843	0.8
1916	1.1		
13 0129	4.8	**28** 0049	5.3
0703	1.6	0653	1.2
SA 1335	4.9	SU 1306	5.5
1945	1.2	1933	0.5
14 0202	5.0	**29** 0136	5.5
0735	1.4	0740	0.8
SU 1408	5.1	M 1350	5.8
2012	1.0	2018	0.2
15 0231	5.1	**30** 0218	5.7
0807	1.1	0824	0.5
M 1438	5.3	TU 1434	6.0
● 2038	0.9	○ 2101	0.1
		31 0259	5.7
		0908	0.4
		W 1518	6.0
		2141	0.2

APRIL

Time	m	Time	m
1 0342	5.7	**16** 0330	5.3
0948	0.5	0917	0.9
TH 1603	5.9	F 1545	5.4
2218	0.5	2131	0.9
2 0424	5.5	**17** 0404	5.3
1025	0.7	0948	0.9
F 1650	5.6	SA 1622	5.3
2249	0.9	2155	1.1
3 0507	5.3	**18** 0440	5.2
1055	1.0	1016	1.0
SA 1737	5.3	SU 1703	5.2
2311	1.3	2220	1.3
4 0550	5.0	**19** 0520	5.0
1120	1.3	1052	1.2
SU 1827	4.9	M 1748	5.1
2337	1.7	2257	1.6
5 0638	4.7	**20** 0606	4.9
1159	1.7	1146	1.4
M 1922	4.5	TU 1841	4.9
		2357	1.9
6 0022	2.1	**21** 0700	4.6
0733	4.4	1306	1.6
TU 1303	2.0	W 1944	4.7
◑ 2023	4.3	◐	
7 0142	2.5	**22** 0142	2.1
0839	4.2	0810	4.5
W 1534	2.2	TH 1443	1.6
2132	4.1	2102	4.6
8 0347	2.5	**23** 0322	2.1
0952	4.2	0935	4.6
TH 1659	2.0	F 1612	1.4
2253	4.2	2220	4.7
9 0457	2.3	**24** 0435	1.9
1109	4.3	1048	4.8
F 1753	1.8	SA 1719	1.1
		2328	4.9
10 0004	4.4	**25** 0532	1.5
0545	2.0	1149	5.1
SA 1211	4.6	SU 1815	0.9
1832	1.5		
11 0049	4.7	**26** 0023	5.2
0626	1.7	0623	1.2
SU 1255	4.8	M 1241	5.4
1904	1.3	1905	0.6
12 0124	4.9	**27** 0110	5.4
0702	1.4	0712	0.9
M 1331	5.0	TU 1328	5.6
1933	1.1	1951	0.5
13 0155	5.1	**28** 0154	5.5
0737	1.2	0800	0.7
TU 1404	5.2	W 1414	5.7
2003	0.9	○ 2034	0.5
14 0226	5.2	**29** 0236	5.6
0811	1.0	0846	0.6
W 1437	5.3	TH 1500	5.7
● 2033	0.9	2114	0.6
15 0258	5.3	**30** 0319	5.5
0845	0.9	0929	0.6
TH 1510	5.3	F 1546	5.6
2103	0.8	2150	0.8

Chart Datum: 2·90 metres below Ordnance Datum (Newlyn). HAT is 6·3 metres above Chart Datum; see 0.19

>> FREE monthly updates from <<
www.reedsalmanac.co.uk
181

SE Scotland

TIME ZONE (UT)
For Summer Time add ONE hour in **non-shaded areas**

LEITH   LAT 55°59′N   LONG 3°11′W
TIMES AND HEIGHTS OF HIGH AND LOW WATERS

Dates in red are **SPRINGS**
Dates in blue are NEAPS

YEAR 2010

MAY

Time	m		Time	m
1 0401	5.4		**16** 0344	5.3
1007	0.8		0943	0.8
SA 1632	5.4		SU 1607	5.4
2220	1.1		2156	1.1
2 0443	5.2		**17** 0424	5.3
1039	1.0		1028	0.9
SU 1718	5.1		M 1652	5.4
2244	1.5		2239	1.3
3 0526	5.0		**18** 0507	5.2
1107	1.3		1117	1.0
M 1805	4.9		TU 1741	5.2
2313	1.8		2328	1.5
4 0610	4.8		**19** 0556	5.1
1142	1.6		1212	1.1
TU 1854	4.6		W 1834	5.0
2356	2.0			
5 0701	4.5		**20** 0026	1.7
1233	1.8		0651	4.9
W 1947	4.4		TH 1314	1.2
			◑ 1935	4.9
6 0058	2.3		**21** 0135	1.9
0758	4.4		0757	4.8
TH 1351	2.0		F 1426	1.3
◓ 2044	4.2		2044	4.8
7 0231	2.4		**22** 0250	1.9
0901	4.3		0912	4.8
F 1545	2.0		SA 1540	1.3
2147	4.2		2155	4.8
8 0357	2.3		**23** 0359	1.8
1006	4.3		1021	4.9
SA 1647	1.9		SU 1645	1.2
2251	4.3		2259	4.9
9 0454	2.1		**24** 0459	1.6
1108	4.4		1123	5.1
SU 1733	1.7		M 1743	1.1
2347	4.5		2356	5.0
10 0541	1.8		**25** 0555	1.4
1201	4.6		1218	5.2
M 1812	1.5		TU 1837	1.0
11 0034	4.7		**26** 0046	5.2
0623	1.6		0649	1.2
TU 1247	4.8		W 1310	5.3
1848	1.3		1924	1.0
12 0114	5.0		**27** 0133	5.3
0702	1.3		0741	1.0
W 1329	5.0		TH 1359	5.4
1923	1.1		○ 2008	0.9
13 0152	5.1		**28** 0218	5.3
0741	1.1		0829	0.8
TH 1408	5.2		F 1447	5.4
1959	1.0		2048	1.0
14 0229	5.3		**29** 0301	5.3
0820	1.0		0913	0.8
F 1446	5.3		SA 1532	5.4
● 2036	1.0		2124	1.1
15 0306	5.3		**30** 0343	5.3
0900	0.8		0952	0.9
SA 1526	5.4		SU 1616	5.2
2115	1.0		2155	1.3
			31 0424	5.2
			1025	1.0
			M 1659	5.1
			2223	1.5

JUNE

Time	m		Time	m
1 0503	5.1		**16** 0456	5.5
1053	1.2		1119	0.6
TU 1740	4.9		W 1730	5.5
2254	1.6		2329	1.2
2 0544	4.9		**17** 0545	5.4
1124	1.4		1208	0.7
W 1823	4.7		TH 1822	5.3
2332	1.8			
3 0628	4.8		**18** 0018	1.4
1204	1.6		0638	5.3
TH 1908	4.5		F 1301	0.9
			1918	5.1
4 0020	2.0		**19** 0110	1.6
0715	4.6		0738	5.1
F 1255	1.7		SA 1357	1.1
◑ 1956	4.4		◓ 2020	4.9
5 0122	2.2		**20** 0211	1.7
0809	4.5		0846	5.0
SA 1358	1.9		SU 1501	1.3
2050	4.3		2125	4.8
6 0237	2.2		**21** 0319	1.8
0907	4.4		0954	4.9
SU 1512	1.9		M 1608	1.4
2147	4.3		2229	4.8
7 0350	2.2		**22** 0428	1.7
1007	4.4		1059	4.9
M 1621	1.8		TU 1713	1.5
2245	4.5		2330	4.8
8 0450	2.0		**23** 0534	1.6
1106	4.5		1202	4.9
TU 1716	1.7		W 1812	1.5
2342	4.6			
9 0542	1.8		**24** 0028	4.9
1203	4.7		0636	1.4
W 1804	1.5		TH 1300	5.0
			1902	1.4
10 0034	4.8		**25** 0120	5.1
0629	1.5		0732	1.2
TH 1255	4.9		F 1352	5.1
1849	1.4		1947	1.3
11 0122	5.1		**26** 0206	5.2
0714	1.3		0820	1.1
F 1342	5.1		SA 1438	5.2
1933	1.2		○ 2026	1.3
12 0205	5.2		**27** 0249	5.2
0801	1.0		0902	1.0
SA 1427	5.3		SU 1520	5.2
● 2019	1.1		2101	1.3
13 0246	5.4		**28** 0328	5.3
0850	0.8		0938	0.9
SU 1511	5.5		M 1559	5.2
2106	1.0		2132	1.3
14 0328	5.5		**29** 0405	5.2
0939	0.6		1008	1.0
M 1556	5.6		TU 1636	5.1
2154	1.0		2202	1.3
15 0411	5.5		**30** 0441	5.2
1029	0.5		1034	1.0
TU 1642	5.6		W 1713	5.0
2242	1.1		2234	1.4

JULY

Time	m		Time	m
1 0517	5.1		**16** 0528	5.7
1102	1.2		1152	0.4
TH 1750	4.9		F 1802	5.5
2307	1.5		2356	1.1
2 0555	5.0		**17** 0619	5.6
1135	1.3		1236	0.7
F 1829	4.7		SA 1854	5.2
2343	1.7			
3 0635	4.8		**18** 0038	1.4
1213	1.5		0714	5.3
SA 1912	4.6		SU 1322	1.1
			◑ 1950	4.9
4 0026	1.9		**19** 0129	1.6
0719	4.7		0819	5.0
SU 1258	1.7		M 1417	1.5
◑ 1959	4.5		2053	4.7
5 0122	2.1		**20** 0240	1.9
0809	4.5		0928	4.8
M 1353	1.9		TU 1531	1.8
2053	4.4		2159	4.6
6 0234	2.2		**21** 0406	1.9
0910	4.4		1039	4.7
TU 1503	2.0		W 1650	1.9
2154	4.4		2307	4.6
7 0353	2.2		**22** 0529	1.8
1017	4.4		1151	4.7
W 1622	1.9		TH 1758	1.9
2257	4.5			
8 0504	2.0		**23** 0014	4.8
1123	4.6		0641	1.6
TH 1734	1.8		F 1255	4.8
2359	4.7		1850	1.7
9 0603	1.7		**24** 0112	4.9
1226	4.8		0734	1.3
F 1827	1.6		SA 1347	5.0
			1932	1.6
10 0055	5.0		**25** 0157	5.1
0657	1.3		0815	1.1
SA 1322	5.1		SU 1429	5.1
1918	1.3		2006	1.4
11 0145	5.2		**26** 0236	5.2
0749	1.0		0850	1.0
SU 1411	5.4		M 1505	5.2
● 2008	1.1		○ 2039	1.3
12 0230	5.5		**27** 0311	5.3
0842	0.6		0920	0.9
M 1457	5.6		TU 1539	5.2
2057	0.9		2110	1.2
13 0313	5.7		**28** 0344	5.3
0932	0.3		0946	0.9
TU 1541	5.8		W 1611	5.2
2145	0.8		2141	1.1
14 0356	5.8		**29** 0416	5.3
1021	0.2		1011	0.9
W 1627	5.8		TH 1643	5.1
2230	0.8		2211	1.2
15 0441	5.8		**30** 0449	5.3
1107	0.2		1037	1.0
TH 1714	5.7		F 1717	5.0
2314	0.9		2240	1.3
			31 0523	5.1
			1103	1.1
			SA 1753	4.9
			2306	1.5

AUGUST

Time	m		Time	m
1 0558	5.0		**16** 0005	1.3
1130	1.3		0649	5.3
SU 1831	4.8		M 1244	1.3
2335	1.7		◐ 1919	4.9
2 0637	4.8		**17** 0050	1.6
1202	1.6		0753	4.9
M 1913	4.6		TU 1331	1.8
			2021	4.6
3 0013	1.9		**18** 0205	2.0
0722	4.6		0904	4.6
TU 1246	1.8		W 1455	2.2
◑ 2003	4.5		2130	4.5
4 0117	2.1		**19** 0358	2.1
0819	4.5		1019	4.5
W 1355	2.1		TH 1634	2.3
2106	4.4		2245	4.5
5 0255	2.2		**20** 0538	1.9
0932	4.4		1140	4.5
TH 1537	2.2		F 1749	2.1
2219	4.4			
6 0434	2.1		**21** 0000	4.7
1051	4.5		0641	1.6
F 1710	2.0		SA 1247	4.7
2330	4.6		1838	1.9
7 0547	1.7		**22** 0058	4.9
1203	4.8		0725	1.4
SA 1813	1.7		SU 1335	4.9
			1914	1.7
8 0033	5.0		**23** 0142	5.1
0646	1.3		0759	1.2
SU 1304	5.2		M 1412	5.1
1905	1.4		1944	1.4
9 0126	5.3		**24** 0217	5.3
0740	0.8		0828	1.0
M 1354	5.5		TU 1444	5.2
1954	1.0		○ 2015	1.2
10 0210	5.7		**25** 0249	5.4
0831	0.4		0853	0.9
TU 1438	5.8		W 1513	5.3
● 2041	0.8		2046	1.1
11 0253	5.9		**26** 0318	5.4
0918	0.1		0918	0.8
W 1522	5.9		TH 1542	5.3
2127	0.6		2117	1.0
12 0336	6.1		**27** 0348	5.4
1004	-0.1		0943	0.8
TH 1606	5.9		F 1612	5.2
2211	0.5		2147	1.0
13 0421	6.1		**28** 0419	5.4
1047	0.0		1008	0.9
F 1651	5.8		SA 1644	5.2
2252	0.7		2211	1.2
14 0507	5.9		**29** 0452	5.3
1128	0.3		1029	1.1
SA 1737	5.5		SU 1718	5.1
2329	0.9		2232	1.3
15 0556	5.7		**30** 0526	5.1
1206	0.8		1048	1.3
SU 1825	5.2		M 1754	4.9
			2255	1.5
			31 0605	4.9
			1113	1.5
			TU 1834	4.7
			2329	1.7

Chart Datum: 2·90 metres below Ordnance Datum (Newlyn). HAT is 6·3 metres above Chart Datum; see 0.19

TIME ZONE (UT)
For Summer Time add ONE hour in **non-shaded areas**

LEITH LAT 55°59′N LONG 3°11′W
TIMES AND HEIGHTS OF HIGH AND LOW WATERS

Dates in red are **SPRINGS**
Dates in blue are NEAPS

YEAR **2010**

SEPTEMBER

Time	m		Time	m
1 0650	4.7	**16**	0136	2.1
1151	1.8		0839	4.5
W 1922	4.6	TH	1417	2.4
◑			2101	4.4
2 0024	2.0	**17**	0355	2.2
0746	4.5		0954	4.4
TH 1257	2.2	F	1612	2.5
2025	4.4		2217	4.4
3 0216	2.2	**18**	0524	1.9
0900	4.4		1117	4.4
F 1513	2.3	SA	1724	2.3
2146	4.4		2333	4.6
4 0417	2.0	**19**	0620	1.7
1026	4.5		1224	4.7
SA 1656	2.1	SU	1810	2.0
2305	4.7			
5 0535	1.6	**20**	0031	4.8
1143	4.8		0659	1.4
SU 1758	1.7	M	1310	4.9
			1845	1.7
6 0010	5.0	**21**	0114	5.1
0632	1.1		0729	1.2
M 1244	5.2	TU	1345	5.1
1847	1.3		1916	1.5
7 0103	5.4	**22**	0149	5.2
0724	0.7		0755	1.1
TU 1332	5.6	W	1415	5.2
1934	1.0		1948	1.2
8 0147	5.8	**23**	0220	5.4
0812	0.3		0820	0.9
W 1416	5.9	TH	1443	5.3
● 2019	0.7	○	2020	1.1
9 0229	6.1	**24**	0250	5.4
0857	0.0		0846	0.9
TH 1458	6.0	F	1511	5.3
2104	0.5		2052	1.0
10 0313	6.2	**25**	0320	5.4
0941	0.0		0912	0.9
F 1541	6.0	SA	1541	5.3
2147	0.4		2121	1.0
11 0358	6.2	**26**	0352	5.4
1022	0.1		0936	1.0
SA 1625	5.8	SU	1613	5.3
2228	0.6		2146	1.1
12 0444	6.0	**27**	0425	5.3
1100	0.5		0956	1.1
SU 1710	5.5	M	1647	5.2
2304	0.9		2207	1.3
13 0534	5.6	**28**	0501	5.2
1134	1.0		1014	1.3
M 1757	5.2	TU	1723	5.0
2337	1.3		2231	1.4
14 0628	5.2	**29**	0542	5.0
1204	1.6		1041	1.6
TU 1849	4.9	W	1804	4.9
			2308	1.7
15 0019	1.7	**30**	0630	4.8
0729	4.8		1121	1.9
W 1248	2.1	TH	1853	4.7
◑ 1950	4.6			

OCTOBER

Time	m		Time	m
1 0010	1.9	**16**	0321	2.2
0727	4.6		0918	4.3
F 1233	2.3	SA	1526	2.6
◑ 1956	4.5		2138	4.4
2 0207	2.1	**17**	0443	2.0
0841	4.5		1033	4.4
SA 1501	2.4	SU	1637	2.4
2119	4.5		2249	4.5
3 0401	1.9	**18**	0537	1.8
1005	4.6		1142	4.6
SU 1633	2.1	M	1727	2.1
2240	4.8		2349	4.7
4 0514	1.5	**19**	0617	1.6
1120	4.9		1231	4.8
M 1733	1.7	TU	1807	1.7
2344	5.1			
5 0611	1.0	**20**	0036	5.0
1219	5.3		0648	1.4
TU 1822	1.4	W	1308	5.0
			1843	1.6
6 0036	5.5	**21**	0114	5.1
0701	0.6		0715	1.2
W 1307	5.6	TH	1340	5.2
1908	1.0		1918	1.2
7 0122	5.9	**22**	0147	5.3
0747	0.3		0743	1.1
TH 1351	5.8	F	1410	5.3
● 1954	0.7		1952	1.2
8 0206	6.1	**23**	0220	5.4
0832	0.2		0812	1.0
F 1433	5.9	SA	1441	5.4
2040	0.5	○	2026	1.1
9 0251	6.1	**24**	0254	5.4
0915	0.2		0841	1.0
SA 1516	5.9	SU	1513	5.4
2125	0.5		2059	1.0
10 0337	6.1	**25**	0328	5.4
0955	0.5		0909	1.1
SU 1559	5.7	M	1547	5.4
2207	0.7		2130	1.1
11 0425	5.8	**26**	0404	5.4
1032	0.8		0935	1.2
M 1644	5.5	TU	1622	5.3
2245	1.0		2200	1.2
12 0515	5.5	**27**	0443	5.3
1103	1.3		1000	1.4
TU 1731	5.2	W	1700	5.2
2319	1.3		2233	1.4
13 0608	5.1	**28**	0527	5.1
1128	1.8		1032	1.7
W 1821	4.9	TH	1743	5.0
2357	1.7		2320	1.5
14 0706	4.8	**29**	0616	5.0
1210	2.2		1120	2.0
TH 1920	4.7	F	1833	4.9
◐				
15 0103	2.0	**30**	0032	1.7
0809	4.5		0714	4.8
F 1326	2.5	SA	1250	2.2
2027	4.5	◑	1935	4.7
		31	0201	1.8
			0824	4.7
		SU	1437	2.3
			2054	4.7

NOVEMBER

Time	m		Time	m
1 0333	1.7	**16**	0432	2.0
0942	4.8		1034	4.4
M 1559	2.1	TU	1635	2.3
2212	4.9		2251	4.6
2 0444	1.4	**17**	0519	1.9
1052	5.0		1132	4.6
TU 1700	1.8	W	1725	2.1
2316	5.2		2345	4.7
3 0542	1.1	**18**	0559	1.7
1151	5.2		1219	4.8
W 1753	1.5	TH	1808	1.8
4 0010	5.5	**19**	0032	4.9
0633	0.8		0633	1.5
TH 1242	5.5	F	1300	5.0
1842	1.1		1847	1.6
5 0100	5.7	**20**	0114	5.1
0721	0.7		0707	1.4
F 1327	5.7	SA	1338	5.2
1931	0.9		1925	1.4
6 0146	5.9	**21**	0153	5.2
0806	0.6		0741	1.3
SA 1410	5.8	SU	1414	5.4
● 2020	0.7	○	2003	1.2
7 0233	5.9	**22**	0231	5.4
0850	0.7		0816	1.2
SU 1454	5.8	M	1450	5.4
2107	0.7		2041	1.1
8 0321	5.8	**23**	0309	5.4
0930	0.9		0852	1.2
M 1538	5.7	TU	1526	5.5
2151	0.8		2121	1.0
9 0409	5.6	**24**	0348	5.5
1006	1.1		0930	1.3
TU 1623	5.5	W	1603	5.4
2231	1.0		2204	1.0
10 0458	5.4	**25**	0430	5.4
1035	1.5		1009	1.4
W 1708	5.3	TH	1644	5.4
2305	1.3		2250	1.1
11 0547	5.1	**26**	0516	5.3
1101	1.8		1052	1.6
TH 1755	5.0	F	1729	5.3
2337	1.6		2340	1.2
12 0638	4.8	**27**	0605	5.2
1139	2.1		1143	1.8
F 1847	4.8	SA	1819	5.1
13 0022	1.9	**28**	0036	1.4
0732	4.6		0700	5.0
SA 1236	2.4	SU	1247	2.0
◑ 1945	4.6	◐	1916	5.0
14 0138	2.1	**29**	0142	1.5
0831	4.4		0803	4.9
SU 1400	2.5	M	1402	2.1
2048	4.5		2027	4.9
15 0328	2.1	**30**	0256	1.5
0932	4.4		0914	4.8
M 1532	2.5	TU	1518	2.0
2151	4.5		2141	5.0

DECEMBER

Time	m		Time	m
1 0407	1.4	**16**	0401	2.1
1022	4.9		1026	4.5
W 1625	1.9	TH	1633	2.3
2248	5.1		2248	4.5
2 0509	1.3	**17**	0504	2.0
1124	5.1		1125	4.6
TH 1725	1.6	F	1730	2.1
2348	5.3		2347	4.7
3 0606	1.2	**18**	0554	1.8
1218	5.3		1219	4.8
F 1822	1.4	SA	1818	1.8
4 0043	5.4	**19**	0040	4.9
0658	1.1		0637	1.7
SA 1308	5.4	SU	1308	5.1
1917	1.2		1902	1.5
5 0134	5.5	**20**	0129	5.1
0745	1.1		0718	1.5
SU 1355	5.5	M	1351	5.3
● 2009	1.0		1946	1.3
6 0223	5.6	**21**	0212	5.3
0829	1.1		0800	1.3
M 1439	5.6	TU	1432	5.4
2057	0.9	○	2030	1.0
7 0311	5.6	**22**	0254	5.5
0909	1.1		0843	1.2
TU 1523	5.5	W	1510	5.5
2141	0.9		2116	0.8
8 0356	5.5	**23**	0335	5.6
0944	1.3		0927	1.1
W 1606	5.5	TH	1550	5.6
2219	1.0		2203	0.7
9 0441	5.3	**24**	0418	5.6
1013	1.5		1012	1.2
TH 1648	5.3	F	1631	5.6
2249	1.2		2250	0.7
10 0524	5.1	**25**	0503	5.6
1040	1.6		1056	1.2
F 1729	5.2	SA	1716	5.6
2315	1.4		2337	0.8
11 0607	4.9	**26**	0550	5.4
1113	1.8		1139	1.4
SA 1812	5.0	SU	1803	5.5
2347	1.6			
12 0651	4.7	**27**	0024	0.9
1155	2.0		0640	5.2
SU 1859	4.8	M	1225	1.6
			1856	5.3
13 0031	1.8	**28**	0114	1.2
0739	4.5		0737	5.0
M 1249	2.2	TU	1320	1.8
◑ 1951	4.6	◑	1958	5.1
14 0128	2.0	**29**	0213	1.4
0831	4.4		0842	4.8
TU 1400	2.4	W	1430	1.9
2048	4.5		2111	5.0
15 0240	2.1	**30**	0324	1.6
0928	4.4		0951	4.8
W 1523	2.4	TH	1549	2.0
2148	4.5		2223	4.9
		31	0438	1.7
			1057	4.8
		F	1704	1.8
			2331	5.0

Chart Datum: 2·90 metres below Ordnance Datum (Newlyn). HAT is 6·3 metres above Chart Datum; see 0.19

SE Scotland

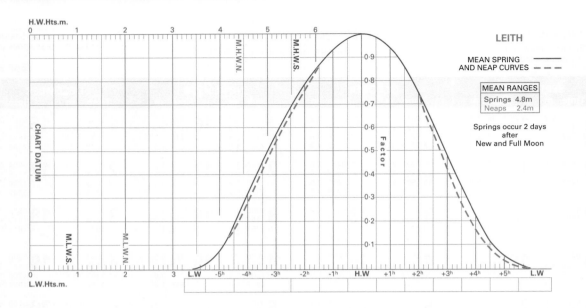

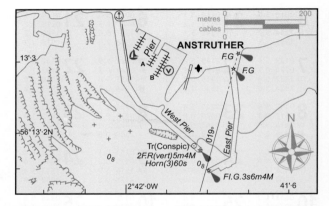

4.9 ANSTRUTHER

Fife 56°13'·15N 02°41'·82W ✳❋♠♠♠♠♠♠♠

CHARTS AC 175, 734; Imray C23, C27.

TIDES +0315 Dover; ML 3·1; Duration 0620

Standard Port LEITH (◄—)

Times				Height (metres)			
High Water		Low Water		MHWS	MHWN	MLWN	MLWS
0300	0900	0300	0900	5·6	4·4	2·0	0·8
1500	2100	1500	2100				
Differences ANSTRUTHER EASTER							
−0018	−0012	−0006	−0008	−0·3	−0·2	0·0	0·0

SHELTER Good, but dangerous to enter in strong E to S winds. Hbr dries; access approx HW±2. Pontoon berths for bilge keel craft only, drying out soft mud.

NAVIGATION WPT 56°12'·59N 02°42'·20W, 019° to ent, 0·60M. Beware FVs and creels in the area. Do not go N of W Pier Lt due to rks extending N & W across the mouth of Dreel Burn.

LIGHTS AND MARKS Conspic tr on W pier. Ldg lts 019°, both FG 7/11m 4M. Pier lts as chartlet. Horn (3) 60s in conspic tr.

R/T Call *Anstruther Hbr* VHF Ch 11 16 (HO) or Forth CG Ch 16 (OT).

TELEPHONE (Code 01333) HM ☎ 310836 (HO); MRCC 450666; Marinecall 09068 969642; Police: 08456 005702, St Andrews

592100; Dr 310352; Ⓗ St Andrews 01334 472327, Kirkaldy 01592 643355;⊖ 0800 595000.

FACILITIES Harbour: wall AB (22 + 8Ⓥ); for 10m LOA: entry £15.29 then £10.37 per day; pontoons (no fin keels, 100 + 8 Ⓥ,check availability with HM) £17.85 then £10.28 per day; Slip, FW, ⬦, ♿, Shwrs 0800-2100; **Services:** D (tanker ☎ 730622), Marine engineer (☎ 01382 541848), ACA, Gas, Gaz,El, Ⓔ, LB. **Town** D, P, SM (☎ 01383 622444), SC (☎ 313492) 🛒, R, Bar, ✉, Ⓑ, ⊶ (bus Cupar or Leuchars), ✈ Edinburgh/Dundee.

ADJACENT HARBOURS AND ANCHORAGE

KIRKCALDY, Fife, **56°06'·80N 03°08'·96W**. AC 741. HW +0345 on Dover, −0005 on Leith; HW −0·1m on Leith; ML 3·2m; Duration 0620. See 4.9. Shelter good except in strong E winds; an emergency refuge. Officially the hbr is closed (no commercial tfc, but some local FVs) and not manned; depths may be less than charted due to silting. The only hbr light is on E Pier head, Fl WG 10s 12m 8M. Small craft should contact Forth Ports Authority ☎ (01333) 426725, Forth Navigation Ch 71 (H24) or Methil Docks Radio Ch 16 14 for advice.

METHIL, Fife, **56°10'·75N 03°00'·55W**. AC 734,741. HW +0330 Dover; −0020 and −0·1 on Leith; ML 3m; Duration 0615. Commercial port unsuitable for leisure/small craft; infrastructure unsafe. Dangerous to enter in bad weather; in emergency call Forth Navigation Ch 71 (H24) or Forth Coastguard Ch 16.

PITTENWEEM, Fife, **56°12'·60N 02°43'·79W**. AC 734. HW +0325 Dover; −0015 and −0·1m on Leith; ML 3m; Duration 0620. Busy fishing hbr, dredged 1-2m, access all tides, but not in onshore winds; seek advice before entering at LW springs. Yachts not encouraged; contact HM for berth at W end of inner hbr, but only for emergency use. Outer hbr dries to rock; is only suitable for temp stop in calm weather. Appr 037° on ldg marks/lts, W cols, both FR 3/8m 5M. Rks to port marked by bn, QR 3m 2M, and 3 unlit bns. E bkwtr lt Fl (2) RG 5s 9m 9/6M, 265°-R-345°-G-055°. **R/T** VHF Ch 11 (0700-2100, Mon-Fri) or Forth CG Ch 16 (other times). HM ☎ (01333) 312591. Facilities: FW, CH, D & P (tanker) (☎ 730622), Gas, 🛒, Bar.

CRAIL, Fife, **56°15'·35N 02°37'·29W**. AC 175. HW +0320 on Dover, −0020 on Leith; HW −0·2m on Leith; ML 3·0m; Duration 0615. Good shelter but only for boats able to take the ground alongside. Appr between S pier and bn on rks to S following ldg line 295°, two W concrete pillars with FR lts, 24/30m 6M. Turn 150° to stbd for ent. Call Forth CG on VHF Ch 16 before entering. HM ☎ (01333) 450820. Facilities: AB, entry £15.29/craft then £10.37/day, El, FW, 🛢, Slip, P. **Village** Bar, R, 🛒, ✉, ⓑ.

ISLE OF MAY, Fife, 56°11′·40N 02°33′·69W. AC 734. HW +0325 on Dover, −0025 on Leith. In settled weather only, and depending on the wind, ⚓ at E or W Tarbert in 4m; landing at Altarstanes. Near the SE tip there is a tiny hbr at Kirkhaven, with narrow, rky ent; yachts can moor fore-and-aft to rings in rks, in about 1-1·5m.

SDs are needed. Beware Norman Rk to N of Island, and Maiden Hair Rk to S. At the summit, a 3 tr on stone ho, Fl (2) 15s 73m 22M. The island, owned by Scottish Natural Heritage (☎ 01334 654038), is a bird/seal-colony sanctuary. Sensitive seasons: (a) breeding birds April to September; (b) breeding seals October to January (c) moulting seals January to March. Land only at Alterstanes or Kirkhaven 0900-1700 UT (not Tuesdays). No overnight accommodation or camping. Avoid marked out areas to minimise disturbance to wildlife and ongoing conservation experiments. Island warden is in residence Easter to September. Contact on VHF CH 16 or 6, or on first landing.

FIFE NESS TO MONTROSE

(AC 190) Fife Ness is fringed by rky ledges, and a reef extends 1M NE to N Carr Rk (dries 1·4m, marked by bn). In strong onshore winds keep to seaward of N Carr ECM lt buoy. From here keep 5ca offshore to clear dangers entering St Andrews B, where there is anch; the little hbr dries, and should not be approached in onshore winds.

Northward from Firth of Forth to Rattray Hd the coast is mostly rky and steep-to, and there are no out-lying dangers within 2M of the coast except those off R Tay and Bell Rk. But in an onshore blow there are few safe havens; both yachts and crews need to be prepared for offshore cruising rather than coast-crawling.

R Tay (AC 1481) is approached from the NE via Fairway buoy; it is dangerous to cut corners from the S. The Bar, NE of Abertay lt buoy, is dangerous in heavy weather, particularly in strong onshore wind or swell. Abertay Sands extend nearly 4M E of Tentsmuir Pt on S side of chan (buoyed); Elbow is a shoal extension eastward. Gaa Sands, running 1·75M E from Buddon Ness, are marked by Abertay lt buoy (Racon) on N side of chan. Passage across Abertay and Gaa Sands is very dangerous. The estuary is shallow, with many shifting sandbanks; Tayport is a good passage stop and best yacht hbr (dries) in the Tay. ▶ *S of* Buddon Ness the W-going (flood) stream begins about HW Aberdeen − 0400, and the E-going at about HW Aberdeen + 0230, sp rates 2kn. ◀

Bell Rk (lt, Racon) lies about 11·5M E of Buddon Ness. ▶ *2M E of Bell Rk the S-going stream begins HW Aberdeen − 0220, and the N-going at HW Aberdeen + 0405, sp rates 1kn. W of Bell Rk the streams begin earlier.* ◀

N from Buddon Ness the coast is sandy. 1·25M SW of Arbroath beware Elliot Horses, rky patches with depth 1·9m, which extend about 5ca offshore. Between Whiting Ness and Scurdie Ness, 9·5M NNE, the coast is clear of out-lying dangers, but is mostly fringed with drying rks up to 1ca off. In offshore winds there is temp anch in SW of Lunan B, off Ethie Haven.

Scurdie Ness (lt, Racon) is conspic on S side of ent to Montrose. Scurdie Rks (dry) extend 2ca E of the Ness. On N side of chan Annat Bank dries up to about 5ca E of the shore, opposite Scurdie Ness (AC 1438). ▶ *The in-going stream begins at HW Aberdeen − 0500, and the outgoing at HW Aberdeen + 0115;* **both streams are very strong, up to 7kn at sp,** *and there is turbulence off the ent on the ebb. The ent is dangerous in strong onshore winds, with breaking seas extending to Scurdie Ness on the ebb. In marginal conditions the last quarter of the flood is best time to enter.* ◀

SE Scotland

4.10 RIVER TAY

Fife/Angus Tayport **(56°27'·10N 02°52'·87W)** ✳✳⚓🐚🌼🌼

CHARTS AC 190, 1481; Imray C23.

TIDES +0401 (Dundee) Dover; ML 3·1; Duration 0610

Standard Port ABERDEEN (→)

Times				Height (metres)			
High Water		Low Water		MHWS	MHWN	MLWN	MLWS
0000	0600	0100	0700	4·3	3·4	1·6	0·6
1200	1800	1300	1900				
Differences BAR							
+0100	+0100	+0050	+0110	+0.9	+0.8	+0.3	+0.1
DUNDEE							
+0140	+0120	+0055	+0145	+1·1	+0·9	+0·3	+0·1
NEWBURGH							
+0215	+0200	+0250	+0335	−0·2	−0·4	−1·1	−0·5
PERTH							
+0220	+0225	+0510	+0530	−0·9	−1·4	−1·2	−0·3

NOTE: At Perth LW time differences give the start of the rise, following a LW stand of about 4 hours.

SHELTER Good in Tay Estuary, but ent is dangerous in strong E/SE winds or on-shore swell. **Tayport** best place for yachts on passage, access HW±4. Hbr partly dries except W side of NE pier; S side has many yacht moorings. **Dundee** commercial dock (Camperdown), gates open HW–2 to HW by request (fee £6 – Fl R lt = no ent/exit). Docks no longer used commercially. Possible moorings off Royal Tay YC. ⚓s as chartlet: the ⚓ off the city is exposed/landing difficult. Off S bank good shelter at Woodhaven and ⚓s from Wormit BC. There are other ⚓s up-river at Balmerino, Newburgh and Inchyra.

NAVIGATION WPT Tay Fairway SWM buoy, 56°28'·30N 02°36'·60W, 239°/1M to Middle Bar buoys. Chan is well buoyed, least depth 5·2m. Keep N of Larick, a conspic disused lt bn.

> Beware strong tidal streams. No passage across Abertay or Gaa Sands; charted depths are unreliable.

LIGHTS AND MARKS See 4.3 and chartlet. 'Abertay' ECM buoy(Racon), at E end of Gaa Sands is a clear visual mark.

R/T *Forth & Tay Navigation Service* VHF Ch **71**; *Dundee Hbr Radio* VHF Ch **12** 16 (H24); local nav warnings, weather, vis and tides on request. Royal Tay YC, Ch M.

TELEPHONE (Code 01382): Forth & Tay Navigation Service (01324) 498584; HM (Dundee) 224121; HM (Perth) (01738) 624056; MRCC (01333) 450666; Marinecall 09068 969642; Tayport Boatowners' Association 553679; Police (Tayport) 542222, (Dundee) 223200; Dr 221953; Ⓗ 223125.

FACILITIES N BANK: Camperdown Dock, AB £19 all LOA, £38 for week; FW, ME, El, C (8 ton); **Victoria Dock**, AB, FW, ME, C (8 ton); **Royal Tay YC** (Broughty Ferry) ☎ 477516, ⚓s free, R, Bar; **Services**: CH, M, L, ME, El, ✕, C (2 ton), ACA. **Dundee City** P, D, CH, 🛒, R, Bar, ✉, Ⓑ, ⛟, ✈.

S BANK: Tayport Hbr AB £6.80, Slip, L, FW, AC; **Wormit Boating Club** ☎ 541400 ⚓s free, Slip, L, FW, 🛒.

ADJACENT HARBOURS

PERTH, Perth & Kinross, **56°22'·89N 03°25'·74W**. AC 1481; OS 53, 58. Tides, see 4.11. FYCA Pilot Handbook needed. Leave Tay Rly bridge about HW Dundee –2 to carry the tide for 16·5M to Perth. Keep clear of coasters which have to travel at speed and are constrained by their draft. Lit chan favours S bank for 9M to Newburgh where caution req'd due to mudbanks mid-stream; keep S of Mugdrum Is. Up-river, power cables clearance 33m and Friarton Bridge 26m. Keep S of Willow Is, past gasworks to Hbr on W bank. Hbr has approx 1·5m. See HM, ☎ (01738) 624056, for berth. VHF Ch 09 16. FW, D & P (cans), all city amenities, ⛟, ✈.

ST ANDREWS, Fife, **56°20'·32N 02°46'·79W**. AC 190. HW –0015 Leith. Small drying hbr 7M S of Tay Estuary /8M NW of Fife Ness. In strong onshore winds breaking seas render appr/ent impossible. Appr at HW±2 on 270°, N bkwtr bn in transit with conspic cathedral tr; no lights. A recce by dinghy is useful. Keep about 10m S of the bkwtr for best water. 8m wide ent to inner hbr (drying 2·5m) has lock gates, usually open, and sliding footbridge; berth on W side. Facilities: FW, SC; all amenities of university town, inc golf course.

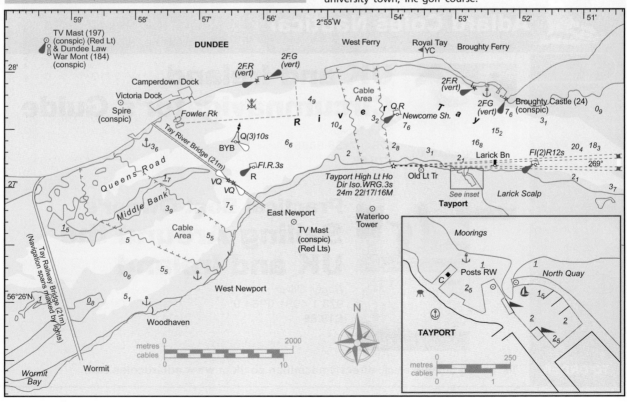

4.11 ARBROATH

Angus **56°33'·22N 02°34'·99W** ❁❁♦♦♦♣♣

CHARTS AC 190, 1438; Imray C23.

TIDES +0317 Dover; ML 2·9; Duration 0620

Standard Port ABERDEEN (→)

Times				Height (metres)			
High Water		Low Water		MHWS	MHWN	MLWN	MLWS
0000	0600	0100	0700	4·3	3·4	1·6	0·6
1200	1800	1300	1900				
Differences ARBROATH							
+0056	+0037	+0034	+0055	+1·0	+0·8	+0·4	+0·2

SHELTER Good, especially in Inner Basin with lock gates, afloat pontoon berths with 2.5m depth maintained. Ent can be dangerous in moderate SE swell. Inside the entrance, turn to starboard and then to starboard again.

NAVIGATION WPT 56°32'·98N 02°34'·21W, 299°/0·5M to ent.

Entry should not be attempted LW±2½. Beware Knuckle rks to stbd and Cheek Bush rks to port on entering.

LIGHTS AND MARKS Ldg lts 299°, both FR 7/13m 5M, or twin trs of St Thomas' ✠ visible between N pier lt ho and W bkwtr bn. Hbr entry sigs: Fl G 3s on E pier = Entry safe. Same lt shows FR when hbr closed, entry dangerous. Siren (3) 60s at E pier lt is occas, for FVs. Inner Basin Lock Gates, FR = closed, FG = open >2.5m over sill.

R/T Ch 11 16.

TELEPHONE (Code 01241) HM 872166; MRCC (01224) 592334 MRCC 01333 452000; Marinecall 09068 969642; Police 872222; Dr 876836.

FACILITIES **Inner Basin** 59 inc ♥, £19/craft, Showers, 🚻, **Pier** AB £13/craft, Slip, FW; **Services:** BY, Slip, L, ME, El, ✕, C (8 ton) Ⓔ, M, Gas, CH. **Town** P, D, 🛒, R, Bar, ✉, Ⓑ, ⇌, ✈ (Dundee).

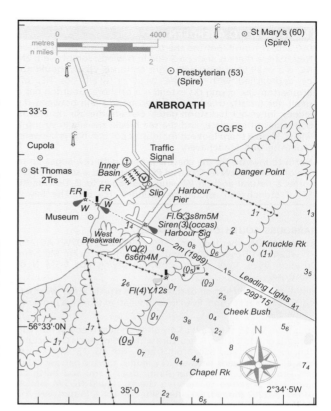

4.12 MONTROSE

Angus **56°42'·19N 02°26'·60W** ❁❁♦♦♦♣♣

CHARTS AC 190, 1438; Imray C23.

TIDES +0320 Dover; ML 2·9; Duration 0645

Standard Port ABERDEEN (→)

Times				Height (metres)			
High Water		Low Water		MHWS	MHWN	MLWN	MLWS
0000	0600	0100	0700	4·3	3·4	1·6	0·6
1200	1800	1300	1900				
Differences MONTROSE							
+0055	+0055	+0030	+0040	+0·5	+0·4	+0·2	0·0

SHELTER Good; yachts are welcome in this busy commercial port. Contact HM for AB, usually available, but beware wash from other traffic. Double mooring lines advised due to strong tidal streams (up to 6kn).

NAVIGATION WPT 56°42'·18N 02°25'·11W, 271°/1.25M to front ldg lt. Beware Annat Bank to N and Scurdie Rks to S of ent chan. In quiet weather best access is LW to LW+1, but in strong onshore winds only safe access would be from HW –2 to HW.

Ent is dangerous with strong onshore winds against any ebb tide when heavy overfalls develop.

LIGHTS AND MARKS See 4.3 and chartlet two sets of ldg lts: Outer 271·5°, both FR 11/18m 5M, front W twin pillars, R bands; rear W tr, R cupola. Inner 265°, both FG 21/33m 5M, Orange △ front and ▽ rear.

R/T VHF Ch 12 16 (H24).

TELEPHONE (Code 01674) HM 672302; MRCC (01333) 450666; Marinecall 09068 969642; Police 01307 302200; Dr 672554.

FACILITIES **N Quay** ☎ 672302, AB £6.50, D (by tanker via HM), FW, ME, El, C (1½ to 40 ton), CH, Gas. **Town** 🛒, R, P, Bar, ✉, Ⓑ, ⇌, ✈ (Aberdeen).

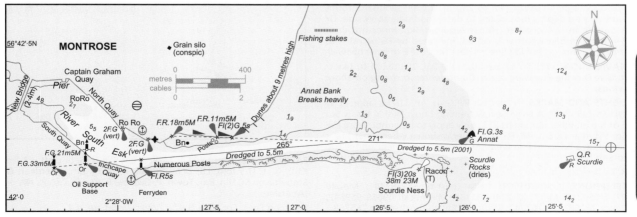

MONTROSE TO ABERDEEN

(AC 210) N from Montrose the coast is sandy for 5M to Milton Ness, where there is anch on S side in N winds. Johnshaven, 2M NE, is a small hbr (dries) with tight entrance, which should not be approached with onshore wind or swell. 5ca NE, off Brotherton Cas, drying rks extend 4ca offshore. Gourdon has a small hbr (mostly dries) approached on ldg line between rky ledges; inner hbr has storm gates. Outside the hbr rks extend both sides of entrance, and the sea breaks heavily in strong E winds. Keep a sharp lookout for lobster pot dan buoys between Montrose and Stonehaven.

North to Inverbervie the coast is fringed with rky ledges up to 2ca offshore. Just N of Todhead Pt is Catterline, a small B which forms a natural anch in W winds, but open to E. Downie Pt, SE of Stonehaven, should be rounded 1ca off. The Bay is encumbered by rky ledges up to 2ca from shore and exposed to the E; anch 6ca E of Bay Hotel or berth afloat in outer hbr.

From Garron Pt to Girdle Ness the coast is mostly steep-to. Fishing nets may be met off headlands during fishing season. Craigmaroinn and Seal Craig (dry) are parts of reef 3ca offshore SE of Portlethen, a fishing village with landing sheltered by rks. Cove B has a very small fishing hbr, off which there is anch in good weather; Mutton Rk (dries 2·1m) lie 1½ca offshore. From Cove to Girdle Ness keep 5ca offshore, avoiding Hasman Rks (dries 3·4m) 1ca off Altens.

Greg Ness and Girdle Ness (lt, Racon), at SE corner of Aberdeen Bay, are fringed by rks. Girdlestone is a rocky patch, depth less than 2m, 2ca ENE of lt ho. A drying patch lies 2ca SE of lt ho. ▶ *Off Girdle Ness the S-going stream begins at HW Aberdeen –0430, and the N-going at HW Aberdeen + 0130, sp rates 2·5kn. A race forms on S-going stream.* ◀

HARBOURS SOUTH OF STONEHAVEN

JOHNSHAVEN, Aberdeenshire, 56°47'·60N 02°20'·07W. AC 210. HW +0245 on Dover; +0045 and +0·4m on Aberdeen; ML 2·7m; Duration 0626. Very small, attractive drying hbr 6·5M N of Montrose.

> Ent impossible in strong onshore winds; strictly a fair weather visit with great caution. Even in calm weather swell is a problem inside the hbr.

Appr from 5ca SE at HW±2½. Conspic W shed at N end of hbr. Ldg marks/lts on 316°: front, R structure with FR 5m; rear is G structure, 20m up the hill and 85m from front, with FG (FR when entry unsafe). Transit leads between rky ledges to very narrow (20m) ent. Turn 90° port into Inner Basin (dries 2·5m) and berth on outer wall or secure to mooring chains, rigged NE/SW. HM ☎ (01561) 362262 (home). Facilities: Slip, AB, ⌁, C (5 ton), FW, 🛒, R, ME, Bar, ✉. Bus to Montrose/Aberdeen.

Berthing Fees: *For details of Rover Ticket see 4.4.*

GOURDON, Aberdeenshire, 56°49'·49N 02°17'·21W. AC 210. HW +0240 on Dover; +0035 on Aberdeen; HW +0·4m on Aberdeen; ML 2·7m; Duration 0620. Shelter good in inner W hbr (dries about 2m; protected by storm gates); access from about mid-flood. E (or Gutty) hbr is rky, with difficult access. Beware rky ledges marked by bn and extending 200m S from W pier end. **A dangerous rk dries on the ldg line** about 1½ca S of pier heads. Ldg marks/lts 358°, both FR 5/30m 5M, 2 W trs; front lt shows G when not safe to enter. W pier hd Fl WRG 3s 5m 9/7M, vis 180°-G-344°-W-354°-R-180°. Essential to keep in W sector until R Ldg Lts are aligned. E bkwtr hd Q 3m 7M. HM ☎ (01569) 762741 (part-time, same as 4.13). Facilities: Slip, FW from standpipe, D, ME, ⌁, M, 🛒, R, Bar.

Berthing Fees: *For details of Rover Ticket see 4.4.*

4.13 STONEHAVEN

Aberdeenshire 56°57'·57N 02°12'·02W ✿✿✿✿≋❀✿

CHARTS AC 210, 1438; Imray C23.

TIDES +0235 Dover; ML 2·6; Duration 0620

Standard Port ABERDEEN (→)

Times				Height (metres)			
High Water		Low Water		MHWS	MHWN	MLWN	MLWS
0000	0600	0100	0700	4·3	3·4	1·6	0·6
1200	1800	1300	1900				
Differences STONEHAVEN							
+0013	+0008	+0013	+0009	+0·2	+0·2	+0·1	0·0

SHELTER Good, especially from offshore winds. Berth in Outer hbr on W side of bkwtr (3m to 2m) or N wall; sandbank forms with varying depths (not <0.6m to date) in middle to W side. Or ⌓ outside in fair weather. Hbr speed limit 3kn. Inner hbr dries 3·4m and in bad weather is closed, indicated by FG(occas) lt as shown. Do not go S of ldg line, to clear rks close S of inner hbr wall.

NAVIGATION WPT 56°57'·69N 02°11'·11W, 258°/0·5M to bkwtr lt. Give Downie Pt a wide berth. *Do not enter in strong on-shore winds.*

LIGHTS AND MARKS N pier Iso WRG 4s 7m 11/7M; appr in W sector, 246°-268°. A large yellow training buoy, Fl(4) Y 12s, is 5ca E of N pier. Inner hbr ldg lts 273° only apply to inner hbr: front FW 6m 5M; rear FR 8m 5M. FG on SE pier is shown when inner hbr is closed by a boom in bad weather. Conspic monument on hill top to S of hbr.

R/T HM VHF Ch 11.

TELEPHONE (Code 01569) HM (part-time) 762741, Mobile 07741050210; MRCC (01224) 592334; Marinecall 09068 969642; Police 762963; Dr 762945; Maritime Rescue Institute ☎ 765768.

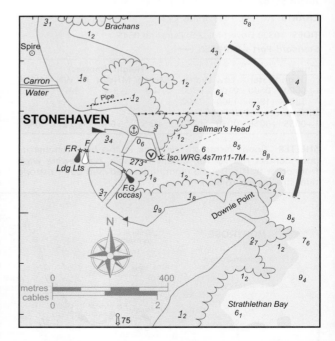

FACILITIES Hbr AB £14.99, L, M, FW, ⌁, Slip (£15, or craft < 3.1m £10), ⌁, C (1·5 ton), LB, D by tanker, Fri early am; **Aberdeen & Stonehaven SC** Slip, Bar. **Town** P, Gas, 🛒, R, Bar, Ⓗ, ✉, Ⓑ, ⇌, ✈ (Aberdeen).

Berthing Fees: *For details of a Rover Ticket see 4.4.*

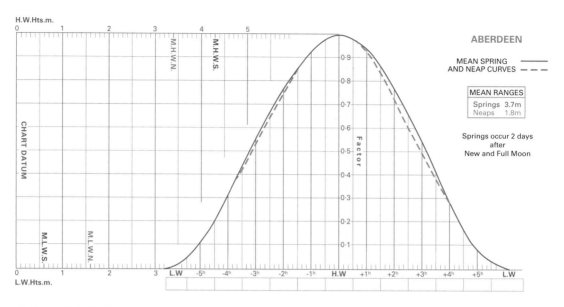

4.14 ABERDEEN

Aberdeenshire **57°08'·70N 02°03'·59W** 🌸🌸🌸🏊🌸🌸

CHARTS AC 210, 1446; Imray C23.

TIDES +0231 Dover; ML 2·5; Duration 0620

SHELTER Good in hbr; open at all tides, but do not enter in strong NE/ESE winds. Call Aberdeen VTS when 3M off for permission to enter VTS area and berthing availability.

> Yachts are not encouraged in this busy commercial port, but usually lie on N side of Albert Basin alongside floating linkspan.

⚓ in Aberdeen Bay gives some shelter from S and W winds. Peterhead is 25M to N; Stonehaven is 13M S.

NAVIGATION WPT Fairway SWM buoy, Mo (A) 5s, Racon, 57°09'·31N 02°01'·96W, 236°/1M to hbr ent. Give Girdle Ness a berth of at least ¼M (more in bad weather). Do not pass close round pier hds. Strong tidal streams and, with river in spate, overfalls. Chan dredged to 6m on ldg line.

LIGHTS AND MARKS Ldg lts 236° (FR = port open; FG = port closed). Traffic sigs at root of N pier:

●	=	Entry prohib
●	=	Dep prohib
● & ●	=	Port closed

R/T Aberdeen VTS VHF Ch **12** 16 (H24).

TELEPHONE (Code 01224) VTS 597000; MRCC 592334; Weather 722334; Marinecall 09068 969642/0839 406189; Police 0845 600 5700.

FACILITIES Services: AB £18/craft for up to 5 days , El, Ⓔ, ME, ACA. **City** all amenities, ⇌, ✈. **Ferries:** Kirkwall and Lerwick (www.northlinkferries.co.uk).

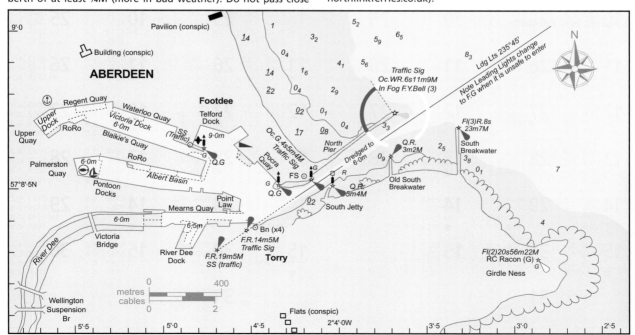

TIME ZONE (UT)
For Summer Time add ONE hour in **non-shaded areas**

ABERDEEN LAT 57°09′N LONG 2°05′W

TIMES AND HEIGHTS OF HIGH AND LOW WATERS

Dates in red are SPRINGS
Dates in blue are NEAPS

YEAR **2010**

JANUARY

Day	Time	m	Day	Time	m
1 F	0114 0714 1329 1945	4.3 1.0 4.4 0.6	16 SA	0203 0746 1402 2015	4.0 1.2 4.2 0.9
2 SA	0203 0801 1413 2033	4.4 0.9 4.5 0.4	17 SU	0236 0818 1433 2047	4.0 1.2 4.2 0.9
3 SU	0252 0846 1459 2121	4.5 0.9 4.6 0.4	18 M	0307 0848 1504 2117	4.0 1.2 4.2 0.9
4 M	0341 0931 1546 2210	4.4 1.0 4.6 0.5	19 TU	0339 0919 1535 2148	3.9 1.2 4.2 1.0
5 TU	0431 1017 1635 2300	4.2 1.1 4.5 0.6	20 W	0412 0950 1609 2221	3.8 1.3 4.1 1.1
6 W	0522 1106 1729 2352	4.0 1.3 4.3 0.9	21 TH	0447 1024 1646 2257	3.7 1.4 4.0 1.2
7 TH ◑	0617 1200 1828	3.8 1.5 4.1	22 F	0527 1103 1729 2339	3.6 1.6 3.8 1.4
8 F	0048 0715 1303 1933	1.2 3.7 1.7 3.8	23 SA ◐	0615 1152 1821	3.5 1.7 3.7
9 SA	0152 0821 1417 2048	1.4 3.6 1.8 3.7	24 SU	0032 0713 1259 1927	1.6 3.4 1.8 3.5
10 SU	0305 0931 1543 2206	1.6 3.6 1.8 3.6	25 M	0141 0822 1422 2045	1.7 3.4 1.9 3.5
11 M	0418 1037 1654 2312	1.7 3.7 1.6 3.7	26 TU	0303 0937 1548 2206	1.7 3.5 1.7 3.6
12 TU	0514 1131 1747	1.6 3.8 1.4	27 W	0422 1045 1659 2317	1.6 3.7 1.4 3.8
13 W	0006 0559 1216 1830	3.8 1.5 3.9 1.3	28 TH	0525 1141 1756	1.4 4.0 1.0
14 TH	0051 0638 1255 1908	3.9 1.4 4.1 1.1	29 F	0014 0616 1230 1846	4.1 1.2 4.2 0.7
15 F	0129 0713 1329 ● 1943	3.9 1.3 4.1 1.0	30 SA	0105 0703 1315 ○ 1933	4.3 0.9 4.5 0.4
			31 SU	0151 0747 1359 2019	4.5 0.8 4.7 0.2

FEBRUARY

Day	Time	m	Day	Time	m
1 M	0236 0830 1442 2104	4.5 0.7 4.7 0.2	16 TU	0240 0824 1439 2049	4.0 1.0 4.3 0.8
2 TU	0320 0911 1526 2148	4.4 0.7 4.7 0.3	17 W	0308 0853 1509 2118	4.0 1.0 4.2 0.8
3 W	0404 0952 1612 2232	4.3 0.9 4.6 0.6	18 TH	0338 0922 1541 2147	3.9 1.1 4.2 1.0
4 TH	0450 1035 1701 2317	4.1 1.1 4.3 0.9	19 F	0410 0954 1616 2219	3.9 1.2 4.0 1.1
5 F ◑	0538 1123 1756	3.8 1.3 4.0	20 SA	0446 1029 1657 2257	3.7 1.3 3.9 1.3
6 SA	0007 0632 1222 1901	1.3 3.6 1.6 3.7	21 SU	0529 1115 1747 2347	3.6 1.5 3.7 1.5
7 SU	0106 0737 1338 2019	1.6 3.4 1.8 3.5	22 M ◐	0626 1219 1856	3.5 1.7 3.5
8 M	0224 0853 1522 2148	1.9 3.4 1.8 3.4	23 TU	0100 0741 1349 2022	1.8 3.4 1.8 3.4
9 TU	0358 1012 1643 2303	1.9 3.5 1.7 3.5	24 W	0237 0905 1529 2152	1.8 3.4 1.6 3.5
10 W	0500 1115 1736 2357	1.8 3.6 1.4 3.6	25 TH	0409 1023 1646 2306	1.7 3.6 1.3 3.8
11 TH	0546 1201 1817	1.6 3.8 1.2	26 F	0513 1123 1742	1.4 3.9 0.9
12 F	0037 0622 1239 1851	3.8 1.4 4.0 1.1	27 SA	0002 0602 1213 1830	4.1 1.1 4.2 0.5
13 SA	0112 0656 1312 1923	3.9 1.3 4.1 0.9	28 SU	0049 0646 1257 ○ 1916	4.3 0.8 4.5 0.2
14 SU	0142 0727 1342 ● 1953	4.0 1.1 4.2 0.8			
15 M	0212 0756 1411 2021	4.0 1.0 4.2 0.8			

MARCH

Day	Time	m	Day	Time	m
1 M	0132 0728 1339 1959	4.4 0.6 4.7 0.1	16 TU	0142 0730 1344 1951	4.0 0.9 4.2 0.7
2 TU	0213 0808 1421 2040	4.5 0.5 4.8 0.1	17 W	0209 0758 1413 2019	4.0 0.9 4.2 0.7
3 W	0254 0847 1504 2121	4.4 0.6 4.7 0.3	18 TH	0238 0827 1444 2048	4.0 0.9 4.2 0.8
4 TH	0334 0927 1549 2201	4.3 0.7 4.5 0.6	19 F	0307 0858 1517 2117	4.0 0.9 4.1 0.9
5 F	0416 1008 1636 2242	4.1 0.9 4.2 1.0	20 SA	0340 0930 1555 2150	3.9 1.0 4.0 1.1
6 SA	0501 1054 1730 2327	3.8 1.2 3.9 1.4	21 SU	0416 1008 1638 2229	3.8 1.1 3.8 1.3
7 SU ◑	0551 1148 1833	3.6 1.5 3.5	22 M	0500 1057 1732 2322	3.7 1.3 3.6 1.5
8 M	0023 0653 1303 1950	1.8 3.4 1.7 3.3	23 TU ◐	0557 1205 1846	3.5 1.5 3.5
9 TU	0143 0810 1455 2122	2.0 3.3 1.8 3.2	24 W	0041 0715 1337 2011	1.8 3.4 1.5 3.4
10 W	0331 0937 1622 2242	2.0 3.3 1.6 3.3	25 TH	0223 0840 1514 2139	1.8 3.4 1.4 3.5
11 TH	0438 1047 1713 2334	1.8 3.5 1.4 3.5	26 F	0353 1000 1627 2250	1.6 3.6 1.0 3.8
12 F	0523 1135 1752	1.6 3.7 1.2	27 SA	0453 1101 1722 2343	1.3 3.9 0.7 4.0
13 SA	0012 0559 1213 1825	3.7 1.4 3.8 1.0	28 SU	0542 1150 1810	1.0 4.2 0.4
14 SU	0045 0631 1245 1855	3.8 1.2 4.0 0.9	29 M	0027 0624 1235 1853	4.2 0.8 4.4 0.2
15 M	0114 0701 1315 ● 1923	3.9 1.0 4.1 0.8	30 TU	0108 0705 1318 ○ 1934	4.3 0.6 4.6 0.2
			31 W	0147 0745 1400 2014	4.4 0.5 4.6 0.3

APRIL

Day	Time	m	Day	Time	m
1 TH	0226 0825 1443 2053	4.3 0.5 4.5 0.5	16 F	0209 0805 1422 2022	4.1 0.8 4.1 0.8
2 F	0305 0905 1528 2131	4.2 0.6 4.3 0.8	17 SA	0242 0840 1500 2056	4.1 0.8 4.1 0.9
3 SA	0345 0947 1616 2210	4.0 0.8 4.0 1.1	18 SU	0317 0918 1542 2133	4.0 0.9 4.0 1.1
4 SU	0428 1031 1709 2254	3.8 1.1 3.7 1.5	19 M	0357 1002 1630 2219	3.9 1.0 3.8 1.3
5 M	0515 1124 1809 2347	3.6 1.4 3.4 1.8	20 TU	0444 1056 1730 2317	3.7 1.1 3.6 1.5
6 TU ◑	0614 1231 1919	3.4 1.6 3.2	21 W ◐	0544 1205 1843	3.6 1.2 3.5
7 W	0100 0725 1404 2039	2.0 3.3 1.7 3.2	22 TH	0035 0659 1329 2000	1.7 3.5 1.2 3.5
8 TH	0238 0846 1539 2159	2.0 3.2 1.6 3.2	23 F	0206 0817 1452 2119	1.7 3.5 1.1 3.6
9 F	0358 1001 1634 2255	1.9 3.3 1.4 3.4	24 SA	0325 0932 1601 2225	1.6 3.7 0.9 3.7
10 SA	0447 1055 1714 2335	1.7 3.5 1.2 3.6	25 SU	0426 1035 1657 2318	1.3 3.9 0.7 3.9
11 SU	0526 1136 1749	1.4 3.7 1.0	26 M	0517 1127 1745	1.1 4.1 0.5
12 M	0009 0559 1211 1819	3.7 1.2 3.8 0.9	27 TU	0002 0602 1214 1829	4.1 0.8 4.3 0.5
13 TU	0040 0630 1243 1849	3.9 1.0 4.0 0.8	28 W	0043 0645 1258 ○ 1910	4.2 0.7 4.4 0.5
14 W	0109 0701 1315 ● 1919	4.0 0.9 4.1 0.7	29 TH	0123 0726 1343 1949	4.2 0.6 4.4 0.6
15 TH	0139 0732 1348 1950	4.0 0.8 4.1 0.7	30 F	0201 0808 1427 2028	4.2 0.6 4.3 0.8

Chart Datum: 2·25 metres below Ordnance Datum (Newlyn). HAT is 4·8 metres above Chart Datum; see 0.19

FREE monthly updates from www.reedsalmanac.co.uk

TIME ZONE (UT)
For Summer Time add ONE hour in **non-shaded areas**

ABERDEEN LAT 57°09'N LONG 2°05'W
TIMES AND HEIGHTS OF HIGH AND LOW WATERS

Dates in red are SPRINGS
Dates in blue are NEAPS

YEAR 2010

MAY

Time	m	Time	m
1 SA 0240 / 0849 / 1513 / 2106	4.1 / 0.7 / 4.1 / 1.0	**16** SU 0222 / 0829 / 1449 / 2044	4.1 / 0.7 / 4.1 / 0.9
2 SU 0320 / 0931 / 1600 / 2145	4.0 / 0.8 / 3.9 / 1.2	**17** M 0302 / 0914 / 1536 / 2128	4.1 / 0.7 / 4.0 / 1.1
3 M 0401 / 1014 / 1650 / 2227	3.9 / 1.0 / 3.6 / 1.5	**18** TU 0346 / 1003 / 1629 / 2217	4.0 / 0.8 / 3.9 / 1.2
4 TU 0446 / 1102 / 1743 / 2315	3.7 / 1.2 / 3.4 / 1.7	**19** W 0436 / 1058 / 1728 / 2315	3.9 / 0.8 / 3.7 / 1.4
5 W 0539 / 1158 / 1842	3.5 / 1.4 / 3.3	**20** TH 0535 / 1202 / 1833	3.8 / 0.9 / 3.6
6 TH 0015 / 0639 / 1307 / 1945	1.9 / 3.4 / 1.5 / 3.2	**21** F 0023 / 0642 / 1312 / 1940	1.5 / 3.7 / 1.0 / 3.6
7 F 0132 / 0746 / 1423 / 2055	1.9 / 3.3 / 1.5 / 3.2	**22** SA 0137 / 0752 / 1423 / 2050	1.6 / 3.7 / 1.0 / 3.6
8 SA 0250 / 0856 / 1532 / 2157	1.9 / 3.3 / 1.5 / 3.3	**23** SU 0249 / 0902 / 1530 / 2155	1.5 / 3.7 / 0.9 / 3.7
9 SU 0354 / 0959 / 1623 / 2246	1.7 / 3.4 / 1.3 / 3.5	**24** M 0355 / 1008 / 1629 / 2250	1.4 / 3.9 / 0.9 / 3.8
10 M 0441 / 1049 / 1703 / 2326	1.5 / 3.6 / 1.2 / 3.6	**25** TU 0452 / 1106 / 1721 / 2338	1.2 / 4.0 / 0.8 / 3.9
11 TU 0521 / 1131 / 1739	1.3 / 3.7 / 1.0	**26** W 0543 / 1157 / 1808	1.0 / 4.1 / 0.8
12 W 0002 / 0557 / 1210 / 1813	3.8 / 1.1 / 3.8 / 0.9	**27** TH 0022 / 0629 / 1246 / 1850	4.0 / 0.8 / 4.1 / 0.8
13 TH 0037 / 0633 / 1248 / 1849	3.9 / 1.0 / 4.0 / 0.9	**28** F 0103 / 0713 / 1332 / 1930	4.1 / 0.7 / 4.1 / 0.9
14 F 0110 / 0710 / 1326 / 1925	4.0 / 0.8 / 4.0 / 0.8	**29** SA 0143 / 0756 / 1417 / 2009	4.1 / 0.7 / 4.0 / 1.0
15 SA 0145 / 0748 / 1406 / 2004	4.1 / 0.7 / 4.1 / 0.9	**30** SU 0222 / 0837 / 1501 / 2047	4.1 / 0.7 / 3.9 / 1.1
		31 M 0301 / 0916 / 1544 / 2124	4.0 / 0.8 / 3.8 / 1.2

JUNE

Time	m	Time	m
1 TU 0340 / 0956 / 1628 / 2203	3.9 / 0.9 / 3.7 / 1.4	**16** W 0337 / 0959 / 1622 / 2211	4.2 / 0.5 / 4.0 / 1.1
2 W 0421 / 1037 / 1712 / 2244	3.8 / 1.1 / 3.5 / 1.5	**17** TH 0427 / 1051 / 1716 / 2302	4.2 / 0.6 / 3.9 / 1.2
3 TH 0505 / 1122 / 1800 / 2331	3.7 / 1.2 / 3.4 / 1.7	**18** F 0521 / 1147 / 1813 / 2359	4.1 / 0.7 / 3.8 / 1.3
4 F 0555 / 1214 / 1852	3.5 / 1.4 / 3.3	**19** SA 0621 / 1246 / 1913	3.9 / 0.8 / 3.7
5 SA 0029 / 0650 / 1312 / 1948	1.8 / 3.4 / 1.4 / 3.3	**20** SU 0103 / 0725 / 1350 / 2017	1.4 / 3.8 / 1.0 / 3.6
6 SU 0135 / 0750 / 1414 / 2049	1.8 / 3.4 / 1.5 / 3.3	**21** M 0213 / 0834 / 1456 / 2123	1.5 / 3.8 / 1.1 / 3.6
7 M 0243 / 0853 / 1515 / 2148	1.8 / 3.4 / 1.4 / 3.4	**22** TU 0326 / 0946 / 1604 / 2225	1.5 / 3.7 / 1.2 / 3.7
8 TU 0345 / 0955 / 1610 / 2240	1.7 / 3.4 / 1.4 / 3.5	**23** W 0434 / 1052 / 1702 / 2319	1.3 / 3.8 / 1.2 / 3.8
9 W 0438 / 1050 / 1658 / 2325	1.5 / 3.6 / 1.2 / 3.7	**24** TH 0532 / 1149 / 1752	1.2 / 3.8 / 1.2
10 TH 0525 / 1138 / 1742	1.3 / 3.7 / 1.1	**25** F 0007 / 0621 / 1240 / 1836	3.9 / 1.0 / 3.9 / 1.1
11 F 0006 / 0608 / 1224 / 1825	3.9 / 1.1 / 3.9 / 1.0	**26** SA 0050 / 0705 / 1326 / 1916	4.0 / 0.9 / 3.9 / 1.1
12 SA 0046 / 0652 / 1309 / 1908	4.0 / 0.9 / 4.0 / 0.9	**27** SU 0130 / 0746 / 1407 / 1953	4.1 / 0.8 / 3.9 / 1.1
13 SU 0126 / 0736 / 1355 / 1952	4.1 / 0.7 / 4.1 / 0.9	**28** M 0207 / 0823 / 1446 / 2029	4.1 / 0.8 / 3.9 / 1.1
14 M 0208 / 0822 / 1442 / 2037	4.2 / 0.5 / 4.2 / 0.9	**29** TU 0243 / 0859 / 1523 / 2103	4.1 / 0.8 / 3.8 / 1.2
15 TU 0251 / 0910 / 1531 / 2123	4.2 / 0.5 / 4.1 / 1.0	**30** W 0318 / 0934 / 1600 / 2137	4.0 / 0.9 / 3.8 / 1.2

JULY

Time	m	Time	m
1 TH 0354 / 1009 / 1637 / 2212	4.0 / 0.9 / 3.7 / 1.3	**16** F 0410 / 1033 / 1653 / 2240	4.4 / 0.4 / 4.1 / 1.0
2 F 0432 / 1045 / 1717 / 2250	3.9 / 1.1 / 3.6 / 1.4	**17** SA 0500 / 1122 / 1745 / 2331	4.3 / 0.6 / 3.9 / 1.2
3 SA 0513 / 1125 / 1801 / 2334	3.7 / 1.2 / 3.5 / 1.6	**18** SU 0556 / 1215 / 1841	4.1 / 0.9 / 3.7
4 SU 0600 / 1212 / 1850	3.6 / 1.4 / 3.4	**19** M 0029 / 0658 / 1315 / 1943	1.4 / 3.9 / 1.2 / 3.6
5 M 0028 / 0653 / 1307 / 1945	1.7 / 3.5 / 1.5 / 3.3	**20** TU 0139 / 0810 / 1424 / 2052	1.5 / 3.7 / 1.4 / 3.5
6 TU 0134 / 0754 / 1410 / 2048	1.8 / 3.4 / 1.6 / 3.4	**21** W 0303 / 0930 / 1543 / 2203	1.6 / 3.6 / 1.5 / 3.6
7 W 0246 / 0901 / 1517 / 2152	1.8 / 3.4 / 1.6 / 3.5	**22** TH 0425 / 1045 / 1650 / 2306	1.5 / 3.6 / 1.5 / 3.7
8 TH 0356 / 1011 / 1622 / 2250	1.6 / 3.5 / 1.5 / 3.6	**23** F 0526 / 1146 / 1741 / 2356	1.3 / 3.7 / 1.4 / 3.8
9 F 0457 / 1113 / 1718 / 2340	1.4 / 3.7 / 1.3 / 3.8	**24** SA 0614 / 1235 / 1824	1.1 / 3.8 / 1.3
10 SA 0550 / 1207 / 1809	1.1 / 3.9 / 1.1	**25** SU 0039 / 0655 / 1316 / 1901	4.0 / 1.0 / 3.9 / 1.2
11 SU 0026 / 0638 / 1257 / 1855	4.0 / 0.8 / 4.1 / 1.0	**26** M 0116 / 0731 / 1351 / 1935	4.1 / 0.8 / 3.9 / 1.1
12 M 0110 / 0725 / 1344 / 1940	4.2 / 0.5 / 4.2 / 0.8	**27** TU 0150 / 0805 / 1425 / 2007	4.1 / 0.8 / 3.9 / 1.1
13 TU 0154 / 0811 / 1431 / 2025	4.4 / 0.3 / 4.3 / 0.8	**28** W 0222 / 0836 / 1457 / 2038	4.2 / 0.8 / 3.9 / 1.1
14 W 0238 / 0858 / 1517 / 2109	4.5 / 0.2 / 4.3 / 0.8	**29** TH 0253 / 0906 / 1528 / 2109	4.2 / 0.8 / 3.9 / 1.1
15 TH 0323 / 0945 / 1605 / 2153	4.5 / 0.2 / 4.2 / 0.9	**30** F 0325 / 0937 / 1600 / 2140	4.1 / 0.9 / 3.8 / 1.2
		31 SA 0358 / 1008 / 1634 / 2213	4.0 / 1.0 / 3.7 / 1.3

AUGUST

Time	m	Time	m
1 SU 0435 / 1042 / 1712 / 2250	3.9 / 1.1 / 3.6 / 1.4	**16** M 0531 / 1142 / 1806 / 2359	4.1 / 1.1 / 3.7 / 1.4
2 M 0516 / 1121 / 1757 / 2336	3.8 / 1.3 / 3.5 / 1.6	**17** TU 0635 / 1240 / 1909	3.8 / 1.5 / 3.5
3 TU 0605 / 1209 / 1851	3.6 / 1.5 / 3.4	**18** W 0111 / 0750 / 1354 / 2022	1.6 / 3.6 / 1.7 / 3.4
4 W 0037 / 0707 / 1314 / 1956	1.7 / 3.5 / 1.7 / 3.4	**19** TH 0249 / 0918 / 1527 / 2142	1.7 / 3.4 / 1.8 / 3.5
5 TH 0157 / 0821 / 1434 / 2109	1.8 / 3.4 / 1.7 / 3.4	**20** F 0418 / 1038 / 1638 / 2250	1.5 / 3.5 / 1.7 / 3.6
6 F 0323 / 0942 / 1556 / 2220	1.7 / 3.5 / 1.6 / 3.6	**21** SA 0516 / 1137 / 1727 / 2341	1.3 / 3.6 / 1.6 / 3.8
7 SA 0437 / 1054 / 1702 / 2318	1.4 / 3.7 / 1.4 / 3.8	**22** SU 0600 / 1221 / 1807	1.1 / 3.8 / 1.4
8 SU 0534 / 1152 / 1754	1.1 / 3.9 / 1.2	**23** M 0021 / 0636 / 1257 / 1840	4.0 / 1.0 / 3.9 / 1.2
9 M 0007 / 0623 / 1242 / 1840	4.1 / 0.7 / 4.2 / 0.9	**24** TU 0055 / 0709 / 1328 / 1912	4.1 / 0.9 / 4.0 / 1.1
10 TU 0053 / 0709 / 1328 / 1924	4.4 / 0.4 / 4.4 / 0.7	**25** W 0126 / 0739 / 1357 / 1942	4.2 / 0.8 / 4.0 / 1.0
11 W 0135 / 0754 / 1412 / 2006	4.6 / 0.1 / 4.5 / 0.6	**26** TH 0156 / 0807 / 1426 / 2011	4.2 / 0.7 / 4.0 / 1.0
12 TH 0218 / 0839 / 1455 / 2048	4.7 / 0.1 / 4.5 / 0.6	**27** F 0225 / 0835 / 1454 / 2040	4.3 / 0.8 / 4.0 / 1.0
13 F 0302 / 0923 / 1539 / 2130	4.7 / 0.1 / 4.4 / 0.7	**28** SA 0255 / 0903 / 1524 / 2109	4.2 / 0.8 / 4.0 / 1.1
14 SA 0347 / 1007 / 1624 / 2213	4.6 / 0.4 / 4.2 / 0.9	**29** SU 0327 / 0932 / 1556 / 2141	4.1 / 0.9 / 3.9 / 1.2
15 SU 0436 / 1052 / 1712 / 2302	4.4 / 0.7 / 4.0 / 1.1	**30** M 0402 / 1003 / 1631 / 2216	4.0 / 1.1 / 3.8 / 1.3
		31 TU 0442 / 1039 / 1712 / 2259	3.8 / 1.3 / 3.7 / 1.5

Chart Datum: 2·25 metres below Ordnance Datum (Newlyn). HAT is 4·8 metres above Chart Datum; see 0.19

SE Scotland

TIME ZONE (UT)
For Summer Time add ONE hour in **non-shaded areas**

ABERDEEN LAT 57°09′N LONG 2°05′W
TIMES AND HEIGHTS OF HIGH AND LOW WATERS

Dates in red are SPRINGS
Dates in blue are NEAPS

YEAR 2010

SEPTEMBER

Time	m		Time	m
1 0531	3.7	**16**	0047	1.6
1125	1.5		0730	3.4
W 1805	3.5		TH 1322	2.0
☽ 2359	1.7		1949	3.4
2 0635	3.5	**17**	0230	1.7
1232	1.8		0858	3.4
TH 1916	3.4		F 1502	2.0
			2112	3.5
3 0123	1.8	**18**	0400	1.6
0756	3.4		1019	3.5
F 1404	1.9		SA 1616	1.9
2036	3.4		2224	3.6
4 0300	1.6	**19**	0454	1.4
0922	3.5		1115	3.6
SA 1538	1.8		SU 1703	1.7
2153	3.6		2315	3.8
5 0419	1.3	**20**	0535	1.2
1038	3.7		1155	3.8
SU 1645	1.5		M 1741	1.5
2256	3.9		2354	3.9
6 0516	0.9	**21**	0609	1.0
1135	4.0		1228	3.9
M 1736	1.2		TU 1815	1.3
2346	4.2			
7 0604	0.6	**22**	0027	4.1
1223	4.3		0639	0.9
TU 1820	0.9		W 1258	4.0
			1845	1.1
8 0030	4.5	**23**	0058	4.2
0649	0.3		0707	0.8
W 1306	4.5		TH 1326	4.1
● 1902	0.7		○ 1914	1.0
9 0113	4.7	**24**	0128	4.3
0732	0.1		0735	0.8
TH 1348	4.6		F 1354	4.1
1943	0.6		1943	1.0
10 0156	4.8	**25**	0157	4.3
0815	0.1		0803	0.8
F 1429	4.5		SA 1422	4.1
2024	0.5		2013	1.0
11 0239	4.8	**26**	0228	4.2
0856	0.2		0831	0.9
SA 1510	4.4		SU 1452	4.1
2105	0.6		2043	1.0
12 0325	4.6	**27**	0301	4.2
0938	0.5		0900	1.0
SU 1553	4.2		M 1523	4.0
2149	0.8		2116	1.1
13 0414	4.4	**28**	0338	4.0
1021	0.9		0932	1.2
M 1639	4.0		TU 1559	3.9
2236	1.1		2152	1.3
14 0509	4.0	**29**	0420	3.9
1109	1.3		1009	1.4
TU 1732	3.8		W 1640	3.8
2333	1.4		2238	1.4
15 0614	3.7	**30**	0511	3.7
1206	1.7		1058	1.6
W 1835	3.6		TH 1734	3.6
☽			2341	1.6

OCTOBER

Time	m		Time	m
1 0619	3.5	**16**	0147	1.7
1208	1.8		0820	3.3
F 1847	3.5		SA 1413	2.1
☽			2027	3.5
2 0106	1.6	**17**	0319	1.7
0740	3.5		0939	3.4
SA 1344	1.9		SU 1535	2.0
2008	3.5		2140	3.6
3 0239	1.5	**18**	0417	1.5
0904	3.6		1036	3.6
SU 1516	1.8		M 1628	1.8
2125	3.7		2236	3.7
4 0355	1.2	**19**	0458	1.3
1018	3.8		1118	3.7
M 1622	1.5		TU 1708	1.6
2229	4.0		2318	3.9
5 0452	0.9	**20**	0533	1.2
1113	4.1		1153	3.9
TU 1712	1.2		W 1743	1.4
2321	4.3		2354	4.0
6 0541	0.6	**21**	0605	1.1
1159	4.3		1224	4.0
W 1757	0.9		TH 1816	1.2
7 0007	4.5	**22**	0027	4.1
0625	0.4		0634	1.0
TH 1242	4.5		F 1254	4.1
● 1839	0.7		1846	1.1
8 0051	4.7	**23**	0100	4.2
0708	0.5		0703	0.9
F 1322	4.5		SA 1323	4.2
1921	0.6		○ 1918	1.0
9 0134	4.8	**24**	0132	4.2
0749	0.3		0733	0.9
SA 1402	4.5		SU 1353	4.2
2002	0.6		1950	1.0
10 0219	4.7	**25**	0206	4.2
0830	0.5		0804	1.0
SU 1443	4.4		M 1425	4.2
2045	0.7		2024	1.0
11 0306	4.5	**26**	0242	4.2
0911	0.8		0837	1.1
M 1525	4.3		TU 1459	4.1
2129	0.9		2100	1.1
12 0356	4.2	**27**	0322	4.1
0953	1.2		0913	1.2
TU 1609	4.1		W 1536	4.1
2217	1.1		2142	1.2
13 0451	3.9	**28**	0408	3.9
1038	1.5		0954	1.4
W 1700	3.8		TH 1620	3.9
2311	1.4		2232	1.3
14 0553	3.6	**29**	0502	3.8
1132	1.8		1046	1.6
TH 1800	3.6		F 1715	3.8
☽			2334	1.4
15 0019	1.6	**30**	0610	3.6
0702	3.4		1155	1.8
F 1243	2.1		SA 1824	3.7
1910	3.5		☽	
		31	0051	1.4
			0724	3.6
			SU 1321	1.9
			1940	3.7

NOVEMBER

Time	m		Time	m
1 0213	1.3	**16**	0313	1.7
0840	3.7		0939	3.5
M 1444	1.8		TU 1533	1.9
2054	3.8		2142	3.6
2 0325	1.1	**17**	0408	1.5
0950	3.8		1031	3.6
TU 1551	1.6		W 1625	1.8
2200	4.0		2234	3.7
3 0424	0.9	**18**	0450	1.4
1046	4.1		1112	3.8
W 1646	1.3		TH 1707	1.6
2256	4.3		2318	3.9
4 0516	0.7	**19**	0527	1.3
1134	4.2		1149	3.9
TH 1734	1.1		F 1745	1.4
2345	4.5		2357	4.0
5 0602	0.6	**20**	0601	1.2
1217	4.4		1223	4.1
F 1819	0.9		SA 1820	1.2
6 0032	4.6	**21**	0034	4.1
0645	0.6		0634	1.1
SA 1259	4.4		SU 1256	4.2
● 1903	0.8		○ 1856	1.1
7 0118	4.6	**22**	0111	4.2
0727	0.7		0709	1.1
SU 1339	4.5		M 1330	4.2
1947	0.7		1933	1.0
8 0205	4.3	**23**	0149	4.2
0808	0.8		0745	1.1
M 1420	4.4		TU 1405	4.3
2030	0.8		2012	0.9
9 0252	4.3	**24**	0230	4.2
0848	1.1		0823	1.1
TU 1501	4.3		W 1442	4.3
2114	0.9		2053	0.9
10 0341	4.1	**25**	0313	4.1
0929	1.3		0904	1.2
W 1545	4.1		TH 1522	4.4
2200	1.1		2138	1.0
11 0433	3.9	**26**	0401	4.0
1012	1.6		0948	1.4
TH 1631	4.0		F 1608	4.1
2249	1.3		2228	1.0
12 0527	3.7	**27**	0455	3.9
1059	1.8		1039	1.5
F 1724	3.8		SA 1701	4.0
2344	1.5		2325	1.1
13 0625	3.5	**28**	0555	3.8
1156	2.0		1139	1.7
SA 1824	3.6		SU 1803	3.9
☽			☽	
14 0049	1.6	**29**	0031	1.2
0727	3.4		0700	3.7
SU 1307	2.1		M 1251	1.7
1928	3.5		1911	3.9
15 0202	1.7	**30**	0141	1.2
0835	3.4		0808	3.7
M 1424	2.1		TU 1405	1.7
2037	3.5		2021	3.9

DECEMBER

Time	m		Time	m
1 0250	1.2	**16**	0255	1.7
0916	3.8		0930	3.5
W 1516	1.6		TH 1527	1.9
2130	4.0		2138	3.5
2 0355	1.1	**17**	0356	1.7
1018	3.9		1026	3.6
TH 1620	1.4		F 1626	1.8
2234	4.1		2237	3.7
3 0452	1.0	**18**	0447	1.6
1111	4.1		1113	3.8
F 1716	1.2		SA 1714	1.6
2330	4.2		2327	3.8
4 0543	1.0	**19**	0531	1.4
1158	4.2		1154	3.9
SA 1807	1.1		SU 1757	1.4
5 0021	4.3	**20**	0012	3.9
0628	1.0		0611	1.3
SU 1242	4.3		M 1233	4.1
● 1853	0.9		1838	1.1
6 0110	4.3	**21**	0055	4.1
0711	1.0		0652	1.2
M 1323	4.4		TU 1311	4.2
1937	0.8		○ 1919	0.9
7 0157	4.3	**22**	0137	4.2
0752	1.1		0732	1.1
TU 1404	4.4		W 1349	4.3
2020	0.8		2002	0.8
8 0242	4.2	**23**	0220	4.3
0831	1.2		0814	1.1
W 1444	4.3		TH 1429	4.4
2102	0.9		2046	0.7
9 0326	4.1	**24**	0305	4.3
0909	1.3		0856	1.1
TH 1524	4.2		F 1511	4.4
2142	1.0		2131	0.7
10 0410	3.9	**25**	0351	4.2
0947	1.5		0939	1.2
F 1605	4.1		SA 1556	4.4
2223	1.2		2218	0.7
11 0455	3.8	**26**	0440	4.1
1026	1.6		1025	1.3
SA 1648	3.9		SU 1645	4.3
2306	1.3		2309	0.8
12 0541	3.6	**27**	0533	4.0
1110	1.8		1117	1.4
SU 1736	3.8		M 1740	4.2
2353	1.5			
13 0631	3.5	**28**	0005	1.0
1202	1.9		0631	3.8
M 1829	3.6		TU 1217	1.6
☽			☽ 1841	4.0
14 0048	1.6	**29**	0107	1.2
0726	3.4		0734	3.7
TU 1307	2.0		W 1325	1.7
1928	3.5		1950	3.9
15 0150	1.7	**30**	0214	1.3
0827	3.4		0842	3.7
W 1418	2.0		TH 1441	1.7
2032	3.5		2105	3.8
		31	0326	1.4
			0951	3.7
			F 1600	1.7
			2219	3.9

Chart Datum: 2·25 metres below Ordnance Datum (Newlyn). HAT is 4·8 metres above Chart Datum; see 0.19

》》 FREE monthly updates from 《《
www.reedsalmanac.co.uk

ABERDEEN TO RATTRAY HEAD

(AC 213) From Aberdeen there are few offshore dangers to Buchan Ness. Drums Links Firing Range lies 8¾M N of Aberdeen; red flags and lights are shown when firing is taking place. R Ythan, 1·75M SSW of Hackley Hd, is navigable by small craft, but chan shifts constantly. 3M North is the very small hbr of Collieston (mostly dries), only accessible in fine weather. 4·75M NNE of Hackley Head lie The Skares, rks (marked by PHM lt buoy) extending 3½ca from S point of Cruden B, where there is anch in offshore winds. On N side of Cruden B is Port Erroll (dries 2·5m).

Buchan Ness (lt, fog sig, Racon) is a rky peninsula. 2ca N is Meikle Mackie islet, close W of which is the small hbr of Boddam (dries). 3ca NE of Meikle Mackie is The Skerry, a rk 6m high on S side of Sandford B; rks on which the sea breaks extend 2ca NNE. The chan between The Skerry and the coast is foul with rks

and not advised. Peterhead is easy to enter in almost all conditions and is an excellent passage port with marina at SW corner of the Bay.

Rattray Bay has numerous submarine pipelines leading ashore to St Fergus Gas Terminal.

For notes on offshore oil/gas installations, see 3.4.

Rattray Hd (with lt, fog sig on The Ron, rk 2ca E of Hd) has rky foreshore, drying for 2ca off. Rattray Briggs is a detached reef, depth 0·2m, 2ca E of lt ho. Rattray Hard is a rky patch, depth 10·7m, 1·5M ENE of lt ho, which raises a dangerous sea during onshore gales. ▶ *Off Rattray Hd the S-going stream begins at HW Aberdeen – 0420, and the N-going at HW Aberdeen + 0110, sp rates 3kn. In normal conditions keep about 1M E of Rattray Hd, but pass 5M off in bad weather, preferably at slack water.* ◀ Conspic radio masts with red lights lie 2·5M WNW and 2·2M W of lighthouse.

4.15 PETERHEAD

Aberdeenshire **57°29′·81N 01°46′·42W** ❀❀❀⚓⚓❀❀

CHARTS AC 213, 1438; Imray C23.

TIDES +0140 Dover; ML 2·3; Duration 0620

Standard Port ABERDEEN (◀——)

Times				Height (metres)			
High Water		Low Water		MHWS	MHWN	MLWN	MLWS
0000	0600	0100	0700	4·3	3·4	1·6	0·6
1200	1800	1300	1900				
Differences PETERHEAD							
–0035	–0045	–0035	–0040	–0·3	–0·2	0·0	+0·1

SHELTER Good in marina (2·8m). A useful passage hbr, also a major fishing and oil/gas industry port. Access any weather/tide.

NAVIGATION WPT 57°29′·44N 01°45′·75W, 314°/0·5M to ent. No dangers. 5kn speed limit in Bay; 4kn in marina. Chan between marina bkwtr and SHM lt buoy is <30m wide.

LIGHTS AND MARKS Power stn chy (183m) is conspic 1·25M S of ent, with Fl W lts H24. Ldg marks 314°, front △, rear ▽ on cols; lts as chartlet. Marina E bkwtr ☆ Fl R 4s 6m 2M; W bkwtr hd, QG 5m 2M, vis 185°-300°. Buchan Ness ☆ Fl 5s 40m 28M is 1·6M S of entr.

R/T All vessels, including yachts, **must** call *Peterhead Harbour Radio* VHF Ch **14** for clearance to enter/depart the Bay.

TELEPHONE (Code 01779) Marina Manager (Bay Authority: www.peterheadport.co.uk) 477868; Hr Control (H24) 483630; MRCC (01224) 592334; Marinecall 09068 969642; Police 472571; Dr 474841; Ⓗ 472316.

FACILITIES Peterhead Bay Marina ☎ 477868, 150 AB £11 up to 6m LOA, + £1 per m thereafter (7 days for price of 5), max LOA 20m; access all tides, 2·3m at ent. Pontoons are 'E' to 'A' from ent. Gas, CH; D from bowser at end of Princess Royal jetty (☆ Oc WRG 4s); R, 🍴 and Ⓘ at caravan site. **Peterhead SC** ☎ (01358) 751340 (Sec); **Services:** Slip, ME, El, Ⓔ, ⚒, C, Gas. **Town** P, 🍴, R, ✉, bus to Aberdeen for ⇌ & ✈.

ADJACENT HARBOUR

BODDAM, Aberdeenshire, **57°28′·47N 01°46′·56W**.
AC 213. HW +0145 on Dover; Tides as 4.15. Good shelter in the lee of Meikle Mackie, the island just N of Buchan Ness, Fl 5s 40m 28M Horn (3) 60s. Inner hbr dries/unlit. Beware rks around Meikle Mackie and to the SW of it. Appr from 1½ca NW of The Skerry. Yachts on S side of outer hbr. All facilities at Peterhead, 2M N.

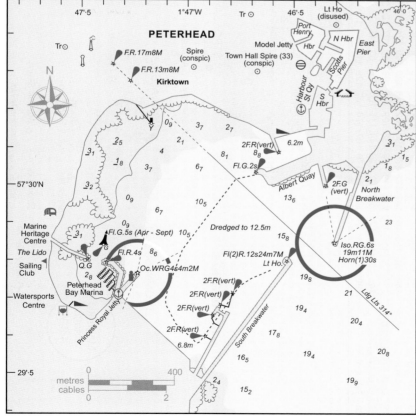

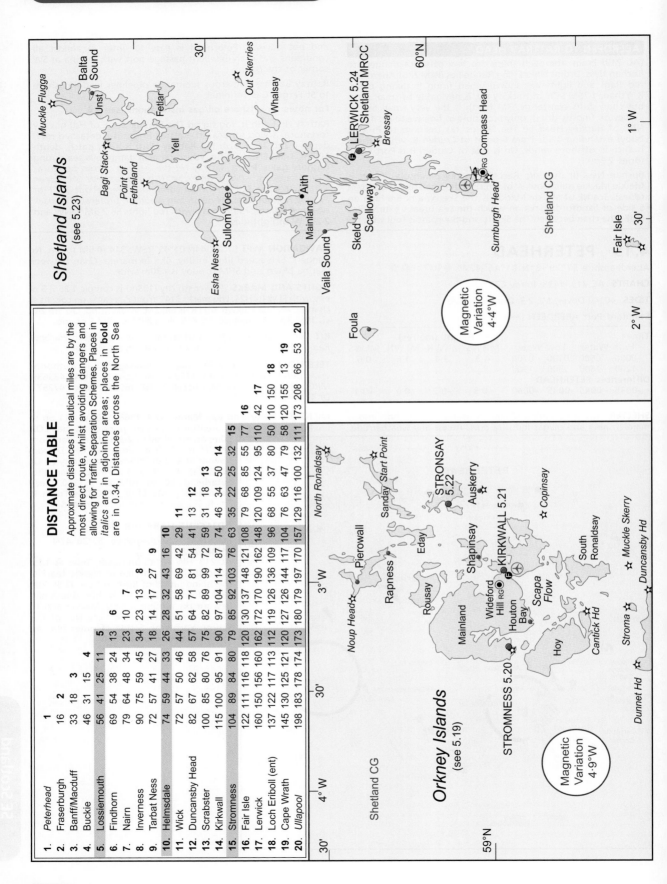

DISTANCE TABLE

Approximate distances in nautical miles are by the most direct route, whilst avoiding dangers and allowing for Traffic Separation Schemes. Places in *italics* are in adjoining areas; places in **bold** are in 0.34, Distances across the North Sea

	1	2	3	4	5	6	7	8	9	10	11	12	13	14	15	16	17	18	19	20
1. *Peterhead*	**1**																			
2. Fraserburgh	16	**2**																		
3. Banff/Macduff	33	18	**3**																	
4. Buckie	46	31	15	**4**																
5. Lossiemouth	56	41	25	11	**5**															
6. Findhorn	69	54	38	24	13	**6**														
7. Nairn	79	64	48	34	23	10	**7**													
8. Inverness	90	75	59	45	34	23	13	**8**												
9. Tarbat Ness	72	57	41	27	18	14	17	27	**9**											
10. Helmsdale	74	59	44	33	26	28	32	43	16	**10**										
11. Wick	72	57	50	46	44	51	58	69	42	29	**11**									
12. Duncansby Head	82	67	62	58	57	64	71	81	54	41	13	**12**								
13. Scrabster	100	85	80	76	75	82	89	99	72	59	31	18	**13**							
14. Kirkwall	115	100	95	91	90	97	104	114	87	74	46	34	50	**14**						
15. Stromness	104	89	84	80	79	85	92	103	76	63	35	22	25	32	**15**					
16. Fair Isle	122	111	116	118	120	130	137	148	121	108	79	68	85	55	77	**16**				
17. Lerwick	160	150	156	160	162	172	170	190	162	148	120	109	124	95	110	42	**17**			
18. Loch Eriboll (ent)	137	122	117	113	112	119	126	136	109	96	68	55	37	80	50	110	150	**18**		
19. Cape Wrath	145	130	125	121	120	127	126	144	117	104	76	63	47	79	58	120	155	13	**19**	
20. *Ullapool*	198	183	178	174	173	180	179	197	170	157	129	116	100	132	111	173	208	66	53	**20**

Shetland Islands

(see 5.23)

Muckle Flugga
Balta Sound
Unst
Out Skerries
Fetlar
Whalsay
Bagi Stack
Yell
Point of Fethaland
LERWICK 5.24
Shetland MRCC
Bressay
Esha Ness
Sullom Voe
Aith
Mainland
Vaila Sound
Skeld
Scalloway
RG Compass Head
Sumburgh Head
Shetland CG
Foula
Fair Isle

Magnetic Variation 4·4°W

60°N
1°W
2°W
30'

Orkney Islands

(see 5.19)

Shetland CG

North Ronaldsay
Start Point
Sanday
Noup Head
Pierowall
STRONSAY 5.22
Auskerry
Copinsay
Rapness
Eday
Shapinsay
KIRKWALL 5.21
Rousay
Wideford Hill RG
Houton Bay
Scapa Flow
South Ronaldsay
Mainland
Muckle Skerry
Hoy
Cantick Hd
Stroma
Duncansby Hd
Dunnet Hd
STROMNESS 5.20

Magnetic Variation 4·9°W

59°N
4°W
3°W
30'

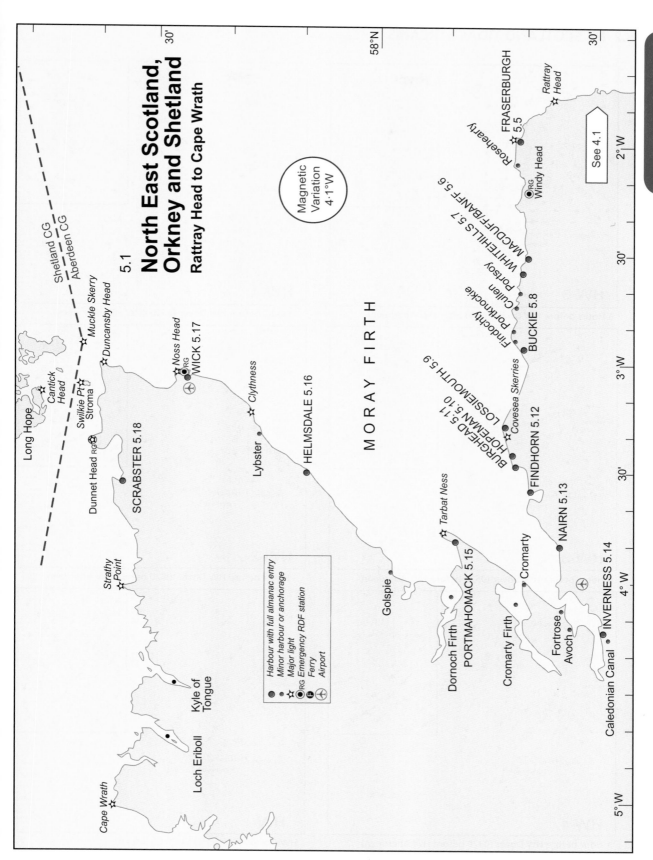

5.1

North East Scotland, Orkney and Shetland

Rattray Head to Cape Wrath

Magnetic Variation 4·1°W

MORAY FIRTH

See 4.1

Harbour with full almanac entry
Minor harbour or anchorage
Major light
RG Emergency RDF station
Ferry
Airport

Long Hope
Cantick Head
Swilkie Pt
Stroma
Muckle Skerry
Duncansby Head
Noss Head RG
WICK 5.17
Clythness
Dunnet Head RG
SCRABSTER 5.18
Strathy Point
Lybster
HELMSDALE 5.16
Kyle of Tongue
Loch Eriboll
Cape Wrath
Golspie
Dornoch Firth
PORTMAHOMACK 5.15
Tarbat Ness
Cromarty Firth
Cromarty
Fortrose
Avoch
Caledonian Canal
INVERNESS 5.14
NAIRN 5.13
FINDHORN 5.12
BURGHEAD 5.11
HOPEMAN 5.10
LOSSIEMOUTH 5.9
Covesea Skerries
BUCKIE 5.8
Findochty
Portknockie
Cullen
Portsoy
WHITEHILLS 5.7
MACDUFF/BANFF 5.6
Windy Head RG
Rosehearty
FRASERBURGH 5.5
Rattray Head

Shetland CG
Aberdeen CG

58°N
30'
30'
30'
30'
2°W
3°W
4°W
5°W

5.2 NE SCOTLAND TIDAL STREAMS

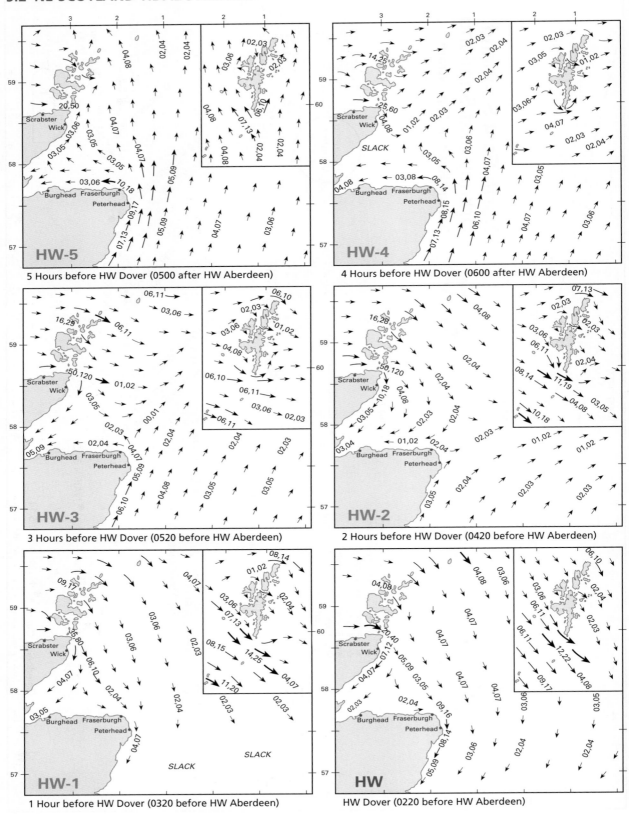

5 Hours before HW Dover (0500 after HW Aberdeen)

4 Hours before HW Dover (0600 after HW Aberdeen)

3 Hours before HW Dover (0520 before HW Aberdeen)

2 Hours before HW Dover (0420 before HW Aberdeen)

1 Hour before HW Dover (0320 before HW Aberdeen)

HW Dover (0220 before HW Aberdeen)

Southward 4.2

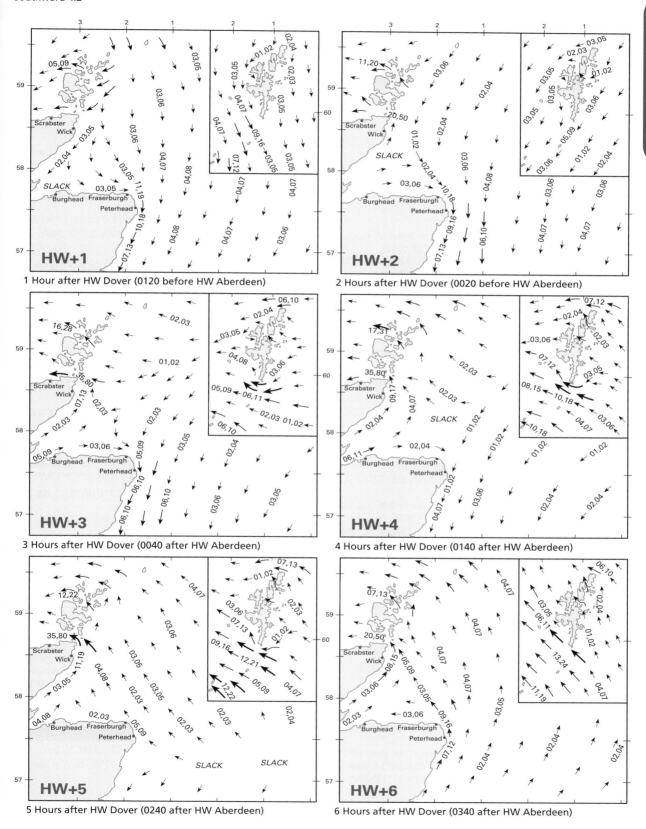

HW+1
1 Hour after HW Dover (0120 before HW Aberdeen)

HW+2
2 Hours after HW Dover (0020 before HW Aberdeen)

HW+3
3 Hours after HW Dover (0040 after HW Aberdeen)

HW+4
4 Hours after HW Dover (0140 after HW Aberdeen)

HW+5
5 Hours after HW Dover (0240 after HW Aberdeen)

HW+6
6 Hours after HW Dover (0340 after HW Aberdeen)

5.3 LIGHTS, BUOYS AND WAYPOINTS

Bold print = light with a nominal range of 15M or more. CAPITALS = place or feature. *CAPITAL ITALICS* = light-vessel, light float or Lanby. *Italics* = Fog signal. ***Bold italics*** = Racon. See 0.2 for Abbreviations.

RATTRAY HEAD TO INVERNESS

Rattray Hd ☆ 57°36'·61N 01°49'·03W Fl (3) 30s 28m **24M**; W twr; ***Racon (M) 15M***; *Horn (2) 45s*.

FRASERBURGH
Fraserburgh Ldg lt 291°; Iso R 2s 12m 9M; 57°41'·57N 02°00'·13W. Rear, 75m from front, Iso R 2s 17m 9M.
Fraserburgh, Balaclava Bkwtr Head ⚡ Fl (2) G 8s 26m 6M; dome on W twr; vis: 178°-326°; 57°41'·51N 01°59'·70W.
Kinnaird Hd ☆ 57°41'·87N 02°00'·26W Fl 5s 25m **22M**; vis: 092°-297°.

MACDUFF, BANFF and WHITEHILLS
Macduff Pier Hd ⚡ Fl (2) WRG 6s 12m W9M, R7M; W twr; vis: shore-G-115°-W-174°-R-210°; 57°40'·25N 02°30'·02W.
Macduff Ldg Lts 127°, Front FR 44m 3M; 57°40'·12N 02°29'·75W. Rear, 60m from front, FR 55m 3M; both Or △ on mast.
Banff Ldg Lts 295°, Front Fl R 4s; 57°40·30N 02°31·36W. Rear, QR; both vis: 210°-345°.
Whitehills Pier Hd ⚡ 57°40'·80N 02°34'·88W Fl WR 3s 7m W9M, R6M; W twr; vis: 132°-R-212°-W-245°.

PORTSOY and FINDOCHTY
Portsoy Pier Ldg Lts 173°, Front Fl G 4s 20m 3M; post; 57°41'·09N 02°41'·40W; Rear Q G 22m 3M; R △ on BW post.
Findochty Middle Pier Ldg Lts 166°, Front FR 6m 3M; 57°41'·90N 02°54'·20W. Rear FR 10m 3M.

BUCKIE
West Muck ⚡ QR 5m 7M; tripod; 57°41'·06N 02°58'·01W.
N Pier 60m from Hd ☆ 57°40'·9N 02°57'·5W Oc R 10s 15m **15M** W twr.

LOSSIEMOUTH, HOPEMAN and BURGHEAD
Lossiemouth S Pier Hd ⚡ Fl R 6s 11m 5M; *Siren 60s;* 57°43'·42N 03°16'·69W.
Covesea Skerries ☆ 57°43'·47N 03°20'·45W Fl WR 20s 49m **W24M, R20M**; W twr; vis: 076° - W - 267° - R - 282°.
Hopeman Ldg Lts 081°, Front,FR 3m; 57°42'·71N 03°26'·18W. Rear, 10m from front, FR 4m.
Burghead N Bkwtr Hd ⚡ Oc 8s 7m 5M; 57°42'·09N 03°30'·03W.

FINDHORN, NAIRN and INVERNESS FIRTH
Findhorn Landfall ⚓ LF 10s 57°43'·00 N 03°38'·94W.
Nairn E Pier Hd ⚡ Oc WRG 4s 6m 5M; 8-sided twr; vis: shore-G-100°-W-207°-R-shore; 57°35'·62N 03°51'·65W
Riff Bank E ⚓ Fl Y 10s 3m 5M 57°38'·38N 03°58'·18W.

SOUTH CHANNEL
Riff Bank S ⚓ Q (6) + L Fl 15s; 57°36'·73N 04°00'·97W.
Chanonry ☆ 57°34'·44N 04°05'·57W Oc 6s 12m **15M**; W twr; vis: 148°-073°.
Munlochy ⚓ L Fl 10s; 57°32'·91N 04°07'·65W .
Petty Bank ⚓ Fl R 5s 57°31'·58N 04°08'·98W.
Meikle Mee ⚓ Fl G 3s 57°30'·26N 04°12'·02W.
Longman Pt ⚓ Fl WR 2s 7m W5M, R4M; vis: 078°-W-258°-R-078°; 57°29'·99N 04°13'·31W.
Craigton Point ⚡ Fl WRG 4s 6m W11M, R7M, G7M; vis: 312° - W - 048° - R - 064° - W - 085° - G - shore; 57°30'·05N 04°14'·09W.
Bridge Centre , Or △; ***Racon (K) 6M***; 57°29'·97N 04°13'·79W.

INVERNESS and CALEDONIAN CANAL
R. Ness Outer ⚓ QR 3m 4M; 57°29'·83N 04°13'·93W.

Emb'kmt H'd ⚡ Fl G 2s 8m 4M; G f'work twr; 57°29'·72N 04°14'·25W.
Clachnaharry, S Tr'ng Wall Hd ⚓ Iso G 4s 5m 2M; tfc sigs; 57°29'·43N 04°15'·86W.

INVERNESS TO DUNCANSBY HEAD
CROMARTY FIRTH and INVERGORDON
Fairway ⚓ L Fl 10s; ***Racon (M) 5M***; 57°39'·96N 03°54'·19W.
Cromarty Bank ⚓ Fl (2) G 10s; 57°40'·66N 03°56'·78W.
Buss Bank ⚓ Fl R 3s 57°40'·97N 03°59'·54W.
Cromarty - The Ness (Lt ho disused W tr 13m); 57°40'·98N 04°02'·20W
Nigg Oil Terminal Pier Hd ⚡ Oc G 5s 31m 5M; Gy twr, floodlit; 57°41'·54N 04°02'·60W.

DORNOCH FIRTH to LYBSTER
Tarbat Ness ☆ 57°51'·88N 03°46'·76W Fl (4) 30s 53m **24M**; W twr, R bands; ***Racon (T) 14-16M***.
Lybster, S Pier Hd ⚡ Oc R 6s 10m 3M; 58°17'·79N 03°17'·41W.
Clyth Ness ☆ Fl (2) 30s 45m 14M; 58°18'·64N 03°12'·74W.

WICK
S Pier Hd ⚡ Fl WRG 3s 12m W12M, R9M, G9M; W 8-sided twr; vis: 253°-G-270°-W-286°-R-329°; *Bell (2) 10s* (occas); 58°26'·34N 03°04'·73W.
Dir lt 288·5° F WRG 9m W10M, R7M, G7M; col, N end of bridge; vis: 283·5°-G-287·2°-W-289·7°-R-293·5°; 58°26'·54N 03°05'·34W
Noss Hd ☆ 58°28'·71N 03°03'·09W Fl WR 20s 53m **W25M, R21M**; W twr; vis: shore-R-191°-W-shore.

DUNCANSBY HEAD TO CAPE WRATH
Duncansby Hd ☆ 58°38'·65N 03°01'·58W Fl 12s 67m **22M**; W twr; ***Racon (T)***.
Pentland Skerries ☆ 58°41'·41N 02°55'·49W Fl (3) 30s 52m **23M**; W twr.
Lother Rock ⚡ Fl 2s 13m 6M; ***Racon (M) 10M***; 58°43'·79N 02°58'·69W.
Swona ⚡ Fl 8s 17m 9M; vis: 261°-210°; 58°44'·25N 03°04'·24W.
Swona N Hd ⚡ Fl (3) 10s 16m 10M; 58°45'·11N 03°03'·10W.
Stroma ☆, Swilkie Point 58°41'·75N 03°07'·01W Fl (2) 20s 32m **26M**; W twr.
Dunnet Hd ☆ 58°40'·28N 03°22'·60W Fl (4) 30s 105m **23M**.

THURSO, SCRABSTER and CAPE WRATH
Thurso Ldg Lts 195°. Front, FG 5m 4M; Gy post; 58°35'·96N 03°30'·76W. Rear, FG 6m 4M; Gy mast.
Scrabster Q. E. Pier Hd ⚡ Fl (2) 4s 8m 8M 58°36'·66N 03°32'·31W.
Strathy Pt ☆ 58°36'·04N 04°01'·12W Fl 20s 45m **26M**; W twr on W dwelling. F.R. on chy 100° 8·5M.
Sule Skerry ☆ 59°05'·09N 04°24'·38W Fl (2) 15s 34m **21M**; W twr; ***Racon (T)***.
North Rona ☆ 59°07'·27N 05°48'·91W Fl (3) 20s 114m **24M**.
Sula Sgeir ⚡ Fl 15s 74m 11M; ☐ structure; 59°05'·61N 06°09'·57W.
Loch Eriboll, White Hd ⚡ Fl WR10s 18m W13M, R12M; W twr and bldg; vis: 030°-W-172°-R-191°-W-212°; 58°31'·01N 04°38'·90W.
Cape Wrath ☆ 58°37'·54N 04°59'·94W Fl (4) 30s 122m **22M**; W twr.

ORKNEY ISLANDS
Tor Ness ☆ 58°46'·78N 03°17'·86W Fl 5s 21m **17M**; W twr.
Cantick Hd (S Walls, SE end) ☆ 58°47'·23N 03°07'·88W Fl 20s 35m 13M; W twr.
SCAPA FLOW and APPROACHES
Long Hope, S Ness Pier Hd ⚡ Fl WRG 3s 6m W7M, R5M, G5M; vis:

Plot waypoints on chart before use

082°-G- 242°-W- 252°-R-082°; 58°48'·05N 03°12'·35W.

Hoxa Head ☆ Fl WR 3s 15m W9M, R6M; W twr; vis: 026°-W-163°-R-201°-W-215°; 58°49'·31N 03°02'·09W.

Nevi Skerry ⚓ Fl (2) 6s 7m 6M; 58°50'·67N 03°02'·70W.

Rose Ness ☆ 58°52'·33N 02°49'·97W Fl 6s 24m 8M; W twr.

Barrel of Butter ⚓ Fl (2) 10s 6m 7M; 58 53'·40N 03°07'·62W.

Cava ☆ Fl WR 3s 11m W10M, R8M; W ○ twr; vis: 351°-W-143°-196°-W-251°-R-271°-R-298°; 58°53'·21N 03°10'·70W .

Houton Bay Ldg Lts 316°. Front ⚓ Fl G 3s 8m. Rear ⚓, 200m from front, FG 16m; vis: 312°- 320°; 58°54'·97N 03°11'·56W.

CLESTRAN SOUND and HOY SOUND

Graemsay Is Hoy Sound Low ☆ Ldg Lts 104°. **Front**, 58°56'·42N 03°18'·60W Iso 3s 17m **15M**; W twr; vis: 070°-255°. **High Rear**, 1·2M from front, Oc WR 8s 35m **W20M, R16M**; W twr; vis: 097°-R-112°-W-163°-R-178°-W-332°; obsc on Ldg line within 0·5M.

Skerry of Ness ☆ Fl WG 4s 7m W7M, G4M; vis: shore -W-090°- G-shore; 58°56'·95N 03°17'·83W.

STROMNESS

Ldg Lts 317°. Front, FR 29m 11M; post on W twr; 58°57'·61N 03°18'·15W. Rear, 55m from front, FR 39m 11M; vis: 307°-327°; H24.

AUSKERRY

Copinsay ☆ 58°53'·77N 02°40'·35W Fl (5) 30s 79m **21M**; W twr.

Auskerry ☆ 59°01'·51N 02°34'·34W Fl 20s 34m **20M**; W twr.

Helliar Holm, S end ☆ Fl WRG 10s 18m W14M, R11M, G11M; W twr; vis: 256°-G-276°-W-292°-R-098°-W-116°-G-154°; 59°01'·13N 02°54'·09W.

Balfour Pier Shapinsay ☆ Fl (2) WRG 5s 5m W3M, R2M, G2M; vis: 270°-G-010°-W-020°-R-090°; 59°01'·86N 02°54'·49W.

KIRKWALL

Thieves Holm, ☆ Q.R8M; 59°01'·09N 02°56'·21W.

Pier N end ☆ 58°59'·29N 02°57'·72W Iso WRG 5s 8m **W15M**, **R13M, G13M**; W twr; vis: 153°-G-183°-W-192°-R-210°.

WIDE FIRTH

Linga Skerry ⚓ Q (3) 10s; 59°02'·39N 02°57'·56W.

Boray Skerries ⚓ Q (6) + L Fl 15s; 59°03'·65N 02°57'·66W.

Skertours ⚓ Q; 59°04'·11N 02°56'·72W.

Galt Skerry ⚓ Q; 59°05'·21N 02°54'·20W.

Brough of Birsay ☆ 59°08'·19N 03°20'·41W Fl (3) 25s 52m **18M**.

Papa Stronsay NE end, The Ness Fl(4)20s 8m 9M; W twr; 59°09'·34N 02°34'·93W.

SANDAY ISLAND and NORTH RONALDSAY

Quiabow ⚓ Fl (2) G 12s; 59°09'·82N 02°36'·30W.

Start Pt ☆ 59°16'·69N 02°22'·71W Fl (2) 20s 24m **18M**.

Kettletoft Pier Hd ☆ Fl WRG 3s 7m W7M, R5M, G5M; vis: 351°-W-011°-R-180°-G-351°; 59°13'·80N 02°35'·86W.

N Ronaldsay ☆ NE end, 59°23'·34N 02°22'·91W Fl 10s 43m **24M**; R twr, W bands; *Racon (T) 14-17M*.

EDAY and EGILSAY

Calf Sound ☆ Fl (3) WRG 10s 6m W8M, R6M, G6M; W twr; vis: shore-R-215°-W-222°-G-301°-W-305°; 59°14'·21N 02°45'·82W.

Backaland Pier ☆ 59°09'·43N 02°44'·88W Fl R 3s 5m 4M; vis: 192°-250°.

Egilsay Graand ⚓ Q (6) + L Fl 15s; 59°06'·86N 02°54'·42W.

WESTRAY and PIEROWALL

Noup Head ☆ 59°19'·86N 03°04'·23W Fl 30s 79m **20M**; W twr; vis: about 335°-282° but partially obsc 240°-275°.

Pierowall E Pier Head ☆ Fl WRG 3s 7m W11M, R7M, G7M; vis: 254°-G-276°-W-291°-R-308°-G-215°; 59°19'·35N 02°58'·53W.

Papa Westray, Moclett Bay Pier Head ☆ Fl WRG 5s 7m W5M, R3M, G3M; vis: 306°-G-341°-W-040°-R-074°; 59°19'·60N 02°53'·52W.

FAIR ISLE

Skadan South ☆, 59°30'·84N 01°39'·16W Fl (4) 30s 32m **22M**; W twr; vis: 260°-146°, obsc inshore 260°-282°.

Skroo ☆ N end 59°33'·13N 01°36'·58W Fl (2) 30s 80m **22M**; W twr; vis: 086·7°-358°.

MAINLAND, SOUTH

Sumburgh Head ☆ 59°51'·21N 01°16'·58W Fl (3) 30s 91m **23M**.

Mousa, Perie Bard ☆ Fl 3s 20m 10M; 59°59'·84N 01°09'·51W.

BRESSAY and LERWICK

Bressay, Kirkabister Ness ☆ 60°07'·20N 01°07'·29W; Fl (2) 20s 32m **23M**.

Maryfield Ferry Terminal ☆ Oc WRG 6s 5m 5M; vis: W008°-R013°-G-111°-008°; 60°09'·43N 01°07'·45W.

North Ness ☆ Iso WG 4s 4m 5M; vis: shore-W-158°-G-216°-W-301°; 60°09'·57N 01°08'·77W

Loofa Baa ⚓ Q (6) + L Fl 15s 4m 5M; 60°09'·72N 01°08'·79W.

Soldian Rock ⚓ Q (6) + L Fl 15s 60°12'·51N 01°04'·73W.

N ent Dir lt 215°, Oc WRG 6s 27m 8M; Y △, Or stripe; vis: 211°-R-214°-W-216°-G-221°; 60°10'·47N 01°09'·53W.

Rova Hd ☆ 60°11'·46N 01°08'·60W Fl (3) WRG 18s 12m W12M, R9M, G9M; W twr; vis: 090°-R-182°-W-191°-G-213°-R-241°-W-261·5°-R-009°-R-040°. Same structure and synchronised: Fl (3) WRG 18s 14m **W16M**, R13M, G13M; vis: 176·5°-R-182°-W-191°-G-196·5°.

Dales Voe ☆ Fl (2) WRG 8s 5m W4M, R3M, G3M; vis: 220°-G-227°-W-233°-R-240°; 60°11'·79N 01°11'·23W.

Hoo Stack ☆ Fl (4) WRG 12s 40m W7M, R5M, G5M; W pylon; vis: 169°-R-180°-W-184°-G-193°-W-169°. Same structure, Dir lt 182°. Fl (4) WRG 12s 33m W9M, R6M, G6M; vis: 177°- R-180°-W-184°-W-187°; synch with upper lt; 60°14'·96N 01°05'·38W.

Mull (Moul) of Eswick ☆ Fl WRG 3s 50m W9M, R6M, G6M; W twr; vis: 028°-R-200°-W-207°-G-018°-W-028°; 60°15'·74N 01°05'·90W.

Inner Voder ⚓ Q (9) 15s; 60°16'·43N 01°05'·18W.

WHALSAY and SKERRIES

Symbister Ness ☆ Fl (2) WG 12s 11m W8M, G6M; W twr; vis: shore-W-203°-G-shore; 60°20'·43N 01°02'·29W.

Suther Ness ☆ Fl WRG 3s 10m W10M, R8M, G7M; vis: shore -W-038°-R-173°-W-206°-G-shore; 60°22'·12N 01°00'·20W.

Bound Skerry ☆ 60°25'·47N 00°43'·72W Fl 20s 44m **20M**; W twr. South Mouth. Ldg Lts 014°. Front, FY3m 2M; 60°25'·33N 00°45'·01W. Rear, FY 12m 2M.

Muckle Skerry ☆ Fl (2) WRG 10s 15m W7M, R5M, G5M; W twr; vis: 046°-W-192°-R-272°-G-348°-W-353°-R-046°; 60°26'·41N 00°51'·84W.

YELL SOUND

S ent, Lunna Holm ☆ Fl (3) WRG 15s 19m W10M,R7M,G7M; W○twr; vis: shore-R-090°-W-094°-G-209°-W-275°-R-shore; 60°27'·34N 01°02'·52W.

Firths Voe ☆, N shore 60°27'·21N 01°10'·63W Oc WRG 8s 9m **W15M**, R10M, G10M; W twr; vis: 189°-W-194°-G-257°-W-261°-R-339°-W-066°.

Linga Is. Dir lt 150° ☆ Q (4) WRG 8s 10m W9M, R9M, G9M; vis: 145°-R-148°-W-152°-G-155°. Q (4) WRG 8s 10m W7M, R4M, G4M; same structure; vis: 052°-R-146°, 154°-G-196°-W-312°; synch; 60°26'·80N 01°09'·13W.

The Rumble Bn ☆ R Bn; Fl 10s 8m 4M; *Racon (O)*; 60°28'·16N 01°07'·26W.

Yell, Ulsta Ferry Term. Bkwtr Hd ☆ Oc RG 4s 7m R5M, G5M; vis: shore-G-354°, 044°-R-shore. Same structure; Oc WRG 4s 5m W8M, R5M, G5M; vis: shore-G-008°-W-036°-R-shore; 60°29'·74N 01°09'·52W.

Toft Ferry Terminal ☆,Dir lt 241° (H24); Dir Oc WRG 10s 8m **W16M**, R10M, G10M; vis: 236° -G-240°-W-242°-R-246°; By day W2M, R1M, G1M. 60°27'·96N 01°12'·34W.

Ness of Sound, W side ⚡ Fl (3) WRG 12s 18m W9M, R6M, G6M; vis: shore-G-345°-W-350°-R-160°-W-165°-G-shore;60°31'·34N 01°11'·28W.

Brother Is. Dir lt 329°. Fl (4) WRG 8s 16m W10M, R7M, G7M; vis: 323·5°-G-328°-W-330°-R-333·5°; 60°30'·95N 01°14'·11W.

Mio Ness ⚡ Q (2) WR 10s 12m W7M, R4M; W ○ twr; vis: 282° - W - 238° - R - 282°; 60°29'·66N 01°13'·68W.

Tinga Skerry ⚡ Q (2) G 10s 9m 5M. W ○ twr; 60°30'·48N 01°14'·86W.

YELL SOUND, NORTH ENTRANCE

Bagi Stack ⚡ Fl (4) 20s 45m 10M; 60°43'·53N 01°07'·54W.

Gruney Is ⚡ Fl WR 5s 53m W8M, R6M; W twr; vis: 064°-R-180°-W-012°; *Racon (T) 14M*; 60°39'·15N 01°18'·17W.

Pt of Fethaland ☆ 60°38'·05N 01°18'·70W Fl (3) WR 15s 65m **W24M, R20M**; vis 080°-R-103°-W-160°-206°-W-340°.

Muckle Holm ⚡ Fl (4) 10s 32m 10M 60°34'·83N 01°16'·01W.

Little Holm ⚡ Iso 4s 12m 6M; W twr; 60°33'·42N 01°15'·88W.

Outer Skerry ⚡ Fl 6s 12m 8M; 60°33'·04N 01°18'·32W.

Quey Firth ⚡ Oc WRG 6s 22m W12M, R8M, G8M; W twr; vis: shore (through S & W)-W-290°-G-327°-W-334°-W-shore; 60°31'·43N 01°19'·58W.

Lamba, S side ⚡Fl WRG 3s 30m W8M, R5M, G5M; W twr; vis: shore-G-288°-W-293°-R-327°-W-044°-R-140°-W-shore. Dir lt 290·5° Fl WRG 3s 24m W10M, R7M, G7M; vis: 285·5°-G-288°-W-293°-W-295·5°; 60°30'·73N 01°17'·84W .

SULLOM VOE

Gluss Is ☆ Ldg Lts 194·7° (H24). **Front**, 60°29'·77N 01°19'·44W F 39m **19M**; □ on Gy twr; H24. **Rear**, 0·75M from front, F 69m **19M**; □ on Gy twr.; H24. Both Lts 9M by day.

Little Roe ⚡ Fl (3) WR 10s 16m W5M, R4M; W structure, Or band; vis: 036°-R-095·5°-W-036°; 60°29'·99N 01°16'·46W.

Skaw Taing ⚡ Ldg Lts 150·5°. Front, Oc WRG 5s 21m W8M, R5M, G5M; Or and W structure; vis: 049°-W-078°-G-147°-W-154°-R-169°-W-288°; 60°29'·10N 01°16'·86W. Rear, 195m from front, Oc 5s 35m 8M; vis: W145°-156°.

Ness of Bardister ⚡ Oc WRG 8s 20m W9M, R6M, G6M; Or &W structure; vis: 180·5°- W-240°- R-310·5°- W-314·5°- G-030·5°; 60°28'·19N 01°19'·63W.

Fugla Ness. Lts in line 212·3°. Rear, 60°27'·25N 01°19'·74W Iso 4s 45m 14M. Common front 60°27'·45N 01°19'·57W Iso 4s 27m 14M; synch with rear Lts. Lts in line 203°. Rear, 60°27'·26N 01°19'·81W Iso 4s 45m 14M.

Sella Ness ☆ Dir lt 133·5° 60°26'·76N 01°16'·66W Oc WRG 10s 19m **W16M**, R3M, G3M; vis: 123·5° -G- 130·5°-Al WG(white phase increasing with brg)-132·5°-W-134·5°-Al WR(R phase inc with brg)-136·5°-R-143·5°; H24. By day Oc WRG 10s 19m W2M, R1M,G1M as above.

EAST YELL, UNST and BALTA SOUND

Whitehill ⚡ Fl WR 3s 24m W9M, R6M; vis: shore-W-163°-R-211°-W-352°-R-shore.

Balta Sound ⚡Fl WR 10s 17m 10M, R7M; vis: 249°-W-008°-R-058°-W-154°; 60°44'·48N 00°47'·56W.

Holme of Skaw ⚡ Fl 5s 8m 8M; 60°49'·87N 00°46'·33W.

Muckle Flugga ☆ 60°51'·32N 00°53'·14W Fl (2) 20s 66m **22M**.

Yell. Cullivoe Bkwtr Hd ⚡Fl (2) WRG 10s 3m 4M; vis: 080°-G- 294°-W-355°-R-080°; 60°41'·91N 00°59'·66W.

Head of Mula ⚡Fl WRG 5s 48m W10M, G7M, R7M; metal framework twr; vis: 292°-G-357°-W-002°-R-157°-W-161·5; 60°44'·48N 00°47'·56W.

MAINLAND, WEST

Esha Ness ☆ 60°29'·34N 01°37'·65W Fl 12s 61m **25M**.

Ness of Hillswick ⚡ Fl (4) WR 15s 34m W9M, R6M; vis: 217°-W-093°-R-114°; 60°27'·21N 01°29'·80W.

Muckle Roe, Swarbacks Minn ⚡ Fl WR 3s 30m W9M, R6M; vis: 314°-W-041°-R-075°-W-137°; 60°20'·98N 01°27'·07W.

W Burra Firth Outer ⚡ Oc WRG 8s 27m W9M, R7M, G7M; vis: 136°-G-142°-W-150°-R-156°. H24; 60°17'·79N 01°33'·56W.

W Burra Firth Inner ☆ 60°17'·78N 01°32'·17W F WRG 9m **W15M**, R9M, G9M; vis: 095°-G-098°-W-102°-105°; H24.

Ve Skerries ⚡ Fl (2) 20s 17m 11M; W twr; *Racon (T) 15M*; 60°22'·36N 01°48'·78W.

Papa Stour Housa Voe Dir lt 228° ⚡ F WRG 2m W9M, R7M, G7M; vis: 219°-G-226°-W-230°-R-239°; 60°19'·58N 01°40'·47W.

Rams Head ⚡ Fl WRG 8s 16m W9M, R6M; G6M; W house; vis: 265°-G-355°-W-012°-R-090°-W-136°, obsc by Vaila I when brg more than 030°; 60°11'·96N 01°33'·47W.

North Havra ⚡ Fl(3) WRG 12s 24m W11M, R8M, G8M; W twr; vis: 001°-G-053·5°-W-060·5°-R-182°, 274°- G-334°-W-337·5°-R -001°; 60°09'·85N 01°20'·31W.

SCALLOWAY

Bullia Skerry ⚡ Fl 5s 5m 5M; steel pillar & platform 60°06'·55N 01°21'·57W.

Point of the Pund ⚡ Fl WRG 5s 20m W7M, R5M, G5M; W twr; vis: 350°-R-090°-G-111°-R-135°-W-140°-G-177°, 267°-W-350°; 60°07'·99N 01°18'·31W.

Whaleback Skerry ⚡ Q; 60°07'·95N 01°18'·90W.

Blacks Ness Pier SW corner ⚡ Oc WRG 10s 10m W11M, G8M, R8M; vis: 052°-G-063·5°-W-065·5°-R-077°; 60°08'·02N 01°16'·59W.

Fugla Ness ⚡ Fl (2) WRG 10s 20m W10M, R7M, G7M; W twr; vis: 014°-G-032°-W-082°-R-134°-W-shore; 60°06'·38N 01°20'·85W.

FOULA

South Ness ☆ 60°06'·75N 02°03'·87W Fl (3) 15s 36m **18M**; W twr; vis: obscured 123°-221°.

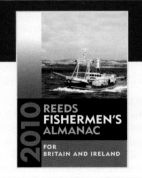

5.4 PASSAGE INFORMATION

Refer to the *N Coast of Scotland Pilot*; the CCC's SDs (3 vols) for N and NE coasts of Scotland; Orkney; and Shetland.

A 'Rover Ticket', £25 from Aberdeenshire and Moray Councils, allows berthing (subject to availability) for one week from arrival at the first harbour. The scheme includes: Johnshaven, Gourdon, Stonehaven, Rosehearty, Banff, Portsoy, Cullen, Portknockie, Findochty, Hopeman and Burghead.

Orkney Marinas charge on a sliding scale (based on 10m LOA): £17·50/day or £80/week. In harbours without a marina, berthing on a pier costs £14 for 4 days or £28 for 14 days. This scheme covers all marinas and piers in the Orkney Islands except St Margaret's Hope (5.19) which is independently run.

More Passage Information is threaded between the harbours in this Area.

MORAY FIRTH: SOUTH COAST

(AC 115, 222, 223) Crossing the Moray Firth from Rattray Hd (lt, fog sig) to Duncansby Hd (lt, Racon) heavy seas may be met in strong W winds. Most hbrs in the Firth are exposed to NE-E winds. For oil installations, see 3.4; the Beatrice Field is 20M S of Wick. ► *Tidal streams attain 3kn at sp close off Rattray Hd, but 5M NE of the Head the NE-going stream begins at HW Aberdeen + 0140, and the SE-going stream at HW Aberdeen – 0440, sp rates 2kn. Streams are weak elsewhere in the Moray Firth, except in the inner part.* ◄

In late spring/early summer fog (haar) is likely in onshore winds. In strong winds the sea breaks over Steratan Rk and Colonel Rk, respectively 3M E and 1M ENE of Fraserburgh. Rosehearty firing range is N & W of Kinnairds Hd (lt); tgt buoys often partially submerged. Banff B is shallow; N of Macduff beware Collie Rks. Banff hbr dries, and should not be approached in fresh NE-E winds, when seas break well offshore; Macduff is a possible alternative.

From Meavie Pt to Scar Nose dangers extend up to 3ca from shore in places. Beware Caple Rk (depth 0·2m) 7½ca W of Logie Hd. Spey B is clear of dangers more than 7½ca from shore; anch here, but only in offshore winds. Beware E Muck (dries) 5ca SW of Craigenroan, an above-water rky patch 5ca SW of Craig Hd, and Middle Muck and W Muck in approach to Buckie; Findochty & Portknockie are 2 and 3.5M ENE. Halliman Skerries (dry; bn) lie 1·5M WNW of Lossiemouth. Covesea Skerries (dry) lie 5ca NW of their lt ho.

The area to the SW of a line between Helmsdale and Lossiemouth is an EU Special Area of Conservation to protect a vulnerable population of bottlenose dolphins. Mariners are advised to proceed at a safe, constant speed through the area and avoid disturbing the dolphins.

Inverness Firth is approached between Nairn and S Sutor. In heavy weather there is a confused sea with overfalls on Guillam Bank, 9M S of Tarbat Ness. The sea also breaks on Riff Bank (S of S Sutor) which dries in places. Chans run both N and S of Riff Bank. ► *Off Fort George, on E side of ent to Inverness Firth (AC1078), the SW-going stream begins HW Aberdeen + 0605, sp rate 2·5kn; the NE-going stream begins at HW Aberdeen – 0105, sp rate 3·5kn. There are eddies and turbulence between Fort George and Chanonry Pt when stream is running hard. Tidal streams in the Inverness Firth and approaches are not strong, except in the Cromarty Fifth Narrows, the Fort George Narrows and the Kessock Road, including off the entrance to the Caledonian Canal.* ◄

There is a firing range between Nairn and Inverness marked, when in operation, by flags at Fort George. Much of Inverness Firth is shallow, but a direct course from Chanonry Pt to Kessock Bridge, via Munlochy SWM and Meikle Mee SHM lt buoys, carries a least depth of 2·1m. Meikle Mee bank dries 0·2m.

5.5 FRASERBURGH

Aberdeenshire 57°41'·50N 01°59'·79W ❋❋⚓⚓✿✿✿

CHARTS AC 115, 222, 1462; Imray C23.

TIDES +0120 Dover; ML 2·3; Duration 0615

Standard Port ABERDEEN (←——)

Times				Height (metres)			
High Water		Low Water		MHWS	MHWN	MLWN	MLWS
0000	0600	0100	0700	4·3	3·4	1·6	0·6
1200	1800	1300	1900				
Differences FRASERBURGH							
–0105	–0115	–0120	–0110	–0·6	–0·5	–0·2	0·0

SHELTER A safe refuge, but ent is dangerous in NE/SE gales. A very busy fishing hbr; yachts are not encouraged but may find a berth in S Hbr (3.2m). FVs come and go H24.

NAVIGATION WPT 57°41'·30N 01°58'·80W, 291°/0·57M to ent. The Outer Ent Chan is maintained to 8·9m and Inner Ent Chan 5.9m. Good lookout on entering/leaving. Yachts can enter under radar control in poor vis.

LIGHTS AND MARKS Kinnairds Hd lt ho, Fl 5s 25m 22M, is 0·45M NNW of ent. Cairnbulg Briggs bn, Fl (2) 10s 9m 6M, is 1·8M ESE of ent. Ldg lts 291°: front Iso R 2s 12m 9M; rear Iso R 2s 17m 9M.

R/T Call on approach VHF Ch 12 16 (H24) for directions/berth.

TELEPHONE (Code 01346) Port Office 515858; Watch Tr 515926; MRCC (01224) 592334; Marinecall 09068 969641; Police 513121; Dr 518088.

FACILITIES Port ☎ 515858, AB £10 (in S Hbr) any LOA, Slip, P (cans), D, FW, CH, ME, El, ⚒, C (30 ton & 70 ton mobile), SM, 🛒, R, Bar; Town ✉, Ⓑ, ⇌, ✈ (bus to Aberdeen).

ADJACENT HARBOURS
ROSEHEARTY, Aberdeen, 57°42'·08N 02°06'·87W. ❋❋⚓✿✿. AC 222, 213. HW Aberdeen –1. E pier and inner hbr dry, but end of W pier is accessible at all tides. Ent exposed in N/E winds; in E/SE winds hbr can be uncomfortable. Ldg marks B/W now (2001) lit on approx 220°; rks E of ldg line. When 30m from pier, steer midway between ldg line and W pier. Port Rae, close to E, has unmarked rks; local knowledge req'd. AB £10 any LOA. *For details of Rover berthing ticket see 5.4.* Town 🛒, R, Bar, ✉. Firing range: for info ☎ (01346) 571634; see also 5.4. **Pennan Bay**, 5M W: ⚓ on sand between Howdman (2·9m) and Tamhead (2·1m) rks, 300m N of hbr (small craft only). **Gardenstown** (Gamrie Bay). Appr from E of Craig Dagerty rk (4m, conspic). Access HW±3 to drying hbr or ⚓ off.

5.6 MACDUFF/BANFF

Aberdeenshire Macduff **57°40'·25N 02°30'·03W** ✵✵⚓⚓🌸🌸
Banff **57°40'·22N 02°31'·27W** ✵✵⚓🌸🌸🌸

CHARTS AC 115, 222, 1462; Imray C23.

TIDES + 0055 Dover; ML 2·0; Duration 0615

Standard Port ABERDEEN (←—)

Times				Height (metres)			
High Water		Low Water		MHWS	MHWN	MLWN	MLWS
0200	0900	0400	0900	4·3	3·4	1·6	0·6
1400	2100	1600	2100				
Differences BANFF							
–0100	–0150	–0150	–0050	–0·4	–0·2	–0·1	+0·2

SHELTER Macduff: Reasonably good, but ent not advised in strong NW winds. Slight/moderate surge in outer hbr with N/NE gales. Hbr ent is 17m wide with 3 basins; approx 2·6m in outer hbr and 2m inner hbr. A busy cargo/fishing port with limited space for yachts. **Banff:** Popular hbr (dries); access HW±4. When Macduff ent is very rough in strong NW/N winds, Banff can be a safe refuge; pontoon berths in both basins. Best to contact HM beforehand. In strong E/ENE winds Banff is unusable.

NAVIGATION WPT 57°40'·48N 02°30'·59W, 127°/0·4M to **Macduff** ent. WPT 57°40'·11N 02°30'·85W, 115°/0·25M to **Banff** ent. Beware Feachie Craig, Collie Rks and rky coast N and S of hbr ent.

LIGHTS AND MARKS Macduff: Ldg lts/marks 127° both FR 44/55m 3M, orange △s. Pier hd lt, Fl (2) WRG 6s 12m 9/7M, W tr; shore-G-115°-W-174°-R-210°, Horn (2) 20s. **Banff:** Fl 4s end of New Quay and ldg lts 295° rear Fl R 2s, front Fl R 4s.

R/T Macduff Ch 12 16 (H24); **Banff** Ch 12.

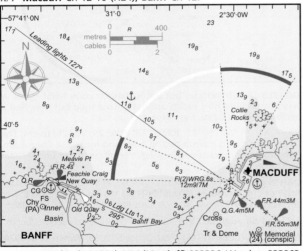

TELEPHONE (Code 01261) HM (**Macduff**) 832236, Watch tr 833962; HM (**Banff**) 815544; MRCC (01224) 592334; Marinecall 09068 969641; Police 812555; Dr (**Banff**) 812027.

FACILITIES Macduff: Hbr £10 any LOA, Slip, P (cans), D, FW, ME, El, ✖, CH. Town 🛒, R, Bar, ✉, ⇌ (bus to Keith). **Banff:** Hbr £10 any LOA, *for details of Rover berthing ticket see 5.4;* ♥ in marina (www.banffmarina.com) in Inner Hbr; FW, 🗲, Slip, toilet block; **Banff SC:** showers. Town, P, D, 🛒, R, Bar, ⇌, Ⓑ, ✈ (Aberdeen).

ADJACENT HARBOURS
PORTSOY, Aberdeenshire, **57°41'·34N 02°41'·59W.** ✵✵⚓🌸🌸. AC 222. HW +0047 on Dover; –0132 and Ht –0·3m on Aberdeen. Small drying hbr; ent exposed to NW/NE'lies. New Hbr to port of ent partially dries; Inner Hbr dries to clean sand. Ldg lts 173°, front Fl G 4s 20m 3M, metal post; rear Q G 22m 3M, R △ on BW post. HM ☎ (01261) 815544. Facilities: few but hosts Scottish Traditional Boat Festival late June/early July. AB £10, *for details of Rover berthing ticket see 5.4,* FW, Slip, 🛒, R, Bar, ✉. **Sandend Bay,** 1·7M W (57°41'N 02°44'·5W). ⚓ on sand E of hbr.

5.7 WHITEHILLS

Aberdeenshire **57°40'·80N 02°34'·87W** ✵✵⚓⚓🌸🌸

CHARTS AC 115, 222; Imray C23.

TIDES +0050 Dover; ML 2·4; Duration 0610

Standard Port ABERDEEN (←—)

Times				Height (metres)			
High Water		Low Water		MHWS	MHWN	MLWN	MLWS
0200	0900	0400	0900	4·3	3·4	1·6	0·6
1400	2100	1600	2100				
Differences WHITEHILLS							
–0122	–0137	–0117	–0127	–0·4	–0·3	+0·1	+0·1

SHELTER Safe. In strong NW/N winds beware surge in the narrow ent and outer hbr, when ent is best not attempted. See HM for vacant pontoon berth.

NAVIGATION WPT 57°41'·98N 02°34'·89W, 180°/1·2M to bkwtr lt. Reefs on S side of chan marked by 2 rusty/white SHM bns. Beware fishing floats. Narrow entrance dredged to 1·8m, Outer Hbr pontoon berths 2.2m and Inner Hbr 1.5m–1·8m.

LIGHTS AND MARKS Fl WR 3s on pier hd, vis 132°-R-212°-W-245°; approach in R sector.

R/T Whitehills Hbr Radio VHF Ch **14** 16.

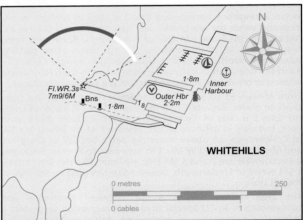

TELEPHONE (Code 01261) HM/Marina ☎ 861291, mobile 07906 135786, www.whitehillsharbour.co.uk; MRCC (01224) 592334; Marinecall 09068 969641; Police Banff 812555; Dr 812027.

FACILITIES Marina (47 + ♥), £15 (decreasing to £30/3nights), Quayside £12, @,Wi-fi, D, 🗲, ME, El, CH; **Town** 🛒, R, Bar, ✉, ⇌ (bus to Keith), ✈ (Aberdeen).

ADJACENT HARBOURS

CULLEN, Moray, **57°41'·63N 02°49'·29W.** ✵⚓🌸🌸. AC 222. HW +0045 on Dover, HW –0135 & –0·3m on Aberdeen; Duration 0555; ML 2·4m. Shelter good, but ent hazardous in strong W/N winds. Appr on 180° toward conspic viaduct and W bn on N pier. Caple Rk, 0·2m, is 5ca NE of hbr. Access HW ±2 approx. Small drying unlit hbr, best for shoal draft. Moor S of Inner jetty if < 1m draft. Beware moorings across inner basin ent. Pontoons in inner hbr (1·8m at HW Np). *For details of Rover berthing ticket see 5.4.* HM ☎ (01261) 842477 (home, part-time). Town 🛒,R,Bar, ✉.

PORTKNOCKIE, Moray, **57°42'·28N 02°51'·79W.** ✵✵⚓🌸🌸🌸. AC 222. HW +0045 on Dover; –0135 and ht –0·3m Aberdeen; ML 2·3m; Duration 0555; access H24. Good shelter in one of the safest hbrs on S side of Moray Firth, but scend is often experienced; care needed in strong NW/N winds. FW ldg lts, on white-topped poles, lead approx 151°, to ent. Orange street lts surround the hbr. Limited ABs on N Quay; most of inner hbr dries. HM ☎ (01542) 840833 (home, p/time); Facilities: Slip, AB; *for details of Rover berthing ticket see 5.4.,* FW, ✖; Dr ☎ 840272. **Town** Ⓑ, P & D, ✉, 🛒, Bar.

ADJACENT HARBOUR (2M ENE of BUCKIE)

FINDOCHTY, Moray, 57°41'·94N 02°54'·29W. AC 222. HW +0045 on Dover, HW −0135 & ht −0·2m on Aberdeen; ML 2·3m; Duration 0550. Ent is about 2ca W of conspic church belfry. 1ca N of ent, leave Beacon Rock (3m high) to stbd. Ldg lts, FR, lead approx 166° into Outer Basin which dries 0·2m and has many rky outcrops; access HW ±2 for 1·5m draft. Ent faces N and is 20m wide; unlit white bn at hd of W pier. Good shelter in inner basin for 100 small craft/yachts on 3 pontoons (the 2 W'ly pontoons dry); possible AB on Sterlochy Pier in 2m; Slip (£10) *for details of Rover berthing ticket see 5.4*. HM ☎ (01542) 832560 (home, part-time), mob 07900 920445. **Town** 🛒, R, Bar, ✉, Ⓑ.

5.8 BUCKIE

Moray 57°40'·84N 02°57'·63W ✿✿✿✿♦♦♦✿✿

CHARTS AC 115, 222, 1462; Imray C23.

TIDES +0040 Dover; ML 2·4; Duration 0550

Standard Port ABERDEEN (◀—)

Times				Height (metres)			
High Water		Low Water		MHWS	MHWN	MLWN	MLWS
0200	0900	0400	0900	4·3	3·4	1·6	0·6
1400	2100	1600	2100				
Differences BUCKIE							
−0130	−0145	−0125	−0140	−0·2	−0·2	0·0	+0·1

SHELTER Good in all weathers.

In strong NNW to NE winds there is a dangerous swell over the bar at hbr ent, which is 24m wide.

Access H24. Berth in No 4 basin as directed by HM.

NAVIGATION WPT 57°41'·3N 02°59'·0W, 125°/0°8M to ent. The recommended track from the WPT is 128° until the 2F.R (vert) and Oc.R. 10s on the N breakwater are in line (096°), thence to the hbr ent. Beware W Muck (QR 5m tripod, 2M), Middle Muck and E Muck Rks, 3ca off shore.

LIGHTS AND MARKS The Oc R 10s 15m 15M, W tr on N bkwtr, 2FG(vert) in line 120° with Iso WG 2s 20m 16/12M, W tr, R top, leads clear of W Muck. Entry sigs on N pier: 3 ● lts = hbr closed. Traffic is controlled by VHF.

R/T VHF Ch 12 16 (H24).

TELEPHONE (Code 01542) HM 831700; MRCC (01224) 592334; Marinecall 09068 969641; Police 08450 6005 700; Dr 831555.

FACILITIES No 4 Basin AB £10.58 or £5.29 <12hrs, 🗑, FW; **Services:** D & P (delivery), BY, ME, El, ✕, CH, Slip, BH (50 tons), C (15 ton), Gas. **Town** 🛒, Bar, Ⓑ, ✉, ▣ at Strathlene caravan site 1·5M E, ⇌ (bus to Elgin), ✈ (Aberdeen or Inverness).

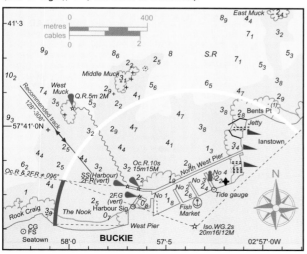

5.9 LOSSIEMOUTH

Moray 57°43'·41N 03°16'·63W ✿✿♦♦♦✿✿✿

CHARTS AC 223, 1462; Imray C23.

TIDES +0040 Dover; ML 2·3; Duration 0605

Standard Port ABERDEEN (◀—)

Times				Height (metres)			
High Water		Low Water		MHWS	MHWN	MLWN	MLWS
0200	0900	0400	0900	4·3	3·4	1·6	0·6
1400	2100	1600	2100				
Differences LOSSIEMOUTH							
−0125	−0200	−0130	−0130	−0·2	−0·2	0·0	0·0

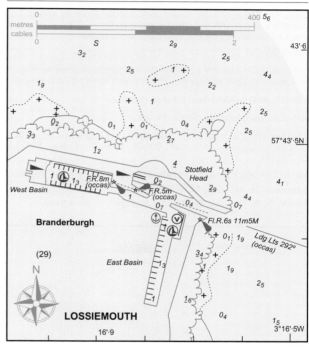

SHELTER Very good in winds from SSE to NW. Pontoon berths in both basins, dredged 2m; access HW±4.

- In N to SE winds >F6 appr can be dangerous, with swell tending to break across hbr mouth and in outer hbr. Residual swell from E to SE can be particularly hazardous.
- Near ent, beware current from R Lossie setting in N'ly direction, causing confused water in N to SE winds at sp.
- Chan and Basins are prone to silting; a vessel drawing 2m would have little clearance at LWS ±2.

NAVIGATION WPT 57°43'·38N 03°16'·09W, 277°/0·3M to ent. Rks to N and S of hbr ent; appr from E.

LIGHTS AND MARKS Covesea Skerries, W lt ho, Fl WR 20s 49m 24M, is 2M W of the hbr ent. Ldg lts 292°, both FR 5/8m; S pier hd Fl R 6s 11m 5M. Traffic sigs: B ● at S pier (● over Fl R 6s) = hbr shut.

R/T VHF Ch 12 16 HO.

TELEPHONE (Code 01343) HM ☎ 813066, mob 07796790481; MRCC (01224) 592334; Marinecall 09068 969641; Police 0845 6005 700; Dr 812277.

FACILITIES Marina (85 + some ✓), ☎ 813066, £20/craft, ▣, &; **Hbr Slip** (£5), ME, El, ✕, C, BH, CH, @, SM ☎ 07989 956698, harbourmaster@lossiemarina.fsnet.co.uk; **Hbr Service Stn** ☎ 813001, Mon-Fri 0800-2030, Sat 0800-1930, Sun 0930-1900, P & D cans, Gas. **Town** 🛒, R, Bar, ✉, Ⓑ, ⇌ (bus to Elgin), ✈ (Inverness).

5.10 HOPEMAN

Moray 57°42'·70N 03°26'·31W ✿✿▲▲✿✿

CHARTS AC 223, 1462; Imray C23.

TIDES +0050 Dover; ML 2·4; Duration 0610;

Standard Port ABERDEEN (◄──)

Times				Height (metres)			
High Water		Low Water		MHWS	MHWN	MLWN	MLWS
0200	0900	0400	0900	4·3	3·4	1·6	0·6
1400	2100	1600	2100				
Differences HOPEMAN							
–0120	–0150	–0135	–0120	–0·2	–0·2	0·0	0·0

SHELTER Once in Inner Basin, shelter good from all winds; but hbr dries, access HW ± 2 (for 1·5m draft). Ent is difficult in winds from NE to SE. A popular yachting hbr with AB.

NAVIGATION WPT 57°42'·66N, 03°26'·59W, 083° to ent, 0·17M.

Dangerous rks lie off hbr ent. Do not attempt entry in heavy weather. Beware lobster pot floats E and W of hbr (Mar-Aug).

LIGHTS AND MARKS See 5.3 and chartlet.

R/T Call Burghead Radio Ch 14 (HX).

TELEPHONE (Code 01343) HM ☎ 835337 (part-time); MRCC (01224) 592334; Marinecall 09068 969641; Police 830222; Dr 543141.

FACILITIES Hbr AB £9, for details of Rover Ticket see 5.4, FW, Slip. Services: CH, ME, Gas, ✕, El, P (cans).
Town 🛒, R, Bar, ✉, Ⓑ, ➔ (bus to Elgin), ✈ (Inverness).

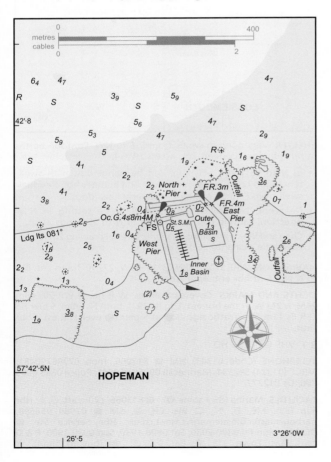

5.11 BURGHEAD

Moray 57°42'·06N 03°30'·02W ✿✿▲✿✿✿

CHARTS AC 223, 1462; Imray C23.

TIDES +0035 Dover; ML 2·4; Duration 0610

Standard Port ABERDEEN (◄──)

Times				Height (metres)			
High Water		Low Water		MHWS	MHWN	MLWN	MLWS
0200	0900	0400	0900	4·3	3·4	1·6	0·6
1400	2100	1600	2100				
Differences BURGHEAD							
–0120	–0150	–0135	–0120	–0·2	–0·2	0·0	0·0

SHELTER One of the few Moray Firth hbrs accessible in strong E winds. 0·6m depth in ent chan and 1·4m in hbr. Go alongside where available and contact HM. Can be very busy with FVs.

NAVIGATION WPT 57°42'·28N 03°30'·39W, 137°/0·28M to N pier lt QR. Access HW ±4. Chan is variable due to sand movement. Advisable to contact HM if entering at LW. 3kn speed limit.

LIGHTS AND MARKS No ldg lts but night ent is safe after identifying the N pier lts: QR 3m 5M and Oc 8s 7m 5M.

R/T Call Burghead Radio VHF Ch 14 12 (HO and when vessel due).

TELEPHONE (Code 01343) HM 835337; MRCC (01224) 592334; Marinecall 09068 969641; Dr 812277.

FACILITIES Hbr AB £9, for details of Rover Ticket see 5.4, FW, AB, C (50 ton mobile), L, Slip, BY, ✕.
Town Bar, ✉, 🛒, Ⓑ, ➔ (bus to Elgin), ✈ (Inverness).

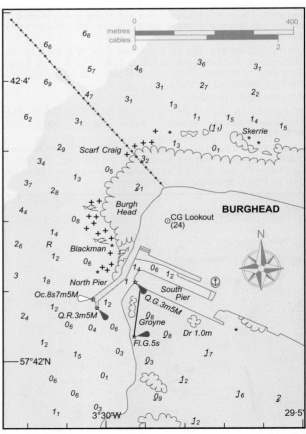

5.12 FINDHORN

Moray **57°39'·64N 03°37'·47W** ❀❀♨♨❀❀❀

CHARTS AC 223; Imray C23.

TIDES +0110 Dover; ML 2·5; Duration 0615

Standard Port ABERDEEN (←—)

Times				Height (metres)			
High Water		Low Water		MHWS	MHWN	MLWN	MLWS
0200	0900	0400	0900	4·3	3·4	1·6	0·6
1400	2100	1600	2100				
Differences FINDHORN							
–0120	–0150	–0135	–0130	0·0	–0·1	0·0	+0·1

SHELTER ⚓ in pool off boatyard or off N pier or dry out alongside, inside piers and ask at YC; or pick up Y ⚓ off N pier.

Do not attempt entry in strong NW/NE winds or with big swell running; expect breakers/surf either side of ent.

NAVIGATION WPT 57°43'·00N 03°38'·94W, SWM Landfall Buoy. Access HW±2. 100m SE of the Landfall Buoy there is 1 Y waiting ⚓ in 4m. From WPT, the bar is marked (Fl R marker) and thence by Fl R or G buoys all of which are moved to suit the channel into the bay, and may be lifted Nov to early Apr. Once past The Ee, turn port inside G buoys. The S part of Findhorn Bay dries extensively.

LIGHTS AND MARKS Unlit. There is a windsock on FS by The Ee. Boatyard building is conspic.

R/T VHF Ch M *Chadwick Base* (when racing in progress). Findhorn BY: Ch 80.

TELEPHONE (Code 01309) Fairways Committee (via BY) 690099; MRCC (01224) 592334; Findhorn Pilot (Derek Munro) 690802, mob 07747 840916; Marinecall 09068 969641; Police 0845 6005000700; Dr 678866/678888; Findhorn BY 690099.

FACILITIES **Royal Findhorn YC** ☎ 690247, M, ⚓ (free), FW, Bar; **Services:** BY, L, M, ⟨D⟩, FW, Slip, C (16 ton), P & D (cans), El, ME, CH, ACA, Gas, ✂.
Town 🛒, R, Bar, ✉, Ⓑ, ⇌ (Forres), ✈ (Inverness).

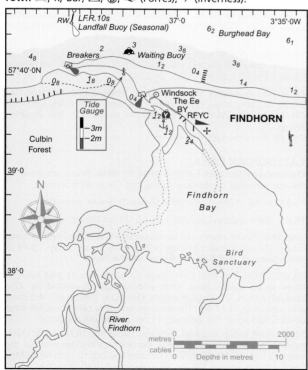

5.13 NAIRN

Highland **57°35'·61N 03°51'·65W** ❀❀♨♨❀❀

CHARTS AC 223, 1462; Imray C23.

TIDES +0110 Dover; ML 2·2; Duration 0615

Standard Port INVERGORDON (—→)

Times				Height (metres)			
High Water		Low Water		MHWS	MHWN	MLWN	MLWS
0100	0700	0000	0700	4·3	3·3	1·6	0·7
1300	1900	1200	1900				
Differences NAIRN							
+0005	–0015	0000	–0015	0·0	0·0	0·0	0·0
McDERMOTT BASE							
+0015	–0005	+0015	0000	–0·1	0·0	+0·1	+0·2

SHELTER Good, but entry difficult in fresh NNE'ly. Pontoons in hbr with ❶ berths. Best entry HW ± 1½. No commercial shipping.

NAVIGATION WPT 57°35'·88N 03°51'·89W, 155°/0·3M to ent. The approach dries to 100m off the pierheads. Inside, the best water is to the E side of the river chan.

LIGHTS AND MARKS Lt ho on E pier hd, Oc WRG 4s 6m 5M, vis shore-G-100°-W-207°-R-shore. Keep in W sector.

R/T None. Ch M (weekends only).

TELEPHONE (Code 01667) Hbr Office 456008; MRCC (01224) 592334; Doctor and Clinic 452096; Marinecall 09068 500451; Police 452222; Dr 453421.

FACILITIES **Nairn Basin** AB £15.28 - 48hrs, Slip (launching £6), AC (110 volts), P(cans), D; **Nairn SC** ☎ 453897, Bar.
Town 🛒, R, Bar, ✉, Ⓑ, ⇌, ✈ (Inverness).

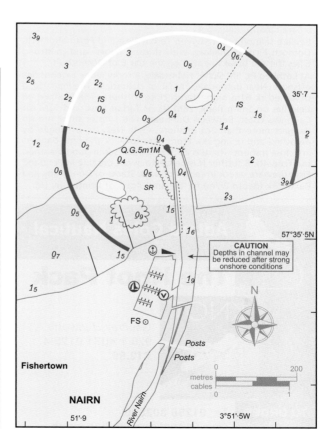

MORAY FIRTH: NORTH WEST COAST

(AC 115) Cromarty Firth (AC 1889, 1890) is entered between the North and South Sutors, both fringed by rks, some of which dry.

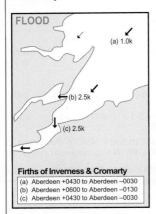

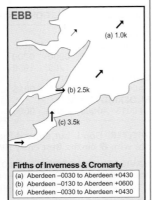

Firths of Inverness & Cromarty (FLOOD)
(a)	Aberdeen +0430 to Aberdeen −0030
(b)	Aberdeen +0600 to Aberdeen −0130
(c)	Aberdeen +0430 to Aberdeen −0030

Firths of Inverness & Cromarty (EBB)
(a)	Aberdeen −0030 to Aberdeen +0430
(b)	Aberdeen −0130 to Aberdeen +0600
(c)	Aberdeen −0030 to Aberdeen +0430

▶ *Off the entrance the in-going stream starts at HW Aberdeen + 0600, and the out-going at HW Aberdeen − 0130, sp rates 1·5 kn, stronger in the narrows between Nigg and Cromarty* ◀ Buss Bank buoy, Fl R 3s, marks the entrance, and there are good sheltered anchorages within the firth. Keep 100m clear of the Nigg Oil Terminal on the north side. A buoyed deepwater channel runs to Invergordon; outside the channel there are shallows and drying banks. Beware large ships and tugs using Invergordon.

The coast NE to Tarbat Ness (lt) is fringed with rocks. Beware Three Kings (dries) about 3M NE of N Sutor. ▶ *Culloden Rk, a shoal with depth of 1·8m, extends 2½ca NE of Tarbat Ness, where stream is weak.* ◀

Beware salmon nets between Tarbat Ness and Portmahomack. Dornoch Firth is shallow, with shifting banks, and in strong E'lies the sea breaks heavily on the bar E of Dornoch Pt.

At Lothbeg Pt, 5M SW of Helmsdale, a rocky ledge extends 5ca offshore. Near Berriedale, 7M NE of Helmsdale, The Pinnacle, a detached rk 61m high, stands close offshore. The Beatrice oil field lies on Smith Bank, 28M NE of Tarbat Ness, and 11M off Caithness coast. Between Dunbeath and Lybster there are no dangers more than 2ca offshore. Clyth Ness (lt) is fringed by detached and drying rks. From here to Wick the only dangers are close inshore. There is anch in Sinclair's B in good weather, but Freswick B further N is better to await the tide in Pentland Firth (beware wreck in centre of bay). Stacks of Duncansby and Baxter Rk (depth 2·7m) lie 1M and 4ca S of Duncansby Hd.

5.14 INVERNESS

Highland 57°29'·73N 04°14'·17W ❄❄❄💧💧💧🌸🌸

CHARTS AC 223, 1077, 1078; Imray C23.

TIDES +0100 Dover; ML 2·7; Duration 0620

Standard Port INVERGORDON (→)

Times				Height (metres)			
High Water		Low Water		MHWS	MHWN	MLWN	MLWS
0100	0700	0000	0700	4·3	3·3	1·6	0·7
1300	1900	1200	1900				
Differences INVERNESS							
+0010	+0015	+0015	+0010	+0·3	+0·2	+0·1	+0·1
FORTROSE							
0000	+0010	+0010	−0010	0·0+0·1		No data	
CROMARTY							
−0005	0000	0000	−0005	0·0	0·0	0·0	0·0
DINGWALL							
+0020	+0015	No data		0·0	+0·1	No data	

SHELTER Good in all weathers. Berth at Inverness Marina (2.5m at CD) or at one of the 2 marinas in the Caledonian Canal, entrance to which can be difficult in strong tidal streams. The sea lock is normally available HW±4 in canal hours; the gates cannot be opened LW±2.

NAVIGATION WPT Meikle Mee SHM By Fl G 3s, 57°30'·25N 04°12'·03W, 250°/0·74M to Longman Pt bn. Inverness Firth is deep from Chanonry Pt to Munlochy SWM buoy, but shoal (2·1m) to Meikle Mee buoy. Meikle Mee partly dries. Beware bird rafts S of Avoch (off chartlet). Tidal streams are strong S of Craigton Pt (E-going stream at sp exceeds 5kn). Ent to R Ness is narrow, dredged to 3m CD. For the entrance to the Caledonian Canal, keep to N Kessock bank until clear of unmarked shoals on S bank. Care must be taken to avoid Carnarc Pt W of R mouth.

LIGHTS AND MARKS Longman Pt bn Fl WR 2s 7m 5/4M, vis 078°-W-258°-R-078°. Craigton Pt lt, Fl WRG 4s 6m 11/7M vis 312°-W-048°-R-064°-W-085°-G-shore. Caledonian Canal ent marked by QR and Iso G 4s on ends of training walls.

R/T Call: *Inverness Hbr Office* VHF Ch 12 (Mon-Fri: 0800 -1700 LT). *Inverness Marina* Ch 12. Caledonian Canal: Ch 74 is used by all stations. Call: *Clachnaharry Sea Lock*; or for office: *Caledonian Canal*.

TELEPHONE (Code 01463) HM 715715; Clachnaharry Sea Lock 713896; Canal Office 233140; MRCC (01224) 592334; Marinecall 09068 969641; Police 715555; Dr 234151.

FACILITIES Inverness Marina (150 inc 20♥), £2.00, ☎ 220501 or 07526 446348, www.invernessmarina.com, D, BH (45 ton), BY, CH, El, ME, 🛢, Wi-fi, dredged to 3m below CD, full disabled access.
City All domestic facilities, ≥, ✈.

CALEDONIAN CANAL
Clachnaharry Sea Lock 57°29'·44N 04°15'·84W. These notes are for the convenience of those entering the Canal at Inverness.

CHARTS AC 1791, 1078. *BWB Skipper's Guide* essential.

TIDES Differences: Clachnaharry +0116 on Dover; see 5.14.

SHELTER Clachnaharry sea lock operates HW±4 (sp) within canal hours. The road and rail swing bridges may cause delays up to 25 mins. Seaport and Caley marinas: see Facilities.

NAVIGATION The 60M Caledonian Canal consists of 38M through three lochs, (Lochs Ness, Oich and Lochy), connected by 22M through canals. It can take vessels 45m LOA, 10m beam, 4m draft and max mast ht 27·4m. The passage normally takes two full days, possibly longer in the summer; 13 hrs is absolute minimum.

Speed limit is 5kn in canal sections. There are 10 swing bridges; road tfc has priority at peak hrs. Do not pass bridges without the keeper's instructions. From Clachnaharry sea lock to Loch Ness (Bona Ferry lt ho) is approx 7M, via Muirtown and Dochgarroch locks.

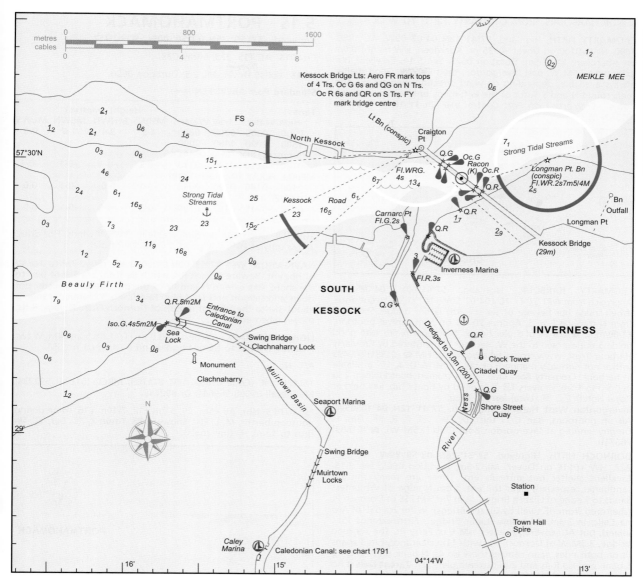

metres / cables
0   800   1600
0   4   8

Kessock Bridge Lts: Aero FR mark tops
of 4 Trs. Oc G 6s and QG on N Trs.
Oc R 6s and QR on S Trs. FY
mark bridge centre

MEIKLE MEE

Craigton Pt

Lt Bn (conspic)

North Kessock

FS

57°30'N

Strong Tidal Streams

Longman Pt. Bn (conspic)
Fl.WR.2s7m5/4M

Fl.WRG. 4s 13.4

Strong Tidal Streams

Kessock Road

Carnarc Pt Fl.G.2s

Kessock Bridge (29m)

Longman Pt

Bn Outfall

Beauly Firth

Inverness Marina

Fl.R.3s

SOUTH KESSOCK

INVERNESS

Q.R.5m2M

Entrance to Caledonian Canal

Iso.G.4s5m2M

Sea Lock

Dredged to 3.0m (2001)

Clock Tower
Citadel Quay

Swing Bridge
Clachnaharry Lock

Monument
Clachnaharry

Muirtown Basin

Shore Street Quay

Seaport Marina

River Ness

Swing Bridge
Muirtown Locks

Station

Town Hall Spire

Caley Marina

Caledonian Canal: see chart 1791

16'   15'   04°14'W   13'

LOCKS All 29 locks are manned and operate early May to early Oct, 0800-1800LT daily. For regulations and *BWS Skipper's Guide* apply: Canal Manager, Muirtown Wharf, Inverness IV3 5LS, ☎ (01463) 233140. www. scottishcanals.co.uk

LIGHTS AND MARKS Chans are marked by posts, cairns and unlit buoys, PHM on the NW side of the chan and SHM on the SE side.

BOAT SAFETY SCHEME Visiting vessels will be checked for apparent dangerous defects eg leaking gas or fuel, damaged electrical cables, taking in water, risk of capsize. £1M 3rd party insurance is required.

R/T Sea locks and main lock flights operate VHF Ch **74** (HO).

TELEPHONE Clachnaharry sea lock (01463) 713896; Canal Office, Inverness (01463) 233140.

FACILITIES Seaport Marina (20+ 20♥), ☎ (01463) 725500, ⊡, FW, D, El, ME, ✕, Gas, Gaz, ▨, C (40 ton), ⚓, ♿. **Caley Marina** (25+25 ♥ £1.50) ☎ (01463) 236539, CH, D, ME, El, ✕, C (20 ton), ACA, Wi-fi.

MINOR HARBOURS IN INVERNESS FIRTH

FORTROSE, Highland, **57°34'·71N 04°08'·04W**. AC 1078. Tides 5.14. HW +0055 on Dover; ML 2·5m; Duration 0620. Small drying unlit hbr, soft silt bottom, well protected by Chanonry Ness to E; access HW±2, limited space. Follow ldg line 296°, Broomhill Ho (conspic on hill to NW) in line with school spire until abeam SPM buoy; then turn W to avoid Craig an Roan rks (1·8m) ESE of ent. Chanonry Pt lt, Oc 6s 12m 15M, obscd 073°-shore. HM ☎ (01381) 620311; Dr ☎ 620909. **Facilities:** AB £5, 4 ⚓, L, M, P, D, Slip, scrubbing grid, Gas, R, ⛟, ⊠, Ⓑ; **Chanonry SC** (near pier) ☎ 01381 621973.

AVOCH, Highland, **57°34'·03N 04°09'·94W**. AC 1078. Tides as Fortrose (1·25M to the ENE). Hbr dries, mostly on the N side, but is bigger than Fortrose; access HW±2. Small craft may stay afloat at nps against the S pier (2FR (vert)). AB may be available on drying pontoons; one ⚓ (max 35ft LOA) off hbr ent. HM ☎ (mobile) 07779 833951. **Facilities**: AB £7, FW, ⊡. **Village**: ⊠, ⛟, R, Bar, P & D (cans), ME.

MINOR HARBOURS FROM CROMARTY FIRTH TO WICK

CROMARTY FIRTH, Highland, **57°41'·18N 04°02'·09W**. AC 1889, 1890. HW +0100 on Dover –0135 on Aberdeen; HW height 0.0m on Aberdeen; ML 2·5m; Duration 0625. See 5.14. Excellent hbr extending 7·5M W, past Invergordon, then 9M SW. Good shelter always available, depending on wind direction. Beware rks and reefs round N and S Sutor at the ent; many unlit oil rig mooring buoys. *Cromarty Firth Port Control* VHF Ch 11 16 13 (H24) ☎ (01349) 852308.

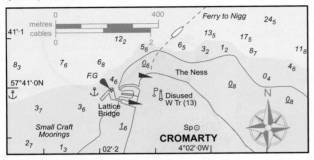

CROMARTY HARBOUR, Highland. **57°41'·00N 04°02'·35W**. Approach from WPT 57°41'·10N 04°02'·50W, 142°/1.3ca to entrance. When inside hbr beware of set towards lattice bridge. Sheltered from N through E to S. Approx 20 AB on 50m central pontoon, £1·00/m. 2 ⚓ 2ca W of S pier hd, or ⚓ in approx 6m with good holding but exposed to the W. Harbour administered by Cromarty Harbour Trust, www.cromartyharbour.org. HM ☎ (01381) 600493 (office not normally manned) or call Ch M/16. D, ⛽, ⎓ available in harbour. **Cromarty Boat Club**, www.cromartyboatclub.org, 2 ⚓ in 0·5m to 1·5m; showers, 🚻, ▣ (owned by Boat Club; key held at Royal Hotel). ✉, 🛒. Local ferry to Nigg.
Invergordon West Harbour Highland. **57°41'·12N 04°10'·05W**. AB on pontoons, Bar, C (3 ton), D, FW, ✉, P, R, 🛒, Gas, L. Dinghy landing at Invergordon Boat Club (1·5M W), ☎ (01863) 766710.

DORNOCH FIRTH, Highland. **57°51'·28N 03°59'·39W**. AC 115, 223. HW +0115 on Dover; ML 2·5m; Duration 0605; see 5.15. Excellent shelter but difficult ent. There are many shifting sandbanks, especially near the ent, from N edge of Whiteness Sands to S edge of Gizzen Briggs. ⚓s in 7m ¾M ESE of Dornoch Pt (sheltered from NE swell by Gizzen Briggs); in 7m 2ca SSE of Ard na Cailc; in 3·3m 1M below Bonar Bridge. Firth extends 15M inland, but AC coverage ceases ¼M E of Ferry Pt. The A9 road bridge, 3·3M W of Dornoch Pt, with 11m clearance, has 3 spans lit on both sides; span centres show Iso 4s, N bank pier Iso G 4s, S bank pier Iso R 4s and 2 midstream piers QY. Tarbat Ness lt ho Fl (4) 30s 53m 24M. Fl R 5s lt shown when Tain firing range active. Very limited facilities at Ferrytown and Bonar Bridge. MRCC ☎ 01224 592334. **Dornoch**: 🛒, P, ✉, Dr, Ⓑ, R, Bar.

GOLSPIE, Highland, **57°58'·71N 03°56'·79W**. AC 223. HW +0045 on Dover; ML 2·3m; Duration 068. See 5.15. Golspie pier projects 60m SE across foreshore with arm projecting SW at the hd, giving shelter during NE winds. Beware The Bridge, a bank (0·3m to 1·8m) running parallel to the shore ¼M to seaward of pier hd. Seas break heavily over The Bridge in NE winds. There are no lts. To enter, keep Duke of Sutherland's Memorial in line 316° with boathouse SW of pier, until church spire in village is in line 006° with hd of pier, then keep on those marks. Hbr gets very congested; good ⚓ off pier. HM ☎ 01431 821692. **Town** Bar, D, Dr, Ⓗ, L, M, P, Gas, ✉, R, ⇌, 🛒, Ⓑ.

LYBSTER, Highland, **58°17'·72N 03°17'·39W**. AC 115. HW +0020 on Dover; HW -0150 sp, -0215 np; HW ht -0·6m on Aberdeen; ML 2·1m; Duration 0620. Excellent shelter in SW corner of inner hbr; AB on W side of pier in about 1·2m. Most of hbr dries to sand/mud and is much used by FVs; no bollards on N wall. Appr on about 350°. Beware rks close on E side of ent; narrow (10m) ent is difficult in strong E to S winds. Min depth 2·5m in ent. S pier hd, Oc R 6s 10m 3M, occas in fishing season. AB £7.00 per week, FW on W quay. Showers/laundry at Waterlines Visitor Centre, 01593 721520. **Town** Bar, D, P, R, 🛒.

5.15 PORTMAHOMACK

Highland **57°50'·25N 03°50'·00W** ❀❀⚓❀❀

CHARTS AC 115, 223; Imray C23.

TIDES +0035 Dover; ML 2·5; Duration 0600

Standard Port ABERDEEN (←—)

Times				Height (metres)			
High Water		Low Water		MHWS	MHWN	MLWN	MLWS
0300	0800	0200	0800	4·3	3·4	1·6	0·6
1500	2000	1400	2000				
Differences PORTMAHOMACK							
–0120	–0210	–0140	–0110	–0·2	–0·1	+0·1	+0·1
MEIKLE FERRY (Dornoch Firth)							
–0100	–0140	–0120	–0055	+0·1	0·0	–0·1	0·0
GOLSPIE							
–0130	–0215	–0155	–0130	–0·3	–0·3	–0·1	0·0

SHELTER Good, but uncomfortable in SW/NW winds. Hbr dries, access only at HW, but good ⚓ close SW of pier.

NAVIGATION WPT 57°53'·00N 03°50'·00W, 180°/2.7M to 1ca W of hbr ent. Beware Curach Rks which lie from 2ca SW of pier to the shore. Rks extend N and W of the pier. Beware lobster pot floats and salmon nets N of hbr. Tain firing & bombing range is about 3M to the W, S of mouth of Dornoch Firth; R flags, R lts, shown when active.

LIGHTS AND MARKS Tarbert Ness lt ho Fl (4) 30s 53m 24M, W twr R bands, is 2·6M to NE of hbr. Pier hd 2 FR (vert) 7m 5M.

R/T None.

TELEPHONE (Code 01862) HM 871705; MRCC (01224) 592334; Marinecall 09068 969641; Dr 892759.

FACILITIES **Hbr**, AB <5m £9, 5-7m £12, 7-10m £16, some drying pontoon berths, M, L, FW. Showers, 🚻. **Town** R, 🛒, Bar, ✉, ⇌ (bus to Tain), ✈ (Inverness).

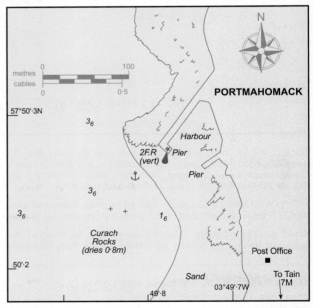

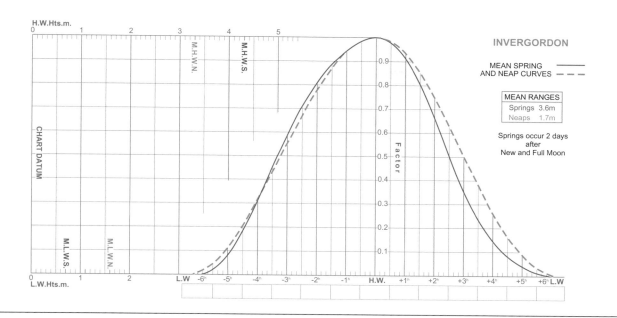

INVERGORDON

MEAN SPRING ————
AND NEAP CURVES ─ ─ ─

MEAN RANGES
Springs 3.6m
Neaps   1.7m

Springs occur 2 days
after
New and Full Moon

INVERGORDON LAT 57°41'N LONG 4°10'W
TIMES AND HEIGHTS OF HIGH AND LOW WATERS

TIME ZONE (UT)
For Summer Time add ONE hour in **non-shaded areas**

Dates in red are **SPRINGS**
Dates in blue are **NEAPS**

YEAR 2010

JANUARY

Time	m		Time	m
1 0611	1.0	**16** 0039	3.9	
1211	4.5	0611	1.2	
F 1846	0.5	SA 1236	4.2	
		1904	0.9	
2 0040	4.4	**17** 0111	3.9	
0659	1.0	0647	1.1	
SA 1259	4.6	SU 1310	4.2	
1934	0.4	1933	0.9	
3 0132	4.4	**18** 0143	3.9	
0742	1.0	0720	1.1	
SU 1347	4.7	M 1344	4.1	
2021	0.3	2002	0.9	
4 0221	4.4	**19** 0214	3.8	
0823	1.0	0747	1.2	
M 1435	4.6	TU 1415	4.0	
2107	0.4	2028	1.0	
5 0310	4.3	**20** 0244	3.7	
0859	1.1	0759	1.3	
TU 1523	4.5	W 1445	3.9	
2152	0.6	2045	1.1	
6 0356	4.1	**21** 0315	3.6	
0933	1.3	0813	1.4	
W 1610	4.3	TH 1516	3.8	
2237	0.9	2046	1.3	
7 0442	3.9	**22** 0350	3.5	
1011	1.5	0841	1.5	
TH 1659	4.1	F 1553	3.7	
◗ 2328	1.2	2106	1.4	
8 0531	3.7	**23** 0431	3.4	
1100	1.7	0921	1.6	
F 1754	3.8	SA 1639	3.6	
		◗ 2149	1.6	
9 0042	1.5	**24** 0523	3.3	
0626	3.5	1028	1.8	
SA 1207	1.9	SU 1738	3.4	
1903	3.6			
10 0214	1.6	**25** 0035	1.7	
0732	3.5	0631	3.3	
SU 1455	1.8	M 1316	1.8	
2022	3.6	1855	3.4	
11 0319	1.6	**26** 0157	1.6	
0845	3.5	0746	3.4	
M 1559	1.6	TU 1443	1.5	
2140	3.6	2019	3.5	
12 0413	1.6	**27** 0300	1.5	
0952	3.7	0855	3.6	
TU 1653	1.4	W 1548	1.2	
2242	3.7	2132	3.7	
13 0455	1.6	**28** 0406	1.3	
1045	3.9	1000	3.9	
W 1736	1.2	TH 1651	0.9	
2329	3.8	2241	4.0	
14 0522	1.5	**29** 0508	1.1	
1127	4.0	1101	4.2	
TH 1810	1.1	F 1745	0.5	
		2341	4.3	
15 0006	3.9	**30** 0600	0.9	
0540	1.4	1156	4.5	
F 1202	4.1	SA 1833	0.2	
● 1838	1.0	○		
		31 0032	4.4	
		0644	0.8	
		SU 1245	4.7	
		1918	0.1	

FEBRUARY

Time	m		Time	m
1 0120	4.5	**16** 0118	4.0	
0724	0.7	0704	0.9	
M 1332	4.8	TU 1321	4.2	
2001	0.1	1935	0.7	
2 0205	4.5	**17** 0147	3.9	
0802	0.7	0735	0.9	
TU 1418	4.8	W 1352	4.1	
2042	0.2	2004	0.8	
3 0248	4.4	**18** 0216	3.9	
0836	0.8	0754	1.0	
W 1503	4.6	TH 1422	4.0	
2121	0.5	2025	1.0	
4 0330	4.2	**19** 0246	3.8	
0908	1.0	0744	1.1	
TH 1547	4.4	F 1453	3.9	
2200	0.9	1957	1.1	
5 0411	3.9	**20** 0319	3.7	
0942	1.3	0805	1.2	
F 1633	4.0	SA 1529	3.8	
◗ 2239	1.3	2019	1.3	
6 0454	3.6	**21** 0358	3.5	
1026	1.6	0840	1.4	
SA 1726	3.7	SU 1613	3.6	
2333	1.7	2059	1.5	
7 0544	3.4	**22** 0448	3.4	
1136	1.8	0929	1.6	
SU 1831	3.4	M 1710	3.4	
		◗ 2157	1.8	
8 0139	1.9	**23** 0554	3.3	
0646	3.3	1253	1.7	
M 1435	1.8	TU 1829	3.3	
1953	3.3			
9 0259	1.8	**24** 0133	1.7	
0754	3.4	0712	3.3	
TU 1545	1.6	W 1423	1.4	
2127	3.4	2000	3.4	
10 0357	1.8	**25** 0248	1.6	
0906	3.5	0826	3.6	
W 1640	1.4	TH 1533	1.1	
2233	3.5	2122	3.6	
11 0442	1.6	**26** 0357	1.3	
1018	3.7	0935	3.9	
TH 1723	1.2	F 1636	0.7	
2317	3.7	2234	4.0	
12 0511	1.5	**27** 0455	1.0	
1107	3.9	1041	4.2	
F 1755	1.0	SA 1728	0.3	
2352	3.8	2330	4.3	
13 0525	1.3	**28** 0542	0.8	
1144	4.1	1138	4.6	
SA 1817	0.9	SU 1814	0.0	
		○		
14 0021	3.9			
0554	1.1			
SU 1217	4.2			
● 1839	0.8			
15 0050	4.0			
0629	1.0			
M 1249	4.2			
1906	0.7			

MARCH

Time	m		Time	m
1 0017	4.5	**16** 0022	4.0	
0624	0.6	0607	0.9	
M 1227	4.8	TU 1222	4.2	
1856	-0.1	1835	0.7	
2 0101	4.6	**17** 0050	4.1	
0702	0.5	0642	0.8	
TU 1313	4.9	W 1255	4.2	
1935	0.0	1907	0.7	
3 0142	4.5	**18** 0120	4.0	
0738	0.5	0715	0.8	
W 1357	4.8	TH 1328	4.2	
2013	0.2	1938	0.7	
4 0222	4.4	**19** 0150	4.0	
0812	0.7	0741	0.9	
TH 1440	4.6	F 1401	4.1	
2049	0.6	2002	0.9	
5 0301	4.2	**20** 0222	3.9	
0845	0.9	0730	1.0	
F 1524	4.3	SA 1435	4.0	
2123	1.0	1928	1.1	
6 0341	3.9	**21** 0256	3.7	
0917	1.2	0745	1.1	
SA 1610	3.9	SU 1514	3.8	
2151	1.4	1954	1.2	
7 0423	3.6	**22** 0337	3.6	
0955	1.5	0821	1.3	
SU 1701	3.5	M 1600	3.6	
◗ 2229	1.8	2037	1.5	
8 0511	3.4	**23** 0429	3.4	
1118	1.8	0918	1.5	
M 1804	3.3	TU 1700	3.4	
		◗ 2142	1.8	
9 0104	2.0	**24** 0534	3.3	
0612	3.3	1238	1.5	
TU 1412	1.7	W 1817	3.3	
1921	3.1			
10 0235	1.9	**25** 0110	1.8	
0719	3.3	0649	3.4	
W 1519	1.5	TH 1407	1.2	
2103	3.2	1947	3.4	
11 0333	1.8	**26** 0242	1.6	
0825	3.4	0802	3.6	
TH 1613	1.3	F 1517	0.9	
2211	3.4	2113	3.6	
12 0418	1.6	**27** 0346	1.3	
0932	3.6	0911	3.9	
F 1656	1.1	SA 1617	0.5	
2252	3.6	2221	4.0	
13 0448	1.5	**28** 0438	1.0	
1031	3.8	1019	4.2	
SA 1726	1.0	SU 1707	0.3	
2325	3.8	2313	4.3	
14 0505	1.3	**29** 0522	0.7	
1113	4.0	1118	4.5	
SU 1806	0.8	M 1751	0.1	
2354	3.9	2357	4.4	
15 0532	1.1	**30** 0602	0.6	
1148	4.1	1207	4.7	
M 1806	0.7	TU 1831	0.0	
●		○		
		31 0038	4.5	
		0640	0.5	
		W 1252	4.7	
		1910	0.1	

APRIL

Time	m		Time	m
1 0117	4.5	**16** 0053	4.1	
0716	0.5	0655	0.8	
TH 1336	4.6	F 1305	4.2	
1946	0.4	1914	0.8	
2 0156	4.3	**17** 0127	4.1	
0752	0.6	0728	0.8	
F 1419	4.4	SA 1342	4.1	
2019	0.7	1942	1.0	
3 0234	4.1	**18** 0202	4.0	
0826	0.9	0754	0.9	
SA 1503	4.1	SU 1422	4.0	
2046	1.1	1922	1.1	
4 0313	3.9	**19** 0241	3.9	
0857	1.1	0757	1.0	
SU 1549	3.8	M 1505	3.8	
2050	1.5	1949	1.3	
5 0355	3.7	**20** 0325	3.7	
0922	1.4	0905	1.2	
M 1640	3.4	TU 1556	3.6	
2119	1.8	2039	1.5	
6 0443	3.4	**21** 0419	3.6	
1133	1.7	1051	1.3	
TU 1738	3.2	W 1656	3.5	
◗ 2237	2.0	◗ 2248	1.8	
7 0541	3.3	**22** 0521	3.5	
1337	1.6	1223	1.2	
W 1845	3.1	TH 1808	3.4	
8 0158	2.0	**23** 0031	1.8	
0645	3.3	0629	3.5	
TH 1442	1.5	F 1346	1.0	
2002	3.2	1930	3.3	
9 0256	1.8	**24** 0224	1.6	
0748	3.4	0739	3.7	
F 1534	1.3	SA 1455	0.8	
2117	3.3	2053	3.7	
10 0340	1.6	**25** 0326	1.3	
0846	3.5	0848	3.9	
SA 1615	1.2	SU 1554	0.6	
2207	3.5	2158	3.9	
11 0411	1.5	**26** 0417	1.1	
0941	3.7	0956	4.1	
SU 1642	1.1	M 1645	0.4	
2244	3.7	2249	4.1	
12 0436	1.3	**27** 0502	0.8	
1029	3.9	1057	4.3	
M 1703	1.0	TU 1729	0.3	
2317	3.9	2334	4.3	
13 0506	1.1	**28** 0543	0.7	
1112	4.0	1148	4.5	
TU 1731	0.8	W 1809	0.4	
2349	4.0	○		
14 0542	0.9	**29** 0014	4.3	
1152	4.1	0622	0.6	
W 1805	0.7	TH 1233	4.5	
●		1846	0.5	
15 0021	4.1	**30** 0053	4.3	
0619	0.8	0700	0.6	
TH 1229	4.2	F 1317	4.4	
1841	0.7	1920	0.7	

Chart Datum: 2·10 metres below Ordnance Datum (Local). HAT is 5·0 metres above Chart Datum; see 0.19

INVERGORDON LAT 57°41'N LONG 4°10'W
TIMES AND HEIGHTS OF HIGH AND LOW WATERS

TIME ZONE (UT)
For Summer Time add ONE hour in **non-shaded areas**

Dates in red are SPRINGS
Dates in blue are NEAPS

YEAR 2010

NE Scotland

MAY				JUNE				JULY				AUGUST			
1 0131 4.2		**16** 0108 4.1		**1** 0226 3.9		**16** 0226 4.3		**1** 0241 3.9		**16** 0301 4.6		**1** 0310 3.8		**16** 0414 4.2	
0737 0.7		0722 0.7		0846 1.0		0856 0.5		0851 1.0		0925 0.3		0846 1.1		1020 1.1	
SA 1400 4.2		SU 1329 4.2		TU 1508 3.7		W 1500 4.1		TH 1519 3.6		F 1534 4.2		SU 1538 3.6		M 1636 3.8	
1951 0.7		1932 1.0		1956 1.4		2050 1.1		2011 1.3		2115 1.0		2035 1.4		◑ 2217 1.4	
2 0209 4.1		**17** 0148 4.1		**2** 0307 3.8		**17** 0314 4.3		**2** 0316 3.8		**17** 0347 4.4		**2** 0342 3.6		**17** 0506 3.8	
0814 0.9		0805 0.8		0919 1.2		0944 0.6		0859 1.1		1008 0.6		0900 1.3		1112 1.5	
SU 1444 3.9		M 1414 4.1		W 1551 3.5		TH 1550 4.0		F 1553 3.5		SA 1618 4.0		M 1614 3.5		TU 1725 3.6	
2011 1.2		2000 1.2		2025 1.5		2129 1.2		2039 1.4		2153 1.2		2110 1.5		2326 1.7	
3 0248 3.9		**18** 0232 4.0		**3** 0349 3.6		**18** 0403 4.2		**3** 0349 3.6		**18** 0435 4.2		**3** 0423 3.5		**18** 0609 3.5	
0850 1.1		0853 0.8		0911 1.3		1034 0.7		0920 1.2		1054 0.9		0932 1.5		1300 1.8	
M 1529 3.7		TU 1503 3.9		TH 1634 3.4		F 1640 3.9		SA 1627 3.4		SU 1704 3.8		TU 1700 3.3		W 1825 3.4	
2013 1.5		2020 1.3		2109 1.6		2214 1.4		2119 1.5		◑ 2239 1.4		◑ 2208 1.7			
4 0330 3.7		**19** 0320 3.9		**4** 0433 3.5		**19** 0454 4.0		**4** 0425 3.5		**19** 0527 3.9		**4** 0515 3.4		**19** 0203 1.7	
0901 1.3		0948 0.9		1002 1.4		1128 0.9		1003 1.4		1151 1.2		1130 1.7		0729 3.4	
TU 1617 3.4		W 1556 3.8		F 1720 3.4		SA 1732 3.7		SU 1705 3.3		M 1756 3.6		W 1801 3.3		TH 1434 1.8	
2047 1.7		2121 1.5		2207 1.8		◑ 2306 1.5		◑ 2212 1.7		2342 1.6				1939 3.4	
5 0417 3.5		**20** 0412 3.9		**5** 0521 3.4		**20** 0549 3.9		**5** 0509 3.4		**20** 0630 3.7		**5** 0057 1.8		**20** 0317 1.5	
1056 1.5		1050 1.0		1122 1.5		1236 1.1		1109 1.5		1327 1.5		0627 3.3		0902 3.4	
W 1709 3.2		TH 1652 3.7		SA 1812 3.2		SU 1830 3.6		M 1756 3.3		TU 1859 3.5		TH 1332 1.7		F 1537 1.7	
2142 1.9		◑ 2232 1.6		2323 1.8				2331 1.8				1919 3.3		2101 3.6	
6 0510 3.4		**21** 0508 3.8		**6** 0616 3.3		**21** 0011 1.6		**6** 0606 3.3		**21** 0213 1.7		**6** 0219 1.5		**21** 0416 1.3	
1236 1.6		1159 1.0		1302 1.5		0653 3.8		1250 1.6		0746 3.5		0756 3.4		1012 3.6	
TH 1806 3.1		F 1754 3.6		SU 1909 3.2		M 1358 1.2		TU 1901 3.3		W 1448 1.5		F 1437 1.5		SA 1628 1.6	
◑ 2316 2.0		2342 1.6				1939 3.6				2013 3.5		2031 3.5		2213 3.8	
7 0608 3.3		**22** 0610 3.7		**7** 0137 1.8		**22** 0233 1.5		**7** 0141 1.7		**22** 0328 1.5		**7** 0320 1.3		**22** 0504 1.1	
1345 1.5		1317 1.0		0715 3.4		0804 3.7		0718 3.4		0908 3.5		0910 3.6		1102 3.8	
F 1907 3.2		SA 1904 3.6		M 1357 1.4		TU 1507 1.2		W 1403 1.5		TH 1550 1.5		SA 1537 1.4		SU 1706 1.5	
				2006 3.4		2051 3.6		2008 3.4		2128 3.6		2134 3.8		2302 4.0	
8 0201 1.9		**23** 0143 1.6		**8** 0233 1.6		**23** 0339 1.4		**8** 0245 1.5		**23** 0429 1.3		**8** 0421 0.9		**23** 0541 0.9	
0708 3.3		0716 3.8		0812 3.5		0919 3.7		0828 3.5		1020 3.6		1018 3.9		1141 3.9	
SA 1435 1.4		SU 1429 0.9		TU 1443 1.4		W 1604 1.2		TH 1458 1.4		F 1642 1.4		SU 1640 1.1		M 1728 1.3	
2008 3.3		2020 3.6		2059 3.5		2155 3.7		2108 3.6		2230 3.8		2235 4.1		2339 4.1	
9 0248 1.7		**24** 0300 1.4		**9** 0319 1.5		**24** 0435 1.2		**9** 0340 1.3		**24** 0519 1.1		**9** 0518 0.6		**24** 0607 0.8	
0804 3.4		0825 3.9		0906 3.6		1026 3.8		0931 3.7		1115 3.8		1119 4.2		1215 4.0	
SU 1512 1.3		M 1530 0.8		W 1530 1.2		TH 1653 1.2		F 1554 1.3		SA 1722 1.4		M 1734 0.9		TU 1744 1.1	
2103 3.5		2127 3.8		2149 3.7		2248 3.9		2204 3.8		2319 4.0		2331 4.4		○	
10 0325 1.5		**25** 0356 1.2		**10** 0406 1.3		**25** 0523 1.0		**10** 0437 1.0		**25** 0559 0.9		**10** 0608 0.2		**25** 0009 4.2	
0856 3.6		0935 4.0		1000 3.8		1122 3.9		1032 3.9		1159 3.9		1211 4.4		0626 0.8	
M 1541 1.2		TU 1623 0.8		TH 1621 1.1		F 1733 1.2		SA 1654 1.1		SU 1749 1.3		TU 1820 0.7		W 1244 4.0	
2151 3.6		2223 3.9		2237 3.9		2334 4.0		2259 4.1		2359 4.1		●		1814 1.0	
11 0359 1.3		**26** 0446 1.0		**11** 0456 1.1		**26** 0605 0.9		**11** 0532 0.8		**26** 0630 0.8		**11** 0022 4.7		**26** 0039 4.3	
0946 3.7		1038 4.1		1053 3.9		1209 4.0		1130 4.1		1236 3.9		0653 0.0		0650 0.7	
TU 1615 1.1		W 1709 0.8		F 1712 1.0		SA 1806 1.1		SU 1748 1.0		M 1810 1.2		W 1258 4.6		TH 1312 4.1	
2233 3.8		2310 4.1		2324 4.0		○		● 2350 4.3		○		1902 0.6		1848 0.9	
12 0437 1.2		**27** 0530 0.9		**12** 0545 0.9		**27** 0014 4.1		**12** 0623 0.5		**27** 0034 4.2		**12** 0109 4.8		**27** 0110 4.2	
1035 3.9		1132 4.2		1144 4.1		0643 0.8		1223 4.3		0657 0.8		0736 -0.1		0718 0.7	
W 1655 1.0		TH 1749 0.8		SA 1800 1.0		SU 1250 3.9		M 1836 0.9		TU 1309 3.9		TH 1343 4.6		F 1339 4.0	
2313 4.0		○ 2353 4.2		●		1835 1.1				1840 1.1		1941 0.6		1921 0.9	
13 0518 1.0		**28** 0610 0.8		**13** 0008 4.2		**28** 0052 4.1		**13** 0039 4.5		**28** 0107 4.2		**13** 0156 4.9		**28** 0140 4.2	
1121 4.0		1219 4.2		0633 0.7		0718 0.8		0711 0.3		0724 0.7		0818 0.0		0748 0.8	
TH 1737 0.9		F 1824 0.9		SU 1233 4.2		M 1328 3.9		TU 1313 4.4		W 1341 3.9		F 1427 4.5		SA 1406 3.9	
2351 4.1				1846 0.9		1904 1.1		1920 0.8		1912 1.0		2018 0.7		1948 1.0	
14 0559 0.9		**29** 0032 4.2		**14** 0053 4.3		**29** 0129 4.1		**14** 0127 4.6		**29** 0140 4.2		**14** 0241 4.8		**29** 0210 4.1	
1204 4.1		0650 0.7		0720 0.6		0751 0.8		0757 0.2		0752 0.8		0859 0.3		0813 0.9	
F 1817 0.9		SA 1302 4.1		M 1321 4.2		TU 1406 3.8		W 1401 4.4		TH 1412 3.9		SA 1510 4.3		SU 1433 3.8	
●		1857 1.0		1929 1.0		1932 1.1		2001 0.8		1942 1.0		2054 0.9		1953 1.1	
15 0029 4.1		**30** 0110 4.1		**15** 0139 4.3		**30** 0205 4.0		**15** 0214 4.6		**30** 0212 4.1		**15** 0327 4.5		**30** 0240 3.9	
0641 0.8		0728 0.8		0808 0.5		0823 0.9		0841 0.2		0819 0.8		0939 0.7		0812 1.1	
SA 1246 4.2		SU 1344 4.0		TU 1411 4.2		W 1443 3.7		TH 1448 4.4		F 1442 3.8		SU 1552 4.1		M 1503 3.7	
1856 0.9		1927 1.1		2011 1.0		1954 1.2		2039 0.9		2003 1.1		2132 1.1		2000 1.3	
		31 0148 4.1								**31** 0241 3.9				**31** 0314 3.8	
		0807 0.9								0839 1.0				0810 1.3	
		M 1426 3.8								SA 1509 3.7				TU 1540 3.6	
		1948 1.2								2013 1.2				2030 1.4	

Chart Datum: 2·10 metres below Ordnance Datum (Local). HAT is 5·0 metres above Chart Datum; see 0.19

TIME ZONE (UT)
For Summer Time add ONE hour in **non-shaded areas**

INVERGORDON LAT 57°41′N LONG 4°10′W
TIMES AND HEIGHTS OF HIGH AND LOW WATERS

Dates in red are **SPRINGS**
Dates in blue are NEAPS

YEAR 2010

SEPTEMBER

#	Time	m	#	Time	m
1	0356 / 0843 / W 1625 / ☽ 2118	3.6 / 1.5 / 3.4 / 1.7	16	0548 / 1236 / TH 1755	3.4 / 2.0 / 3.5
2	0449 / 0935 / TH 1726	3.4 / 1.7 / 3.3	17	0147 / 0707 / F 1414 / 1906	1.7 / 3.3 / 2.0 / 3.4
3	0033 / 0601 / F 1307 / 1844	1.7 / 3.3 / 1.8 / 3.4	18	0256 / 0845 / SA 1514 / 2024	1.5 / 3.4 / 1.8 / 3.6
4	0159 / 0733 / SA 1424 / 2000	1.5 / 3.4 / 1.6 / 3.6	19	0351 / 0951 / SU 1603 / 2140	1.3 / 3.6 / 1.7 / 3.8
5	0303 / 0856 / SU 1528 / 2108	1.1 / 3.6 / 1.4 / 3.9	20	0437 / 1037 / M 1640 / 2230	1.1 / 3.8 / 1.5 / 4.0
6	0403 / 1006 / M 1626 / 2211	0.8 / 4.0 / 1.1 / 4.2	21	0512 / 1113 / TU 1701 / 2305	1.0 / 4.0 / 1.3 / 4.1
7	0458 / 1104 / TU 1716 / 2310	0.4 / 4.3 / 0.9 / 4.6	22	0533 / 1144 / W 1717 / 2336	1.0 / 4.1 / 1.2 / 4.2
8	0547 / 1153 / W 1759 / ●	0.1 / 4.5 / 0.6	23	0549 / 1212 / TH 1748 / ○	0.8 / 4.2 / 1.0
9	0001 / 0631 / TH 1237 / 1840	4.8 / 0.0 / 4.7 / 0.5	24	0006 / 0615 / F 1239 / 1823	4.3 / 0.8 / 4.2 / 0.9
10	0048 / 0712 / F 1306 / 1918	4.9 / 0.0 / 4.8 / 0.5	25	0038 / 0647 / SA 1306 / 1858	4.3 / 0.7 / 4.2 / 0.9
11	0134 / 0752 / SA 1401 / 1956	4.9 / 0.1 / 4.6 / 0.6	26	0110 / 0719 / SU 1334 / 1928	4.2 / 0.8 / 4.1 / 1.0
12	0219 / 0831 / SU 1442 / 2033	4.8 / 0.5 / 4.4 / 0.8	27	0142 / 0747 / M 1404 / 1944	4.1 / 1.0 / 4.0 / 1.1
13	0304 / 0909 / M 1524 / 2112	4.5 / 1.0 / 4.1 / 1.1	28	0216 / 0739 / TU 1436 / 1940	4.0 / 1.2 / 3.9 / 1.3
14	0352 / 0946 / TU 1607 / 2200	4.1 / 1.3 / 3.9 / 1.5	29	0254 / 0741 / W 1515 / 2010	3.9 / 1.4 / 3.7 / 1.4
15	0445 / 1031 / W 1656 / ☽ 2330	3.7 / 1.7 / 3.6 / 1.7	30	0339 / 0818 / TH 1603 / 2108	3.7 / 1.6 / 3.6 / 1.6

OCTOBER

#	Time	m	#	Time	m
1	0434 / 0916 / F 1704 / ◐	3.5 / 1.9 / 3.5	16	0114 / 0632 / SA 1337 / 1830	1.7 / 3.3 / 2.1 / 3.5
2	0013 / 0546 / SA 1234 / 1818	1.6 / 3.4 / 1.9 / 3.5	17	0221 / 0755 / SU 1439 / 1938	1.5 / 3.3 / 1.9 / 3.5
3	0138 / 0714 / SU 1411 / 1933	1.4 / 3.4 / 1.7 / 3.7	18	0315 / 0907 / M 1527 / 2041	1.4 / 3.5 / 1.8 / 3.7
4	0243 / 0839 / M 1515 / 2042	1.0 / 3.7 / 1.5 / 4.0	19	0359 / 0955 / TU 1604 / 2133	1.3 / 3.7 / 1.6 / 3.9
5	0342 / 0949 / TU 1608 / 2147	0.7 / 4.0 / 1.2 / 4.3	20	0430 / 1032 / W 1627 / 2216	1.2 / 3.9 / 1.4 / 4.0
6	0436 / 1044 / W 1655 / 2246	0.4 / 4.3 / 0.9 / 4.6	21	0447 / 1105 / TH 1651 / 2255	1.1 / 4.1 / 1.2 / 4.2
7	0524 / 1131 / TH 1738 / ● 2339	0.2 / 4.6 / 0.7 / 4.8	22	0508 / 1135 / F 1724 / 2333	1.0 / 4.2 / 1.1 / 4.2
8	0607 / 1214 / F 1819	0.1 / 4.7 / 0.6	23	0541 / 1205 / SA 1801 / ○	0.9 / 4.3 / 1.0
9	0026 / 0648 / SA 1255 / 1858	4.9 / 0.2 / 4.7 / 0.6	24	0008 / 0618 / SU 1236 / 1838	4.3 / 0.9 / 4.3 / 1.0
10	0112 / 0727 / SU 1335 / 1937	4.8 / 0.4 / 4.6 / 0.7	25	0044 / 0654 / M 1307 / 1912	4.3 / 1.0 / 4.2 / 1.0
11	0157 / 0804 / M 1415 / 2016	4.6 / 0.8 / 4.4 / 0.9	26	0120 / 0725 / TU 1341 / 1943	4.2 / 1.1 / 4.1 / 1.1
12	0243 / 0839 / TU 1456 / 2058	4.3 / 1.1 / 4.1 / 1.2	27	0158 / 0758 / W 1416 / 2004	4.1 / 1.3 / 4.0 / 1.2
13	0332 / 0907 / W 1539 / 2150	4.0 / 1.5 / 3.9 / 1.5	28	0240 / 0730 / TH 1457 / 2055	3.9 / 1.4 / 3.9 / 1.3
14	0424 / 0923 / TH 1628 / ◐ 2332	3.7 / 1.9 / 3.7 / 1.7	29	0328 / 0813 / F 1547 / 2226	3.8 / 1.6 / 3.7 / 1.4
15	0523 / 1040 / F 1725	3.4 / 2.1 / 3.5	30	0425 / 0941 / SA 1647 / ◐ 2350	3.6 / 1.9 / 3.7 / 1.4
			31	0532 / 1145 / SU 1754	3.5 / 1.9 / 3.7

NOVEMBER

#	Time	m	#	Time	m
1	0109 / 0650 / M 1338 / 1905	1.3 / 3.6 / 1.8 / 3.8	16	0222 / 0752 / TU 1436 / 1950	1.6 / 3.4 / 1.9 / 3.6
2	0218 / 0812 / TU 1451 / 2015	1.0 / 3.7 / 1.5 / 4.0	17	0302 / 0848 / W 1516 / 2043	1.5 / 3.6 / 1.7 / 3.7
3	0319 / 0922 / W 1547 / 2122	0.8 / 4.0 / 1.3 / 4.2	18	0328 / 0936 / TH 1549 / 2131	1.4 / 3.8 / 1.5 / 3.9
4	0413 / 1018 / TH 1636 / 2224	0.6 / 4.2 / 1.0 / 4.4	19	0351 / 1017 / F 1623 / 2217	1.3 / 4.0 / 1.4 / 4.0
5	0501 / 1106 / F 1721 / 2319	0.5 / 4.4 / 0.8 / 4.6	20	0428 / 1056 / SA 1702 / 2301	1.2 / 4.1 / 1.2 / 4.1
6	0545 / 1150 / SA 1803 / ●	0.5 / 4.5 / 0.7	21	0511 / 1133 / SU 1742 / ○ 2342	1.1 / 4.2 / 1.1 / 4.2
7	0007 / 0626 / SU 1231 / 1844	4.6 / 0.6 / 4.6 / 0.7	22	0553 / 1210 / M 1823	1.1 / 4.3 / 1.0
8	0053 / 0704 / M 1311 / 1925	4.6 / 0.8 / 4.5 / 0.8	23	0023 / 0634 / TU 1246 / 1905	4.2 / 1.1 / 4.3 / 1.0
9	0138 / 0740 / TU 1350 / 2007	4.4 / 1.0 / 4.3 / 0.9	24	0104 / 0712 / W 1324 / 1947	4.2 / 1.2 / 4.3 / 1.0
10	0224 / 0811 / W 1430 / 2051	4.2 / 1.3 / 4.2 / 1.1	25	0146 / 0742 / TH 1404 / 2032	4.2 / 1.3 / 4.2 / 1.0
11	0311 / 0821 / TH 1513 / 2143	3.9 / 1.6 / 4.0 / 1.4	26	0232 / 0749 / F 1448 / 2123	4.0 / 1.4 / 4.1 / 1.1
12	0401 / 0837 / F 1559 / 2253	3.7 / 1.8 / 3.8 / 1.6	27	0323 / 0833 / SA 1537 / 2220	3.9 / 1.6 / 4.0 / 1.1
13	0452 / 0927 / SA 1651 / ◐	3.5 / 2.0 / 3.6	28	0416 / 0952 / SU 1631 / ◐ 2321	3.8 / 1.7 / 3.9 / 1.2
14	0014 / 0548 / SU 1045 / 1749	1.7 / 3.3 / 2.1 / 3.5	29	0514 / 1102 / M 1730	3.7 / 1.8 / 3.9
15	0126 / 0649 / M 1341 / 1850	1.7 / 3.3 / 2.0 / 3.5	30	0030 / 0619 / TU 1211 / 1836	1.2 / 3.6 / 1.8 / 3.8

DECEMBER

#	Time	m	#	Time	m
1	0145 / 0731 / W 1416 / 1947	1.2 / 3.7 / 1.7 / 3.9	16	0140 / 0744 / TH 1421 / 1957	1.7 / 3.4 / 1.8 / 3.5
2	0252 / 0845 / TH 1524 / 2059	1.1 / 3.8 / 1.4 / 4.0	17	0226 / 0840 / F 1510 / 2052	1.6 / 3.6 / 1.7 / 3.6
3	0350 / 0949 / F 1620 / 2207	1.0 / 4.0 / 1.2 / 4.2	18	0308 / 0930 / SA 1555 / 2143	1.5 / 3.8 / 1.5 / 3.8
4	0442 / 1042 / SA 1709 / 2305	1.0 / 4.2 / 1.0 / 4.3	19	0353 / 1018 / SU 1641 / 2233	1.4 / 3.9 / 1.3 / 4.0
5	0527 / 1128 / SU 1754 / ● 2355	0.9 / 4.3 / 0.9 / 4.3	20	0444 / 1104 / M 1728 / 2321	1.3 / 4.1 / 1.1 / 4.1
6	0608 / 1211 / M 1836	1.0 / 4.4 / 0.8	21	0535 / 1147 / TU 1814 / ○	1.2 / 4.3 / 0.9
7	0040 / 0645 / TU 1251 / 1917	4.3 / 1.1 / 4.4 / 0.8	22	0007 / 0623 / W 1230 / 1900	4.2 / 1.1 / 4.4 / 0.8
8	0124 / 0718 / W 1329 / 1958	4.2 / 1.2 / 4.3 / 0.9	23	0053 / 0706 / TH 1313 / 1945	4.3 / 1.1 / 4.4 / 0.7
9	0207 / 0747 / TH 1408 / 2038	4.0 / 1.3 / 4.2 / 1.0	24	0140 / 0747 / F 1356 / 2030	4.3 / 1.1 / 4.4 / 0.7
10	0249 / 0801 / F 1447 / 2117	3.9 / 1.4 / 4.1 / 1.2	25	0227 / 0824 / SA 1441 / 2116	4.2 / 1.2 / 4.4 / 0.7
11	0332 / 0814 / SA 1528 / 2151	3.7 / 1.6 / 3.9 / 1.4	26	0315 / 0859 / SU 1527 / 2201	4.1 / 1.3 / 4.3 / 0.8
12	0414 / 0852 / SU 1611 / 2200	3.5 / 1.7 / 3.7 / 1.6	27	0402 / 0939 / M 1615 / 2249	4.0 / 1.4 / 4.2 / 1.0
13	0459 / 0944 / M 1658 / ◐ 2302	3.4 / 1.9 / 3.6 / 1.7	28	0451 / 1029 / TU 1707 / ◐ 2346	3.8 / 1.5 / 4.0 / 1.2
14	0548 / 1053 / TU 1753	3.3 / 2.0 / 3.5	29	0545 / 1129 / W 1807	3.7 / 1.7 / 3.8
15	0036 / 0645 / W 1306 / 1856	1.7 / 3.3 / 2.0 / 3.4	30	0102 / 0647 / TH 1250 / 1920	1.7 / 3.6 / 1.7 / 3.7
			31	0227 / 0800 / F 1506 / 2042	1.4 / 3.6 / 1.6 / 3.8

Chart Datum: 2·10 metres below Ordnance Datum (Local). HAT is 5·0 metres above Chart Datum; see 0.19

5.16 HELMSDALE

Highland 58°06'·83N 03°38'·89W ❀❀⌂⌂❀❀

CHARTS AC 115, 1462; Imray C23.

TIDES +0035 Dover; ML 2·2; Duration 0615

Standard Port WICK (→)

Times				Height (metres)			
High Water		Low Water		MHWS	MHWN	MLWN	MLWS
0000	0700	0200	0700	3·5	2·8	1·4	0·7
1200	1900	1400	1900				
Differences HELMSDALE							
+0025	+0015	+0035	+0030	+0·4	+0·3	+0·1	0·0

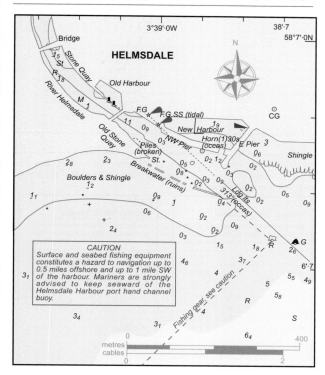

SHELTER Good, except in strong E/SE'lies. AB on NW pier, approx 1m. 80m of pontoon berths through HM. Limited depths at LWS.

NAVIGATION WPT 58°06'·59N 03°38'·39W, 313°/0·35M to ent; ldg marks are black masts with Or □ topmarks.

• Surface and seabed fishing gear, hazardous to navigation, extends up to 0.5M offshore and 1.0M SW of hbr.
• Essential to pass seaward of Hbr Chan PHM.
• Beware spate coming down river after heavy rain. Shoals both sides of chan and bar build up when river in spate.

LIGHTS AND MARKS See 5.3 and chartlet.

R/T VHF Ch 13 16.

TELEPHONE (Code 01431) HM 821692 (Office), 821386 (Home); MRCC (01224) 592334; Police 821222; Marinecall 09068 969641; Dr 821221, or 821225 (Home).

FACILITIES Hbr AB <5m £9, 5m-7m £12, 7m-10m £16, M (See HM), FW, Slip. **Town** P, D, Gas, ⚒, R, Bar, ✉, Ⓑ (Brora), ➤.

5.17 WICK

Highland 58°26'·38N 03°04'·72W ❀❀❀⌂❀

CHARTS AC 115, 1462; Imray C23, C68.

TIDES +0010 Dover; ML 2·0; Duration 0625. Wick is a Standard Port. Daily tidal predictions are given below.

Standard Port WICK (→)

Times				Height (metres)			
High Water		Low Water		MHWS	MHWN	MLWN	MLWS
0000	0700	0200	0700	3·5	2·8	1·4	0·7
1200	1900	1400	1900				
Differences DUNCANSBY HEAD							
–0115	–0115	–0110	–0110	–0·4	–0·4	No data	

SHELTER Good, except in strong NNE to SSE winds, to await right conditions for W-bound passage through the Pentland Firth (see 5.4). Berth where directed in the Outer Harbour, 2·4m, or in marina in Inner Harbour, 2·0m. NB: The River Hbr (commercial) is leased and must not be entered without prior approval.

NAVIGATION WPT 58°26'·18N 03°03'·39W, 284°/0·72M to S pier. From the N, open up hbr ent before rounding North Head so as to clear drying Proudfoot Rks.

> Hbr ent is dangerous in strong E'lies as craft have to turn 90° to port at the end of S pier.

On S side of bay, unlit bn, 300m ENE of LB slip, marks end of ruined bkwtr.

LIGHTS AND MARKS S pier lt, Fl WRG 3s 12m 12/9M, 253°-G-270°-W-286°-R-329°, Bell (2) 10s (fishing). Ldg lts, both FR 5/8m, lead 234° into outer hbr. Traffic signals:

B ● (●) at CG stn on S Head = hbr closed by weather.
B ● (●) at S pier head = caution; hbr temp obstructed.

R/T VHF Ch 14 16 (Mon-Fri 0800-1700).

TELEPHONE (Code 01955) HM 602030; MRCC (01224) 592334; Police 603551; Ⓗ 602434, 602261.

FACILITIES Poss temporary AB on pontoons in Outer Harbour. **Wick Marina** (Inner Harbour) 70 inc 15 ❶ dredged to 2·0m; £15/craft up to 10m; max 25m LOA; BH, shower block 50m from marina. **Fish Jetty** D, FW, CH; **Services:** ME, El, ✖, Slip, Gas, C (15/100 ton). **Town** P, ⚒, R, Bar, ✉, Ⓑ, ➤, ✈.

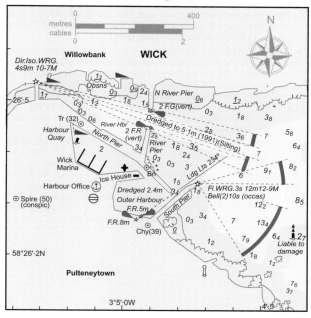

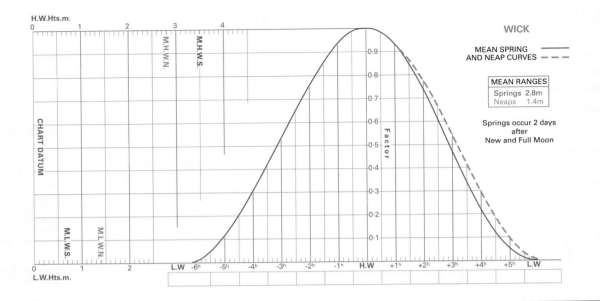

PENTLAND FIRTH

(AC 2162, 2581) ▶ *This potentially dangerous chan should only be attempted with moderate winds (less than F4), good vis, no swell and a fair np tide. In such conditions it presents few problems. A safe passage depends on a clear understanding of tidal streams and correct timing. The Admiralty Tidal Stream Atlas for Orkney and Shetland (NP 209) gives large scale vectors and is essential. Even in ideal conditions the races off Duncansby Hd, Swilkie Pt (N end of Stroma), and Rks of Mey (Merry Men of Mey) must be avoided as they are always dangerous to small craft. Also avoid the Pentland Skerries, Muckle Skerry, Old Head, Lother Rock (S Ronaldsay), and Dunnet Hd on E-going flood. For passages across the Firth see CCC SDs for Orkney.* ◀

At E end the Firth is entered between Duncansby Hd and Old Hd (S Ronaldsay), between which lie Muckle Skerry and the Pentland Skerries. Near the centre of Firth are the Islands of Swona (N side) and Stroma (S side). Outer Sound (main chan, 2·5M wide) runs between Swona and Stroma; Inner Sound (1·5M wide) between Stroma and the mainland. Rks of Mey extend about 2ca N of St John's Pt. The W end of the Firth is between Dunnet Hd and Tor Ness (Hoy).

▶*Tide flows strongly around and through the Orkney Islands. The Pentland Firth is a dangerous area for all craft, tidal flows reach 12 knots between Duncansby Head and S Ronaldsay. W of Dunnet Hd and Hoy is less violent. There is little tide within Scapa Flow. Tidal streams reach 8-9kn at sp in the Outer Sound, and 9-12kn between Pentland Skerries and Duncansby Hd. The resultant dangerous seas, very strong eddies and violent races should be avoided by yachts at all costs.*

The E-going stream begins at HW Aberdeen + 0500, and the W-going at HW Aberdeen – 0105. **Duncansby Race** extends ENE towards Muckle Skerry on the SE-going stream, but by HW Aberdeen – 0440 it extends NW from Duncansby Hd. Note: HW at Muckle Skerry is the same time as HW Dover. A persistent race off **Swilkie Pt**, at N end of Stroma, **is very dangerous with a strong W'ly wind over a W-going stream.** The most dangerous and extensive race in the Firth is *Merry Men of Mey. It forms off*

St John's Pt on W-going stream at HW Aberdeen – 0150 and for a while extends right across to Tor Ness with heavy breaking seas even in fine weather. ◀

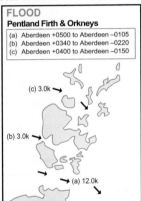

FLOOD
Pentland Firth & Orkneys

| (a) Aberdeen +0500 to Aberdeen –0105 |
| (b) Aberdeen +0340 to Aberdeen –0220 |
| (c) Aberdeen +0400 to Aberdeen –0150 |

(c) 3.0k
(b) 3.0k
(a) 12.0k

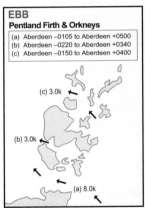

EBB
Pentland Firth & Orkneys

| (a) Aberdeen –0105 to Aberdeen +0500 |
| (b) Aberdeen –0220 to Aberdeen +0340 |
| (c) Aberdeen –0150 to Aberdeen +0400 |

(c) 3.0k
(b) 3.0k
(a) 8.0k

Passage Westward: This is the more difficult direction due to prevailing W winds. ▶ *Freswick B, 3·5M S of Duncansby Hd, is a good waiting anch; here an eddy runs N for 9 hrs. Round Duncansby Hd close in at HW Aberdeen –0220, as the ebb starts to run W. Take a mid-course through the Inner Sound to appr the Rks of Mey from close inshore. Gills Bay is a temp anch if early; do not pass Rks of Mey until ebb has run for at least 2 hrs. Pass 100m N of the Rks (awash).*◀

Passage Eastward: ▶ *With a fair wind and tide, no race forms and the passage is easier. Leave Scrabster at local LW+1 so as to be close off Dunnet Hd not before HW Aberdeen +0340 when the E-going flood starts to make. If late, give the Hd a wide berth. Having rounded the Rks of Mey, steer S initially to avoid being set onto the rky S tip of Stroma, marked by unlit SCM bn.*◀ Then keep mid-chan through the Inner Sound and maintain this offing to give Duncansby Hd a wide berth.

TIME ZONE (UT)
For Summer Time add ONE hour in **non-shaded areas**

WICK   LAT 58°26'N   LONG 3°05'W
TIMES AND HEIGHTS OF HIGH AND LOW WATERS

Dates in red are **SPRINGS**
Dates in blue are NEAPS

YEAR 2010

JANUARY

Day	Time	m	Day	Time	m
1 F	0459 / 1123 / 1732 / 2356	1.0 / 3.7 / 0.6 / 3.6	16 SA	0530 / 1155 / 1802	1.1 / 3.5 / 0.9
2 SA	0545 / 1210 / 1820	0.9 / 3.8 / 0.4	17 SU	0027 / 0601 / 1228 / 1833	3.2 / 1.1 / 3.5 / 0.8
3 SU	0046 / 0629 / 1257 / 1908	3.6 / 0.9 / 3.8 / 0.4	18 M	0059 / 0632 / 1259 / 1904	3.2 / 1.1 / 3.5 / 0.8
4 M	0135 / 0713 / 1343 / 1957	3.6 / 0.9 / 3.8 / 0.5	19 TU	0131 / 0702 / 1330 / 1934	3.2 / 1.1 / 3.4 / 0.9
5 TU	0224 / 0758 / 1431 / 2047	3.4 / 1.0 / 3.7 / 0.6	20 W	0202 / 0733 / 1403 / 2006	3.1 / 1.1 / 3.4 / 1.0
6 W	0313 / 0844 / 1522 / 2141	3.3 / 1.2 / 3.5 / 0.8	21 TH	0235 / 0806 / 1438 / 2040	3.0 / 1.2 / 3.3 / 1.1
7 TH	0405 / 0936 / 1618 / ☽2241	3.1 / 1.3 / 3.4 / 1.1	22 F	0313 / 0842 / 1518 / 2119	2.9 / 1.4 / 3.1 / 1.2
8 F	0500 / 1043 / 1720 / 2347	3.0 / 1.5 / 3.2 / 1.3	23 SA	0359 / 0928 / 1608 / ◑2212	2.9 / 1.5 / 3.0 / 1.4
9 SA	0602 / 1206 / 1830	2.9 / 1.6 / 3.0	24 SU	0456 / 1035 / 1712 / 2331	2.8 / 1.6 / 2.9 / 1.5
10 SU	0100 / 0710 / 1337 / 1948	1.4 / 2.9 / 1.5 / 3.0	25 M	0605 / 1216 / 1829	2.8 / 1.6 / 2.9
11 M	0209 / 0819 / 1448 / 2058	1.4 / 3.0 / 1.4 / 3.0	26 TU	0057 / 0719 / 1343 / 1950	1.5 / 2.9 / 1.5 / 2.9
12 TU	0303 / 0917 / 1539 / 2153	1.4 / 3.1 / 1.3 / 3.1	27 W	0212 / 0829 / 1452 / 2103	1.4 / 3.0 / 1.2 / 3.1
13 W	0346 / 1004 / 1620 / 2238	1.3 / 3.3 / 1.1 / 3.1	28 TH	0313 / 0929 / 1547 / 2204	1.2 / 3.3 / 0.9 / 3.3
14 TH	0423 / 1045 / 1657 / 2318	1.3 / 3.4 / 1.0 / 3.2	29 F	0404 / 1022 / 1636 / 2256	1.1 / 3.5 / 0.6 / 3.5
15 F	0457 / 1121 / ●2354	1.2 / 3.4 / 3.2 (1730 0.9)	30 SA	0449 / 1110 / 1722 / ○2345	0.9 / 3.7 / 0.4 / 3.6
			31 SU	0532 / 1156 / 1806	0.8 / 3.9 / 0.2

FEBRUARY

Day	Time	m	Day	Time	m
1 M	0031 / 0613 / 1241 / 1850	3.7 / 0.7 / 3.9 / 0.2	16 TU	0034 / 0608 / 1236 / 1835	3.2 / 0.9 / 3.5 / 0.7
2 TU	0116 / 0653 / 1326 / 1933	3.6 / 0.7 / 3.9 / 0.3	17 W	0102 / 0637 / 1305 / 1904	3.2 / 0.9 / 3.5 / 0.7
3 W	0159 / 0733 / 1410 / 2016	3.5 / 0.8 / 3.8 / 0.5	18 TH	0131 / 0706 / 1336 / 1932	3.2 / 0.9 / 3.4 / 0.8
4 TH	0242 / 0814 / 1456 / 2101	3.3 / 1.0 / 3.6 / 0.8	19 F	0202 / 0737 / 1409 / 2003	3.1 / 1.0 / 3.3 / 1.0
5 F	0327 / 0858 / 1547 / ◐2151	3.1 / 1.2 / 3.3 / 1.1	20 SA	0236 / 0812 / 1448 / 2039	3.0 / 1.1 / 3.2 / 1.1
6 SA	0417 / 0955 / 1646 / 2255	2.9 / 1.4 / 3.0 / 1.4	21 SU	0318 / 0853 / 1536 / 2124	2.9 / 1.3 / 3.0 / 1.3
7 SU	0516 / 1126 / 1800	2.8 / 1.5 / 2.8	22 M	0411 / 0953 / 1640 / ◐2239	2.8 / 1.4 / 2.8 / 1.5
8 M	0018 / 0628 / 1321 / 1930	1.6 / 2.8 / 1.5 / 2.7	23 TU	0522 / 1146 / 1805	2.7 / 1.5 / 2.8
9 TU	0149 / 0751 / 1440 / 2048	1.6 / 2.8 / 1.4 / 2.8	24 W	0032 / 0646 / 1327 / 1935	1.5 / 2.8 / 1.3 / 2.8
10 W	0251 / 0858 / 1529 / 2142	1.5 / 3.0 / 1.2 / 2.9	25 TH	0159 / 0806 / 1440 / 2053	1.4 / 2.9 / 1.0 / 3.0
11 TH	0334 / 0947 / 1607 / 2224	1.4 / 3.1 / 1.1 / 3.0	26 F	0302 / 0911 / 1534 / 2152	1.2 / 3.2 / 0.7 / 3.3
12 F	0409 / 1027 / 1640 / 2301	1.3 / 3.3 / 0.9 / 3.1	27 SA	0350 / 1005 / 1620 / 2242	1.0 / 3.5 / 0.4 / 3.5
13 SA	0440 / 1103 / 1710 / 2334	1.1 / 3.4 / 0.8 / 3.2	28 SU	0432 / 1052 / 1703 / ○2327	0.8 / 3.7 / 0.2 / 3.6
14 SU	0510 / 1135 / ●1739	1.0 / 3.4 / 0.7			
15 M	0004 / 0539 / 1206 / 1807	3.2 / 0.9 / 3.5 / 0.7			

MARCH

Day	Time	m	Day	Time	m
1 M	0512 / 1137 / 1745	0.6 / 3.9 / 0.1	16 TU	0514 / 1139 / 1737	0.8 / 3.4 / 0.6
2 TU	0010 / 0551 / 1221 / 1825	3.6 / 0.5 / 3.9 / 0.2	17 W	0004 / 0542 / 1209 / 1805	3.2 / 0.8 / 3.4 / 0.6
3 W	0051 / 0630 / 1304 / 1905	3.6 / 0.5 / 3.9 / 0.3	18 TH	0033 / 0612 / 1240 / 1833	3.2 / 0.7 / 3.4 / 0.7
4 TH	0130 / 0709 / 1347 / 1944	3.5 / 0.6 / 3.7 / 0.6	19 F	0102 / 0643 / 1313 / 1903	3.2 / 0.8 / 3.3 / 0.8
5 F	0210 / 0748 / 1431 / 2023	3.3 / 0.8 / 3.4 / 0.9	20 SA	0134 / 0716 / 1348 / 1935	3.2 / 0.8 / 3.2 / 0.9
6 SA	0250 / 0830 / 1519 / 2105	3.1 / 1.0 / 3.1 / 1.2	21 SU	0209 / 0752 / 1430 / 2013	3.1 / 1.0 / 3.1 / 1.1
7 SU	0336 / 0922 / 1616 / ◐2202	2.9 / 1.3 / 2.8 / 1.5	22 M	0250 / 0837 / 1521 / 2101	3.0 / 1.1 / 2.9 / 1.3
8 M	0432 / 1053 / 1731 / 2331	2.8 / 1.5 / 2.6 / 1.7	23 TU	0344 / 0943 / 1628 / ◐2221	2.8 / 1.2 / 2.8 / 1.5
9 TU	0546 / 1254 / 1907	2.7 / 1.5 / 2.6	24 W	0456 / 1138 / 1755	2.7 / 1.3 / 2.7
10 W	0119 / 0713 / 1417 / 2028	1.7 / 2.7 / 1.3 / 2.7	25 TH	0018 / 0622 / 1312 / 1925	1.5 / 2.8 / 1.1 / 2.8
11 TH	0228 / 0829 / 1505 / 2120	1.6 / 2.8 / 1.2 / 2.8	26 F	0142 / 0743 / 1421 / 2039	1.4 / 2.9 / 0.8 / 3.0
12 F	0311 / 0920 / 1541 / 2200	1.4 / 3.0 / 1.0 / 2.9	27 SA	0242 / 0849 / 1514 / 2134	1.1 / 3.2 / 0.6 / 3.2
13 SA	0345 / 1001 / 1612 / 2234	1.2 / 3.1 / 0.9 / 3.1	28 SU	0328 / 0943 / 1559 / 2221	0.9 / 3.4 / 0.3 / 3.4
14 SU	0416 / 1036 / 1641 / 2306	1.1 / 3.2 / 0.7 / 3.1	29 M	0410 / 1031 / 1640 / 2304	0.7 / 3.6 / 0.2 / 3.5
15 M	0445 / 1108 / ●1709 / 2335	0.9 / 3.3 / 0.7 / 3.2	30 TU	0450 / 1116 / 1722 / ○2344	0.5 / 3.7 / 0.2 / 3.5
			31 W	0529 / 1159 / 1759	0.5 / 3.8 / 0.3

APRIL

Day	Time	m	Day	Time	m
1 TH	0023 / 0608 / 1242 / 1837	3.5 / 0.5 / 3.7 / 0.4	16 F	0004 / 0550 / 1218 / 1807	3.3 / 0.7 / 3.3 / 0.7
2 F	0102 / 0648 / 1325 / 1914	3.4 / 0.6 / 3.5 / 0.7	17 SA	0038 / 0625 / 1255 / 1841	3.3 / 0.7 / 3.3 / 0.8
3 SA	0139 / 0728 / 1408 / 1951	3.3 / 0.7 / 3.2 / 1.0	18 SU	0112 / 0703 / 1336 / 1918	3.2 / 0.7 / 3.2 / 0.9
4 SU	0218 / 0810 / 1455 / 2030	3.1 / 0.9 / 3.0 / 1.3	19 M	0151 / 0746 / 1422 / 2001	3.1 / 0.8 / 3.0 / 1.1
5 M	0301 / 0903 / 1551 / 2120	2.9 / 1.1 / 2.7 / 1.5	20 TU	0236 / 0838 / 1517 / 2056	3.0 / 0.9 / 2.9 / 1.3
6 TU	0354 / 1022 / 1701 / ◐2240	2.8 / 1.3 / 2.5 / 1.7	21 W	0331 / 0954 / 1626 / ◑2220	2.9 / 1.0 / 2.7 / 1.4
7 W	0503 / 1202 / 1826	2.6 / 1.4 / 2.5	22 TH	0442 / 1129 / 1747 / 2357	2.8 / 1.0 / 2.7 / 1.4
8 TH	0020 / 0623 / 1331 / 1947	1.7 / 2.6 / 1.4 / 2.6	23 F	0602 / 1249 / 1906	2.8 / 0.9 / 2.8
9 F	0145 / 0741 / 1425 / 2043	1.6 / 2.7 / 1.1 / 2.7	24 SA	0113 / 0717 / 1355 / 2014	1.3 / 2.9 / 0.7 / 2.9
10 SA	0234 / 0839 / 1504 / 2124	1.4 / 2.8 / 1.0 / 2.8	25 SU	0214 / 0822 / 1448 / 2108	1.1 / 3.1 / 0.5 / 3.1
11 SU	0312 / 0923 / 1536 / 2200	1.2 / 3.0 / 0.9 / 3.0	26 M	0303 / 0918 / 1534 / 2155	0.9 / 3.3 / 0.4 / 3.2
12 M	0344 / 1000 / 1607 / 2232	1.0 / 3.1 / 0.7 / 3.1	27 TU	0347 / 1008 / 1615 / 2238	0.7 / 3.4 / 0.4 / 3.3
13 TU	0415 / 1035 / 1636 / 2303	0.9 / 3.2 / 0.7 / 3.2	28 W	0429 / 1055 / 1655 / ○2319	0.6 / 3.5 / 0.4 / 3.4
14 W	0446 / 1108 / ●1705 / 2333	0.8 / 3.3 / 0.6 / 3.2	29 TH	0510 / 1140 / 1734 / 2358	0.5 / 3.5 / 0.5 / 3.4
15 TH	0517 / 1142 / 1735	0.7 / 3.3 / 0.6	30 F	0552 / 1223 / 1812	0.5 / 3.4 / 0.7

Chart Datum: 1·71 metres below Ordnance Datum (Newlyn). HAT is 4·0 metres above Chart Datum; see 0.19

WICK LAT 58°26'N LONG 3°05'W

TIMES AND HEIGHTS OF HIGH AND LOW WATERS

TIME ZONE (UT)
For Summer Time add ONE hour in **non-shaded areas**

Dates in red are **SPRINGS**
Dates in blue are **NEAPS**

YEAR **2010**

MAY

Time	m		Time	m
1 SA 0036/0633/1307/1849	3.4/0.6/3.3/0.9	**16** SU 0018/0614/1244/1827	3.3/0.6/3.3/0.8
2 SU 0114/0714/1350/1926	3.3/0.7/3.1/1.1	**17** M 0058/0658/1329/1911	3.2/0.6/3.2/0.9
3 M 0152/0757/1435/2005	3.1/0.9/2.9/1.3	**18** TU 0141/0748/1419/1959	3.2/0.6/3.1/1.1
4 TU 0234/0846/1526/2050	3.0/1.0/2.7/1.4	**19** W 0229/0845/1516/2055	3.2/0.7/2.9/1.2
5 W 0322/0947/1625/2152	2.8/1.1/2.5/1.5	**20** TH 0324/0954/1620/2206	3.1/0.8/2.8/1.3
6 TH 0421/1101/1733/2312	2.7/1.2/2.5/1.6	**21** F 0429/1109/1728/2325	3.0/0.8/2.8/1.3
7 F 0529/1216/1844	2.6/1.2/2.5	**22** SA 0539/1219/1837	3.0/0.8/2.8
8 SA 0032/0638/1323/1947	1.5/2.6/1.1/2.6	**23** SU 0037/0648/1324/1941	1.3/3.0/0.7/2.9
9 SU 0138/0741/1412/2036	1.4/2.7/1.0/2.7	**24** M 0143/0754/1421/2039	1.1/3.1/0.7/3.0
10 M 0227/0833/1452/2117	1.3/2.8/0.9/2.9	**25** TU 0239/0855/1509/2129	1.0/3.2/0.7/3.1
11 TU 0307/0918/1527/2153	1.1/2.9/0.8/3.0	**26** W 0329/0950/1553/2215	0.9/3.2/0.7/3.2
12 W 0344/0959/1601/2229	1.0/3.1/0.8/3.1	**27** TH 0415/1040/1634/2257	0.7/3.3/0.7/3.3
13 TH 0419/1039/1635/2304	0.8/3.2/0.7/3.2	**28** F 0459/1126/1714/2337	0.7/3.3/0.8/3.3
14 F 0455/1119/1710/2340	0.7/3.2/0.7/3.3	**29** SA 0541/1210/1752	0.6/3.2/0.9
15 SA 0534/1200/1747	0.6/3.3/0.7	**30** SU 0016/0622/1252/1829	3.3/0.6/3.1/1.0
		31 M 0054/0702/1333/1906	3.3/0.7/3.0/1.1

JUNE

Time	m		Time	m
1 TU 0132/0742/1414/1943	3.2/0.8/2.9/1.2	**16** W 0133/0745/1414/1952	3.4/0.4/3.2/0.9
2 W 0211/0824/1458/2023	3.1/0.9/2.8/1.3	**17** TH 0221/0838/1506/2042	3.4/0.5/3.1/1.0
3 TH 0253/0909/1545/2108	3.0/1.0/2.6/1.4	**18** F 0313/0937/1602/2139	3.3/0.6/3.0/1.1
4 F 0340/1003/1638/2206	2.9/1.1/2.6/1.5	**19** SA 0411/1040/1700/2247	3.2/0.7/2.9/1.2
5 SA 0434/1104/1736/2318	2.8/1.2/2.5/1.5	**20** SU 0513/1145/1802	3.1/0.8/2.8
6 SU 0534/1208/1836	2.7/1.2/2.6	**21** M 0000/0619/1252/1906	1.3/3.0/0.9/2.8
7 M 0029/0636/1308/1934	1.5/2.7/1.1/2.7	**22** TU 0115/0730/1355/2010	1.2/3.0/1.0/2.9
8 TU 0133/0737/1401/2026	1.4/2.7/1.1/2.8	**23** W 0224/0839/1451/2107	1.1/3.0/1.0/3.0
9 W 0227/0833/1447/2113	1.2/2.8/1.0/2.9	**24** TH 0321/0939/1538/2157	1.0/3.0/1.0/3.1
10 TH 0314/0925/1529/2156	1.1/3.0/0.9/3.1	**25** F 0410/1031/1620/2242	0.9/3.1/1.0/3.2
11 F 0357/1014/1610/2238	0.9/3.1/1.0/3.2	**26** SA 0453/1116/1659/2323	0.8/3.1/1.0/3.3
12 SA 0439/1101/1652/2320	0.7/3.2/0.8/3.3	**27** SU 0533/1158/1736	0.7/3.1/1.0
13 SU 0523/1147/1735	0.6/3.3/0.8	**28** M 0001/0610/1237/1811	3.3/0.7/3.1/1.0
14 M 0003/0608/1235/1819	3.4/0.6/3.3/0.8	**29** TU 0038/0646/1314/1846	3.3/0.7/3.1/1.0
15 TU 0047/0655/1324/1905	3.5/0.4/3.3/0.8	**30** W 0113/0720/1350/1919	3.3/0.7/3.0/1.1

JULY

Time	m		Time	m
1 TH 0147/0755/1426/1953	3.2/0.8/2.9/1.1	**16** F 0207/0819/1446/2019	3.6/0.3/3.2/0.9
2 F 0223/0831/1504/2030	3.1/0.9/2.8/1.2	**17** SA 0255/0909/1535/2108	3.5/0.5/3.1/1.0
3 SA 0302/0910/1545/2112	3.0/1.0/2.7/1.3	**18** SU 0347/1005/1627/2208	3.3/0.8/2.9/1.2
4 SU 0345/0957/1633/2206	2.9/1.1/2.6/1.4	**19** M 0446/1109/1725/2327	3.1/1.0/2.8/1.3
5 M 0436/1056/1729/2321	2.8/1.2/2.6/1.5	**20** TU 0554/1219/1831	2.9/1.2/2.8
6 TU 0537/1203/1831	2.7/1.3/2.7	**21** W 0056/0712/1335/1943	1.3/2.8/1.3/2.8
7 W 0039/0644/1310/1935	1.5/2.7/1.3/2.8	**22** TH 0221/0831/1440/2050	1.2/2.8/1.3/3.0
8 TH 0149/0753/1411/2034	1.3/2.8/1.2/2.9	**23** F 0320/0933/1529/2143	1.1/2.9/1.2/3.1
9 F 0249/0858/1505/2128	1.2/2.9/1.1/3.1	**24** SA 0405/1023/1609/2228	0.9/3.0/1.2/3.2
10 SA 0340/0955/1554/2217	0.9/3.1/1.0/3.3	**25** SU 0444/1105/1645/2308	0.8/3.1/1.1/3.3
11 SU 0427/1047/1640/2303	0.7/3.3/0.9/3.4	**26** M 0518/1143/1718/2344	0.7/3.1/1.0/3.4
12 M 0513/1136/1724/2349	0.5/3.4/0.8/3.6	**27** TU 0551/1217/1750	0.7/3.1/0.9
13 TU 0559/1224/1808	0.3/3.5/0.7	**28** W 0017/0622/1250/1821	3.4/0.6/3.1/0.9
14 W 0034/0644/1312/1851	3.7/0.2/3.4/0.7	**29** TH 0049/0652/1321/1852	3.4/0.7/3.1/0.9
15 TH 0120/0731/1359/1935	3.7/0.2/3.4/0.8	**30** F 0121/0722/1352/1922	3.3/0.7/3.0/1.0
		31 SA 0152/0753/1424/1955	3.3/0.8/3.0/1.1

AUGUST

Time	m		Time	m
1 SU 0226/0825/1459/2030	3.2/0.9/2.9/1.2	**16** M 0323/0926/1552/2135	3.3/1.0/3.0/1.2
2 M 0304/0902/1541/2113	3.0/1.1/2.8/1.3	**17** TU 0421/1028/1649/2302	3.1/1.1/2.9/1.4
3 TU 0350/0948/1633/2214	2.9/1.3/2.7/1.5	**18** W 0532/1148/1759	2.8/1.5/2.8
4 W 0449/1059/1737/2352	2.8/1.4/2.7/1.5	**19** TH 0048/0659/1319/1919	1.4/2.7/1.5/2.8
5 TH 0603/1228/1850	2.7/1.4/2.8	**20** F 0217/0824/1429/2032	1.3/2.8/1.5/2.9
6 F 0120/0723/1346/2002	1.4/2.8/1.4/2.9	**21** SA 0311/0923/1516/2127	1.1/2.9/1.4/3.1
7 SA 0231/0839/1450/2104	1.2/2.9/1.2/3.1	**22** SU 0351/1008/1553/2210	1.0/3.0/1.2/3.2
8 SU 0326/0940/1541/2157	0.9/3.1/1.1/3.3	**23** M 0425/1046/1625/2247	0.8/3.1/1.1/3.3
9 M 0414/1033/1626/2246	0.6/3.3/0.9/3.6	**24** TU 0455/1119/1655/2320	0.7/3.2/1.0/3.4
10 TU 0458/1121/1708/2332	0.3/3.5/0.7/3.7	**25** W 0524/1151/1725/2352	0.7/3.2/0.9/3.5
11 W 0542/1207/1750	0.2/3.6/0.6	**26** TH 0553/1220/1755	0.6/3.2/0.9
12 TH 0017/0625/1252/1831	3.9/0.1/3.6/0.6	**27** F 0022/0621/1249/1824	3.5/0.6/3.2/0.9
13 F 0102/0708/1335/1912	3.9/0.2/3.5/0.6	**28** SA 0052/0649/1318/1853	3.4/0.7/3.2/0.9
14 SA 0146/0752/1418/1953	3.8/0.3/3.4/0.8	**29** SU 0122/0717/1348/1924	3.3/0.8/3.1/1.0
15 SU 0233/0836/1503/2039	3.6/0.6/3.2/1.0	**30** M 0155/0747/1421/1958	3.2/1.0/3.0/1.1
		31 TU 0233/0821/1501/2038	3.1/1.1/2.9/1.3

Chart Datum: 1·71 metres below Ordnance Datum (Newlyn). HAT is 4·0 metres above Chart Datum; see 0.19

FREE monthly updates from
www.reedsalmanac.co.uk

WICK LAT 58°26'N LONG 3°05'W
TIMES AND HEIGHTS OF HIGH AND LOW WATERS

TIME ZONE (UT)
For Summer Time add ONE hour in **non-shaded areas**

Dates in red are SPRINGS
Dates in blue are NEAPS

YEAR **2010**

NE Scotland

SEPTEMBER

Time	m		Time	m
1 0319	3.0	**16**	0511	2.7
0903	1.3		1112	1.7
W 1550	2.8		TH 1725	2.8
◑ 2134	1.4			
2 0418	2.8	**17**	0031	1.4
1008	1.5		0641	2.7
TH 1655	2.8		F 1253	1.7
2321	1.5		1848	2.8
3 0537	2.7	**18**	0158	1.3
1200	1.6		0805	2.7
F 1816	2.8		SA 1407	1.6
			2004	2.9
4 0101	1.4	**19**	0248	1.1
0705	2.8		0900	2.9
SA 1329	1.5		SU 1453	1.4
1934	2.9		2100	3.1
5 0214	1.1	**20**	0325	1.0
0824	3.0		0942	3.0
SU 1434	1.3		M 1528	1.3
2041	3.2		2142	3.2
6 0308	0.8	**21**	0356	0.9
0925	3.2		1018	3.1
M 1523	1.0		TU 1559	1.1
2136	3.4		2218	3.3
7 0354	0.5	**22**	0425	0.8
1015	3.4		1050	3.2
TU 1606	0.8		W 1628	1.0
2224	3.7		2251	3.4
8 0437	0.3	**23**	0453	0.7
1101	3.6		1120	3.3
W 1647	0.7		TH 1658	0.9
● 2310	3.9		○ 2322	3.5
9 0519	0.1	**24**	0521	0.7
1144	3.7		1149	3.3
TH 1727	0.5		F 1728	0.8
2355	4.0		2353	3.5
10 0601	0.1	**25**	0549	0.7
1226	3.7		1217	3.3
F 1808	0.5		SA 1757	0.8
11 0039	3.9	**26**	0024	3.4
0641	0.3		0617	0.8
SA 1308	3.6		SU 1247	3.3
1848	0.6		1828	0.9
12 0124	3.8	**27**	0057	3.4
0722	0.5		0646	0.9
SU 1348	3.4		M 1318	3.3
1930	0.8		1900	1.0
13 0210	3.5	**28**	0132	3.3
0803	0.8		0717	1.0
M 1431	3.3		TU 1352	3.2
2014	1.0		1936	1.1
14 0259	3.2	**29**	0211	3.1
0848	1.2		0752	1.2
TU 1518	3.1		W 1431	3.1
2110	1.2		2019	1.2
15 0358	3.0	**30**	0259	3.0
0946	1.5		0836	1.4
W 1614	2.9		TH 1521	3.0
◑ 2241	1.4		2120	1.3

OCTOBER

Time	m		Time	m
1 0401	2.8	**16**	0605	2.6
0944	1.6		1158	1.8
F 1627	2.9		SA 1805	2.8
◑ 2307	1.4			
2 0522	2.8	**17**	0114	1.4
1140	1.6		0724	2.7
SA 1749	2.9		SU 1323	1.7
			1919	2.9
3 0040	1.2	**18**	0209	1.2
0649	2.8		0823	2.8
SU 1307	1.5		M 1416	1.5
1908	3.0		2019	3.0
4 0151	1.0	**19**	0249	1.1
0804	3.0		0907	3.0
M 1410	1.3		TU 1455	1.4
2015	3.2		2105	3.1
5 0245	0.7	**20**	0321	1.0
0903	3.2		0943	3.1
TU 1500	1.1		W 1528	1.2
2111	3.5		2144	3.3
6 0331	0.5	**21**	0351	0.9
0952	3.4		1016	3.2
W 1543	0.9		TH 1600	1.1
2201	3.7		2219	3.3
7 0413	0.3	**22**	0420	0.8
1036	3.6		1047	3.3
TH 1624	0.7		F 1631	1.0
● 2248	3.9		2252	3.4
8 0454	0.3	**23**	0449	0.8
1118	3.7		1118	3.4
F 1705	0.6		SA 1703	0.9
2333	3.9		○ 2326	3.5
9 0535	0.3	**24**	0519	0.8
1159	3.7		1148	3.4
SA 1746	0.6		SU 1735	0.9
10 0018	3.8	**25**	0000	3.4
0614	0.5		0549	0.9
SU 1240	3.6		M 1220	3.4
1828	0.6		1808	0.9
11 0103	3.7	**26**	0037	3.4
0654	0.7		0621	1.0
M 1320	3.5		TU 1254	3.4
1911	0.8		1845	0.9
12 0149	3.4	**27**	0116	3.3
0734	1.0		0657	1.1
TU 1401	3.3		W 1331	3.3
1957	1.0		1926	1.0
13 0239	3.2	**28**	0159	3.2
0816	1.3		0737	1.2
W 1447	3.2		TH 1413	3.2
2053	1.2		2014	1.1
14 0336	2.9	**29**	0250	3.0
1024	1.6		0826	1.4
TH 1541	3.0		F 1504	3.1
◑ 2212	1.4		2119	1.2
15 0445	2.7	**30**	0353	2.9
1024	1.8		0934	1.6
F 1648	2.9		SA 1608	3.0
2347	1.4		◑ 2251	1.2
		31	0509	2.9
			1113	1.6
			SU 1725	3.0

NOVEMBER

Time	m		Time	m
1 0013	1.1	**16**	0106	1.4
0626	2.9		0727	2.8
M 1235	1.5		TU 1319	1.7
1839	3.1		1923	2.9
2 0121	1.0	**17**	0159	1.3
0737	3.1		0820	2.9
TU 1340	1.4		W 1412	1.5
1946	3.3		2018	3.0
3 0218	0.8	**18**	0239	1.2
0836	3.2		0902	3.1
W 1433	1.2		TH 1455	1.4
2046	3.5		2104	3.1
4 0306	0.6	**19**	0315	1.1
0926	3.4		0940	3.2
TH 1520	1.0		F 1532	1.2
2139	3.6		2145	3.2
5 0349	0.5	**20**	0348	1.0
1011	3.5		1014	3.3
F 1604	0.8		SA 1607	1.1
2228	3.7		2224	3.3
6 0431	0.6	**21**	0421	1.0
1054	3.6		1049	3.4
SA 1647	0.7		SU 1643	1.0
● 2315	3.7		○ 2303	3.4
7 0512	0.6	**22**	0454	1.0
1136	3.7		1124	3.5
SU 1731	0.7		M 1719	0.9
			2342	3.4
8 0001	3.7	**23**	0529	1.0
0552	0.8		1200	3.5
M 1217	3.6		TU 1757	0.9
1814	0.7			
9 0047	3.5	**24**	0023	3.4
0631	1.0		0606	1.0
TU 1257	3.5		W 1238	3.5
1859	0.8		1838	0.8
10 0133	3.3	**25**	0106	3.4
0711	1.2		0647	1.1
W 1338	3.4		TH 1318	3.5
1944	1.0		1923	0.9
11 0220	3.1	**26**	0152	3.3
0751	1.4		0731	1.2
TH 1421	3.3		F 1402	3.4
2033	1.1		2013	0.9
12 0311	2.9	**27**	0244	3.2
0835	1.6		0820	1.3
F 1509	3.1		SA 1453	3.3
2132	1.3		2113	1.0
13 0409	2.8	**28**	0342	3.1
0931	1.7		0919	1.5
SA 1606	3.0		SU 1551	3.2
◑ 2243	1.4		◑ 2225	1.0
14 0513	2.7	**29**	0448	3.0
1046	1.8		1035	1.5
SU 1712	2.9		M 1659	3.2
2358	1.4		2339	1.0
15 0622	2.7	**30**	0556	3.0
1207	1.8		1154	1.5
M 1820	2.9		TU 1808	3.2

DECEMBER

Time	m		Time	m
1 0047	1.0	**16**	0049	1.4
0702	3.0		0716	2.8
W 1305	1.4		TH 1316	1.7
1916	3.3		1920	2.9
2 0148	1.0	**17**	0148	1.4
0805	3.2		0813	2.9
TH 1408	1.3		F 1416	1.5
2022	3.3		2020	3.0
3 0242	0.9	**18**	0237	1.3
0900	3.3		0901	3.1
F 1503	1.1		SA 1505	1.4
2121	3.4		2112	3.1
4 0330	0.9	**19**	0319	1.2
0950	3.4		0943	3.2
SA 1553	1.0		SU 1547	1.2
2215	3.5		2200	3.2
5 0414	0.9	**20**	0358	1.2
1035	3.5		1024	3.4
SU 1639	0.9		M 1627	1.0
● 2304	3.5		2244	3.3
6 0455	0.9	**21**	0436	1.1
1118	3.6		1104	3.5
M 1723	0.8		TU 1707	0.9
2350	3.5		○ 2328	3.4
7 0536	1.0	**22**	0516	1.0
1159	3.6		1144	3.6
TU 1806	0.8		W 1749	0.7
8 0034	3.4	**23**	0012	3.5
0614	1.1		0556	1.0
W 1239	3.6		TH 1226	3.7
1847	0.8		1831	0.6
9 0117	3.3	**24**	0058	3.5
0651	1.2		0638	1.0
TH 1318	3.5		F 1308	3.7
1928	0.9		1916	0.6
10 0159	3.2	**25**	0144	3.4
0728	1.3		0722	1.0
F 1358	3.4		SA 1352	3.6
2008	1.0		2004	0.7
11 0241	3.0	**26**	0232	3.3
0805	1.4		0807	1.1
SA 1439	3.3		SU 1440	3.6
2051	1.2		2055	0.8
12 0327	2.9	**27**	0323	3.2
0846	1.5		0856	1.3
SU 1524	3.1		M 1532	3.4
2139	1.3		2154	0.9
13 0417	2.8	**28**	0419	3.1
0937	1.6		0955	1.4
M 1615	3.0		TU 1632	3.3
◑ 2238	1.4		◑ 2301	1.0
14 0514	2.7	**29**	0520	3.0
1045	1.7		1110	1.5
TU 1714	2.9		W 1738	3.2
2344	1.4			
15 0615	2.7	**30**	0011	1.2
1203	1.7		0625	3.0
W 1817	2.9		TH 1232	1.5
			1850	3.1
		31	0121	1.2
			0734	3.0
			F 1351	1.4
			2006	3.2

Chart Datum: 1·71 metres below Ordnance Datum (Newlyn). HAT is 4·0 metres above Chart Datum; see 0.19

5.18 SCRABSTER

Highland 58°36'·61N 03°32'·61W ✿✿✿❀△△✿✿✿

CHARTS AC 1954, 2162, 1462; Imray C68.

TIDES -0240 Dover; ML 3·2; Duration 0615

Standard Port WICK (←—)

Times				Height (metres)			
High Water		Low Water		MHWS	MHWN	MLWN	MLWS
0200	0700	0100	0700	3·5	2·8	1·4	0·7
1400	1900	1300	1900				
Differences SCRABSTER							
–0255	–0225	–0240	–0230	+1·5	+1·2	+0·8	+0·3
GILLS BAY							
–0150	–0150	–0202	–0202	+0·7	+0·7	+0·6	+0·3
STROMA							
–0115	–0115	–0110	–0110	–0·4	–0·5	–0·1	–0·2
LOCH ERIBOLL (Portnancon)							
–0340	–0255	–0315	–0255	+1·6	+1·3	+0·8	+0·4
KYLE OF DURNESS							
–0350	–0350	–0315	–0315	+1·1	+0·7	+0·4	–0·1
SULE SKERRY (59°05'N 04°24'W)							
–0320	–0255	–0315	–0250	+0·4	+0·3	+0·2	+0·1
RONA (59°08'N 05°49'W)							
–0410	–0345	–0330	–0340	–0·1	–0·2	–0·2	–0·1

SHELTER Very good except for swell in NW and N winds. Yachts usually lie in the Inner (0·9–1·2m) or Centre Basins (0·9–2·7m). ⚓ is not advised.

- A good hbr to await the right conditions for E-bound passage through Pentland Firth (see 5.4).
- Beware floating creel lines in W of hbr.

NAVIGATION WPT 58°36'·58N 03°32'·09W, 278°/0·25M to E pier lt. Can be entered H24 in all weathers. Beware FVs and the Orkney ferries.

LIGHTS AND MARKS No ldg marks/lts but entry is simple once the conspic ice plant tr and/or pier lts have been located. Do not confuse hbr lts with the shore lts of Thurso.

R/T Call HM VHF Ch 12 16 (H24) for berthing directions, before entering hbr. From the W reception is very poor due to masking by Holborn Head.

TELEPHONE (Code 01847) HM 892779, Mobile 07803 290366, www.scrabster.co.uk; MRCC (01224) 592334; Marinecall 09068 969641; Police 893222; Dr 893154.

FACILITIES Hbr AB £8.00 (£35/week), FW, D, P (cans), ME, EI, C (15, 30 & 99 ton mobiles), Slip, CH, ⬧; **Pentland Firth YC** M, R, Bar, Showers (keys held by Duty HM). **Thurso** 🛒, R, Bar, ✉, Ⓑ, ⇌, ✈ (Wick). **Ferries:** Stromness; 3/day; 1½ Hrs; Northlink (www.northlinkferries.co.uk). Faroe Islands (Torshavn); weekly (seasonal); 12 Hrs; Smyril (www.smyril.co.uk). Bergen; weekly (seasonal); 16 Hrs; Smyril.

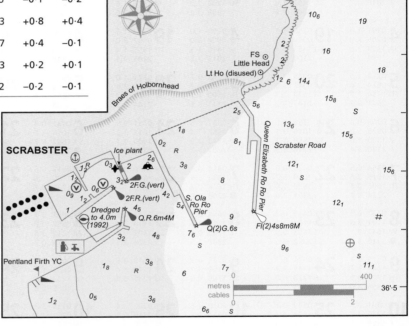

ANCHORAGES BETWEEN SCRABSTER AND CAPE WRATH
KYLE OF TONGUE, Highland, **58°31'·97N 04°22'·67W** (ent). AC 2720, 1954. HW +0050 on Ullapool; HW ht –0·4m; see 5.18. The Kyle runs about 7M inland.

- *Entry (see 5.4) should not be attempted in strong N winds.*

⚓ at Talmine (W of Rabbit Is) protected from all but NE winds; at Skullomie Hr, protected from E'lies; off Mol na Coinnle, a small bay on SE side of Eilean nan Ron, protected from W and N winds; off S of Rabbit Is, protected from W to N winds. No ldg lts/marks. Facilities: Limited 🛒 at Talmine (½M from slip) or at Coldbachie (1½M from Skullomie).

LOCH ERIBOLL, Highland, **58°32'·58N 04°37'·48W**. AC 2076. HW –0345 on Dover; ML 2·7m. See 5.18. Enter between Whiten Hd and Klourig Is in W sector of White Hd lt. See 5.3.

In SW winds fierce squalls funnel down the loch.

Yachts can enter Rispond Hbr, access approx HW ± 3, and dry out alongside; no lts/marks and very limited facilities. Good ⚓s at: Rispond Bay on W side of loch, ent good in all but E winds, in approx 5m; off Portnancon in 5·5m; at the head of the loch; Camus an Duin and in bays to N and S of peninsula at Heilam on E side of loch. Beware numerous marine farms in the S half of the loch.

PENTLAND FIRTH TO CAPE WRATH

(AC 1954) Dunnet B, S of Dunnet Hd (lt) gives temp anch in E or S winds, but dangerous seas enter in NW'lies. On W side of Thurso B is Scrabster sheltered from S and W. ► *Between Holborn Hd and Strathy Pt the E-going stream begins at HW Ullapool –0150, and the W-going at HW Ullapool + 0420, sp rates 1·8kn. Close to Brims Ness off Ushat Hd the sp rate is 3kn, and there is often turbulence.* ◄

SW of Ushat Hd the Dounreay power stn is conspic, near shore. Dangers extend 2½ca seaward off this coast.► *Along E side of Strathy Pt (lt) an eddy gives almost continuous N-going stream, but there is usually turbulence off the Pt where this eddy meets the main E or W stream.* ◄ Several small bays along this coast give temp anch in offshore winds, but should not be used or approached with wind in a N quarter.

Kyle of Tongue is entered from E through Caol Raineach, S of Eilean nan Ron, or from N between Eilean Iosal and Cnoc Glass. There is no chan into the kyle W of Rabbit Is, to which a drying spit extends 0·5M NNE from the mainland shore. Further S there is a bar across entrance to inner part of kyle. There are anchs on SE side of Eilean nan Ron, SE side of Rabbit Is, off Skullomie, or S of Eilean Creagach off Talmine. Approach to the latter runs close W of Rabbit Islands, but beware rks to N and NW of them.

Loch Eriboll (AC 2076) provides secure anchs, but in strong winds violent squalls blow down from mountains. Eilean Cluimhrig lies on W side of entrance; the E shore is fringed with rks up to 2ca offshore. At White Hd (lt) the loch narrows to 6ca. There are chans W and E of Eilean Choraidh. Best anchs in Camas an Duin (S of Ard Neackie) or in Rispond B close to entrance (but not in E winds, and beware Rispond Rk which dries).

The coast to C Wrath is indented, with dangers extending 3ca off the shore and offlying rks and Is. Once a yacht has left Loch Eriboll she is committed to a long and exposed passage until reaching Loch Inchard. The Kyle of Durness is dangerous if the wind or sea is onshore. ► *Give Cape Wrath a wide berth when wind-against-tide which raises a severe sea.* ◄ A firing exercise area extends 8M E of C. Wrath, and 4M offshore. When in use, R flags or pairs of R lts (vert) are shown from E and W limits, and yachts should keep clear.

ORKNEY ISLANDS

(AC 2249, 2250) The Islands are mostly indented and rocky, but with sandy beaches especially on NE sides. ►*Pilotage is easy in good vis, but in other conditions great care is needed since tides run strongly. For details refer to* **Clyde Cruising Club's Orkney Sailing Directions** *and the* **Admiralty Tidal Atlas NP 209.** *When cruising in Orkney it is essential to understand and use the tidal streams to the best advantage, avoiding the various tide races and overfalls, particularly near sp.* ◄

A good engine is needed since, for example, there are many places where it is dangerous to get becalmed. Swell from the Atlantic or North Sea can contribute to dangerous sea conditions, or penetrate to some of the anchorages. During summer months winds are not normally unduly strong, and can be expected to be Force 7 or more on about two days a month. But in winter the wind reaches this strength for 10-15 days per month, and gales can be very severe in late winter and early spring. Cruising conditions are best near midsummer, when of course the hours of daylight are much extended.

Stronsay Firth and Westray Firth run SE/NW through the group. The many good anchs include: Deer Sound (W of Deer Ness); B of Firth, B of Isbister, and off Balfour in Elwick B (all leading from Wide Firth); Rysa Sound, B of Houton, Hunda Sound (in Scapa Flow); Rousay Sound; and Pierowall Road (Westray). Plans for some of these are on AC 2622. There is a major oil terminal and prohibited area at Flotta, on the S side of Scapa Flow.

► *Tide races or dangerous seas occur at the entrances to most of the firths or sounds when the stream is against strong winds. This applies particularly to Hoy Sound, Eynhallow Sound, Papa Sound (Westray), Lashy Sound, and North Ronaldsay Firth. Also off Mull Head, over Dowie Sand, between Muckle Green Holm and War Ness (where violent turbulence may extend right across the firth), between Faraclett Head and Wart Holm, and off Sacquoy Hd. Off War Ness the SE-going stream begins at HW Aberdeen + 0435, and the NW-going at HW Aberdeen – 0200, sp rates 7kn.* ◄

5.19 ORKNEY ISLANDS

The Orkney Islands number about 70, of which some 24 are inhabited. They extend 5 to 50M NNE from Duncansby Hd, are mostly low-lying, but Hoy in the SW of the group reaches 475m (1560ft). Coasts are rocky and much indented, but there are many sandy beaches. A passage with least width of about 3M runs NW/SE through the group. The islands are separated from Scotland by the Pentland Firth, a very dangerous stretch of water. The principal island is Mainland (or Pomona) on which stands Kirkwall, the capital. For inter island ferries see www.orkneyferries.co.uk.

Severe gales blow in winter and early spring. The climate is mild but windy, and very few trees grow. There are LBs at Longhope, Stromness and Kirkwall.

CHARTS AC 2162, 2250 and 2249, at medium scale. For larger scale charts, see under individual hbrs. Imray C68.

TIDES Wick (5.17) is the Standard Port. Tidal streams are strong, particularly in Pentland Firth and in the islands' firths and sounds.

SHELTER/MARINA CHARGES There are piers (fender board advised) at all main islands. See 5.4 for details of berthing charges in marinas or on piers throughout the Orkney Islands (except St Margaret's Hope). Some of the many ⚓s are listed below:

MAINLAND Scapa Bay: good except in S winds. No yacht berths alongside pier due to heavy hbr traffic. Only ents to Scapa Flow are via Hoy Snd, Hoxa Snd or W of Flotta.
St Marys (Holm/Ham): 58°53'·80N 02°54'·50W; N side of Kirk Sound; ⚓ in B of Ayre or berth E side of Pier, HW±4. P & D (cans), ✉, Bar, R, Bus to Kirkwall & Burwick Ferry.

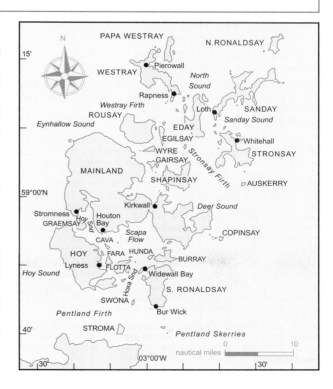

Kirk Sound (E ent): ⚓ N of Lamb Holm; beware fish cages.

Deer Sound: ⚓ in Pool of Mirkady or off pier on NW side of sound; very good shelter, no facilities.

Hunda Sound: good ⚓ in all winds.

SOUTH RONALDSAY/BURRAY St Margaret's Hope/Water Sound: ❀❀❀✿✿❀❀. Ldg Lts, F.G, 174°. ⚓ in centre of bay; or AB £7/day at pier (but limited space and keep clear of ferry berth on S side of pier), beware salmon farm. HM ☎ 01856 831440, mob 07879 688040; Dr 831206. FW, P & D (cans), ⛟, R, Bar, ✉, Bus Kirkwall, Vehicle ferry to Gill's Bay/Caithness.

Widewall Bay: ⚓ sheltered except SW'lies.

FLOTTA 58°50'·20N 03°07'·90W; berth on Sutherland Pier, SW of oil terminal. HM ☎ 01856 701411. P & D (cans), ⛟, ✉.

HOY Long Hope: 58°48'·07N 03°12'·25W; ⚓ E of Pier, used by ferry, or berth on pier (safest at slack water). 2 ⚲'s < 18 tonnes close to Pier. ☎ 01856 701263; Dr 701209. Facilities: FW, P & D (cans), ✉, ⛟, Bar.

Lyness: 58°50'·20N 03°11'·40W; berth on Pier; avoid disused piles; ⚓ in Ore Bay. HM ☎ 01856 791387. FW, P & D (cans), Bar, ✉. Beware fish cages.

Pegal Bay: good ⚓ except in strong W winds.

ROUSAY Wyre Sound: 59°09'·40N 02°44'·70W; ⚓ E of Rousay Pier or berth on it ✉, ⛟, R. Piermaster ☎ 01856 821261.

EDAY Fersness Bay: good holding, sheltered from S winds. Dr ☎ 01857 622243.

Backaland Bay: 59°09'·40N 02°44'·70W: berth on Pier clear of ferry; Piermaster ☎ 01856 622282; or ⚓ to NW. Beware cross tides. FW, P & D, ⛟, ✉.

Calf Sound: ⚓ in Carrick B; good shelter from SW-NW'lies.

PAPA WESTRAY Bay of Moclett 58°21'·40N 02°26'·30W: Good ⚓ but open to S. Pier . Piermaster ☎ 01857 644259;

South Wick: ⚓ off the old pier or ESE of pier off Holm of Papa. Backaskaill: P & D (cans), ⛟, ✉.

SANDAY Loth Bay: 59°11'·50N 02°41'·80W; berth on Pier clear of ferry. Piermaster ☎ 01857 600227; Beware strong tides.

Kettletoft Bay: 59°13'·90N 02°35'·80W; ⚓ in bay or berth on Pier, very exposed to SE'lies. HM ☎ (01857) 600227, Dr 600221; P & D (cans), FW, Gas, ✉, Ⓑ, hotel.

North Bay: on NW side of island, exposed to NW.

Otterswick: good ⚓ except in N or E winds.

NORTH RONALDSAY South Bay: 58°21'·40N 02°26'·30W; ⚓ in middle of bay or berth on Pier. Piermaster ☎ 01857 633239; open to S & W and swell. ⛟, ✉.

Linklet Bay: ⚓ off jetty at N of bay, open to E.

NAVIGATION From the mainland, appr from Scrabster to Stromness and Scapa Flow via Hoy Mouth and Hoy Sd. From the Moray Firth keep well E of the Pentland Skerries if going N to Kirkwall. If bound for Scapa Flow via Hoxa Sd, keep close to Duncansby Hd, passing W of the Pentland Skerries and between Swona and S Ronaldsay. Keep clear of Lother Rk (dries 1·8m) off SW tip of S Ronaldsay. Time this entry for slack water in the Pentland Firth (about HW Aberdeen –1¾ and +4). Beware of tankers off Flotta oil terminal and in S part of Scapa Flow, where are the remains of the German WW1 Battle Fleet; classified as Historic Wrecks (see 0.31) protected, but authorised diving allowed.

Elsewhere in Orkney navigation is easy in clear weather, apart from the strong tidal streams in all the firths and sounds. Beware races and overfalls off Brough of Birsay (Mainland), Noup Head (Westray) and Dennis Head (N Ronaldsay). Keep a good lookout for the many lobster pots (creels).

LIGHTS AND MARKS The main hbrs and sounds are well lit; for details see 5.3. Powerful lts are shown offshore from Cantick Hd, Graemsay Island, Copinsay, Auskerry, Kirkwall, Brough of Birsay, Sanday Island, N Ronaldsay and Noup Hd.

R/T Orkney Hbrs Navigation Service (call: *Orkney Hbr Radio*, Ch 09 11 20 16 (H24)) covers Scapa Flow and apprs, Wide Firth, Shapinsay Sound and Kirkwall Bay.

TELEPHONE Area Code for islands SW of Stronsay and Westray Firths is 01856; islands to the NE are 01857.

MEDICAL SERVICES Doctors are available at Kirkwall, Stromness, Rousay, Hoy, Shapinsay, Eday, S and N Ronaldsay, Stronsay, Sanday and Westray (Pierowall); Papa Westray is looked after by Westray. The only hospital (and dentist) are at Kirkwall. Serious cases are flown to Aberdeen (1 hour).

MARINE FARMS Fish cages/farms approx 30m x 50m may be found anywhere in sheltered waters within anchoring depths. Some are well buoyed, others are marked only by poles. Too many to list but the following will show the scale of the operations:

Beware **salmon cages** (may be marked by Y buoys/lts) at:

Kirkwall Bay	Toy Ness (Scapa Flow)
Rysa Sound	St Margaret's Hope
Bring Deeps	Backaland Bay (Eday)
Pegal Bay (Hoy)	Hunda Sound
Lyrawa Bay	Kirk Sound
Ore Bay (Hoy)	Carness Bay
Widewall Bay (S Ronaldsay)	Bay of Ham
	Bay of London (Eday)

Beware **oysters and longlines** at:

Widewall Bay	Bay of Firth
Swanbister Bay	Damsay Sound
Water Sound	Millburn Bay (Gairsay)
Hunda Sound	Pierowall
Deer Sound	Bay of Skaill (Westray)
Inganess Bay	Longhope

MINOR HARBOURS IN THE ORKNEY ISLANDS

HOUTON BAY, Mainland, **58°54'·85N 03°11'·33W**. AC 35, 2568. HW –0140 on Dover, –0400 on Aberdeen; HW ht +0·3m on Kirkwall; ML 1·8m; Duration 0615. ⚓ in the bay in approx 5·5m at centre, sheltered from all winds. Ent is to the E of Holm of Houton; ent chan dredged 3·5m for 15m each side of ldg line. Keep clear of shipping/ferries plying to Flotta. Ldg lts 316°: front Fl G 3s 8m, rear FG 16m; both R △ on W pole, B bands. Ro Ro terminal in NE corner marked by Iso R 4s with SHM Fl G on edge of ldg line. Bus to Kirkwall; Slip close E of piers. Yachtsmen may contact **M.Grainger** ☎ 01856 811397 for help.

SHAPINSAY, Orkney Islands, **59°01'·97N 02°54'·10W**. AC 2249, 2584. HW –0015 on Dover, –0330 on Aberdeen; HW ht –1·0m on Aberdeen. Good shelter in Elwick Bay off Balfour on SW end of island in 2·5-3m. Enter bay passing W of Helliar Holm which has lt Fl WRG 10s on S end. Keep mid-chan. Balfour Pier lt Q WRG 5m 3/2M; vis 270°-G-010°-W-020°-R-090°. Piermaster ☎ 01856 711358; Tides in The String reach 5kn at sp. Facilities: FW, P & D (cans), ✉, shop, Bar.

AUSKERRY, Orkney Islands, **59°02'·02N 02°34'·65W**. AC 2250. HW –0010 on Dover, -0315 on Aberdeen, HW ht -1m on Aberdeen. Small island at ent to Stronsay Firth with small hbr on W side. Safe ent and good shelter except in SW winds. Ent has 3·5m; 1·2m alongside pier. Yachts can lie secured between ringbolts at ent and the pier. Auskerry Sound and Stronsay Firth are dangerous with wind over tide. Auskerry lt at S end, Fl 20s 34m 18M, W tr. No facilities.

PIEROWALL, Westray, **59°19'·32N 02°58'·51W**. AC 2250, 2622. HW –0135 on Dover; ML 2·2m; Duration 0620. See 5.22. The bay is a good ⚓ in 2-7m and well protected. Marina pontoons in deep water alongside pier at Gill Pt. From S, beware Skelwick Skerry rks, and from the N the rks extending approx 1ca off Vest Ness. The N ent via Papa Sound needs local knowledge; tide race on the ebb. A dangerous tide race runs off Mull Hd at the N of Papa Westray. Lights: E Pier Hd Fl WRG 3s 7m 11/7M. W Pier Hd 2 FR (vert) 4/6m 3M. VHF Ch 16. HM ☎ (01857) 677216. **Marina** ☎ 07810 465784 AB £15/craft, FW, ⚡. Facilities: P & D (cans), Gas, Bar, ✉, Ⓑ, R, ⛟. Dr ☎ (01857) 677209.

RAPNESS: 58°14'·90N 02°51'·50W, berth on Pier clear of Ro-Ro. Piermaster ☎ 01857 677212; Open to SSW.

5.20 STROMNESS

Orkney Islands, Mainland **58°57'·78N 03°17'·72W** ❀❀🐚⚓⚓❀❀❀

CHARTS AC 2249, 2568; Imray C68.

TIDES −0145 Dover; ML 2·0; Duration 0620

Standard Port WICK (←)

Times				Height (metres)			
High Water		Low Water		MHWS	MHWN	MLWN	MLWS
0000	0700	0200	0700	3·5	2·8	1·4	0·7
1200	1900	1400	1900				
Differences STROMNESS							
−0225	−0135	−0205	−0205	+0·1	−0·1	0·0	0·0
ST MARY'S (Scapa Flow)							
−0140	−0140	−0140	−0140	−0·2	−0·2	0·0	−0·1
BURRAY NESS (Burray)							
+0005	+0015	+0015	+0015	−0·2	−0·3	−0·1	−0·1
WIDEWALL BAY (S Ronaldsay)							
−0155	−0155	−0150	−0150	+0·1	−0·1	−0·1	−0·3
BUR WICK (S Ronaldsay)							
−0100	−0100	−0150	−0150	−0·1	−0·1	+0·2	+0·1
MUCKLE SKERRY (Pentland Firth)							
−0025	−0025	−0020	−0020	−0·9	−0·8	−0·4	−0·3

SHELTER Very good. Northern Lights Board have sole use of pier near to ldg lts. Marina in N of hbr; or ⚓ where shown.

NAVIGATION WPT 58°56'·93N 03°17'·00W, 317°/0·9M to front ldg lt.

- Entry from the W should not be attempted with strong wind against tide due to heavy overfalls.
- If entering against the ebb, stand on to avoid being swept onto Skerry of Ness.
- Tides in Hoy Sound are >7kn at springs. No tidal stream in hbr.

LIGHTS AND MARKS For Hoy Sound, ldg lts 104° on Graemsay Is: front Iso 3s 17m 15M, W tr; rear Oc WR 8s 35m 20/16M, ldg sector is 097°-R-112°. Skerry of Ness, Fl WG 4s 7m 7/4M; shore-W-090°-G-shore. Hbr ldg lts 317°, both FR 29/39m 11M (H24), W trs, vis 307°-327°. Stromness Marina ent. Fl(2)R 5s.

R/T VHF Ch 14 16 (0900-1700 LT). (See also 5.21.)

TELEPHONE (Code 01856) HM 850744; Fuel 851286; MRCC 01595 692976; Marinecall 09068 969641; Police 850222; Dr 850205; Dentist 850658.

FACILITIES Stromness Marina: ☎ 07810 465825, 10❿ £16.50/craft, ⬒, FW, Showers, 🚻, ⚒, El, Ⓔ, ME, C (mobile, 30 ton), P & D (0800-2100 ☎ 8851286), Slip. **Town** FW, D, 🛒, R, Bar, Gas, ✉, ▣, Ⓑ, ⇋ (Ferries to Scrabster, bus to Thurso), ✈ (Kirkwall). Yachtsmen may contact for help/advice: **Orkney Marinas** ☎ 871313 or **Piermaster** ☎ 850744.

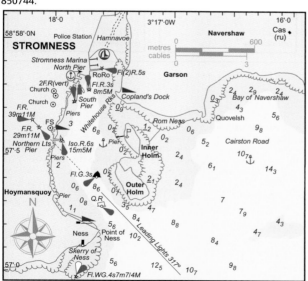

5.21 KIRKWALL

Orkney Islands, Mainland **58°59'·30N 02°57'·70W** ❀❀❀🐚⚓⚓❀❀❀

CHARTS AC 2250, 2249, 2584, 1553; Imray C68.

TIDES −0045 Dover; ML 1·8; Duration 0620

Standard Port WICK (←)

Times				Height (metres)			
High Water		Low Water		MHWS	MHWN	MLWN	MLWS
0000	0700	0200	0700	3·5	2·8	1·4	0·7
1200	1900	1400	1900				
Differences KIRKWALL							
−0042	−0042	−0041	−0041	−0·5	−0·4	−0·1	−0·1
DEER SOUND							
−0040	−0040	−0035	−0035	−0·3	−0·3	−0·1	−0·1
TINGWALL							
−0200	−0125	−0145	−0125	−0·4	−0·4	−0·1	−0·1

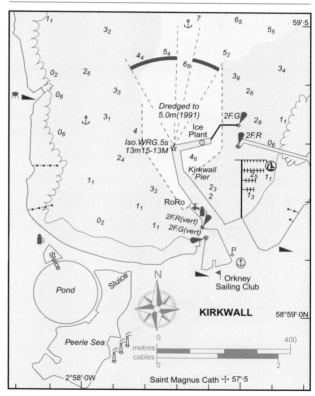

SHELTER Good except in N winds or W gales when there is a surge at the ent. Berth in marina on E of main pier, or SW end of main pier in inner hbr (very full in Jun/Jul). Safe ⚓ between pier and Crow Ness Pt. RoRo terminal in NW of bay.

NAVIGATION WPT 59°01'·37N 02°57'·10W, 188°/2·2M to pier hd lt. Appr in W sector of pier hd lt. Bay is shoal to SW.

LIGHTS AND MARKS See 5.3 and chartlet. Appr with St Magnus Cathedral (conspic) brg about 185°.

R/T *Kirkwall Hbr Radio* VHF Ch 14 16 (0800-1700 LT). Orkney Hbrs Navigation Service, call: *VTS Orkney* Ch 09 11 20 16 (0915–1715).

TELEPHONE (Code 01856) HM 872292; Port Office 873636; Fuel 873105; MRCC (01595) 692976; Weather 873802; Marinecall 09068 969641; Police 872241; Dr 888000 (Ⓗ).

FACILITIES Kirkwall Marina ☎ 871313 (berths 07810 465835), 71 inc ❿ £16.50/craft. **Pier** P & D (HO ☎ 872292), FW, CH, C (mob, 25 ton), slip; **N and E Quays** M; **Orkney SC** ☎ 872331, M, L, C, AB (£15/4days), Slip. **Town** @ Library & Support Training Orkney (HO) P, D, ME, El, ⚒, CH, 🛒, 🍴, Gas, R, Bar, Ⓑ, ▣, ✉, Ferries to Scrabster, Aberdeen and Shetland, ✈.

5.22 STRONSAY

Orkney Islands, Stronsay 59°08'·57N 02°36'·01W ✿✿❀✿✿

CHARTS AC 2250, 2622; Imray C68.

TIDES As Dover; ML 1·7; Duration 0620

Standard Port WICK (◄——)

Times				Height (metres)			
High Water		Low Water		MHWS	MHWN	MLWN	MLWS
0000	0700	0200	0700	3·5	2·8	1·4	0·7
1200	1900	1400	1900				
Differences WHITEHALL (Stronsay)							
–0030	–0030	–0025	–0030	–0·1	0·0	+0·2	+0·2
LOTH (Sanday)							
–0052	–0052	–0058	–0058	–0·1	0·0	+0·3	+0·4
EGILSAY (Rousay Sound)							
–0125	–0125	–0125	–0125	–0·1	0·0	+0·2	+0·1
KETTLETOFT PIER (Sanday)							
–0030	–0025	–0025	–0025	0·0	0·0	+0·2	+0·2
RAPNESS (Westray)							
–0205	–0205	–0205	–0205	+0·1	0·0	+0·2	0·0
PIEROWALL (Westray)							
–0150	–0150	–0145	–0145	+0·2	0·0	0·0	–0·1

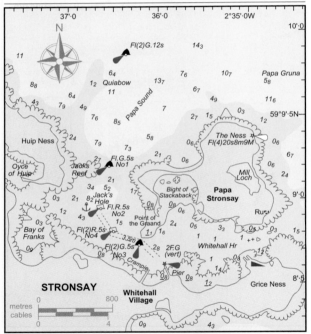

SHELTER Good from all winds. Good ⚓ between seaward end of piers, or berth on outer end of W pier and contact HM. The extended E pier head is berth for Ro-Ro ferry. There are many other sheltered ⚓s around the bay.

NAVIGATION WPT 59°09'·82N 02°36'·31W, Quiabow SHM lt buoy, 189°/6·5ca to No 1 lt buoy. 800m NE of Huip Ness is Quiabow, a submerged rk. Jack's Reef extends 400m E from Huip Ness, and is marked by No 1 SHM lt buoy. A bank extends 350m SW from Papa Stronsay. Crampie Shoal is in mid-chan, marked by No 3 buoy. The buoyed chan to Whitehall pier is dredged 3·5m. Spit to E of Whitehall pier extends 400m N. The E ent is narrow and shallow and should not be attempted.

LIGHTS AND MARKS See chartlet.

R/T See Kirkwall.

TELEPHONE (Code 01857) Piermaster 616317; MRCC (01595) 692976; Marinecall 09068 969641; Police (01856) 872241; Dr 616321.

FACILITIES **W Pier** M, L, AB; **Main (E) Pier** M, L, FW, AB clear of ferry. **Village (Whitehall)** P, D, 🛒, Bar, ✉, Ⓑ, ⚉ (Ferry to Scrabster, bus to Thurso), ✈.

SHETLAND ISLANDS

(AC 3281, 3282, 3283) ► *These Islands mostly have bold cliffs and are relatively high, separated by narrow sounds through which the tide runs strongly, so that in poor vis great care is needed. Avoid sp tides, swell and wind against tide conditions. The tidal flow around the Shetland Islands rotates as the cycle progresses. When the flood begins, at –0400 HW Dover, the tidal flow is to the E, at HW Dover it is S, at Dover +0300 it is W, and at –0600 Dover it is N.*◄

Although there are many secluded and attractive anchs, remember that the weather can change very quickly, with sudden shifts of wind. Also beware salmon fisheries and mussel rafts (unlit) in many Voes, Sounds and hbrs. Lerwick is the busy main port and capital; other hbrs are Scalloway, Vaila Sound and Balta Sound. Refer to the CCC's *Shetland Sailing Directions.*

► *Coming from the S, beware a most violent and dangerous race (roost) off Sumburgh Hd (at S end of Mainland) on both streams. Other dangerous areas include between Ve Skerries and Papa Stour; the mouth of Yell Sound with strong wind against N-going stream; and off Holm of Skaw (N end of Unst). Tidal streams run mainly NW/SE and are not strong except off headlands and in the major sounds; the Admiralty Tidal Atlas NP 209 gives detail. The sp range is about 2m.*◄

The 50M passage from Orkney can conveniently be broken by a stop at Fair Isle (North Haven). ► *Note that races form off both ends of the Is, especially S (Roost of Keels).*◄

Recommended Traffic Routes: NW-bound ships pass to the NE (no closer than 10M to Sumburgh Hd) or SW of Fair Isle; SE-bound ships pass no closer than 5M off N Ronaldsay (Orkney). Lerwick to Bergen, Norway, is about 210M.

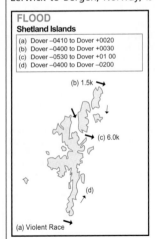

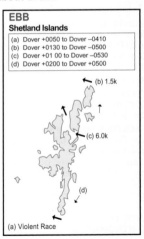

5.23 SHETLAND ISLANDS

The Shetland Islands number about 100 islands, holms and rks with fewer than 20 inhabited. Lying 90 to 150M NNE of the Scottish mainland, the biggest island is Mainland with Lerwick (5.24), the capital, on the E side. Scalloway, the only other town and old capital, is on the W side. At the very S is Sumburgh airport, with other airstrips at Baltasound, Scalsta and Tingwall. Two offlying islands of the Shetland group are Fair Isle, 20M SSW of Sumburgh Hd and owned by the NT for Scotland, and Foula, 12M WSW of Mainland. There are LBs at Lerwick and Aith. The MRCC is at Lerwick, ☎ (01595) 692976, with an Auxilliary Stn at Fair I.

CHARTS AC: medium scale 3281, 3282, 3283; larger scale 3271, 3272, 3292, 3293, 3294, 3295, 3297, 3298.

TIDES Standard Port Lerwick. Tidal streams run mostly N-S or NW-SE; in open waters to the E and W they are mostly weak. Rates >6kn can cause dangerous disturbances at the N and S extremities of the islands and in the two main sounds (Yell Sound and BlueMull/Colgrave Sounds). Keep 3M off Sumburgh Head to clear a dangerous race (Röst) or pass close inshore.

SHELTER Weather conditions are bad in winter; yachts should only visit Apr–Sept. Around mid-summer it is daylight H24. Some small marinas are asterisked* below (see www.visitshetland.com); they may have room for visitors. Of the many ⚓s, the following are safe to enter in most conditions:

MAINLAND (anti-clockwise from Sumburgh Head)

Grutness Voe: 1·5M N of Sumburgh Hd, a convenient passage ⚓, open to NE. Beware 2 rocks awash in mid-ent.

Pool of Virkie*: 59°53'N 01°17W; Close N of Grutness Voe. Ness Boating Club Marina ☎ 01950 477260, AB (pontoon 1⚑< 1m £10/craft/week, slip, ⟲, FW, toilet. Shallow and narrow/entrance, otherwise ⚓ Grutness Voe.

Cat Firth: excellent shelter, ⚓ in approx 6m. Facilities: ✉ (Skellister), FW, 🛒 (both at Lax Firth).

Grunna Voe: off S side of Dury Voe, good shelter and holding, ⚓ in 5-10m; beware prohib ⚓ areas. Facilities: 🛒, FW, ✉ (Lax Firth).

Whalsay*: 60°20'·60N 01°01'·60W; Fishing hbr with small marina at Symbister welcomes visitors. FW, D, AB (pontoon or pier 20⚑s) £7.17/craft/4 days, ⟲, ME, FW, D, P, toilet/showers, 🛒, R, Bar, ✉.

Out Skerries*: 60°25'N 00°45'W; Pier (£2/craft/night); Small Boat Marina (£7.17/craft/4 days). ⟲, FW, D (by arrangement), toilet/showers, 🛒, ✉. Good ⚓ at Bruray.

South of Yell Sound*: Tides –0025 on Lerwick. W of Lunna Ness, well protected ⚓s with good holding include: Boatsroom Voe, W Lunna Voe (small hotel, FW), Colla Firth* and Dales Voe. No facilities.

Sullom Voe: Tides –0130 on Lerwick. 6·5M long deep water voe, partly taken over by the oil industry. ⚓ S of the narrows. Facilities at Brae: FW, 🛒, ✉, D, ME, El, ✕, Bar.

Hamna Voe: Tides –0200 on Lerwick; very good shelter. Ldg line 153° old house on S shore with prominent rock on pt of W shore 3ca within ent. Almost land-locked; ⚓ in 6m approx, but bottom foul with old moorings. Facilities: ✉ (0·5M), Vs, D (1·5M), L (at pier).

Ura Firth: NE of St Magnus Bay, ⚓ off Hills Wick on W side or in Hamar Voe (no facilities) on E side, which has excellent shelter/good holding in all weathers. Facilities: **Hills Wick** FW, ✉, D, ME, El, ✕, 🛒, R, Bar.

Busta Voe: N of Swarsbacks Minn; AB ⚑s at Delting Boating Club's 52-berth marina; ☎ 01806 522479.

Olna Firth: NE of Swarbacks Minn, beware rk 1ca off S shore which dries. ⚓ in firth, 4-8m or in Gon Firth or go alongside pier at Voe. Facilities: (Voe) FW, 🛒, D, ✉, Bar.

Swarbacks Minn*: a large complex of voes and isles SE of St Magnus Bay. Best ⚓ Uyea Sound or Aith Voe, both well sheltered and good holding. No facilities.

Aith Voe*: 60°17'·3N 01°22·3W; Good shelter from all directions. FW, D, AB depth LW 1.2m (pontoon2 ⚑s) otherwise on Pier access H24, ⟲, FW, slip, ME, ✕, toilet/showers (leisure centre), 🛒, R, Bar, ✉.

Vaila Sound: on SW of Mainland, ent via Easter Sound (do not attempt Wester Sound); very good shelter, ⚓ N of Salt Ness in 4-5m in mud. See WALLS* overleaf: FW, 🛒, ✉.

Gruting Voe*: HW –0150 on Lerwick, ⚓ in main voe or in Seli, Scutta or Browland* voes. Facilities: 🛒 and ✉ at Bridge of Walls (head of Browland Voe).

Hamna Voe*: 60°06·3'N 01°20·3W (West Burra) Entered between Fugla Ness and Alta Ness. Open to the NW; good shelter in small marina. Limited facilities in small village.

YELL Mid Yell Voe*: 60°36'N 01°03·4W; tides –0040 on Lerwick,

enter via S Sd or Hascosay Sd, good ⚓ in wide part of voe 2·5-10m. Berth at marina £5/week or Pier £7.17/4 days/craft. Facilities: ✉, FW at pier on S side, D, 🛒, ME, ✕, El.

Basta Voe: good ⚓ above shingle bank in 5-15m; good holding in places. Facilities: FW, 🛒, Hotel, ✉.

Blue Mull Sound/Cullivoe*: 60°42'N 00°59'·7W; Hbr with small craft marina depth 1.2m AB £5/craft/day. FW, D, AB pier 20⚑s £7.17/craft/4 days, ⟲, ME, FW, D, P,toilet/showers, 🛒, R, Bar, ✉. ⚓ off pier and slip. D, FW, 🛒.

Burra Voe*: 60°29'·8N 01°02'·4W; Entrance to voe has 2.5m bar. Good ⚓ at head of voe. AB at small marina £5/visit or on Pier £12/visit , FW, toilets ⟲, 🛒, Bar ✉.

FOULA: Ham Voe on E side has tiny hbr/pier, unsafe in E'ly; berth clear of mailboat. Avoid Hoevdi Grund, 2M ESE.

NAVIGATION A careful lookout must be kept for marine farms, mostly marked by Y buoys and combinations of Y lts. Clyde CC's *Shetland Sailing Directions and Anchorages* are essential for visitors. Local magnetic anomalies may be experienced.

Note: There are two Historic Wrecks (*Kennemerland* and *Wrangels Palais*) on Out Skerries at 60°25'·2N 00°45'·0W and 60°25'·5N 00°43'·3W (see 0.31).

LIGHTS AND MARKS See 5.3. Powerful lighthouses at Fair I, Sumburgh Hd, Kirkabister Ness, Bound Skerry, Muckle Flugga, Pt of Fethaland, Esha Ness and Foula.

R/T For Port Radio services see 5.24. No Coast Radio Station.

TELEPHONE (Code 01595; 01806 for Sullom Voe) MRCC 692976; Sullom Voe Port Control (01806) 242551, 📠 242237; Weather 692239; Forecaster (01806) 242069; Sumburgh Airport (01950) 460654.

FACILITIES All stores obtainable in Lerwick and Scalloway. Elsewhere in Shetland there is little available and yachts should be well provisioned for extended offshore cruising.

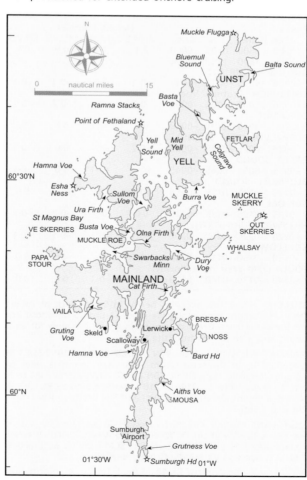

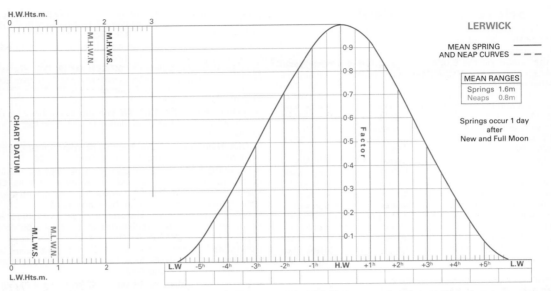

LERWICK

MEAN SPRING ———
AND NEAP CURVES – – –

MEAN RANGES
Springs 1.6m
Neaps 0.8m

Springs occur 1 day after New and Full Moon

5.24 LERWICK

Shetland Is, Mainland 60°09'·26N 01°08'·42W ❀❀❀♒♒✿✿

CHARTS AC 3283, 3272, 3271.

TIDES –0001 Dover; ML 1·4; Duration 0620

Standard Port LERWICK (←)

Times				Height (metres)			
High Water		Low Water		MHWS	MHWN	MLWN	MLWS
0000	0600	0100	0800	2·1	1·7	0·9	0·5
1200	1800	1300	2000				
Differences FAIR ISLE							
–0006	–0015	–0031	–0037	+0·1	0·0	+0·1	+0·1
SUMBURGH (Grutness Voe)							
+0006	+0008	+0004	–0002	–0·3	–0·3	–0·2	–0·1
DURY VOE							
–0015	–0015	–0010	–0010	0·0	–0·1	0·0	–0·2
BURRA VOE (YELL SOUND)							
–0025	–0025	–0025	–0025	+0·2	+0·1	0·0	–0·1
BALTA SOUND							
–0055	–0055	–0045	–0045	+0·2	+0·1	0·0	–0·1
BLUEMULL SOUND							
–0135	–0135	–0155	–0155	+0·5	+0·2	+0·1	0·0
SULLOM VOE							
–0135	–0125	–0135	–0120	0·0	0·0	–0·2	–0·2
HILLSWICK (URA FIRTH)							
–0220	–0220	–0200	–0200	–0·1	–0·1	–0·1	–0·1
SCALLOWAY							
–0150	–0150	–0150	–0150	–0·5	–0·4	–0·3	0·0
FOULA (23M West of Scalloway)							
–0140	–0130	–0140	–0120	–0·1	–0·1	0·0	0·0

SHELTER Good. HM allocates berths in Small Dock or Albert Dock. FVs occupy most alongside space. ⚓ prohib for about 2ca off the waterfront. Gremista marina in N hbr, is mainly for local boats, and is about 1M from the town.

NAVIGATION WPT 60°05'·97N 01°08'·62W, 010°/3·5M to Maryfield lt, in W sector. From S, Bressay Sound is clear of dangers. From N, WPT 60°11'·60N 01°07'·88W, 215°/1·34M to N ent Dir lt (Oc WRG 6s, 214°-W-216°). Beware Soldian Rk (dries), Nive Baa (0·6m), Green Holm (10m) and The Brethren (two rocks 2m and 1·5m).

LIGHTS AND MARKS Kirkabister Ness, Fl (2) 20s 32m 23M; Cro of Ham, Fl 3s 3M; Maryfield, Oc WRG 6s, 008°-W-013°; all on Bressay. Twageos Pt, L Fl 6s 8m 6M. Loofa Baa SCM lt bn, as on chartlet. 2 SHM lt buoys mark Middle Ground in N Hbr.

R/T Lerwick Harbour VHF Ch **12** 16 (H24) for Vessel Information

Service. Other stns: *Sullom Voe Hbr Radio* broadcasts traffic info and local forecasts on request Ch **14** 12 20 16 (H24).

TELEPHONE (Code 01595) HM 692991; MRCC 692976; Weather 692239; Police 692110; Dr 693201.

FACILITIES Hbr Slip, M, P, D, L, FW, ME, ✗, Gas; **Lerwick Hbr Trust** ☎ 692991, Ⓥ pontoons £0.60, 🛢, M, FW, D, P, ♿ ramps/toilet; **Lerwick Boating Club** ☎ 692407, L, C, Bar, ▣; **Services:** ME, El, Ⓔ, ✗, Slip, BY, CH, SM, Gas, ACA. **Town** 🍴, R, Bar, ✉, Ⓑ, @, **Ferries:** Aberdeen via Kirkwall; daily; overnight; North Link (www.northlinkferries.co.uk), ✈. See www.shetland.news.co.uk and www.lerwickboating.co.uk.

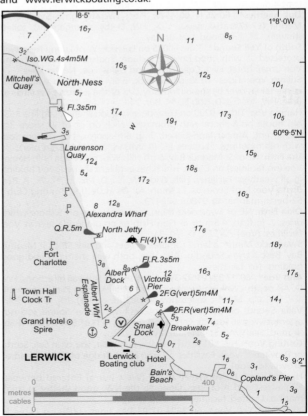

TIME ZONE (UT)
For Summer Time add ONE hour in **non-shaded areas**

LERWICK LAT 60°09'N LONG 1°08'W
TIMES AND HEIGHTS OF HIGH AND LOW WATERS

Dates in red are SPRINGS
Dates in blue are NEAPS

YEAR **2010**

NE Scotland

JANUARY

Time	m		Time	m
1 0442	0.7	**16** 0518	0.8
1057	2.3	1133	2.2
F 1714	0.4	SA 1749	0.6
2336	2.3		
2 0529	0.7	**17** 0006	2.0
1145	2.4	0549	0.8
SA 1801	0.3	SU 1205	2.2
		1819	0.6
3 0027	2.3	**18** 0039	2.0
0614	0.7	0619	0.8
SU 1233	2.4	M 1236	2.2
1848	0.3	1850	0.6
4 0117	2.2	**19** 0110	2.0
0658	0.7	0649	0.8
M 1321	2.4	TU 1306	2.1
1936	0.3	1921	0.6
5 0205	2.1	**20** 0141	1.9
0744	0.7	0721	0.8
TU 1410	2.3	W 1337	2.1
2025	0.4	1954	0.7
6 0252	2.0	**21** 0214	1.9
0831	0.8	0756	0.9
W 1501	2.2	TH 1413	2.0
2117	0.6	2030	0.8
7 0342	1.9	**22** 0253	1.8
0923	0.9	0836	1.0
TH 1555	2.1	F 1456	1.9
◗ 2217	0.8	2112	0.8
8 0436	1.8	**23** 0339	1.8
1029	1.0	0925	1.0
F 1658	1.9	SA 1547	1.8
2330	0.9	◑ 2204	0.9
9 0539	1.8	**24** 0434	1.7
1203	1.0	1033	1.1
SA 1813	1.8	SU 1650	1.8
		2316	1.0
10 0046	1.0	**25** 0541	1.7
0651	1.8	1210	1.1
SU 1327	1.0	M 1807	1.7
1931	1.8		
11 0151	1.0	**26** 0044	1.0
0757	1.9	0659	1.8
M 1432	0.9	TU 1330	1.0
2040	1.8	1934	1.8
12 0245	1.0	**27** 0155	1.0
0854	2.0	0809	1.9
TU 1523	0.8	W 1433	0.8
2135	1.9	2044	1.9
13 0330	0.9	**28** 0254	0.9
0942	2.1	0906	2.0
W 1605	0.8	TH 1527	0.6
2219	2.0	2143	2.1
14 0409	0.9	**29** 0345	0.7
1022	2.1	0957	2.2
TH 1643	0.7	F 1616	0.4
2258	2.2	2236	2.2
15 0445	0.9	**30** 0432	0.6
1059	2.2	1046	2.3
F 1716	0.6	SA 1702	0.2
● 2333	2.0	○ 2325	2.2
		31 0515	0.5
		1133	2.4
		SU 1746	0.1

FEBRUARY

Time	m		Time	m
1 0011	2.3	**16** 0011	2.0
0557	0.5	0554	0.6
M 1219	2.5	TU 1211	2.2
1829	0.1	1820	0.5
2 0056	2.2	**17** 0039	2.0
0638	0.5	0623	0.6
TU 1304	2.4	W 1239	2.1
1913	0.2	1849	0.5
3 0138	2.1	**18** 0106	1.9
0720	0.5	0655	0.6
W 1348	2.3	TH 1309	2.1
1957	0.4	1920	0.6
4 0220	2.0	**19** 0137	1.9
0803	0.6	0728	0.7
TH 1434	2.2	F 1343	2.0
2042	0.6	1954	0.7
5 0303	1.9	**20** 0212	1.9
0850	0.8	0807	0.8
F 1524	2.0	SA 1423	1.9
◗ 2132	0.8	2033	0.8
6 0350	1.8	**21** 0254	1.8
0949	0.9	0853	0.9
SA 1621	1.8	SU 1513	1.8
2237	1.0	2121	0.9
7 0448	1.7	**22** 0348	1.7
1130	1.0	0956	1.0
SU 1740	1.7	M 1619	1.7
		◑ 2229	1.0
8 0010	1.1	**23** 0456	1.7
0609	1.7	1133	1.0
M 1313	1.0	TU 1742	1.6
1916	1.6		
9 0132	1.1	**24** 0018	1.0
0734	1.7	0623	1.7
TU 1423	0.9	W 1311	0.9
2032	1.7	1922	1.7
10 0231	1.0	**25** 0143	1.0
0838	1.8	0749	1.8
W 1513	0.8	TH 1419	0.7
2123	1.8	2035	1.8
11 0317	1.0	**26** 0243	0.8
0926	1.9	0850	2.0
TH 1552	0.7	F 1513	0.5
2203	1.9	2131	2.0
12 0354	0.9	**27** 0331	0.7
1005	2.0	0941	2.1
F 1625	0.6	SA 1559	0.3
2238	1.9	2220	2.1
13 0427	0.8	**28** 0414	0.5
1040	2.1	1029	2.3
SA 1655	0.5	SU 1643	0.1
2310	2.0	○ 2305	2.2
14 0457	0.7		
1113	2.1		
SU 1724	0.5		
● 2341	2.0		
15 0526	0.6		
1143	2.2		
M 1752	0.5		

MARCH

Time	m		Time	m
1 0455	0.4	**16** 0458	0.5
1114	2.4	1114	2.1
M 1725	0.1	TU 1720	0.4
2348	2.2	2338	2.0
2 0535	0.3	**17** 0528	0.5
1158	2.4	1143	2.1
TU 1806	0.1	W 1749	0.4
3 0028	2.2	**18** 0006	2.0
0615	0.3	0558	0.5
W 1241	2.4	TH 1213	2.1
1846	0.2	1819	0.4
4 0107	2.1	**19** 0034	2.0
0656	0.4	0631	0.5
TH 1324	2.3	F 1245	2.0
1927	0.4	1851	0.5
5 0145	2.0	**20** 0105	1.9
0738	0.5	0707	0.6
F 1408	2.1	SA 1320	2.0
2008	0.6	1926	0.6
6 0224	1.9	**21** 0140	1.9
0824	0.7	0748	0.6
SA 1455	1.9	SU 1403	1.9
2052	0.8	2006	0.7
7 0308	1.8	**22** 0221	1.8
0921	0.8	0837	0.7
SU 1551	1.7	M 1456	1.7
◗ 2149	1.0	2056	0.9
8 0401	1.7	**23** 0315	1.7
1059	0.9	0942	0.8
M 1706	1.5	TU 1606	1.6
2327	1.1	◑ 2207	1.0
9 0518	1.6	**24** 0428	1.6
1247	0.9	1117	0.8
TU 1856	1.5	W 1734	1.6
10 0103	1.1	**25** 0003	1.0
0703	1.6	0558	1.6
W 1359	0.8	TH 1253	0.7
2011	1.6	1912	1.6
11 0208	1.0	**26** 0126	0.9
0810	1.7	0727	1.7
TH 1448	0.7	F 1359	0.5
2058	1.7	2019	1.8
12 0253	0.9	**27** 0223	0.7
0858	1.8	0829	1.9
F 1525	0.6	SA 1452	0.3
2135	1.8	2111	1.9
13 0329	0.8	**28** 0310	0.6
0937	1.9	0920	2.1
SA 1556	0.5	SU 1537	0.2
2208	1.8	2157	2.0
14 0400	0.7	**29** 0352	0.4
1012	2.0	1007	2.2
SU 1625	0.5	M 1620	0.1
2240	1.9	2240	2.1
15 0429	0.6	**30** 0433	0.3
1044	2.0	1052	2.3
M 1652	0.4	TU 1700	0.1
● 2310	2.0	○ 2320	2.1
		31 0513	0.3
		1136	2.2
		W 1740	0.2
		2358	2.1

APRIL

Time	m		Time	m
1 0554	0.3	**16** 0536	0.4
1219	2.2	1150	2.0
TH 1819	0.3	F 1752	0.4
2 0035	2.1	**17** 0007	2.0
0635	0.3	0613	0.4
F 1302	2.1	SA 1227	2.0
1858	0.5	1827	0.5
3 0112	2.0	**18** 0041	2.0
0718	0.4	0653	0.4
SA 1346	1.9	SU 1308	1.9
1938	0.7	1907	0.6
4 0151	1.9	**19** 0119	1.9
0804	0.6	0738	0.5
SU 1433	1.7	M 1356	1.8
2020	0.9	1951	0.7
5 0233	1.8	**20** 0204	1.8
0900	0.7	0832	0.6
M 1525	1.6	TU 1456	1.7
2111	1.0	2046	0.8
6 0323	1.7	**21** 0302	1.7
1023	0.8	0938	0.6
TU 1632	1.5	W 1606	1.6
◗ 2238	1.1	◗ 2159	0.9
7 0427	1.6	**22** 0415	1.7
1158	0.8	1105	0.6
W 1812	1.4	TH 1726	1.6
		2340	0.9
8 0015	1.1	**23** 0539	1.7
0610	1.5	1228	0.5
TH 1313	0.8	F 1850	1.6
1926	1.5		
9 0127	1.0	**24** 0058	0.8
0727	1.6	0700	1.7
F 1407	0.7	SA 1333	0.4
2016	1.6	1953	1.7
10 0216	0.9	**25** 0157	0.7
0818	1.7	0803	1.9
SA 1446	0.6	SU 1426	0.3
2056	1.7	2044	1.8
11 0254	0.8	**26** 0245	0.6
0900	1.8	0856	2.0
SU 1518	0.5	M 1512	0.3
2131	1.8	2130	1.9
12 0326	0.7	**27** 0329	0.4
0936	1.9	0945	2.1
M 1547	0.5	TU 1555	0.2
2204	1.9	2212	2.0
13 0357	0.6	**28** 0412	0.3
1010	1.9	1032	2.1
TU 1616	0.4	W 1636	0.3
2235	1.9	○ 2252	2.0
14 0429	0.5	**29** 0454	0.3
1043	2.0	1117	2.1
W 1647	0.4	TH 1716	0.3
● 2305	2.0	2330	2.1
15 0502	0.4	**30** 0536	0.3
1116	2.0	1201	2.0
TH 1719	0.4	F 1755	0.4
2335	2.0		

Chart Datum: 1·22 metres below Ordnance Datum (Local). HAT is 2·5 metres above Chart Datum; see 0.19

TIME ZONE (UT)
For Summer Time add ONE
hour in **non-shaded areas**

LERWICK LAT 60°09'N LONG 1°08'W
TIMES AND HEIGHTS OF HIGH AND LOW WATERS

Dates in red are SPRINGS
Dates in blue are NEAPS

YEAR 2010

MAY

Time	m	Time	m
1 0008	2.0	**16** 0600	0.4
0618	0.3	1217	1.9
SA 1245	1.9	SU 1813	0.5
1834	0.6		
2 0046	2.0	**17** 0027	2.0
0702	0.4	0644	0.4
SU 1328	1.8	M 1306	1.9
1913	0.7	1857	0.6
3 0125	1.9	**18** 0111	2.0
0749	0.5	0733	0.4
M 1414	1.7	TU 1359	1.8
1955	0.8	1946	0.7
4 0207	1.8	**19** 0201	1.9
0840	0.6	0828	0.4
TU 1502	1.6	W 1457	1.7
2043	0.9	2041	0.8
5 0254	1.7	**20** 0259	1.8
0942	0.7	0930	0.5
W 1556	1.5	TH 1559	1.7
2148	1.0	◑ 2145	0.8
6 0348	1.6	**21** 0405	1.8
1052	0.8	1042	0.5
TH 1706	1.4	F 1706	1.6
◔ 2308	1.0	2304	0.8
7 0453	1.5	**22** 0516	1.7
1201	0.7	1157	0.5
F 1826	1.5	SA 1817	1.6
8 0021	1.0	**23** 0023	0.8
0622	1.5	0630	1.8
SA 1302	0.7	SU 1303	0.5
1924	1.5	1920	1.7
9 0121	0.9	**24** 0128	0.7
0727	1.6	0736	1.8
SU 1350	0.7	M 1359	0.4
2009	1.6	2014	1.8
10 0208	0.8	**25** 0222	0.6
0814	1.7	0834	1.9
M 1429	0.6	TU 1448	0.4
2048	1.7	2103	1.9
11 0247	0.7	**26** 0311	0.5
0856	1.7	0927	1.9
TU 1505	0.5	W 1533	0.5
2124	1.8	2148	1.9
12 0324	0.6	**27** 0357	0.4
0935	1.8	1018	2.0
W 1540	0.5	TH 1615	0.5
2159	1.9	○ 2230	2.0
13 0401	0.5	**28** 0441	0.4
1013	1.9	1105	2.0
TH 1616	0.4	F 1656	0.5
2234	2.0	2310	2.0
14 0439	0.4	**29** 0524	0.4
1052	2.0	1149	1.9
F 1653	0.5	SA 1736	0.6
● 2310	2.0	2349	2.0
15 0518	0.4	**30** 0607	0.4
1133	2.0	1231	1.9
SA 1732	0.5	SU 1816	0.7
2347	2.0		
		31 0028	2.0
		0649	0.4
		M 1312	1.8
		1854	0.7

JUNE

Time	m	Time	m
1 0107	1.9	**16** 0107	2.1
0731	0.5	0726	0.2
TU 1353	1.7	W 1355	1.9
1933	0.8	1937	0.6
2 0146	1.9	**17** 0158	2.0
0814	0.6	0817	0.3
W 1435	1.6	TH 1447	1.8
2014	0.8	2027	0.7
3 0228	1.8	**18** 0251	2.0
0900	0.6	0911	0.4
TH 1519	1.6	F 1540	1.7
2100	0.9	2121	0.7
4 0312	1.7	**19** 0348	1.9
0951	0.7	1012	0.5
F 1608	1.5	SA 1637	1.7
◑ 2159	0.9	◑ 2225	0.8
5 0403	1.6	**20** 0450	1.8
1050	0.7	1122	0.5
SA 1704	1.5	SU 1739	1.6
2310	0.9	2345	0.8
6 0500	1.6	**21** 0600	1.8
1151	0.7	1232	0.6
SU 1812	1.5	M 1844	1.7
7 0019	0.9	**22** 0102	0.8
0609	1.6	0712	1.8
M 1248	0.7	TU 1335	0.7
1913	1.6	1945	1.7
8 0118	0.9	**23** 0207	0.7
0719	1.6	0818	1.8
TU 1339	0.7	W 1430	0.7
2001	1.7	2041	1.8
9 0208	0.8	**24** 0302	0.6
0813	1.7	0918	1.8
W 1425	0.7	TH 1518	0.7
2045	1.8	2131	1.9
10 0253	0.7	**25** 0351	0.5
0902	1.8	1010	1.9
TH 1508	0.6	F 1602	0.7
2127	1.9	2216	2.0
11 0337	0.6	**26** 0435	0.5
0948	1.9	1056	1.9
F 1551	0.6	SA 1643	0.7
2208	2.0	○ 2258	2.0
12 0420	0.5	**27** 0516	0.4
1035	1.9	1138	1.9
SA 1634	0.6	SU 1722	0.7
● 2250	2.1	2336	2.0
13 0505	0.4	**28** 0554	0.4
1123	2.0	1216	1.9
SU 1719	0.5	M 1759	0.7
2334	2.1		
14 0550	0.3	**29** 0013	2.0
1213	2.0	0631	0.4
M 1804	0.6	TU 1253	1.8
		1833	0.7
15 0019	2.1	**30** 0049	2.0
0637	0.2	0707	0.5
TU 1304	2.0	W 1328	1.8
1849	0.6	1908	0.7

JULY

Time	m	Time	m
1 0123	1.9	**16** 0144	2.2
0742	0.5	0756	0.2
TH 1403	1.7	F 1425	1.9
1942	0.8	2005	0.6
2 0158	1.9	**17** 0233	2.1
0818	0.6	0845	0.4
F 1440	1.7	SA 1512	1.8
2019	0.8	2053	0.7
3 0237	1.8	**18** 0325	2.0
0858	0.7	0939	0.5
SA 1520	1.6	SU 1602	1.7
2102	0.9	◑ 2151	0.8
4 0320	1.7	**19** 0423	1.9
0943	0.7	1043	0.7
SU 1606	1.6	M 1700	1.7
◑ 2156	0.9	2313	0.9
5 0410	1.7	**20** 0533	1.8
1039	0.8	1202	0.8
M 1659	1.6	TU 1809	1.7
2312	1.0		
6 0509	1.6	**21** 0047	0.8
1148	0.8	0655	1.7
TU 1802	1.6	W 1317	0.9
		1922	1.7
7 0030	0.9	**22** 0201	0.8
0618	1.6	0811	1.7
W 1253	0.8	TH 1418	0.9
1910	1.7	2026	1.8
8 0133	0.9	**23** 0259	0.7
0734	1.7	0914	1.8
TH 1351	0.8	F 1509	0.8
2009	1.8	2120	1.9
9 0228	0.7	**24** 0346	0.6
0836	1.8	1002	1.8
F 1444	0.8	SA 1552	0.8
2100	1.9	2205	2.0
10 0318	0.6	**25** 0425	0.5
0931	1.9	1043	1.9
SA 1534	0.7	SU 1630	0.7
2148	2.0	2244	2.1
11 0406	0.4	**26** 0501	0.5
1023	2.0	1120	1.9
SU 1622	0.6	M 1704	0.7
● 2235	2.1	○ 2320	2.1
12 0453	0.3	**27** 0534	0.4
1113	2.1	1154	1.9
M 1707	0.5	TU 1737	0.7
2322	2.2	2353	2.1
13 0539	0.2	**28** 0606	0.4
1203	2.1	1226	1.9
TU 1752	0.5	W 1808	0.6
14 0009	2.3	**29** 0025	2.1
0624	0.1	0637	0.5
W 1251	2.1	TH 1258	1.9
1835	0.5	1838	0.6
15 0057	2.3	**30** 0055	2.1
0710	0.1	0707	0.5
TH 1338	2.0	F 1328	1.8
1919	0.5	1910	0.7
		31 0126	2.0
		0739	0.6
		SA 1400	1.8
		1943	0.7

AUGUST

Time	m	Time	m
1 0200	1.9	**16** 0300	2.0
0813	0.7	0905	0.7
SU 1435	1.8	M 1526	1.8
2022	0.8	◑ 2124	0.8
2 0240	1.8	**17** 0357	1.8
0852	0.8	1005	0.9
M 1518	1.7	TU 1621	1.7
2108	0.9	2251	0.9
3 0328	1.8	**18** 0510	1.7
0939	0.9	1134	1.0
TU 1609	1.7	W 1734	1.7
◑ 2210	1.0		
4 0427	1.7	**19** 0039	0.9
1042	0.9	0645	1.6
W 1709	1.7	TH 1301	1.1
2343	1.0	1902	1.7
5 0537	1.6	**20** 0154	0.9
1212	1.0	0806	1.7
TH 1823	1.7	F 1406	1.1
		2011	1.8
6 0105	0.9	**21** 0250	0.7
0704	1.7	0902	1.8
F 1328	1.1	SA 1455	0.9
1939	1.8	2104	1.9
7 0209	0.8	**22** 0332	0.7
0819	1.8	0944	1.8
SA 1429	0.8	SU 1535	0.8
2039	1.9	2146	2.0
8 0303	0.6	**23** 0407	0.6
0917	1.9	1021	1.9
SU 1521	0.7	M 1609	0.7
2131	2.1	2223	2.1
9 0351	0.4	**24** 0438	0.5
1009	2.0	1054	2.0
M 1607	0.6	TU 1641	0.7
2219	2.2	○ 2256	2.1
10 0437	0.2	**25** 0508	0.5
1058	2.1	1126	2.0
TU 1651	0.5	W 1711	0.6
● 2306	2.3	2328	2.1
11 0521	0.1	**26** 0536	0.5
1144	2.2	1155	2.0
W 1733	0.4	TH 1740	0.6
2352	2.4	2357	2.1
12 0604	0.1	**27** 0604	0.5
1229	2.2	1224	2.0
TH 1815	0.4	F 1809	0.6
13 0037	2.4	**28** 0025	2.1
0647	0.1	0633	0.5
F 1313	2.1	SA 1251	2.0
1856	0.4	1840	0.6
14 0123	2.3	**29** 0055	2.1
0731	0.3	0703	0.6
SA 1355	2.0	SU 1321	1.9
1940	0.5	1914	0.7
15 0210	2.2	**30** 0128	2.0
0816	0.5	0736	0.7
SU 1439	1.9	M 1354	1.9
2027	0.7	1951	0.8
		31 0207	1.9
		0813	0.8
		TU 1434	1.8
		2036	0.9

Chart Datum: 1·22 metres below Ordnance Datum (Local). HAT is 2·5 metres above Chart Datum; see 0.19

LERWICK LAT 60°09'N LONG 1°08'W
TIMES AND HEIGHTS OF HIGH AND LOW WATERS

TIME ZONE (UT)
For Summer Time add ONE hour in **non-shaded areas**

Dates in red are SPRINGS
Dates in blue are NEAPS

YEAR **2010**

NE Scotland

SEPTEMBER

Day	Time m	Time m	Time m	Time m		Day	Time m	Time m	Time m	Time m
1 W	0255 1.8	0857 0.9	1525 1.8	☽2136 1.0		**16** TH	0447 1.6	1103 1.2	1658 1.7	
2 TH	0356 1.7	0959 1.0	1629 1.7	2306 1.0		**17** F	0021 0.9	0629 1.6	1237 1.2	1835 1.7
3 F	0512 1.7	1142 1.1	1747 1.7			**18** SA	0134 0.9	0747 1.7	1343 1.1	1946 1.8
4 SA	0044 0.9	0647 1.7	1313 1.0	1915 1.8		**19** SU	0226 0.8	0837 1.8	1432 1.0	2037 1.9
5 SU	0151 0.7	0805 1.8	1414 0.9	2020 2.0		**20** M	0306 0.7	0915 1.8	1510 0.9	2118 2.0
6 M	0245 0.5	0901 2.0	1503 0.7	2112 2.1		**21** TU	0339 0.6	0950 1.9	1543 0.8	2154 2.1
7 TU	0332 0.3	0950 2.1	1547 0.6	2159 2.3		**22** W	0408 0.6	1022 2.0	1613 0.7	2227 2.1
8 W	0416 0.2	1036 2.2	1629 0.5	●2245 2.4		**23** TH	0436 0.5	1053 2.1	1642 0.6	○2258 2.2
9 TH	0459 0.1	1120 2.3	1710 0.4	2330 2.5		**24** F	0503 0.5	1122 2.1	1712 0.6	2327 2.2
10 F	0540 0.1	1202 2.2	1752 0.4			**25** SA	0532 0.5	1150 2.1	1742 0.6	2356 2.2
11 SA	0015 2.5	0621 0.2	1243 2.2	1833 0.4		**26** SU	0601 0.6	1217 2.1	1815 0.6	
12 SU	0100 2.4	0703 0.4	1323 2.1	1917 0.5		**27** M	0027 2.1	0632 0.6	1247 2.1	1850 0.7
13 M	0147 2.2	0746 0.6	1405 2.0	2005 0.7		**28** TU	0103 2.0	0705 0.7	1321 2.0	1930 0.8
14 TU	0237 2.0	0833 0.8	1451 1.9	2103 0.8		**29** W	0143 2.0	0744 0.9	1401 1.9	2017 0.9
15 W	0334 1.8	0930 1.0	1545 1.8	☽2236 0.9		**30** TH	0234 1.8	0831 1.0	1453 1.8	2118 0.9

OCTOBER

Day	Time m	Time m	Time m	Time m		Day	Time m	Time m	Time m	Time m
1 F	0340 1.7	0936 1.1	1601 1.8	☽2245 0.9		**16** SA	0548 1.6	1153 1.2	1750 1.7	
2 SA	0459 1.7	1120 1.1	1723 1.8			**17** SU	0054 0.9	0703 1.7	1305 1.1	1906 1.8
3 SU	0022 0.8	0632 1.7	1253 1.0	1851 1.8		**18** M	0149 0.9	0756 1.7	1357 1.0	1959 1.9
4 M	0129 0.7	0746 1.9	1352 0.9	1956 2.0		**19** TU	0230 0.8	0837 1.8	1437 0.9	2042 2.0
5 TU	0222 0.5	0840 2.0	1441 0.8	2049 2.2		**20** W	0303 0.7	0913 1.9	1511 0.8	2120 2.0
6 W	0309 0.4	0927 2.1	1525 0.6	2137 2.3		**21** TH	0333 0.7	0947 2.0	1542 0.7	2154 2.1
7 TH	0353 0.3	1011 2.2	1607 0.5	●2223 2.4		**22** F	0401 0.6	1019 2.1	1613 0.7	2227 2.1
8 F	0435 0.2	1053 2.3	1648 0.4	2308 2.5		**23** SA	0431 0.6	1049 2.1	1646 0.6	○2300 2.2
9 SA	0516 0.3	1133 2.3	1731 0.4	2354 2.4		**24** SU	0501 0.6	1119 2.2	1720 0.6	2333 2.2
10 SU	0557 0.4	1213 2.3	1814 0.4			**25** M	0533 0.7	1150 2.2	1755 0.6	
11 M	0040 2.3	0638 0.6	1253 2.2	1859 0.5		**26** TU	0008 2.1	0607 0.7	1223 2.2	1834 0.7
12 TU	0128 2.1	0720 0.8	1334 2.1	1948 0.7		**27** W	0048 2.1	0645 0.8	1300 2.1	1917 0.7
13 W	0218 2.0	0805 1.0	1420 2.0	2046 0.8		**28** TH	0133 2.0	0727 0.9	1342 2.0	2007 0.8
14 TH	0313 1.8	0859 1.1	1513 1.9	☽2207 0.9		**29** F	0228 1.9	0818 1.0	1436 1.9	2108 0.8
15 F	0418 1.7	1020 1.2	1618 1.8	2340 1.0		**30** SA	0334 1.8	0923 1.1	1544 1.9	☽2226 0.8
						31 SU	0447 1.8	1051 1.1	1701 1.9	2353 0.8

NOVEMBER

Day	Time m	Time m	Time m	Time m		Day	Time m	Time m	Time m	Time m
1 M	0608 1.8	1221 1.0	1822 1.9			**16** TU	0050 0.9	0704 1.7	1306 1.1	1910 1.8
2 TU	0100 0.7	0718 1.9	1324 0.9	1929 2.0		**17** W	0140 0.9	0753 1.8	1355 1.0	2000 1.9
3 W	0156 0.6	0813 2.0	1416 0.8	2025 2.2		**18** TH	0219 0.8	0834 1.9	1435 0.9	2043 2.0
4 TH	0245 0.5	0900 2.1	1503 0.7	2116 2.3		**19** F	0253 0.8	0911 2.0	1512 0.8	2122 2.0
5 F	0330 0.4	0945 2.2	1547 0.6	2204 2.3		**20** SA	0327 0.8	0946 2.1	1548 0.8	2200 2.1
6 SA	0412 0.4	1027 2.3	1631 0.5	●2252 2.4		**21** SU	0401 0.7	1020 2.2	1624 0.7	○2238 2.1
7 SU	0454 0.5	1108 2.3	1715 0.5	2339 2.3		**22** M	0436 0.7	1054 2.2	1702 0.6	2317 2.2
8 M	0535 0.6	1149 2.3	1800 0.5			**23** TU	0513 0.7	1130 2.2	1742 0.6	2358 2.1
9 TU	0026 2.2	0616 0.7	1230 2.2	1845 0.6		**24** W	0552 0.8	1208 2.2	1824 0.6	
10 W	0113 2.1	0658 0.9	1312 2.2	1933 0.7		**25** TH	0042 2.1	0633 0.8	1249 2.1	1910 0.6
11 TH	0200 1.9	0742 1.0	1356 2.1	2026 0.8		**26** F	0131 2.0	0719 0.9	1335 2.1	2000 0.6
12 F	0249 1.8	0830 1.1	1445 2.0	2126 0.9		**27** SA	0225 2.0	0809 1.0	1428 2.1	2056 0.7
13 SA	0342 1.7	0930 1.2	1538 1.9	☽2235 0.9		**28** SU	0324 1.9	0907 1.1	1529 2.0	☽2200 0.7
14 SU	0446 1.7	1045 1.2	1642 1.9	2347 1.0		**29** M	0427 1.8	1015 1.1	1637 2.0	2316 0.7
15 M	0602 1.7	1201 1.2	1804 1.8			**30** TU	0535 1.8	1138 1.0	1750 2.0	

DECEMBER

Day	Time m	Time m	Time m	Time m		Day	Time m	Time m	Time m	Time m
1 W	0028 0.7	0644 1.9	1253 1.0	1901 2.0		**16** TH	0034 1.0	0658 1.8	1304 1.1	1906 1.8
2 TH	0130 0.7	0743 2.0	1354 0.9	2003 2.1		**17** F	0128 1.0	0751 1.8	1358 1.0	2003 1.8
3 F	0223 0.7	0836 2.1	1447 0.8	2100 2.2		**18** SA	0214 0.9	0835 1.9	1444 0.9	2051 1.9
4 SA	0311 0.7	0924 2.1	1535 0.7	2154 2.2		**19** SU	0257 0.9	0916 2.1	1526 0.8	2136 2.0
5 SU	0355 0.7	1010 2.2	1621 0.6	●2244 2.2		**20** M	0338 0.8	0955 2.1	1608 0.7	2221 2.1
6 M	0438 0.7	1053 2.3	1706 0.5	2331 2.2		**21** TU	0419 0.8	1035 2.2	1649 0.6	○2305 2.1
7 TU	0520 0.7	1134 2.3	1750 0.5			**22** W	0500 0.8	1116 2.3	1732 0.5	2350 2.2
8 W	0015 2.1	0600 0.8	1215 2.3	1833 0.6		**23** TH	0542 0.7	1158 2.3	1815 0.5	
9 TH	0058 2.1	0640 0.9	1255 2.2	1916 0.6		**24** F	0037 2.2	0625 0.7	1242 2.3	1900 0.4
10 F	0139 2.0	0720 0.9	1335 2.1	1959 0.7		**25** SA	0125 2.1	0709 0.8	1328 2.3	1947 0.5
11 SA	0220 1.9	0759 1.0	1416 2.0	2043 0.8		**26** SU	0214 2.0	0755 0.8	1418 2.2	2037 0.5
12 SU	0303 1.8	0842 1.1	1459 1.9	2131 0.9		**27** M	0305 2.0	0844 0.9	1511 2.1	2132 0.6
13 M	0349 1.7	0933 1.1	1547 1.9	☽2228 1.0		**28** TU	0359 1.9	0941 1.0	1610 2.0	☽2236 0.7
14 TU	0443 1.7	1042 1.2	1641 1.8	2332 1.0		**29** W	0459 1.8	1053 1.0	1718 2.0	2352 0.8
15 W	0550 1.7	1159 1.2	1751 1.8			**30** TH	0607 1.8	1224 1.0	1835 1.9	
						31 F	0104 0.9	0715 1.9	1339 0.9	1949 1.9

Chart Datum: 1·22 metres below Ordnance Datum (Local). HAT is 2·5 metres above Chart Datum; see 0.19

OTHER HARBOURS IN THE SHETLAND ISLANDS

BALTA SOUND, Unst, **60°44'·32N 00°48'·12W**. AC 3293. HW −0105 on Dover; ML 1·3; Duration 0640. See 5.24. Balta Sound is a large almost landlocked inlet with good shelter from all winds. Beware fish farms and bad holding on kelp. Safest and main entry is via S Chan between Huney Is and Balta Is; inner chan marked by two PHM lt buoys. N Chan is deep but narrow; keep to Unst shore. ⚓ off Sandisons Wharf (2FG vert) in approx 6m or enter marina close W (one Ⓥ, very shallow); pier has Oc WRG 10s 5m 2M, 272°-G-282°-W-287°-R-297°. VHF Ch 16; 20 (HO or as required). Facilities: BY, FW, D, El, ME, ✕; Hotel by pier. **Baltasound village**, Bar, R, 🛒, ✉.

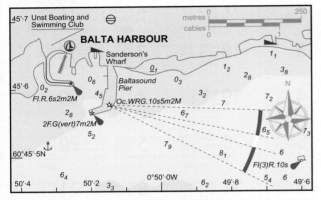

FOULA, Shetland Islands, **60°08'·02N 02°02'·92W** (Ham Voe). AC 3283. HW −0150 on Dover; ML 1·3m. See 5.24. Foula is 12M WSW of Mainland. Highest ground is 416m. S Ness lt ho, Fl (3) 15s, is at the S tip. Beware Foula Shoal (7·6m) and Hœvdi Grund (1·4m), respectively 4·3M E and 2M SE of Ham Voe.

Ham Voe is a narrow inlet on the E coast with a quay; rks on both sides. Two R ▲ ldg marks, approx 270°, are hard to see. ☆ 2 FG (vert) on pierhead. Berthing or landing is only possible in settled weather with no swell. Take advice from mail boat skipper out of Walls and call Foula, ☎ (01595) 753222. Small ✈. No other facilities.

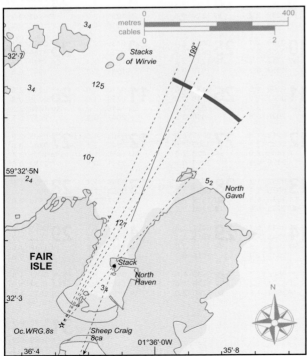

SCALLOWAY, Mainland, **60°08'·02N 01°16'·59W**. AC 3294. HW −0200 on Dover; ML 0·9m; Duration 0620. See 5.24. A busy fishing port; good shelter and ⚓ in all weathers. Care is needed negotiating the islands in strong SW'lies. The N Chan is easier and safer than the S Chan, both are well lit and marked. Castle and warehouse (both conspic) lead 054° through S Chan. Dir Oc WRG 10s on hbr quay leads 064·5° into hbr. Hbr lts as chartlet. Ⓥ pontoon in 3m off SBC is best option; marina close N or new marina in E Voe (though mostly full of local boats). ⚓s in hbr 6–10m or in Hamna Voe (W Burra). Call *Scalloway Hbr Radio* VHF Ch **12** 09 16 (Mon-Fri 0600-1800; Sat 0600-1230LT). Piermaster ☎ (01595) 880574. **Facilities: Scalloway Boat Club** (SBC) ☎ 880409 welcomes visitors; AB (free), Bar. **Town** Slip, P, D, FW, SM, BY, CH, C, El, ME, ✕, ✉,R, 🛒, Bar.

VAILA SOUND (WALLS), Mainland, **60°13'·65N 01°33'·87W**. AC 3295. Tides approx as Scalloway (above); see 5.24. Appr to E of Vaila island (do not attempt Wester Sound) in the W sector (355°-012°) of Rams Head lt, Fl WRG 8s 16m 9/6M. Gruting Voe lies to the NE. Enter Easter Sound and go N for 1·5M, passing E of Linga islet, to Walls at the head of Vaila Voe. Navigate by echo sounder. Beware fish farms. Temporary AB on Bayhaa pier (covers). Close E of this, AB £1 on pontoon of Peter Georgeson. **Marina**: Sec ☎ (01595) 809273, FW. **Walls Regatta Club** welcomes visitors; showers, Bar, Slip. **Village**: P & D (cans), 🛒, ✉.

SKELD, Mainland, **60°09'·65N 01°27'W**. AC 3283, 3294. Tides approx as Scalloway (above); see 5.24. Appr from Skelda Voe. 1M S of ent which is subject to heavy seas and swell in strong S'lies. Beware Braga Rk (dries 2m) and drying rock 1ca S of it. At E of ent also Snap Rk (dries 3.5m) with isolated rocks inshore. **Marina** offers good shelter as virtually landlocked, welcomes visitors; 8Ⓥ £10/craft/week; James Scott ☎ (01595) 860287, FW, ⌐▷, showers, P & D (cans), Bus to Lerwick 2/daily.

FAIR ISLE, Shetland Islands, **59°32'·37N 01°36'·21W** (North Haven). AC 3299. HW −0030 on Dover; ML 1·4m; Duration 0620. See 5.24 Good shelter in North Haven, except in NE winds. AB on pier or ⚓ in approx 2m. Beware strong cross-tides in the apprs; beware also rocks all round Fair Isle, particularly in S Haven and South Hbr which are not recommended. Ldg marks 199° into North Haven: front, Stack of N Haven (only visible as a dark 'tooth' sticking up from the jumble of blocks which form the bkwtr) in transit with conspic summit of Sheep Craig (rear). Dir lt into N Haven, Oc WRG 8s 10m 6M, vis 204°-G-208°-W-211°-R-221°. Other lts: At N tip, Skroo Fl (2) 30s 80m **22M**, vis 086·7°-358°, Horn (3) 45s. At S tip, Skadan Fl (4) 30s 31m **22M**, vis 260°-146°, but obscd close inshore from 260°-282°, Horn (2) 60s. **Facilities:** 🛒, ✉ at N Shriva, ✈ and a bi-weekly mail boat (*Good Shepherd*) to Shetland.